LONDON

SECRET AND HIDDEN PLACES

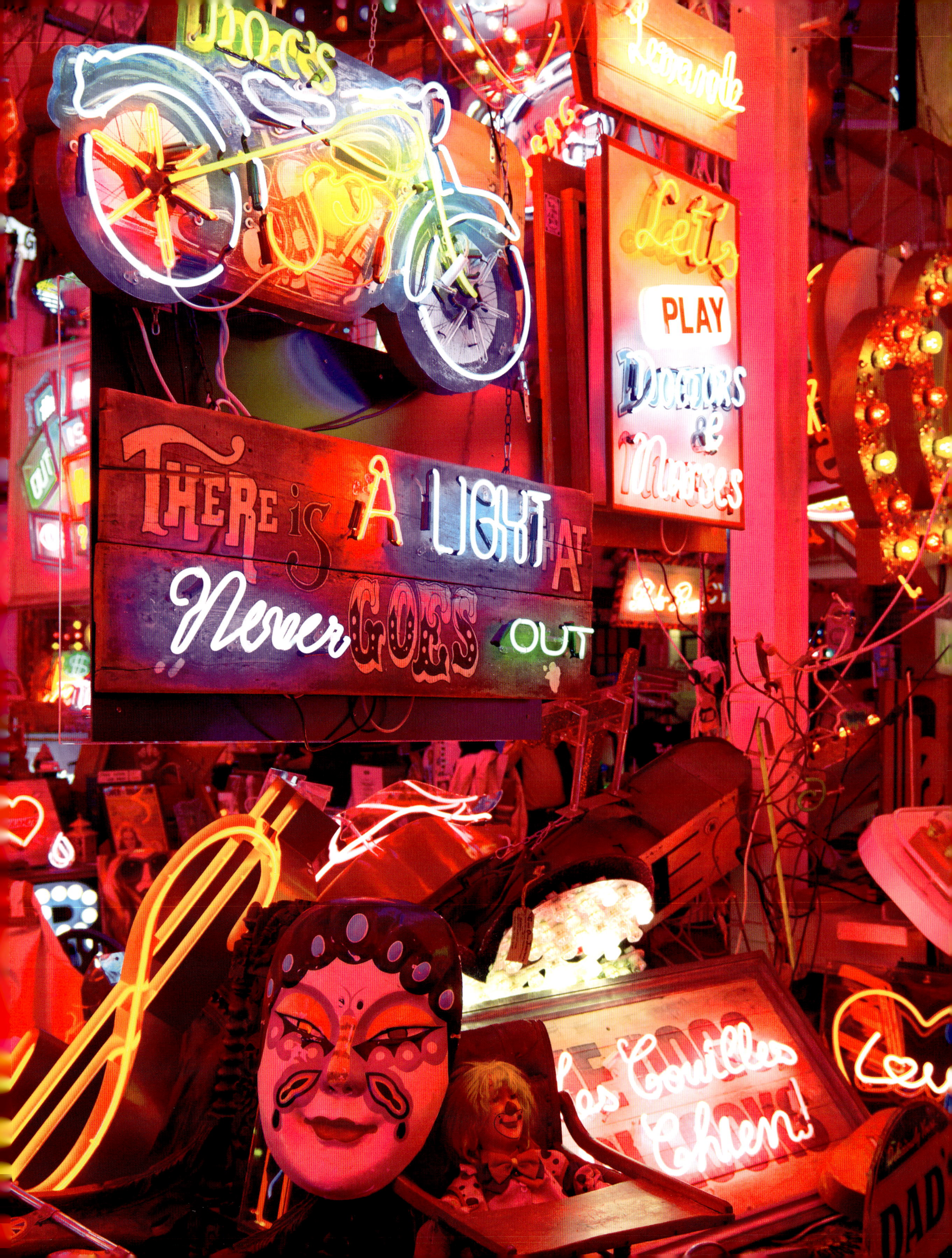
THERE is A LIGHT
Never GOES OUT
Let's
PLAY
Doctors & Nurses
Couilles
Chien!

Peter Dazeley
TEXT BY MARK DALY

LONDON

SECRET AND HIDDEN PLACES

FRANCES
LINCOLN

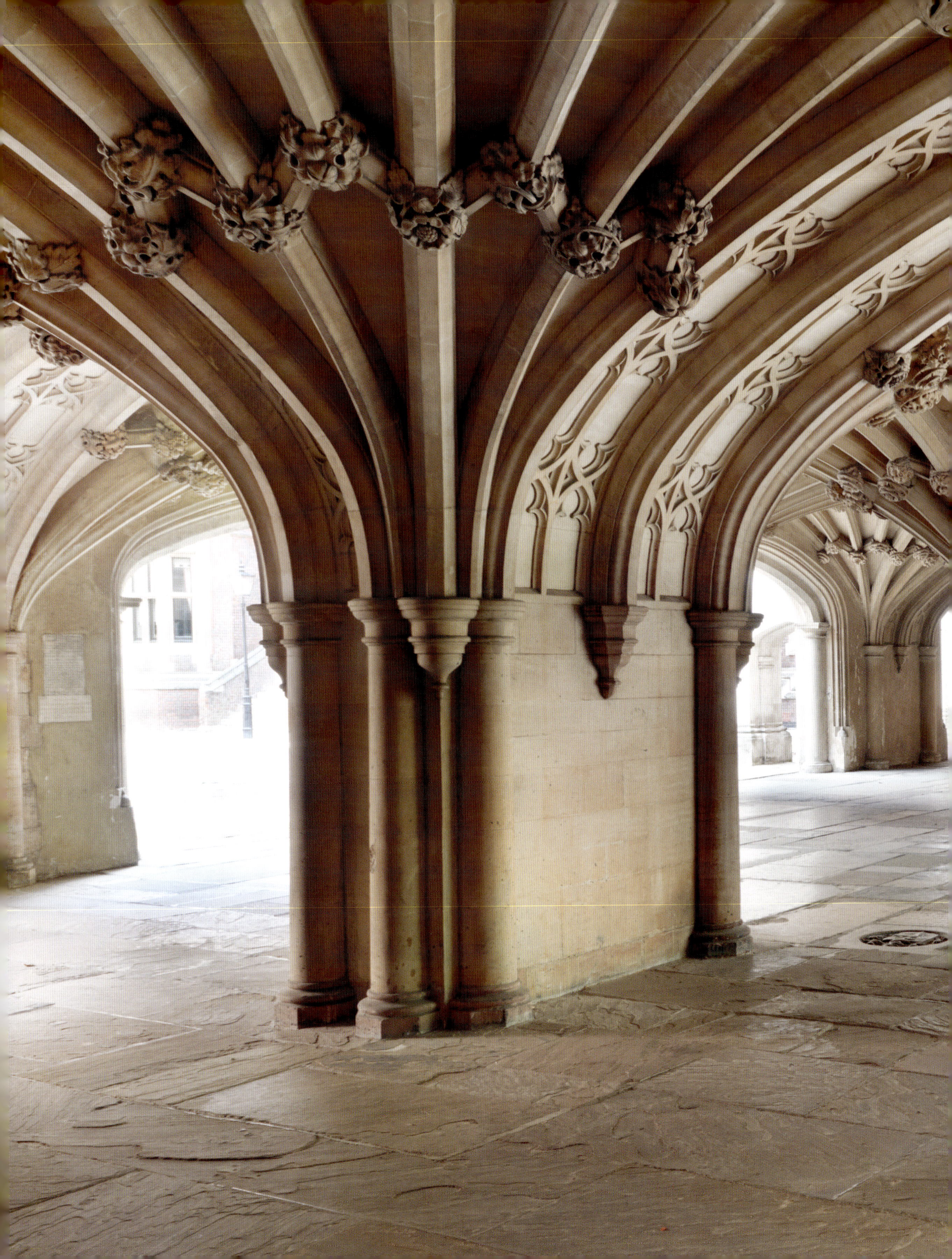

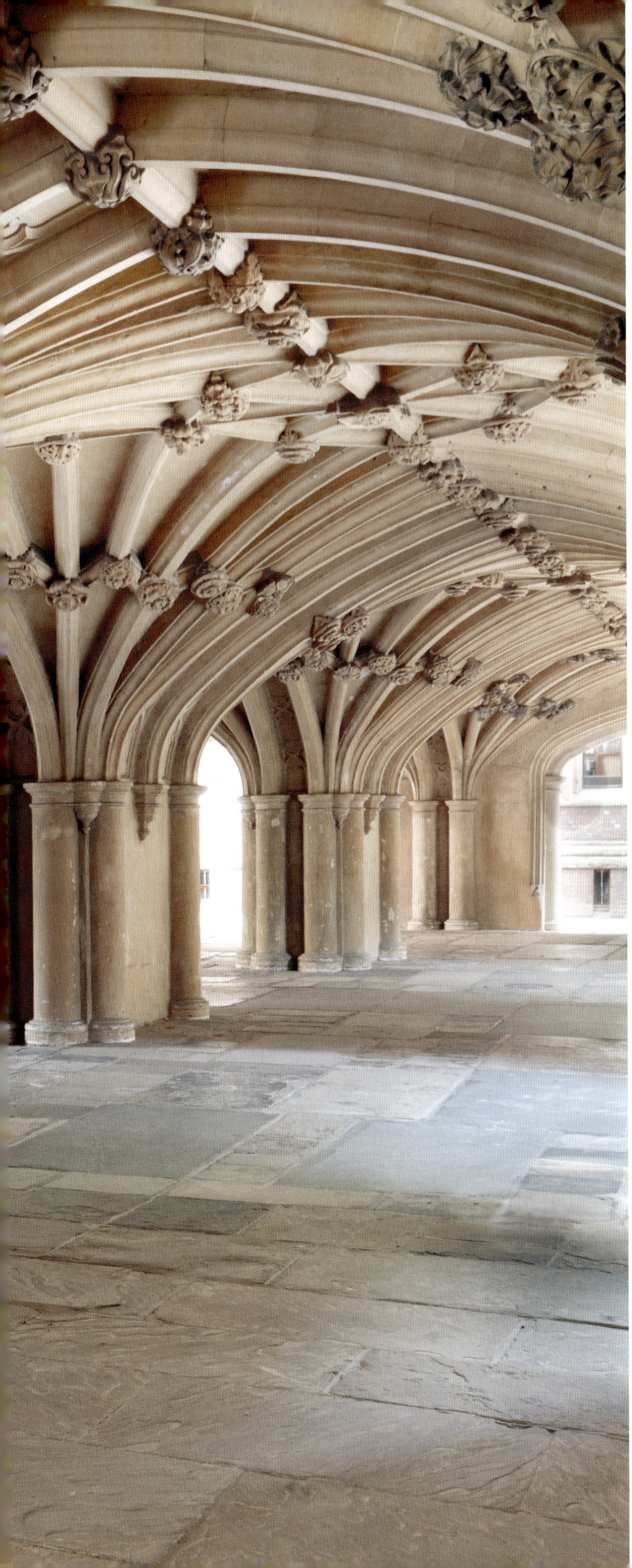

Contents

Title page God's Own Junkyard.
Left The Undercroft, Lincoln's Inn.

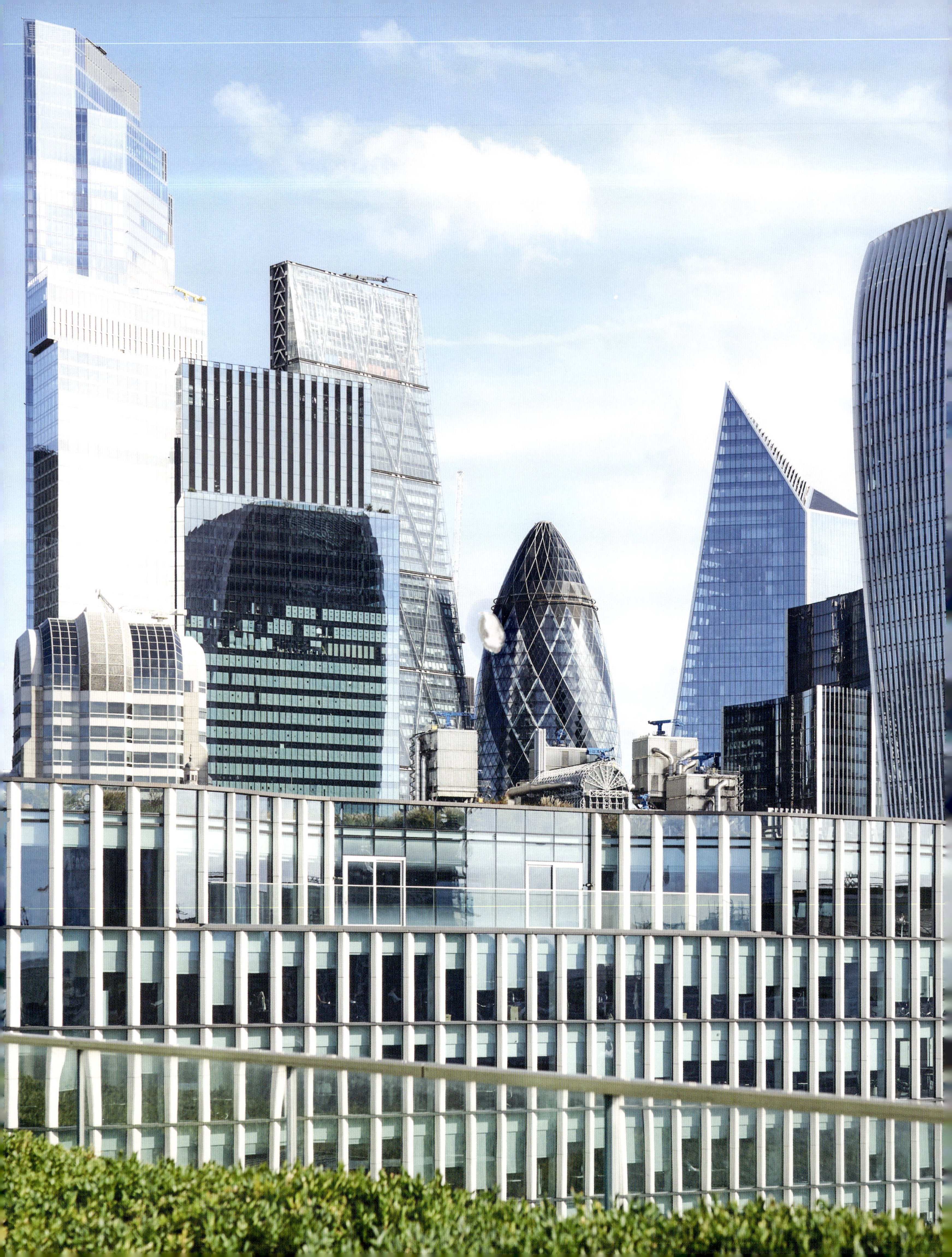

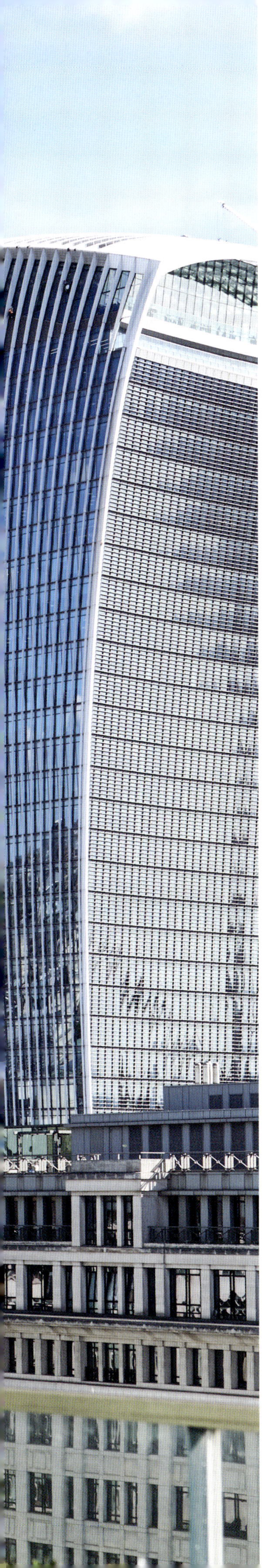

Introduction

The view of the London skyline from Swan Lane.

The first principle of information-gathering, applied by secret intelligence agencies worldwide, is to learn everything about all subjects by scrutinizing the outside. Analyze carefully before going inside discretely.

Peter Dazeley's business is fine upfront photography, not espionage, although he does follow that classic outside-inside approach to gather London's secrets.

This collection adds to locations previously described in *London Explored*, *Unseen London* and *London Uncovered*, over 90 places in total.

London's jagged skyline is constantly evolving, shown by this cluster of City skyscrapers that have sprung up in recent years. It includes Tower 42, 22 Bishopgate, the Gherkin at 30 St Mary Axe, the Walkie Talkie of 20 Fenchurch Street and other high-risers, but it most significantly shows the gilded urn of flames on top of the Monument marking the Great Fire of 1666. Beyond this lie many of the subjects found in this book: some in subterranean places, others down dark, narrow alleyways, in an urban woodland or open parkland. Many live out on the street in plain sight.

St Paul's Cathedral is not glimpsed here, a notable absence given the rules and regulations devoted to protecting views of the City's greatest landmark. It was rated as London's highest building until 1962. Its absence is explained by the special perspective gained from the rooftop terrace of a building in Swan Lane, at the ninth level, aiming westwards and away from the river. An inside view of St Paul's is shown on the cover of this book, part of the Dean's Staircase in the south-west bell tower, eighty-eight steps arranged helically and cantilevered in a geometrical illusion of lightness and space. It was famously deployed in the film of *Harry Potter and the Prisoner of Azkaban*.

Elsewhere, hard-to-classify, and soon to be visible, lies the Hatton Garden Heist Hole. This uprooted chunk of criminality is held in a secret store, poised to go on display in the Museum of London at its new home at West Smithfield. It is a relic of the notorious £14 million robbery at the

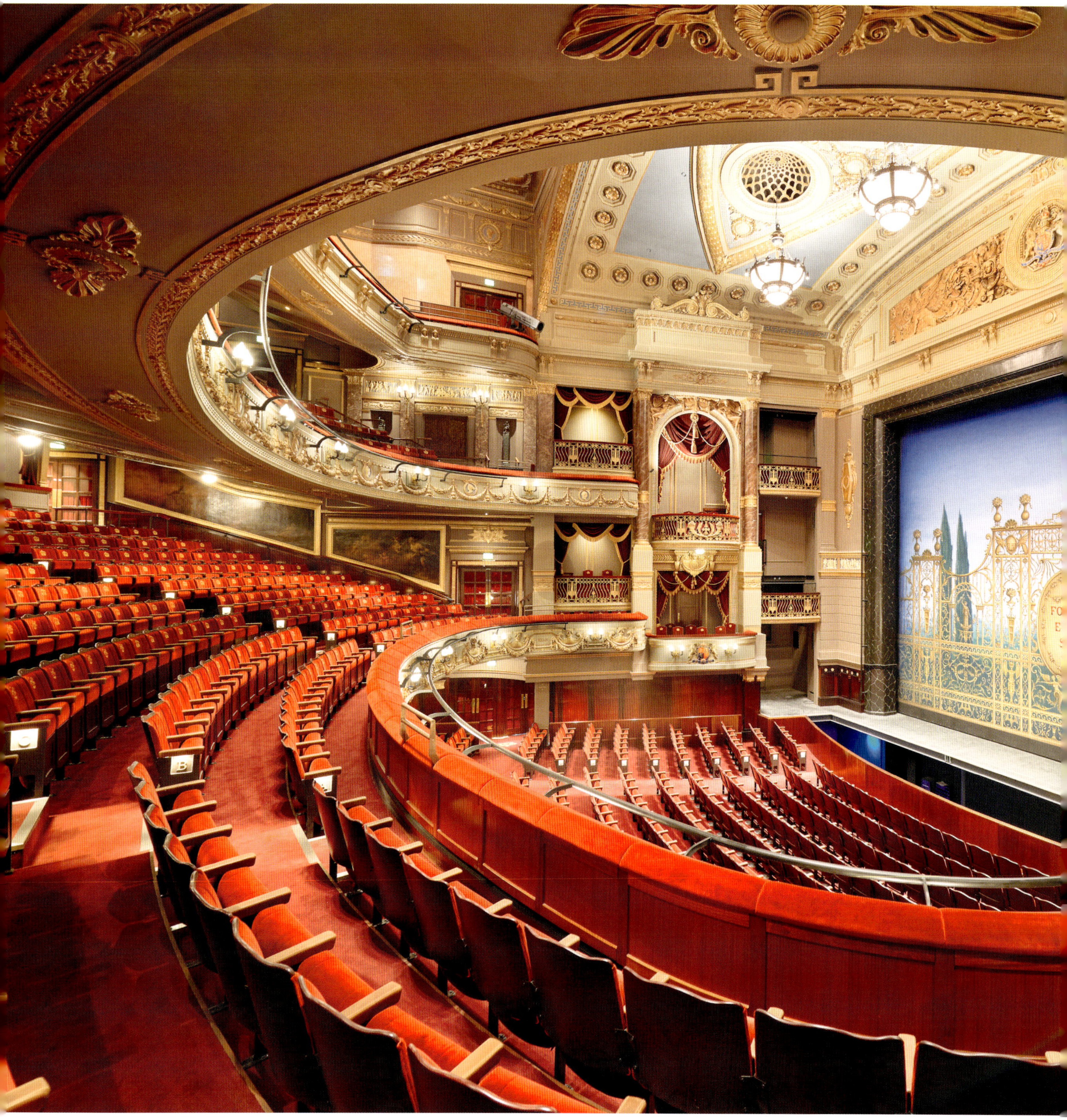

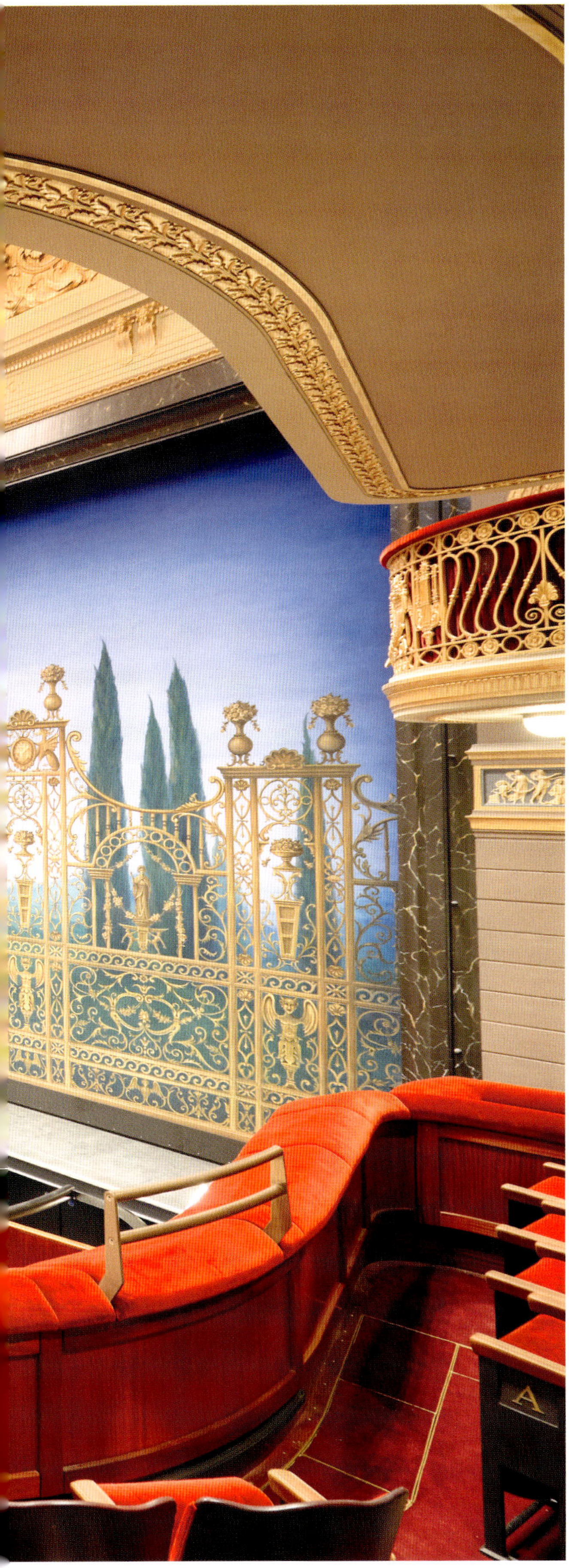

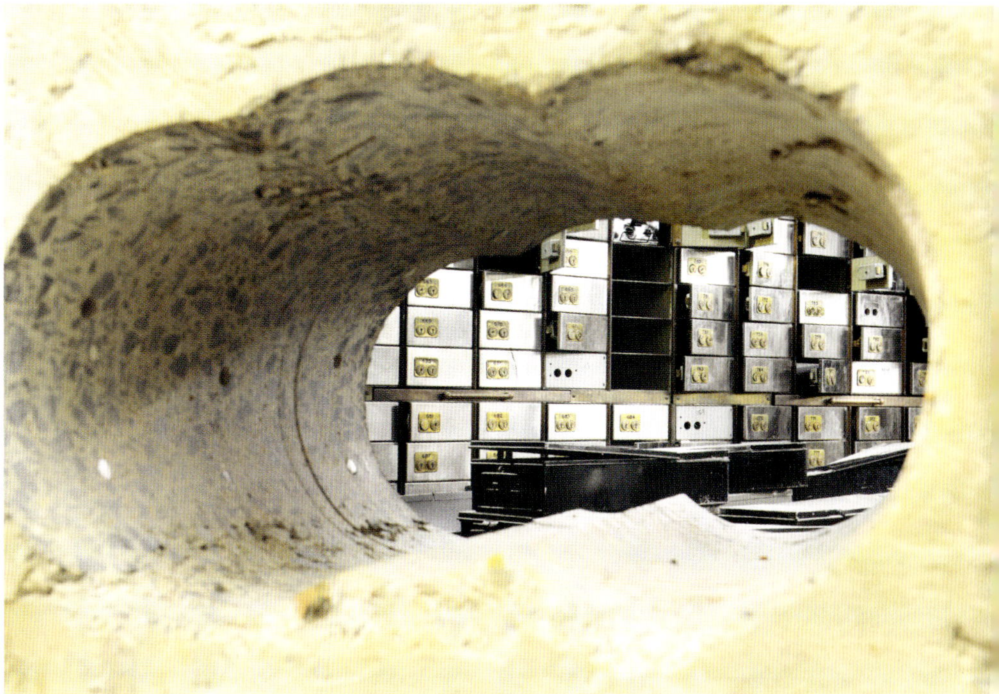

Hatton Garden Safe Deposit in 2015. The plan is to relocate the strong room, armoured door, hundreds of deposit boxes and even the concrete wall of the chamber complete with the drilled hole.

Contrast this with a legendary London location with history going back to about 1663, pre-dating the Fire and the Monument. The Theatre Royal Drury Lane continues its business following a £60-million restoration completed in 2021. Described in Dazeley's *London Theatres* as 'the greatest story ever told in the West End', Drury Lane now seats 1,900 in an auditorium with restored to original Regency style. Over time, four buildings have housed a theatre at this place, the continuity of location staking the claim to it being the world's oldest theatre site in continuous use. Its two royal boxes date back to the time of George III, who was on antagonistic terms with his son. After an altercation between the King and Prince Regent during a night at the theatre, the new building was designed with separate areas, designated the King's side and the Prince's side, with separate entrances and boxes each adorned with the respective royal crest, either a crown or Prince of Wales' feathers. This view shows the King's box from the Prince's side.

A note on access. Many of the places profiled here are open to visitors. Some require tickets and bookings, and some are subject to restricted timings or seasonal openings. In every case, a check is essential before making moves to visit. A few locations are not open to public view.

Opposite The £60m refurbishment of Sir Andrew Lloyd Webber's Theatre Royal Drury Lane.

Above The hole cut during the Hatton Garden Safe Deposit robbery.

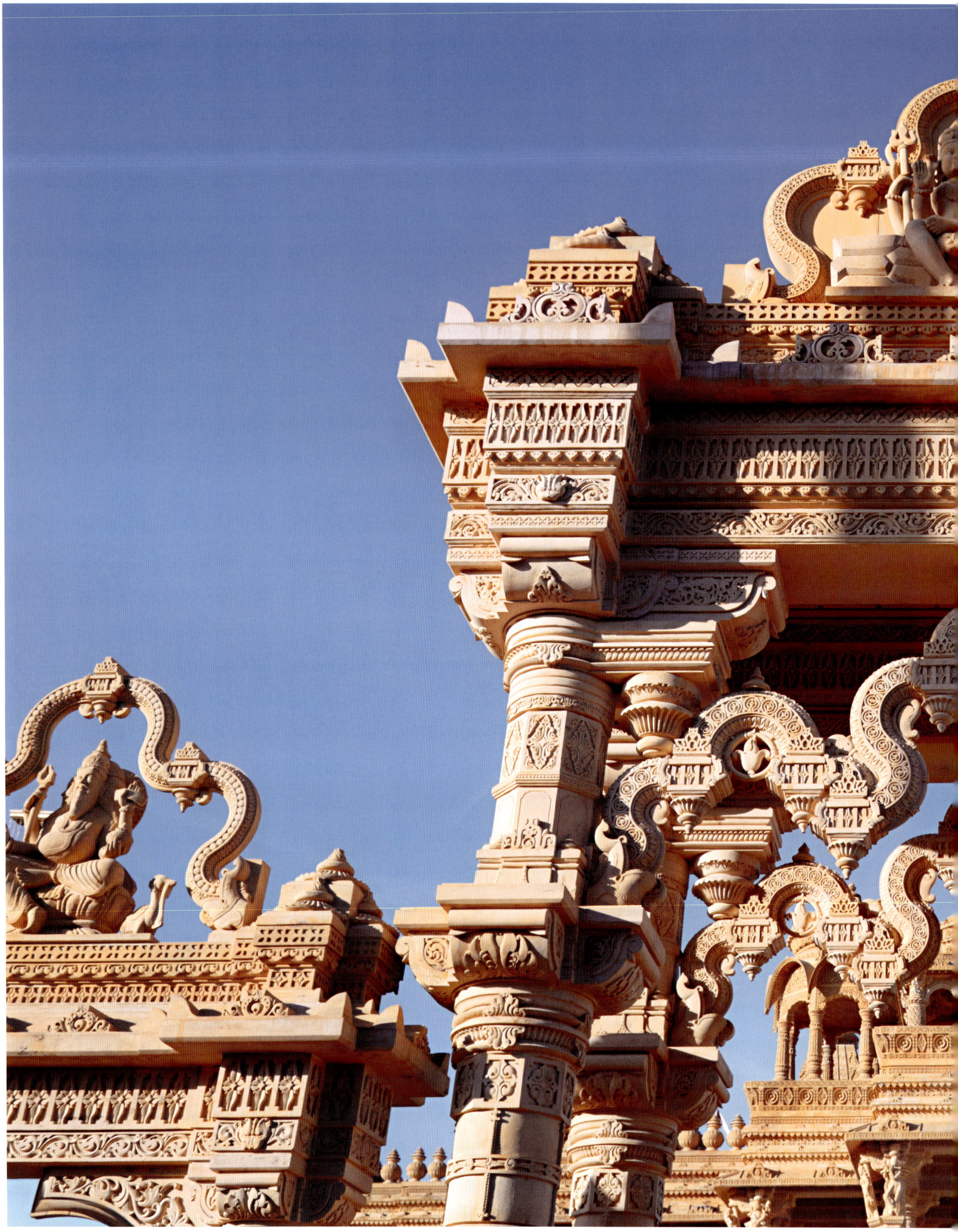

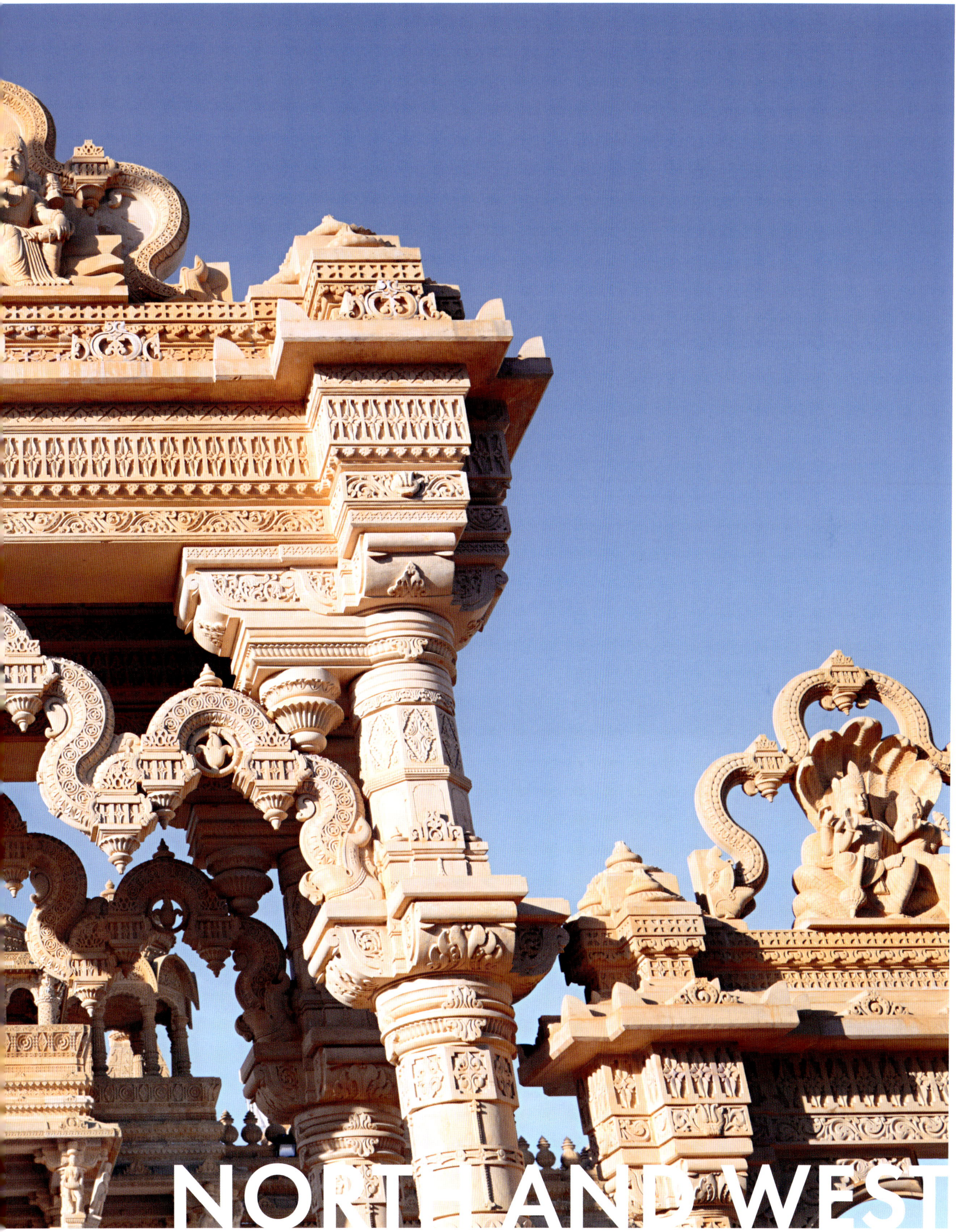

NORTH AND WEST

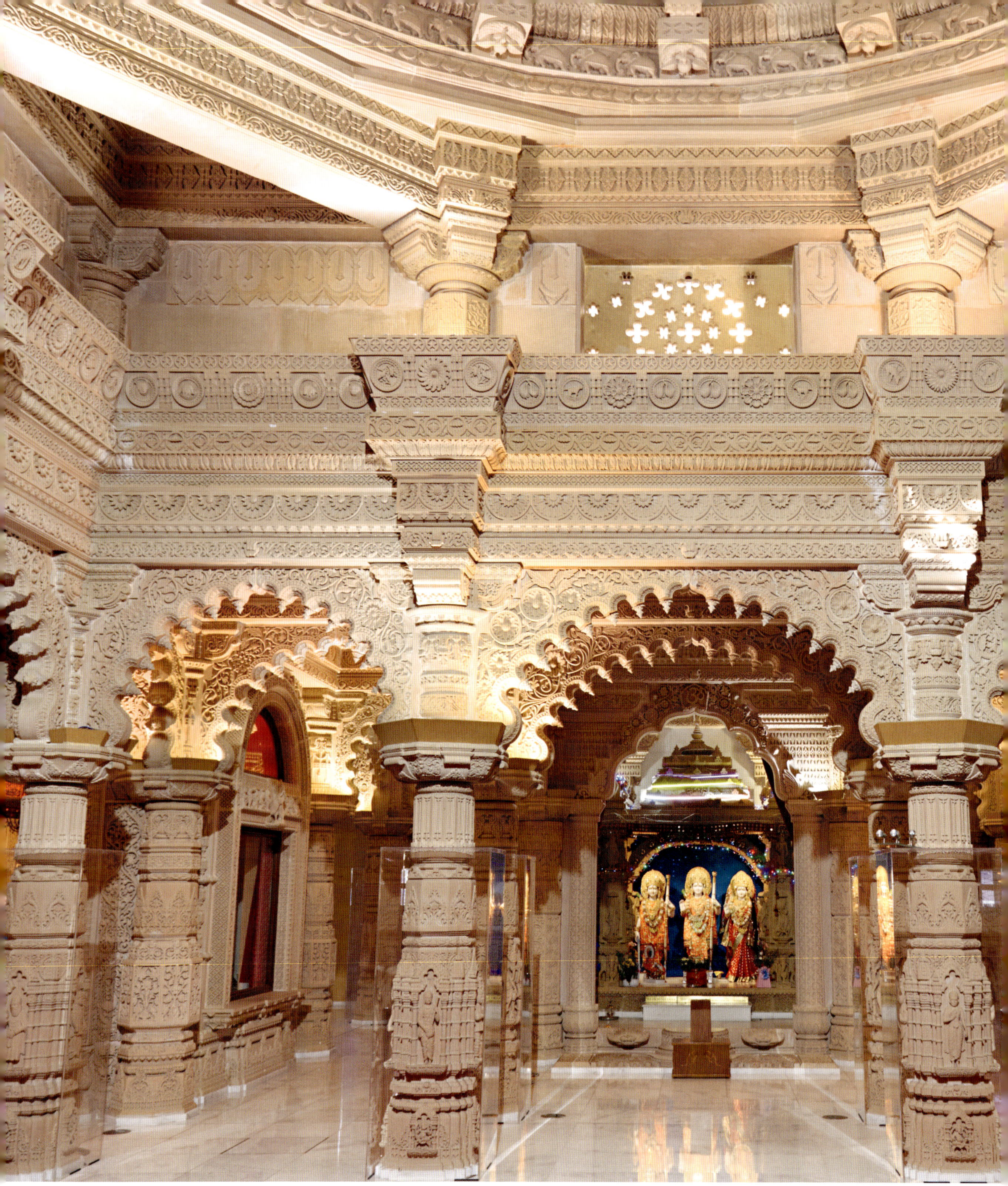

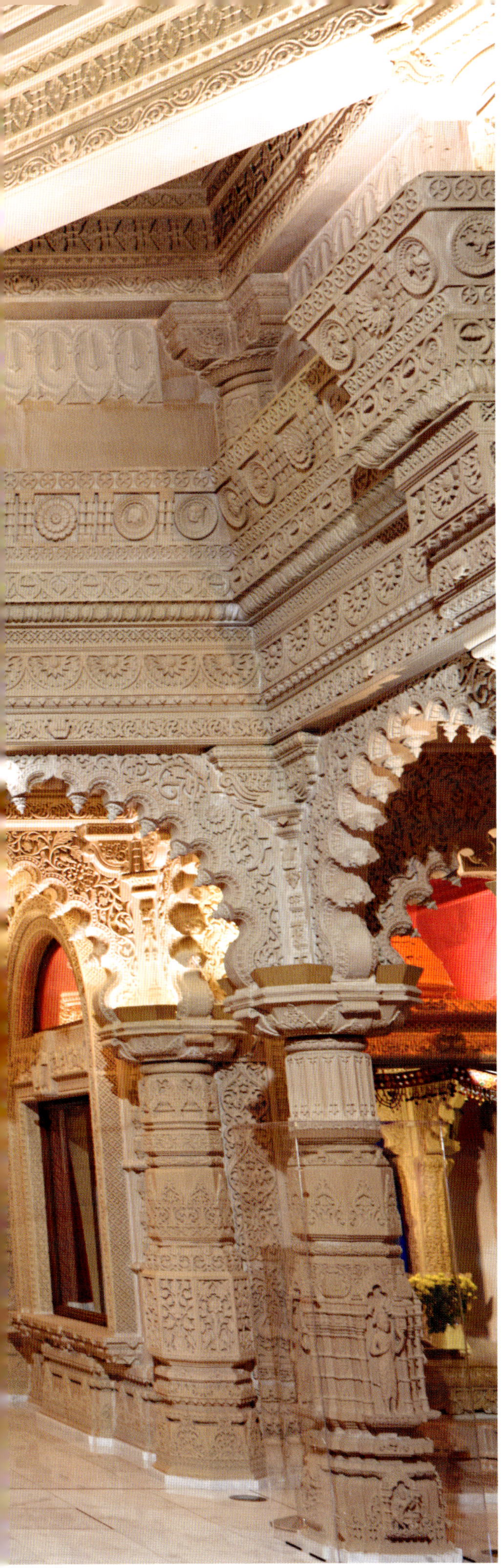

Shri Sanatan Hindu Mandir

Previous page The temple entrance, aligned to the east, is framed by a separate archway.

Left The view into the temple from the main entrance. Shri Ram Darbar is glimpsed.

The architecture of the Shri Sanatan Hindu Temple in Wembley has impressed thousands with its dazzling decorative complexity since its completion in 2010. Its intricately carved bright sand-coloured walls and domes are established as an unmistakable landmark on the Ealing Road.

Construction of the Shri Sanatan Mandir, like all Hindu Temples, is based on the scripture of the Shilpa Shastras, which contain design rules and standards. According to this tradition, it is laid out on numerical and geometrical principles based on a grid. The temple is close to square in plan, aligned with its main doors facing to the east.

For the first-time visitor, the most striking impression is made by numerous intricate forms of carving, which cover not only the exterior and interior walls, but also the ceilings and the pillars supporting the domes. The patterns have been derived from Hindu legends such as the *Mahabharata, Ramayana* and *Shrimad Bhagavatam*. Carvings also recognize non-Hindus Mother Teresa and Guru Nanak. Each of the 210 pillars depicts a famous event from Hindu scripture. Elsewhere on the stonework, rosettes, feathers and leaves are all hand-carved. The only unadorned surface is the smooth expanse of marble floor.

Many of the component pieces were carved in limestone in the small town of Sola in the state of Gujarat, before being shipped to UK and assembled. Yellow Jaisalmer limestone is seen on the exterior

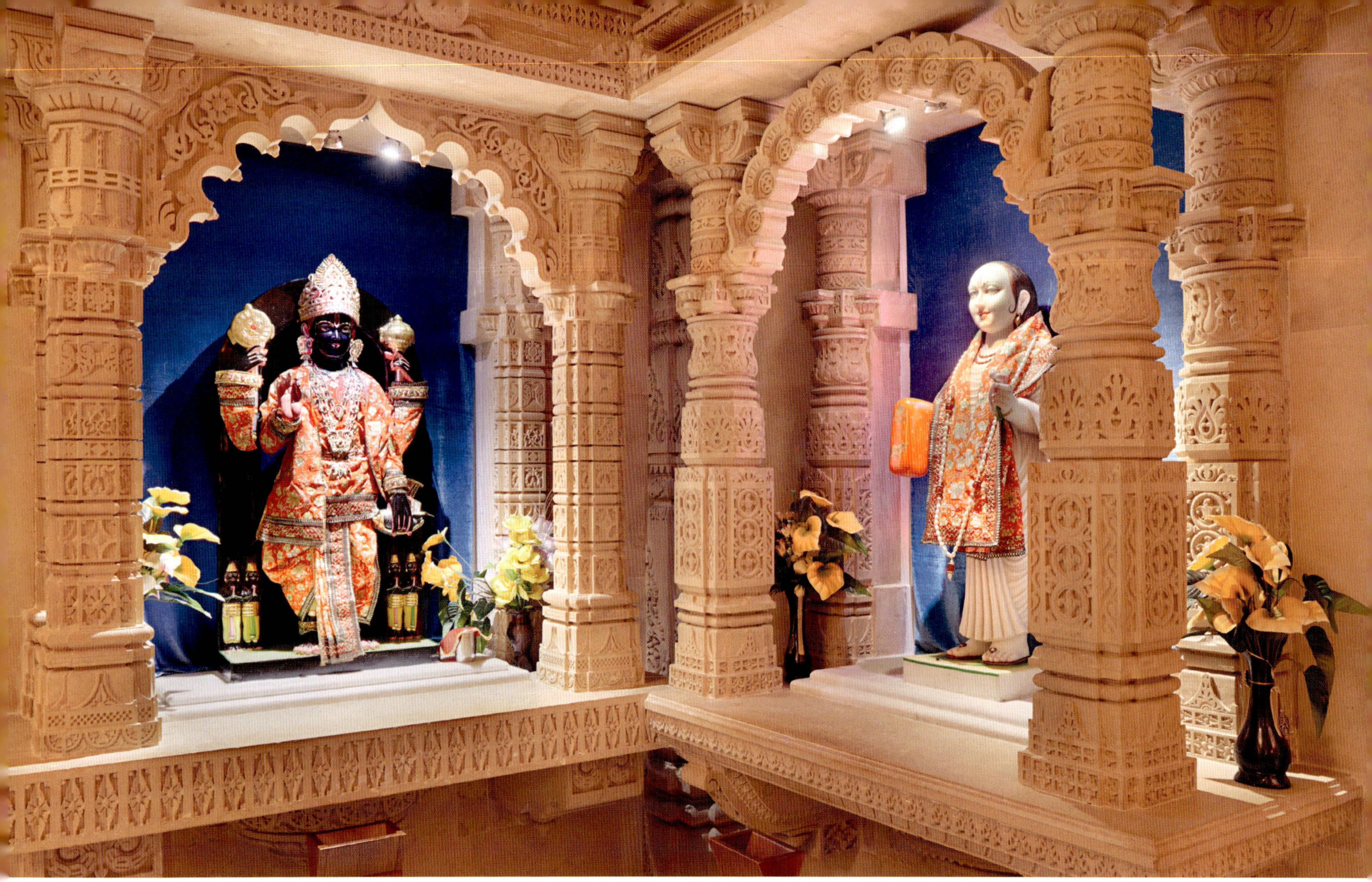

Only copper, silver or gold is permitted in construction.

and pink Bansipahad marble inside, all the stone coming from India. The architectural style is described as being in the Northern Indian tradition. No architect's name is associated with the temple.

There are eleven inner temples and eighteen sanctums housing forty-one *murtis*, including the following deities: Shri Ganeshji, Shri Jalaram Bapa, Shri Hanumanji, Shri Sahajanand Swami, Shri Amba Mataji, Shri Simandhar Swami, Shri Radha Krishna, Shri Ram Darbar, Shri Shrinathji, Shri Tirupati Balaji and Shri Shiv Parivar.

No underlying structural steel framework was used in the temple, nor is there even a single small subsidiary metallic beam or bolt anywhere. For spiritual reasons, iron-based materials are considered inauspicious in Hindu culture. All masonry is designed to be self-load-bearing. Only copper, silver or gold is permitted in construction, and there is indeed gold here at the highest point of the temple, in the gold-plated adornment on the spires, properly known as Dhaja Dand. Measured here, the temple is 66 ft (20 m) high. The Shri Sanatan Mandir at Wembley Temple covers 2.4 acres (1 ha).

The Shri Sanatan Hindu Mandir was constructed over fourteen years using funds raised by the charity Shri Vallabh Nidhi UK. It opened in the summer of 2010 with the Pran Prathistha ceremony to infuse spirit into the statues. The BBC reported then that its construction had cost £16 million.

CONTACT INFORMATION

Shri Sanatan Hinu Mandir,
Ealing Road, Wembley, HA0 4TA
https://svnuk.com/wembley-temple/

Above Gods and goddesses depicted inside the temple include Shri Ranchod Raiji (left); more than forty-one deities and spiritual preceptors are represented.

Opposite, above and below Two types of limestone are used for the interior and exterior; the colour on the outside is described as yellow.

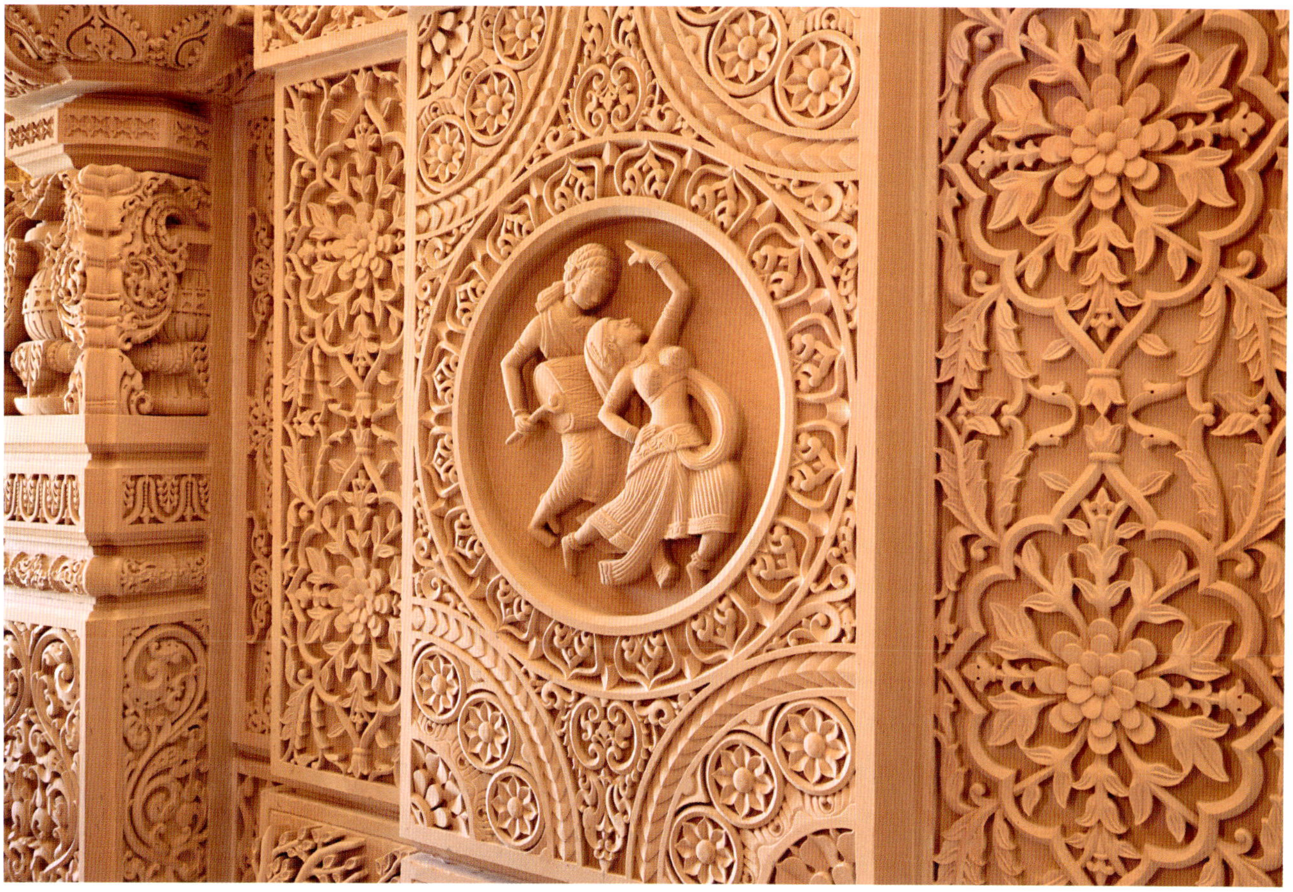

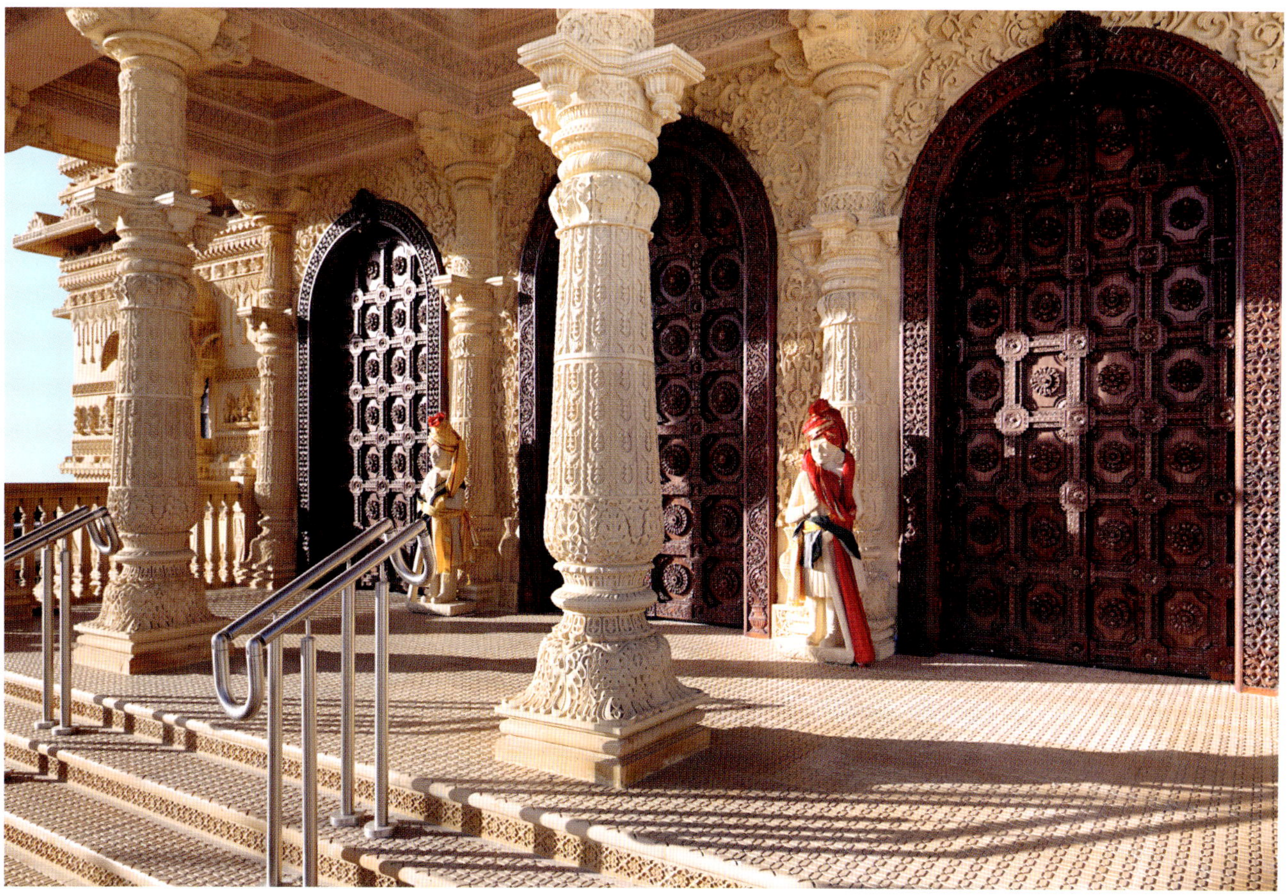

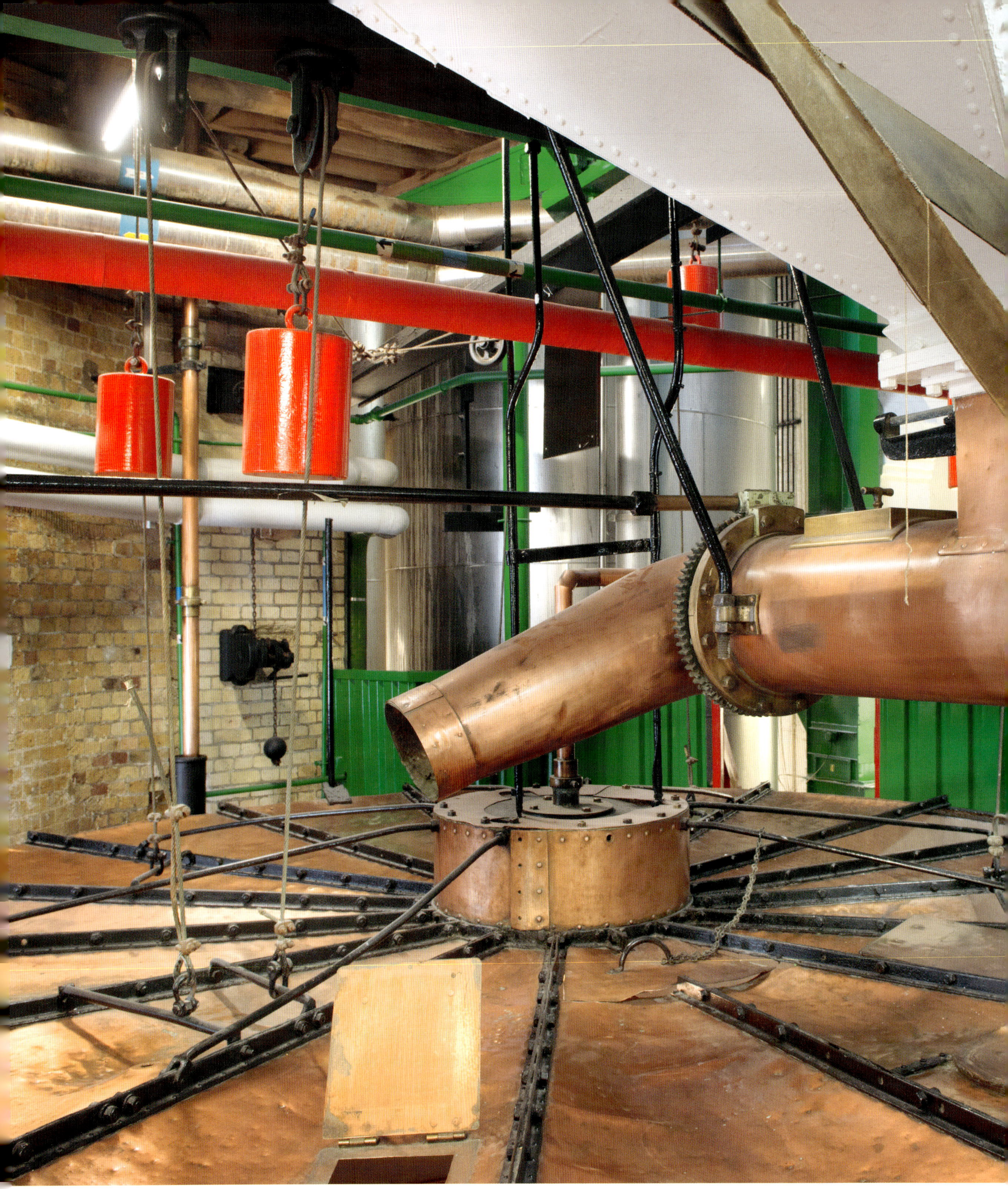

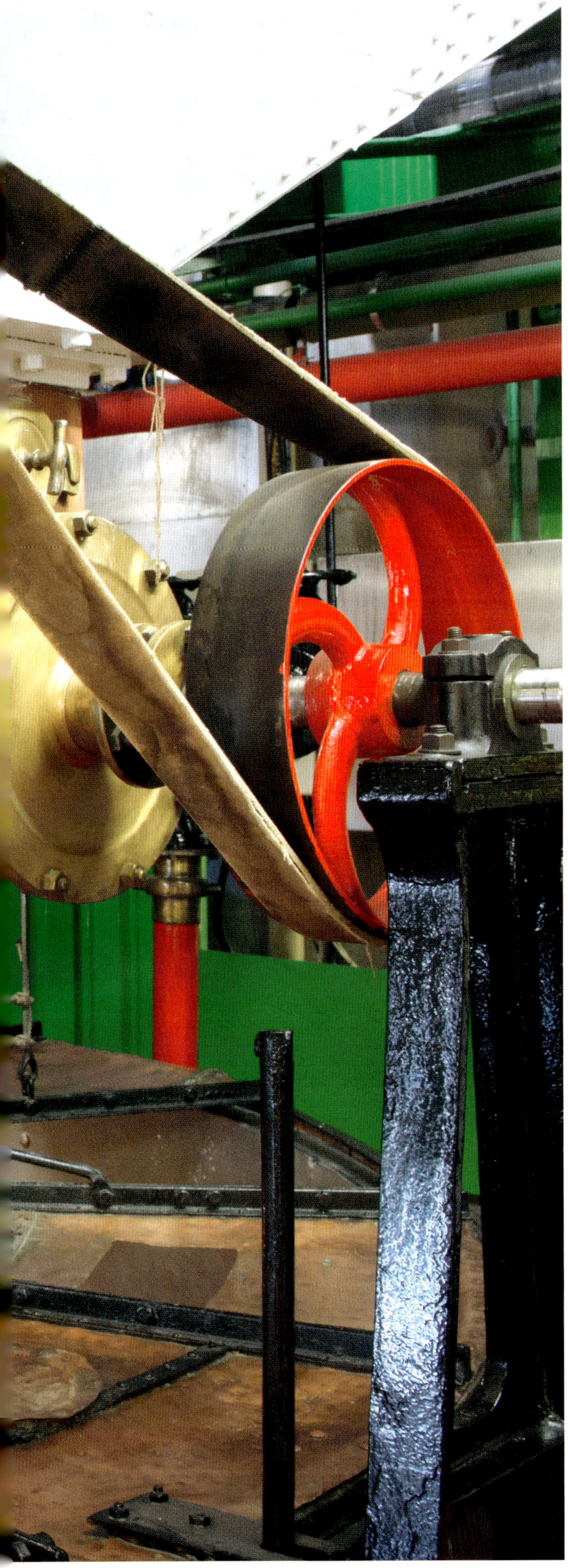

The old mash tun used for mixing ground malt with water for 125 years until 1993.

Fuller's Griffin Brewery

At Chiswick, under the sign of the Griffin, is Fuller's Brewery, the place where London Pride best bitter is made. Fuller's Griffin Brewery operates under the ownership of Asahi Group, which acquired the brewery from London's last big independent, Fuller, Smith & Turner, in 2019. It is London's oldest brewery in continuous production. Fuller's now separately runs its estate of nearly 400 pubs and hotels across London and the south of England.

'Beside the Thames since 1845' is the slogan, although this riverside site can be traced back to a domestic brewery in the garden of the stately home Bedford House on Chiswick Mall, when it was common for large households to brew their own beer. Close by, a cottage brewhouse was operated by the local Urlin family, both of these places being active in the 1660s. They were acquired and brought together as a commercial operation by Thomas Mawson in 1701. Thomas Mawson is still honoured today in the shape of the Mawson Arms, the pub located on the brewery site.

The Fuller family started to take a share in the brewery in 1829 and the partnership of John Bird Fuller, Henry Smith and John Turner took over in 1845. Descendants of these partners continued to manage and direct beer production until the Asahi acquisition of the brewery. The name Griffin, a mythical lion-eagle which is a guardian of treasure, was first applied to the brewery at Chiswick in 1816 and officially trademarked in 1892. Chiswick was

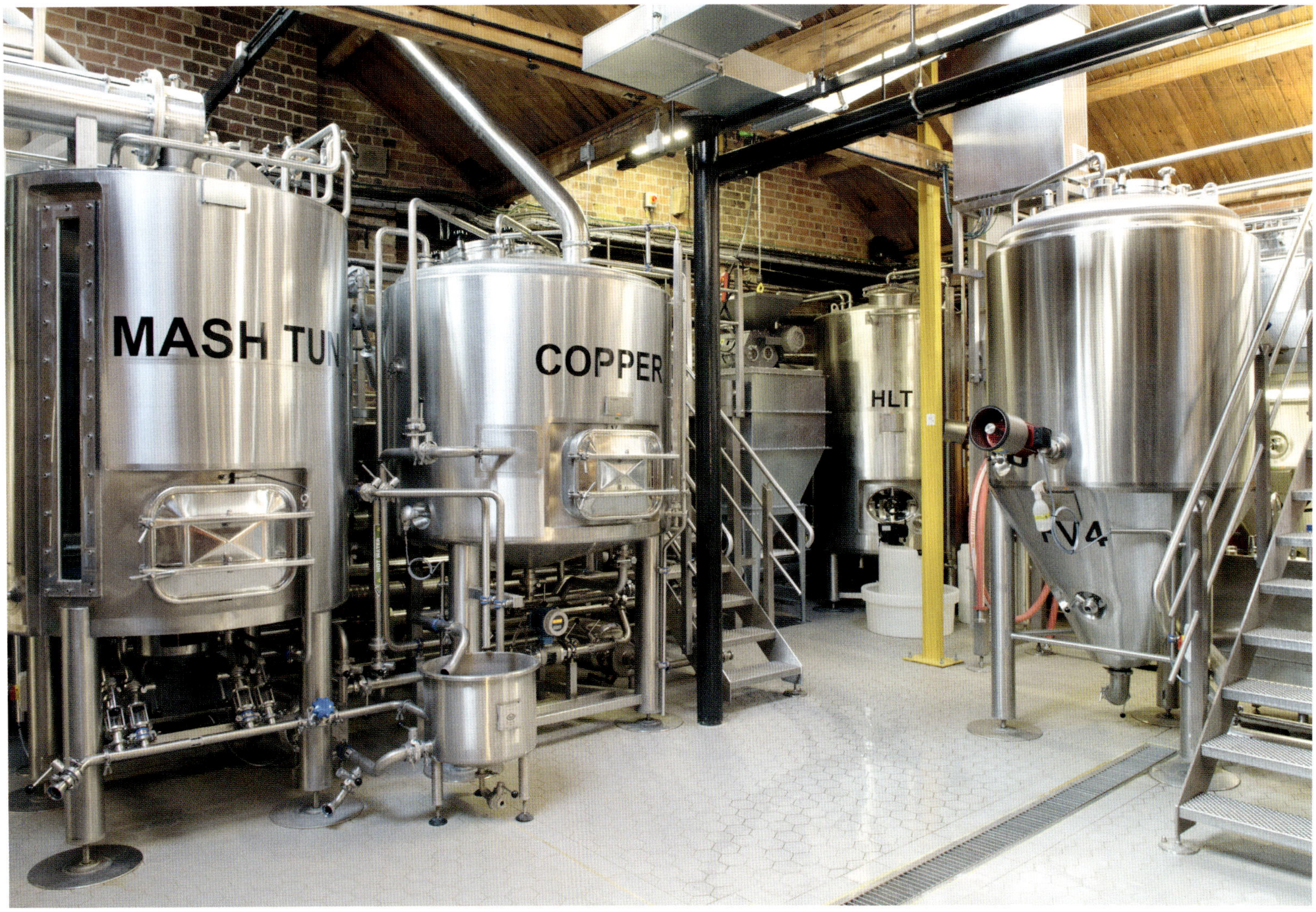

The pilot brewery for development and small-scale brewing.

once a village and the Griffin brewery was first supplied from boats on the Thames, with much of its output transported away by river. Later, a fleet of steam wagons was introduced. Unlike many breweries, the Griffin was never rail connected. By the late 1950s, London's road system and traffic levels had grown to the point that the major A4 arterial road had been cut through yards from the brewery gates. Fuller's Griffin Brewery became a prominent London landmark glimpsed by thousands of travellers.

The brewhouse at Chiswick holds gleaming stainless steel fermenters and twin mash tuns with a production capacity of more than 63 million pints each year, largely computer-controlled with robots handling the sorting and stacking of casks. In places, however, legacies from the old brewery remain – an ancient mash tun and an old London copper dating from the nineteenth century can still be seen, and across the cobbled yard is the former brewer's house, famous for its covering of wisteria, grown from the first plant of its type in England in 1816. The hock cellar, named after a style of harvest ale, also dates from this period. It is an old storeroom, which now serves as a showcase for Fuller's memorabilia and is a highlight on guided tours of the brewery.

In the early 1970s, when a time came to choose between new and old, Fuller's made a crucial decision about its brewing operations as consumer taste was approaching a turning point. The British market had been dominated by keg beers of increasing blandness made by filtration and pasteurization and pumped by carbon dioxide. This gave a stable, transportable product and led to the domination of the big seven brewers: Bass, Allied Whitbread, Watney, Scottish & Newcastle, Courage and Guinness. Fuller's were poised to renew their worn-out plant at that time and considered switching entirely to keg and bottled beer.

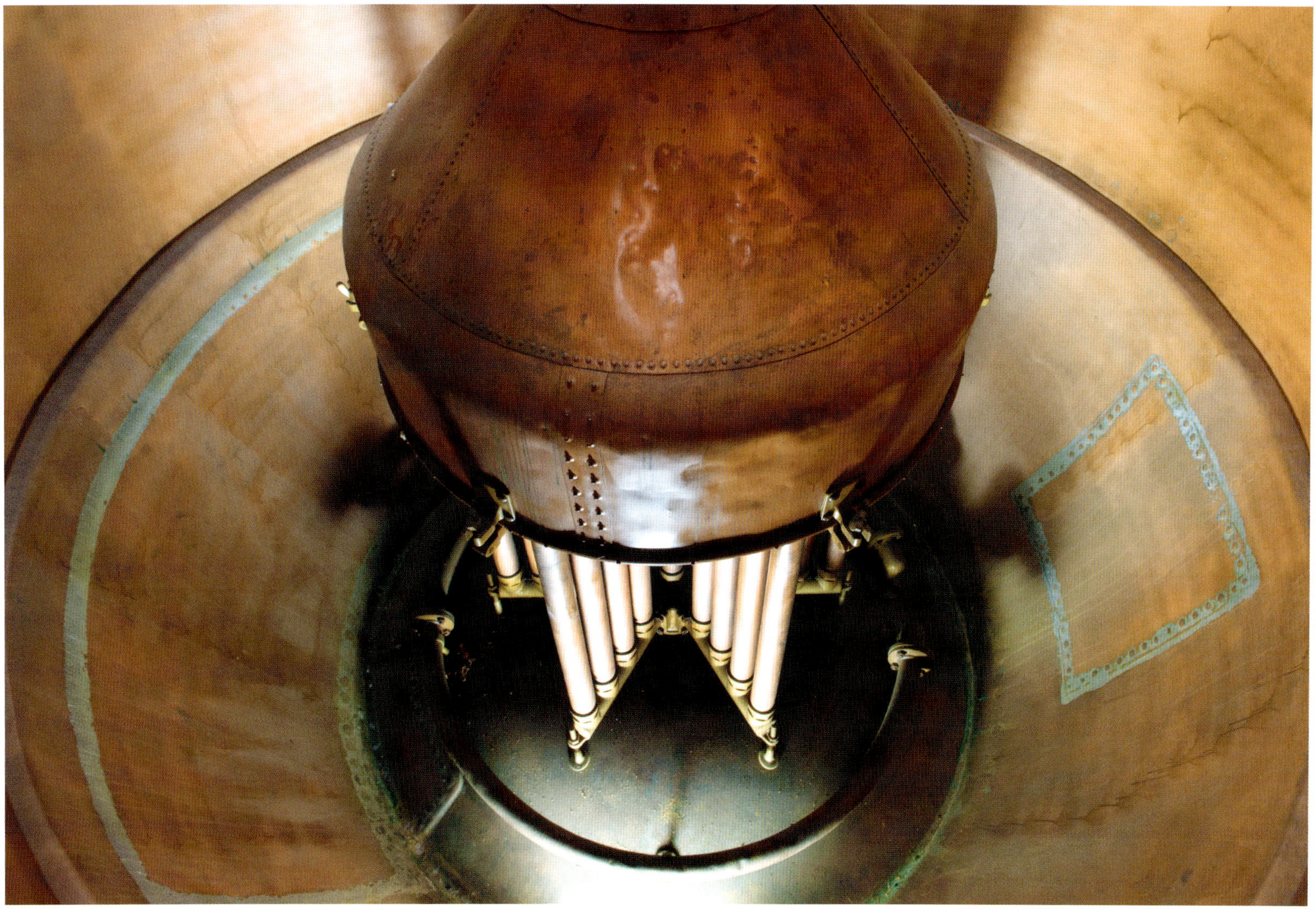

A heating element in the old London copper.

Against this notion came the Campaign for Real Ale (CAMRA), which tapped a growing public desire for a change in taste and supported smaller brewers. Fuller's decided to re-equip to efficiently brew mainly draught cask beers, and increased their home market and export sales. Between 1975 and 1986 much of the brewery was demolished, the landmark brick chimney removed and a new brewhouse and warehouse added.

In 1989 the big brewers were forced by counter-monopoly legislation to divest themselves of some of their pubs and at the same time permit their tenants to buy cask-conditioned ale from outside sources. This again favoured brewers such as Fuller's, which received an increase in orders and was able to more easily expand its own portfolio of pubs. Fuller's reputation as an authentic brewer for the real beer enthusiast has grown, and its range comprises 75 per cent cask ale, a lager and some keg beers, now produced by much-improved processes. London Pride, named for the hardy flower that grew in the rubble left by the Blitz, remains the flagship ale.

Fuller's launched a pilot brewery in its shop at the Griffin Brewery in 2018 to make some experimental beers in smaller quantities, about ten barrels per brew, which can be cask or keg or packaged in bottles. The first of these was dubbed Beer One, a particularly strong ale at 7 per cent alcohol by volume.

CONTACT INFORMATION

Fuller's Griffin Brewery,
Chiswick Lane, W4 2QB
https://www.fullersbrewery.co.uk/

Harrow School

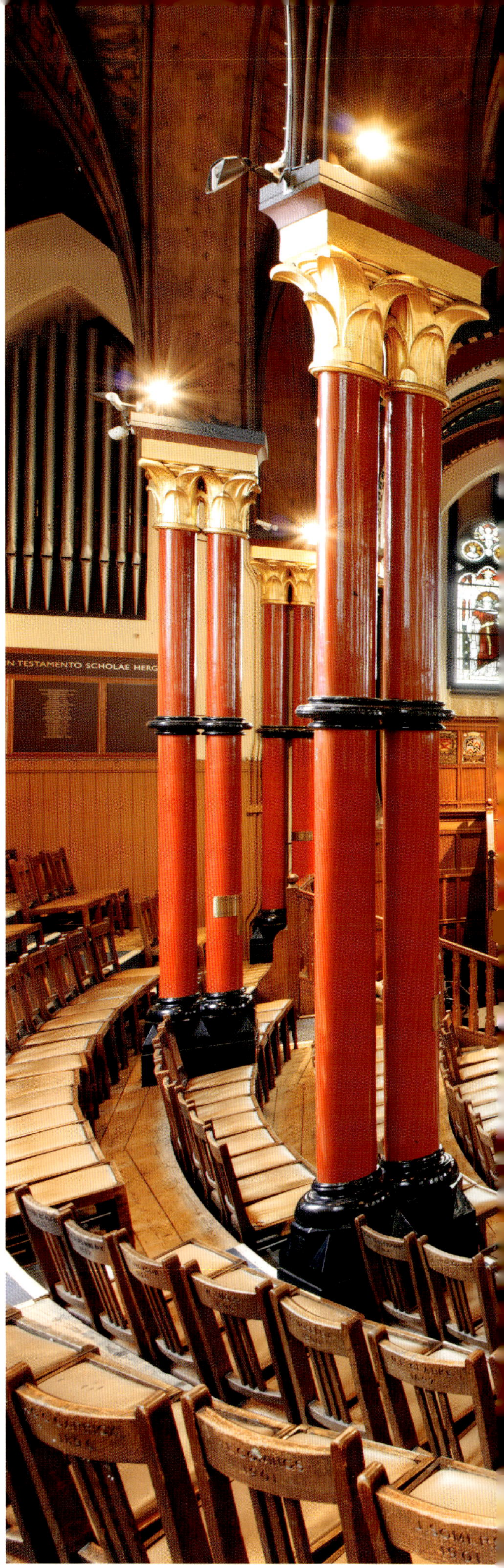

The Speech Room.

Harrow School, a boys' independent public school known usually just as 'Harrow', is located at Harrow on the Hill High Street, in north-west London. Although a school seems to have existed in the locale since 1243, it was not until 1572 that Harrow School was officially founded by a yeoman-farmer John Lyon, under a Royal Charter of Elizabeth I, and the schoolhouse was completed in 1615. One of the nine public schools reformed and regulated by the Public School Act (1868), Harrow usually has around 800 students, who live in a dozen boarding houses on a full-time basis, and whose school uniform features morning suits, top hats, straw hats and canes.

Celebrated alumni include seven British Prime Ministers, including Palmerston, Baldwin and Churchill, and also Jawaharlal Nehru, the first Prime Minister of India, and members of both houses of the UK Parliament. The literary world is represented by Trollope and Byron, and Harrow School's theatrical talent includes Edward and James Fox, and Benedict Cumberbatch. Old soldiers include Field Marshal Alexander, as well as the 7th Earl of Cardigan (who disgraced himself at Balaclava) and twenty recipients of the VC.

Harrow School's famous Fourth Form occupies the entire ground floor of the original seventeenth-century schoolhouse. The internal walls of the room are lined with moulded and fielded black panelling rising to a height of 7 ft (2 m), and, beginning with a T. Basil in 1701, generations of boys have carved their

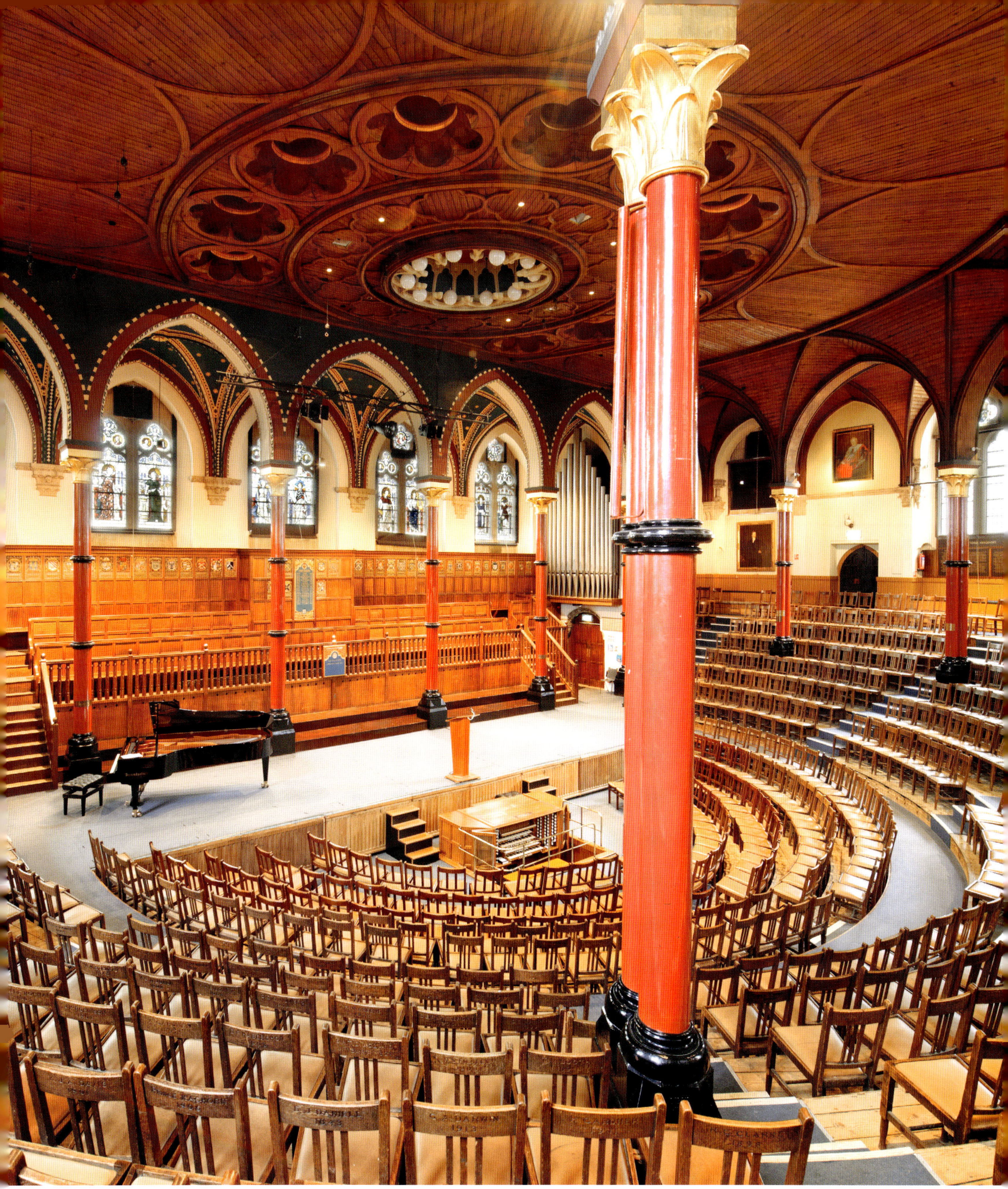

names into the wood. Standing in the middle of the west wall is a stone fireplace from the same era, with an eared surround, a central panel in the head and a cornice with carved brackets. Seventeenth-century chairs with flat-topped desks were positioned in tiers on both sides of the room, with a canopied Headmaster's seat at one end from where enthroned 'beaks' (teachers) could survey their pupils, while an usher seated in an armchair at the other end likely did his best to maintain order. On an outside wall is a plaque honouring the future Earl of Shaftesbury, who, the story goes, upon seeing a pauper's funeral, burned with 'shame and indignation', and was inspired to serve the poor and oppressed.

With so many former pupils undeniably associated with the uppermost levels of the British establishment, and its association with power and leadership, Harrow may seem a lofty hidden establishment, but it also has a human scale. Despite the magnificence of the panels, chandeliers, stained glass windows and Jacobean furniture of the Alex Fitch Room, a poignant story lies behind its creation. Alex Fitch was killed in the First World War at the age of nineteen, shortly after leaving Harrow. In consideration of his happy days at the school, his mother used the family wealth to construct a memorial in his memory. Initially, she suggested building an indoor swimming pool (a rarity at that time). Harrow, however, courteously declined, reportedly on the grounds her idea was a touch vulgar. Undeterred, Mrs Fitch proposed a grand room for entertaining, with that suggestion being accepted. Constructed from floorboards and wood panelling formerly from an Tudor ship, the room has a serenity magnified by the elegance of a bygone age. Stained-glass windows depict Queen Elizabeth I granting the school's charter to John Lyon, while another window displays the arms of sovereigns who have been to the school, including those of Queen Victoria, who visited in 1848, and Queen Elizabeth II in 1971. But taking precedence over these monarchs is a portrait of the young Alex Fitch hanging above the stone fireplace. The light illuminating his portrait has never been extinguished.

In what is called Old Schools Building, the Old Speech Room was built between 1819 and 1821. By 1871, however, the school governors and headmaster resolved to celebrate the tercentenary of John Lyon's charter with the construction of a hall capable of seating entire school. Designed by the architect William Burges, the red-brick building has a semi-circular shape whose straight eastern front runs parallel to the High Street. A north tower was added in 1919, before the attachment of a south tower in 1925, the bell of which summons the school to the chapel and the speech room. With its tiered seating, the room's interior resembles an amphitheatre, with a timber boarding ceiling, the vaulting of which is supported on pointed arches at the top of fourteen paired columns, decorated in red, blue and gold. The principal windows in the auditorium are grand in scale, with semi-circular heads and an intricate design of arches and roundels. The chamber's purpose was to imbue pupils with confidence through the art of public speaking, with many an aspirant orator later making his mark in parliament. As Lord Byron wrote of the Speech Room in his poem, 'On a Distant View of the Village and School of Harrow on the Hill': 'I once more view the room with spectators surrounded.'

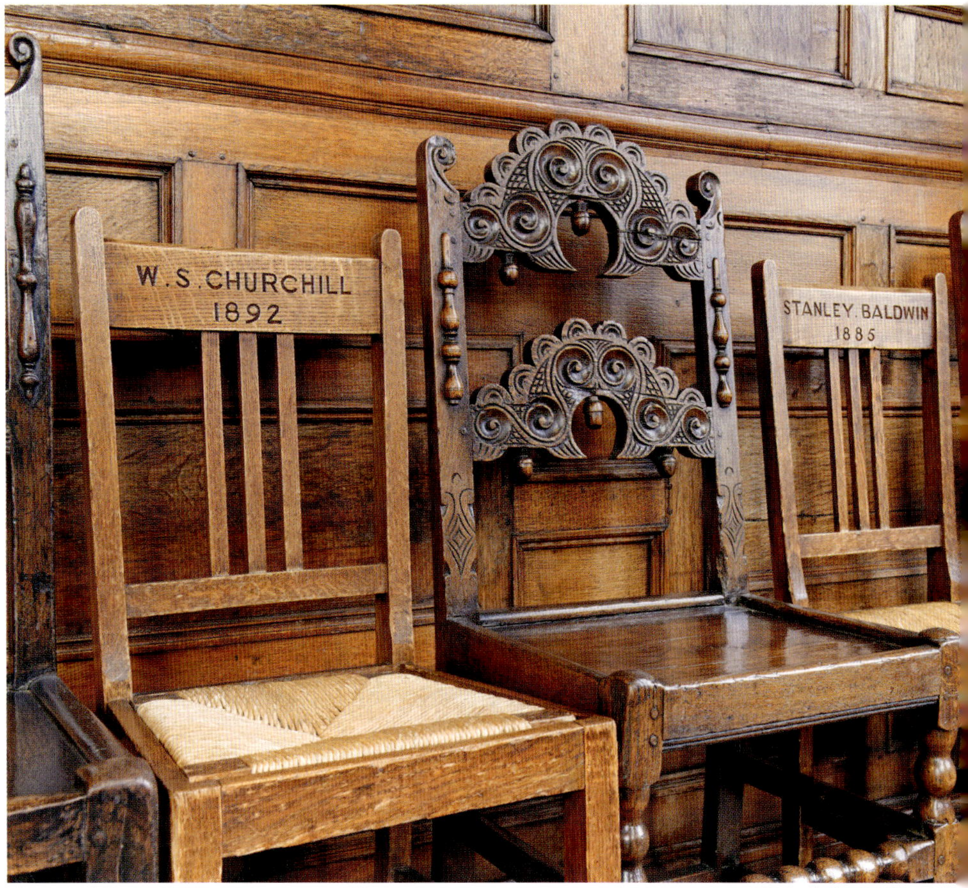

Above Pupils' chairs in the Alex Fitch Room.

Opposite, above Rackets court. Harrow also has courts for squash and fives, and of course tennis. The school claims that squash was invented there some time after 1830, when boys discovered that a punctured rubber ball that squashed on impact produced a game with a great variety of shots. Rackets is a faster game, using a hard white rubber ball.

Opposite, below The famous Fourth Form, with boys' names carved throughout, and birching block in right-hand corner.

CONTACT INFORMATION

Harrow School,
5 High Street, Harrow on the Hill, Middlesex, HA1 3HP
https://www.harrowschool.org.uk/

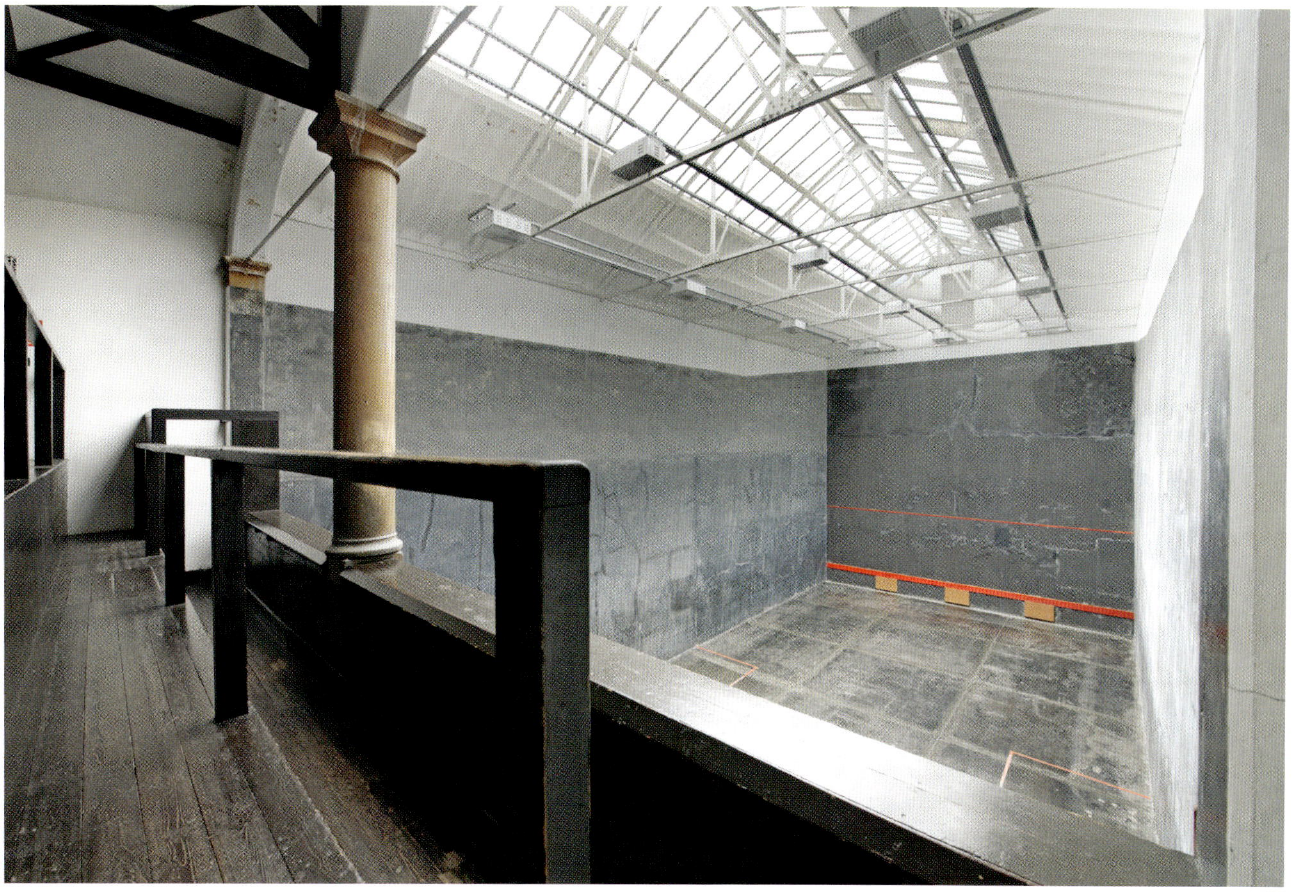

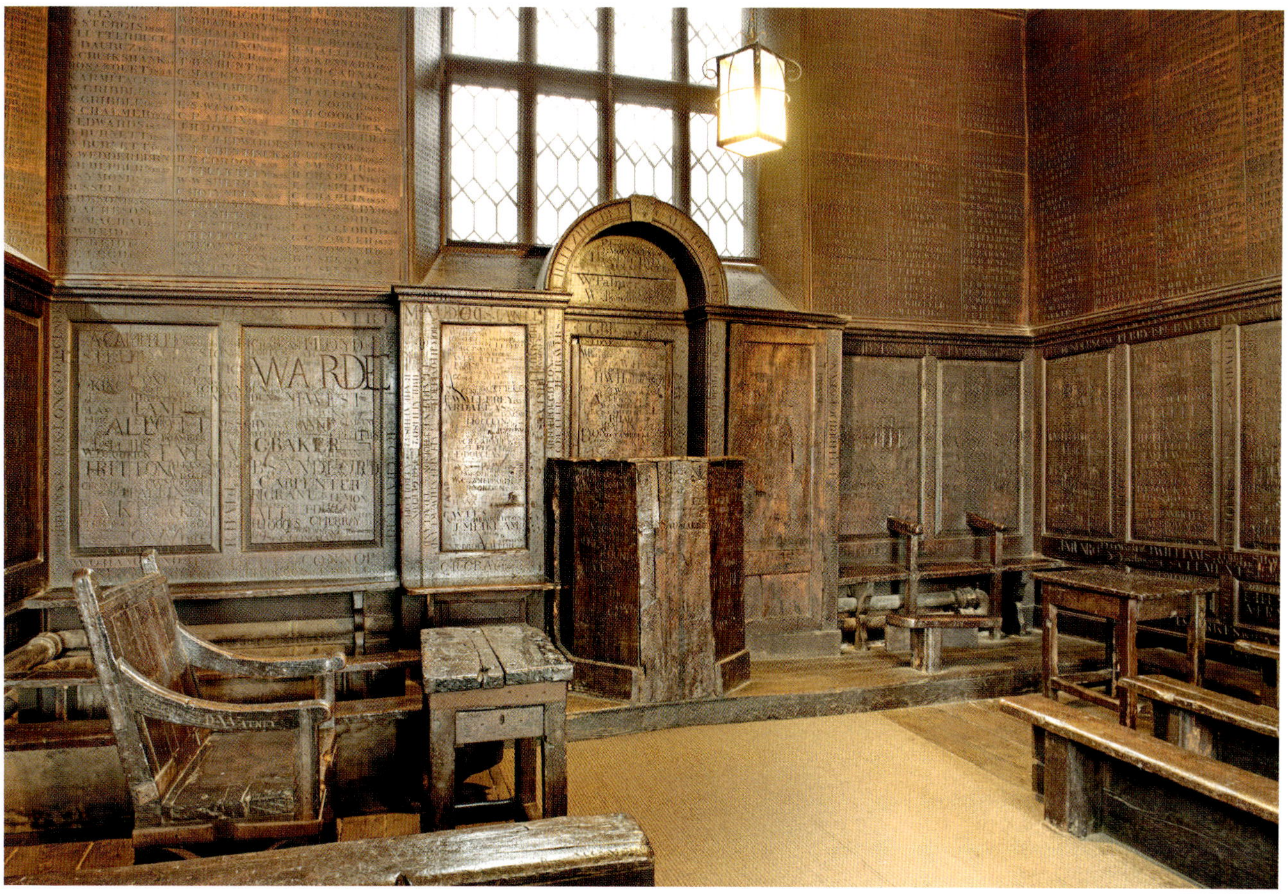
WARDE

Museum of Brands

The Museum of Brands is a mosaic of many things: tins, toys and games, packets, paper, products and puzzles, all assembled across a long timeline. The man who brought it all together, consumer historian Robert Opie, once identified the supermarket as the true gallery of commercial art, a place where thousands of designs are on display at any moment. Given such widespread exposure, there may have seemed little scope for a museum devoted to everyday consumer items, but the Robert Opie collection soon gained a special fascination. 'I was struck by the idea that I should save the packaging which would otherwise surely disappear forever,' writes Opie. 'The collection offers evidence of a dynamic commercial system that delivers thousands of desirable items from all corners of the world. It is a feat arguably more complex than sending man to the Moon, but one still taken for granted.'

The museum does not give much space to exploring cerebral notions of the crossover of advertising into art, but plays it straight with a collection of more than 12,000 products, and specifically of the packaging that encloses them. There is a twist, however, as the result turns out to be a very cleverly curated social history of Britain.

A visitor is invited to enter the 'Time Tunnel' – a corridor of cabinets – and experience the first blossoming of advertising and branding during the Victorian age. There are mugs illustrated with images of Florence Nightingale and even of Crimea, as well

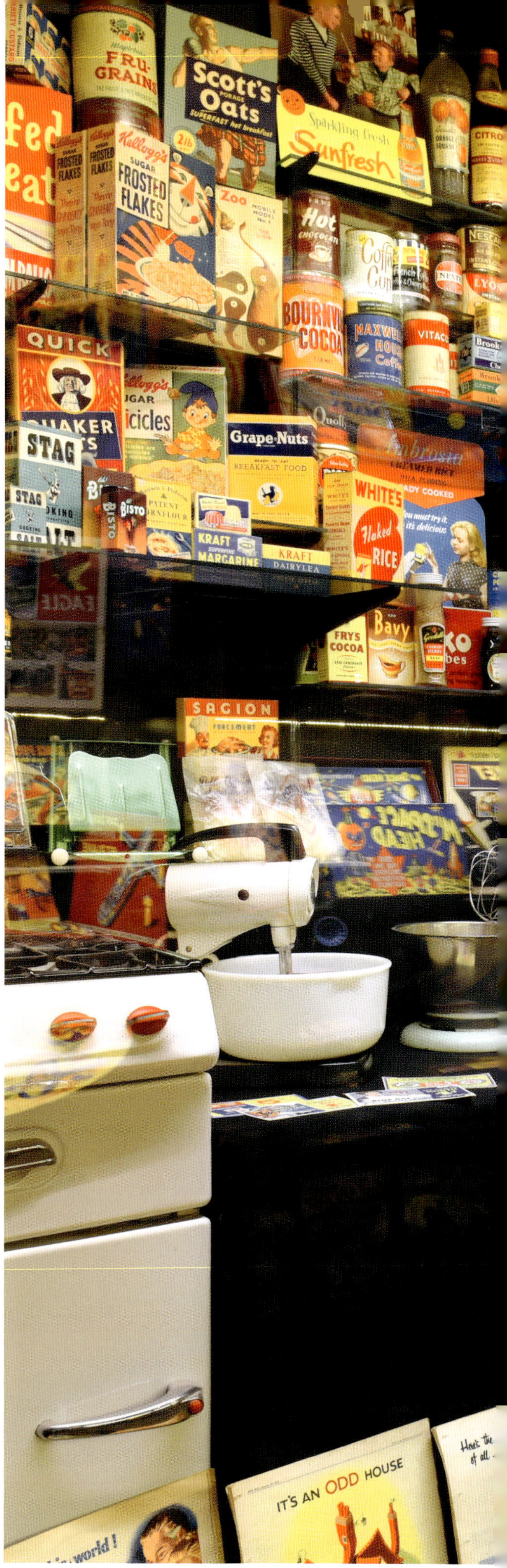

1950s-era packaging and products on display at the Museum of Brands.

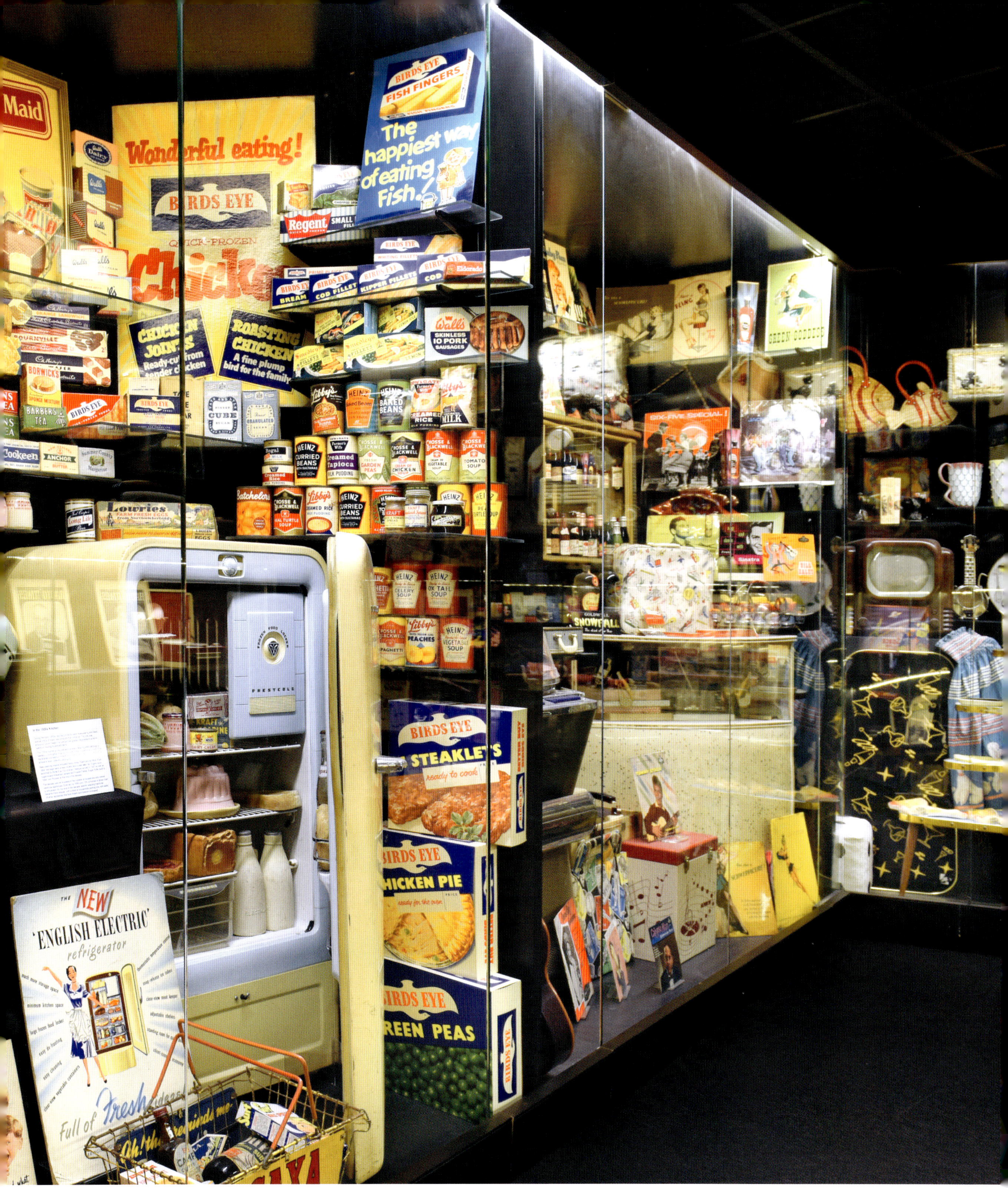
Maid
Wonderful eating!
BIRDS EYE
QUICK-FROZEN
BIRDS EYE FISH FINGERS
The happiest way of eating Fish!
CHICKEN JOINTS Ready-cut from tender chicken
ROASTING CHICKEN A fine plump bird for the family
Regent
Wall's SKINLESS 10 PORK SAUSAGES
HEINZ BAKED BEANS
HEINZ CURRIED BEANS
Batchelors
Libby's
Cookeen
ANCHOR
BORWICKS
Lowries FARM FRESH EGGS
FRESTCOLD
SIX-FIVE SPECIAL
GREEN GODDESS
SNOWFALL
BIRDS EYE STEAKLETS ready to cook
BIRDS EYE
HICKEN PIE
ready for the oven
BIRDS EYE
REEN PEAS
THE NEW 'ENGLISH ELECTRIC' refrigerator
Full of Fresh

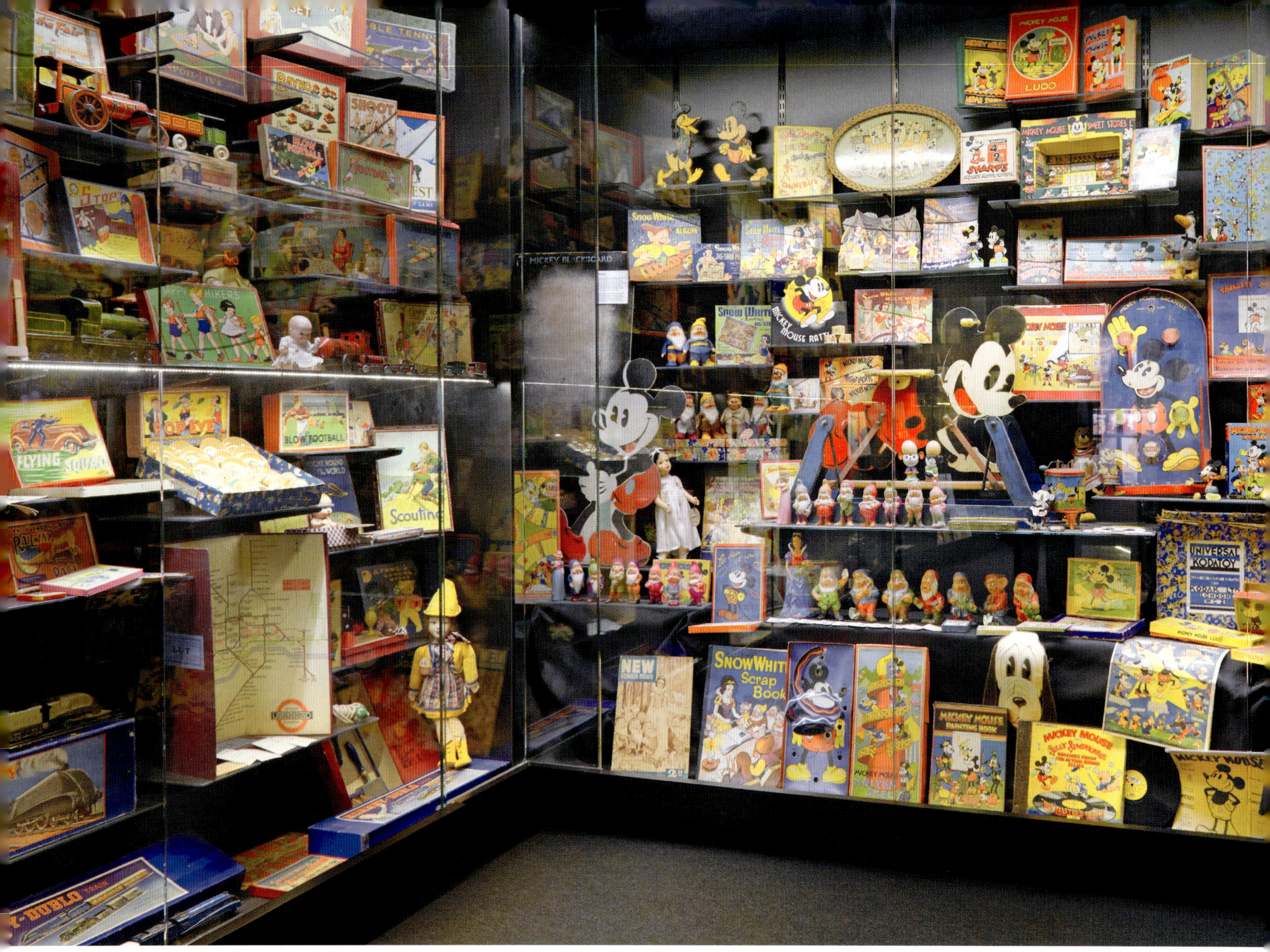

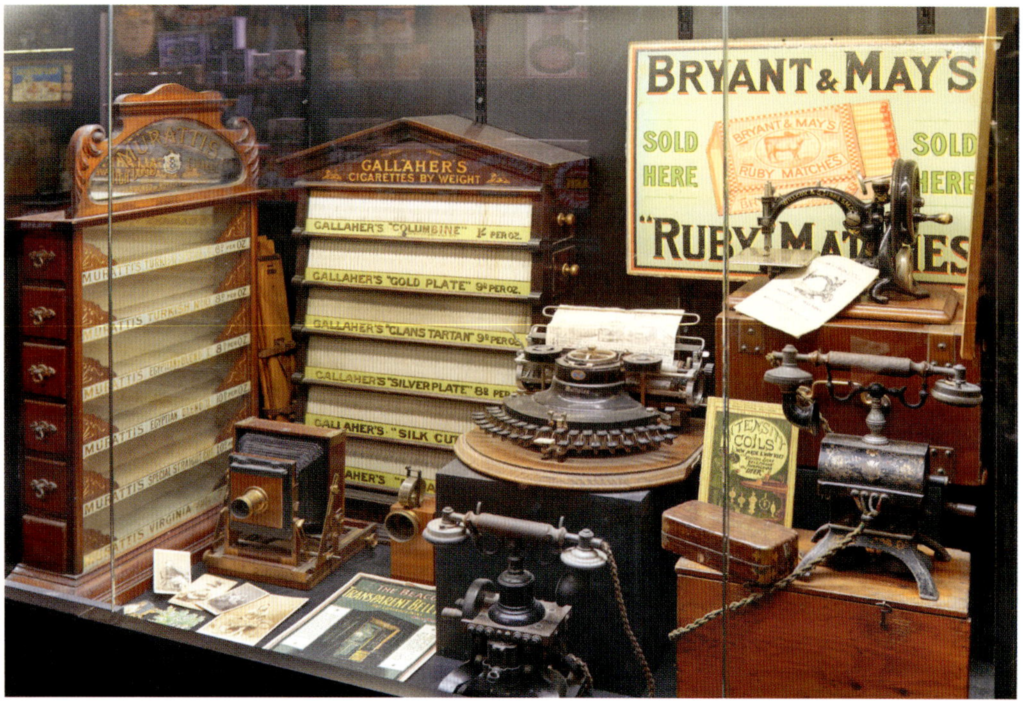

Above A selection of toys and games, including beloved cartoon characters from the 1930s.

Right Victorian-era technology on display, as well as a case for selling cigarettes by weight.

Chocolate boxes and matchboxes became canvases for a growing art form.

as plates with images of Queen Victoria and her consort, Albert. The arrival of colour printing provided the impact for the labelling and branding seen in Colman's mustard and Bird's custard packages. Newspapers and magazines were proliferating, and the Valentine's card arrived alongside the first jigsaw puzzles, then known as dissected puzzles. A milestone was the Great Exhibition of 1851, a monument to the very promotion of Britain itself. Chocolate boxes and matchboxes became canvases for a growing art form, and there is a reminder that the packaging for household soaps and cleaning products might have been designed to appeal to servants as much as masters.

Robert Opie, who had collected packaging since childhood, was working as a market researcher in the 1970s and gaining a special awareness of products. He created an exhibition at the Victoria & Albert Museum in 1975 – 'The Pack Age: A Century of Wrapping It Up' – with around 3,000 items, and the exhibition drew an attendance of 80,000 people in a few weeks. He later said that he resisted the word 'museum' for what he had assembled, but the collection went on to form the basis of the first Museum of Brands, Packaging and Advertising, which opened at Gloucester Docks in 1984. The ever-growing collection was moved to London in 2005 and to its present location on Lancaster Road in 2015, with space quadrupled.

The space has enabled a historical continuity that spans 170 years. The 'Time Tunnel' continues through the Edwardian years, charting the fads of roller skating and table tennis, the first era of motoring and designs in the Art Noveau style of the times.

The cleverness of the exhibition lies in taking threads and themes through the ages, especially in printed ephemera. Jigsaw puzzles and board games are punctuation marks for a whole century, one example being an astonishing game called Sanctions, released just after the end of the First World War with a nod to the post-armistice arrangements. There are also later games based on TV series of the 1960s, such as *Doctor Who* and *The Flintstones*. One display is completely devoted to Dan Dare and another to *Thunderbirds*.

Shredded Wheat, promoted with the slogan 'Busy folk prefer this breakfast', was colourfully packaged with an illustration of the Art Deco factory at Welwyn Garden City where it was produced on the box. Food products and brands are the most recognizable packages in the collection and the word 'iconic', overused but unavoidable, must be applied to thousands of these exhibits.

The evolution of toy packaging is likewise traced across time, particularly well represented during the 1930s, but it is not all kids' stuff. One of the most important platforms for branding was clearly cigarette sales, here unflinchingly explored, from a case designed to sell cigarettes by weight through the coming of the filter tip to the marketable virtues of the king-size cigarettes of the 1950s, and finishing with a rare pack of Three Castles.

Historical events are placed as markers throughout to provide perspective, particularly the dates of wars, the Festival of Britain, coronations, jubilees and regal weddings, and there is a strong impression that the Royal Family are sometimes consumed as a brand through memorabilia.

There is even a nod to the notion of the medium becoming the message in the shape of a bank of TV sets and in a display of transistor radios, which opened another pathway for advertising through sound and vision. The 'Time Tunnel' continues into the 1980s and beyond with electronic games displacing cardboard and counters.

The museum inevitably harnesses nostalgia and self-identification on the part of the visitors, who are invited to share their thoughts with the museum under the Brand Memories programme. The museum has a garden, a café and a gift shop.

CONTACT INFORMATION

Museum of Brands,
111–117 Lancaster Road, Notting Hill, W11 1QT
https://museumofbrands.com/

Emery Walker House

William Morris may be the foremost name in the Arts & Crafts movement, which transformed decorative style and design in late-Victorian times. Emery Walker's name is less recognized, although his collaboration and friendship with Morris made him an important figure in the movement. With Morris and others, he founded the Arts & Craft Exhibition Society. A printer, engraver and expert typeface designer by trade, with particular skill as a photographer, he influenced and advised Morris on the creation of the Kelmscott Press. Kelmscott House was Morris's house at Upper Mall, Hammersmith, along the riverside from where Walker made his home. The press published a series of more than fifty titles in a high aesthetic style, some illustrated by artist Edward Burne-Jones. This was at the heart of the Gothic Revival, following William Morris's interests in furniture, fabrics and wallpaper design, and craft manufacture.

Emery had joined the Society for Protection of Ancient Buildings (SPAB), established by Morris. They were friends who had met through the newly emerging Social Democratic Federation, a forerunner of the Labour Party. After Morris's death, Emery Walker continued in printing and publishing with a partnership in The Doves Press, based at 1 Hammersmith Terrace (named after the pub close by at 16 Upper Mall). The Doves Press is credited with the finest work in the Arts & Crafts tradition, influencing typography and book design across Europe and America.

The drawing room with a portrait of Emery Walker over the fireplace. The black basalt teapot is by Spode, and other pieces on the table belonged to Dante Gabriel Rossetti. The carpet is by Morris & Co.

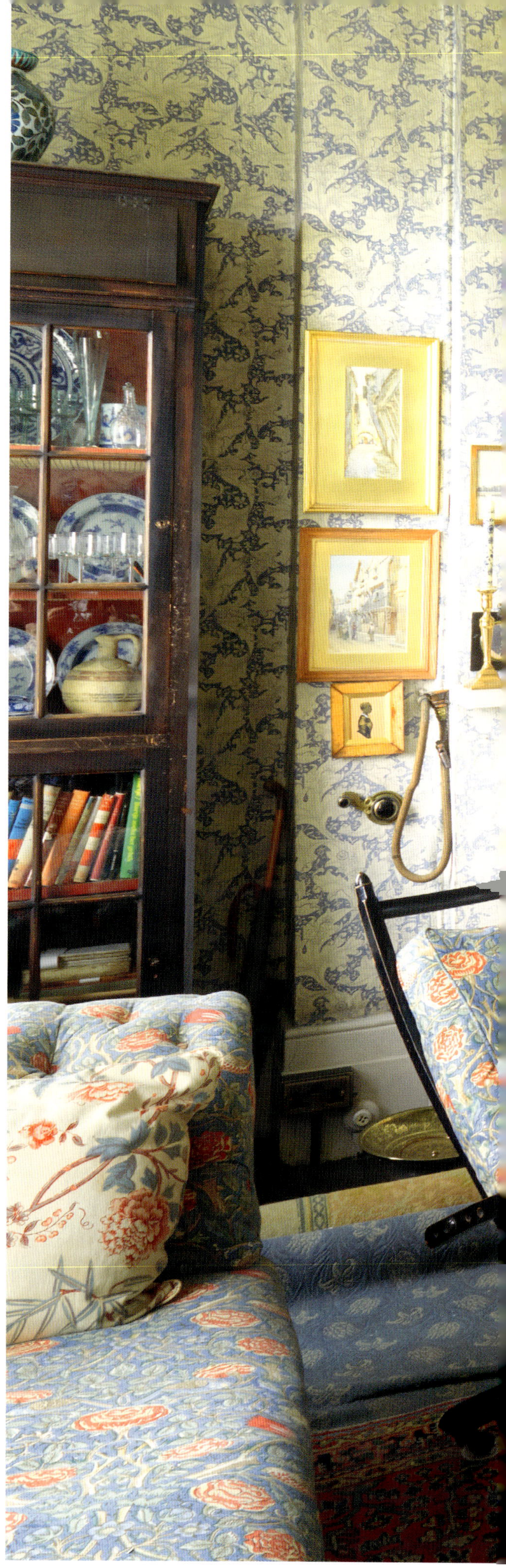

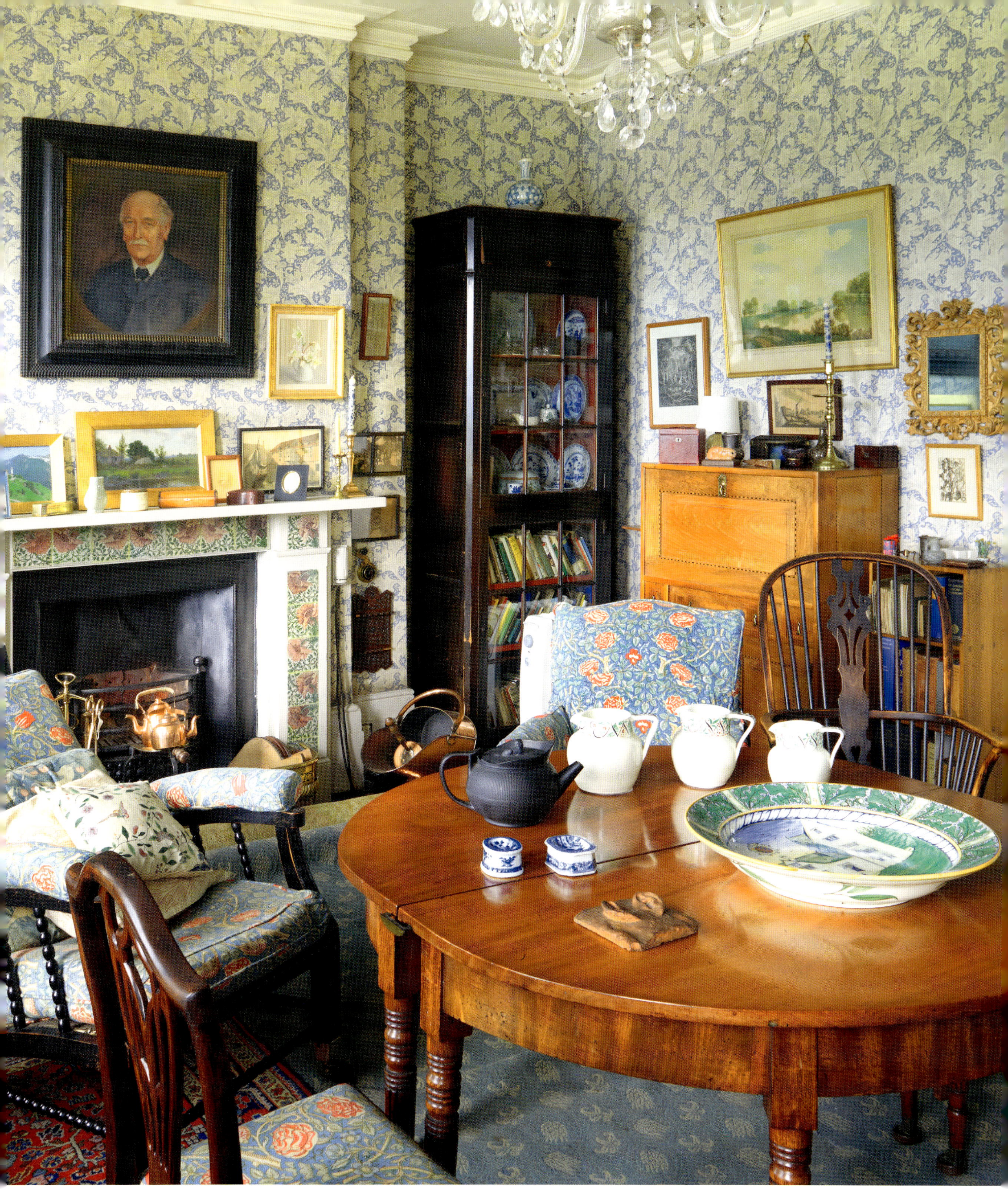

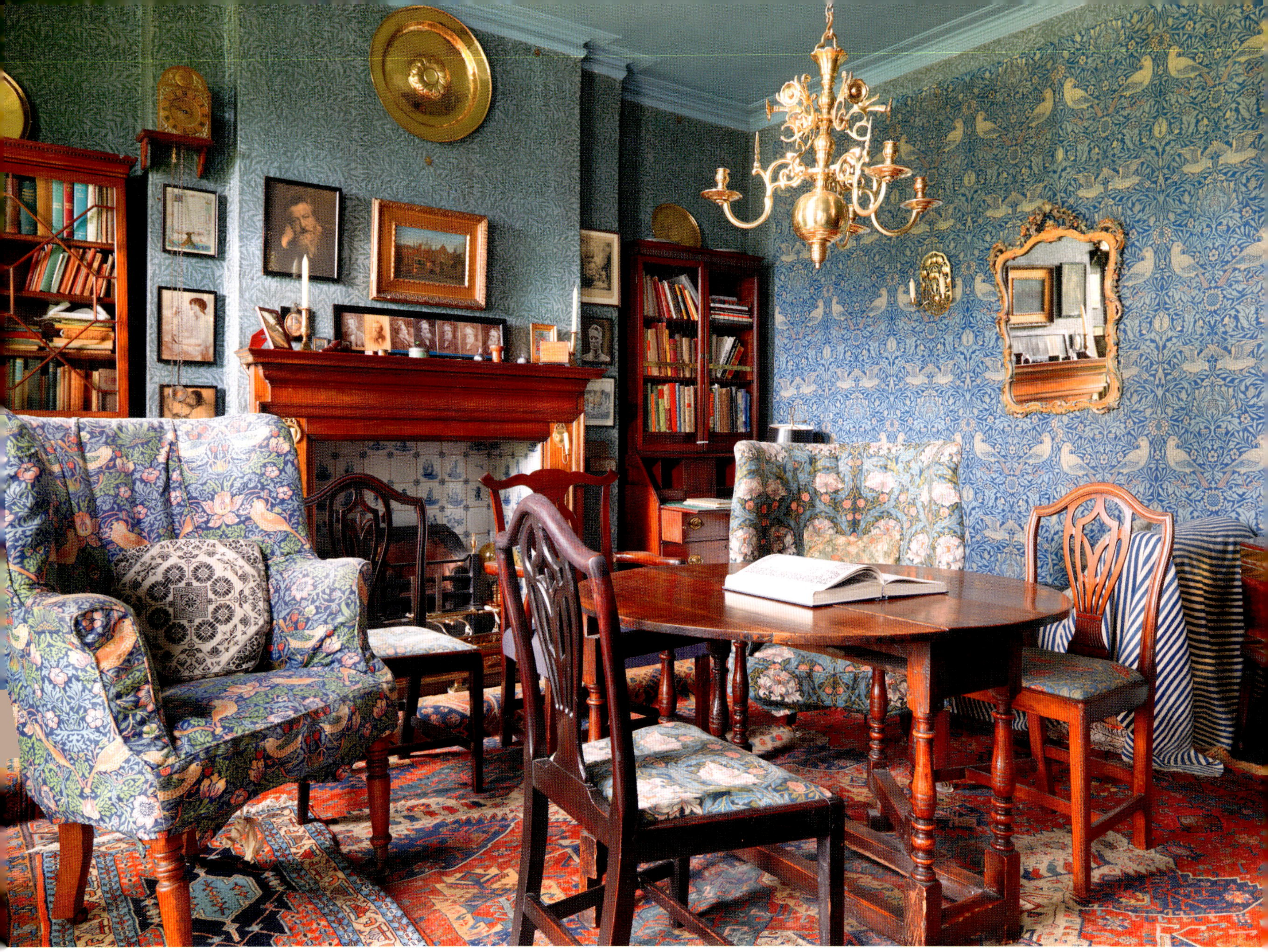

Above The dining room. The wall to the right is covered by Morris & Co.'s 'Bird' woollen hanging, handblocked wallpaper 'Willow', by Morris & Co.

Right The conservatory houses a vine reputedly grown from a cutting taken from William Hogarth's house in Chiswick. The steps lead to the river through a garden retaining a Victorian layout.

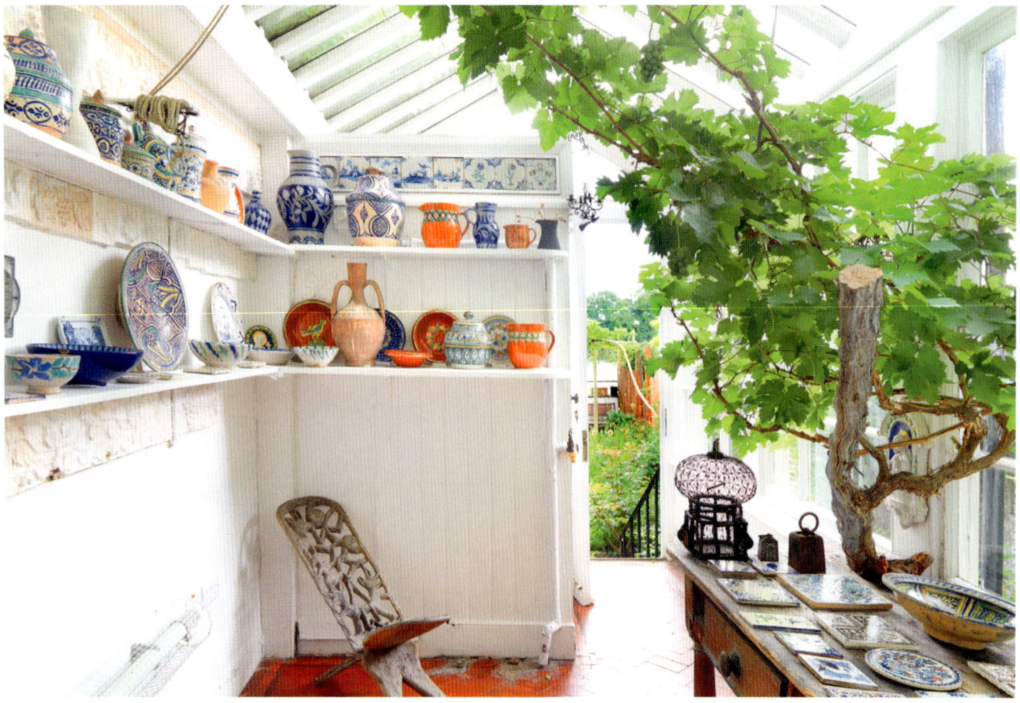

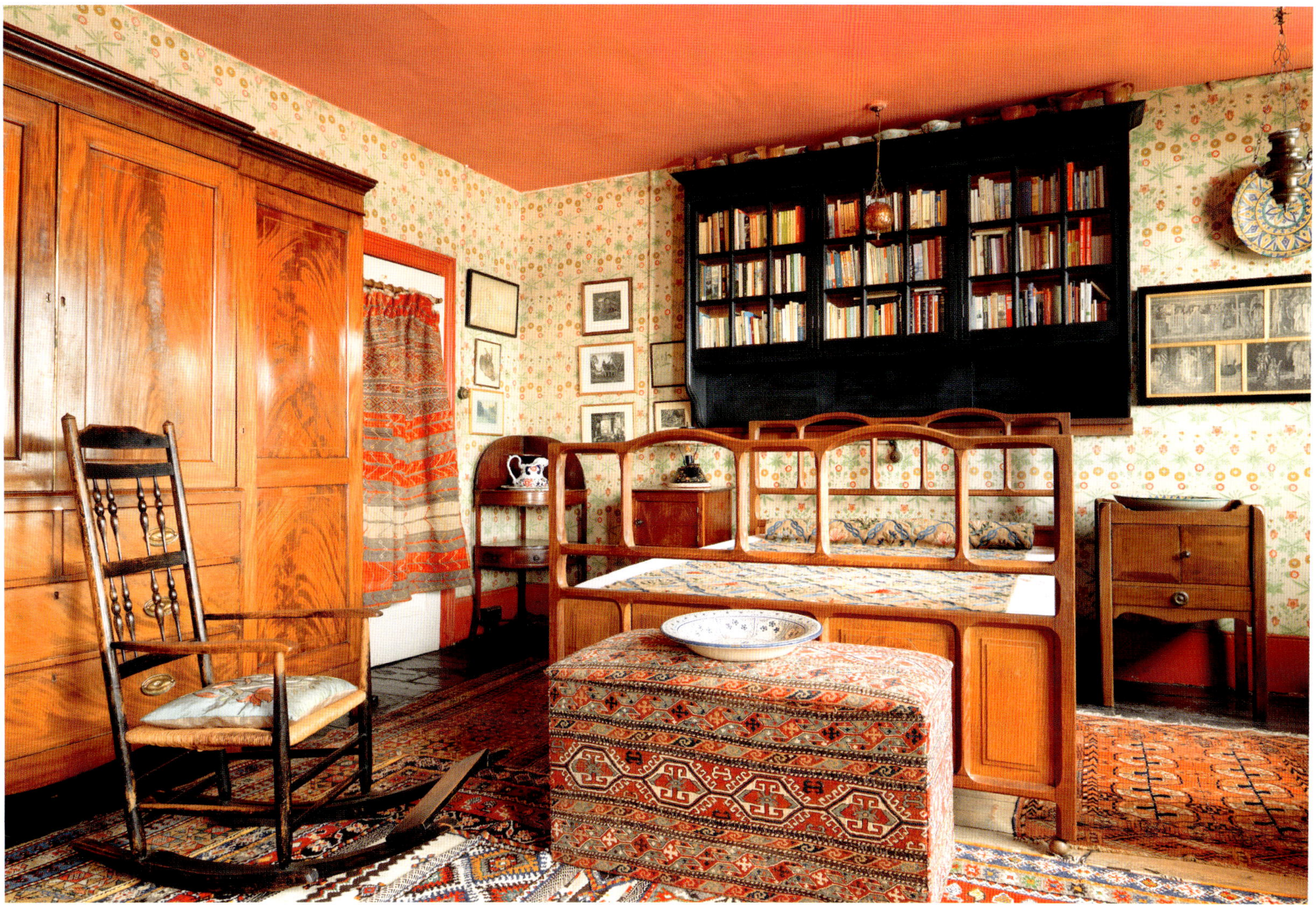

The main bedroom, with round-seated chairs from Morris & Co.'s 'Sussex' range, first made in about 1865.

When Walker died in 1933 the house was maintained by his daughter Dorothy Walker and then by her companion Elizabeth de Hass. It was handed over to the Emery Walker Trust in 1999. Only minor changes had been made to the house since it was completed in the 1760s. It was found to survive exactly as decorated and furnished for Walker, using wallpapers, textiles and furniture by Morris and other members of the Arts & Crafts movement, and can claim to be the most authentic Arts & Crafts home in Britain. There is William Morris linoleum in the kitchen, woollen hangings in the dining room, carpet in the dining room and furniture throughout. A drawer in Walker's desk contains personal mementos of Morris, his spectacles and pens and a cutting of his hair.

The blue plaque on the outside wall describes Sir Emery Walker as a typographer and antiquary, recognizing his scholarly knowledge of historic book design and production. The house is part of a Georgian terrace built with its back facing the Thames in a place that has seen a particular concentration of art, artists and creativity. Emery Walker lived first in 3 Hammersmith Terrace from 1879 to 1903. Sculptor, lithographer and typographer Eric Gill had a studio in Hammersmith Terrace and later the painter Victor Passmore lived there. May Morris, Morris's youngest daughter, an embroiderer and designer, ran the embroidery department of Morris & Co. from 8 Hammersmith Terrace and lived there for a time. Eric Ravilious lived in Upper Mall. J.W.M. Turner lived on Upper Mall and sketched Hammersmith Bridge under construction in 1827.

CONTACT INFORMATION

Emery Walker House,
7 Hammersmith Terrace, W6 9TS
https://www.emerywalker.org.uk/

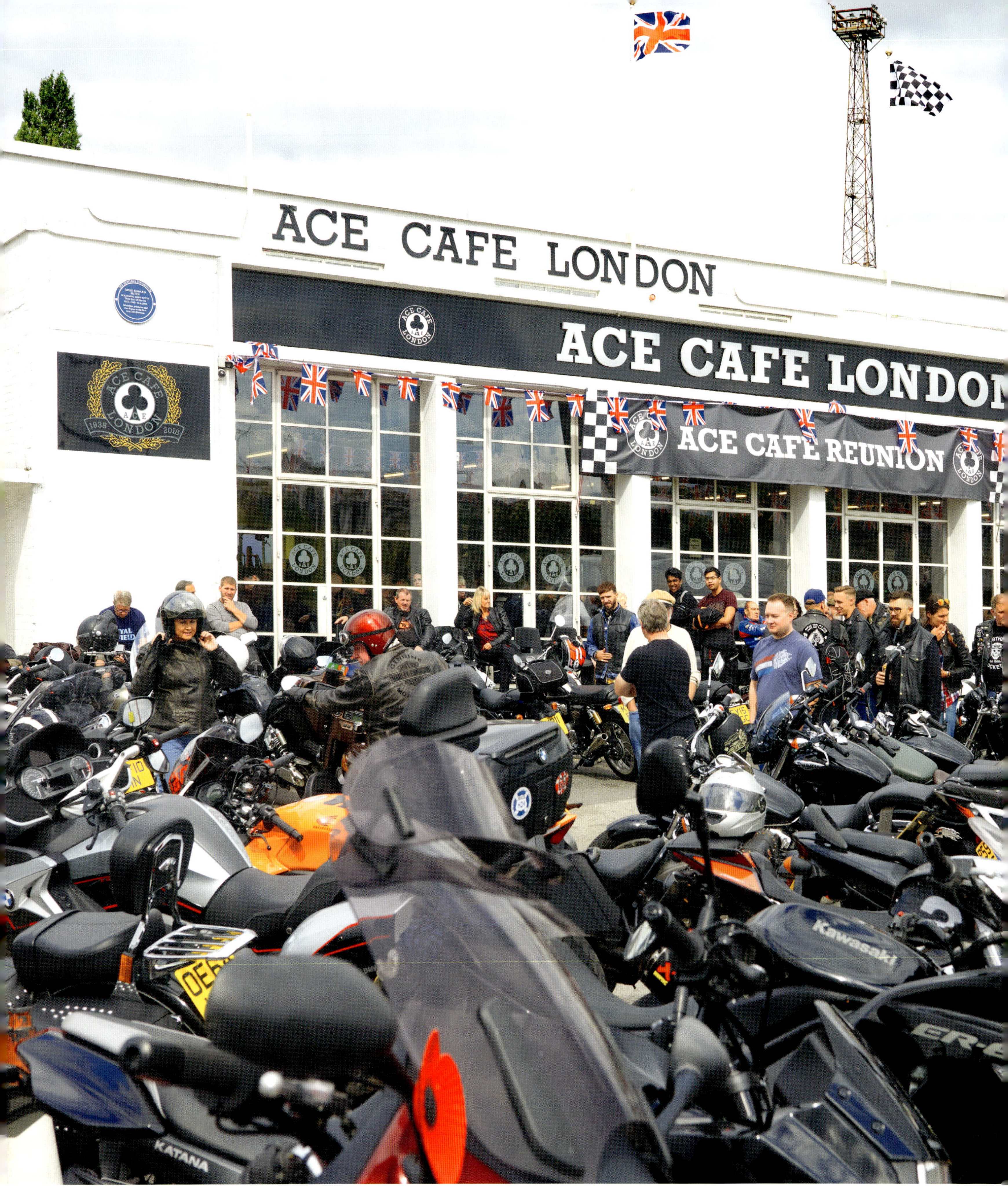
ACE CAFE LONDON
ACE CAFE LONDON
ACE CAFE REUNION
ACE CAFE LONDON 1938 2018
Kawasaki
KATANA

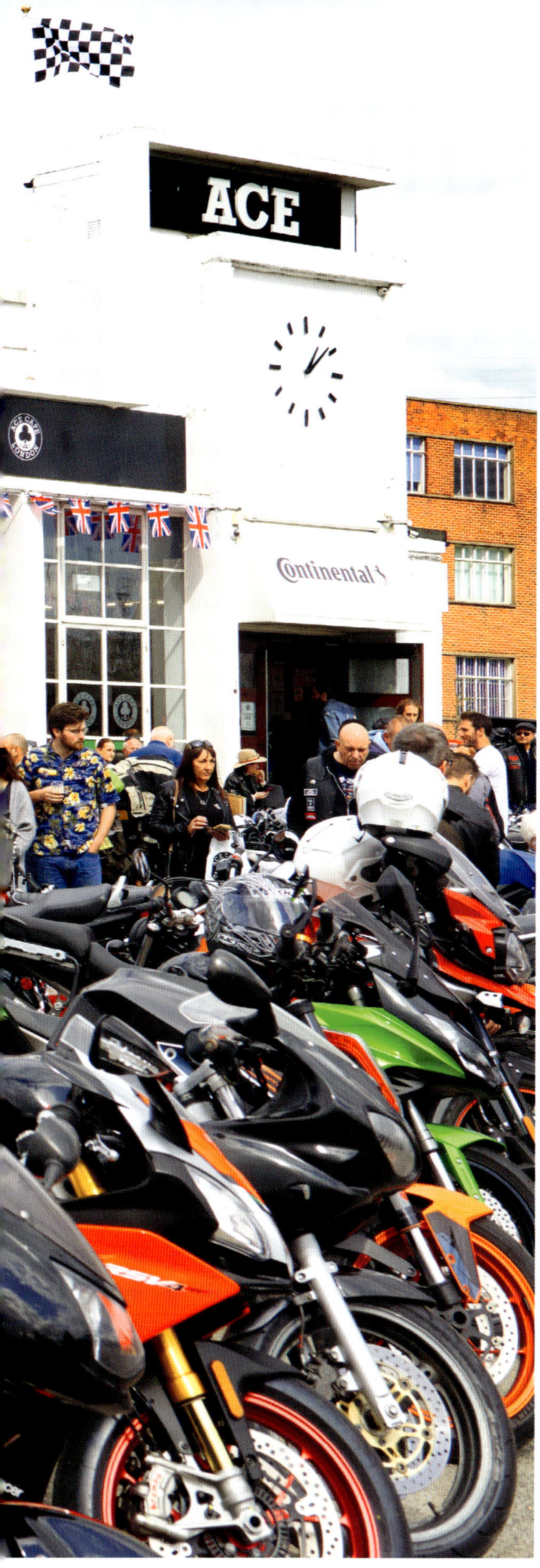

The Ace Café Reunion Weekend, on the North Circular Road, London NW10. A popular hangout for rockers, bikers and petrolheads.

Ace Café

Motorcyclists gather today at the Ace Café on the old North Circular Road at Stonebridge, and so do classic car owners, rock 'n' rollers and film crews in search of a good background. In its latest form, the Ace Café has been described as a heritage site, a retro-culture theme bar and a restaurant licensed for music, dancing and even wedding ceremonies. All this builds on the once-notorious original Ace Café and its lively history.

The first Ace arrived in 1938 alongside the recently completed North Circular as an ultra-modern roadhouse establishment. It was joined by a filling station with garage workshops adjacent, and business was brisk in the months before the outbreak of war. The café was badly damaged by bombing in 1940 and replaced by a larger building completed in 1948, and by the early 1950s, some 2,000 meals were being served each day. In the busy location trade was good and road transport was growing on the main route that skirted central London in the years before the motorway. The Ace operated as a twenty-four-hour transport café in an area of west London where industry was strong. Alongside lorry drivers, mechanics and workmen, motorcyclists in their protective clothing were not unwelcome.

The phenomena of what followed has long fascinated social historians. Motorcycles were cheap transport in the 1950s and the Teddy Boy subculture that emerged after the war quickly picked up on this, and on the rock 'n' roll music coming from the US.

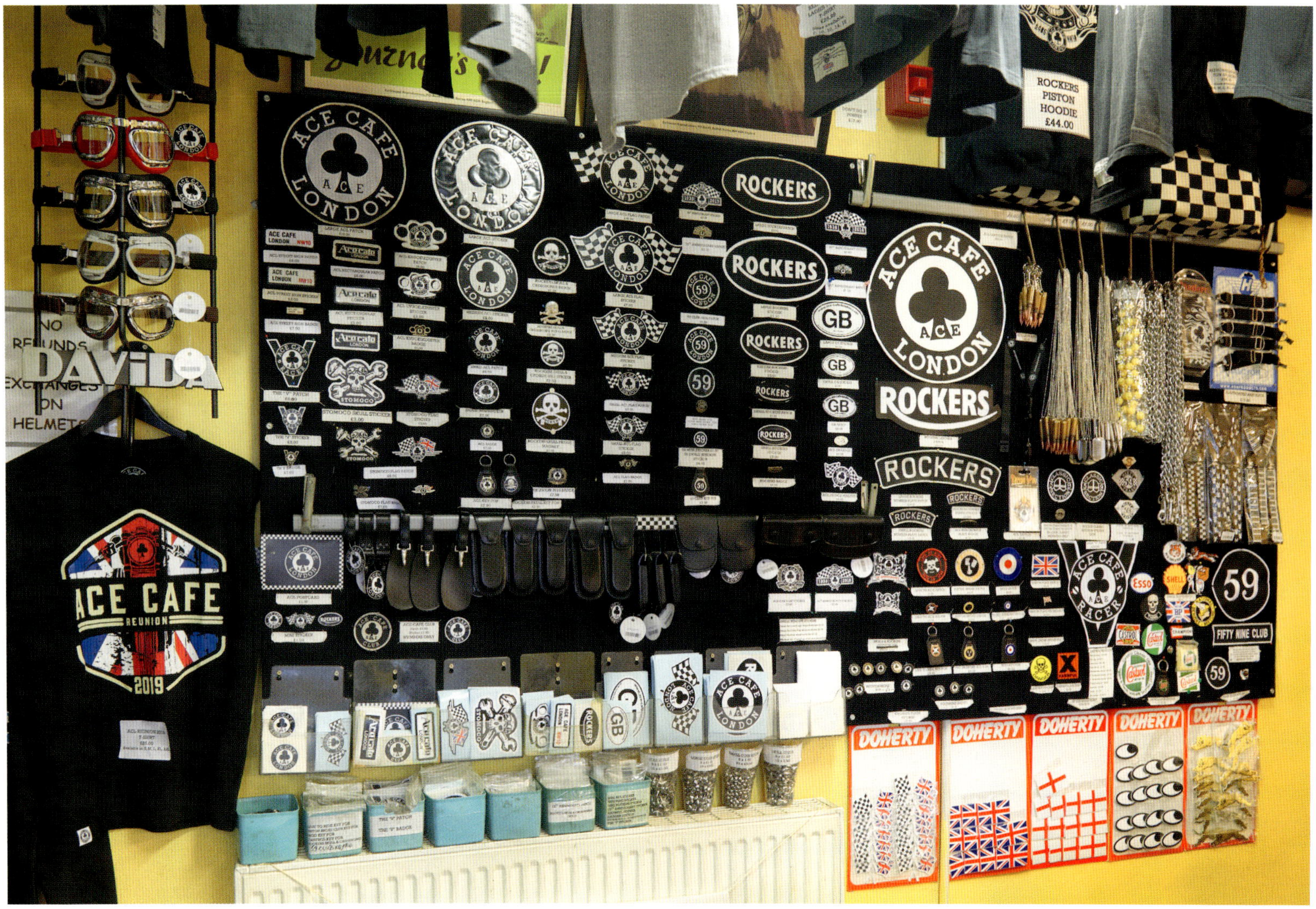

Badges and souvenirs on display and available to purchase.

The confluence of these elements, and a dash of spirit of rebellion, led to the emergence of the riders described as ton-up boys going in search of 100 mph on the roads of Britain. These were later known as rockers, and the Ace Café was an adopted home for many of them. The A406, the North Circular Road, was their sphere of operations.

It is best to imagine the Ace in its peak years, which, measured by motorcycle sales and registrations, were 1959 and 1960. With 'Apache' or 'Shaking All Over' playing on the café jukebox, the leather-clad regulars would stir their cups of tea (with the spoons that were reputedly chained to the tables) while considering their next step and examining the machinery standing outside. This would have typically been a collection of larger-capacity Triumphs, BSAs or Nortons, some modified to single-seat café racers. What followed sometimes was a racing blast by two or ten or twenty riders, often to the Busy Bee Café 18 miles (13 km) around the North Circular on to the Watford bypass.

According to several veterans of the old Ace Café, there was another tradition: insert sixpence in the jukebox, select record, then sprint to the bike for a burst out to the Iron Bridge bends, about a mile and half east of the Ace at Neasden, turn at the roundabout, and aim to return before the record finished playing.

The Ace Café became the destination for thousands of motorcyclists in the 1960s, the point of meeting and departure for countless roads runs. Attrition was high during those years and the accident rate and wildness of rocker culture generated much critical comment in newspapers. Later headlines condemned the conflict between rockers and scooter-borne mods at seaside towns in 1964, but the age of the rocker was soon to fade. The year 1969 marked three key events: the introduction

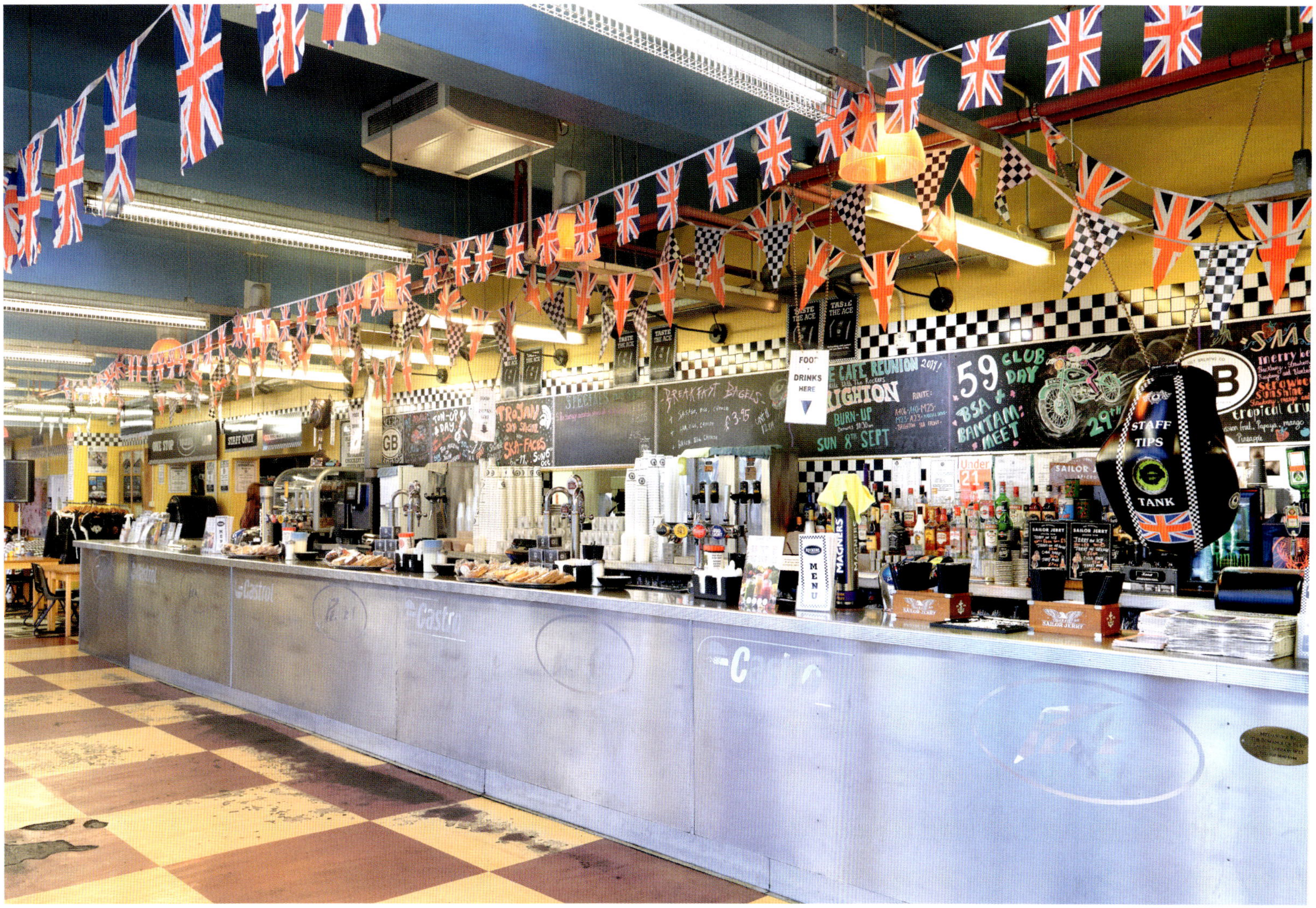

The main bar of the Ace Café London.

of the Honda CB750 four-cylinder, the Japanese motorcycle that toppled the ascendancy of the big British bike, and the release of the feature film *Easy Rider*, which charted quite another direction in the culture. In a changing world, the rockers had undeniably lost the juice. The Ace Café closed that November.

The building remained intact and served at times as a bookmakers' office, workshop for a tyre depot and vehicle delivery centre. The position of the North Circular shifted into a multi-lane realignment to relieve traffic congestion between Hanger Lane and Neasden, leaving the Ace on the old A406 in a quieter place with some grassy space in front and the River Brent behind.

A new breed of motorcyclist emerged, some old rockers returned to their roots, and the Ace Café was not forgotten. A revival reunion meeting on the site in September 1994 was attended by thousands, and further reunions were held in the 1990s. In 2000 a restoration started and the café was reopened in August 2001 in the shape of a bar-restaurant, the One-Stop Rockers Shop, with a stage and dancefloor. It was licensed for the first time. The strength of the Ace Café legend has translated into a brand, and cafés have been opened in China, Finland, Spain, Switzerland and the US.

The Ace Café London opens throughout the week at 7.30 a.m.; closing times vary, generally 22.30 p.m., sometimes later.

CONTACT INFORMATION

Ace Café London,
Ace Corner, North Circular Road, NW10 7UD
https://london.acecafe.com/

Sambourne House

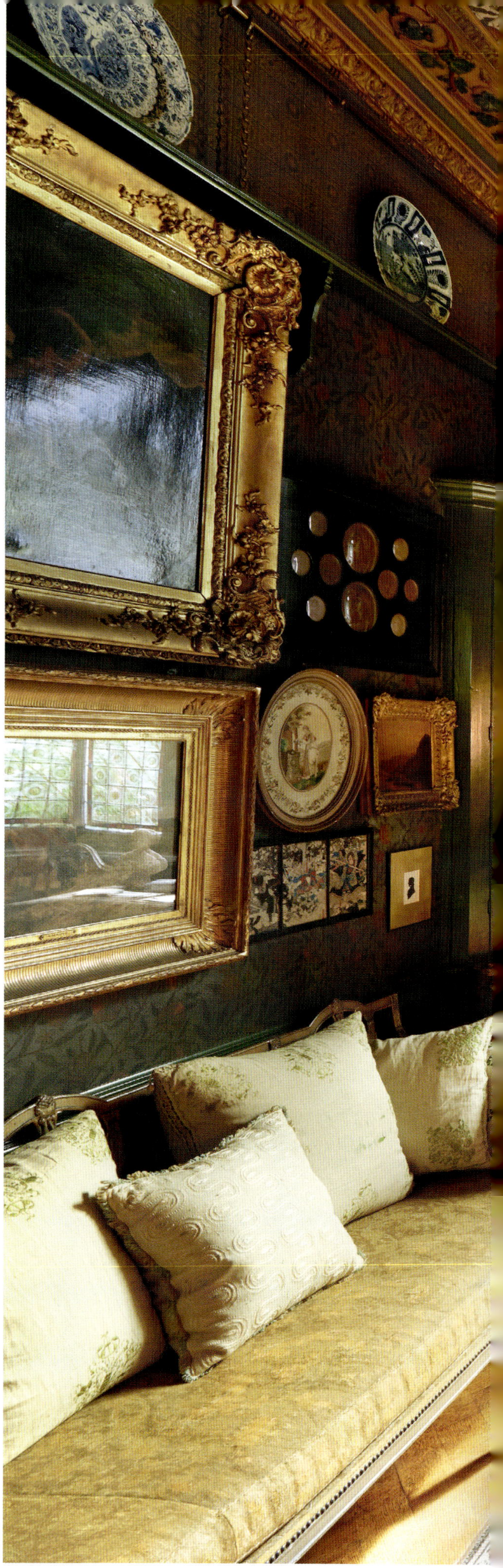

The morning room where Marion Sambourne wrote letters and entertained during the day.

A truly historic meeting was held at 18 Stafford Terrace, Kensington, on Guy Fawkes Night in 1957, hosted by Lady Anne Rosse and attended by the poet John Betjeman, the artist John Piper and thirty others. That evening it was agreed to launch a society dedicated to the protection and appreciation of Victorian architecture and arts and the first meeting of the newly formed Victorian Society followed in February 1958 in the drawing room of the same house.

The house itself was a reflection of the movement and an inspiration. Lady Rosse had taken charge of 18 Stafford Terrace from her mother, who had acquired the family home after the death of her bachelor brother Roy in 1946. He had lived there for most of his life and continuously since the death of his mother in 1914. Roy Sambourne, a man of some inertia, had thrown nothing away. The reach-back across time had enabled the almost miraculous preservation of a house that had first been decorated in the style of the Victorian Aesthetic Movement in the 1870s and updated in the 1890s.

Lady Rosse, who used 18 Stafford Terrace as an occasional townhouse and for entertaining, had done much to repair bomb damage to the building and preserve the decorative schemes at a time in the 1950s, when Victorian things were generally despised. Unmodernized Victorian houses were particularly out of favour. The furniture and effects of the house had next to no value at the time. The

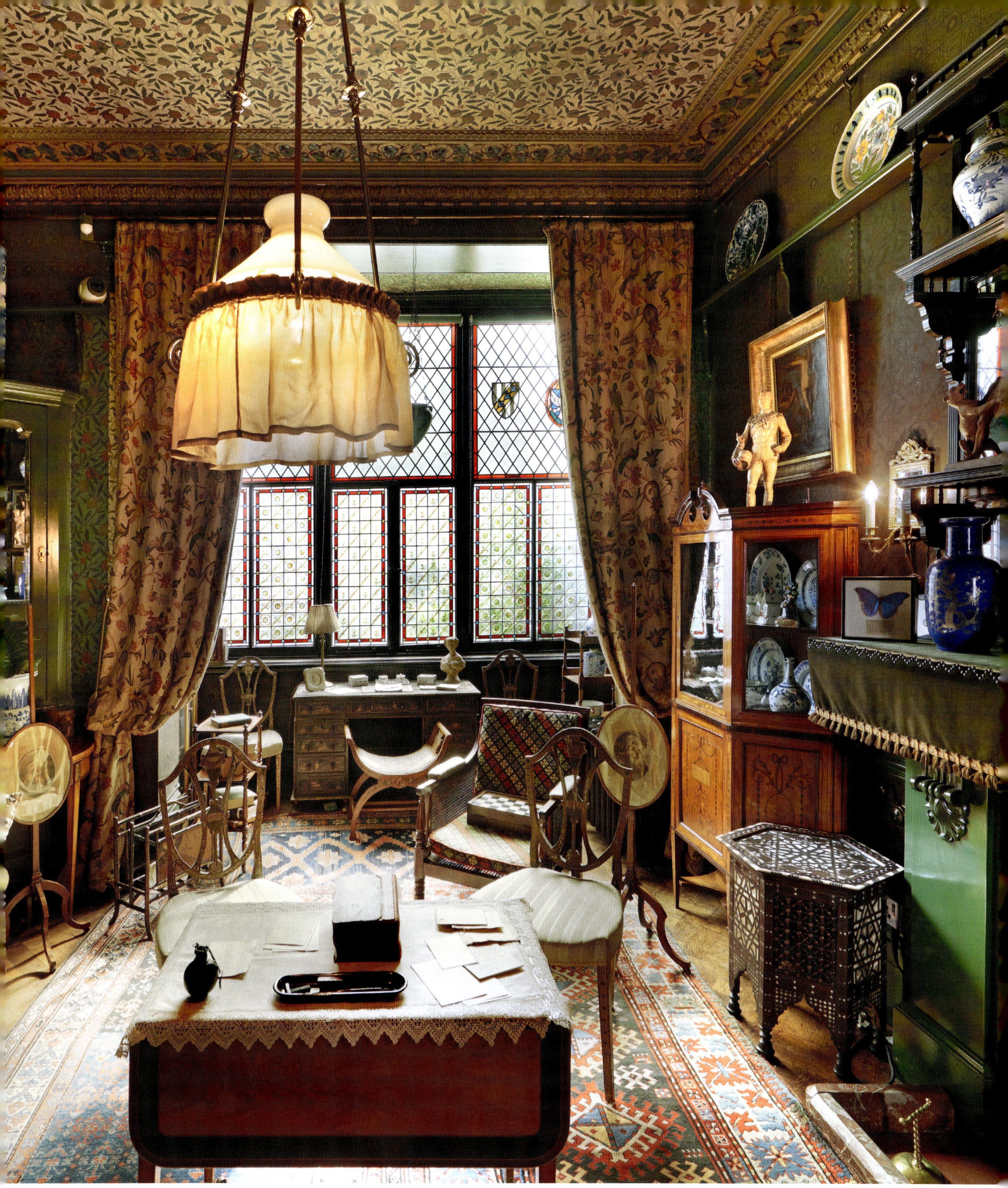

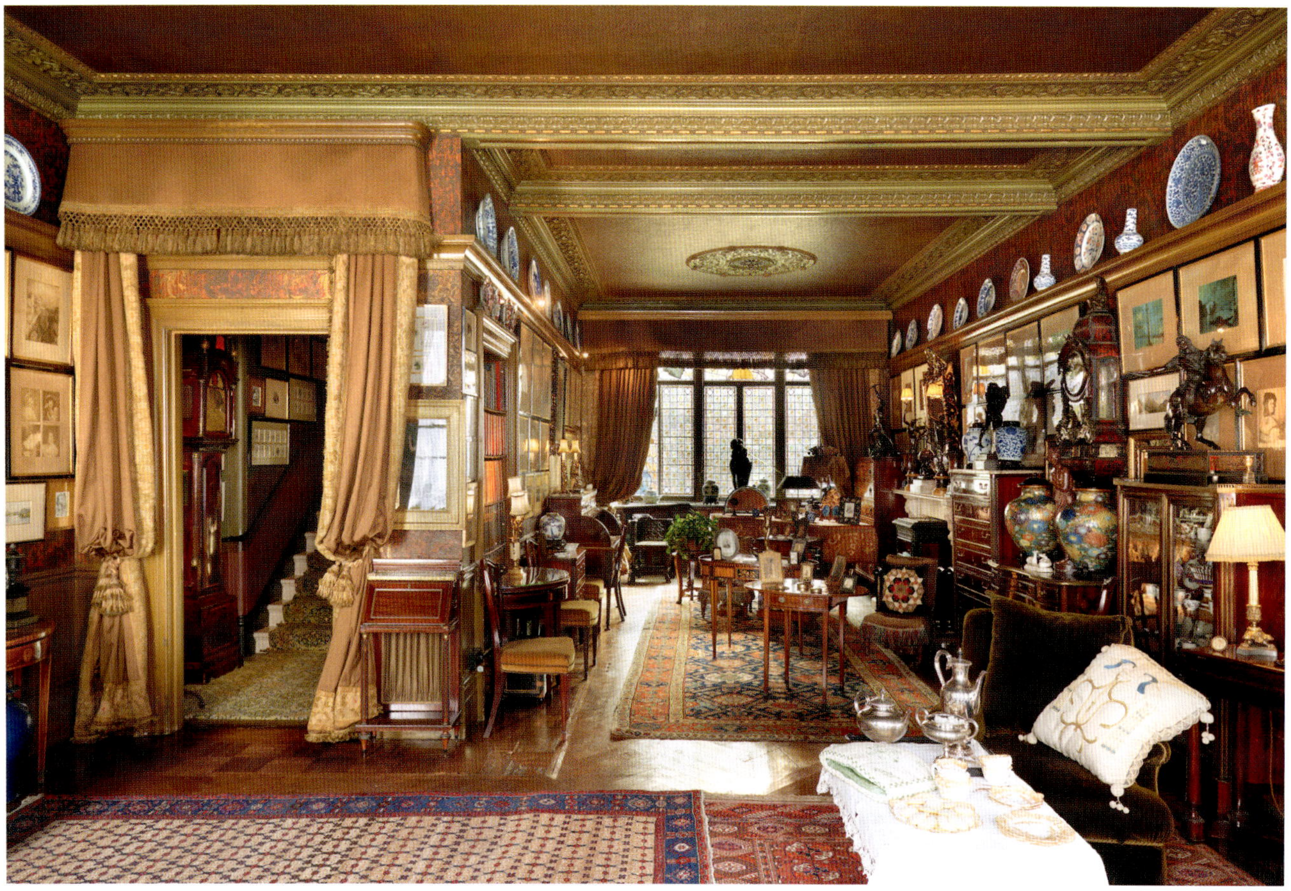

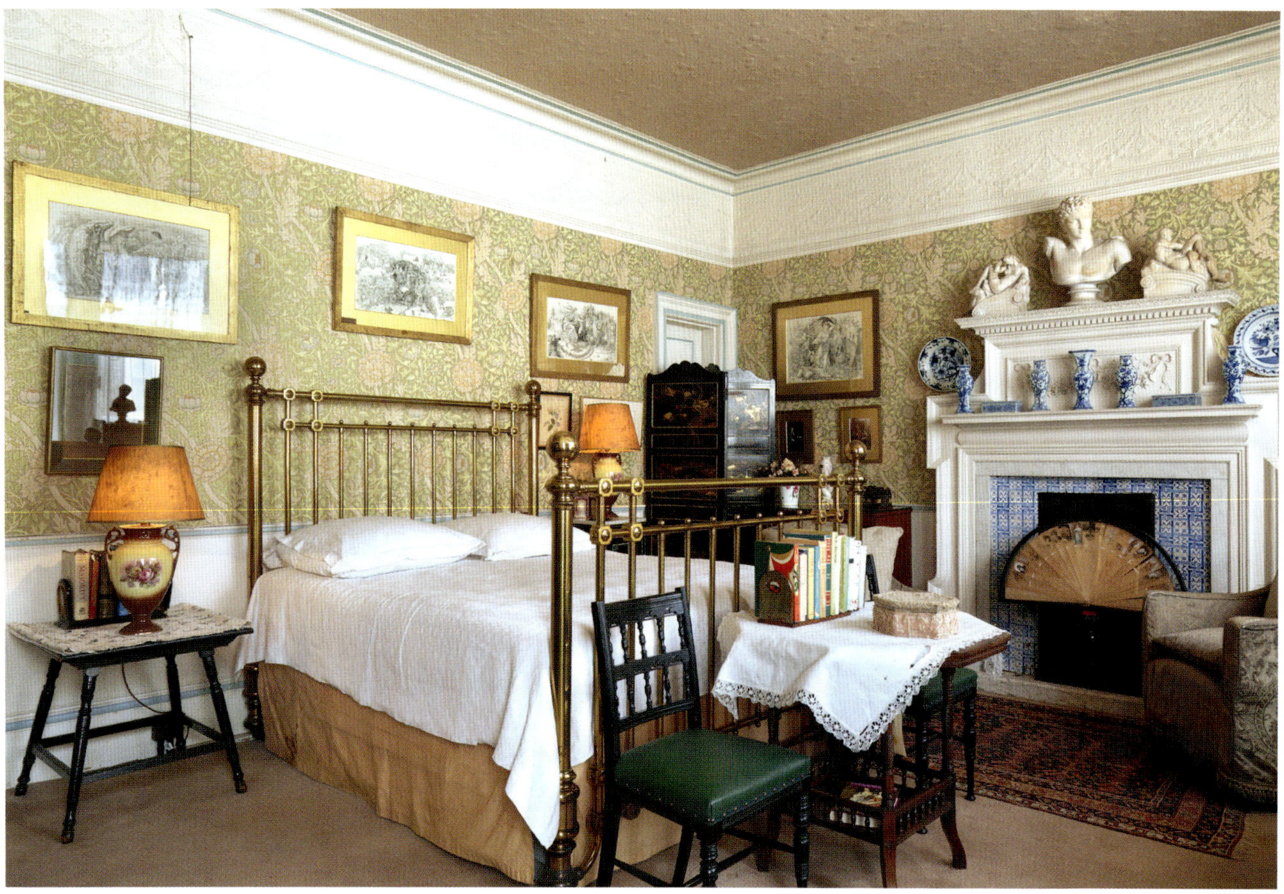

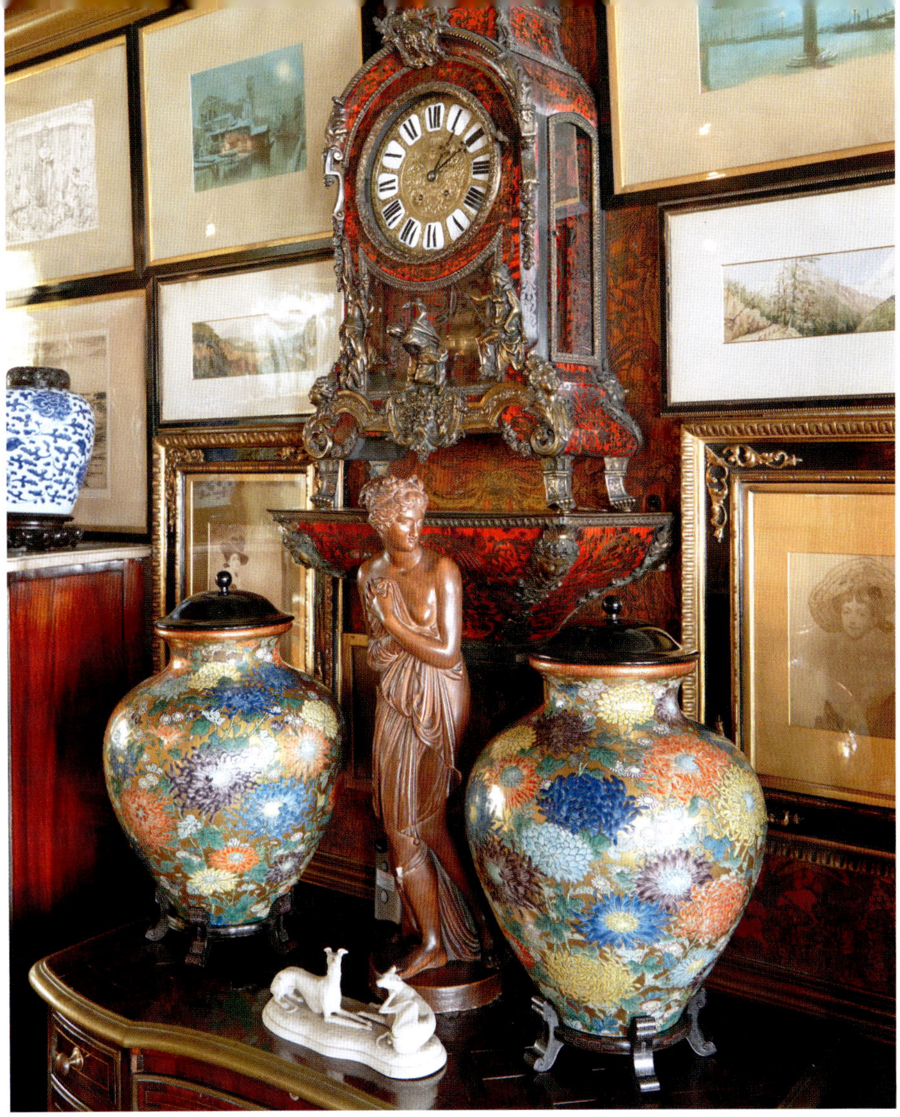

Opposite The opulent drawing room, which occupies the whole of the first floor of the house (above); the master bedroom features an impressive fireplace that was installed in 1887 – it contains antique Dutch tiles and is topped with a classical bust and two small reproductions of Michelangelo's *Night* and *Day* (below).

Above An Andre-Charles Boulle clock in the style of Louis XIV.

Victorian Society was fighting against the tide in its early years, failing to prevent the demolition of Euston Arch and the London Coal Exchange, but through its efforts many buildings which had previously been scorned eventually started to gain respect.

Lady Rosse's ancestors, Linley and Marion Sambourne, had come to 18 Stafford Terrace in 1875. It was one of a recently completed street of three-storey terrace townhouses developed on the Phillimore Estate to the north of Kensington High Street, at that time on the edge of London. Linley Sambourne was an illustrator and cartoonist working for the satirical magazine *Punch*, starting as junior to Sir John Tenniel. He also illustrated several books including an edition of Charles Kingsley's *The Water-Babies* and Hans Christian Andersen fairy tales. Linley was also a photographer. Many of his pictures and photographs are hung at 18 Stafford Terrace. His wife Marion was the daughter of a stockbroker and the couple had two children. The style and decorative ideas for the house are believed to have come from Linley, who was aware of the Aesthetic Movement and the relatively avant-garde trend it represented, taking objects from Japan, China and the Middle East. The house was generously decorated with stained glass in some windows, William Morris wallpaper and crowded with a great deal of furniture and ornaments. It seemed that every wall was covered with pictures. An inventory recorded that 225 framed pictures were hung on the walls and that there were 66 upright chairs in the house.

Diaries kept by Marion Sambourne have left a detailed account of life in the house between 1881 and 1914. The diaries describe a classic social life of the Victorian middle class, with four indoor servants and a groom employed. There were trips to the theatre to see Henry Irving and Ellen Terry in *Macbeth*, and Gilbert and Sullivan operettas, a journey to Paris to see the newly built Eiffel Tower, holidays in Ramsgate, musical evenings, a growing interest in the new art of photography and the coming of the bicycle.

It would be misleading to call 18 Stafford Place a perfect time capsule of 1875 because some of the house had been modernized before the century turned. Electricity had started to replace gas lighting inside the house in 1896 and the Sambournes had updated much of the decoration in the 1890s. Later, Lord and Lady Rosse had installed modern plumbing and redecorated some parts of the house. Yet much of the fabric of the original place has remained intact. It has served as a setting for several films, including the 1985 feature *A Room with a View*.

After the death of Lord Rosse in 1979, it was decided to open 18 Stafford Terrace to public view. It was first run as the Linley Sambourne Museum by the Victorian Society and is now under the ownership of the Royal Borough of Kensington and Chelsea. It is now known as Sambourne House. The Victorian Society continues to work to save Victorian and Edwardian buildings from needless destruction or disfigurement and has a formal role in the planning system through the Secretary of State's arrangements for handling heritage applications under Direction 2015.

CONTACT INFORMATION

Sambourne House,
18 Stafford Terrace, Kensington, W8 7BH
https://www.rbkc.gov.uk/museums/sambourne-house

New West End Synagogue

It is impossible to attribute the New West End Synagogue in Bayswater to a single architectural style, although it unmistakably belongs to the late-Victorian period, when neo-gothicism boomed and red brick and terracotta were being liberally applied to both sacred and secular buildings. There is also a suggestion of Moorish Revivalism, and other influences on the building have been described as Saracenic, Byzantine, Assyrian, Neo-Grecian, Orientalist and Romanesque. Most commentators and architectural writers quickly settle on the word 'eclectic'.

The consecration of the synagogue in 1879 came at a time of growing self-confidence for the Jewish community in London. Judaism in early-nineteenth-century Britain had undergone a cautious emancipation into social acceptability. Scholars have described how an English form of Judaism had first evolved. In the words of a past president of the New West End, 'the United Synagogue was the Anglican Church, Jewish division', with some Jewish ministers of the time wearing clerical collars and preferring the title 'Reverend'. Synagogues built early in the century had been much in the Christian style. In case of the New West End Synagogue, however, the interior in particular was created as lavishly and exotically Jewish.

A key event had been the appointment of the first Jewish Member of Parliament, Baron Lionel de Rothschild, in 1858, and he became a main patron of

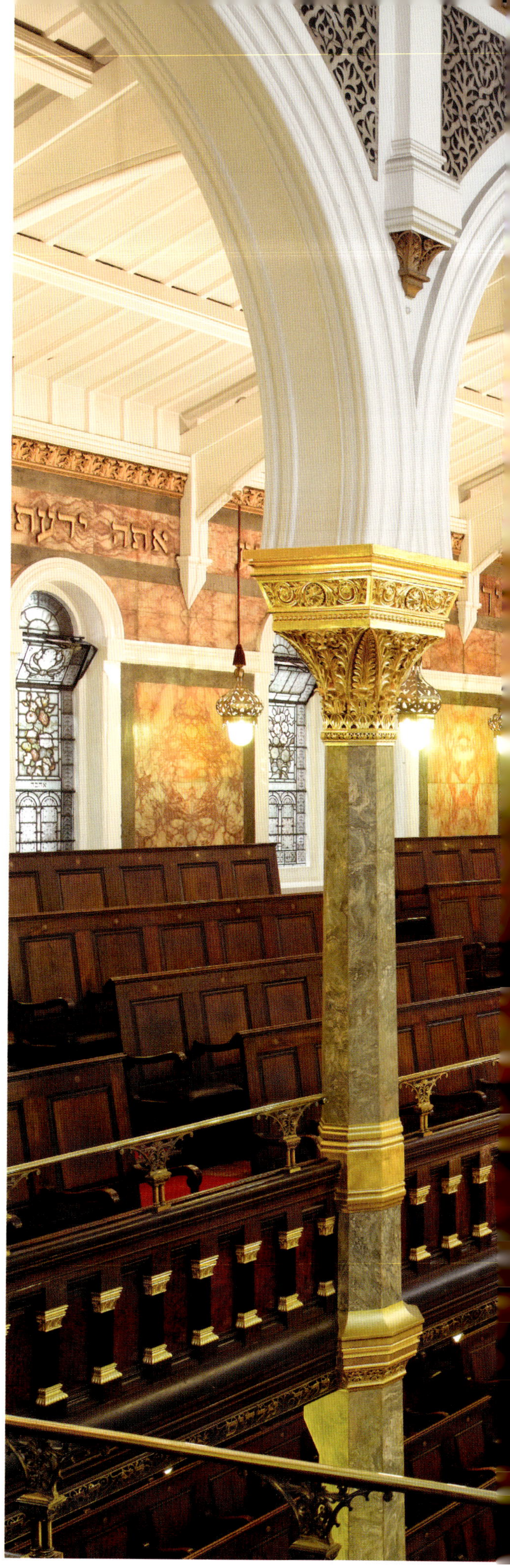

The Ark flanked by menorahs, with the rose window behind and the almemar (pulpit) in the foreground.

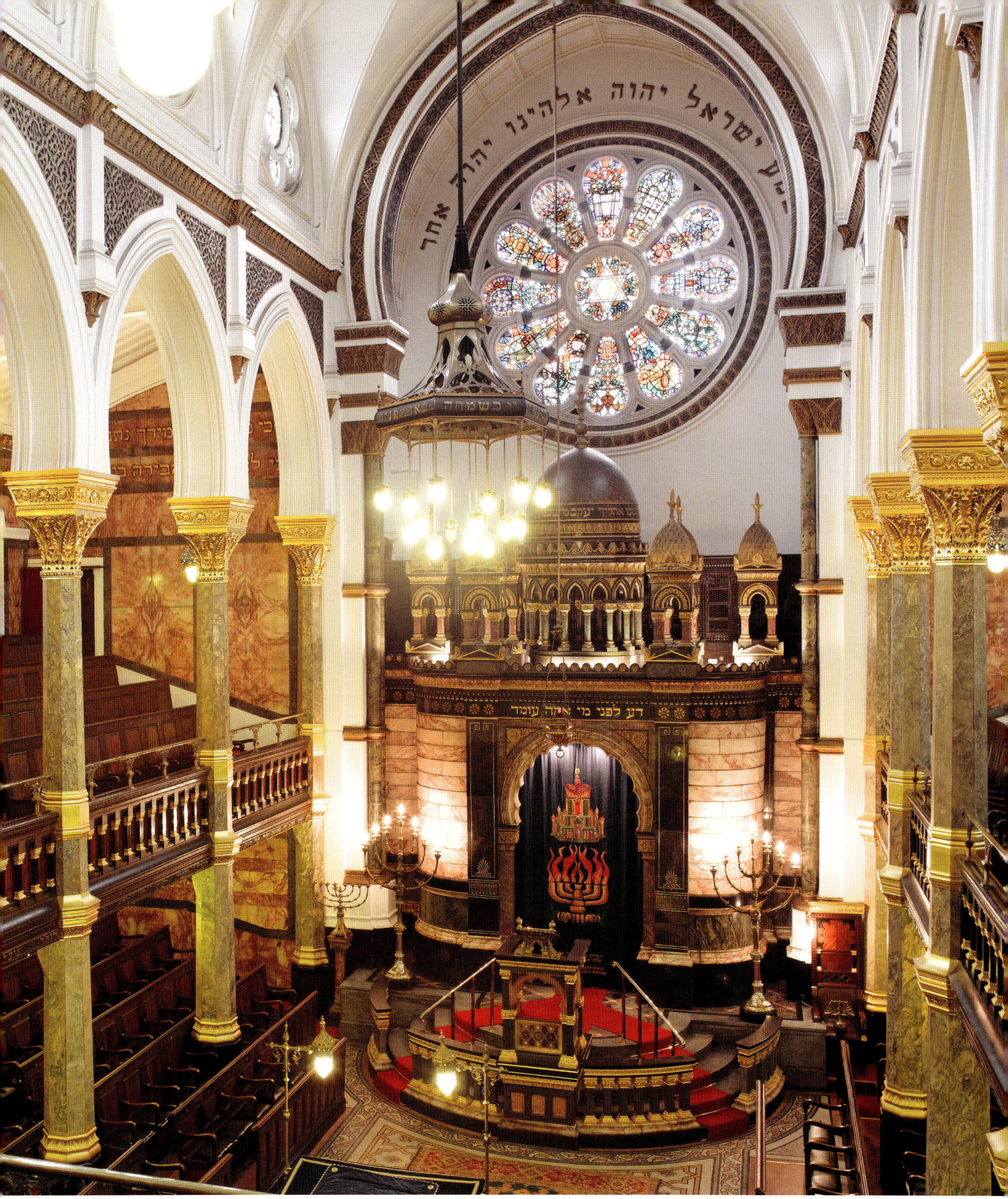
ישראל יהוה אלהינו יהוה אחד
דע לפני מי אתה עומד

The bimah *is supported by forty-nine columns, each of which is decorated differently.*

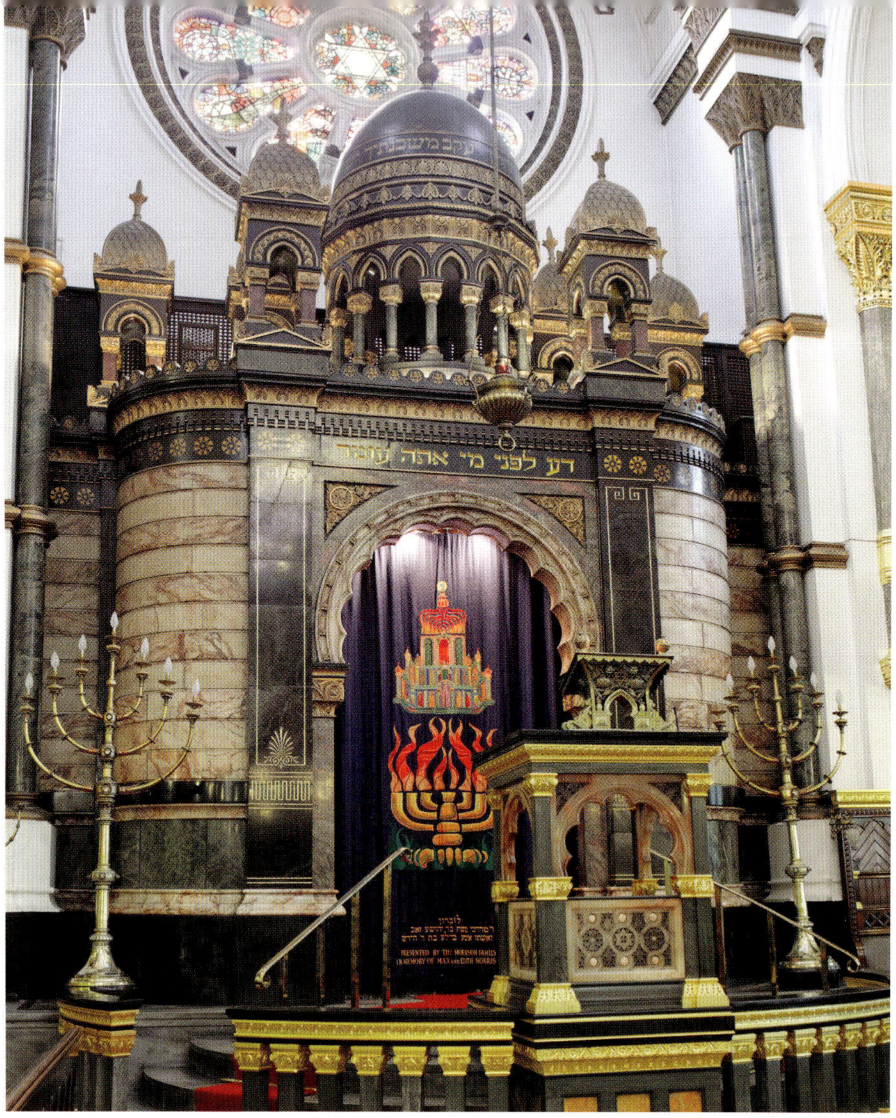

the new synagogue, making a grant towards the purchase of the site in Bayswater, an area where many prosperous and prominent members of the community had settled. Another force behind the building was banker Samuel Montagu, later Lord Montagu. Leaders selected the architect George Audsley, who had already designed a synagogue in Liverpool, which had pioneered an emphatically Jewish cultural style. Rothschild laid the New West End Synagogue foundation stone in 1877.

The Ark is made of marble and alabaster, topped with a canopy comprising a gilded cupola and minarets. High behind in the west wall is a rose window, one of two in the synagogue, which are the clearest examples of straightforward gothicism in the design. The equally lavish pulpit is placed centrally.

Some forty stained-glass side windows are by Nathaniel Westlake, and these date from 1905. However, for the most part, the synagogue remains in its original condition, with the exception of a few later additions in the form of alabaster wall linings and smoothly executed marble coverings for the iron columns. As in almost every religious building in Britain, there is a memorial for members of congregation who died in two World Wars.

Several detailed features are almost rendered unseen by the complexity and sheer opulence of the decoration. The *bimah* (the central platform from where the reading is done) is supported by forty-nine columns, each of which is decorated differently. High in the prayer hall, the spandrels (the curved areas above the arches) are filled with marble panels, each of them again with different design of embellishment.

Patron Samuel Montagu was a man of considerable girth. From the start, his seat in the front row to the left of the Ark had the centre armrest removed, and it remains that way today. Just 130 years after the foundation stone was laid, the synagogue received Grade I listing. In 2007, English Heritage raved in its recommendation for listing, citing mostly the quality and diversity of the interior decoration, and its historical significance. It even noted the brass fittings of the lighting system. Electrical lighting was introduced to the synagogue before the nineteenth century was done, and it is rated as one of the most complete late Victorian examples remaining.

Above Facing the Ark, with scrolls behind and cupola and minarets above.

Opposite, above Torah scrolls.

Opposite, below The Ark flanked by menorahs, with the rose window behind and the almemar (pulpit) in the foreground.

CONTACT INFORMATION

New West End Synagogue
St Petersburgh Place, W2 4JT
https://www.newwestend.org.uk/

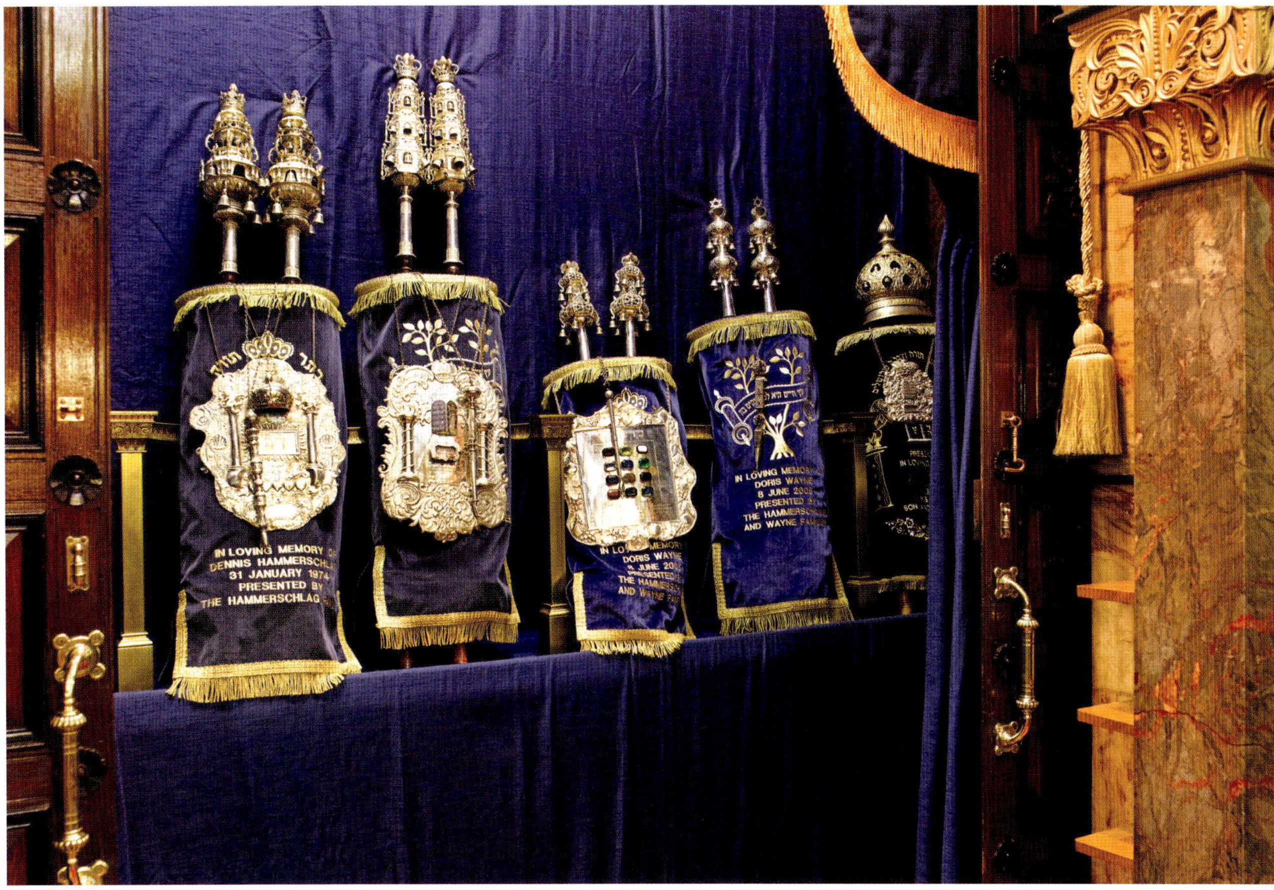
IN LOVING
DENNIS
31 JANUARY
PRESENTED BY
THE HAMMERSCHLAG
IN LOVING
DORIS WAYNE
8 JUNE
PRESENTED
AND WAYNE

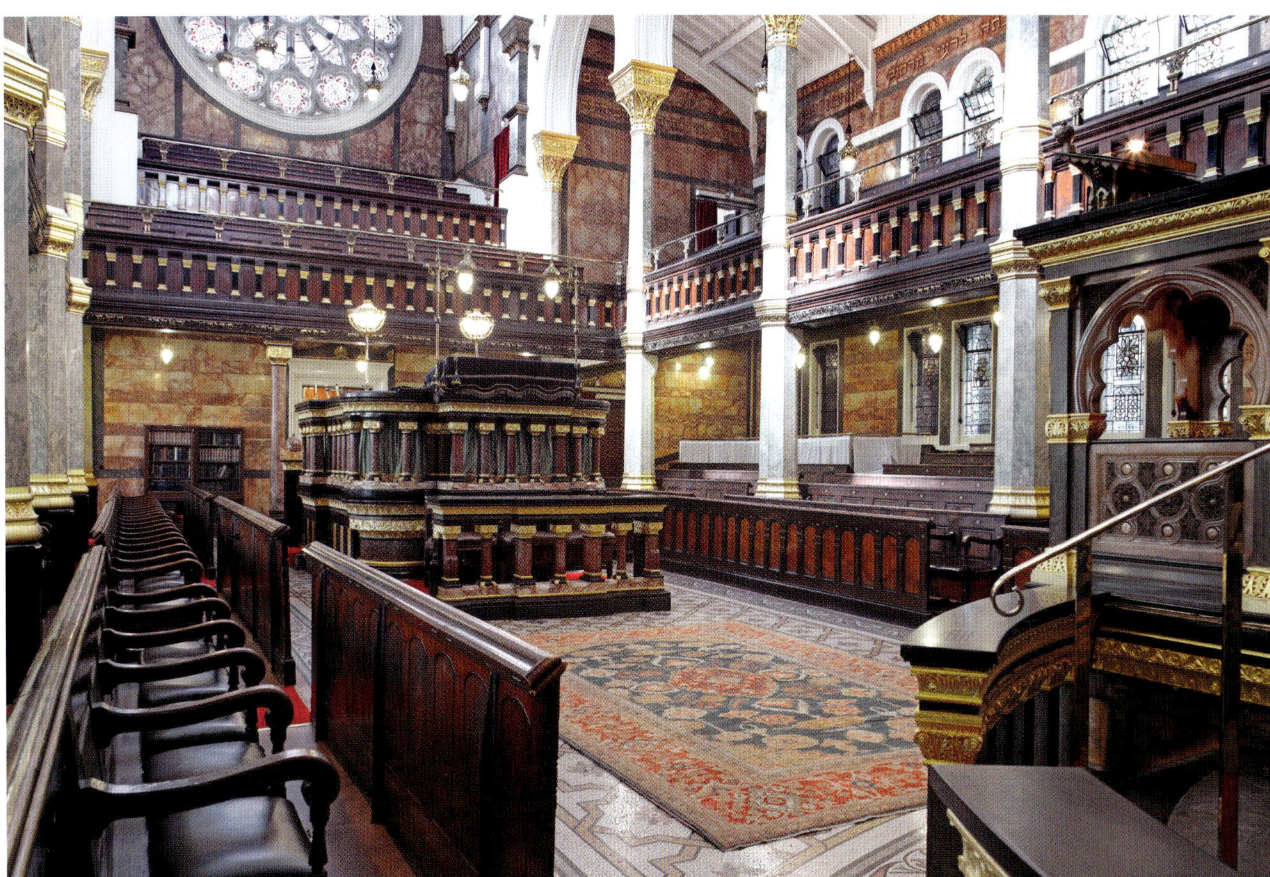

Pitzhanger Manor & Gallery

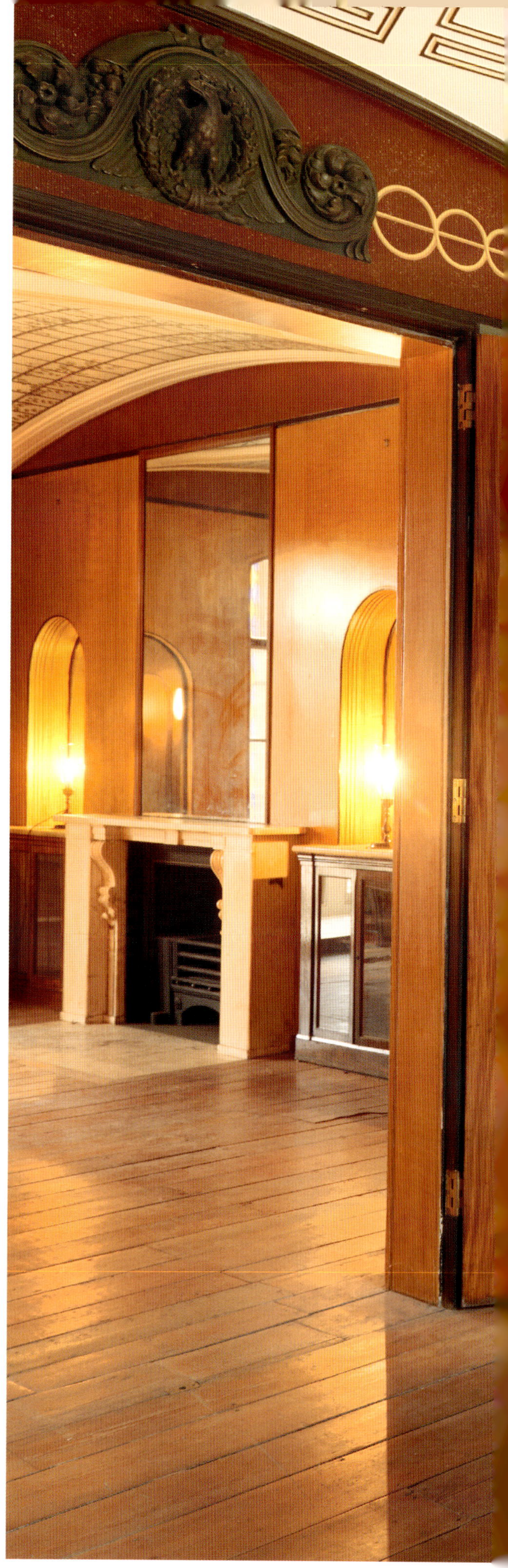

The breakfast room is decorated with Greek key designs on the ceiling and the fireplace.

Sir John Soane is acclaimed as one of the greatest of British architects, although his legacy in bricks and mortar is relatively meagre, as many of his finest buildings have been lost. Pitzhanger Manor in Ealing, once his country home, survived largely intact and relatively unmolested but with much hidden away and forgotten for years under layers of paint and ugly Victorian additions. It served in obscurity as a public library, museum and cultural centre until it fully re-emerged after restoration in 2019 with several Soane features reinstated and the Victorian wing removed. With layers of paint unpeeled, and an analysis of the original finishes, the rooms have regained Soane's original striking colour schemes and decoration.

Ealing was a village separated from London by more than 8 miles (13 km) of countryside in 1800, when John Soane was well-established as a leading architect. He had been appointed architect and surveyor of the Bank of England and had designed several country houses across England. Soane purchased the house known as Pitzhanger Manor with the intention of making it a showcase for his collection of antiquities and to exhibit his abilities as a designer. He had most of the original house demolished and made a new main block with a façade inspired by the Arch of Constantine in Rome, built of yellow London brick and Portland stone. Four Ionic columns are topped with statuary of draped female figures. The design is informed throughout by Soane's

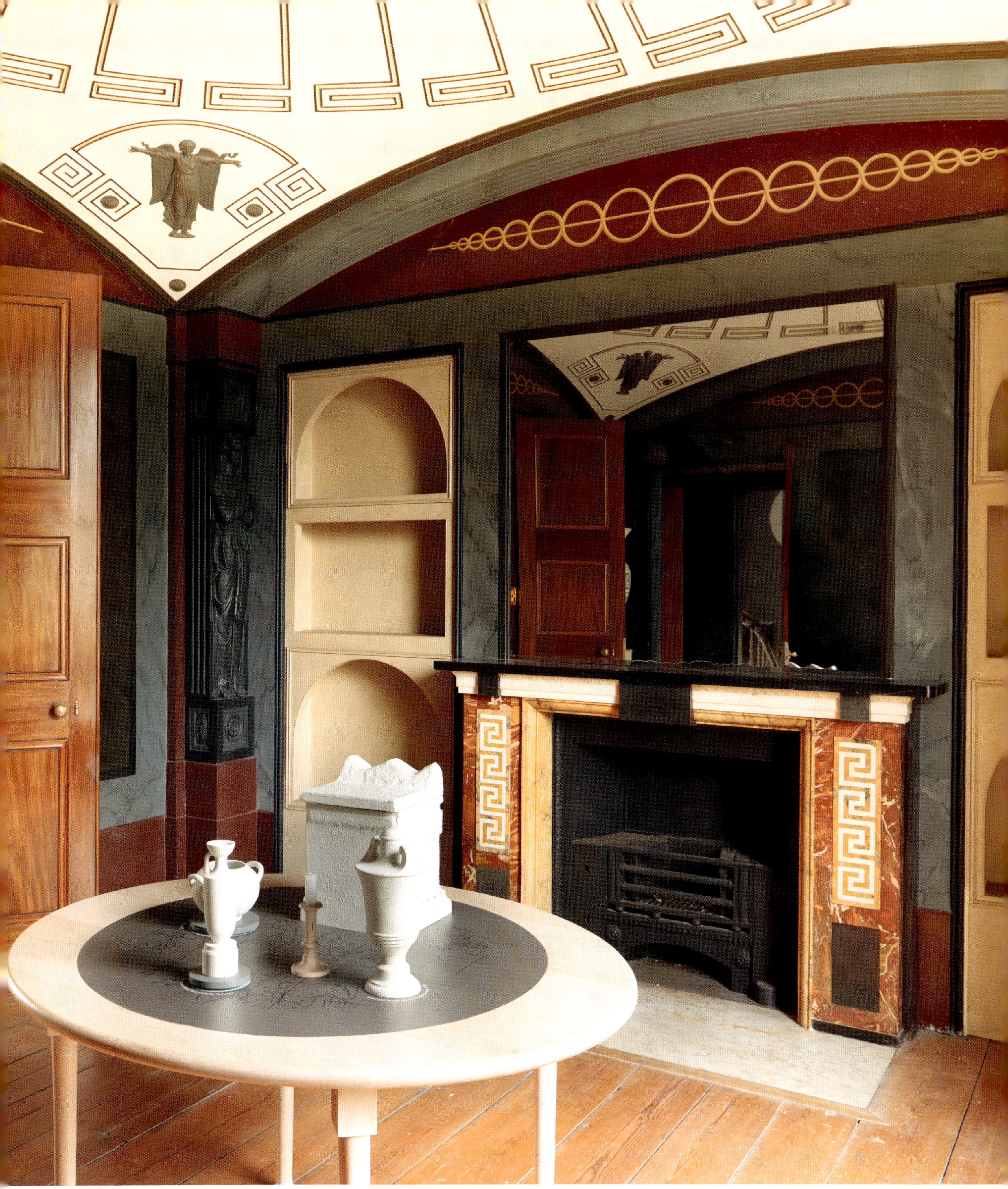

sometimes idiosyncratic take on classicism and clever arrangement of light and space to make the house seem larger than it really is. There are ceramic statues painted to take on the appearance of bronze and areas of plasterwork that are painted as veined marble.

The house is entered by a dark vestibule resembling a vaulted tunnel, which emerges into a tall, naturally lighted hall. The walls are marbled, and the light takes on the warmth of the amber glass of the internal windows on the landing above. The light comes from the top of the house, where there is a large, glass-sided roof lantern. The breakfast room presents itself with an almost theatrical flourish with a ceiling resembling a draped canopy decorated with Greek key designs, which are repeated around the fireplace.

The only part of the house that Soane had retained from the original manor building was a wing designed by architect George Dance, a neoclassical pioneer, for whom Soane had worked as an apprentice aged fifteen in 1768. This wing held some special significant for Soane, possibly because as a pupil he may have worked on it, and for his own house he transformed it into the eating room and upper drawing room. Soane's choice of decoration for the upper drawing room was a vivid Chinese wallpaper and he repainted the Dance-designed ceiling in a matching palette. The wallpaper and colours were recreated after analysis in the restoration.

Soane was a bright boy who rose spectacularly from a modest background, his father being described as a either a bricklayer or a builder. Soane himself is said to have worked as a hod-carrier for his older brother as a thirteen-year-old. The honours and acclaim he later won did not prevent a great disappointment for Soane, and Pitzhanger Manor itself tells the story of an unfulfilled dream. As well as making a showcase for his architectural skills and his collection of art and antiquities, he planned that Pitzhanger would become home to an architectural dynasty by way of his two sons. It was soon clear that neither had any interest in following their father's profession and a rift developed between Soane and his sons. Soane's wife Eliza found Pitzhanger Manor isolated and exhausting to manage alongside a London home. The house was subsequently sold on by Soane in 1812. He already owned a house in Lincoln's Inn when he bought Pitzhanger Manor and he transferred his extensive collection of artefacts to London and expanded the house there.

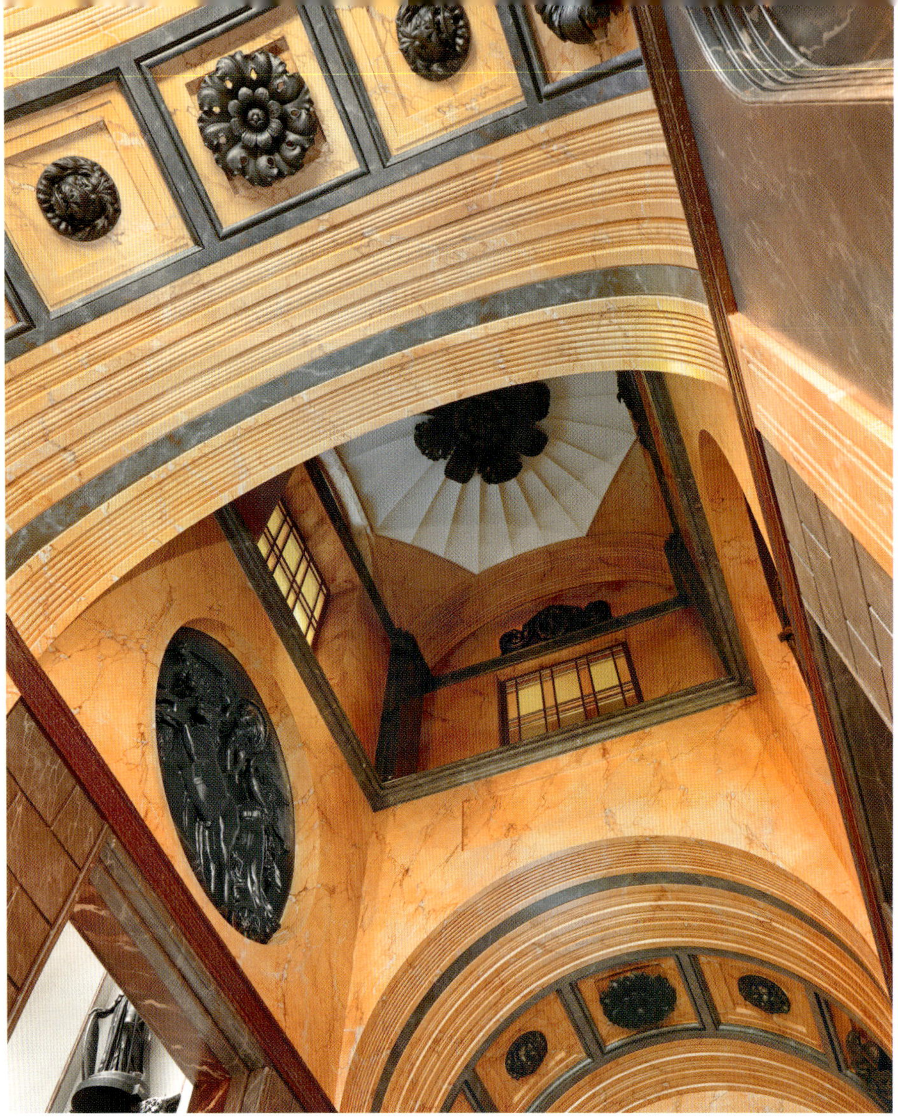

The contrast today between the interior of the two houses is compelling: Pitzhanger, with empty niches and devoid of ornament and furniture, and 13 Lincoln's Inn Fields, known as the Sir John Soane Museum, with densely packed and some seemingly chaotic rooms overflowing with exhibits. It might have been different. In 1802, Eliza Soane had bought a series of eight paintings by William Hogarth, *The Rakes Progress*, and the intention was to display them at Pitzhanger. The small drawing room with its plain red wall was designed to show off paintings, although this might not seem to be a good setting for scenes of Hogarthian debauchery. The Hogarths migrated to Lincoln's Inn, where they can be seen today in the picture room along with a hundred other paintings. At Pitzhanger Manor, the carefully calibrated restoration offers a clear, uncluttered look at the essence of Soane's style.

Above The ceiling of the impressive marbled entrance hall.

Opposite, above The upper drawing room, decorated with hand-painted Chinese wallpaper.

Opposite, below The staircase viewed from the upper landing.

CONTACT INFORMATION

Pitzhanger Manor & Gallery,
Mattock Lane, W5 5EQ
https://www.pitzhanger.org.uk/

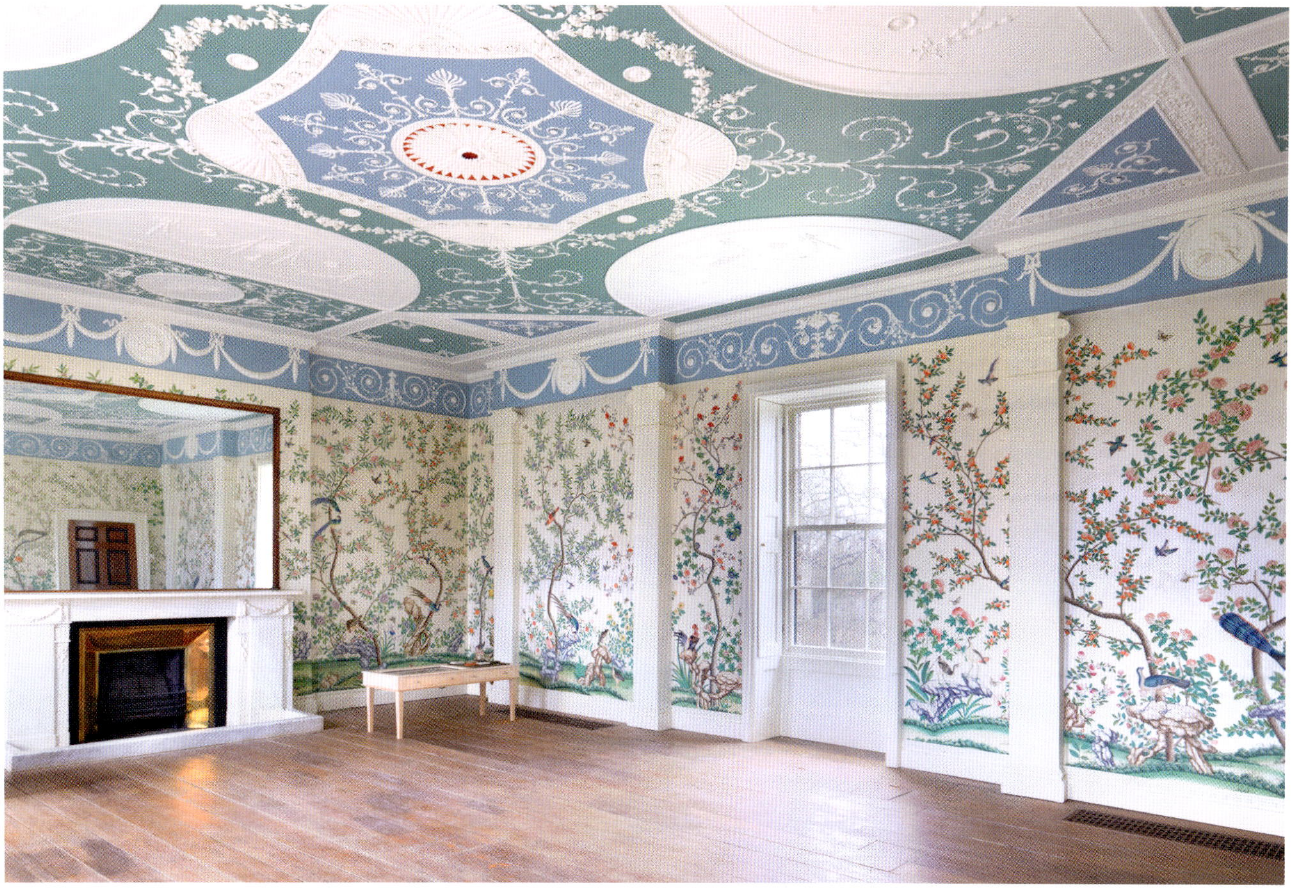

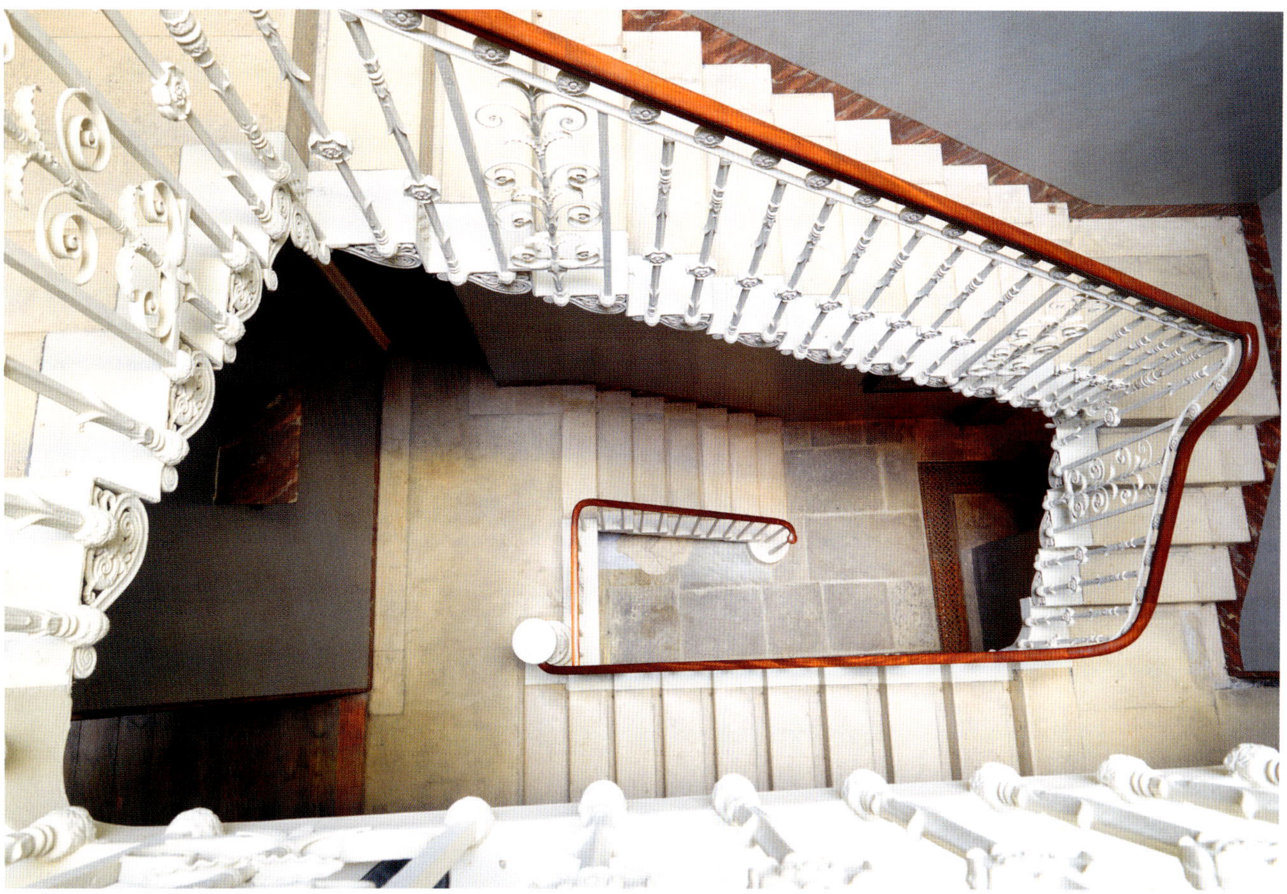

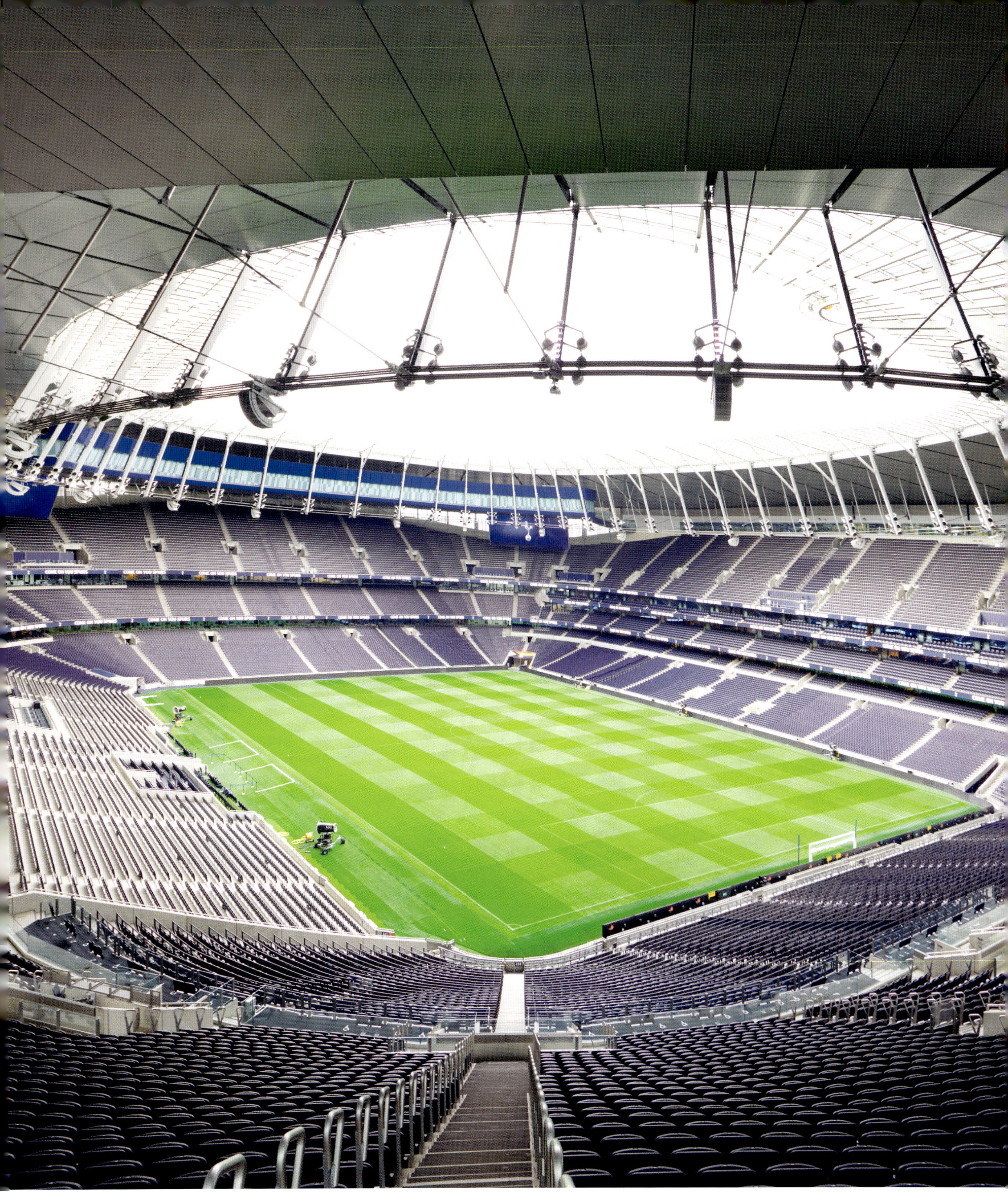

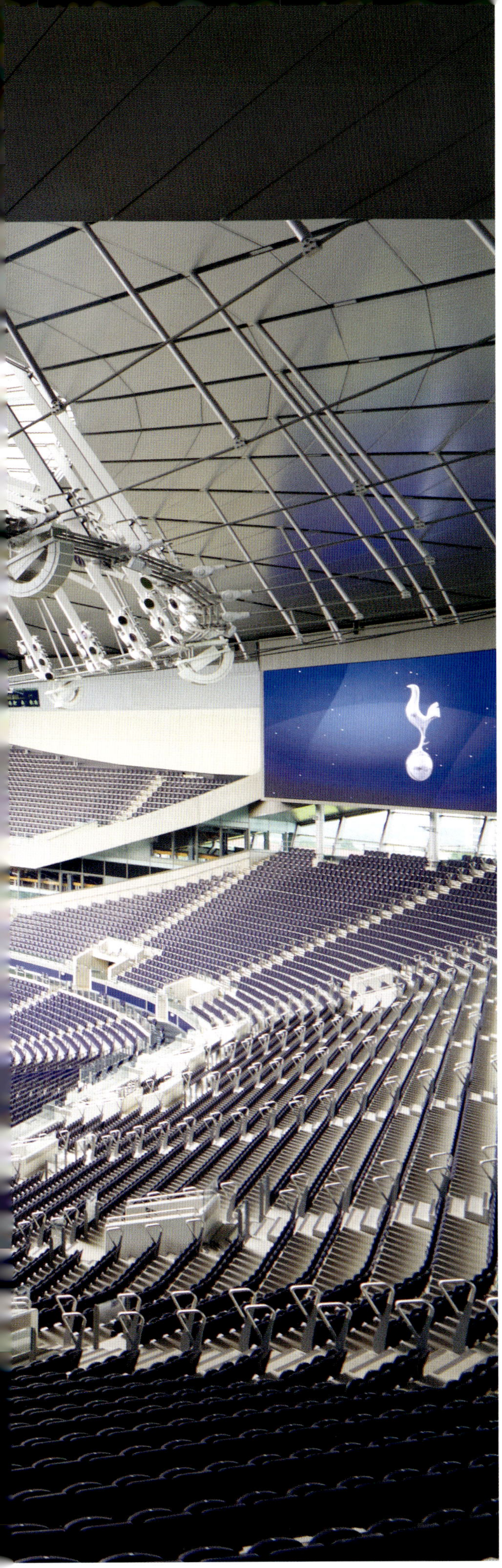

The south-west corner looking north. The South Stand to the right is a defining feature of the stadium.

Tottenham Hotspur Stadium

Tottenham Hotspur Stadium is a colossus in every respect. Capacity is 62,850, the biggest club ground in London. And Tottenham, familiarly known as Spurs, is a truly great football club owning a history studded with glory. The showpiece arena has been operational since 2019, close to the centre of the old White Hart Lane ground where all the glory was made.

Now the challenge at Tottenham is to make the football live up to the architecture. Sometimes criticised for living a legacy of greatness rather than building on it, Spurs went seventeen years from 2008 without winning a major trophy. Then UEFA Europa League victory came in 2025, its first European title won in forty-one years. It came while Spurs returned its lowest ever Premiership finish and points tally.

The spectacular structure soars over a suburban high street landscape with a curving skin of glass and metal. It has been described as a dynamic veil. It covers a bowl of terraced seating with the single tier south end stand accommodating 17,500 home fans which is the defining feature of the stadium. It connects with memory of the old Park Lane end at White Hart Lane, a continuity of the Spurs spirit. Terraces are set at a 35-degree slope, the steepest that stadium design regulations allow. Sections have been fitted with safety bars, poised to allow for safe standing of spectators if changes in law permit. The pitch is glimpsed as a simple perfectly flat rectangle of grass, which is only half the story. It is part of a retractable system. The football pitch sits above a

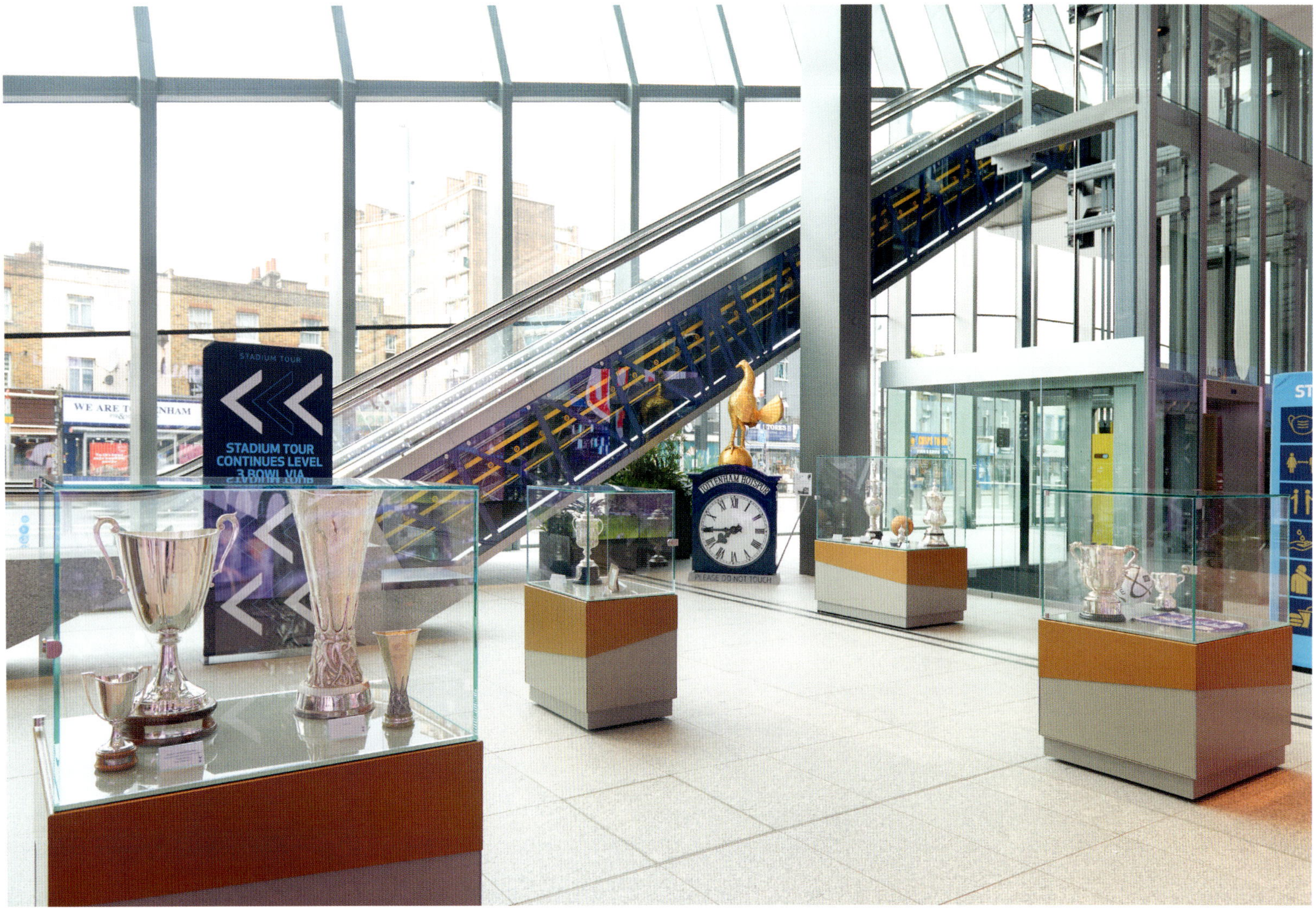

The West Atrium with trophy cabinets on display, Tottenham High Road visible beyond.

second playing surface, an American National Football League NFL field of artificial turf. The real turf football pitch is mounted on three giant steel trays carried on wheels and rails. Driven by electric motors, the pitch slides under the south stand to expose the NFL field. The changeover takes 25 minutes. It is a feature unique in British football and enables Tottenham Hotspur to host two NFL games each year.

The pitch can be kept in top condition when it is stored underground in the pitch pocket beneath the South Stand and Park Lane Square with the application of grow lights, watering systems and robotic mowers. Under the north stand, six lighting rigs are hidden which can be run out to maintain the pitch when it is in place.

Superlatives abound. The longest bar, the biggest club shop in Europe, and the widest indoor digital LED display anywhere is found in the West Atrium. There are thirty-two lifts and seven escalators, a microbrewery and a kart track. Sometimes the stadium is given over to concerts by major artists and to boxing matches.

In recent years, the Premiership has leaned towards predictability, with Manchester, Liverpool and certain other London clubs generally inhabiting the first four places. Measured across time Spurs have averaged fifth place, and this stadium has been built with trophies in mind.

CONTACT INFORMATION

782 High Road, N17 0BX

https://www.tottenhamhotspur.com/

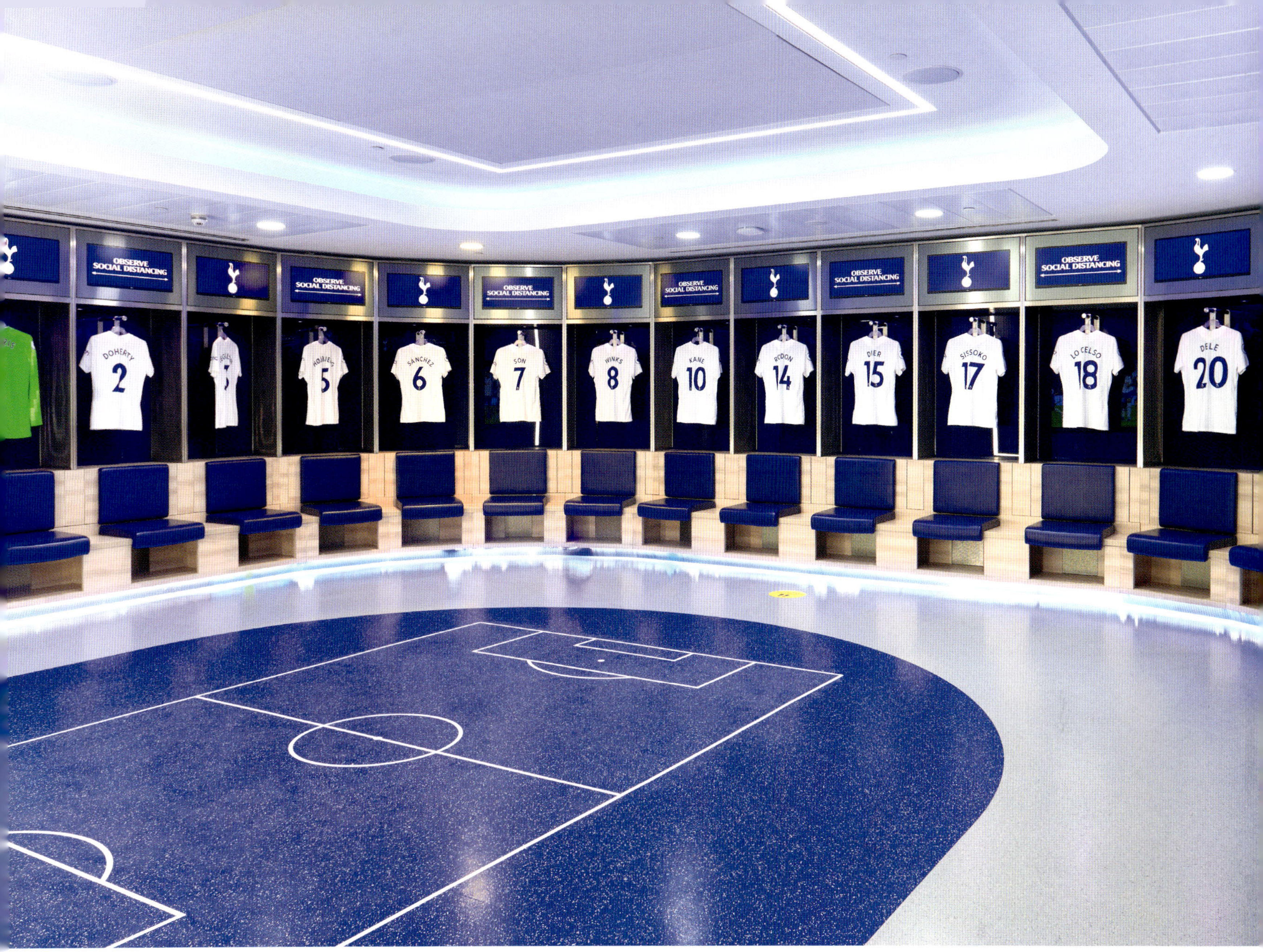

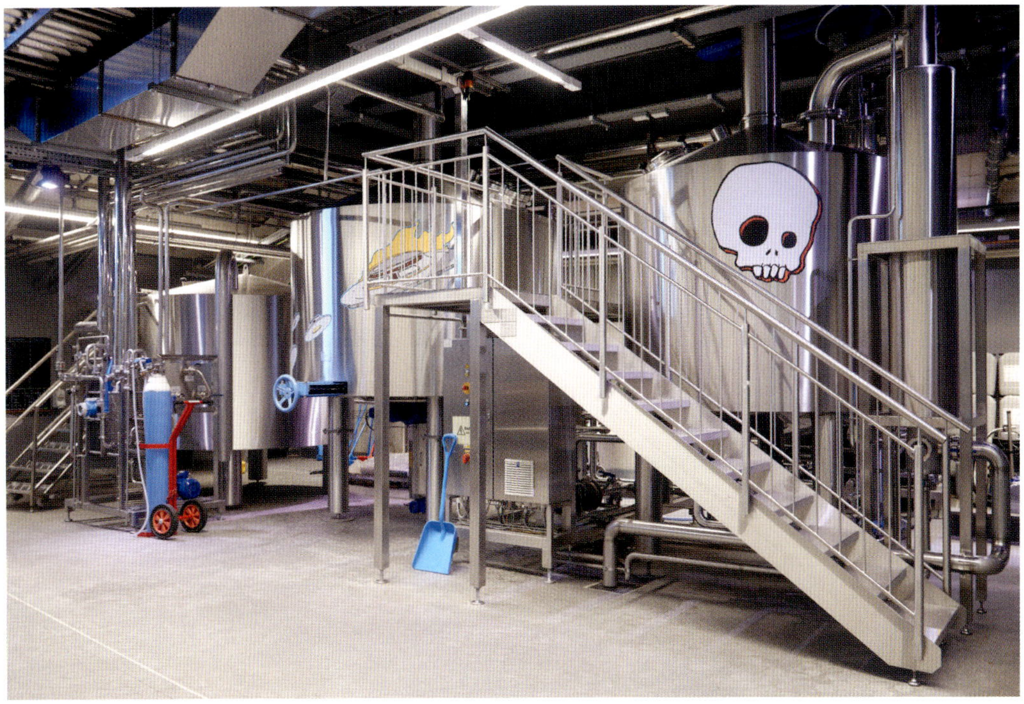

Above The home dressing room is the inner sanctum.

Left Beavertown craft brewery lives under the South Stand.

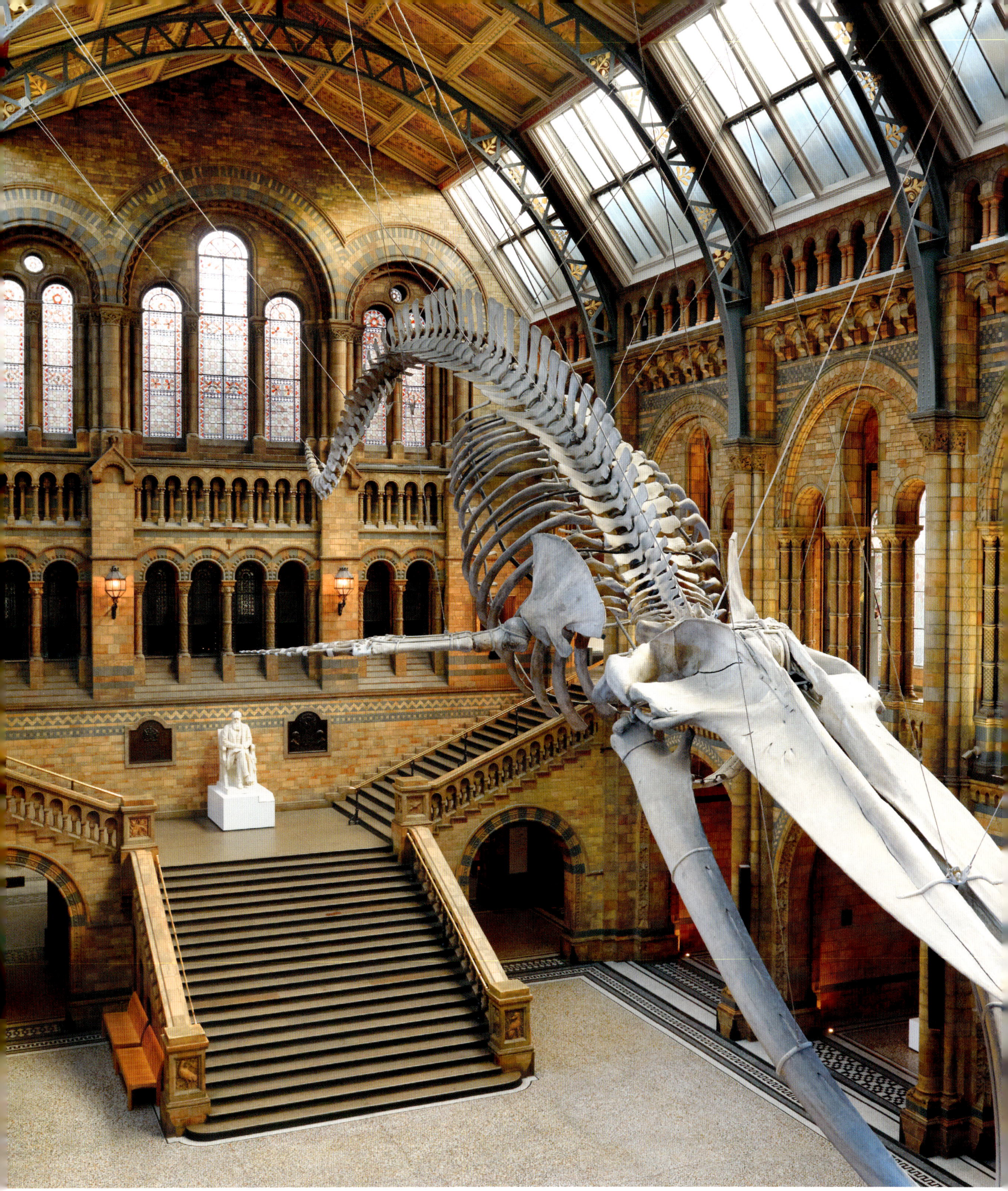

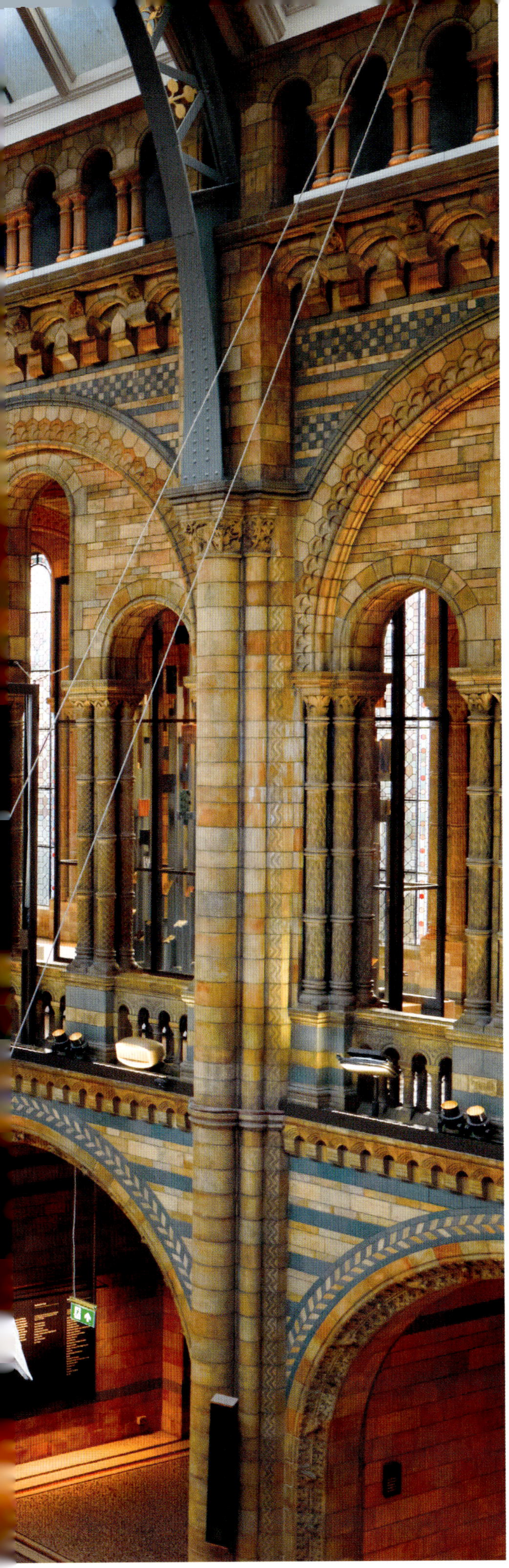

Natural History Museum

Hope, the blue whale, whose skeleton was mounted in the Hintze Hall in 2017.

South Kensington is intensively educational, home to the Science Museum and the Victoria & Albert Museum, as well as that favourite of school parties, the Natural History Museum.

This palace of knowledge for the history of life on Earth was opened in 1881, one of the first buildings in England to have a terracotta-clad front concealing an iron frame. The Natural History Museum's architect, Alfred Waterhouse, worked closely with the first superintendent of the museum, Richard Owen, on the building's design. Owen, a biologist and palaeontologist, provided the specimens to enable the architect to develop the decorative mouldings. Terracotta mouldings outside and in enabled the extensive depictions of flora and fauna. According to the museum, 'From the imposing gargoyles on the façade to the most delicate interior detail, every element of Waterhouse's design pays homage to the natural world.' Its imagery reflected the prevailing scientific state of awareness.

A visitor generally enters through the Hintze Hall, most famous perhaps for being home to 'Dippy the Diplodocus', whose bones hung from the ceiling until January 2017. When Dippy was despatched on a tour of Britain, the dinosaur's skeleton was replaced by the bones of a blue whale named Hope, the largest animal to have ever lived. The hall, refurbished and reopened by Prince William in July 2017, has huge stone arches along its length, underneath which are alcoves containing various animal skeletons, display panels and other exhibits. These include the remains of a gem-filled

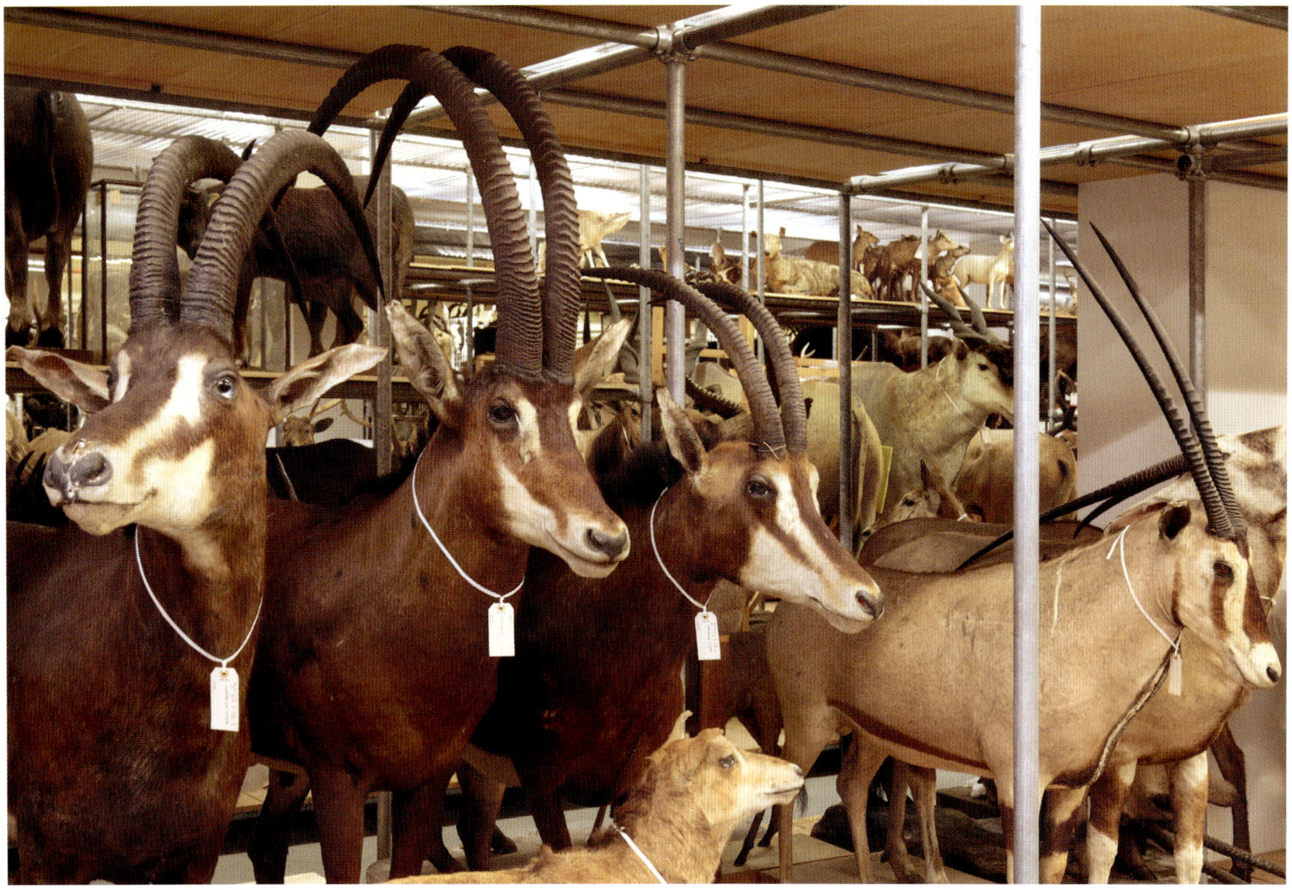

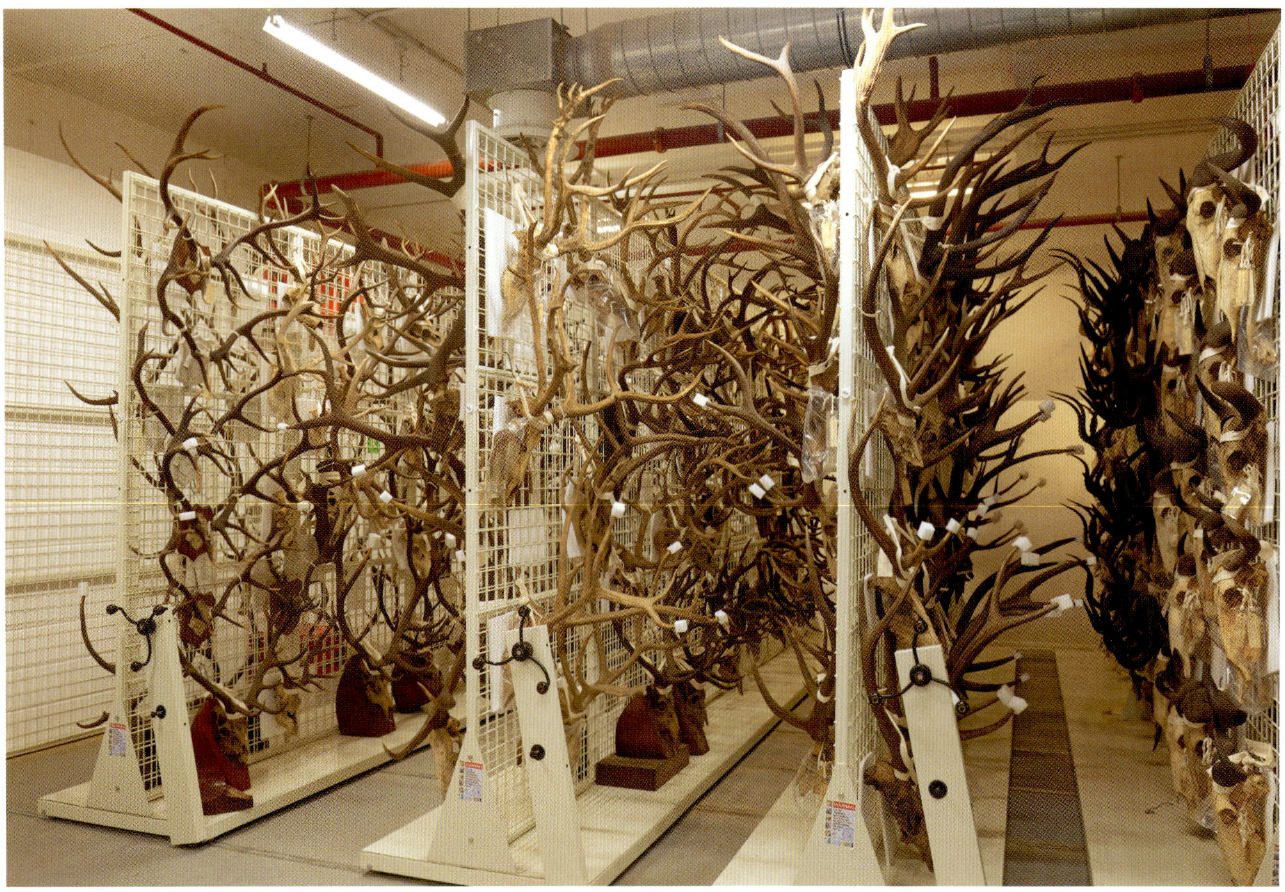

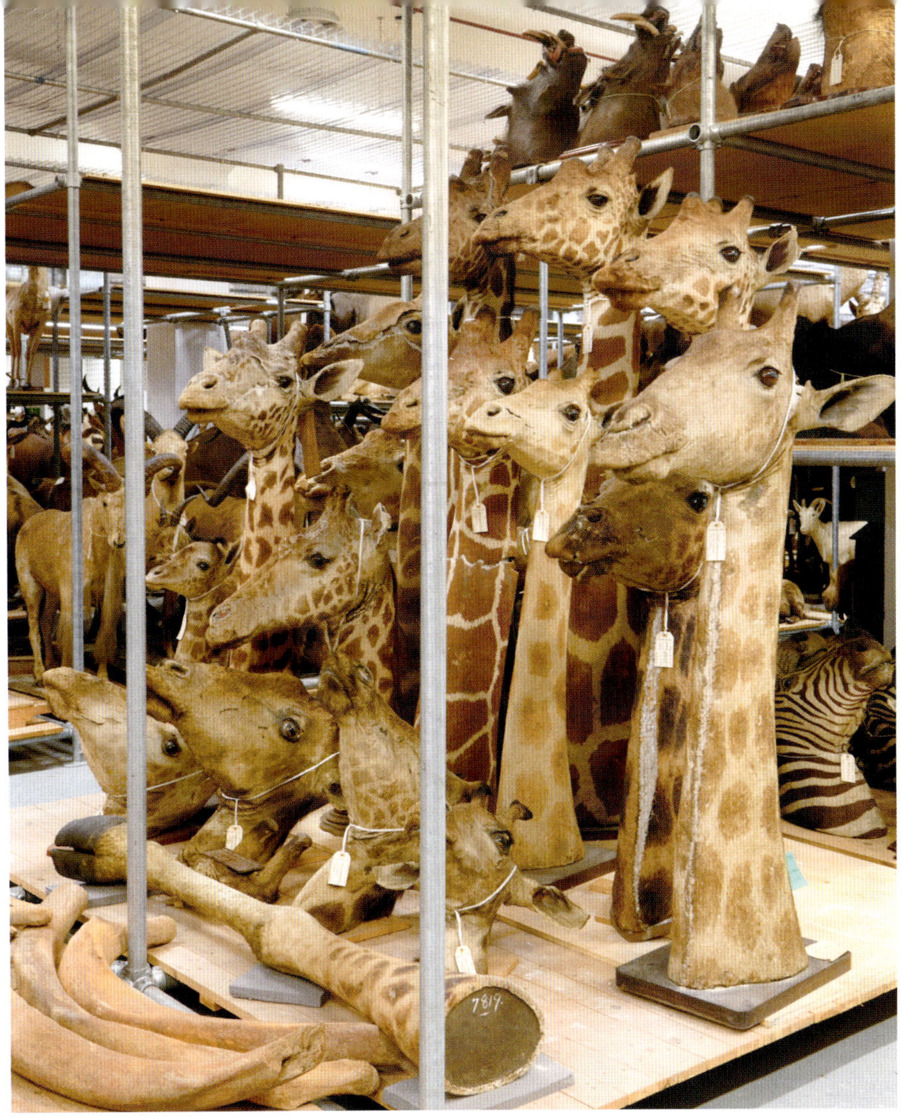

Opposite Taxidermy specimens of sable antelope, giant sable antelope and East African oryx members of the subfamily *Hippotraginae* (above); reference skulls of deer and antelope (below). Both images show specimens located at the Natural History Museum's storage facility.

Above A giraffe audience comprising taxidermy heads of Rothschild's reticulated and Masai giraffes, held at the storage facility of the Natural History Museum.

meteorite that dates back to the dawn of the solar system and remains of an Ice Age American mastodon. These have been chosen to show just some of the huge number of fossils, bones and other remains of flora, fauna and naturally occurring materials the museum has in its collections, most of which are not on display.

The museum has more than 5,000 fragments from some 2,000 individual meteorites, for instance; more than 250,000 fossil mammals in its palaeontology collection; and fossilized plants, algae and fungi dating from the last 3.5 billion years of Earth's history in its palaeobotany collection, including an estimated 6 million plant specimens collected between the 1600s and today. It claims 80 million specimens spanning 4.5 billion years of history, dating from the formation of the solar system to the present day.

Dominating the Hintze Hall is an imposing flight of stairs that lead up to the museum's first floor, on which there is a statue of a seated Charles Darwin. His *On the Origin of Species*, published in 1859, was based on his collection of thousands of specimens while voyaging in the HMS *Beagle* between 1831 and 1836. Many of these specimens are on display and behind the scenes at the museum.

There is a painting on the same stairwell of Alfred Russel Wallace, who developed the theory of natural selection at much the same time as Darwin; the two were friends and corresponded to share their ideas and learn from each other. A statue of Wallace is also found on the third floor of the museum. He is immortalized here carrying a butterfly net, a nod to the time he spent in Indonesia and the Malay archipelago, collecting specimens.

Away from the Hintze Hall's ground floor, the museum is divided into four colour-coded zones, a guide for the visitor who wishes to focus on a particular subject. These areas contain galleries devoted to geology, mineralogy, botany and zoology.

The stone arches of the Hintze Hall feature ornate carvings, including representations of small monkeys, birds and rams. The roof is a gilded canopy depicting diverse plants from across the world of 'economic, medicinal and horticultural importance', including tea and coffee, aloe and opium. Above the entrance on the first floor is a cut-away of a giant sequoia tree. The tree, which was felled in 1891, is believed to have been 1,335 years old, sequoias being among the longest-living species on the planet.

Throughout the building are other details, not all connected with natural history. A wall plaque featuring the design of a secret agent descending by parachute is dedicated to 'The Spirit of Resistance', to the men and women of the Special Operations Executive (SOE), a British spy network that undertook dangerous work during the Second World War. Between 1942 and 1945, SOE 'Station XVb' occupied three sealed galleries of the museum, known as the Demonstration Room, housing the specialized and secret military equipment that served as teaching aids for SOE staff. A workshop here for the sabotage branch modelled explosive devices disguised as pieces of coal and even dead rats.

The full importance of the Natural History Museum is not obvious to the casual visitor to Cromwell Road, yet it has more than 300 scientists and researchers working around the world to further develop knowledge of Earth's flora and fauna.

CONTACT INFORMATION

The Natural History Museum,
Cromwell Road, SW7 5BD
https://www.amnh.org/

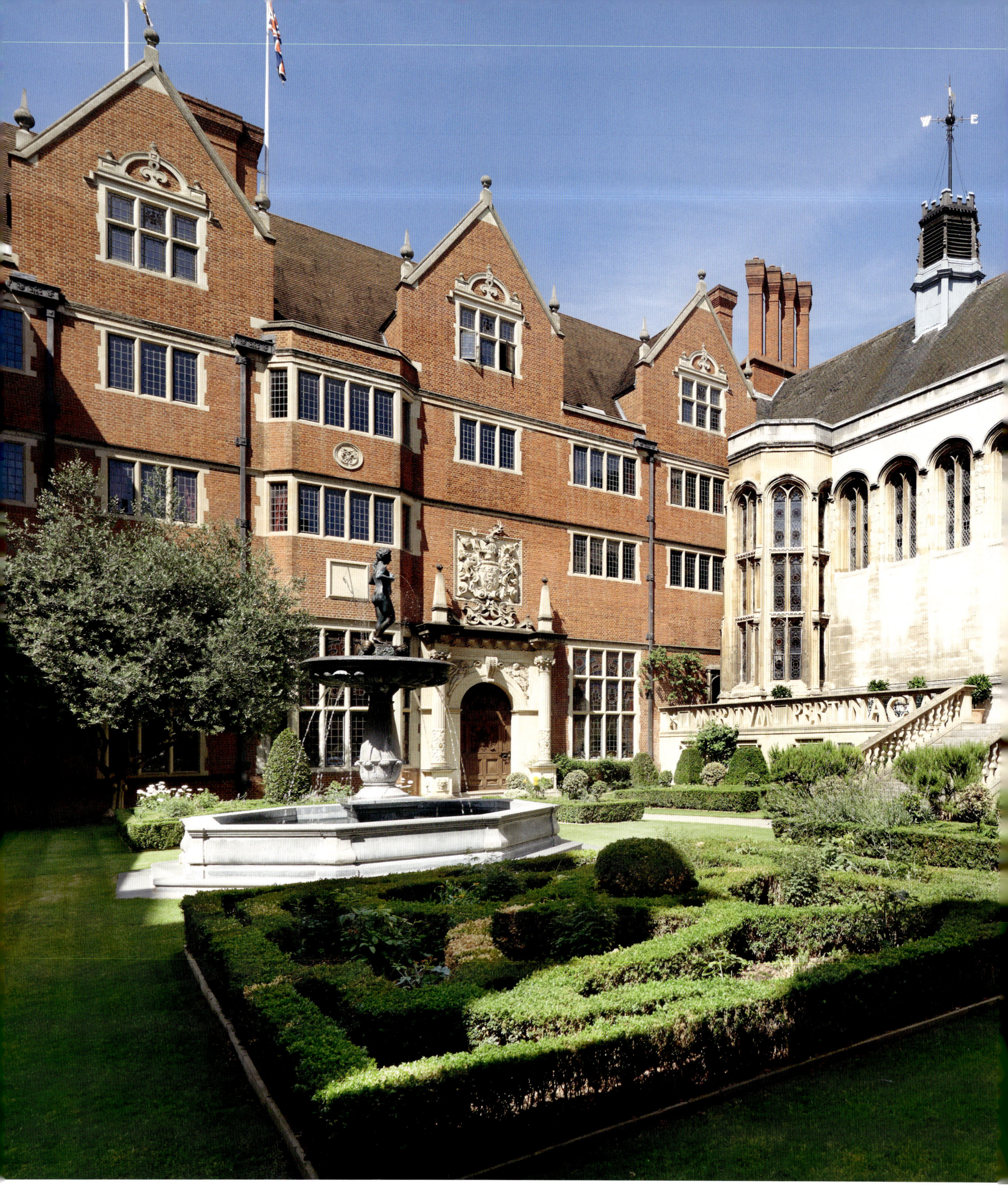

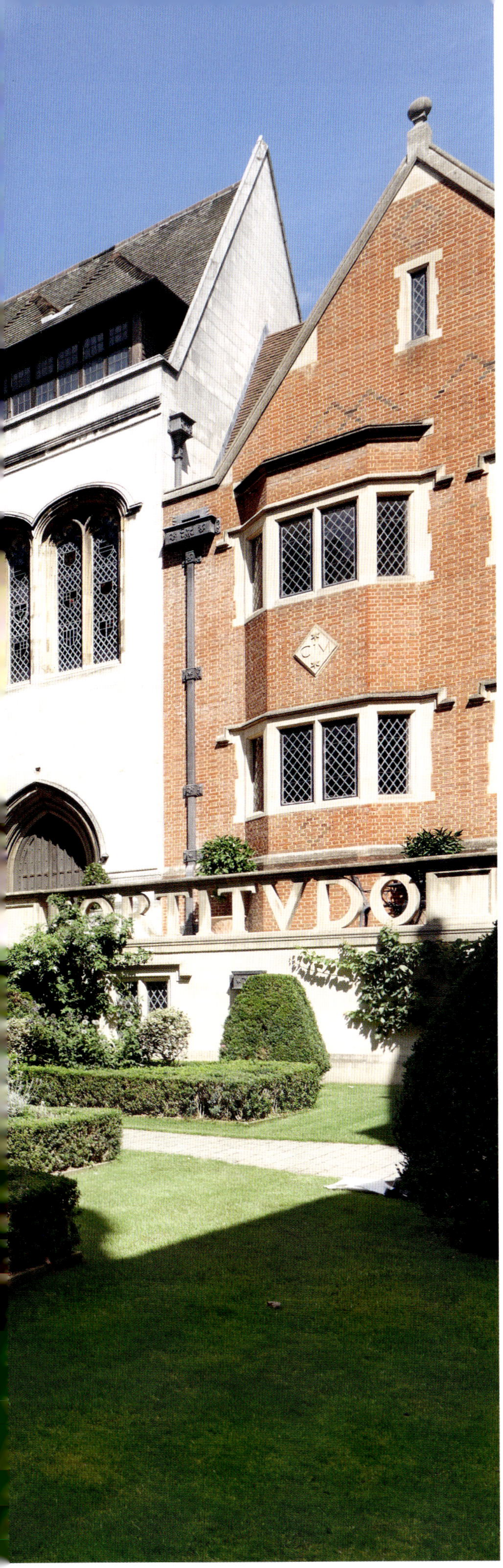

The Elizabethan Garden at Crosby Moran Hall was designed by the Marchioness of Salisbury. One of its features is an ornamental fountain of Diana by Neil Simmons, derived from one at Nonsuch Palace in Surrey.

Crosby Moran Hall

A grand palace by the River Thames in Chelsea, Crosby Moran Hall has been described by English Heritage as 'the most important surviving secular domestic medieval building in London'.

It is the thirty-year achievement of businessman and philanthropist Dr Christopher Moran, chairman of Co-operation Ireland, who has made it his life's work to put London's only domestic medieval building to have survived the Great Fire of 1666, Crosby Moran Hall, back into its historical context in terms of architecture. As a passionate and knowledgeable enthusiast of the Tudor, Elizabethan and early Stuart periods and a collector of Old Master pictures, high-status furniture, silver and gold, arms and armour, and tapestry of these ages, he launched a project unlike any other restoration programme in London – the final aim being to reinstate the art and architecture of the Tudor, Elizabethan and early Stuart periods here. This rebuilding and restoration of Crosby Moran Hall incorporates a Tudor and Elizabethan mansion constructed over a period of 150 years. Its true history spans 500 years and started in the City of London.

A wealthy merchant, Sir John Crosby, commissioned at Bishopsgate his great house, Crosby Place, between 1466 and 1475. It was afterwards occupied by Richard Plantagenet, Duke of Gloucester – later Richard III – at the time of the disappearance of the princes in the Tower. With this connection, Crosby Place generates several mentions in Shakespeare's *Richard III*. Sir Thomas More owned the house, by that time a

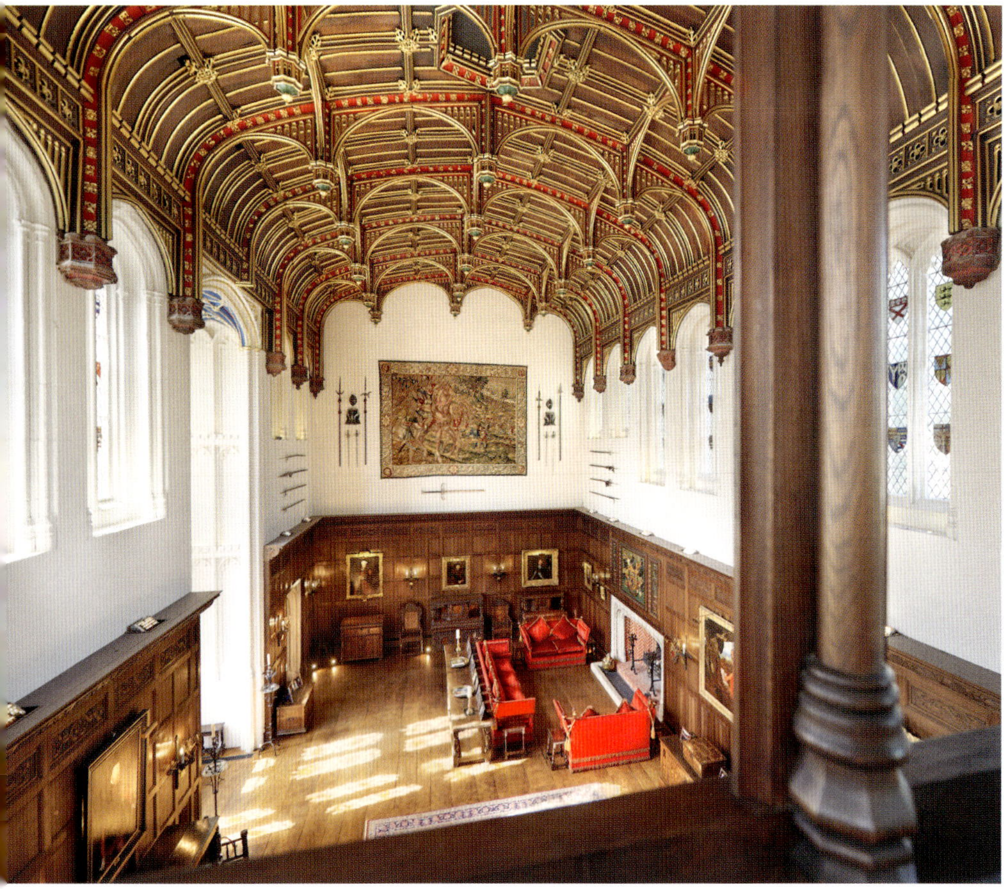

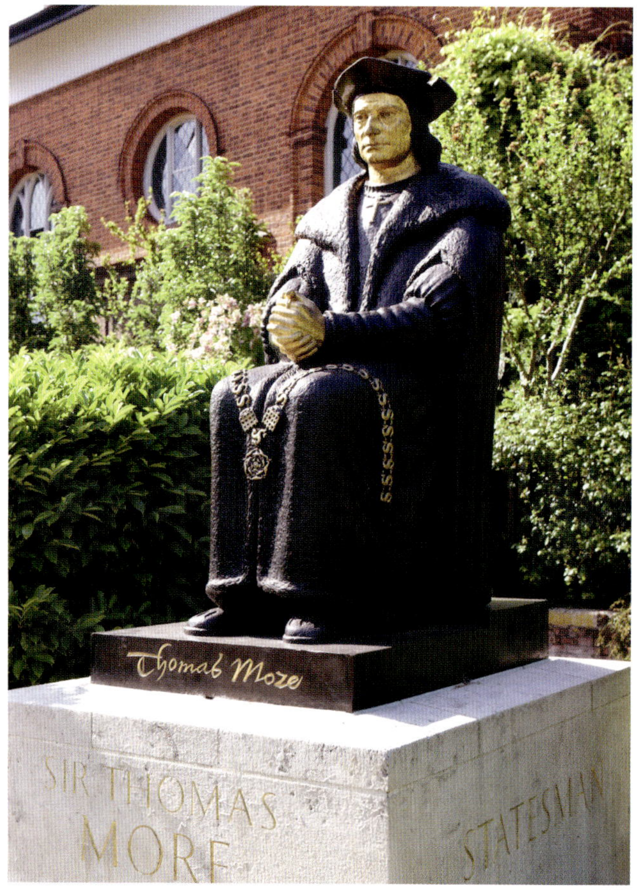

Above A view over the original Great Hall from the balcony.

Above right A statue of Sir Thomas More outside Chelsea Old Church, close to Crosby Moran Hall.

Right The original Great Hall at Crosby Moran Hall.

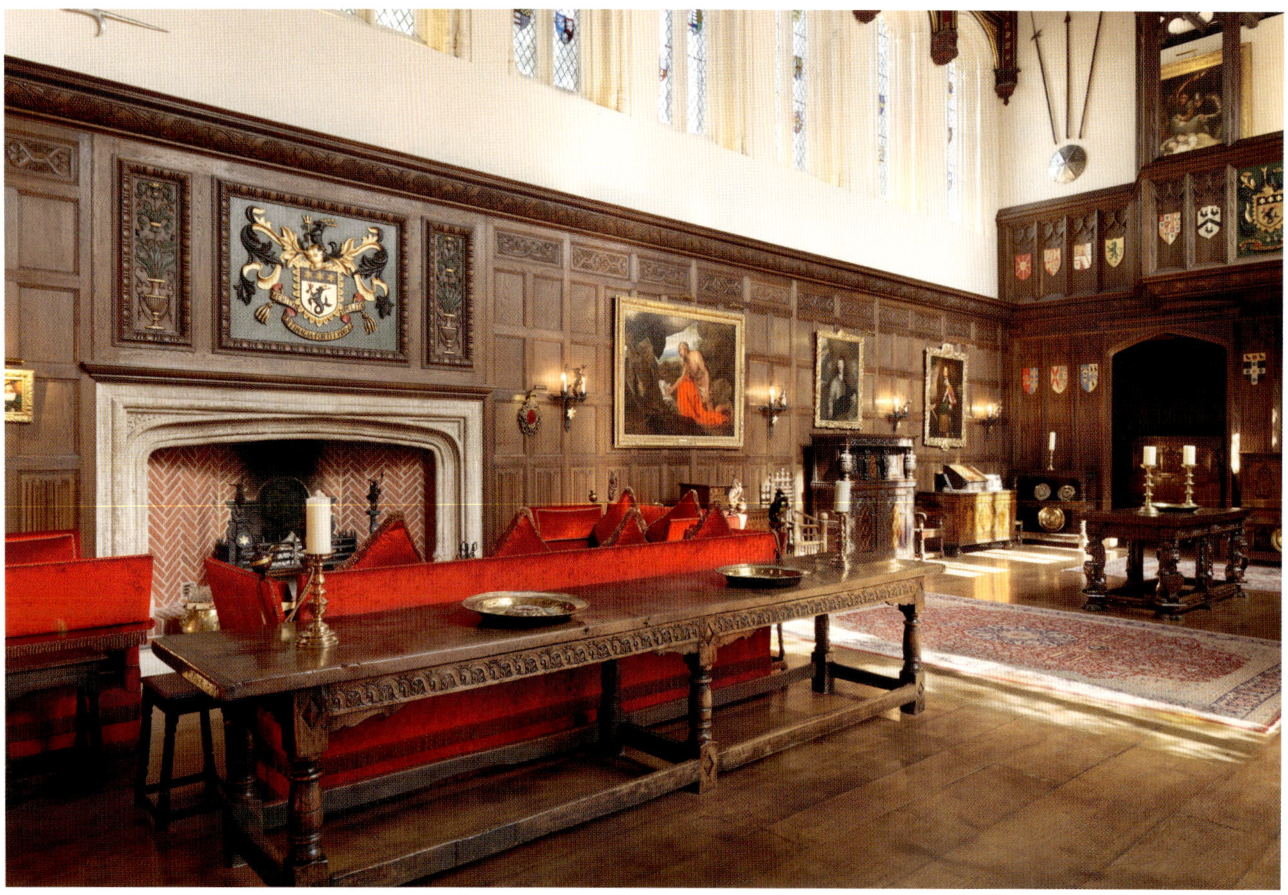

Each of the five floors is furnished with Moran's impressive collection of fifteenth-, sixteenth- and early seventeenth-century furniture.

palace, while he served Henry VIII. It was described by Stowe in his 1603 Survey of London as 'of stone and timber, very large and beautiful, and the highest at that time in London'. Catherine of Aragon, Henry VIII, Elizabeth I, Sir Walter Raleigh, the poet Mary Sidney and Shakespeare have all dined, lodged or visited there. Lord Mayor Sir John Spencer further beautified the grand rooms while Crosby Hall served as his Mansion House. It operated as head office of the East India Company from 1621 to 1638. At that time, the hall served as a meeting place and warehouse, and by Victorian times, it had become a cavernous restaurant.

In 1908 the Chartered Bank of India, Australia and China bought the Bishopsgate site to build a new London headquarters, which put the hall under threat of demolition. Crosby Hall was saved on an early wave of preservation and conservationism awareness and, in a remarkable feat of engineering, it was dismantled, its parts numbered and re-erected in 1910 on a plot in Chelsea owned by the London County Council, the site of Thomas More's country manor of the 1520s. The Queen Mother opened Crosby Hall here in 1926.

This was the Crosby Hall in Chelsea that Christopher Moran was able to acquire out of public ownership in 1988. After purchasing the renamed Crosby Moran Hall and its attendant buildings, Moran commenced eight years of planning, design and expert consultation with Britain's leading architectural historians and scholars. Moran initially invested over £1 million to stabilize the hall's fifteenth-century Reigate stone, which had begun to crumble. Since then, he has invested more than £50 million into the restoration effort alone. The west of the courtyard is a dining room constructed entirely of stone in the Tudor and Elizabethan style. The quadrangle was completed with a red-brick wing facing the river on Cheyne Walk, inspired by elements of Hampton Court Palace and Hengrave Hall and advised by English Heritage.

Fitting out required the commissioning of stained glass, the application of wood and stone carving, marquetry, the making of fireplaces and fine detailing, such as the recreation of embellished bronze door locks. For the dining chamber, a 55-ft (17-m) table was cut from a single piece of oak and seats forty-four people. Each of the five floors are furnished with Moran's impressive collection of fifteenth-, sixteenth- and early seventeenth-century high-status English furniture, arms and armour, tapestries and paintings by artists Van Dyck, Dobson, Eworth, Gheeraerts, Hilliard, Cranach and Holbein. The main rooms are the council chamber (where the king would have held his council), long gallery above, dining chamber, libraries, chapel, billiard room, museum and, most impressively, the Great Hall with its original, magnificent ceiling and soaring, gilded oriel window.

The completed courtyard encloses an Elizabethan knot garden designed by the Dowager Marchioness of Salisbury and is authentic with its plants, trees and layout matching those that had existed in the sixteenth century. Its fountain, bearing a statue of the goddess Diana, is based on the fountain design for the lost Nonsuch Palace of Henry VIII in Surrey. The terrace over the garden, inspired by Rushton, received a stone balustrade carved in the shape of Moran's motto: *Meritum Pertinacia Fortitudo Fidelitas*.

Following medieval tradition, the chapel, with a side Lady Chapel and Mortuary Chapel, is being completed under the Great Hall, with a fan-vaulted ceiling. Under guidance from Westminster Abbey, the chapel will include a rare Cosmati floor, including appropriate stones sourced from Italy in the pattern that was last used 500 years ago. It will also include stained-glass windows to the east and west, and the Lady Chapel will include a window looking across the roses of the knot garden. Several reports have said that Christopher Moran's intention is to leave the house to a charitable trust for cultural or educational use.

CONTACT INFORMATION

Crosby Moran Hall,
Cheyne Walk, Chelsea, SW3 5AZ

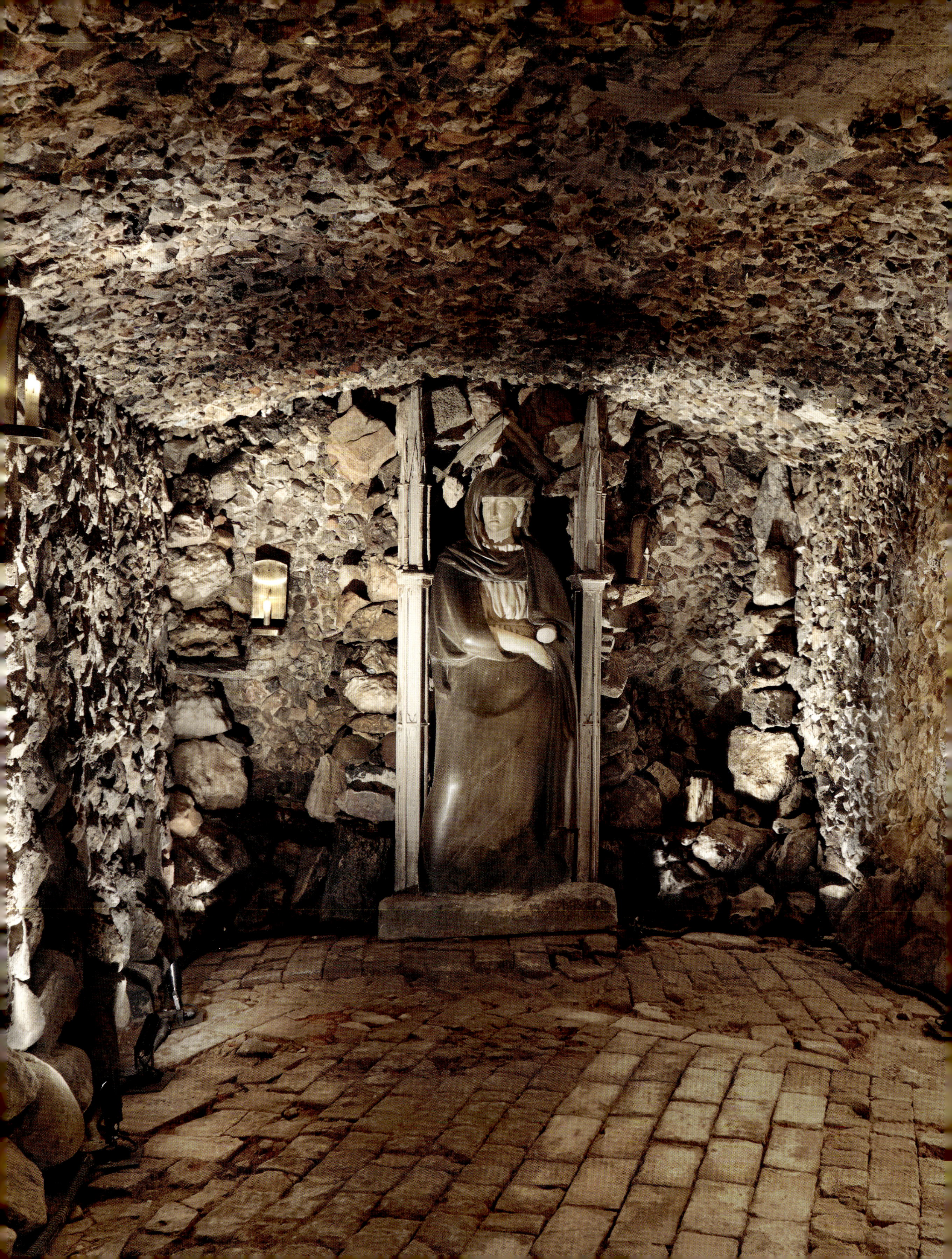

Pope's Grotto

This statue of unknown origin is one of the grotto's several enigmas, possibly the Roman goddess Pudicitia, representing chastity and modesty.

Alexander Pope, eighteenth-century poet, essayist, satirist, translator and pioneering garden designer, created a mysterious encrusted grotto, which survives under the site of his long-demolished house in Twickenham. Today a school stands above the grotto, which is not open for casual visiting but can be explored on certain scheduled days.

Pope came to Twickenham in 1719. Made prosperous by rewards from his translation of Homer's *Iliad*, he was able to build a substantial three-storey house facing the Thames. Across a roadway, he rented several acres of land to create an early landscaped garden. House and garden were linked by a tunnel he commissioned, which remains under the A310 road to Richmond. By 1725, a grotto had been created in the brick basement of the house, forming the entrance of the tunnel. Pope had embellishments added until his death in 1744. Flints, quartz, shells, ammonite, coral, a slab of basalt taken from the Giant's Causeway in Ireland, all line the walls. There are glass pieces, minerals, ceramics and religious and secular imagery. Remains of rustic arcades and columns can be glimpsed, and there were once mirrors and a lens working as a *camera obscura* to illuminate the vaults.

Pope is recognized as a master of rhyming couplets in iambic pentameters. His most famous work is *The Rape of the Lock* and his poetry is most widely recognized in proverbs. 'Fools rush in where angels fear to tread', 'A little learning is a dangerous thing' and 'To err is human, to forgive divine' all come from one poem, *An Essay on Criticism*. The notion 'eternal sunshine of the spotless mind' belongs to Pope.

The sheer curiosity of the grotto is made stranger by the challenge of understanding its inspiration, partly lost across time. Pope may have seen grottoes in travels to Italy or, if not, was aware of decorated chambers through his aesthetic interests stemming from ancient Rome. Pope described later additions to the grotto as forming a museum of mining and geology. A further complication is that some statuary was added after Pope's death by the subsequent owner. Extensive study is needed to uncover the true context for the creation of the chambers.
A symposium exploring the links between the grotto, garden design and eighteenth-century literature has been hosted by the Pope's Grotto Preservation Trust, the group responsible for its continuing restoration and for the scheduling of open days.

CONTACT INFORMATION

Pope's Grotto,
Radnor House Independent School,
21 Cross Deep, Twickenham, TW1 4QG
https://popesgrotto.org.uk/

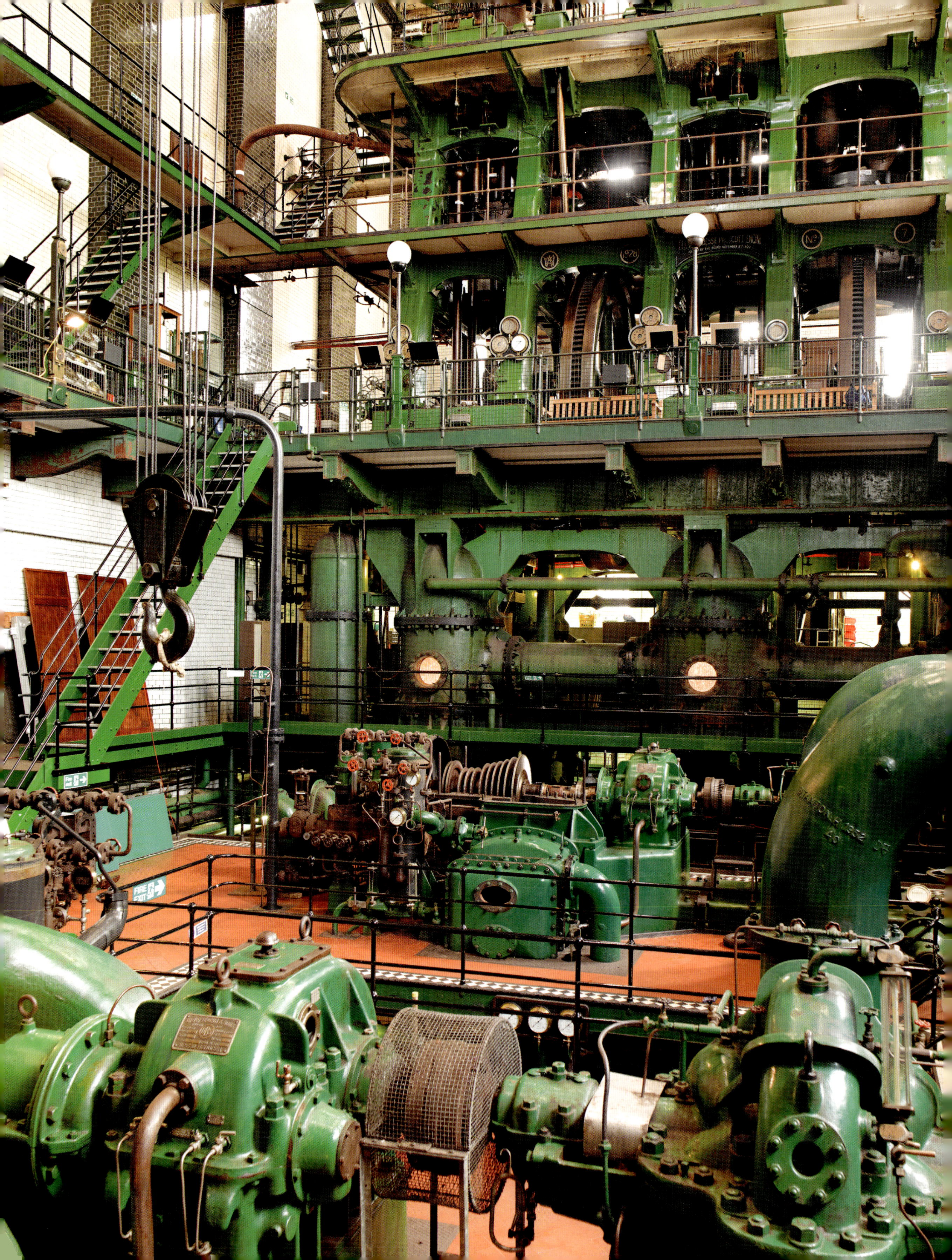

Kempton Steam Museum

The triple-expansion engine is laid out on four storeys, with a turbine of equal rating on the left, together with the hook of the crane which was used to assemble the engines.

Kempton Steam Museum qualifies as a true cathedral of steam, with a monumental engine house containing colossal pieces of machinery in the form of two triple-expansion engines, the largest ever made in the UK.

These engines have also been described as being among the most sophisticated reciprocating steam engines ever built, coming at a time when pistons reached their peak of efficiency and started to be bettered by electric motors and turbines. For good measure, Kempton also has its own pair of early turbines displayed in the museum between the triple-expansion engines.

Kempton Park Works, once owned by the Metropolitan Water Board, was a water treatment and pumping station supplying water to reservoirs in north-west London. This rather distant arrangement followed the 1852 Metropolis Water Act ruling that drinking water from the Thames had to come from above the tidal reaches of the river. The MWB was well-established with feeds from the upper Thames above Teddington Lock, but when it needed to expand its capacity at Kempton during the mid-1920s, the decision was taken to commission new triple-expansion engines, numbered Kempton 6 and 7, from Worthington Simpson of Newark, each rated at just over 1,000 horsepower.

The tall Engine House, in red brick with Portland stone facing, has been attributed to Henry Stilgoe, chief engineer of the MWB, and is lined with glazed bricks and quarry tiles. An overhead travelling crane, which remains in place, was used to assemble the engine from components shipped by rail from Nottinghamshire in loads not greater than 16 tonnes. Yet each finished engine weighs between 800 and 1,000 tonnes. Triple expansion is particularly efficient engine architecture, at the expense of some complexity and bulkiness. Steam was provided by six moving-grate boilers. It flows through three cylinders of progressively increased diameter, with carefully calculated timings of valve cut-off. Superheaters and condensers add to the steam's effectiveness as it travels through the engine.

The first triple at Kempton was named *The Sir William Prescott*, after the MWB Chairman, and the second after his wife *The Lady Bessie Prescott*. The official opening of the new engine house was in October 1929, and the engines ran from that date until 1980, generally being operated alternatively. They pumped about 38 million gallons of water each day across a distance of 12 miles (19 km) to reservoirs at Maiden Lane, Shoot-Up Hill, Fortis Green and Bishops Wood.

Provision for further increase in capacity had been made, with a space left for a third engine of the same type to be placed between the original pair, but the plan was changed in favour of a pair of steam turbines made by Fraser and Chalmers, driving centrifugal pumps through David Brown

They pumped about 38 million gallons of water each day across a distance of 12 miles to reservoirs at Maiden Lane, Shoot-Up Hill, Fortis Green and Bishops Wood.

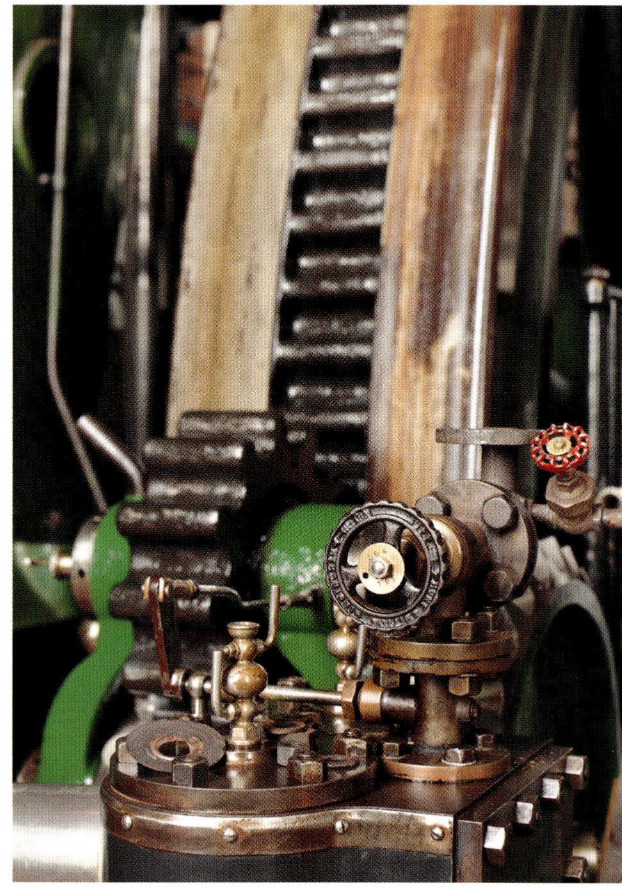

gearboxes. Although the turbines were only a fraction of the size and weight of the reciprocating engines, on paper their power was at least equal and their efficiency far greater, yet they do not seem to have fulfilled their promise and they were not extensively used. One of the turbines is now partly dismantled for display at Kew.

When Kempton was at its coal-fired peak, a considerable infrastructure was built up to support all the steam engines in operation at the works. A narrow-gauge railway was built from Hampton, where the MWB had a riverside wharf and took delivery of coal. Coal was shipped to Kempton from there, or from a connection to the standard-gauge railway yard nearby, and tipped into an automatic boiler feed conveyer. There are plans to revive and reinstate the railway on the original track-bed on land now owned by Thames Water.

The pumping station Engine House at Kempton Park has been designated as a Statutory National Monument. The steam engines are now a museum operated by Kempton Great Engines Trust, who have restored *The Sir William Prescott* to running order.

Right The starting system is itself a small steam engine, which engages with the flywheel.

Right, below Clocking in at Kempton time card machine.

Opposite, above The instrument panel for the two turbines at Kempton: engines number 8 and 9.

Opposite, below The lower level of the four-storey Kempton engine, showing pump valve chambers.

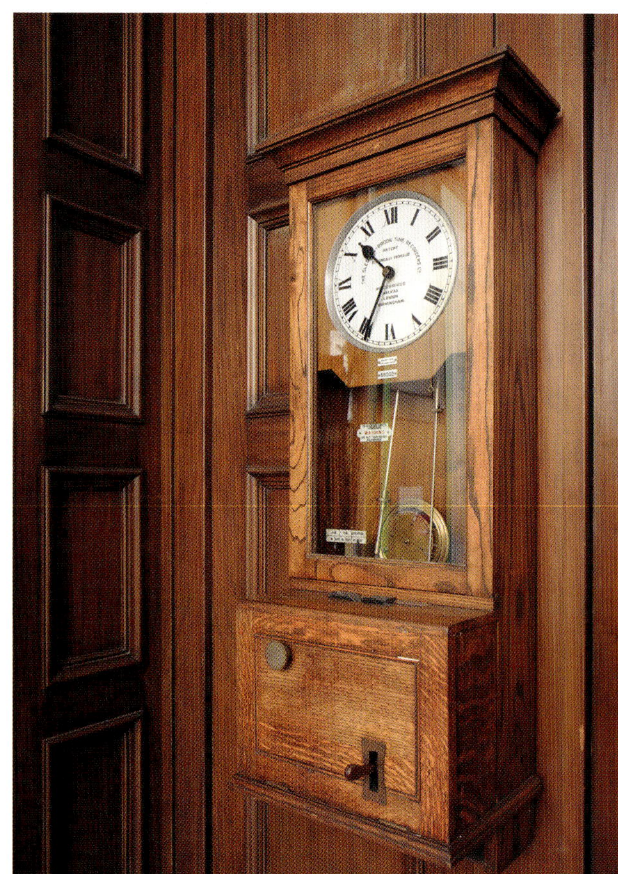

CONTACT INFORMATION

Kempton Steam Museum,
Snakey Lane, Hanworth, TW13 7ND
https://kemptonsteam.org/

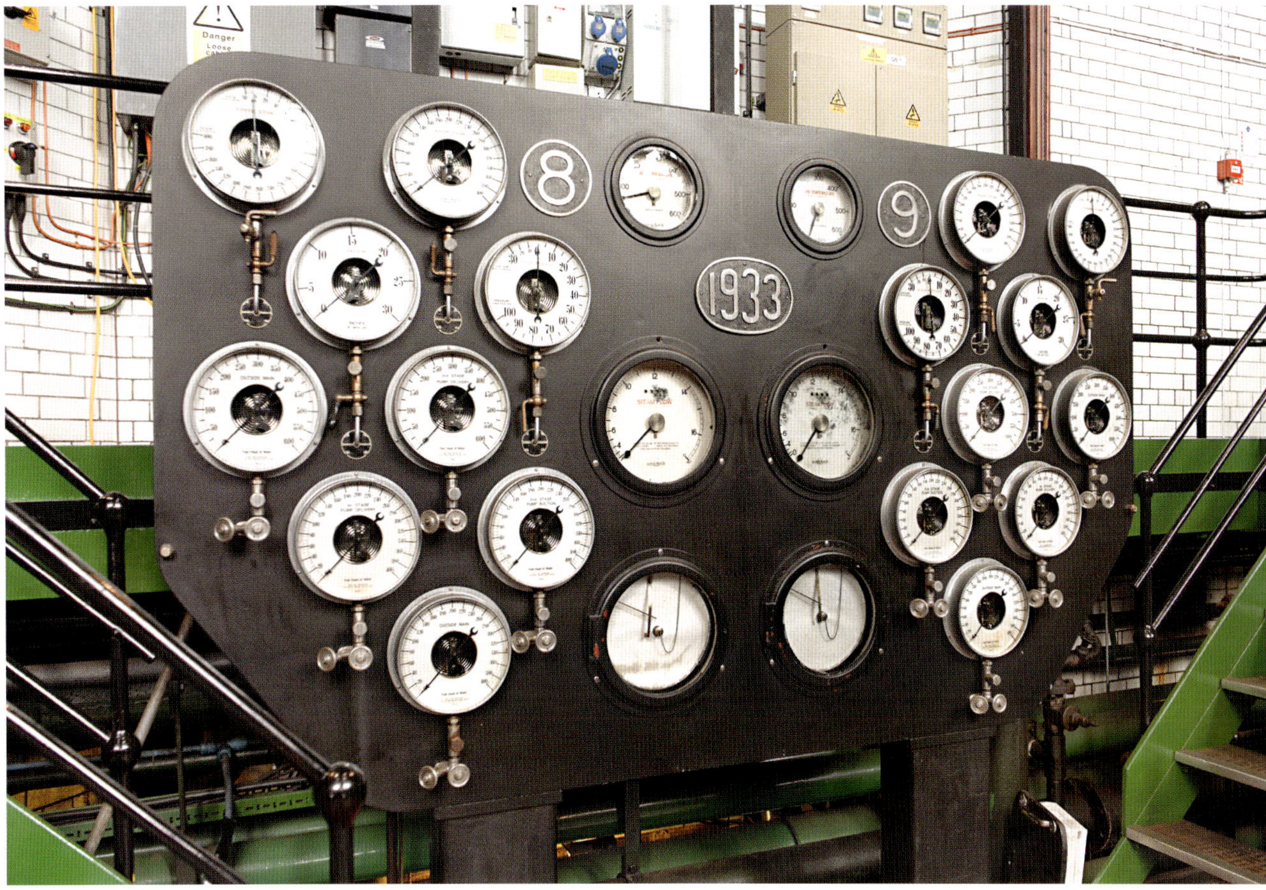
8
1933
9

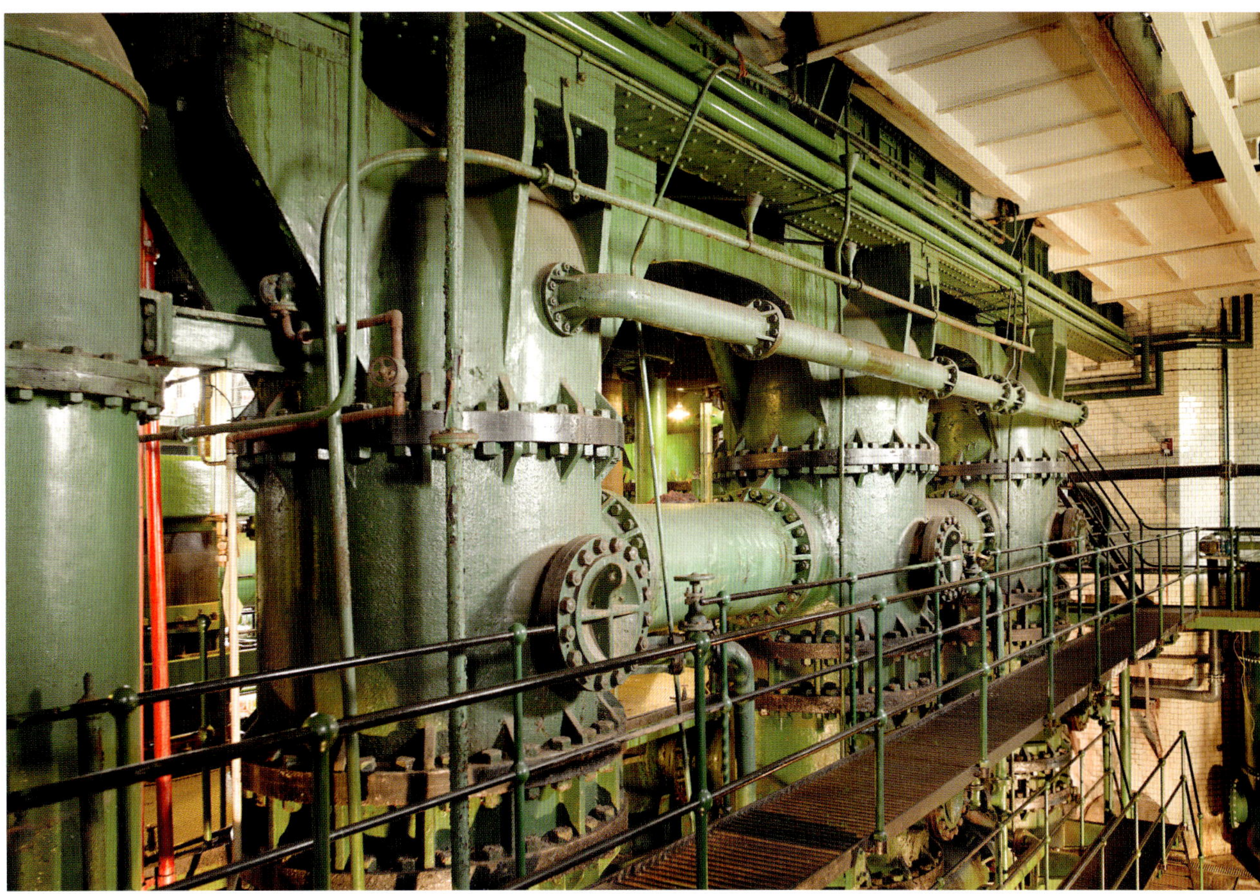

Keats House

John Keats, arguably the greatest of English Romantic poets, drew inspiration from classical mythology, from nature, from notions of love and mortality. His time as a poet spanned less than six years, during which he produced no fewer than sixty poems, some of them remarkable in richness of imagery, sensuality of language and mastery of verse form. In the background lay the northern suburbs of London 'where Keats' life as a poet began and where much of his greatest poetry would be written', in the words of biographer Nicholas Rowe. It was an area he knew well, and a house in Hampstead was John Keats' last real home, now restored as Keats House, a memorial and museum.

A Londoner by birth, he was raised in Moorgate, where his family operated a livery stable attached to The Swan and Hoop pub. At the start of the 1800s, the city was beginning to edge northwards into the countryside and John Keats was sent to Enfield for his schooling. He became a medical apprentice in Edmonton before going to Guy's Hospital to study to be an apothecary surgeon.

In 1816, he turned away from his medical career and the following year, as his first poems were published, he moved with his brothers to lodgings at Well Walk in Hampstead. The move was most likely prompted by a search for a healthier environment; his brother Tom was beginning to show signs of tuberculosis, a disease which dogged the Keats family. Hampstead was a village yet to be connected to London on its southern side, while open to the heath to the north. At that time

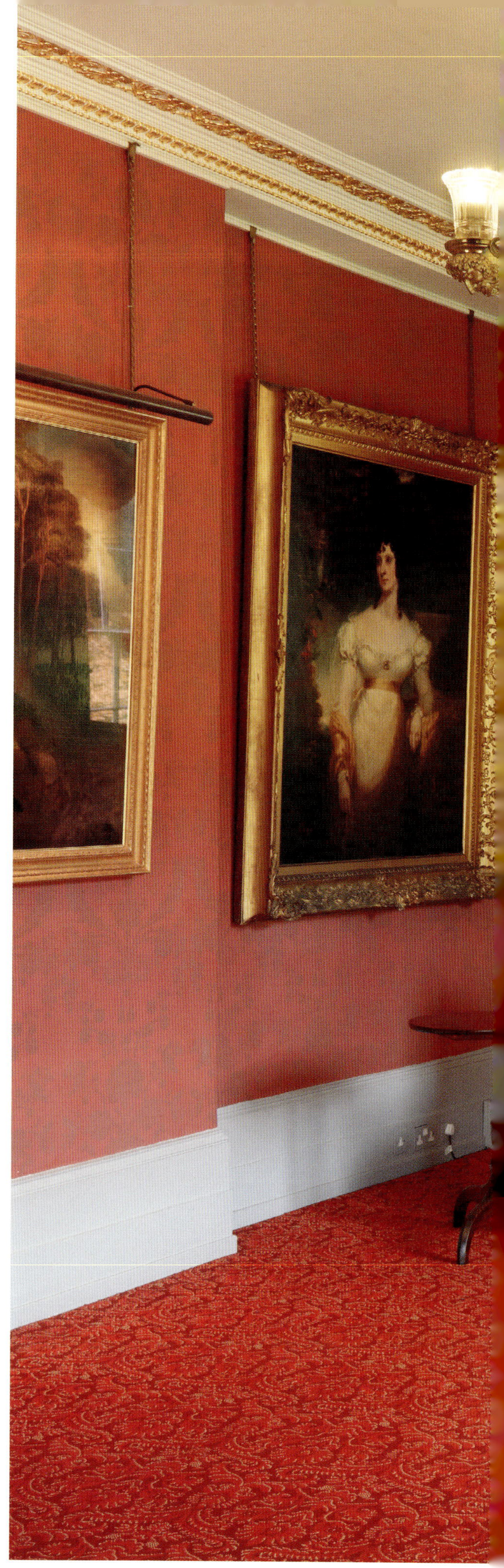

The Chester Room, which was used for entertaining, was an 1839 addition to the original house.

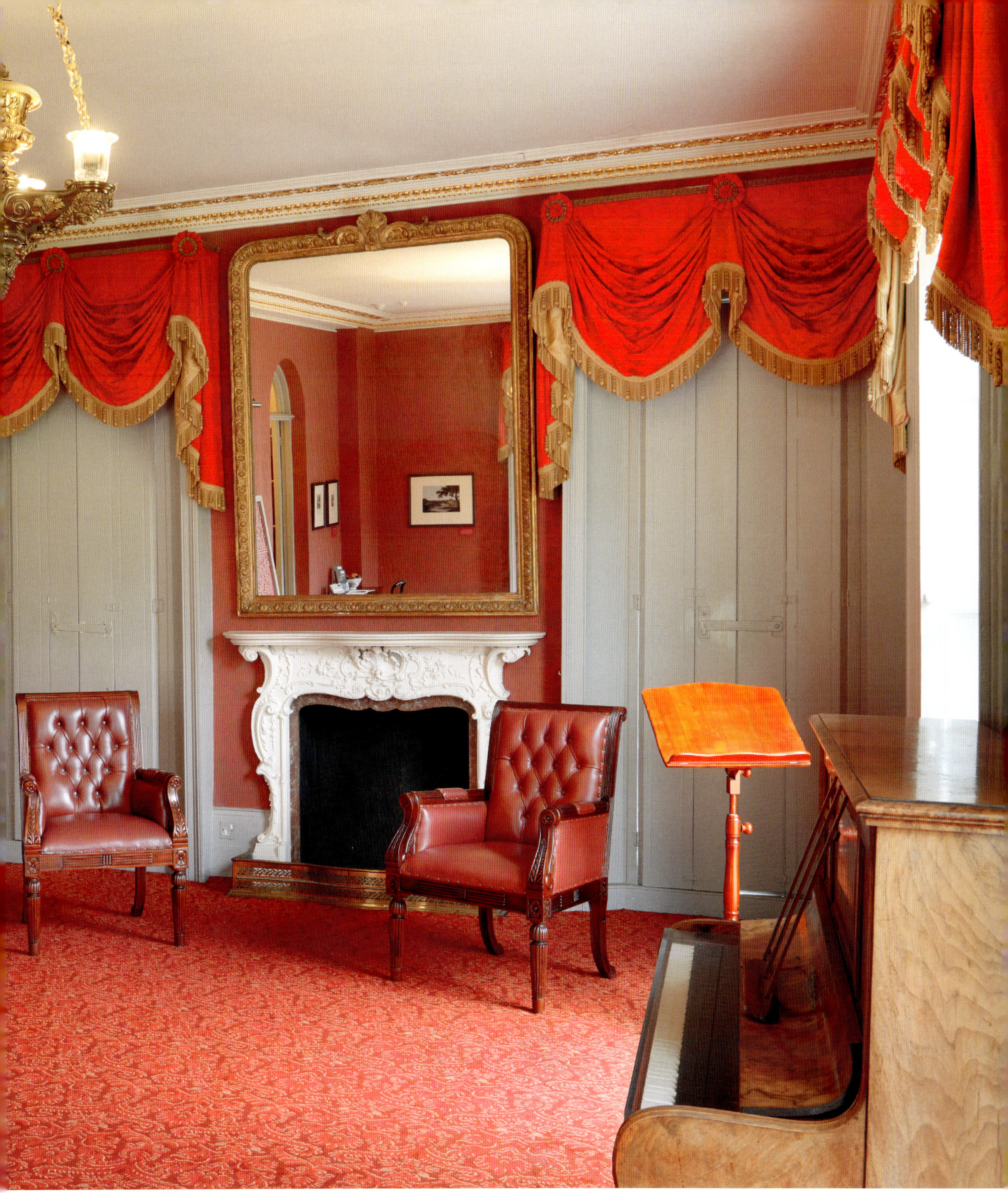

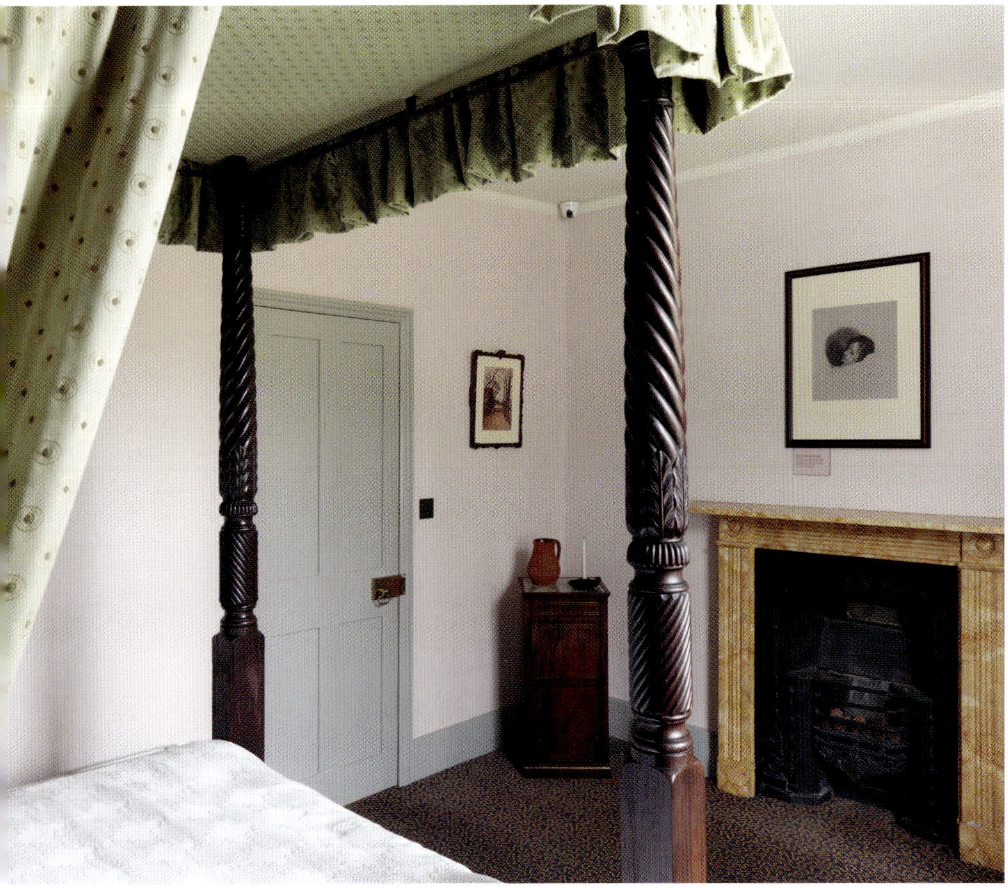

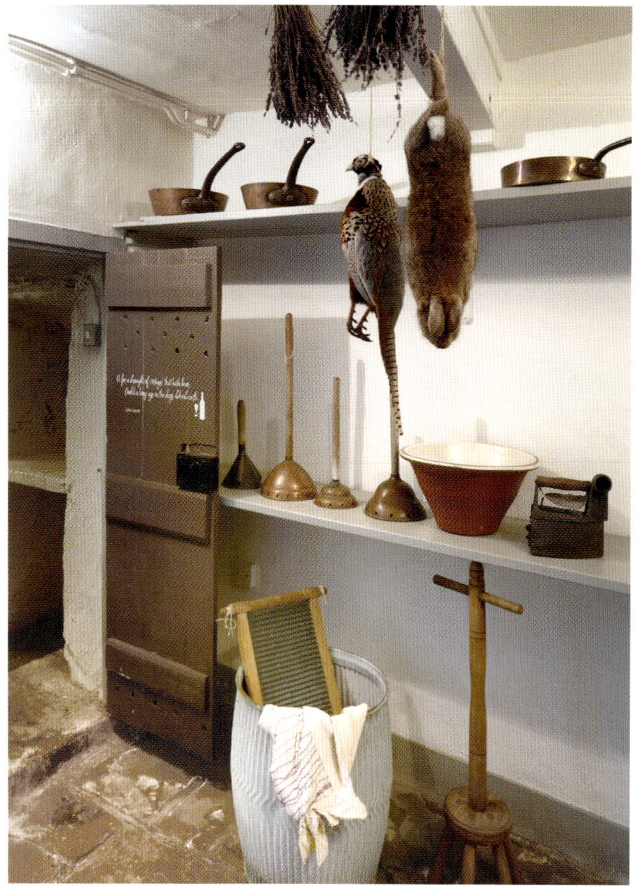

Above Keats' bedroom where he first realized he had consumption (tuberculosis), the illness that he died from in 1821.

Above right The cellar and wine store.

Right the parlour, where Keats wrote his greatest and most enduring poetry.

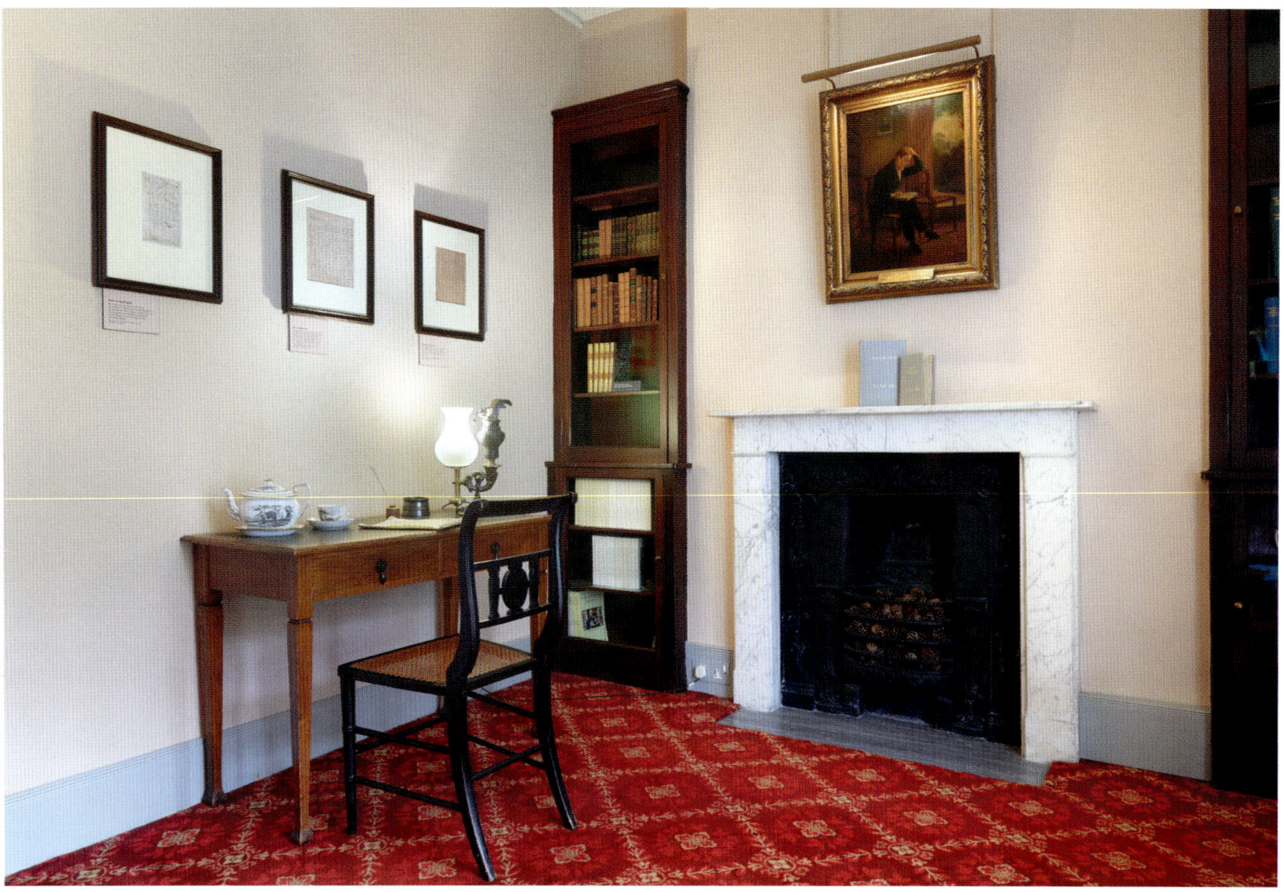

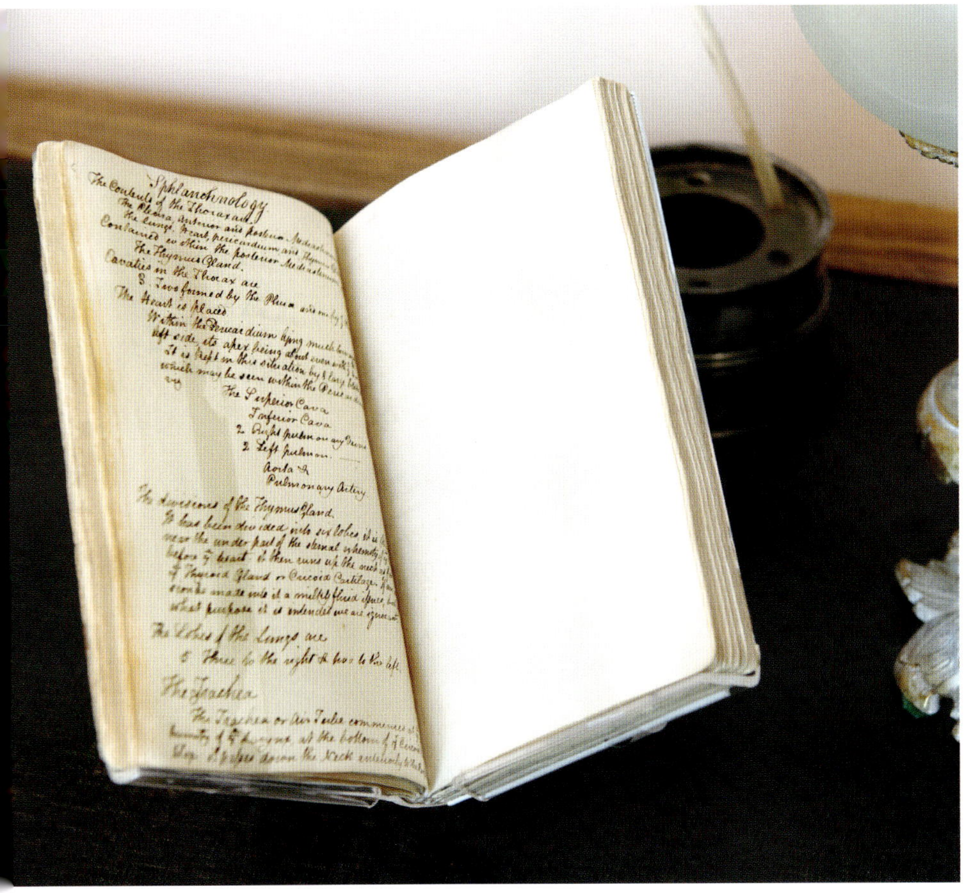

Keats' incredibly neat medical notebook dated 1816, the year he finished his studies and dedicated himself to poetry.

it was starting to become a fashionable place, and several houses were being built along its country lanes. One of these was Wentworth Place, a house divided into two residences, one part-owned by Charles Brown, a merchant and supporter of the arts. When Tom Keats died, Brown invited John Keats to share the rooms at Wentworth Place. This is the building now known as Keats House.

In 1819, the house was surrounded by a garden planted with fruit trees and vegetables, with open fields lying beyond. Tradition says that 'Ode to a Nightingale' was composed under a plum tree here in April or May when Keats was inspired by birdsong; this is based on an account by Charles Brown.

More certain is the fact that the Brawne family had moved into the house that comprised the other side of Wentworth Place around this time. The eldest daughter, Fanny Brawne, met Keats in the garden, a friendship developed and an engagement was arranged between them.

Keats did not come from an aristocratic, prosperous or landed family, which set him apart from other poets of the time, but neither was he born into poverty as sometimes suggested. He enjoyed no particular privilege, yet received a good education in a progressive environment and he travelled quite widely in Britain during his short life. For him, there were to be no Grand Tour or European sojourns as there were for Byron, Shelley and Wordsworth, although his last weeks were spent in Italy for the sake of his health. He died there aged twenty-five in 1821. There had been little positive recognition by critics during his lifetime and there was little sense of preciousness attached to Wentworth Place for years after his death.

Wentworth Place was bought by the actress Eliza Jane Chester in 1838, who ordered the combining of the two houses into a single dwelling and added a drawing room to the eastern side of the building. The house continued as a residence into the twentieth century until it was proposed to demolish it to make way for the development of a row of flats. A growing appreciation of the quality of Keats' poetry had come during the late-nineteenth century and a memorial committee was formed to save the house. Fundraising of £10,000, much of it coming from the US where Keats' reputation was high, saved the house, which subsequently became a museum. A building was added to the side to contain a collection of books, letters and artefacts, and part of this was used as a Hampstead branch library. The house was restored by the London Borough of Camden in the 1970s. In 1998, the City of London took over responsibility for Keats House and completed a programme of conservation and internal restoration. The result is a homely series of rooms describing the time in 1819 when Keats and Charles Brown shared one side of the house and the Brawne family lived next door. By far the grandest room is the Chester Entertaining Room, the drawing room added by Eliza Jane Chester. The cosy bedroom with pale pink walls is poignant because it is the place where Keats was first seized by a tubercular cough and immediately made his own prognosis.

CONTACT INFORMATION

Keats House,
10 Keats Grove, Hampstead, NW3 2RR
https://www.cityoflondon.gov.uk/things-to-do/attractions-museums-entertainment/keats-house

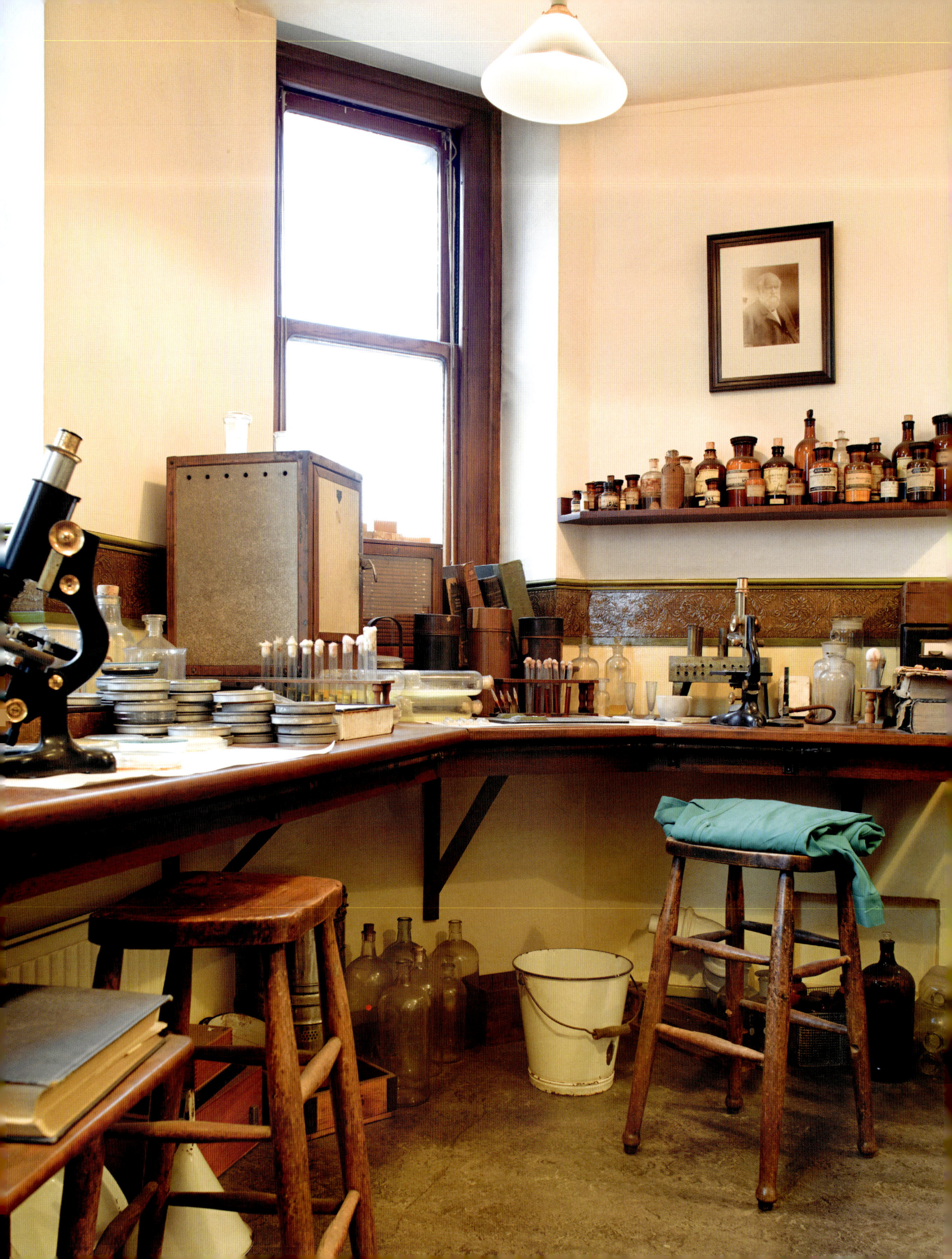

Alexander Fleming Museum

The original laboratory was described as musty, dusty and cramped. Fleming worked in this second-floor room for fourteen years.

A room in St Mary's Hospital Paddington is one of London's smallest museums and one of the most compelling. The Alexander Fleming Museum is the place where penicillin was discovered on 3 September 1928.

Alexander Fleming, Professor of Bacteriology at St Mary's, returned from holiday to find a dish containing a bacteria sample had been left on the bench. He noticed that the sample had been contaminated by a fungus and growth of the bacteria had been inhibited. Fleming said to his colleague Merlin Pryce: 'That's funny.'

Part of the legend of the discovery of penicillin is that fungus mould spore had blown in through an open window, but a visit to the museum nails that myth and others. The museum captures the reality of a simply equipped laboratory with its narrow and cluttered wooden bench, Zeiss microscope, slide cabinet and glass sample dishes. When the laboratory was recreated *in situ* and refitted in 1993, sixty years after Fleming left it, great care was taken to make it as authentic as possible. The apparatus was assembled from relics saved in St Mary's bacteriology department. One of the greatest challenges was finding correct 4-inch glass petri dishes to the original pattern, and after an extensive search a few were discovered in old public health laboratory store. Old photographs of the laboratory, which Fleming occupied from 1919 to 1933, show a framed picture on the side wall. This same picture, a signed photograph of the pioneer of immunology Élie Metchnikoff, was found, and hangs in exactly the same place today.

Fleming had previously worked at the laboratory of a military hospital, observing the limitations of antiseptics when applied to wound infections, as they destroyed white blood cells, a natural defence against bacteria, faster than they destroyed microbes.

Displays in adjacent rooms illustrate other chapters of the penicillin story, including how a team at Oxford University devised a way of purifying and stabilizing penicillin to make it into the antibiotic that changed medicine.

CONTACT INFORMATION

Alexander Fleming Museum,
St Mary's Hospital, Praed Street, W2 1NY
https://www.imperial.nhs.uk/about-us/what-we-do/fleming-museum

Paddock War Rooms

Some of London's most secret government and military sites turn out, on declassification, to have barely been used. A leading example is the underground bunker codenamed Paddock at Dollis Hill in north London. It was built at the start of the Second World War as a contingency against the destruction of the main Cabinet War Rooms in Whitehall, but it appears that there was never any operational cause for ministers to deploy there. It was occupied by staff only twice, in brief exercises lasting for a couple of days.

On one of those occasions, 3 October 1940, it was visited by Prime Minister Winston Churchill in what he described as a 'dress rehearsal' for Central Government War Headquarters dispersal. This was the high point of its melancholy, dust-gathering seventy-year history. Churchill had a considerable aversion to austere secret buildings, and described Paddock as 'a useless piece of folly'. He did not believe that the Cabinet could ever work there. By contrast, the main Cabinet War Rooms in central London were used more than a hundred times during the war. The Prime Minister, who enjoyed creature comforts, preferred the luxury of Downing Street close by. At Paddock there was no accommodation, and the dispersal plan was to house the Prime Minister and staff above ground in Neville Court, a requisitioned block of unfortified civilian flats in a nearby suburban street. The logic of this is hard to fathom.

Paddock was excavated in secrecy alongside the Post Office Research Station at Dollis Hill, a massive office and laboratory block. A late decision about the dispersal of key sites had launched construction in the grounds of the Dollis Hill site in 1939, and Paddock was completed a few days before the start of the Battle of Britain in June 1940. When Paddock was conceived, there seemed to be a compelling need for it. Expert studies, based on the notion that 'the bomber will always get through', had anticipated complete destruction of vast areas of central London in any forthcoming war.

It was a three-level structure, with basements 40 ft (12 m) below the surface. Thirty-seven rooms in all were built along central spines, including offices for the Cabinet, a map room, teleprinter space, possibly a broadcast studio and a private office for the PM. The surface building for Paddock has been demolished, but two of the three original entrances remain, one of which now lies incongruously at the end of a garden between two private houses. Underground, many of the rooms and the diesel-powered emergency generating and ventilation plant remain intact, but derelict. Massively engineered entrances, which once held blast doors, can be seen, but the thick concrete slab ceilings for both basement levels are now concealed.

It was called Paddock merely because that word appeared on a randomly compiled list of non-descriptive codenames. After the Churchill visit, just one

The generator room.

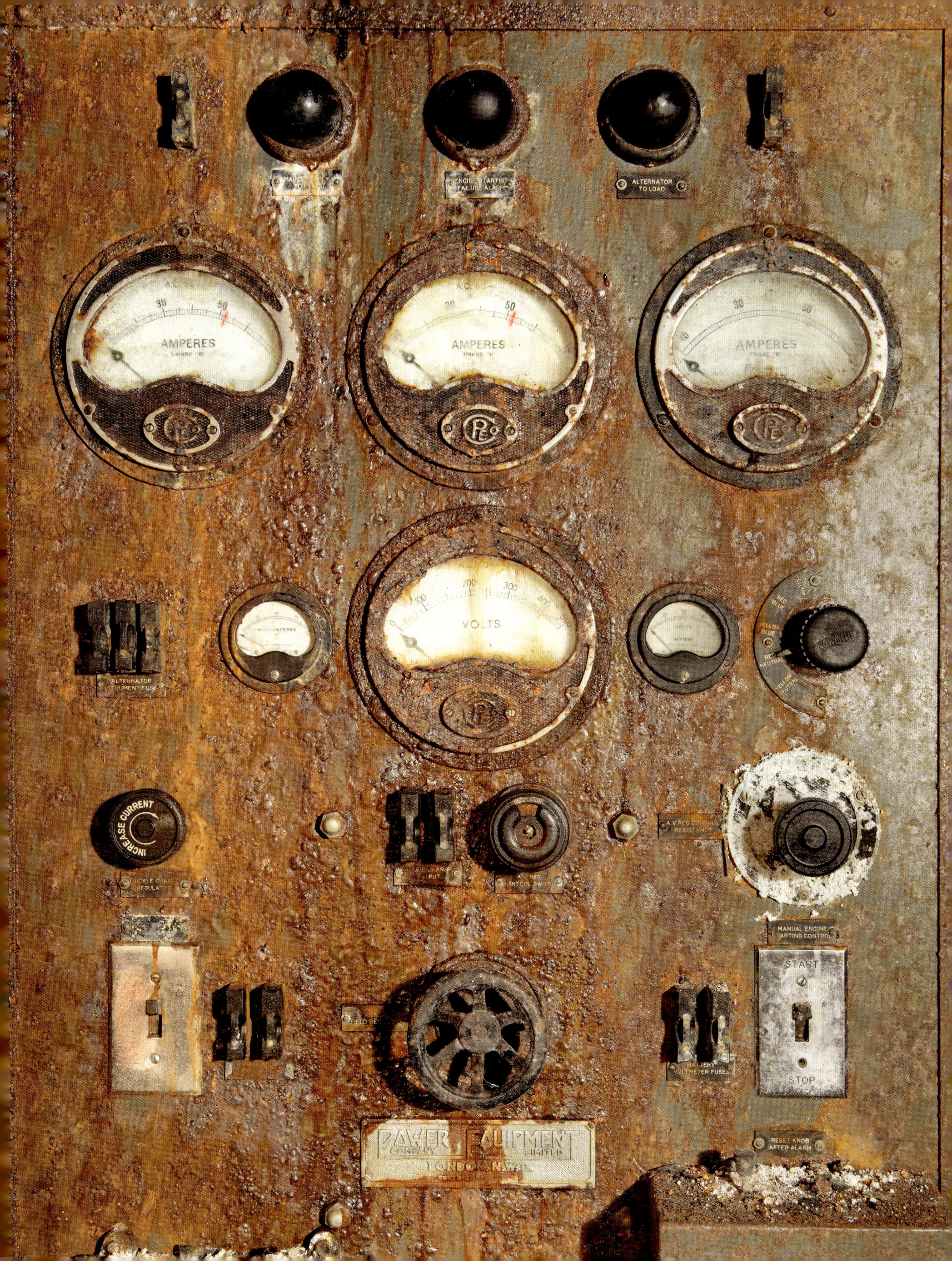
ALTERNATOR TO LOAD
AMPERES
AMPERES
AMPERES
VOLTS
INCREASE CURRENT
MANUAL ENGINE STARTING CONTROL
START
STOP
BATTERY VOLTMETER FUSE
RESET KNOB AFTER ALARM
POWER EQUIPMENT
COMPANY LIMITED

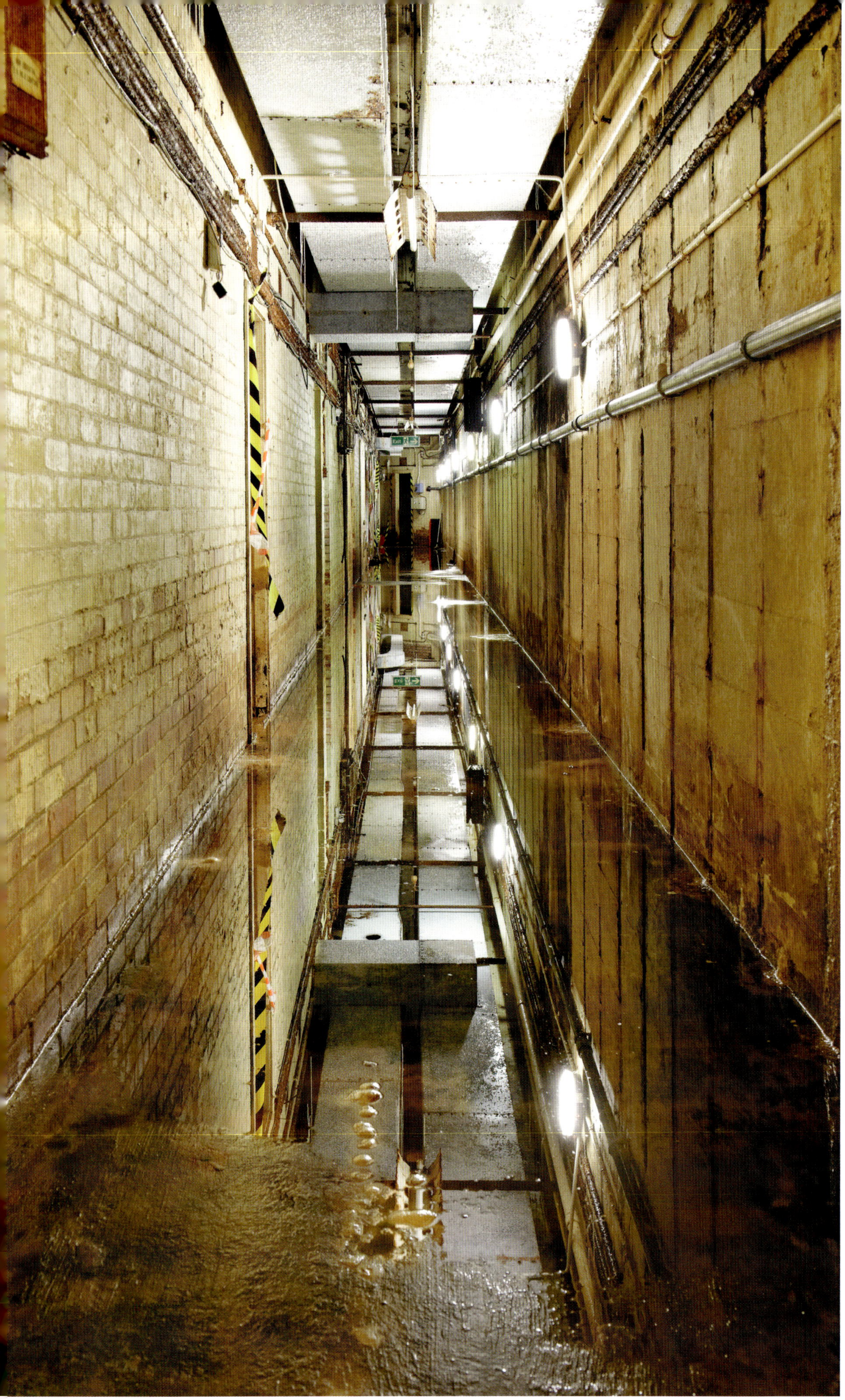

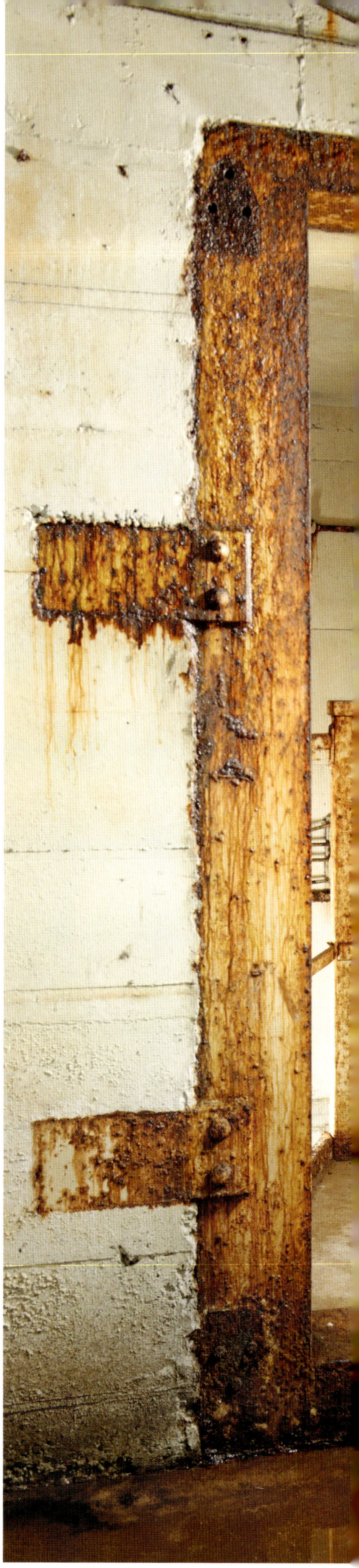

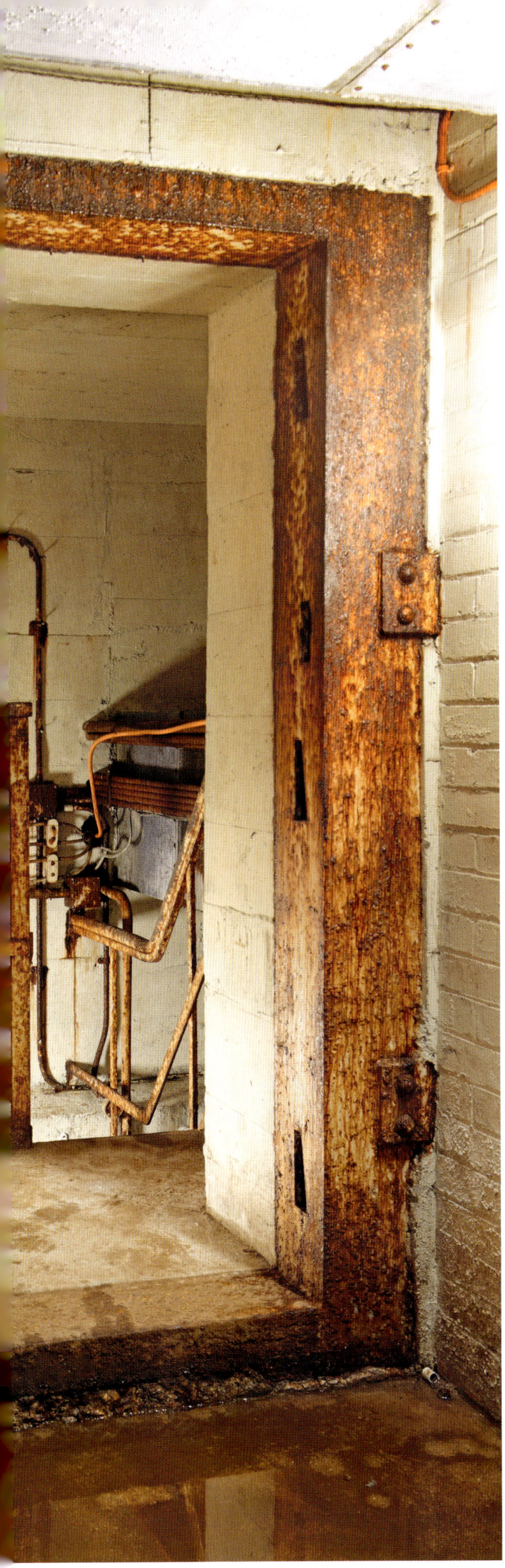

Far left The lower spine corridor.

Left The emergency staircase.

further meeting was conducted there: a presentation given to impress the visiting Australian Prime Minister Robert Menzies in March 1941.

As it emerged that the bunker was unlikely to be used, much equipment was moved out to other sites. Only a skeleton guard of Army personnel remained. Paddock was officially closed in late 1944, even as V-2 rockets descended on London.

Above ground, in the main Post Office building at Dollis Hill, a far more profound contribution to the conduct of the war came in the form of the first programmable computer, designed and constructed by Post Office engineer Tommy Flowers. This was Colossus, destined for Bletchley Park for crucial code-breaking duties. It is said that some of the prototype circuit boards for the Colossus were stored in the Paddock rooms for years afterwards, but the Post Office did not make much significant use of the underground facility.

Although a new series of secret buildings were developed in Britain after 1949 for Cold War use, no subsequent use was ever found for Paddock. It had been designed around comparatively vulnerable manual and electro-mechanical communications systems with surface landlines. Later, cable tunnels were driven deeper in central London and the telecommunications links were made tougher. But Paddock remained a well protected bunker, at least, and local authorities were charged to find sites for regional seats of government and other secret facilities in the age of nuclear war. As late as 1981 there was a suggestion that Paddock might be revived as a war room, but the Greater London Council found that water seepage had taken its toll on the lower basement. Telecommunications research at Dollis Hill had ended by 1976 and the main Research Station building was converted into apartments. A housing association acquired the rest of the site, and developed new homes where the bunker surface building once stood. Paddock bunker is listed, preserved and maintained, and has recently been opened to visitors on one or two occasions each year.

CONTACT INFORMATION

Paddock War Rooms,
109 Brook Rd, Neasden, NW2 7DZ

The Queen's Club

The Queen's Club is a grassy green enclave almost hidden at the end of a residential street in red-bricked West Kensington. Dating from 1886, it claims to be the first multi-purpose sports complex to be built anywhere in the world. Today it is exclusively home to the racquet sports: tennis, squash and rackets, but over time it has hosted more than twenty major sports, including football, cricket and rugby. It tapped into the late-Victorian flowering of competitive sport and was once the home ground of Corinthian F.C., the princes of amateur football.

Lawn tennis is the sport most closely associated with the Queen's Club. The Lawn Tennis Association, the governing body of British tennis, owned the Queen's Club between 1953 and 2007. Looming fears that redevelopment of the site would greatly exceed its value as a sports club led to it being sold to its members. This protected the future of the Queen's Club Championships, the annual men's tournament held on grass since 1890, which is a precursor to Wimbledon and the unofficial warm-up for top players. The twelve grass courts at Queen's are rated as the best anywhere, possibly superior to those at Wimbledon itself.

Two rare sports played at Queens are rackets and real tennis, both games being played in substantial enclosed courts.

Rackets started in the eighteenth century, when it was played by the gentlemen inmates of two of London's debtors' prisons: King's Bench in Southwark

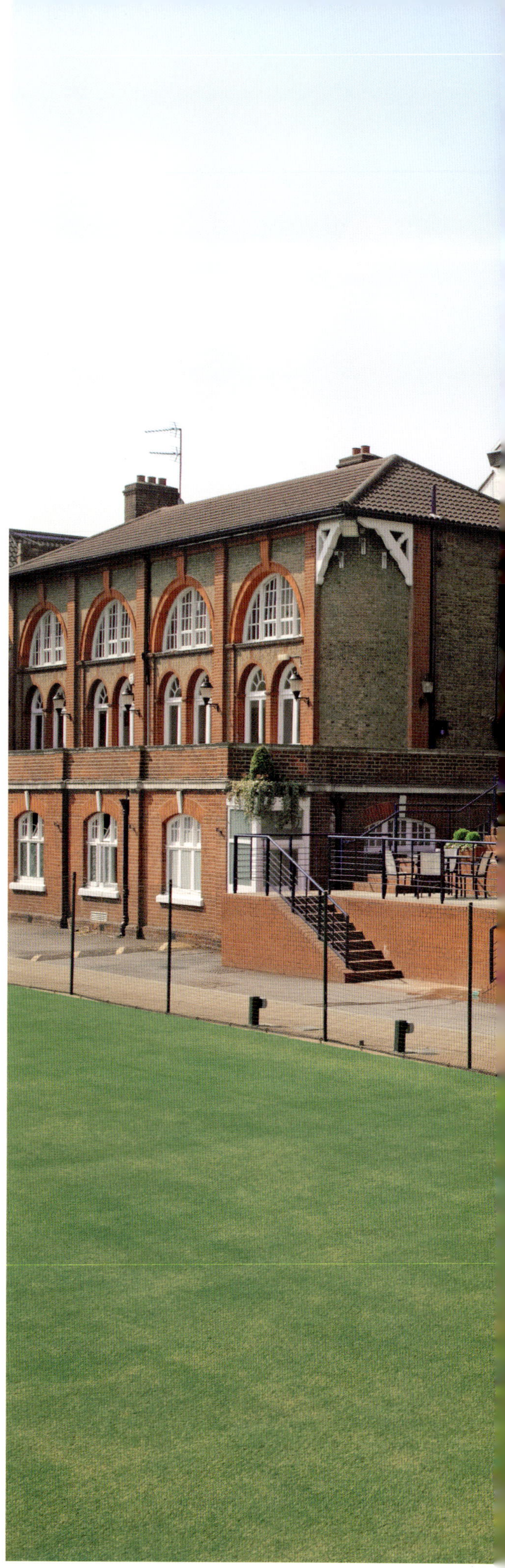

Centre court and clubhouse, best known as venue for the Queen's Club Championship.

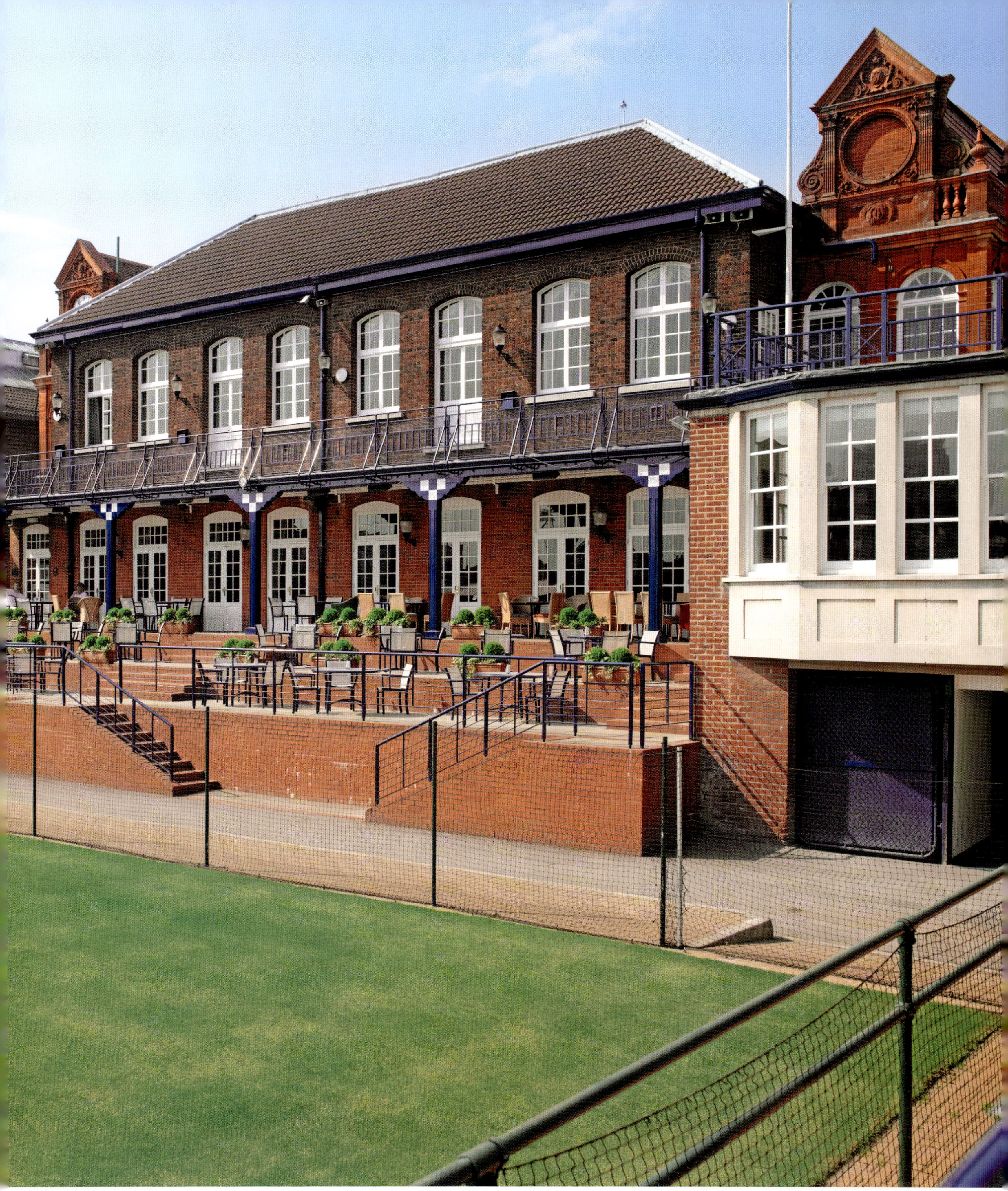

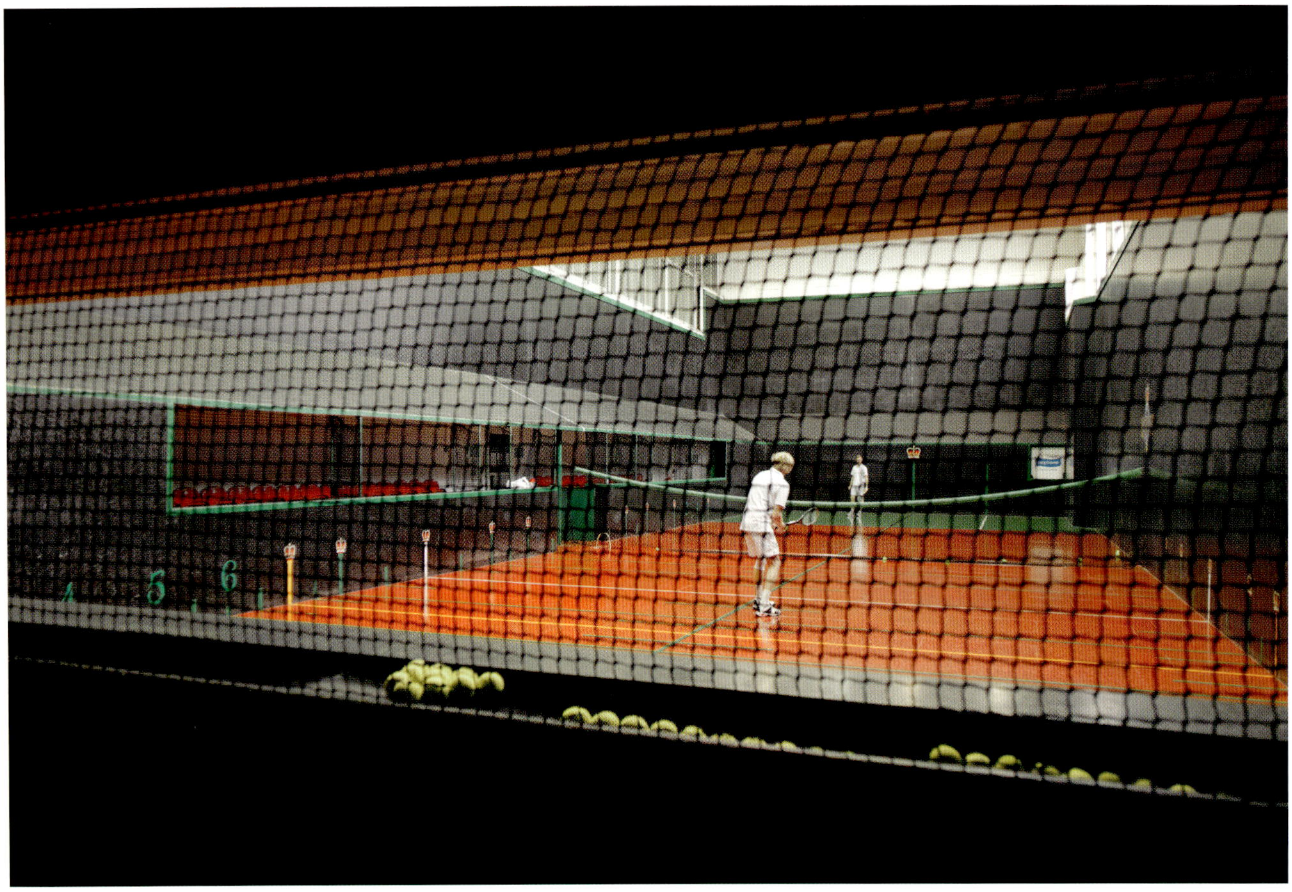

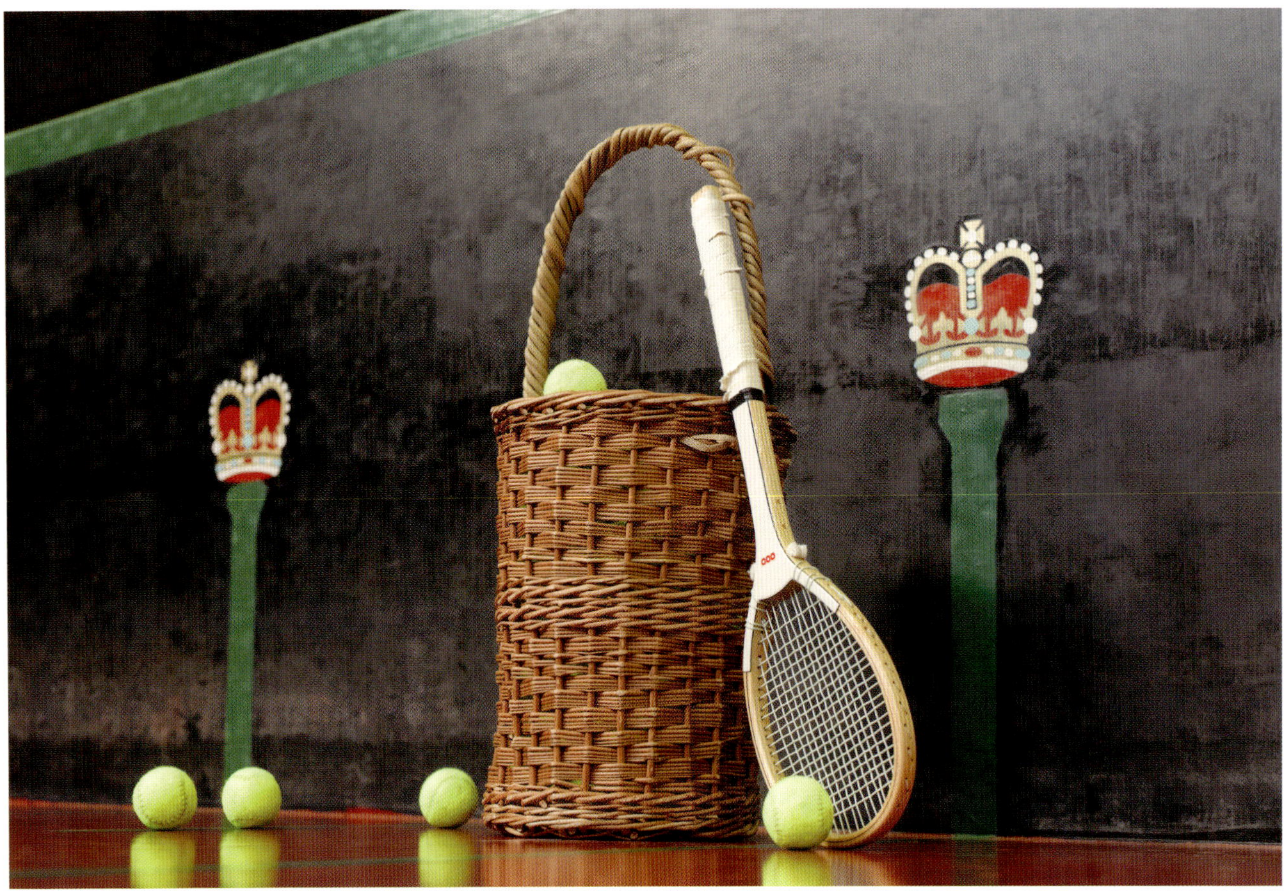

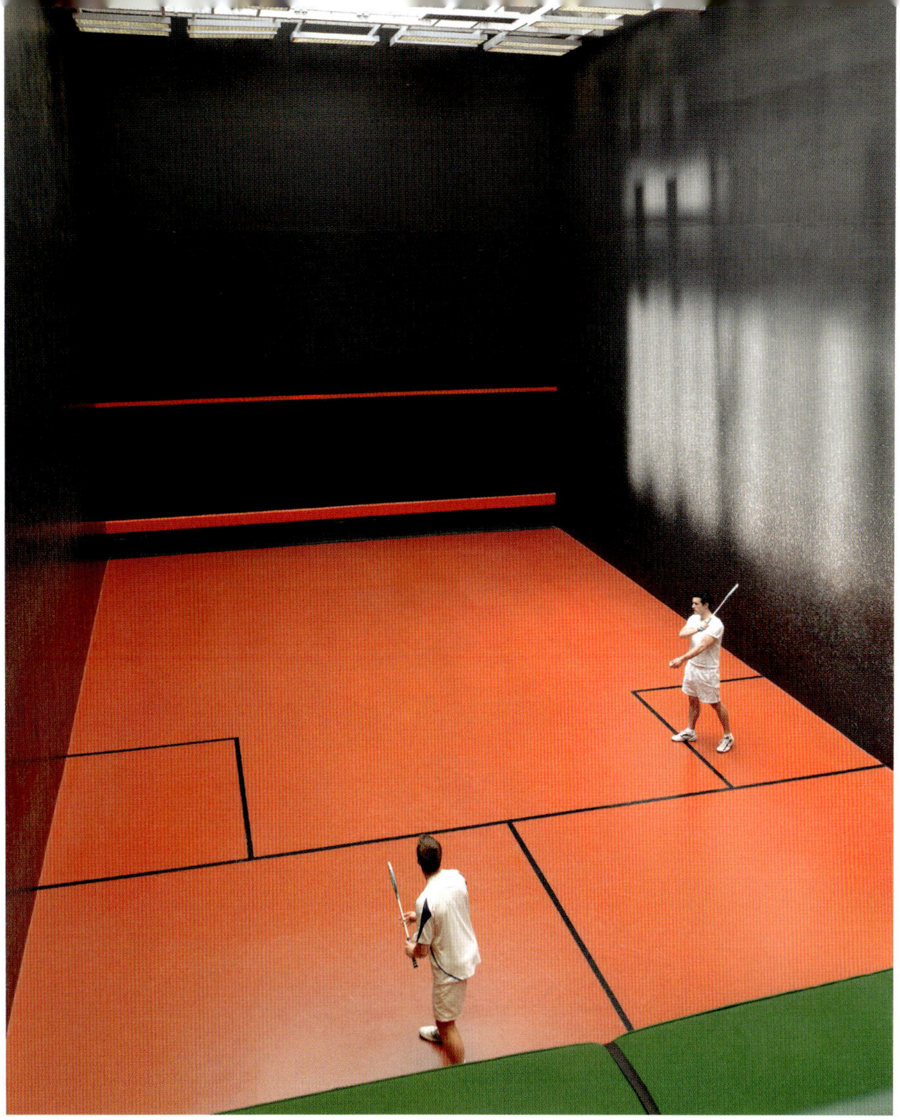

Opposite, above Real tennis court from the dedans.

Opposite, below The real tennis racquet is asymmetrical, and the hand-made balls are heavy.

Above A game of rackets in progress, photographed from the balcony.

and Fleet in Clerkenwell, and it exploited the prisons' most essential features: the walls. The strangely skewed rules of such institutions permitted certain privileges, and there were four courts at King's Bench. Well-bred prisoners had spiced up the handball game fives by using tennis racquets. The game migrated to public schools, with Harrow being the first to gain a court. Queen's rackets courts date from 1880, by which time the code of the game had been established, based on a four-wall 30 × 60-ft (9 × 18-m) enclosed court, with a ceiling no less than 30 ft (9 m) high.

The wooden racquet is called a bat, and is used to hit a hard white ball that can travel at up to 180 mph (290 km/h). Some elements of the sport resemble squash, which began as an off-shoot of rackets, although the scoring system differs and the rules of the two sports have diverged substantially.

Queen's is also the national headquarters of real tennis, hosting the British Open every year. Real tennis is a precursor of lawn tennis, and its supporters claim that it has the oldest continuous annual world championship in sport, at over 250 years. A measure of the game's rarity is there are only forty-seven courts in the world, and two of those are at Queen's. The sport is known as *jeu de paume* in France (originally being played with the hand rather than with a racquet), 'court tennis' in the United States and 'royal tennis' in Australia.

Its heyday was in the sixteenth and seventeenth centuries, being played by members of the royalty in France and England. It became known as real tennis after the derived game of lawn tennis became the more widely known sport. Though similar in certain respects, with the same scoring system, two bounces of the ball does not bring necessarily bring the point to an end. Real tennis is claimed to be a more complex and technical sport, and the court is wider and longer than that for lawn tennis, enclosed by four walls – three of which have sloping roofs, known as penthouses – and a ceiling lofty enough to contain all but the highest lobs. There is also a buttress called a tambour, which intrudes into the playing area, and off which shots may be played. Points can be won by hitting the ball into certain spaces below the penthouses. The hand-made real tennis balls are heavier than those for lawn tennis, and ground strokes are favoured, which may be the reason that the wooden racquets for this sport are asymmetrical.

In 1908 Queen's Club hosted three events during the first London Olympics Games: rackets, covered court tennis (indoor tennis) and real tennis. This combination was not deemed successful for future Olympics.

For thirty years, the annual Oxford and Cambridge University rugby and football matches and athletics challenges took place at the Club, sometimes drawing as many as 10,000 spectators. As these events outgrew the Club's facilities, they found new homes at Twickenham, Wembley and White City. The increasingly popular game of lawn tennis took over the grounds of the Club, and there are twelve grass courts today.

CONTACT INFORMATION

The Queen's Club
Palliser Road, W14 9EQ
https://www.queensclub.co.uk/

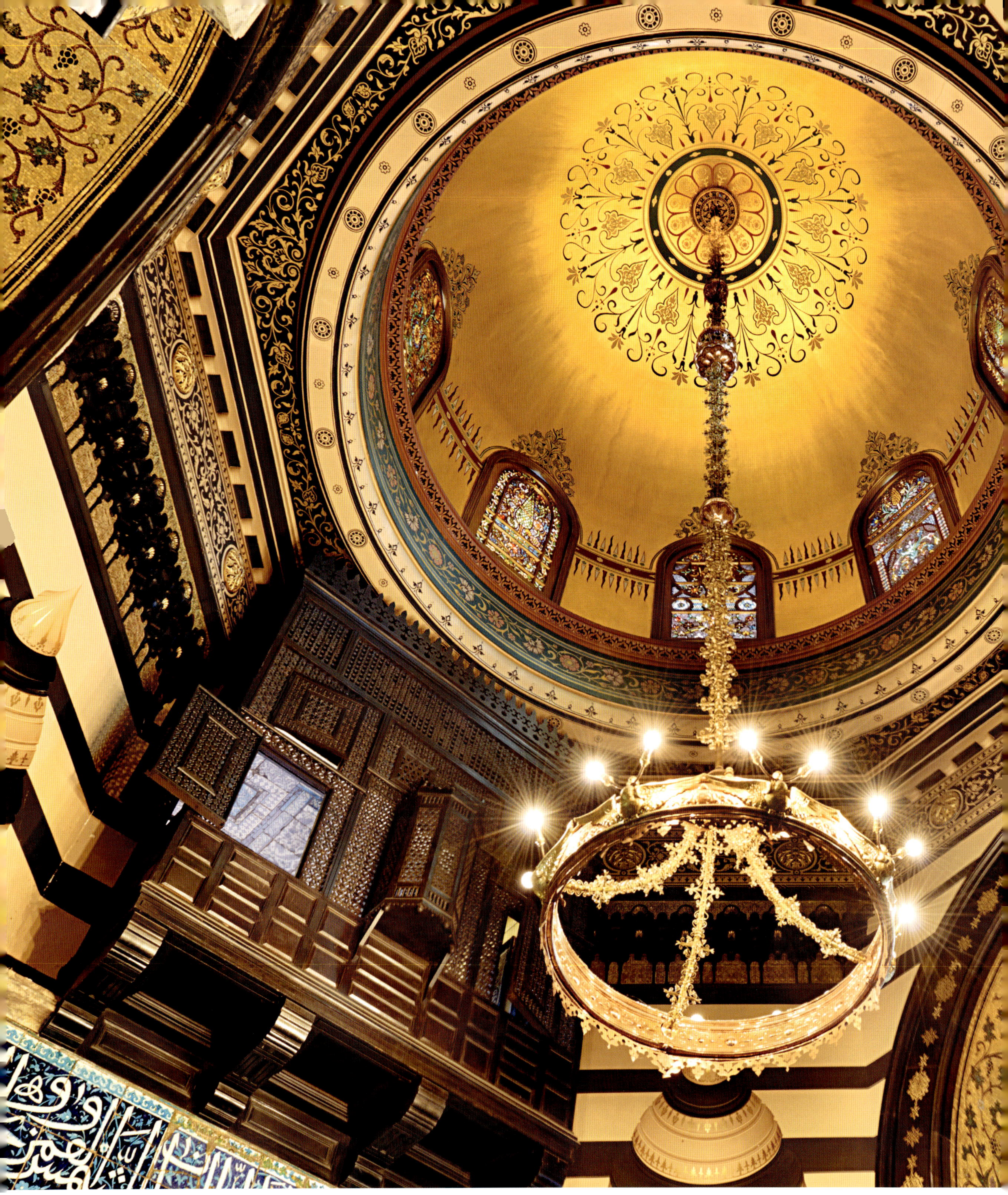

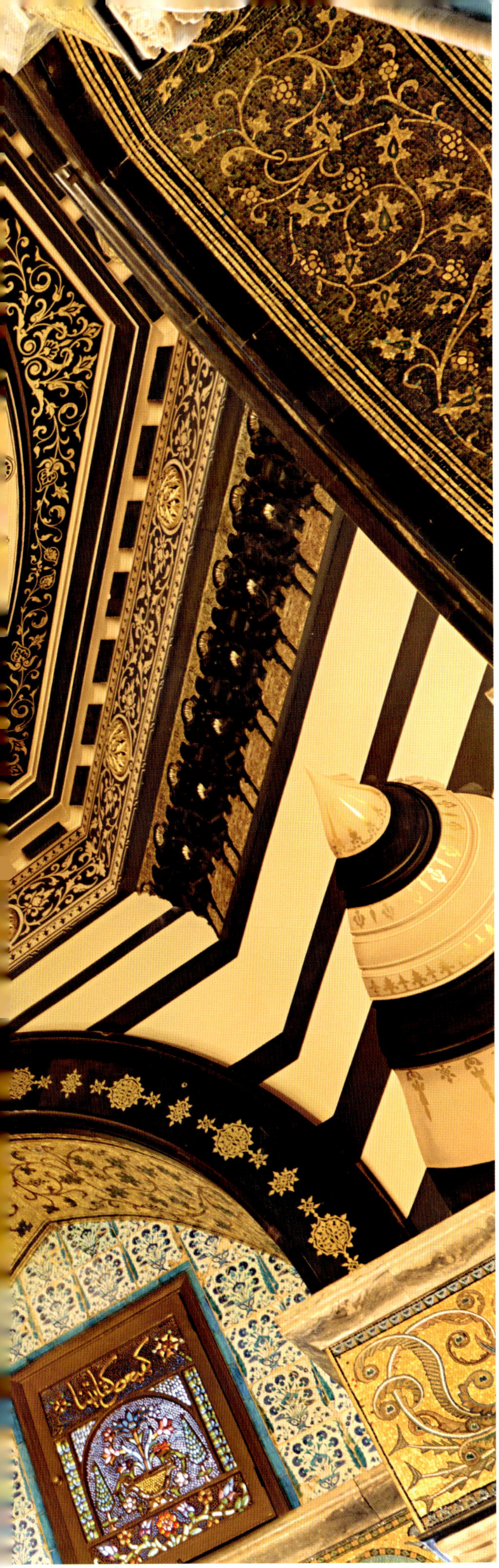

The dome of the Arab Hall is gilded with tiles, mostly from Damascus.

Leighton House Museum

The best-known picture by the Victorian painter Lord Frederic Leighton is *Flaming June*, a sleeping classical maiden reproduced on thousands of cards and posters, but the artist's own house at 12 Holland Park Road also deserves recognition as a great creation. Built in stages over thirty years behind plain unadorned red-brick exterior walls, it was at first a modestly sized house with six rooms. It was designed as a studio-home – a place to live and paint – and the walls were soon hung with Leighton's own paintings and others by his peers. The house was ready for occupation in 1866, and was to set a style for the studio-home among Victorian London painters, and indeed for a particular Holland Park circle of artists.

The architect for Leighton's house was his friend George Aitchison, and they worked again together in 1879 to create a further wing. This included the spectacular Arab Hall, inspired by a room in the twelfth-century Arab-Norman castle at Zisa, near Palermo. The space rises into a high gilded dome, and the walls are decorated with 600 individual tiles – mostly from Damascus and dating from the sixteenth century – with a lattice window from Egypt. The supporting columns, mosaic frieze, screens and some stained glass were made by contemporary leading artists. A pool with a fountain was set in a Victorian mosaic floor.

Leighton House decor included red flocked wallpaper, ebony cabinetry and paintings and prints

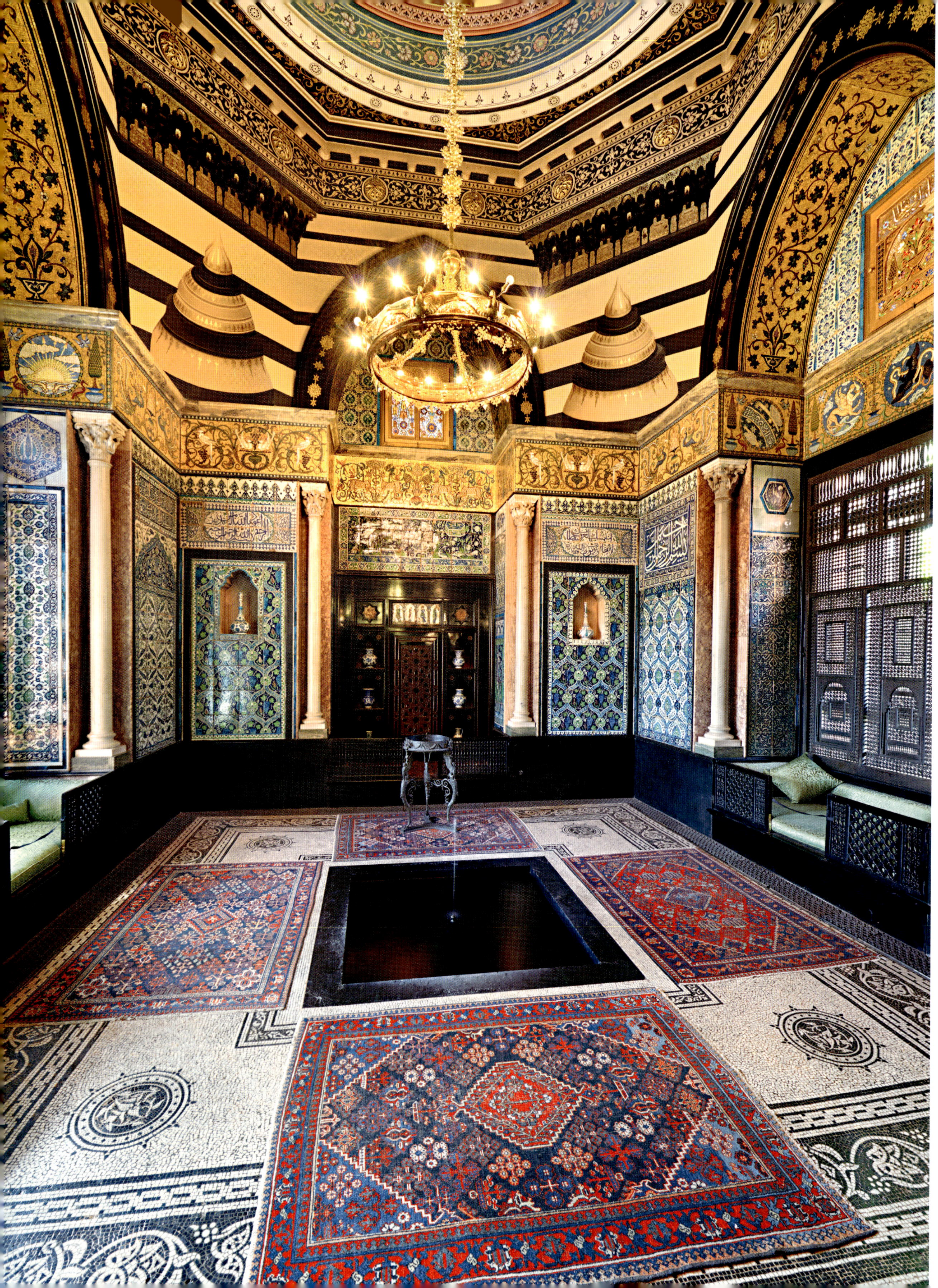

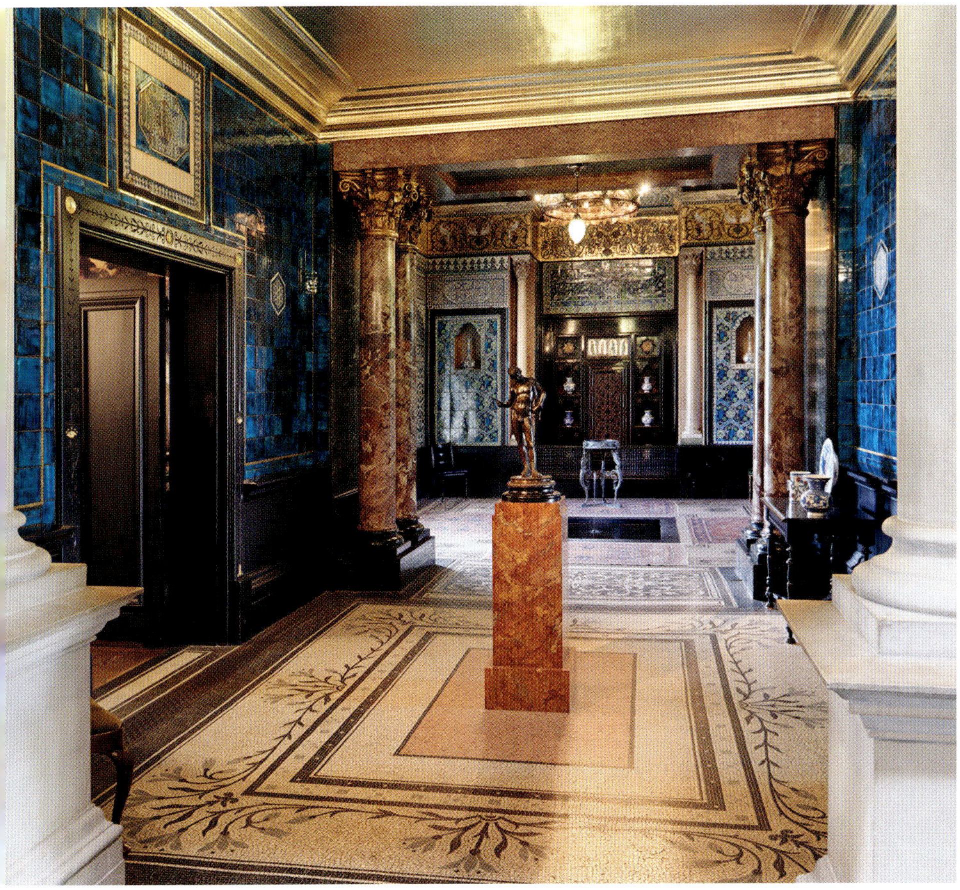

Leighton House decor included red flocked wallpaper, ebony cabinetry and paintings and prints by great European artists including Tintoretto and Corot.

Opposite The mosaics and marbles for the Arab Hall were all sourced in London.

Above The Narcissus Hall, with bronze figure by Leighton. Iridescent blue tiles by Victorian craftsmen represent the waters in which Narcissus observed his reflection.

by great European artists, including Tintoretto and Corot. The house was expanded eventually to ten rooms, the last addition being the Silk Room, a gallery space lined with green silk to display the collection of contemporary paintings, including pictures by John Everett Millais, George Frederic Watts and John Singer Sargent.

Frederic Leighton was an enigmatic and contradictory character, devoted to an artistic life, but tempered by distinct Victorian attitudes. He was well-connected and achieved considerable fame, being appointed President of the Royal Academy in 1878 and serving diligently, working from from his desk in the library until his death in 1896. The dining room was well-used as he entertained generously, and musical soirées were regularly held in the large studio. But there was no guest bedroom, his own bedroom was modest and simple and his bed was small. Leighton lived in the house alone, save for his servants, for three decades. Aside from the splendid entrance hall and staircase, Leighton House has a second side entrance and stairs, where the artists' female models, who were to pose nude, were taken directly to the studio. The house was sometimes opened to poor members of the public, generally when the artist was away travelling and collecting.

Leighton's death came shortly after he was raised to the peerage. Most of his collections of fine art and furniture were sold at auction soon after his death and dispersed. Attempts were made to preserve the house through the Leighton House Committee. It was not until 1926 that Kensington Borough Council purchased the freehold for £2,750. The house was difficult to exploit and protect usefully, but the Arab Hall and Narcissus Hall survived largely intact. Parts of the decoration came to be covered in emulsion and lining paper and strip lighting was fitted. Between 2008 and 2010 Leighton House was closed for extensive refurbishment and restoration at a cost of £1.6 million and returned close to the state it was in Leighton's day, with many pieces of furniture and textiles reproduced and original paintings and pieces loaned back for display. Some 550 books of 23.5 carat gold leaf were needed to restore the dome in the Arab Room.

CONTACT INFORMATION

Leighton House Museum,
12 Holland Park Road, W14 8LZ

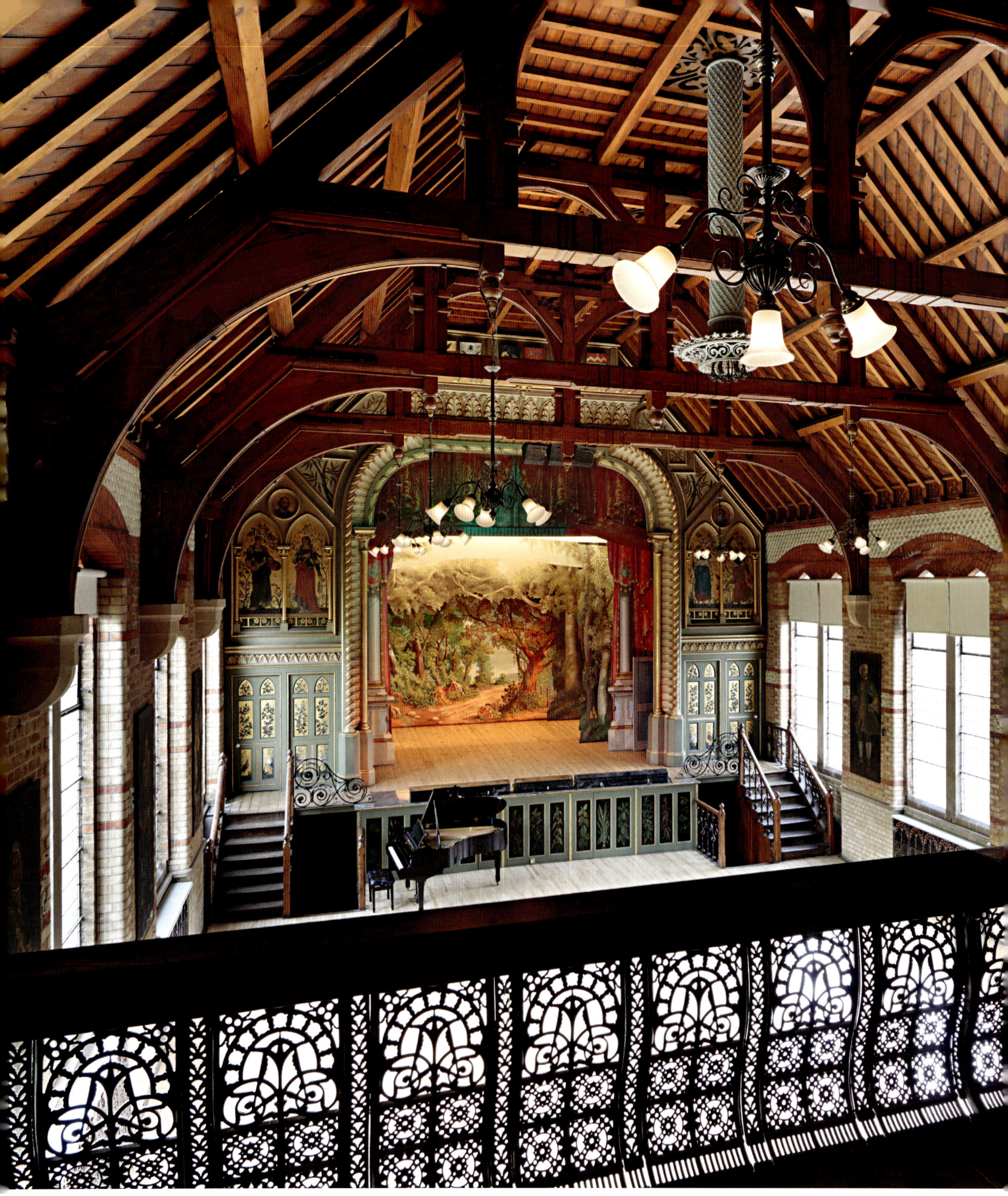

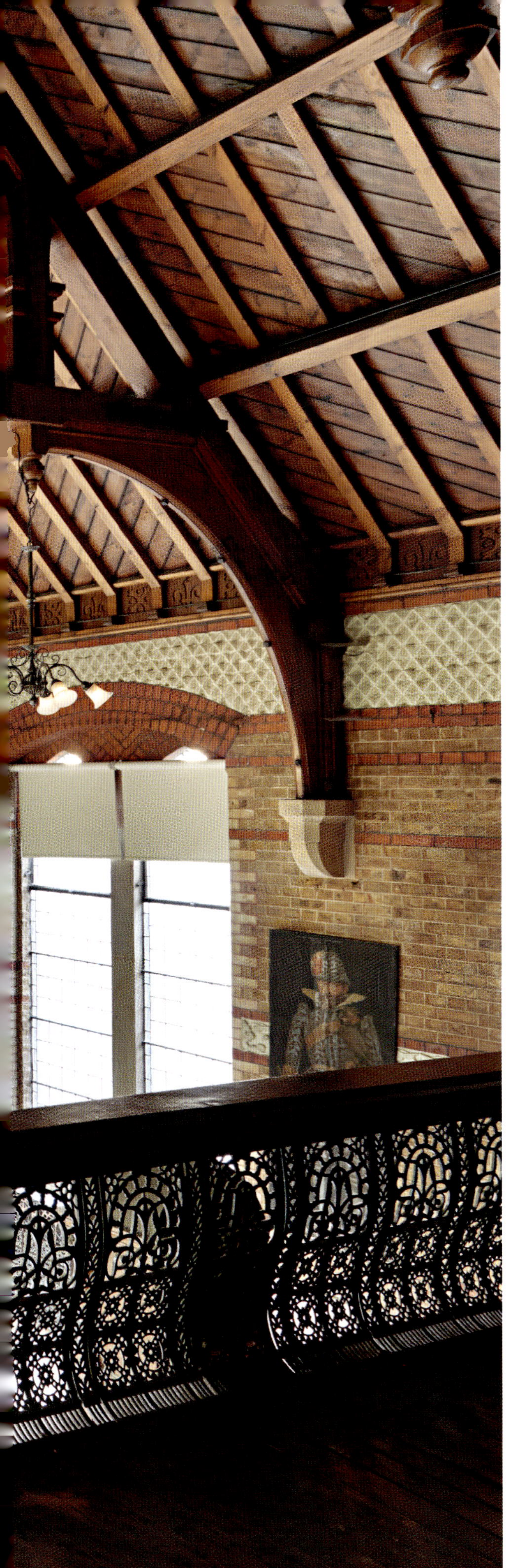

Normansfield Theatre

Normansfield could originally seat at least 350, and includes a stepped gallery with an ornate iron front.

The marvel of Normansfield is how an 1879 proscenium stage theatre survived unaltered in a time capsule, to be restored and reopened 125 years later. The theatre is a tribute to the medical pioneer Dr John Haydon Langdon Down, who gave his name to the congenital chromosomal imbalance known as Down's Syndrome. At Teddington in south-west London, he had commissioned a sanatorium called Normansfield, developed from 1868 as a home for the learning-disabled, and licensed as a private asylum with classrooms, workshops and a farm. Dr Langdon Down's progressive views on treatment valued the role of drama, music and entertainment as a therapeutic tool, and in June 1879 an entertainment hall was opened.

The proscenium is richly coloured and gilded and is surrounded by elaborately decorated panels on all sides. Four doors – two functional and two false – flank the stage. These were expertly painted, as were the panels on the riser at the front of the stage. Some researchers have attributed certain of these pictures to Marianne North, the notable botanical painter whose pictures are displayed at Kew, although that has not been established beyond doubt. Above the doors are four Pre-Raphaelite paintings presenting the muses Tragedy, Painting, Music and Comedy; the artist is unknown.

Displayed on the walls are six wooden panels with paintings of figures in period costume. These are characters from Gilbert and Sullivan's *Ruddigore*, and

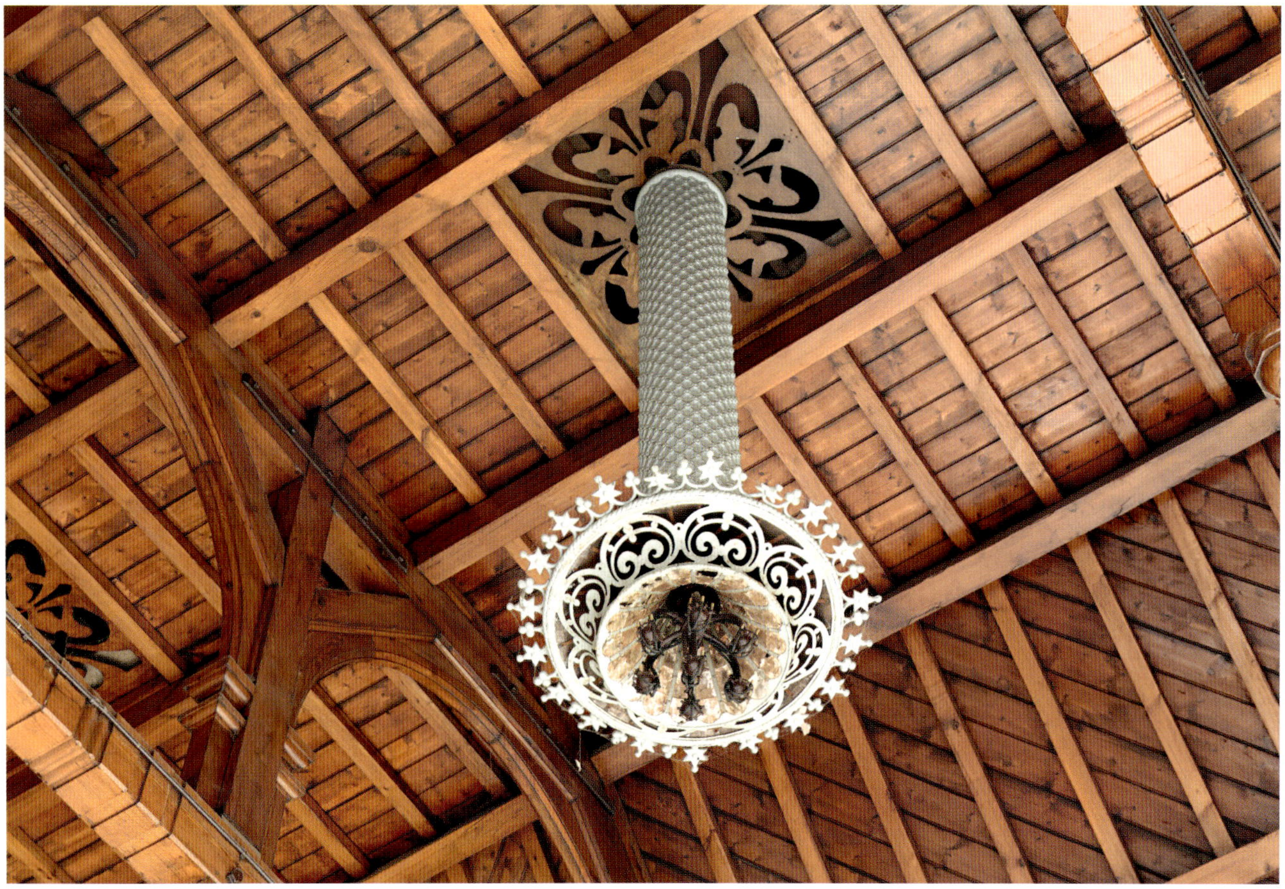

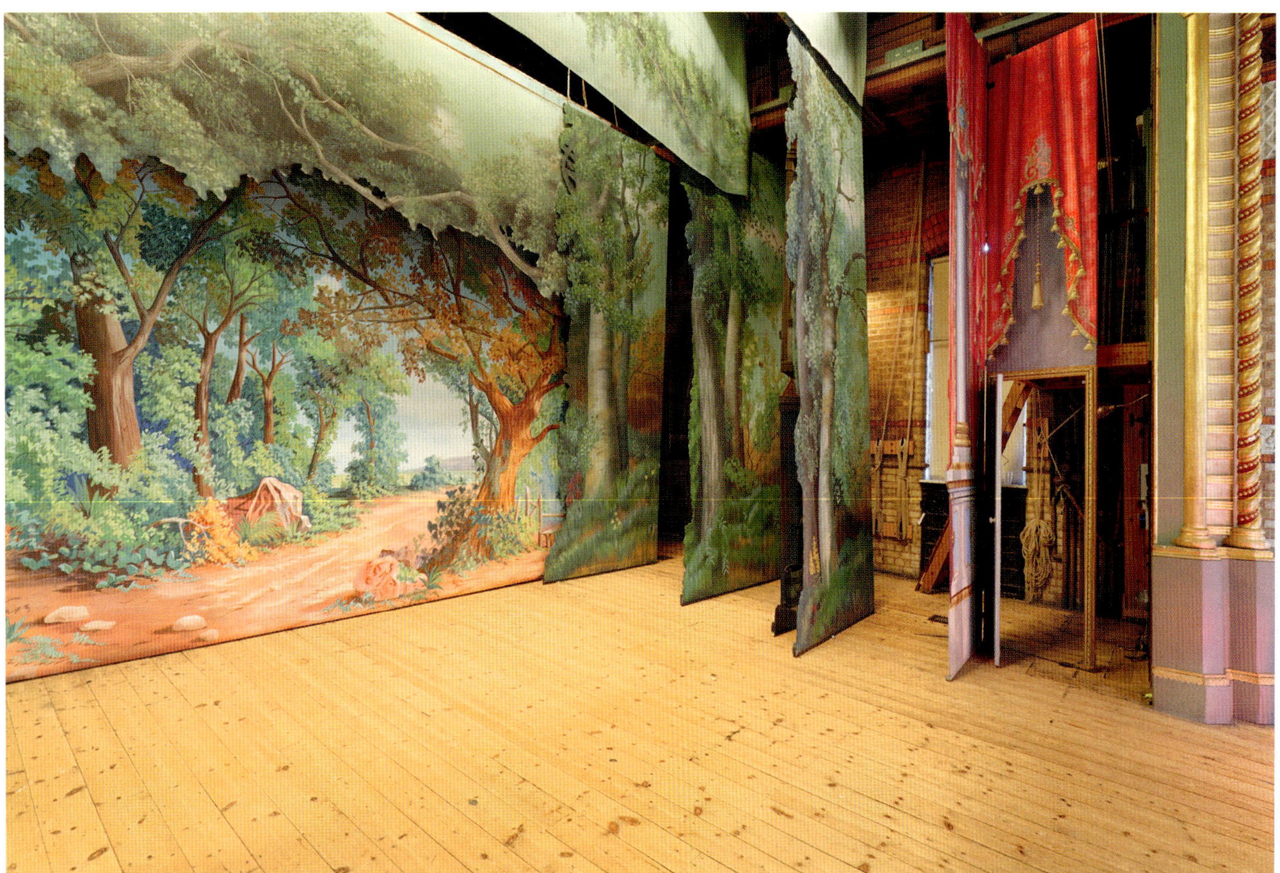

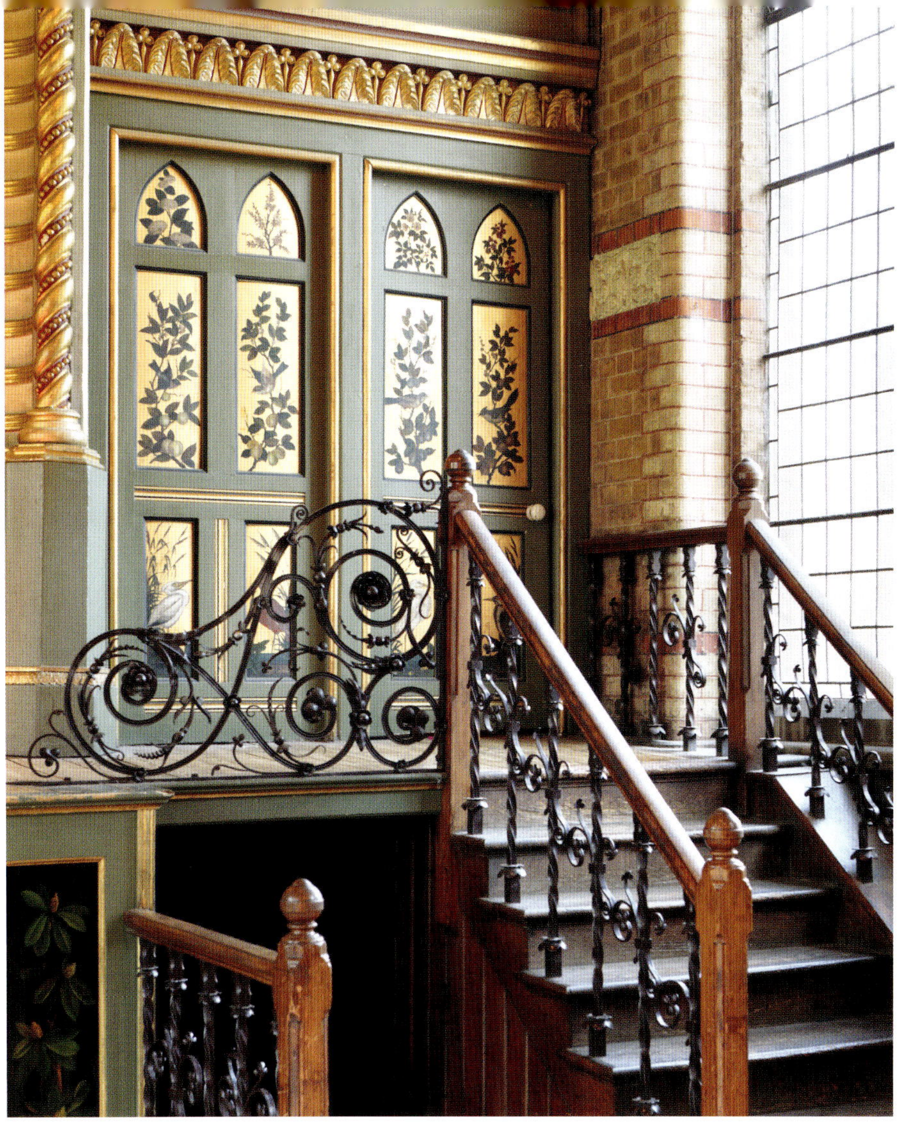

Opposite, above The pendant 'sun burner', a combined gas chandelier and ventilator, as installed in 1879.

Opposite, below The woodland scene on this backcloth is framed with profiled wing flats as an avenue to lead the eye; the hinged wing painted with classical column is part of a false proscenium.

Above The wrought iron and painted panels – attributed to Victorian biologist Marianne North – lend an Arts & Crafts feeling.

came from the original Savoy Theatre production of the operetta, where they functioned in the production as swivelling doors, although no explanation of why they came to Normansfield has been uncovered.

Normansfield's scene-changing system and its collection of stock scenery are rare surviving examples of the apparatus and illusion of theatre that started to disappear at the end of nineteenth century. In addition, more than eighty painted flats have survived, depicting landscapes, gardens, palaces, baronial halls or splendid rooms, capable of creating a setting for a range of plays from melodrama to pantomime, together with backcloths and borders to frame the scene. Theatrical scenery of the time tended to have a short life, pieces being remodelled or scrapped. New systems of overhead scenery-changing were introduced in the commercial theatre shortly after this, but Normansfield did not update its scenic groove system or scenery. When the most ambitious theatrical productions, staged at Normansfield by an amateur company drawn from staff and friends, came to an end around 1908, a long hibernation began of the stage and scenery.

For Normansfield as a medical care institution the running costs started to exceed the income from fees after 1945, and the National Health Service took it over in June 1951. It was then known as Normansfield Hospital. At this time the stage was rarely used for any kind of performance, but the hall remained in use for therapeutic group sessions, meetings and as a badminton court. Some damage was inflicted on the wooden panels. The fragile disused scenery was stored unseen, but everything remained intact and not quite forgotten.

Normansfield Hospital continued to develop until the end of the 1960s, but afterwards changes in healthcare policy and programmes such as Care in the Community were to be introduced, and the hospital was steadily run down. Long before the closure, in the early 1980s, a Theatre Project Committee started negotiations about preservation with the health authorities, which continued for more than ten years. The Friends of Normansfield, the Theatres Trust, the Greater London Council, English Heritage and Richmond Council were all eventually engaged. When Normansfield closed as a hospital in 1997, the scenery was removed and stored for conservation, and much of the site used to build new housing. As a part of permission to develop the housing, Laing Homes restored the hall and stage with as few changes as possible. Some of the scenery was replicated and returned. The building, still known as Normansfield Theatre, is now owned and managed by the Down's Syndrome Association as the Langdon Down Centre, which includes a Museum of Learning Disability and the historical archive material of Dr Langdon Down.

CONTACT INFORMATION

Normansfield Theatre,
Langdon Down Centre, 2a Langdon Park,
Teddington, TW11 9PS
https://langdondowncentre.org.uk/

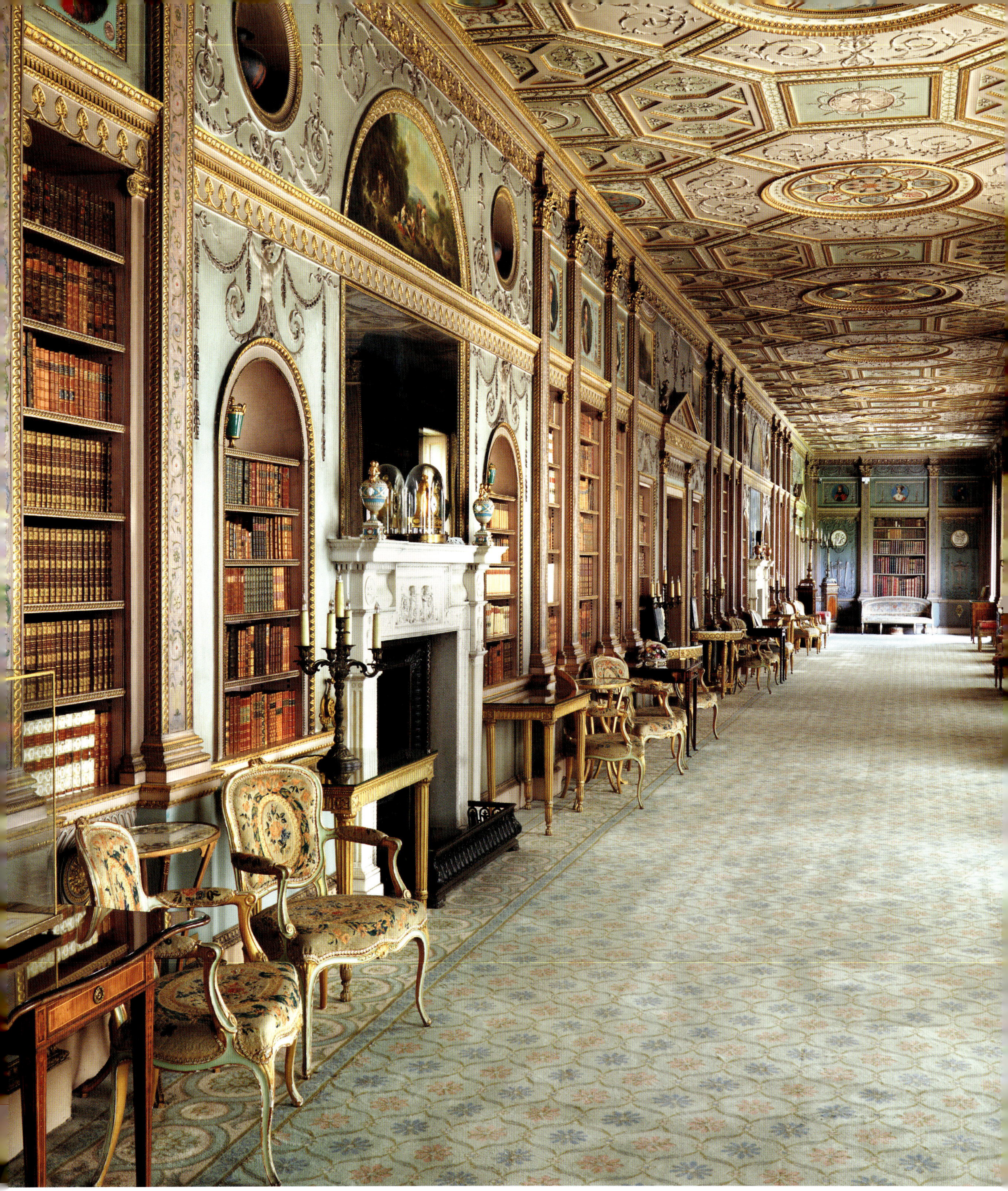

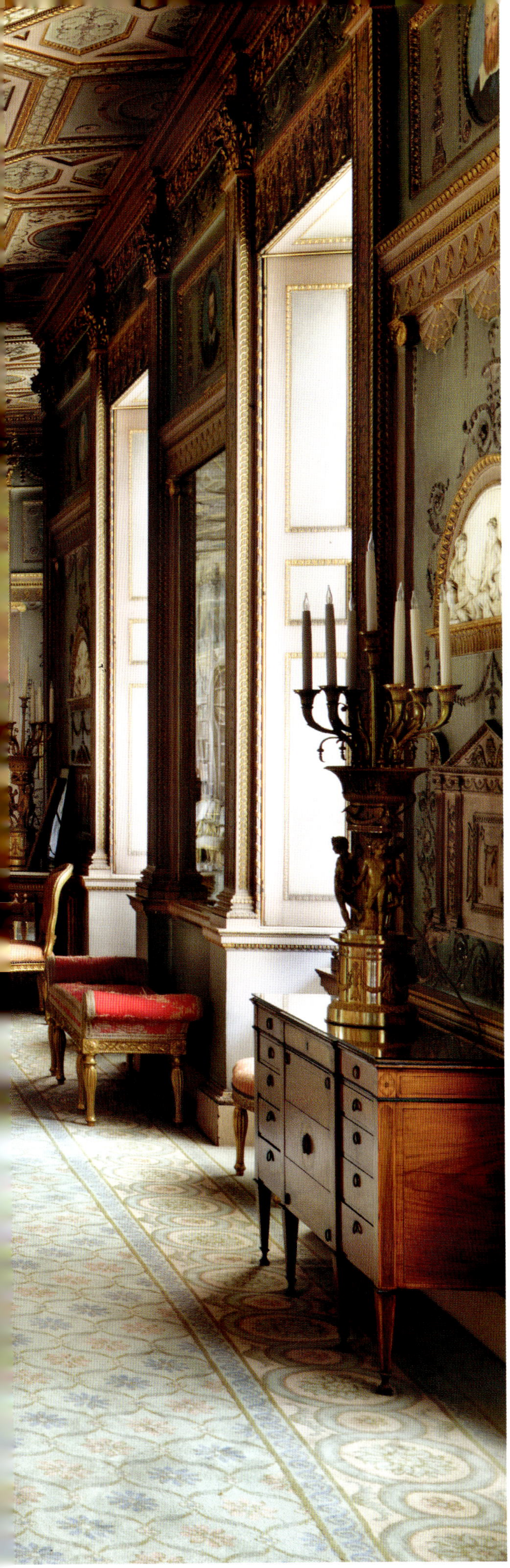

Syon House

Roundels of the Percy family run the length of the Long Gallery, with portraits of dukes and duchesses on one side, and the Earls of Northumberland on the other.

Syon House, which belongs to the Duke of Northumberland, is famous for a series of beautiful and civilized rooms, and also as a focus of turbulent and violent events in British history.

Scottish architect and designer Robert Adam was commissioned to create a series of neo-classical interiors at Syon House in 1762. Filled with statues and artefacts shipped from Italy, it was one of the architect-designer's first commissions and defined a style for new grand houses being built for the remainder of the century.

At Syon House, Adam was required to rework a Tudor mansion building which had existed since 1550, with dated and worn interiors, set in unfashionable formal landscape. He was not permitted to change the interior layout, but applied neo-classical decoration and clever design techniques to modernize and vary the sense of proportion of the rooms.

The Great Hall was made to suggest a Roman basilica with Doric columns, black-and-white marble flooring, and statues and busts, including Socrates and Claudius. The room leads to an inner courtyard garden in Italianate style. The Ante Room to the Great Hall forms a colourful contrast and houses further Roman statues and gilded trophy panels inspired by the Villa Madama in Rome.

The State Dining Room has Corinthian columns, decorated in white and gold, and the room's walls have something of a rose hue.

Princess Victoria was instructed here on court manners by Duchess Charlotte Florentia.

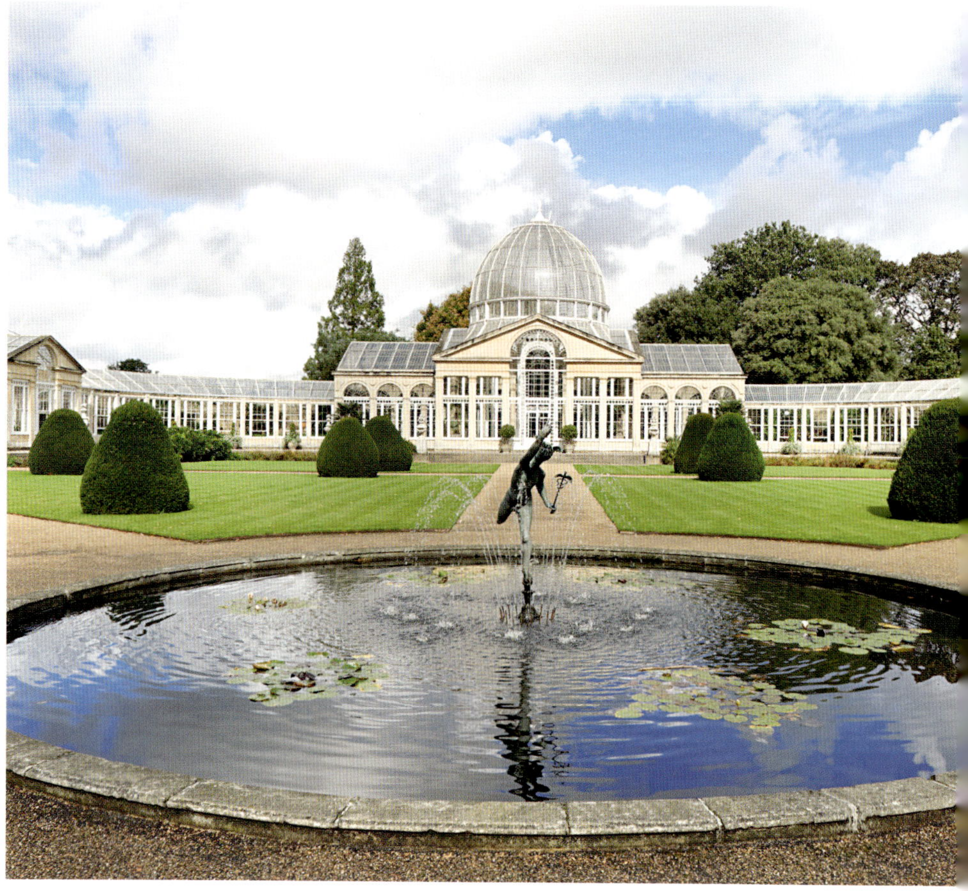

The Red Drawing Room, an antechamber to the Long Gallery, has scarlet wall hangings of Spitalfields silk, set off by a red carpet patterned with a honeysuckle design; artworks include Sir Peter Lely's portrait of Charles I, reputedly painted at Syon.

In the Long Gallery, Adam replaced the former heavily wood-panelled Tudor space with a design featuring sixty-two Corinthian pilasters, gilded and painted, along with classical trailing stucco mouldings. Roundels of the Percy family run the length of the room, with portraits of dukes and duchesses on one side, and the Earls of Northumberland on the other. The gallery also has two hidden turret rooms, or closets, at either end, one of which is decorated with colourfully painted stucco and complete with a mechanical singing-bird timepiece.

Syon Park's 200 acres (80 ha) of parkland were reworked by Lancelot 'Capability' Brown to include what is known as a serene pleasure garden, containing a long ornamental lake. A large Conservatory, with a total frontage of 230 ft (70 m) and a glass dome 125 ft (38 m) wide, was designed and housed the 3rd Duke of Northumberland's exotic flowers, becoming an inspiration for London's Crystal Palace.

The earlier history of Syon was turbulent and violent, mostly in connection with King Henry VIII. Syon Abbey had first existed at this place, and closed during the Dissolution when its spiritual advisor Richard Reynolds was hanged, drawn and quartered for denying the royal supremacy of the King. Henry VIII's fifth wife Catherine Howard was imprisoned at Syon before her execution. Syon was to come into the possession of Edward Seymour, Duke of Somerset, whose sister Jane had been Henry VIII's third queen. Seymour had the house rebuilt around elements of the abbey before his own execution in 1552; Syon passed to John Dudley, 1st Duke of Northumberland, whose son Guildford married the Nine Day Queen, Lady Jane Grey. Nominated as successor by the dying Edward VI, she was cajoled into accepting the Crown by the 1st Duke in Syon's Long Gallery. Shortly after this, she walked to the scaffold, followed by her husband and father-in-law. Syon was acquired by Henry Percy, 9th Earl of Northumberland, in 1594, and has remained in the family ever since.

Princess Victoria, who frequently stayed at Syon House over a period of six years, was instructed here on court manners by Duchess Charlotte Florentia. Princess Victoria's bedroom at Syon House and that of her mother, the Duchess of Kent is preserved.

Syon House is claimed to be the last great 'country' house in private hands remaining in London, a curious definition made possible by its lying 8 miles (13 km) from the centre of the capital, but within the bounds of Greater London.

CONTACT INFORMATION

Syon House,
Syon Park, Brentford, TW8 8LG
https://syonpark.co.uk/

Above Syon House's Conservatory was built for the Duke of Northumberland's rare tropical plant collection.

Opposite, above The Round Closet, adorned with a mechanical singing bird.

Opposite, below The Great Hall is modelled on a Roman basilica, adorned with classical statuary, including a replica of the third-century sculpture *The Dying Gaul* in black marble.

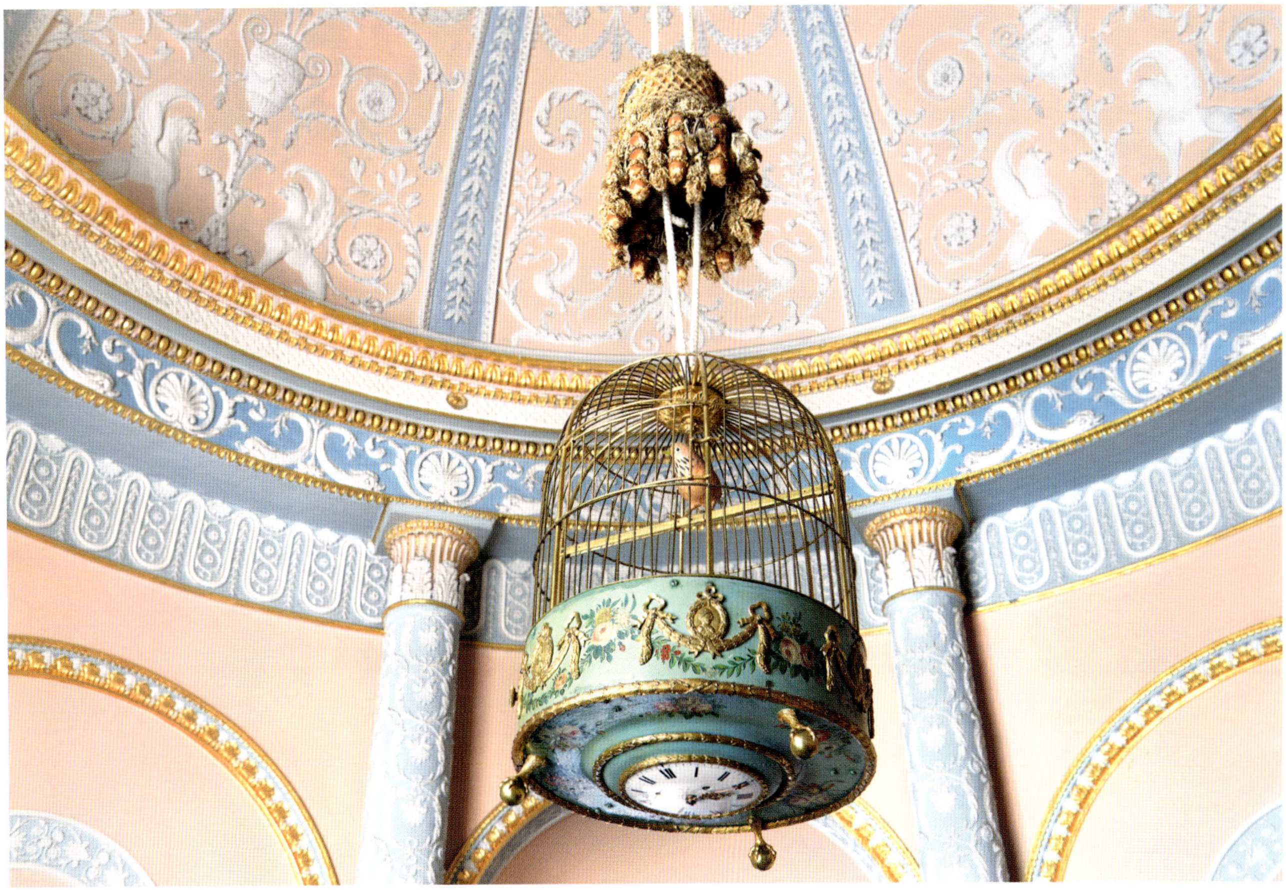

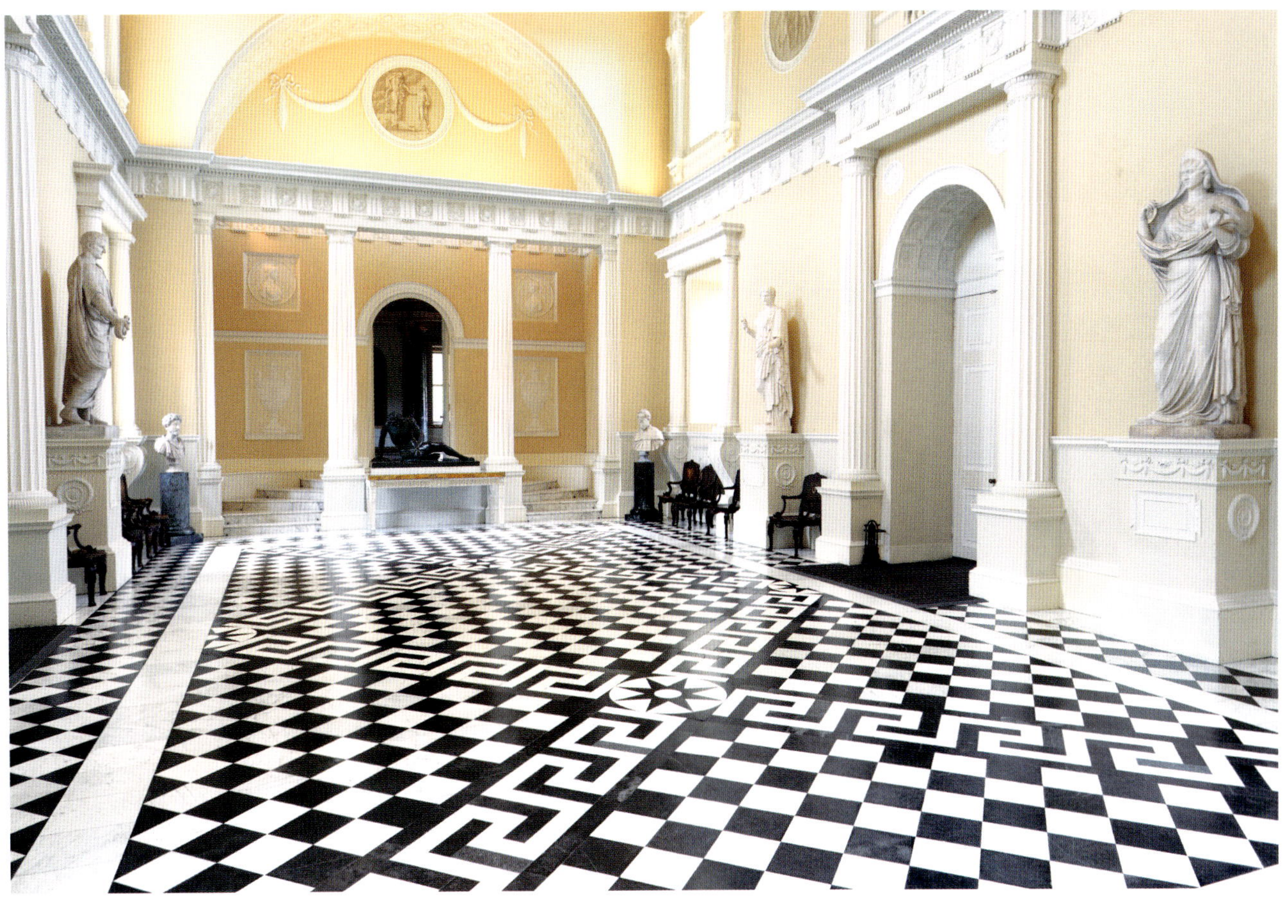

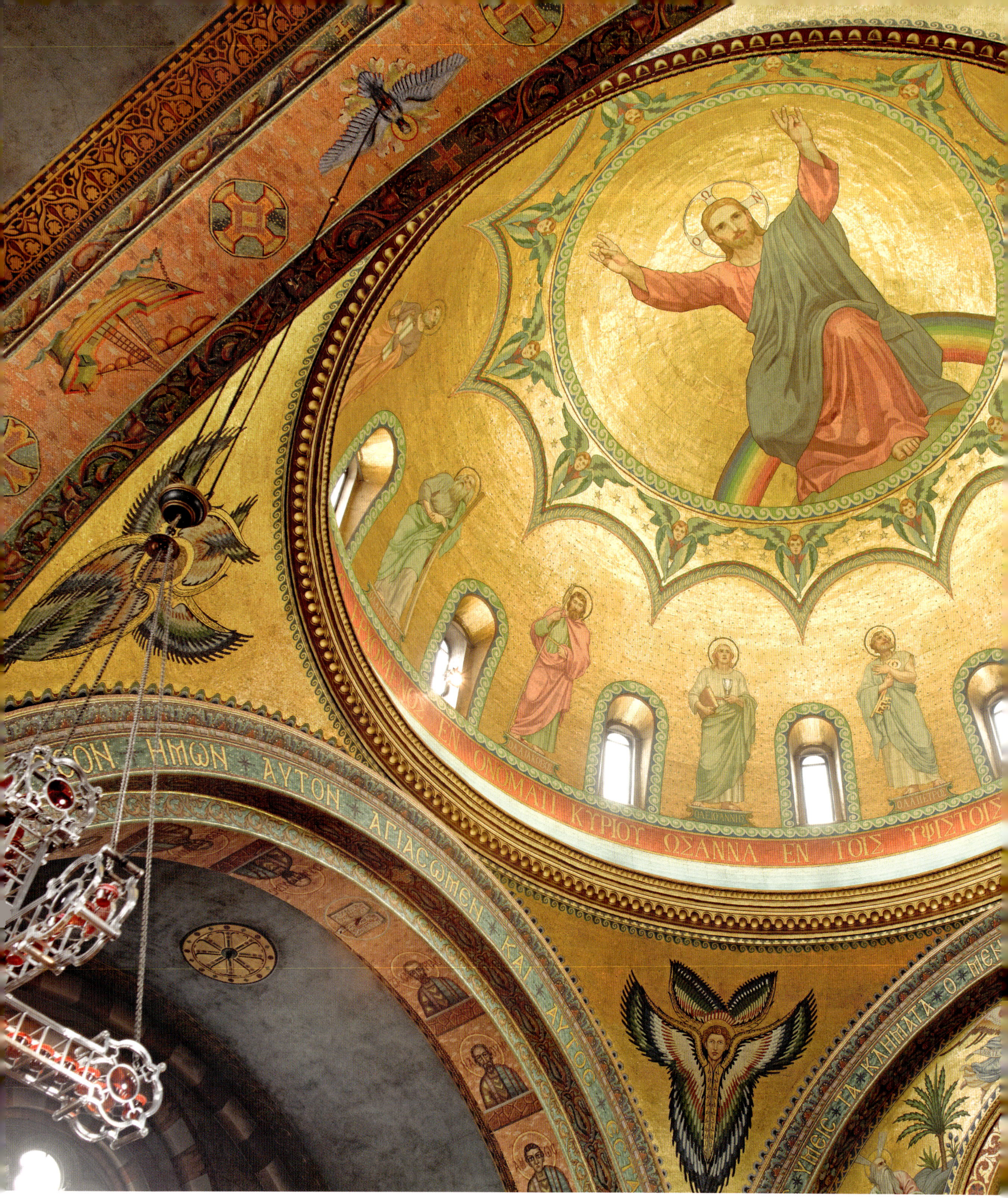
ΗΜΩΝ ΑΥΤΟΝ
ΕΝ ΟΝΟΜΑΤΙ ΚΥΡΙΟΥ ΩΣΑΝΝΑ ΕΝ ΤΟΙΣ ΥΨΙΣΤΟΙΣ

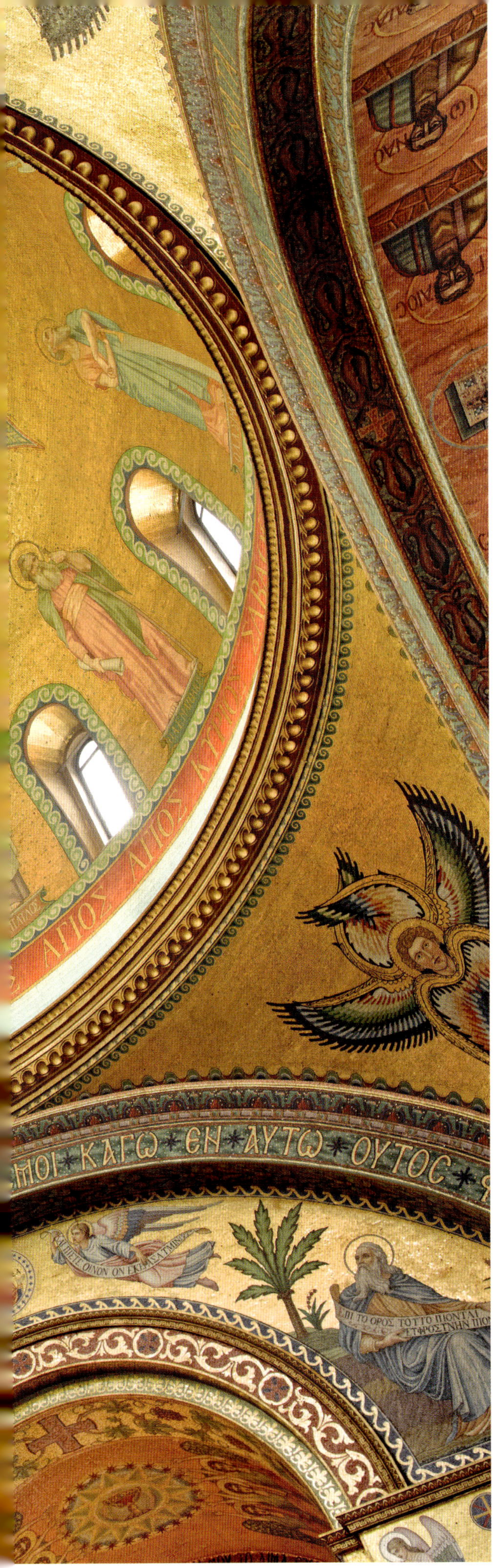

St Sophia's Greek Orthodox Cathedral

Christ Pantocrator, the iconographic image of the Almighty surrounded by the twelve Apostles, looks down from the dome.

A recurring theme in this book is a conventional building, meriting barely a second glance from a passerby, containing a marvellous interior. St Sophia's Greek Orthodox Cathedral in Moscow Road, Bayswater, is a fine example.

It was consecrated in 1883, and its exterior is modestly neo-Byzantine in style. This architectural form was the subject of a revival at the time, and was being applied to new churches in different denominations, including the Catholic Westminster Cathedral. The Cathedral of St Sophia has nicely detailed yellow-and-red brickwork, and is a well-proportioned cruciform, but only the copper domed roof hints at higher design.

This is revealed in the spectacular interior, in an exotic Eastern Orthodox style, much of which is embellished with mosaics. Green, black, white and pink marble panels line the walls.

The iconostasis (the screen that separates the nave from the sanctuary) is an elaborate walnut structure embellished with twenty-two images. To fully appreciate the beauty of the church it may be necessary to have some knowledge of iconography, especially the placement of each icon. It also helps to have an understanding of significance of the holy doors in the iconostasis, but the mystery of the Orthodox Church is palpable. In the high dome is the image of Christ Pantocrator, one of the oldest images in Christianity. The mosaic floor bears the coat of arms of the Byzantine Empire: the double-headed eagle.

In the high dome is the image of Christ Pantocrator, one of the oldest images in Christianity.

There had been a Greek church in London since 1677, and a stone from the very first is preserved in St Sophia's. St Sophia's foundation and its location owed much to the growing Greek colony in the years following the nineteenth-century War of Independence, and the prosperous Greek merchants trading from London.

St Sophia's was designed by John Oldrid Scott, from the famous family of architects (son of Sir George Gilbert Scott, uncle of Sir Giles Gilbert Scott) and work was started in 1877. The church was elevated to the status of a cathedral in 1922.

In 1926 the Cathedral trustees commissioned the Russian artist Boris Anrep to create a further set of mosaics, depicting the incarnation of Christ and the mystery the Eucharist. Anrep was invited to decorate further sections of the cathedral between 1932 and 1956, including full-length figures of the Major Prophets and busts of the Minor Prophets. In the west arch he depicted St Nicholas and St Christopher with Christ, both protectors of the seafarers and travellers, resonant with a congregation historically associated with shipping and trading.

For a while during in the Second World War, when the Greek government was in exile in London, St Sophia's was designated the cathedral of the Greek nation. During the Blitz, bombs destroyed buildings a few metres away across the street, and St Sophia's suffered blast damage that was not repaired until after the war.

CONTACT INFORMATION

St Sophia's Greek Orthodox Cathedral,
Moscow Road, W2 4LQ
https://www.stsophia.org.uk/

Right Detail of cathedral seating.

Far right Icon stand positioned in the nave.

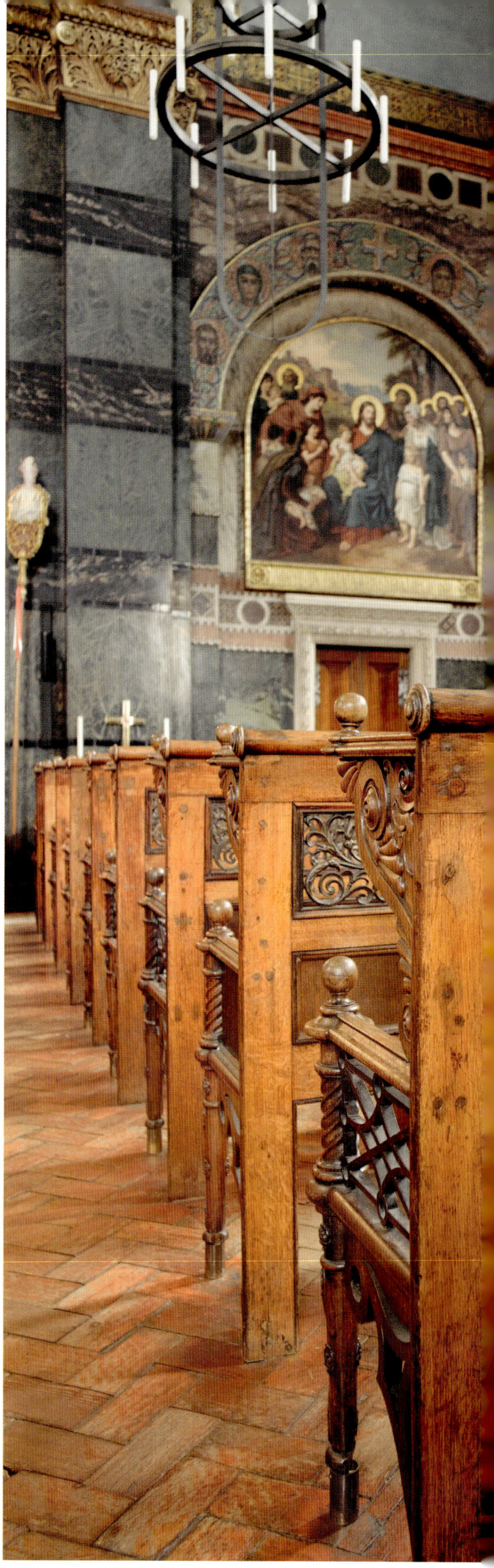

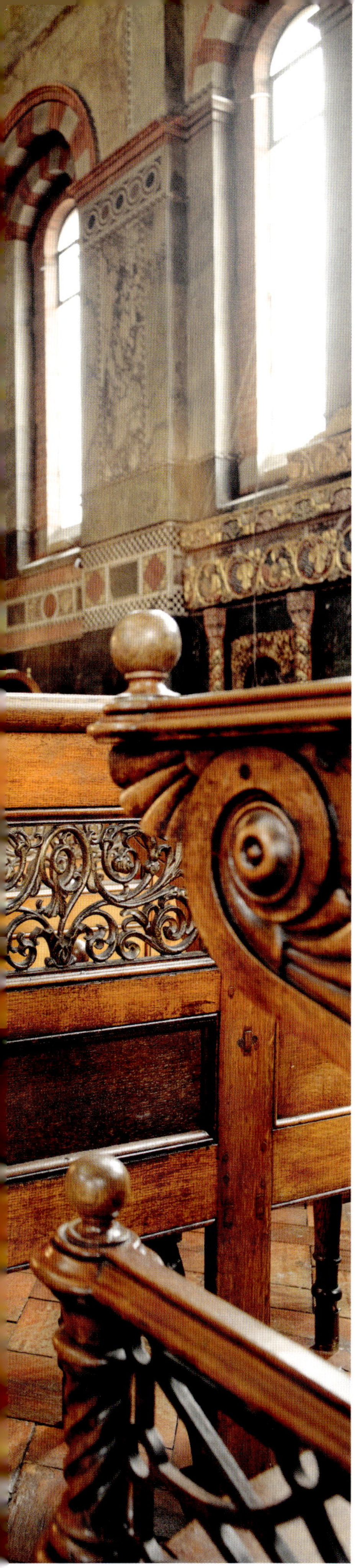

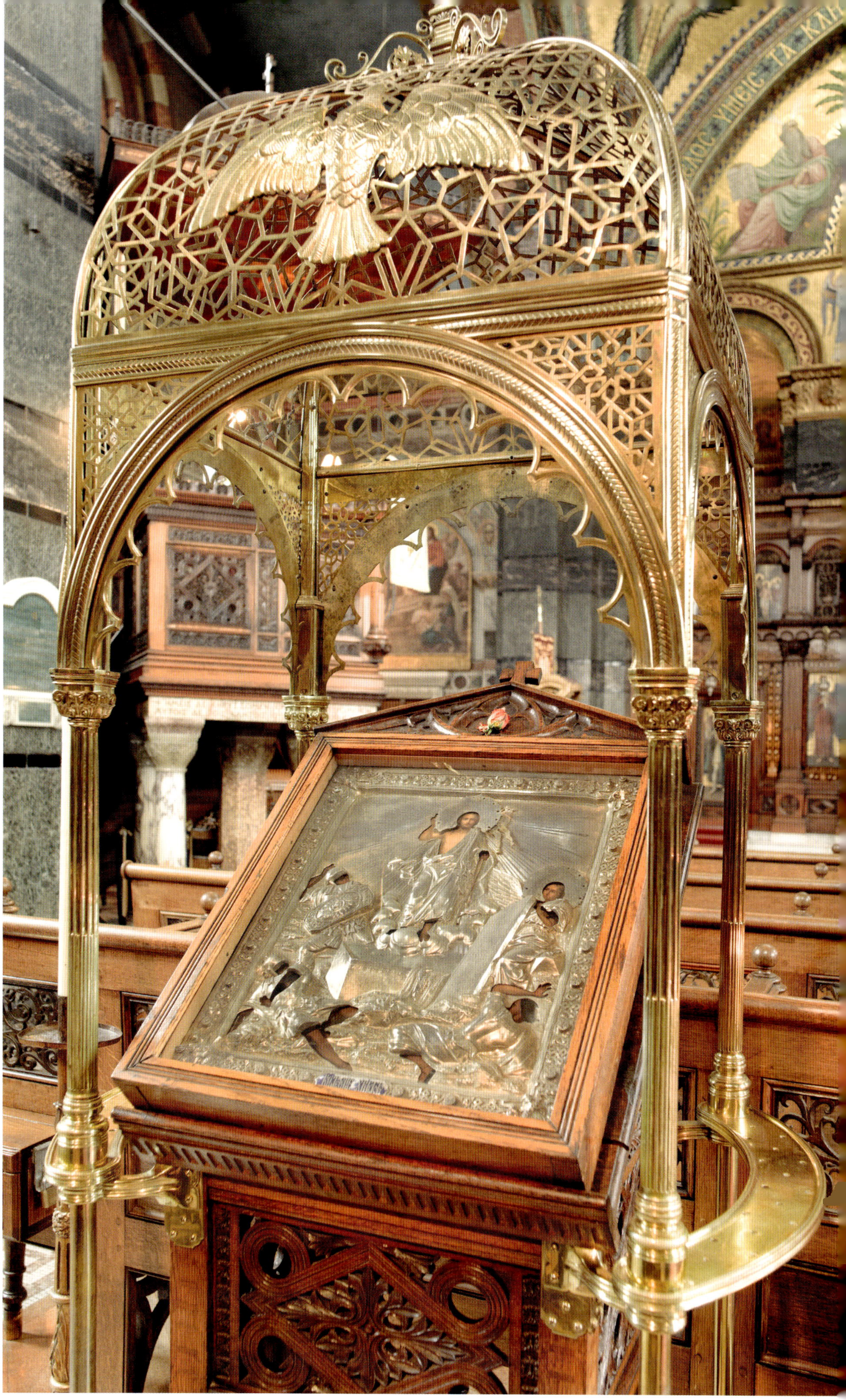

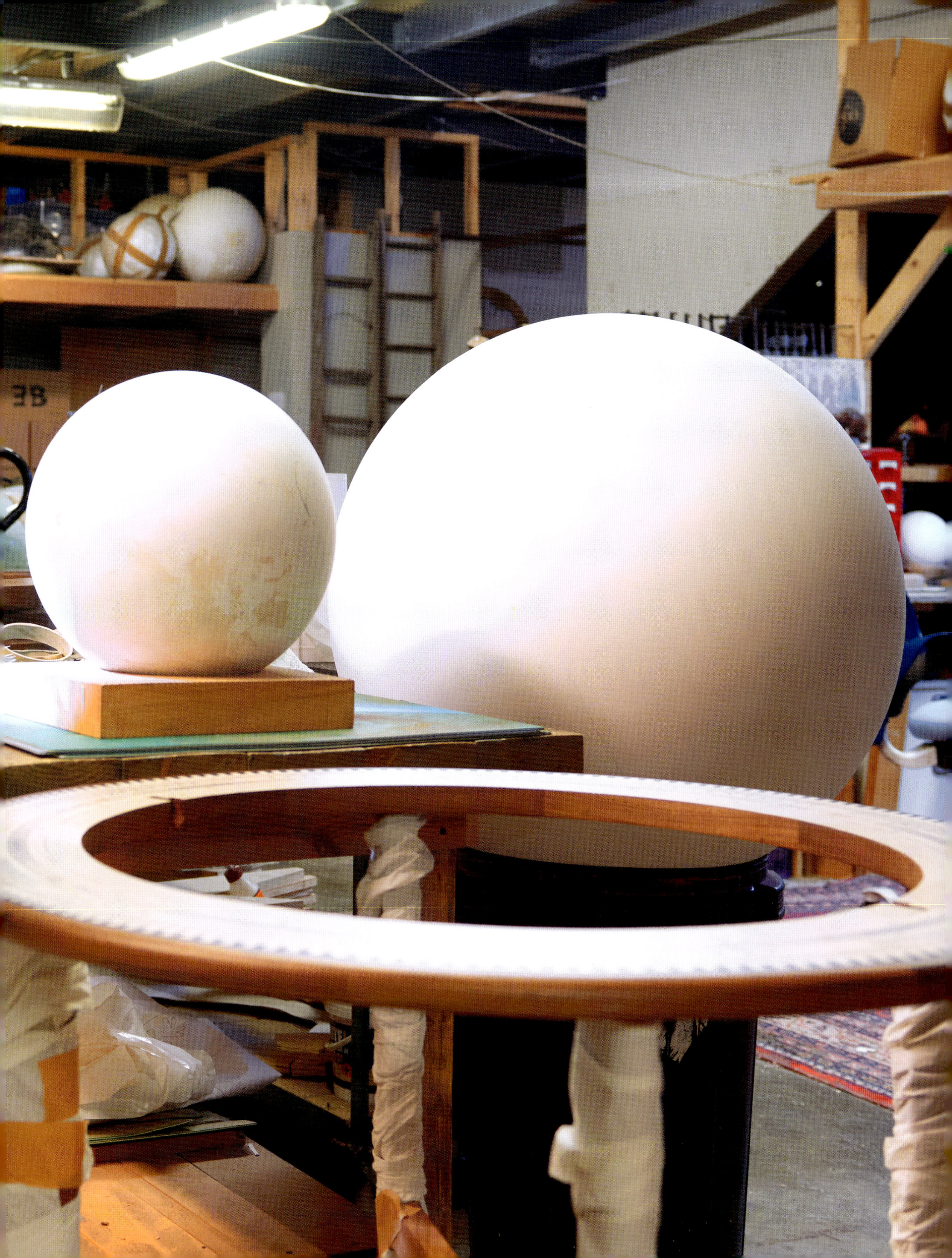

Bellerby & Co. Globemakers

Large floor-standing globe spheres and base.

The studios of Bellerby & Co. in Stoke Newington is home to a rare craft: the business of bespoke globemaking.

London has a history of making fine globes, a tradition that faded over the course of the last century. When Peter Bellerby in 2008 sought a gift for his father's 80th birthday, he was inspired to look for a classic artisan globe. He found only fragile antiques or poor-quality modern renderings and wondered: 'How difficult can it be to make a ball and put a map on it?'

Almost two years later he had his globe. He says he had no intention of setting up a company. Along the way, Peter Bellerby went a considerable distance to re-invent and update the craft and artistry of globemaking. Creating the most perfect sphere from two half-globe moulds required application of advanced precision tooling from Formula 1 fabricators. Fibreglass and modern resin replaced plaster of Paris. Modern mapping was applied. Cartographers and illustrators and woodworkers were recruited and globemakers trained.

Bellerby & Co. now employs at least twenty-five people in its studio-workshop in N16, where exquisite traditional painting and assembly skills meet modern materials. In-house cartographers create the maps, highlighting places, features and routes to the customers' preferences. Clever processing is applied to turn flat maps into the shaped 'gores' to fit on the globe. Before the twelve or twenty-four gores are cut, some paint is applied by the illustrators. Every mistake so far is potentially multiplied by π, and applying the gores to the sphere requires exceptional skill, says Peter Bellerby, who himself spent eighteen months perfecting techniques of laying paper when it is wet and stretchable.

Next, the illustrators return and more watercolour is painted before finishes are applied. More magic may be added, such as invisible lead weighting to bring a spinning globe smoothly to rest. Woodworkers craft and fit the bases. Desktop or floor-standing sizes range from 4¾ in (12 cm) to 50 in (127 cm) in diameter. The studio is not open to visitors.

CONTACT INFORMATION

Bellerby & Co. Globemakers,
7 Bouverie Mews, N16 0AE
https://bellerbyandco.com/

Strawberry Hill House & Garden

Strawberry Hill House at Twickenham, the building which is held to have pioneered the Gothic Revival style in England, is surprisingly light, airy and elegant. Some architectural historians argue that it has a style better described as a whimsical alternative to rococo. Whatever the definition, Strawberry Hill is fascinating place to visit and has recently been restored mostly to its original state, as conceived by its creator Horace Walpole.

Between 1747 and 1797, Walpole transformed a villa known as Chopp'd Straw Hall into a castle-cathedral, complete with towers, battlements and stained glass, all against the grain of prevailing classicism in contemporary architecture. He made additions to the building in stages, without an overarching plan. Walpole drew on illustrated references to rose windows, pointed arches and medieval churches for features and design details inside and out.

The library's carved bookcases were inspired by some doors in Old St Paul's Cathedral; the ceiling of the Holbein Chamber is modelled on the Queen's Dressing Room at Windsor, while the fireplace is based on a tomb at Canterbury Cathedral. The design for the pierced screen was inspired by a choir screen at Rouen Cathedral. Gothic arches from Prince Arthur's tomb in Worcester Cathedral were an inspiration for the decoration of the walls of the hall and staircase.

The Gallery was the main room for entertaining, and the restoration starting in 2007 has returned the

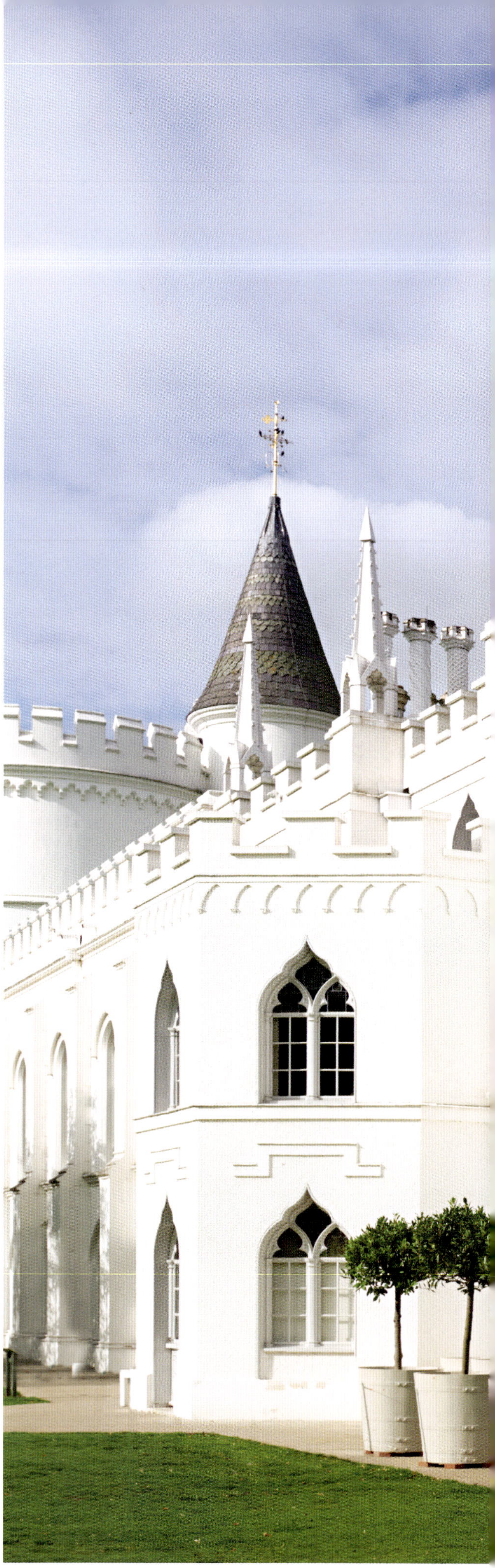

Part castle, part cathedral, no Corinthian columns, no classical symmetry: the exterior's once-dull rendering has been white-limewashed back to its original appearance.

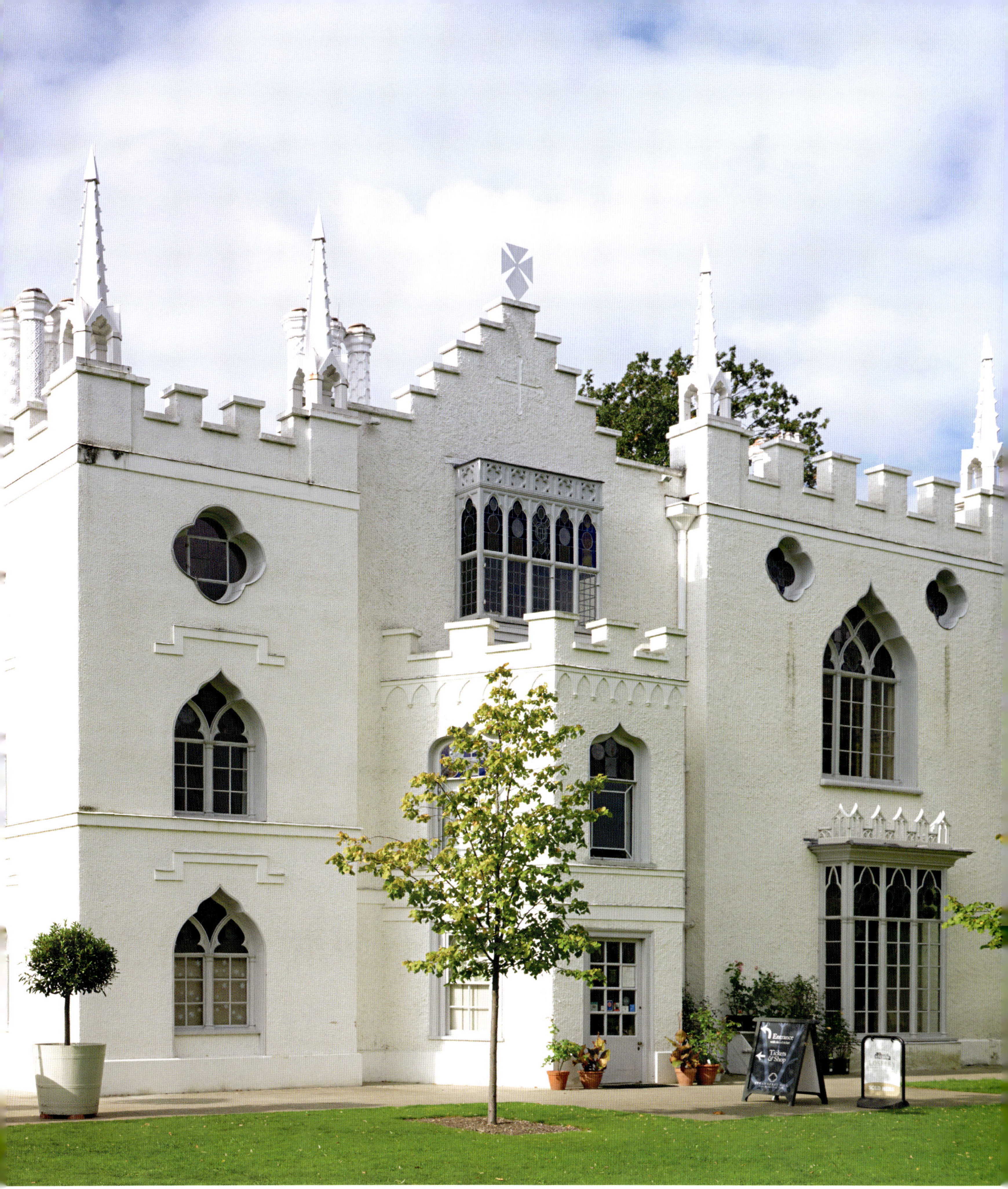
Entrance
Tickets & Shop

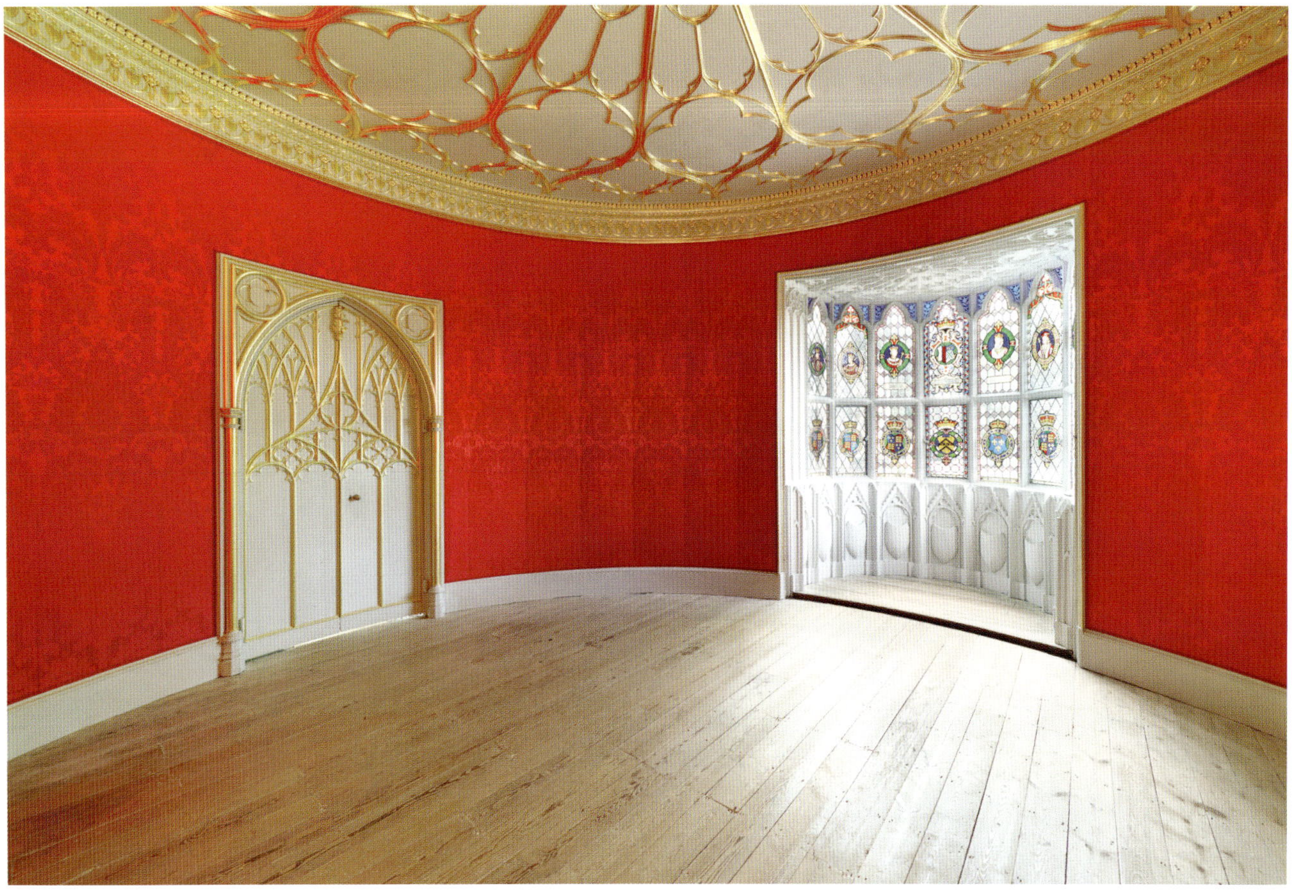

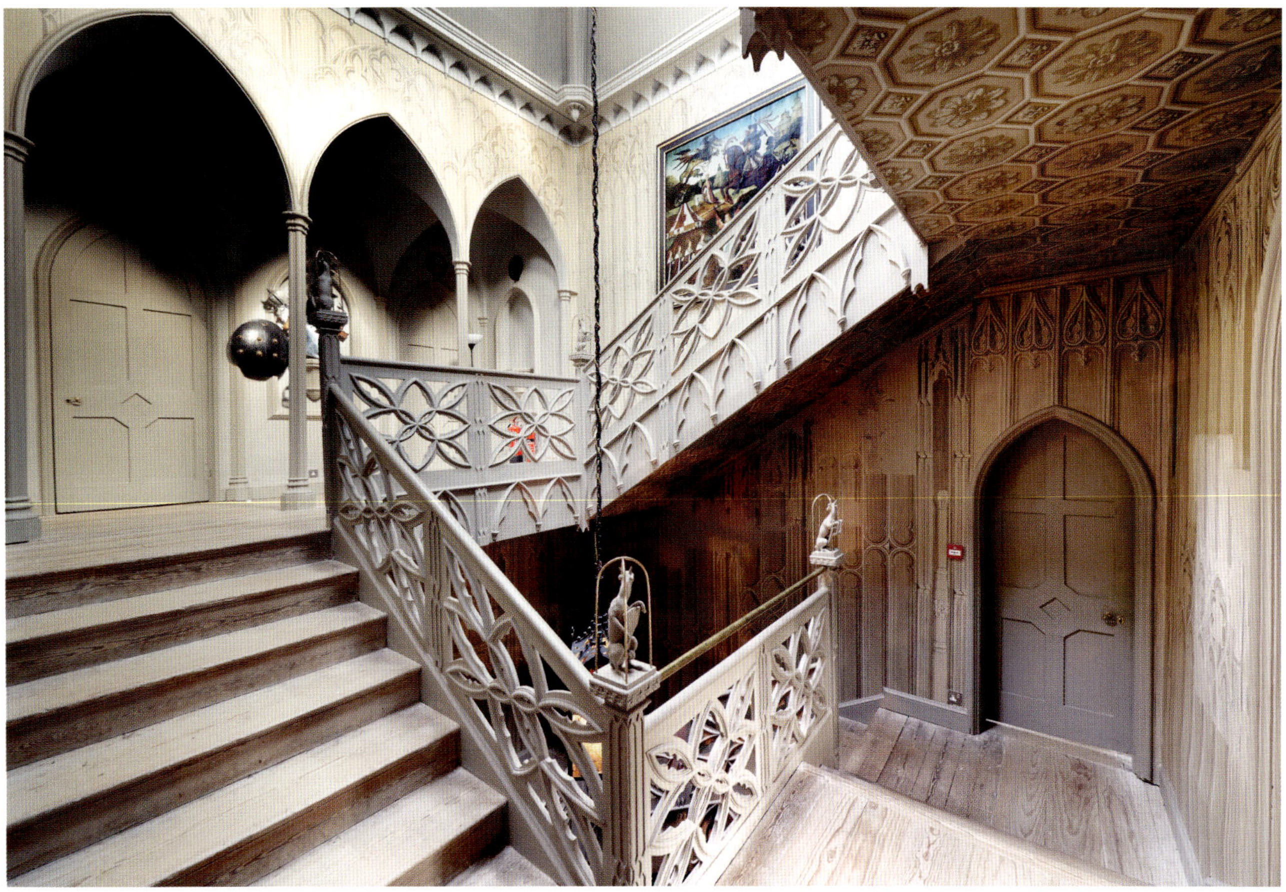

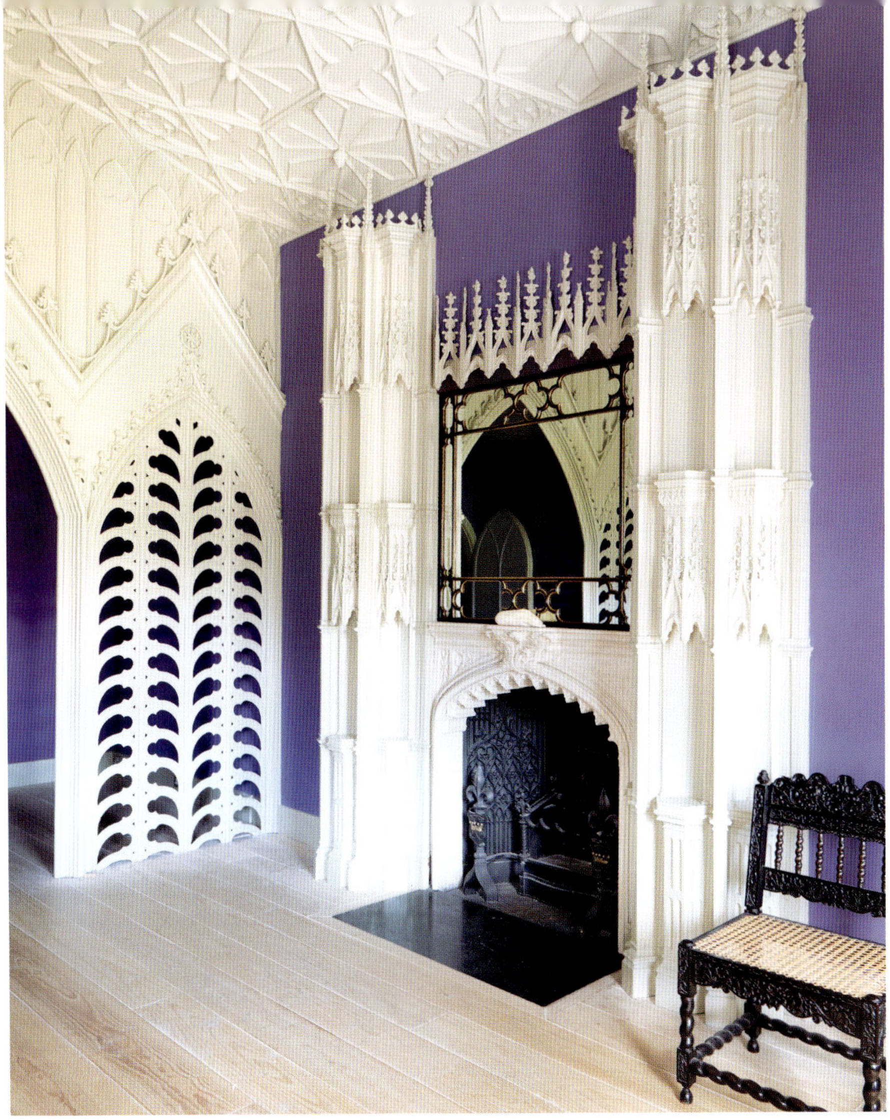

Opposite, above The Round Room is hung with scarlet silk. The ceiling design is based on a round window in Old St Paul's Cathedral.

Opposite, below The hall and staircase, intended to generate gothic gloom.

Above The Holbein Room once held paintings by the master. The ceiling is embossed papier mâché, the fireplace inspired by a tomb in Canterbury Cathedral.

window heights to their original dimensions. The high gothic dado which surrounds the room was also renovated. The ceiling, with its *papier mâché* moulding, has been restored and re-gilded, and the walls are hung with crimson damask.

A lost element of Strawberry Hill is Walpole's collection, which was once housed in the room known as The Tribune. Comprising hundreds of pictures, statues, ceramics, vases and *objets d'art*, it was dispersed in a great sale of 1842. The current location of many of the objects is known, and the Strawberry Hill Collection Trust together with the Strawberry Hill Trust is seeking to return the objects sold to the house.

Descriptions applied to Strawberry Hill have ranged from fairy-tale to eccentric to romantic; its creator Horace Walpole was an antiquarian, author, collector and Whig politician, son of the first British Prime Minister Robert Walpole. He was a dilettante rich enough to indulge fully his imagination, and he described Strawberry Hill as a 'plaything'. His novel *The Castle of Otranto*, published in 1764, prefigured the forthcoming 'Gothick' idiom, including such elements as cursed noblemen, supernatural events, monks, princesses, romantic love, violent death and a dark castle. A visitor to Strawberry Hill today might struggle to make the connection, but Walpole certainly intended the house to be a gothic experience, requiring a walk through a supposedly gloomy hall and up the darkened grey stairway before emerging into the bright and colourful chambers above. He did coin the word 'gloomth' in a letter ('one has satisfaction in imprinting the gloomth of abbeys and cathedrals on one's house') but to the modern eye the spaces do not seem to qualify. The restoration has even returned the exterior to its original gleaming lime-washed white finish; it was once described as resembling a wedding cake.

Strawberry Hill did not suffer too badly after Walpole's death. The house devolved upon the Waldegrave family, certain extensions and additions were made, and some rooms open today have retained the later nineteenth- and twentieth-century details. From 1925, it was a training college for teachers, now St Mary's University, and the gallery was once used as a lecture theatre. Now the university mostly has its own buildings on the Strawberry Hill site. Although the fabric of the house was largely intact, much decay was found during the restoration. This was launched in 2007, with £9 million Heritage Lottery funding, greatly enabled by Strawberry Hill being one of the best-documented houses anywhere. Walpole wrote copiously about his gothic castle and commissioned a set of drawings and paintings to record its changes, all of which were available to the restorers, who are steadily opening more of Walpole's rooms to visitors.

CONTACT INFORMATION

Strawberry Hill House & Garden,
268 Waldegrave Road, Twickenham, TW1 4ST
https://www.strawberryhillhouse.org.uk/

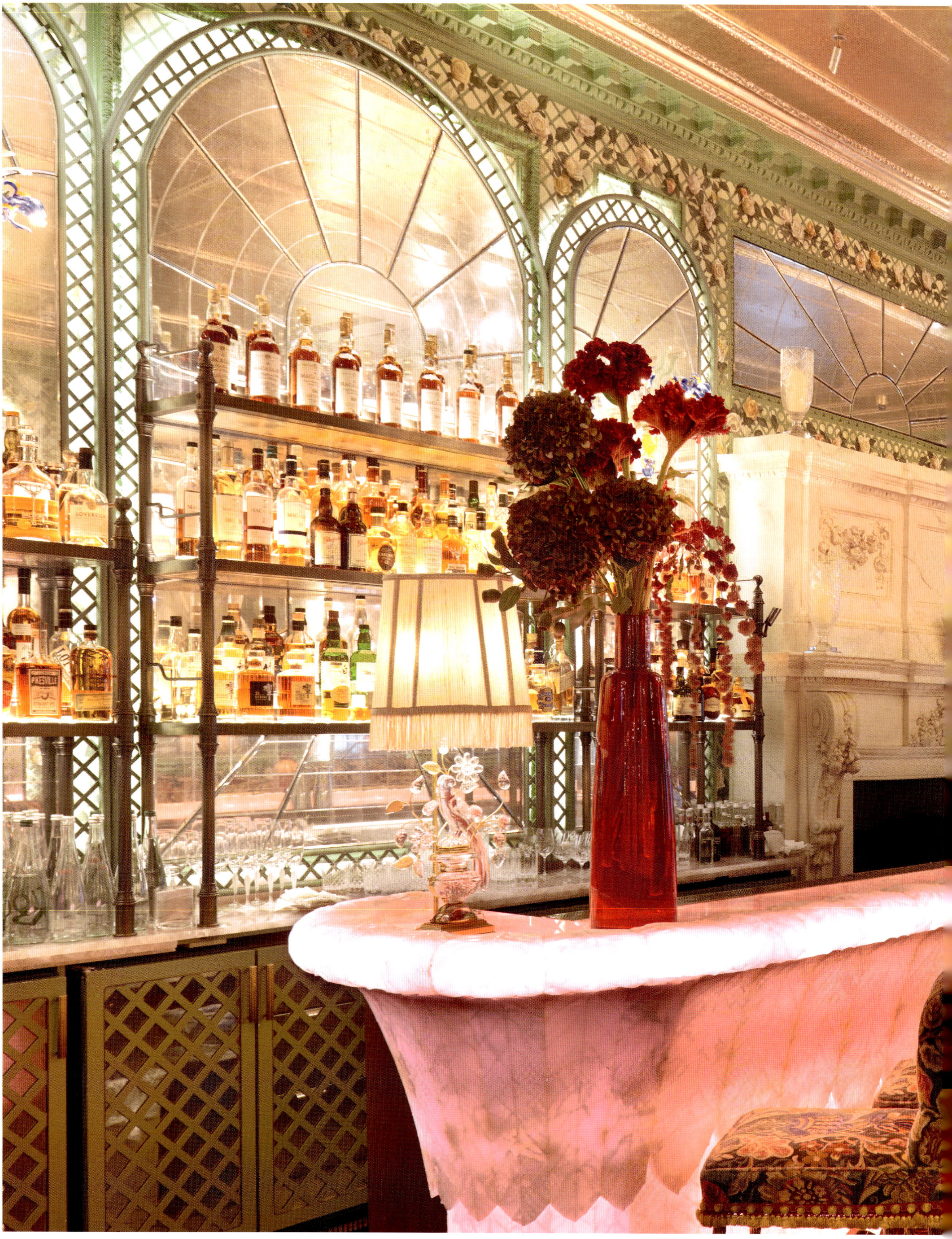
PIKESVILLE

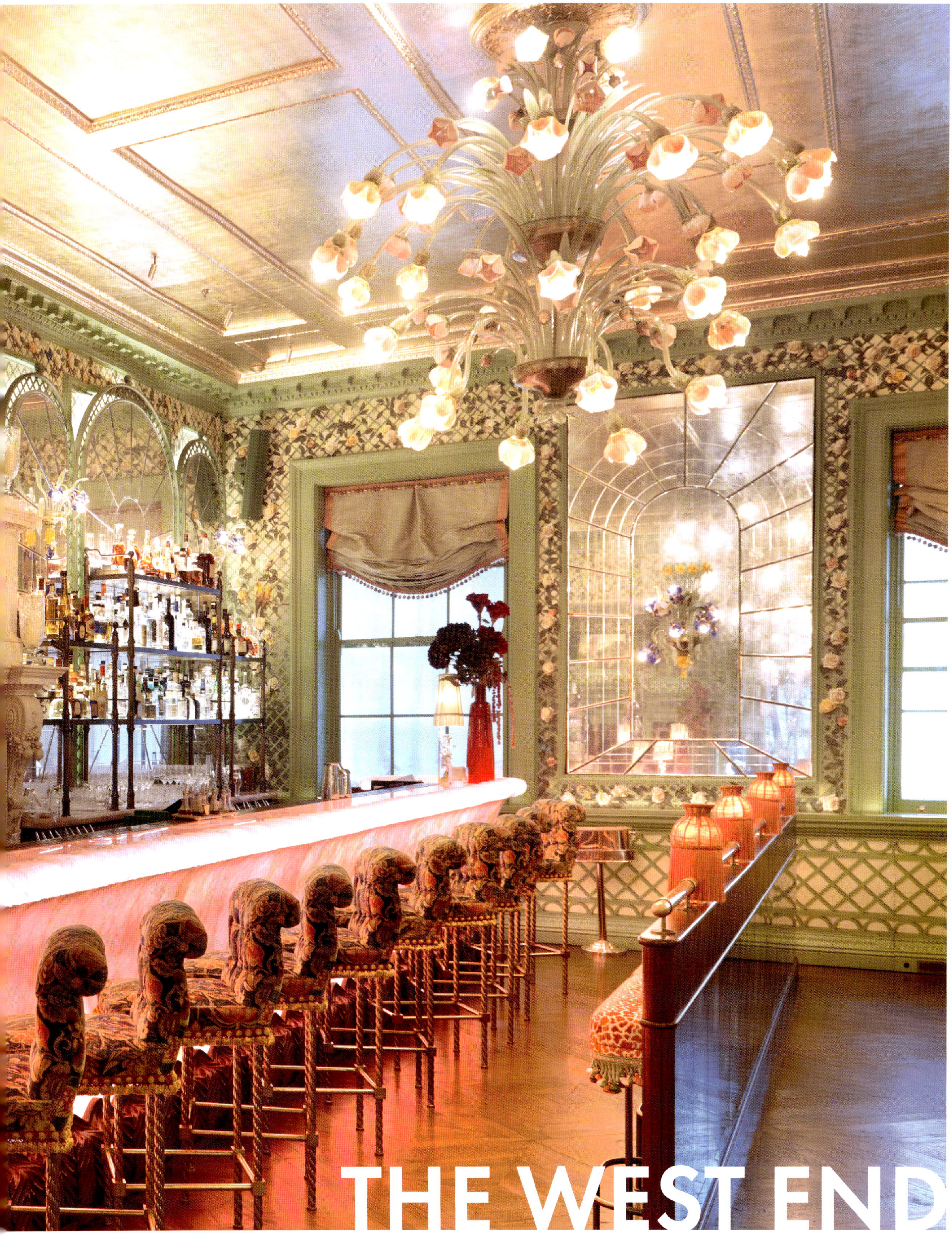

THE WEST END

Annabel's

Annabel's club is spread across four floors of an eighteenth-century townhouse in Berkeley Square. Its seven bars, four restaurants, private dining rooms, cigar salon and garden terrace are all decorated in a lavish maximalist style. In the basement lies a nightclub with dancefloor and stage, a place described by the operators as a seductive decadent paradise.

Annabel's owner, Richard Caring, fashion tycoon and restaurateur, commissioned interior designer Martin Brudnizki to transform the house with decorative themes of flora and fauna running throughout the building. The result left seemingly every surface painted, carpeted, tiled, papered or mirrored, with decorations from floor to ceiling inspired by creatures wild and gardens exotic. The theme is followed through to the Jungle Room, the Elephant Room and the Rose Room. The subterranean nightclub was inspired by the style of the painting *Adam and Eve in the Garden of Eden* by Johann Wenzel Peter, its hydraulic dance floor rising to make a stage as faux palm trees made of brass and glass vibrate to the beat of music.

Real trees on the garden terrace evoke a verdant woodland glade or a Georgian orangery, with seats and tables surrounded by extensive plantings. This can be experienced inside or out – the terrace is topped with a powered retractable steel-and-glass roof, designed by renowned steel designers, architects and engineers, Waagner Biro.

Previous page The Rose Room bar at Annabel's.

Right Illuminated amber onyx counter, silver elephants under the shelves and cavorting creatures on the lamps in the Jungle Room bar.

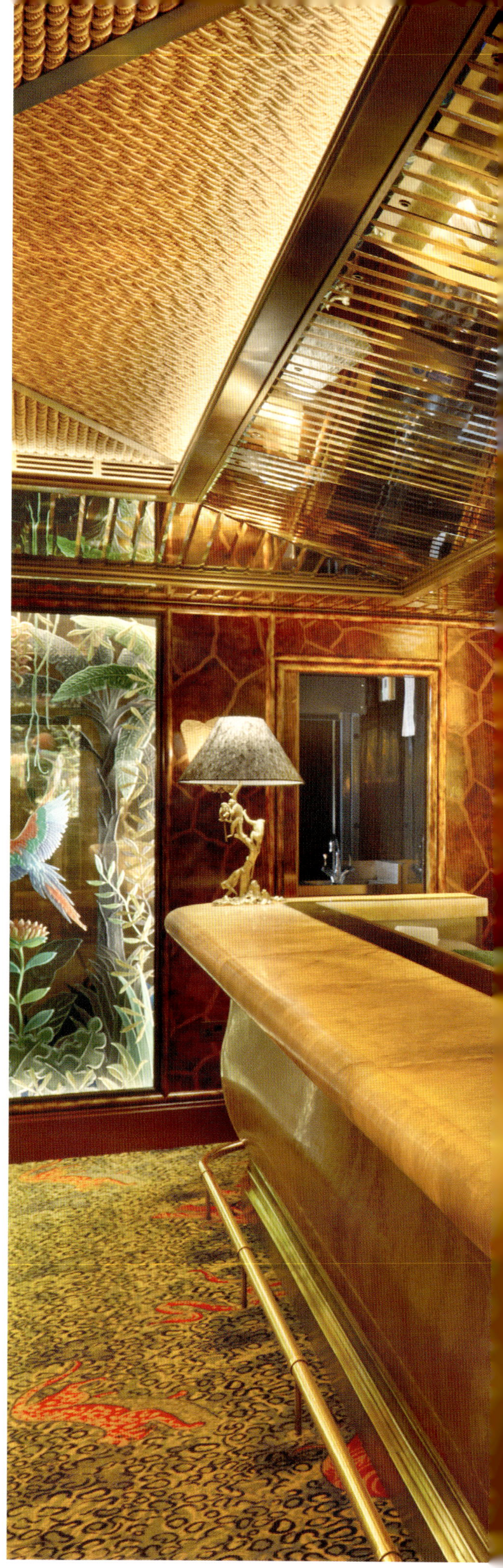

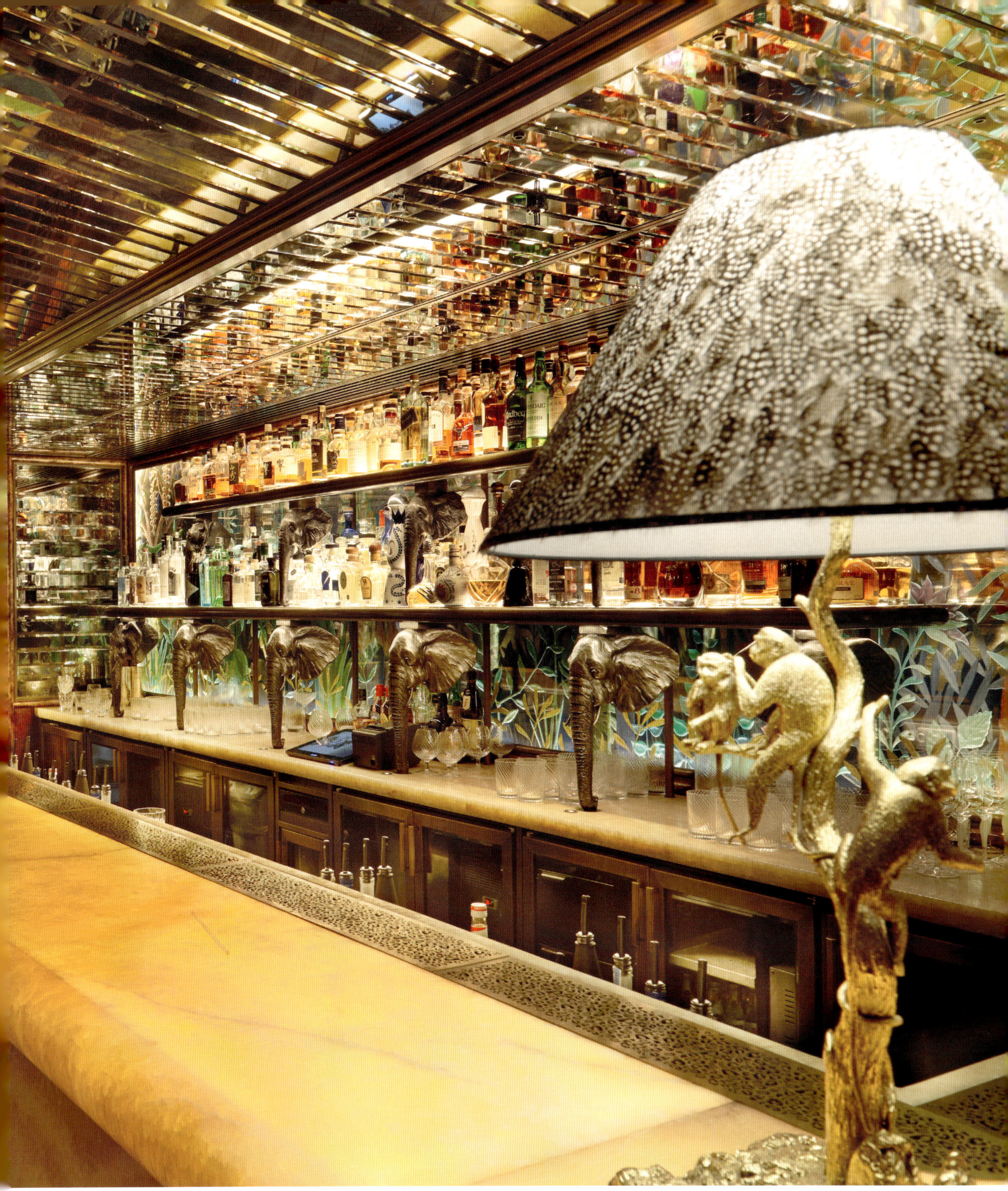

It was the exotic frivolity of the Ladies' Powder Room that generated the most headlines when Annabel's reopened in 2018. Thousands of handmade silk flowers line the ceiling and hand-carved basins of pink onyx in the shape of oyster shells are fitted with gold swan taps, while the walls are covered in embroidered fabric, and the floor and lower walls are made of pink and grey marble.

The Legacy Bar in the basement, reserved for a special higher tier of membership, has a green agate tiled floor, antique mirror-glass walls and hangings including work by Modigliani, Léger and Chagall. In the reception hall, illumination is provided by floor-to-ceiling chandeliers and visitors are greeted with a painting by Pablo Picasso dating from 1937, once known as *The Girl with the Red Beret and Pompom*. This was purchased for more than £20 million by the club owner and was boldly re-christened *Annabel*. A grand, open-well stone staircase with fine ironwork from the 1740s remains and the stairwell is finished entirely in white as a soothing contrast to the rest of the decor. In the void flies a sculpture of Pegasus with a unicorn's horn, suspended from a hot-air balloon.

Annabel's opened in 1963 just as London began to get hip. Mark Birley, a well-connected, well-born and artistically inclined businessman, started it in the basement of 44 Berkeley Square, under the floors of the Clermont Club, London's first licenced casino. Birley's then wife, Lady Annabel Vane-Tempest-Stewart, who lent her name to the club, has said this quickly became the most hedonistic address in London. Annabel's club forged a style of its own, managing to be both old-exclusive and modern-eclectic. A place where aristocrats and visiting Hollywood players rubbed shoulders with contemporary rock stars and occasionally a member of the Royal Family, and where music met film and fashion in the spirit of the changing age. Frank Sinatra was an early member, John Wayne, Elizabeth Taylor and the Beatles and the Rolling Stones were visitors, and later Jack Nicholson, Kate Moss, Naomi Campbell, Diana Princess of Wales and Madonna. Birley's eye was for a decorative style that evoked a cosy English country house with his own collection of animal paintings and prints; at candlelit tables guests ate dinner seated on banquettes trimmed in red velvet; there were intimate nooks and the tiny dancefloor hidden at the back of the club was dimly lit. There was no real cabaret, but occasionally performers such as Ray Charles and Ella Fitzgerald played one-night stands. An unverifiable claim is that it is the only nightclub ever attended by the late Queen Elizabeth II, who drank a martini there in 2003.

Annabel's relocated to 46 Berkeley Square in 2018, having moved a few paces from number 44, to become no longer enclosed in a basement, much expanded and also no longer nocturnal. The club is open from 7.30 a.m. to 3 p.m. during weekdays. It remains a private members club, although it is sometimes home to launches and prestige parties and gatherings. The membership is described as 'diverse, eclectic and cosmopolitan', a 'hand-picked alchemy of like-minded people'.

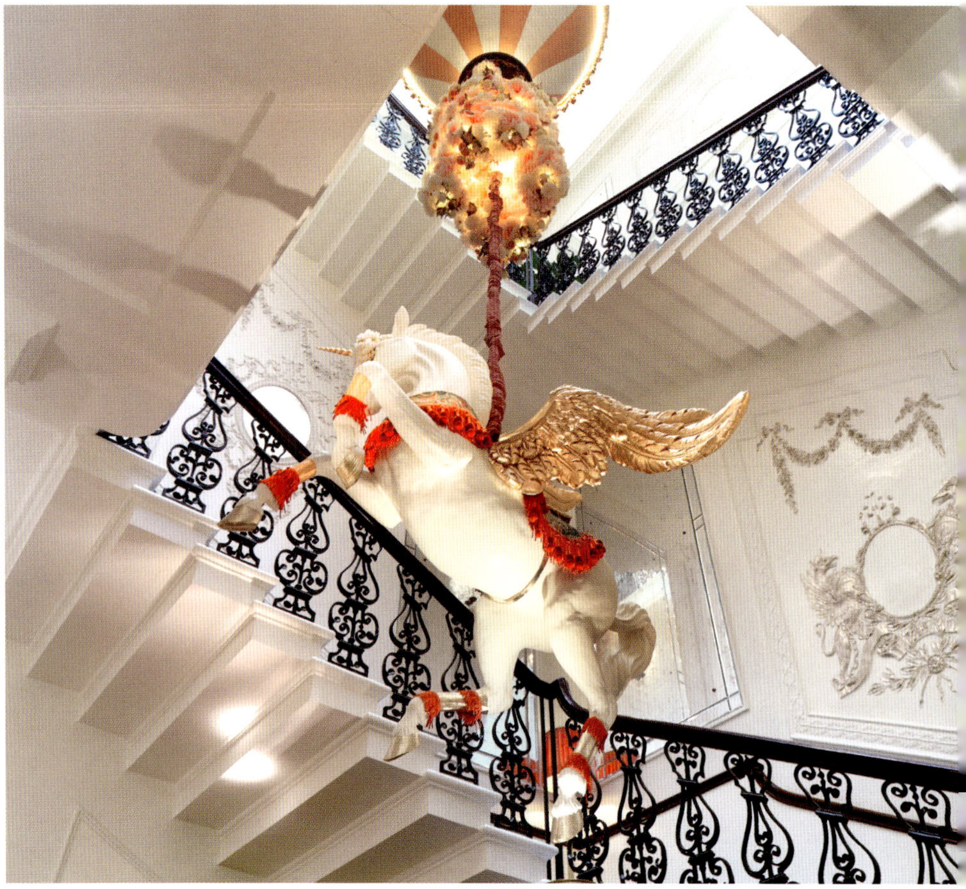

Above Pegasus flies as a unicorn under a hot-air balloon; the staircase dates from the 1740s.

CONTACT INFORMATION

Annabel's,
46 Berkeley Square, W1J 5AT
https://annabels.co.uk/

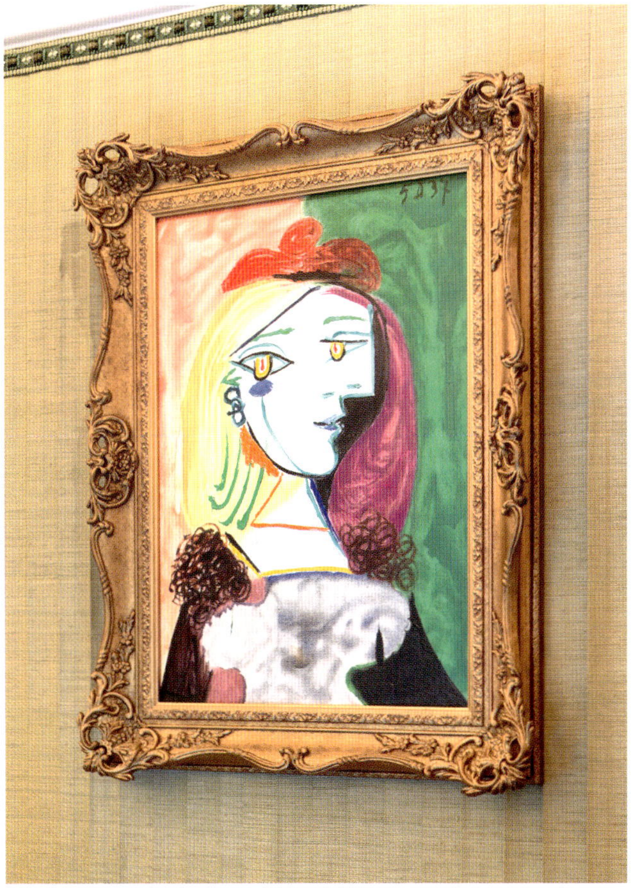

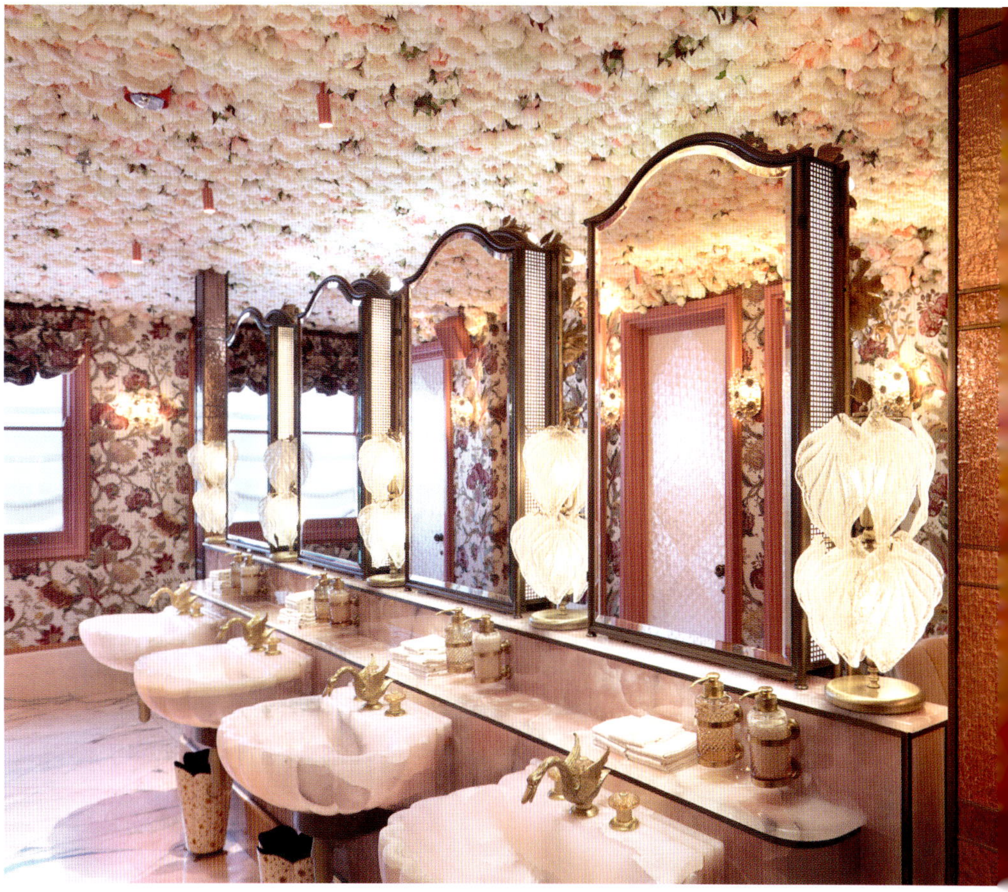

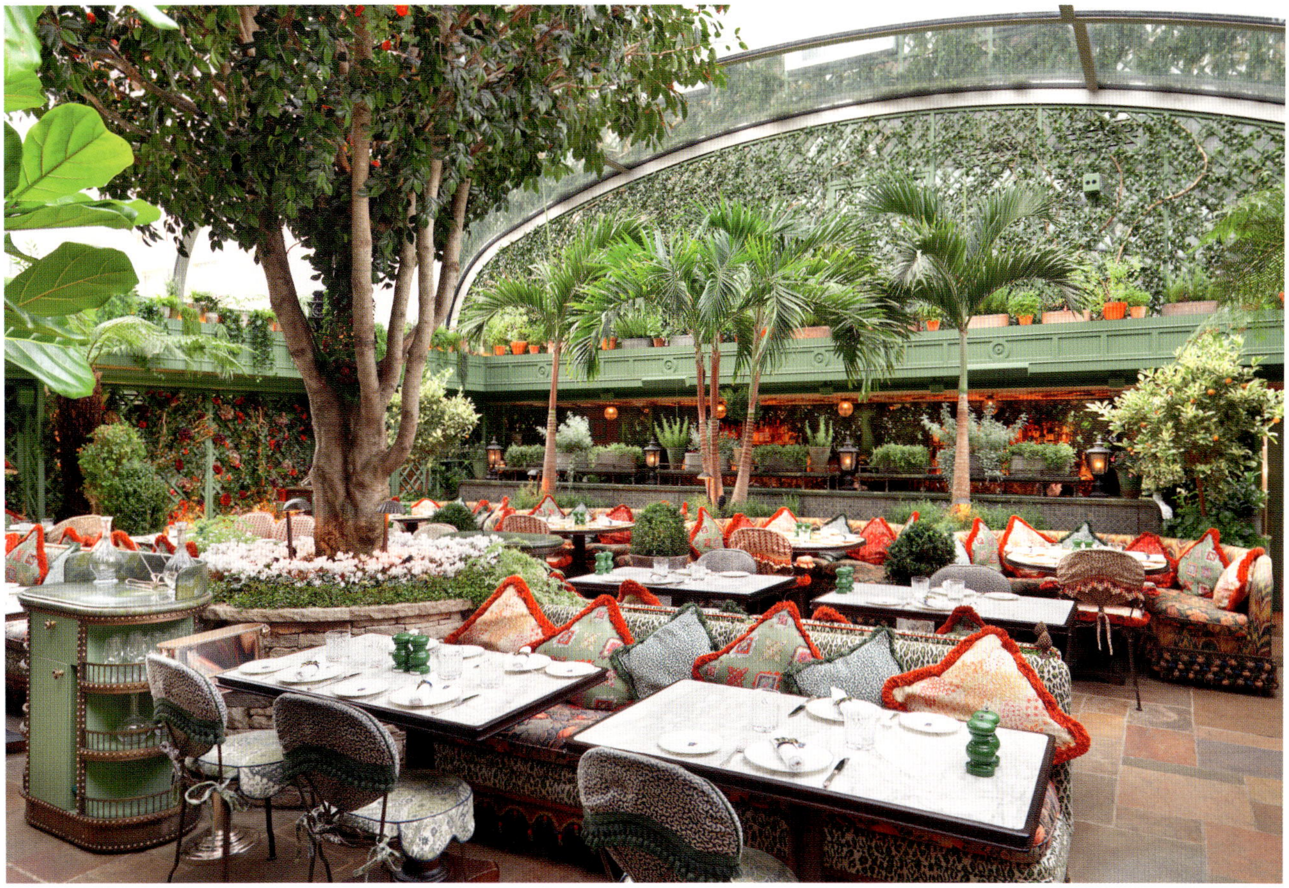

Top left Picasso's *The Girl with a Red Beret and Pompom* in the reception became *Annabel* in 2018.

Above The ladies' powder room with gold swan taps and basins hand-carved from pink onyx.

Left The spectacular, secluded garden dining area, covered by a masterpiece in engineering: a one-of-a-kind retractable glass roof.

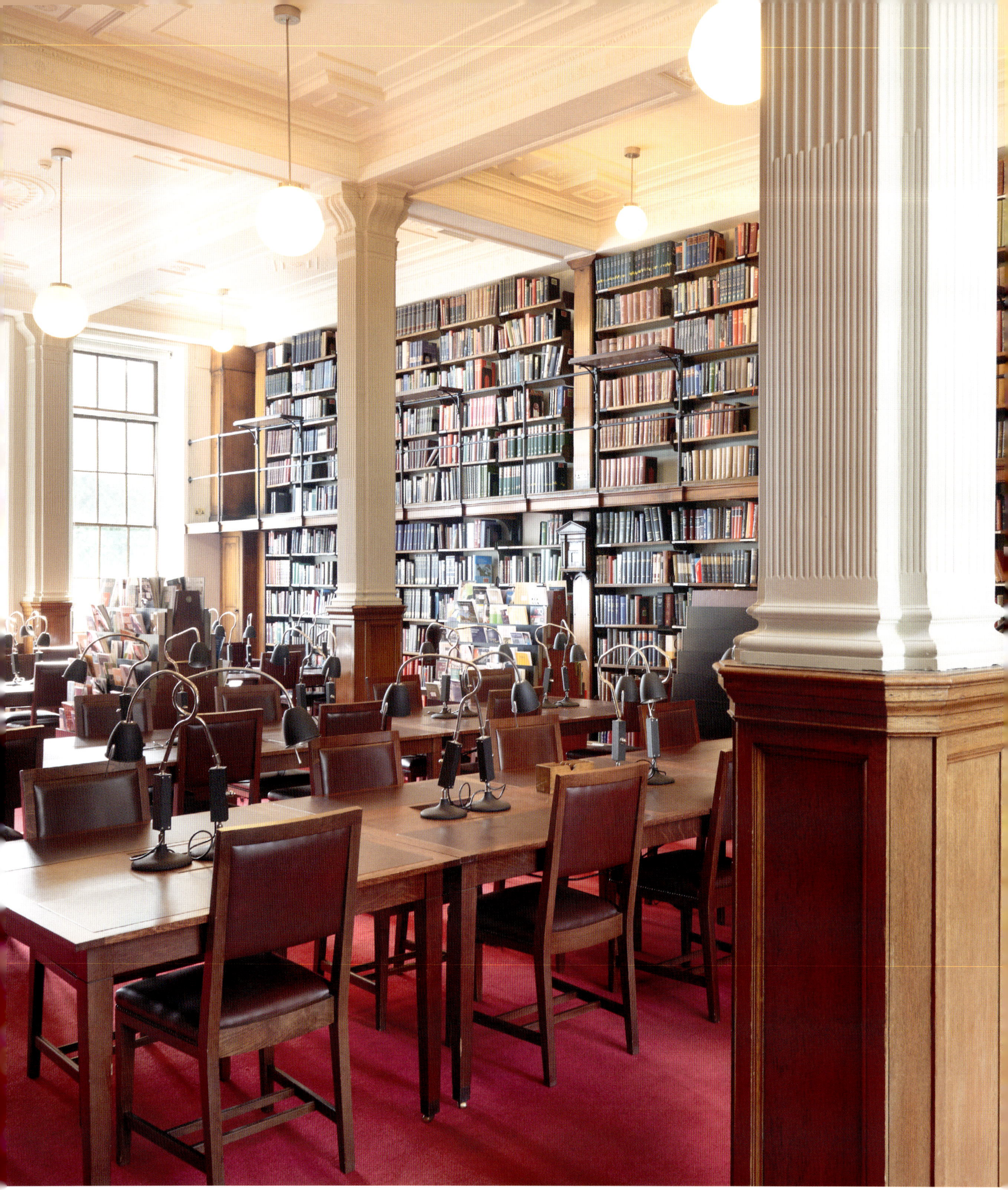

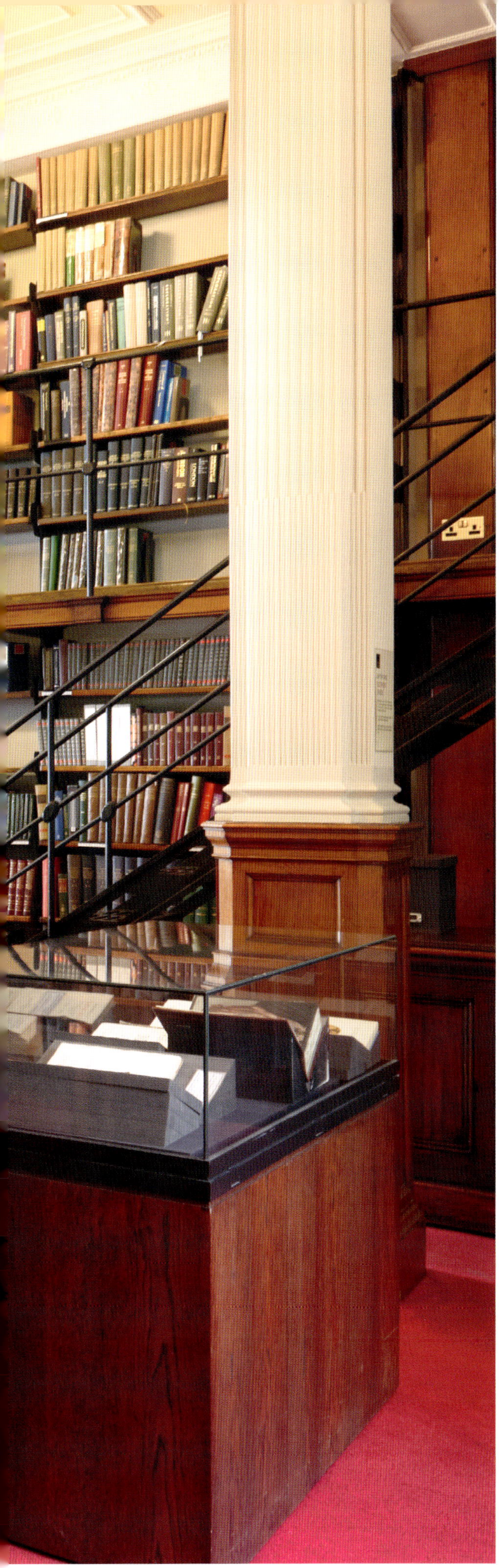

The London Library

Sir Stephen Fry once said of the reading room: 'What gyms can do for your body, this magical place can do for your mind.'

The London Library can be described as a marvel in multiple dimensions. It occupies a fine location in the corner of one of London's historic squares, where its narrow façade hides a complex of rooms and spaces spreading behind, below, to the side and above. It thrives as a subscription library in an age when the use of hardcopy books has supposedly declined. It carries accumulated layers of its own history and legends. The London Library holds more than a million books on its shelves, which measure some 17 miles (27 km), more than the length of the Circle line.

Based in a house on St James's Square since 1845, the library building was entirely rebuilt between 1896 and 1898 with a traditional Portland stone frontage concealing an advanced construction for the Victorian age. It incorporated a space-efficient metal frame for three new floors of bookstacks behind. These dense 1890s bookstacks, with utilitarian exposed beams, columns and grille floors, remain the most famous feature of the library. More bookstacks, this time with opaque glass floors, were added in 1922, and a further six-floor wing was built in 1934. With extra additions in the 1990s and 2000s, its entire ground-floor plan now combines seven buildings between the square and Duke Street behind.

Visitors first enter the double-height issue hall and then the lofty galleried reading room on the first floor. Stairs rise to the shelf levels behind. There are more reading spaces and a writers' room providing 140

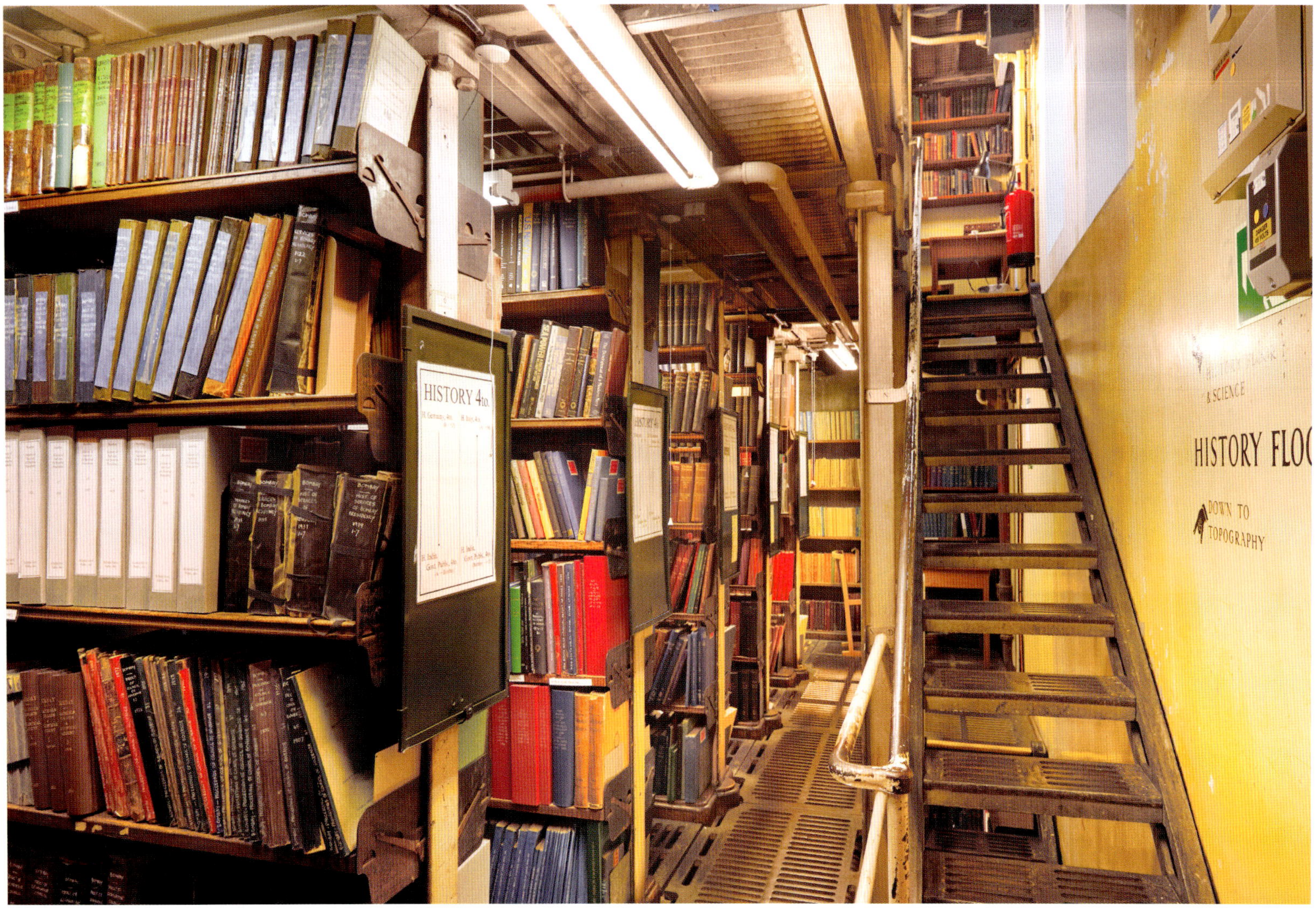

The history floor features an extensive collection, including works on monarchs, historical events and topics such as feudalism, international relations and chivalry.

desks in total, including an art room for large books, a tiled lightwell covered to make a study area and an elegant committee room with a transplanted Adam fireplace. In the labyrinthine basement lies a modern roller racking system for periodicals, alongside original copies of *The Times* newspaper spanning 200 years.

The standard Dewey Decimal Classification is not used in the London Library, which has its own system. There are still ancient finger signs to aid navigation around the stacks and some members say that simply browsing is the best experience, although its digital online catalogue is now rated as a powerful instrument. An increasing amount of its space can be described as virtual through its digital connectivity. In every respect, it is a serious, functional library, strong in history, literature, biography, art, philosophy and religion. There are French, German, Italian, Spanish and Russian collections.

Many direct connections can be made to writers across the literary spectrum and across time. Joseph Conrad, George Eliot, Henry James, George Bernard Shaw, Virginia Woolf, Rudyard Kipling, E.M. Forster, John Betjeman, Siegfried Sassoon, Agatha Christie and Harold Pinter all belonged to the London Library. Tennyson was an early president of the library. T.S. Eliot, a member since 1918, was president between 1952 and 1965, a role later occupied by Sir Tom Stoppard and Sir Tim Rice, and now Helena Bonham Carter.

Sometimes membership, fact and fiction overlap. Member Sir Arthur Conan Doyle deployed Dr John Watson to the library for an intensive study of Chinese pottery in the Sherlock Holmes story *The Adventure of the Illustrious Client*. Recent research has shown that Bram Stoker used his membership to borrow and study titles such as *Transylvania* and *Round About the Carpathians* during the seven years it took him to write

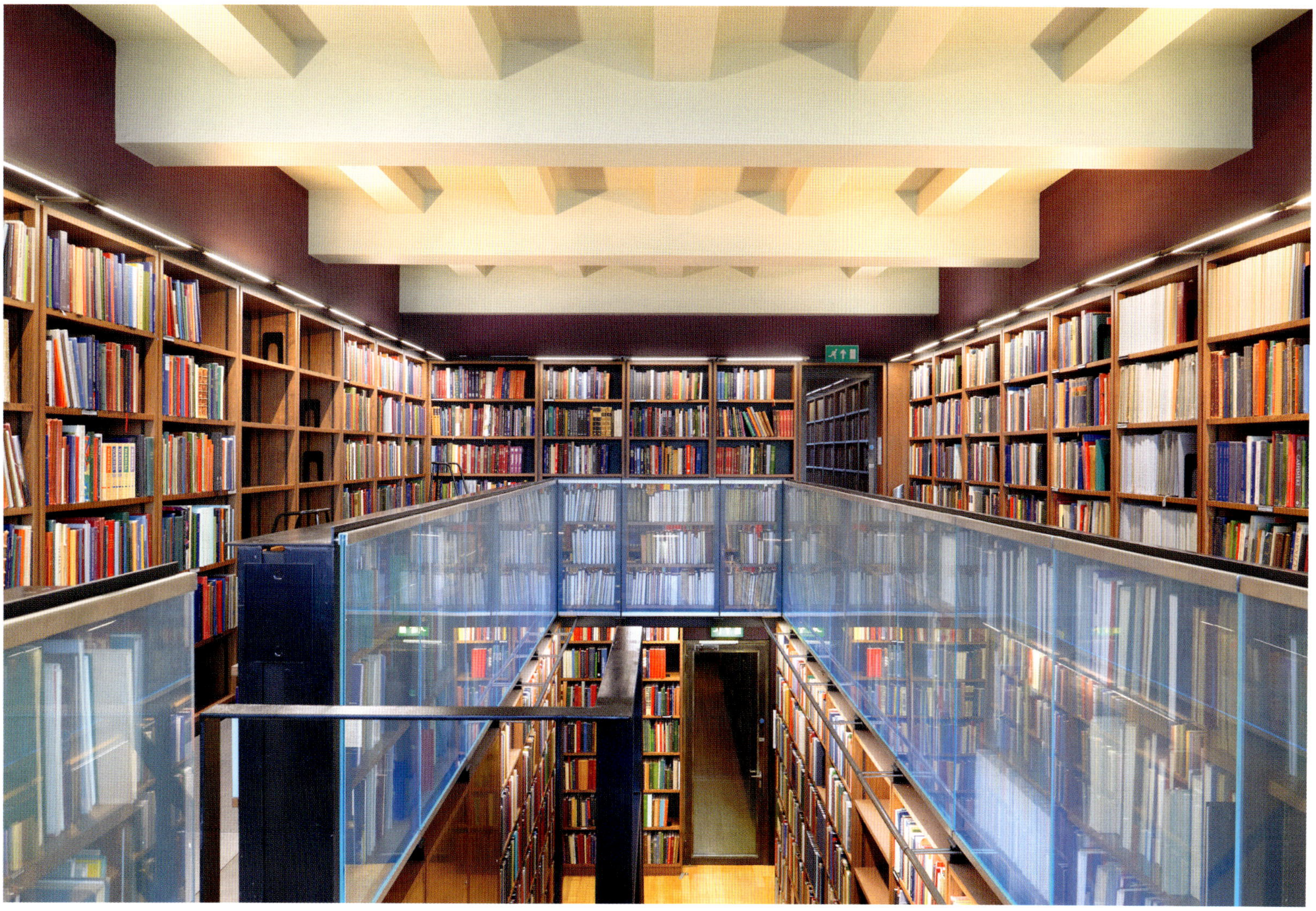

The art room displays works on the fine and applied arts, including painting, sculpture and architecture, as well as on topics such as aesthetics, artistic anatomy and colour.

Dracula. It is not clear if Ian Fleming was a member, but he made sure that James Bond was, as Fleming equips his agent with *Burke's General Armory*, stamped 'Property of the London Library', when he is assigned to tackle the villain Blofeld in *On Her Majesty's Secret Service*.

Thomas Carlyle, the philosopher and historian who wrote an account of the French Revolution, is credited with doing much to launch the London Library after his frustration with the British Museum Library, which did not lend books. Carlyle shipped two cartloads of books on the French Revolution taken from the library to help Charles Dickens write *A Tale of Two Cities*.

Antonia Byatt set the opening chapter of *Possession* in the reading room. It is reported that the 2017 Nobel laureate Kazuo Ishiguro discovered a copy of Harold Laski's *The Dangers of Being a Gentleman* here and was inspired to write *The Remains of the Day*.

The library's warren-like spaces are more smoothly connected than before following refurbishing and rebuilding, but a fine eccentricity remains. Even outside at street level, a sharp-eyed observer might see that the façade, which is asymmetrical, creates an illusion. In 1896 the architect took what was the narrowest house in the square and made it look older and wider than it is. The frontage appears to go under the cornice of the neighbouring building, which dates from the 1730s. It is a hint that more lies behind. To see more, it is sometimes possible to go inside the library during certain evenings by booking in advance.

CONTACT INFORMATION

London Library,
14 St James's Square, SW1Y 4LG
https://www.londonlibrary.co.uk/

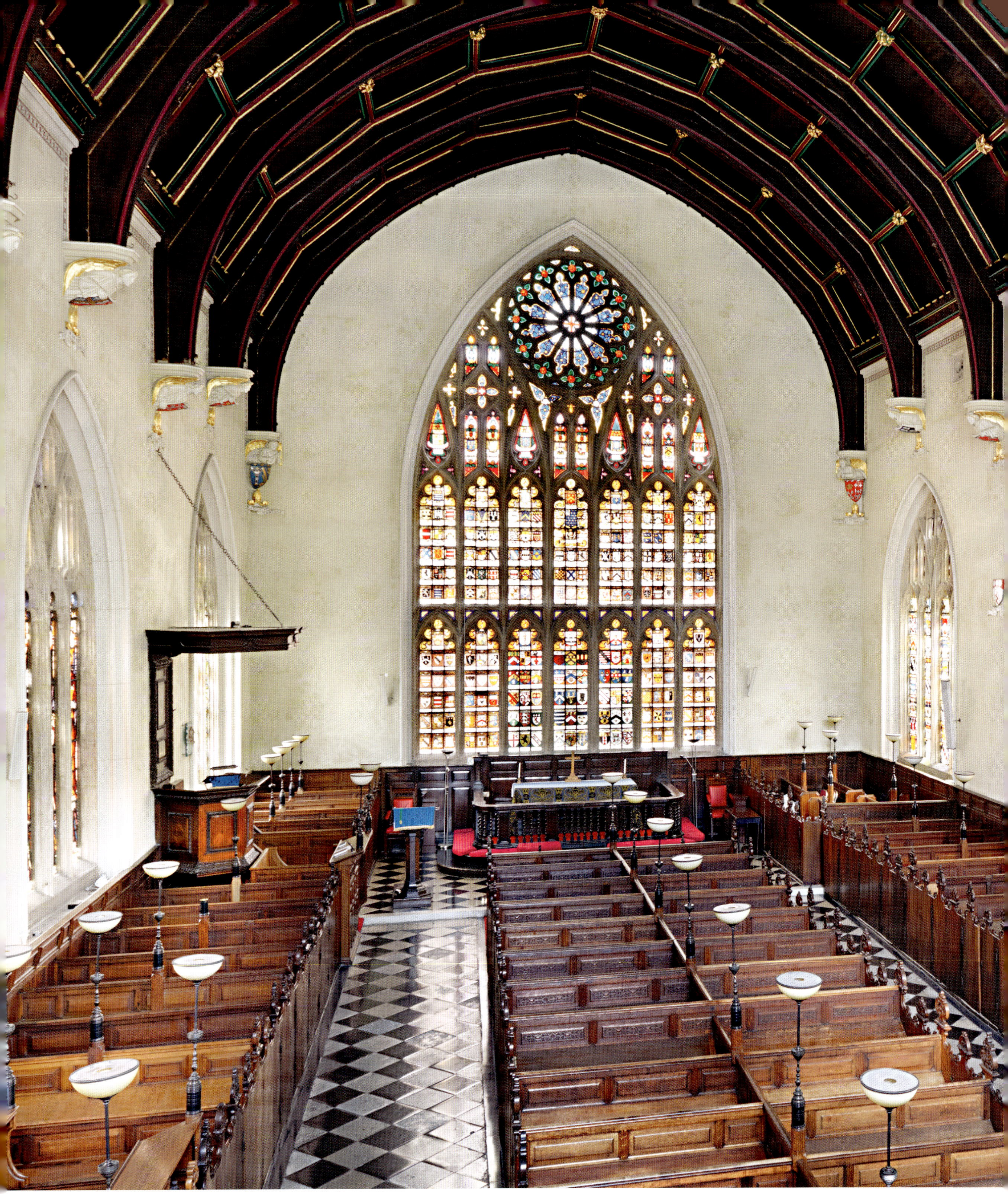

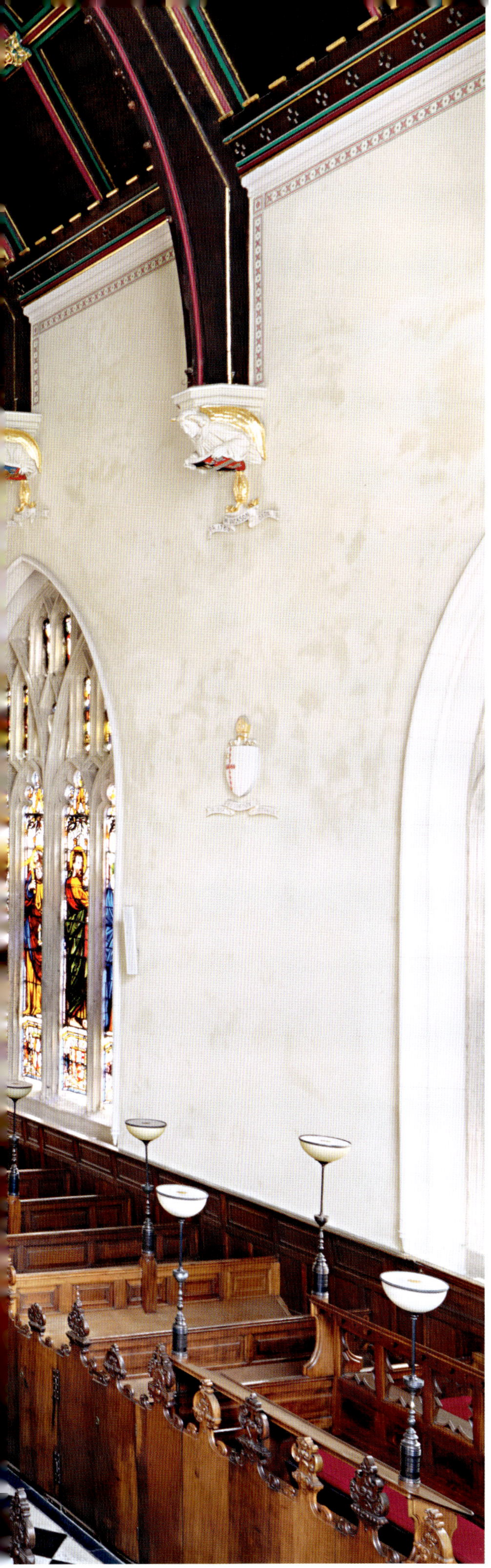

The Honourable Society of Lincoln's Inn

The Chapel dates back to 1620, but has seen many repairs and restorations.

London's four Inns of Court – the Honourable Societies of Lincoln's Inn, Gray's Inn, Middle Temple and Inner Temple – are the professional associations for for all barristers in England and Wales, each with a long hisory. The Lincoln's Inn sits behind a fine brick wall on Chancery Lane, and it is easy for visitors to go inside the precincts around the squares and gardens. The group of buildings comprising Lincoln's Inn span more than 500 years, from Tudor through Georgian to mid-Victorian Tudor Revival. To enter the main buildings – the Great Hall, Old Hall and Library – it is necessary to book a tour and set aside some time, for there is plenty of history to be unlocked.

Lincoln's Inn began as a legal centre in around 1311, when Henry de Lacy, 3rd Earl of Lincoln bequeathed it to London's legal fraternity. Thomas More was a student there between 1496 and 1502. The Old Hall of Lincoln's Inn would have been known to More, and much of the stone and brick of the fabric visible today dates from that time. The Hall was enlarged in the seventeenth century, with an internal wooden screen added. Later work was ill-judged, particularly the addition of an eighteenth-century plaster ceiling over the fine timbers supporting the roof which, together with other alterations, weakened the walls. Between 1924 and 1928 it was painstakingly rebuilt, removing the plaster barrel vault, and restoring the interior to something closer to its original appearance. The Old Hall was regularly used as a functional courtroom, notably as a court of chancery before the Royal Courts of Justice opened in 1882.

The next oldest part of Lincoln's Inn is its Gatehouse on Chancery Lane, built between 1517 and 1521. It is a four-storey tower with diagonal lines of inky brick, and its oak gates date from 1564. It was the brainchild of Sir Thomas Lovell, a Lincoln's Inn treasurer and veteran of the Battle of Bosworth Field, who supervised the construction, and paid the bill. Lovell's coat of arms adorns the gatehouse, alongside those of Henry VIII and the 3rd Earl of Lincoln, whose dragon insignia carried particular status, being rendered in purple, a costly colour in Tudor times.

In the nineteenth century, membership of Lincoln's Inn had greatly expanded, and a new dining hall was constructed. Known as the Great Hall, or New Hall, it was designed by architect Philip Hardwick, whose initials are etched into the brickwork. The foundation stone was laid in 1843, and the hall was opened two years later, incorporating a new main entrance gatehouse on Serle Street. Dominating the north wall of the hall is a vast fresco whose title is *Justice*, by George Frederic Watts, with depictions including Moses and Confucius, while Norman Hepple's oil painting *Short Adjournment* is a tribute to an era when the majority of Court of Appeal judges were Lincoln's Inn members.

The Honourable Society of Lincoln's Inn claims that its collection of books is the oldest library in continuous use in London. Lincoln's Inn Library was first mentioned in 1471. The present library building, an iron-galleried masterpiece, is part of the mid-nineteenth-century building works. It contains 150,000 volumes. As well as housing a unique collection of rare books, it is also a functioning modern legal library, and the only Inns of Court library to survive Second World War bombing.

Stone Buildings, a set of lawyers offices known as chambers, was constructed during the 1770s in the distinct style of the time, contrasting with the red brick elsewhere. Although Lincoln's Inn was more fortunate than the other Inns of Court during the war, Stone Buildings was hit and badly damaged, and this damage was subsequently repaired. A rare London relic is a remaining mark of the first Blitz, as the front of No. 10 Stone Buildings still shows damage inflicted during an air raid of December 1917. A disc, set into the road outside, marks the spot where the bomb exploded.

An early Lincoln's Inn Chapel is first mentioned in records from the reign of Henry VI; the foundation stone of its successor was laid by John Donne, poet and priest, and Preacher of Lincoln's around 1620. The vast space of the Chapel's seventeenth-century fan-vaulted undercroft, where benchers and members were once laid to rest, is a place where today's bewigged and gowned barristers pause to chat.

The Chapel bell, which is tolled at noon whenever a bencher dies, was reputedly immortalized by John Donne in the line 'therefore never send to know for whom the bell tolls; it tolls for thee'. Harder still to prove is the legend that playwright Ben Jonson worked as a young man as a bricklayer on the wall and gatehouse, but Lincoln's Inn does not need to scratch around for history. Notable members have included Walpole, Pitt the Younger, Gladstone, and Margaret Thatcher, fifteen Prime Ministers in all.

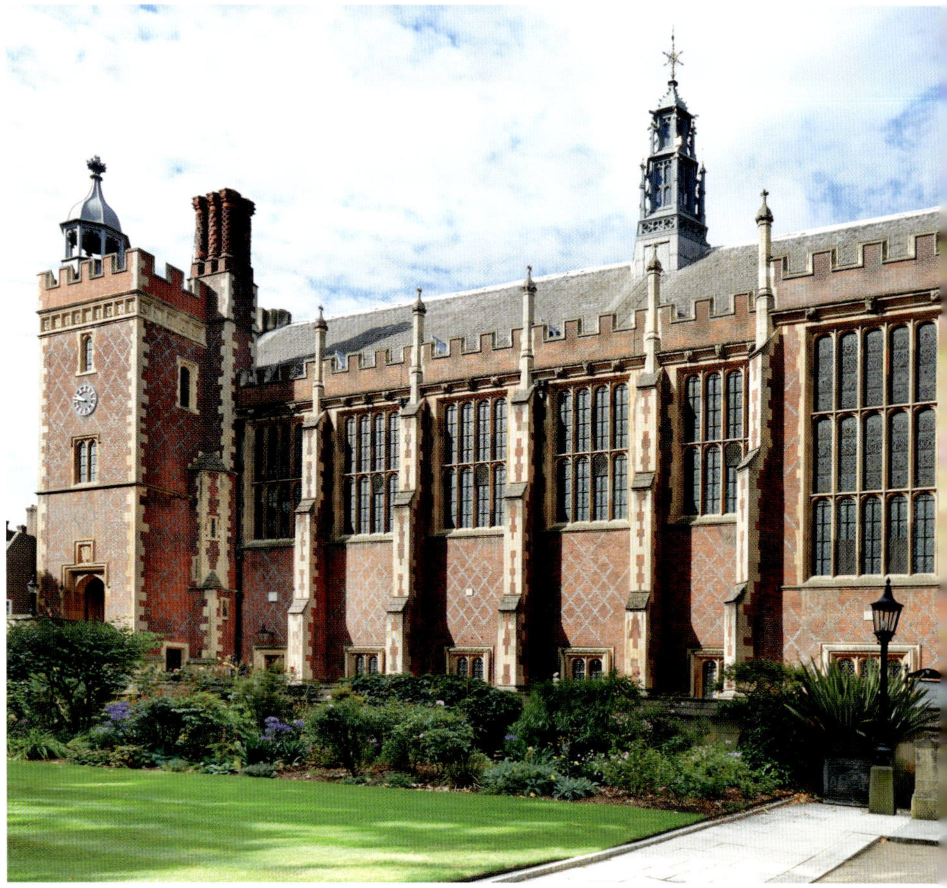

Above The Great Hall, or New Hall, designed by Philip Hardwick, was opened by Queen Victoria on 30 October 1845.

Opposite, above Lincoln's Inn Library is claimed to be the oldest library in continuous use in London.

Opposite, below Portraits and crests adorn the walls of the Great Hall.

CONTACT INFORMATION

The Honourable Society of Lincoln's Inn, Lincoln's Inn Fields, WC2A 3TL
https://www.lincolnsinn.org.uk/

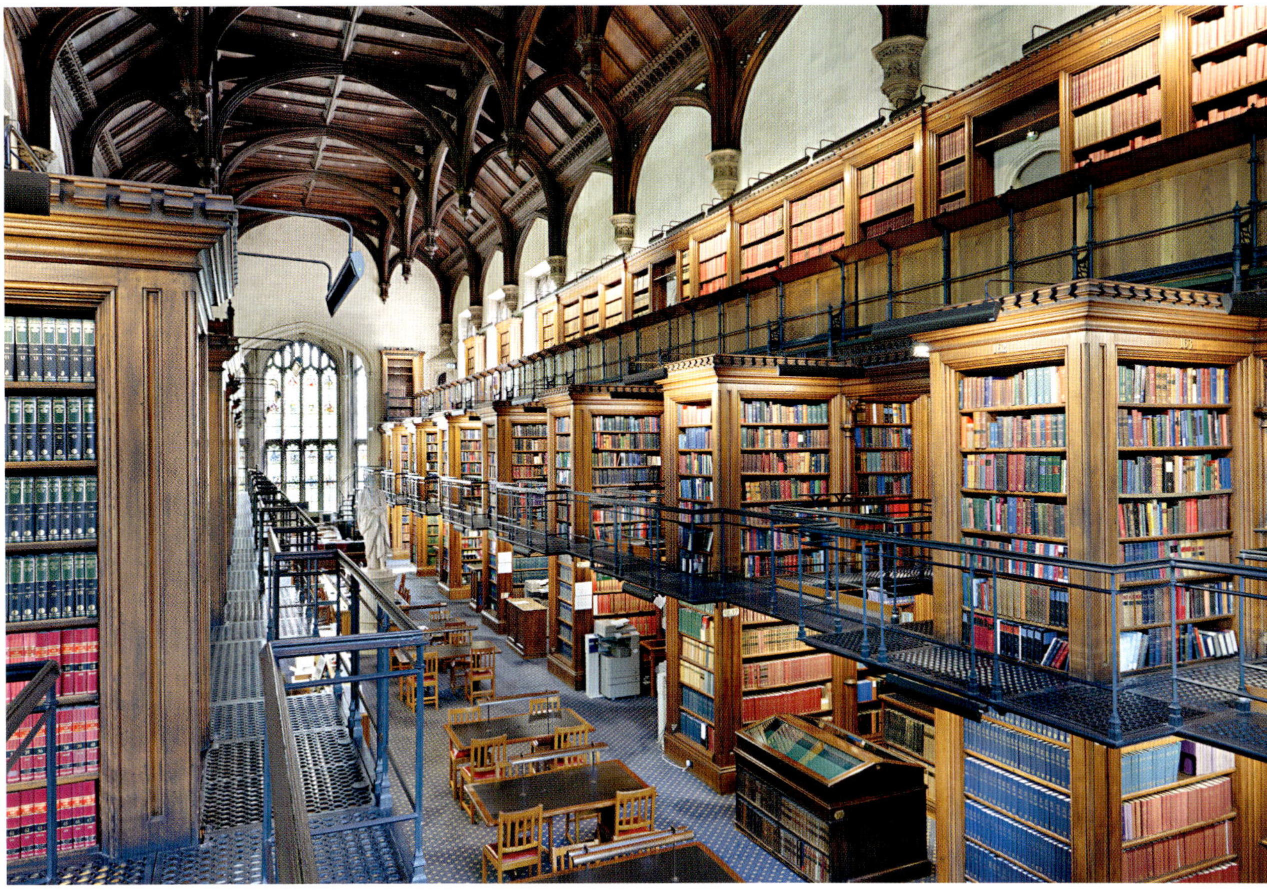

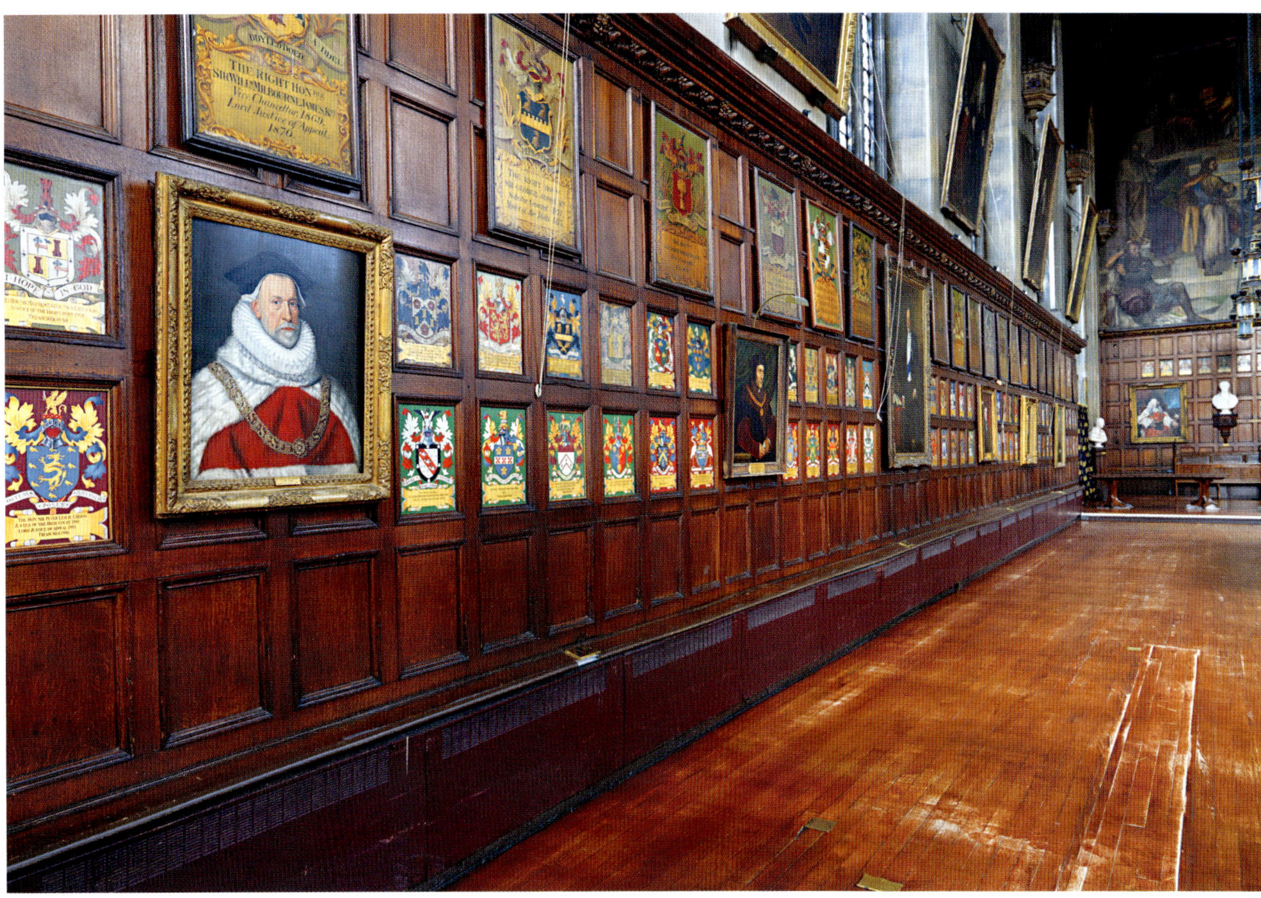

John Lobb Ltd

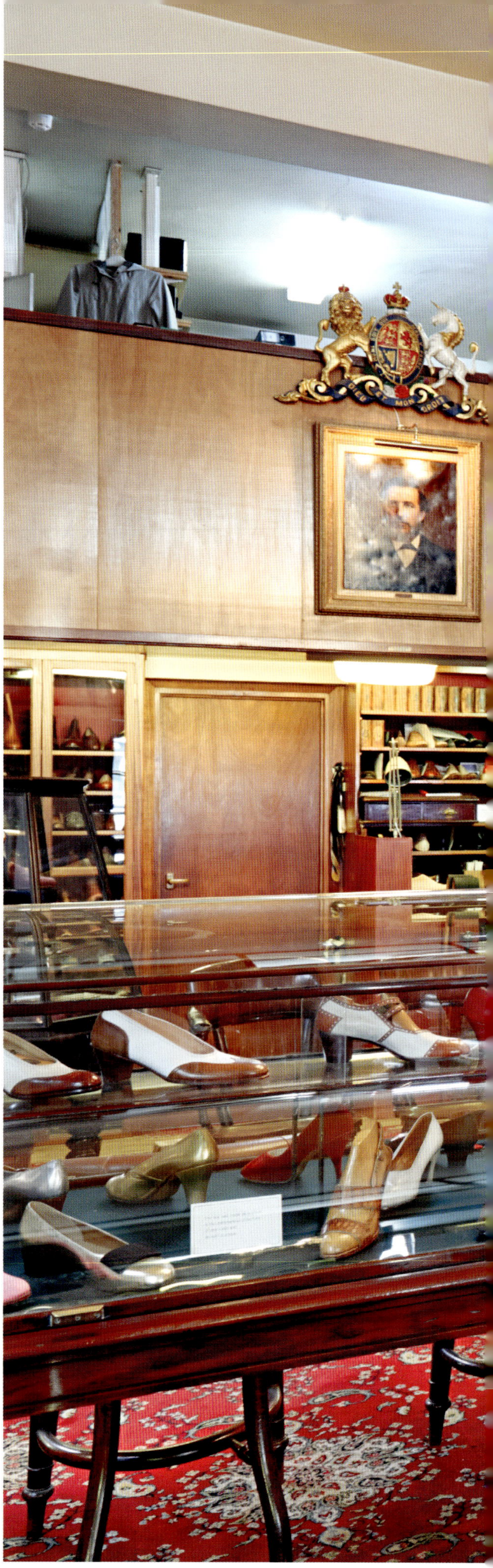

The ground floor showroom displaying Royal Warrants as Bootmaker to HM Queen Elizabeth II, HRH the Duke of Edinburgh and HRH the Prince of Wales.

At Lobb a pair of shoes can cost £4,000, but it is acknowledged as representing the pinnacle of the shoemaker's art.

The styles offered by Lobb may be recognizably classic, but the descriptions denote something special. Shoes made to the outline that most would describe as loafers can be 'Norwegian slipper with raised lake and lace through quarters and tassels'. The Derby styles bespoke at Lobbs are curiously named 'navvy shoes' and it is possible to order a 'two-tone plain golosh Oxford'. Whether you wish for calf, cordovan, patent, kangaroo, ostrich or snakeskin, Lobb advises that its extensive catalogue is merely a guide. 'We can make any style', the company says.

In the workrooms at St James's, which flank the wood-panelled shop area, the 'last-maker' uses maple, beech or hornbeam to reflect the shape of the foot; the 'clicker' cuts the uppers from eight pieces of leather; and the 'closer', who sews, assembles the uppers around the last. The sole and heel pieces come from the misleadingly named 'rough stuff' department, which shapes the thicker pieces of leather. Including the 'pattern-maker', 'socker' and 'polisher', all the thirty-or-so craftsmen and women are apprentice-served. The first pair of shoes for a new customer will take six months or more from the moment the fitter takes the measurements to delivery; after the last has been established, subsequent orders take three months.

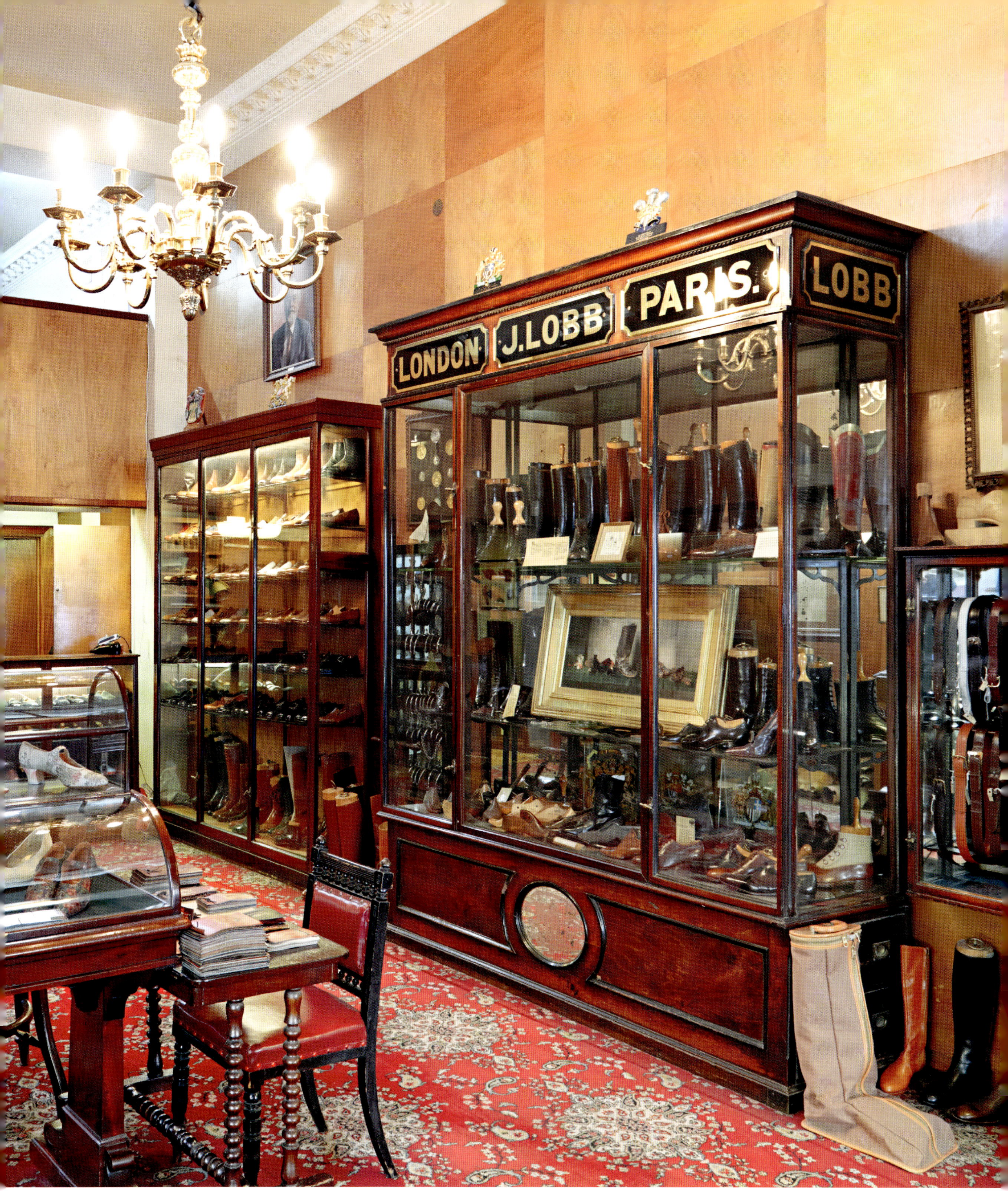
LONDON
J.LOBB
PARIS.
LOBB

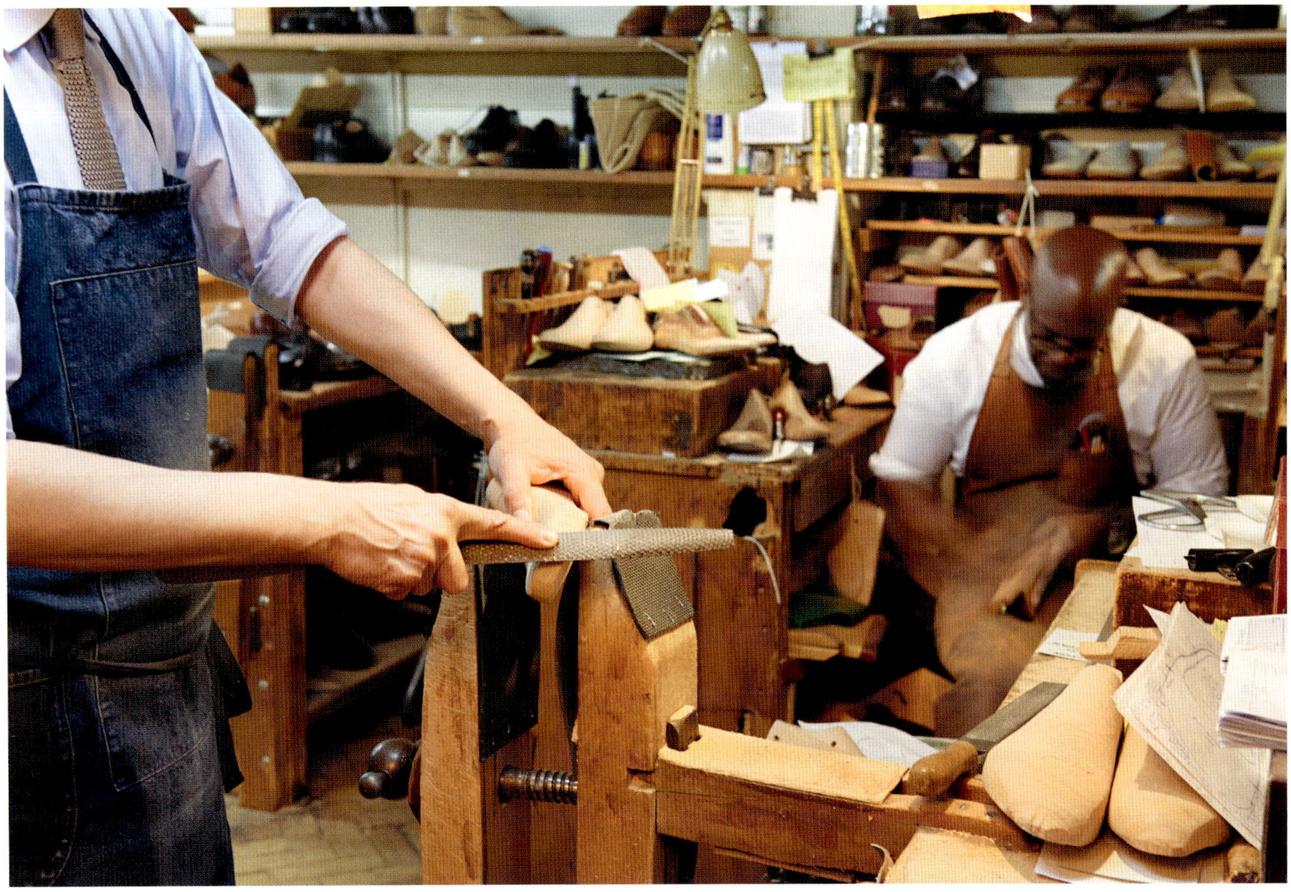

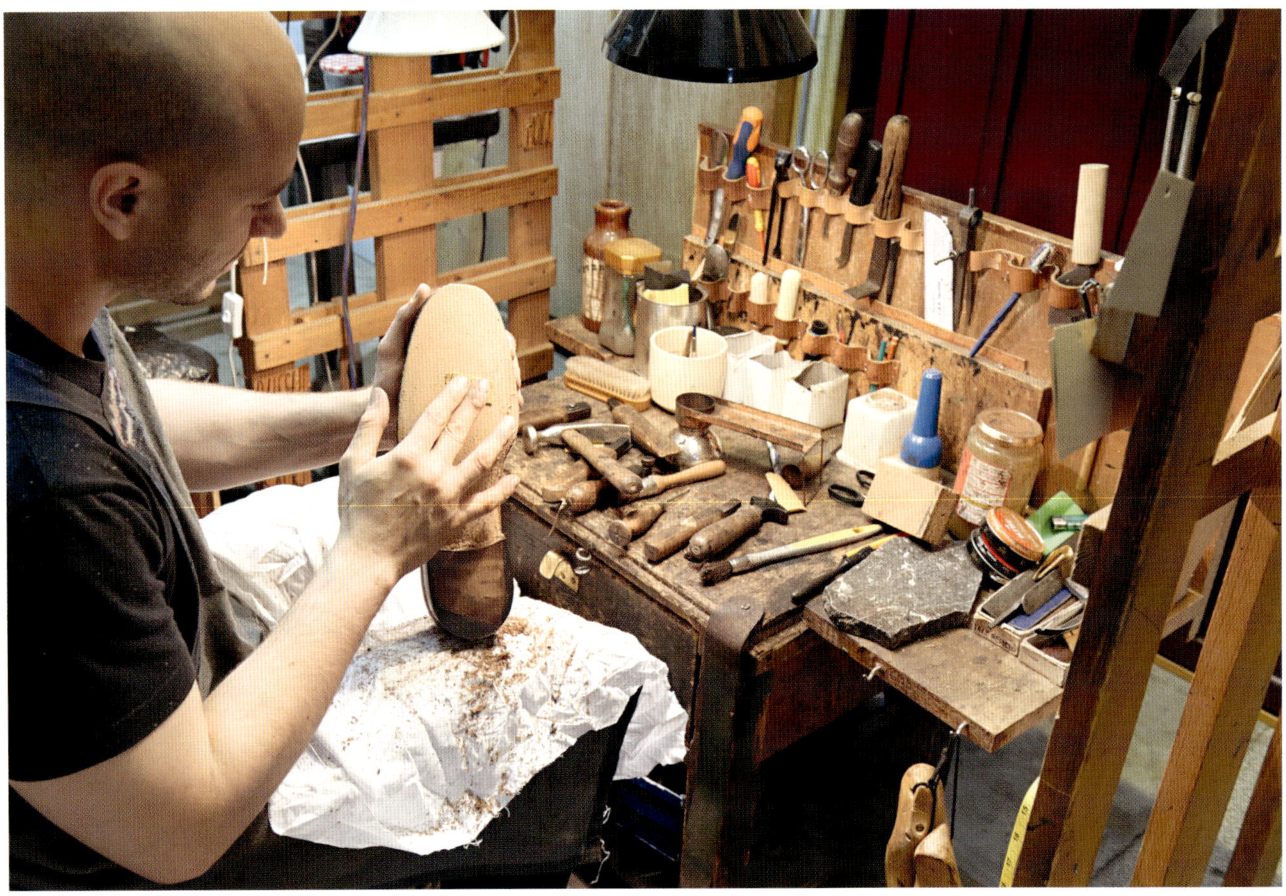

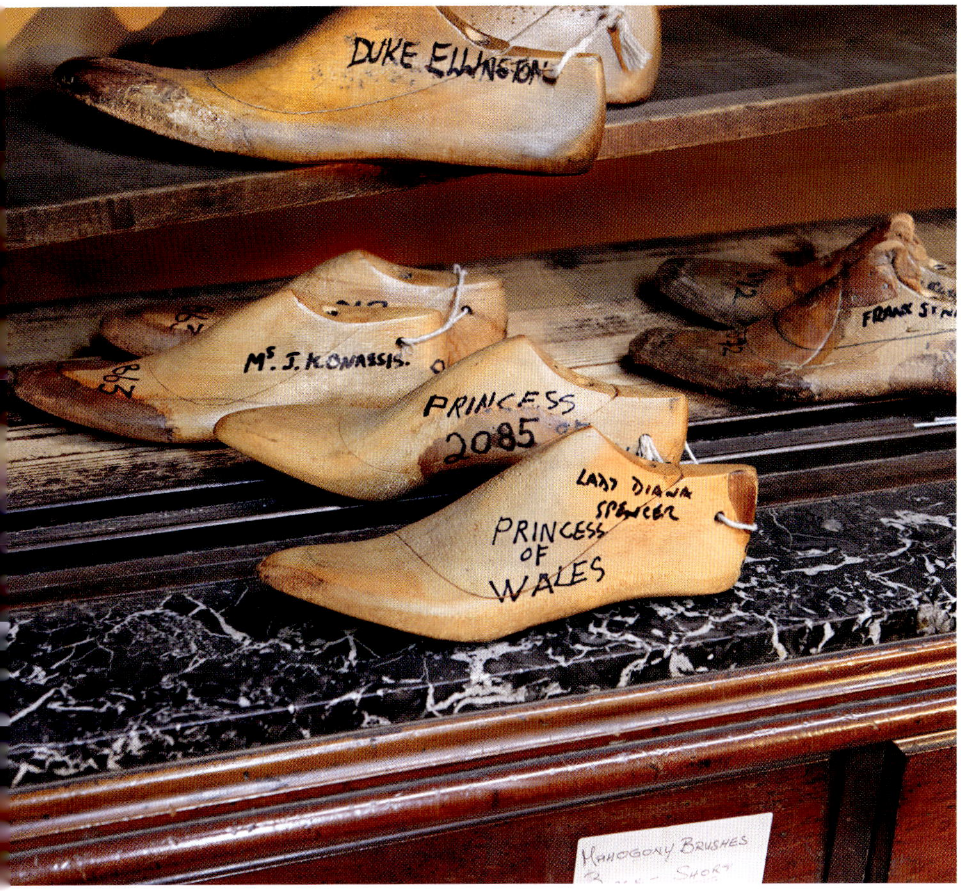

The first pair of shoes for a new customer will take six months or more from the moment the fitter takes the measurements to delivery.

Opposite, above The 'last-maker' carves the mould.

Opposite, below Repairs are part of the service.

Above The lasts of illustrious clients – Duke Ellington, Jacqueline Onassis, Frank Sinatra and Diana, Princess of Wales.

In the shop, display cases provide a history of style in bespoke shoes.

The first floor office of John Lobb has ledgers listing orders from illustrious, famous customers, and very rich customers. They list Princess Diana, Fred Astaire, Frank Sinatra and Mick Jagger. The basement houses rack upon rack of lasts, while some of them are displayed in cases in the showroom, among them the lasts for Queen Victoria from 1898 and, more recently, Duke Ellington, and Aristotle and Jacqueline Onassis.

The Lobb company history from modest beginnings to high achievement has elements of epic legend. Cornish-born John Lobb, despite being made lame by a childhood fall, walked to London in search of his bootmaking fortune. He had completed an apprenticeship to a shoemaker in Fowey, and was recognized as a good craftsman in the days before all shoes were lasted and sewn on machines. But when Lobb entered the premises of London's leading bootmakers of the time, Thomas's of St James's, and offered his skills, he was ejected. Disillusioned, Lobb travelled to Australia on the strength of reports of gold being discovered and prospected for a while. He then shrewdly switched to making boots for prospectors and miners. This included a special hollow-heeled design for concealment of gold. John Lobb established a good business in Sydney. He despatched footwear to the London Exhibition of 1861, winning a gold medal, and two years later received a Royal Warrant to the Prince of Wales as bootmaker. Lobb sold up in Australia in 1866 and set up business in London. His first St James's shop opened in 1880 alongside the fashionable hat makers, gun makers, wine merchants, tobacconists and gentlemen's clubs of the street.

The company has experienced turbulent times. No. 55 St James's Street, the shop founded by John Lobb, was destroyed by bombing in 1944, forcing a move across the road to No. 26 and then in 1962, when the Economist tower block was built, the business moved again to No. 9 St James's Street, an address once occupied by Lord Byron.

This is where the business resides today. The family continuity has remained unbroken across five generations. John Hunter Lobb is Chairman. Luxury goods manufacturer Hermès trades under the name John Lobb for some of its ranges of shoes, but the Lobb shop in St James's Street remains in the hands of the Lobb family. There are stores today in St James's Street where an ocean-going yacht can be commissioned or chartered, but nowhere more exclusive or truer to the spirit of that street than John Lobb, bootmaker.

CONTACT INFORMATION

John Lobb Ltd,
9 St James's Street, SW1A 1EF
https://www.johnlobb.com/

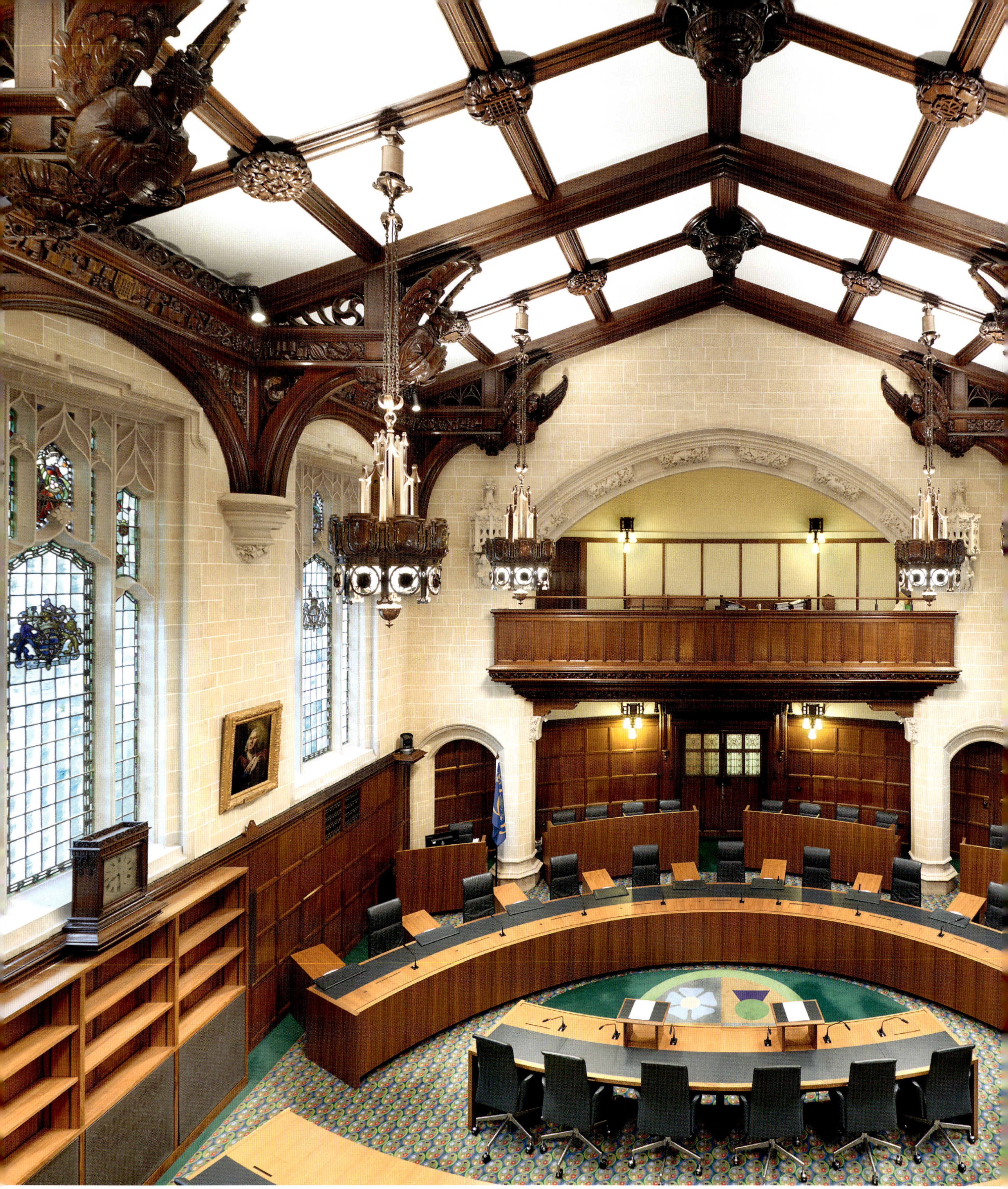

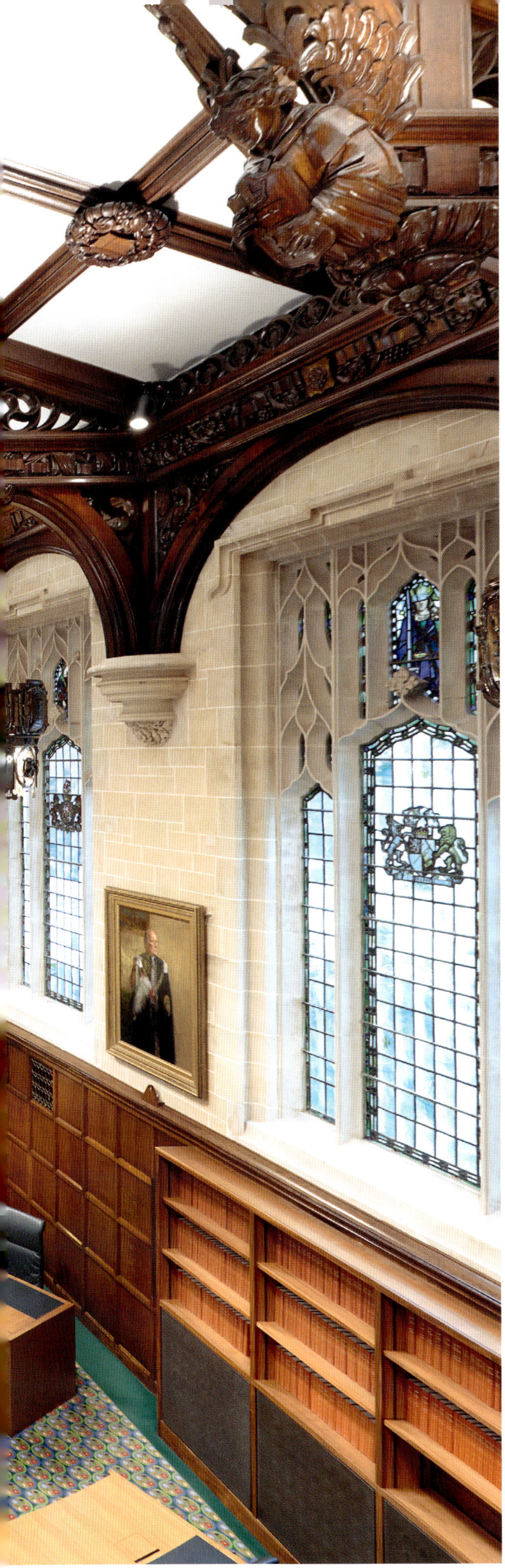

In Courtroom 1 of the Supreme Court, the original hammerbeam roof evokes a medieval hall; nine seats for nine of the eleven justices are seen here; usually, a panel of five judges hears cases.

The Supreme Court and Royal Courts of Justice

The positioning of the new UK Supreme Court, which started work on the west side of Parliament Square in October 2009, was functional and symbolic. Its distance from Parliament marked the separation of the judicial and legislative roles of the House of Lords. The full-time judges who were the Law Lords had done business in a warren of rooms in the Houses of Parliament; the Supreme Court justices who succeeded them were housed in a purpose-converted building which had once been Middlesex Guildhall.

At one time seven court rooms for Middlesex Crown Court and 100 cells were located here, but the conversion for the Supreme Court resulted in three court rooms, all without a dock, witness stand or jury room. In the Supreme Court, there is no prosecution or defence; appellants and respondents are represented by lawyers. The environment is 'designed to encourage an atmosphere of learned debate', according to the official profile. Judges and lawyers do not have to wear court dress, the proceedings are routinely filmed and all courts are open to public access when in session.

Court Room 1 was once Middlesex Council Chamber and retains a hammerbeam roof in the spirit of a medieval great hall. Courts 2 and 3 are original Quarter Session/Crown Court rooms. The Judicial Committee of the Privy Council works in Court 3 with jurisdiction over final legal appeals of thirty countries and territories in the British Commonwealth.

The Supreme Court is the final place of appeal in the UK for civil cases, and for criminal cases from

England, Wales and Northern Ireland. Scottish architect James Gibson designed the building, which was completed in 1913. Architectural authority Pevsner called it Art Noveau Gothic, detecting a strong influence of Arts & Crafts style. When the Supreme Court plans were announced in 2006 there was some controversy from conservation groups because it was a rare example of a largely unmolested Edwardian interior, and the revisions proposed for the Supreme Court were extensive, most significant being a triple height galleried law library. In some places the result was a fusion between old and new, with original carved pew ends being restored and reused on new public seating. Public art was applied to the project, Sir Peter Blake designed carpets with symbols representing the four nations of the United Kingdom, letter sculptors provided carved quotes on screens and panels and the Japanese designer Tomoko Azumi designed the new courtroom furniture.

The Royal Courts of Justice on the Strand were planned and commissioned in the 1860s but construction did not start until 1873 and building work was spread over eight years. The building was opened by Queen Victoria in December 1882. These dates enable architectural historians to place the building right at the end of London's great Gothic Revival cycle, which produced the Palace of Westminster, St Pancras station, the Albert Memorial and numerous churches. The idea of a secular public building made to evoke a vaulted medieval gothic cathedral was becoming anachronistic, and the Royal Courts of Justice, widely known as the Law Courts, was the last in that tradition. Its most impressive feature, the Great Hall, is effectively a vast thirteenth-century nave.

Continuous expansion has been the underlying trend at the Law Courts and over the course of a century the rooms have multiplied. In 2017, signs in the building indicated courtrooms numbered past 100, and the total of all rooms exceeds 1,000. This required expansion into the basement areas and beyond, with the addition of whole new blocks. The first was the West Green Building, followed by the Queens Building, the and Thomas More Building. The separate Rolls Building nearby in Fetter Lane acquired in 1999 is also counted as part of the Law Courts. Despite the modern additions, the core of the Royal Courts remains close to its original state while restored, cleaned and updated in places. The ecclesiastical style is applied throughout, and except for the portraits and statues of judges, there is little to show that any of this is at the heart of a legal complex. In order to understand its purpose, it is necessary to enter one of the many of surrounding courtrooms during a trial, and in most cases visitors can do this.

The Royal Courts of Justice, designed as an instrument of modernization and reform, houses the High Court and the Court of Appeal of England and Wales. These handle high-level civil cases, divorce, property, inheritance, bankruptcy, company disputes, maritime law and certain criminal cases on appeal.

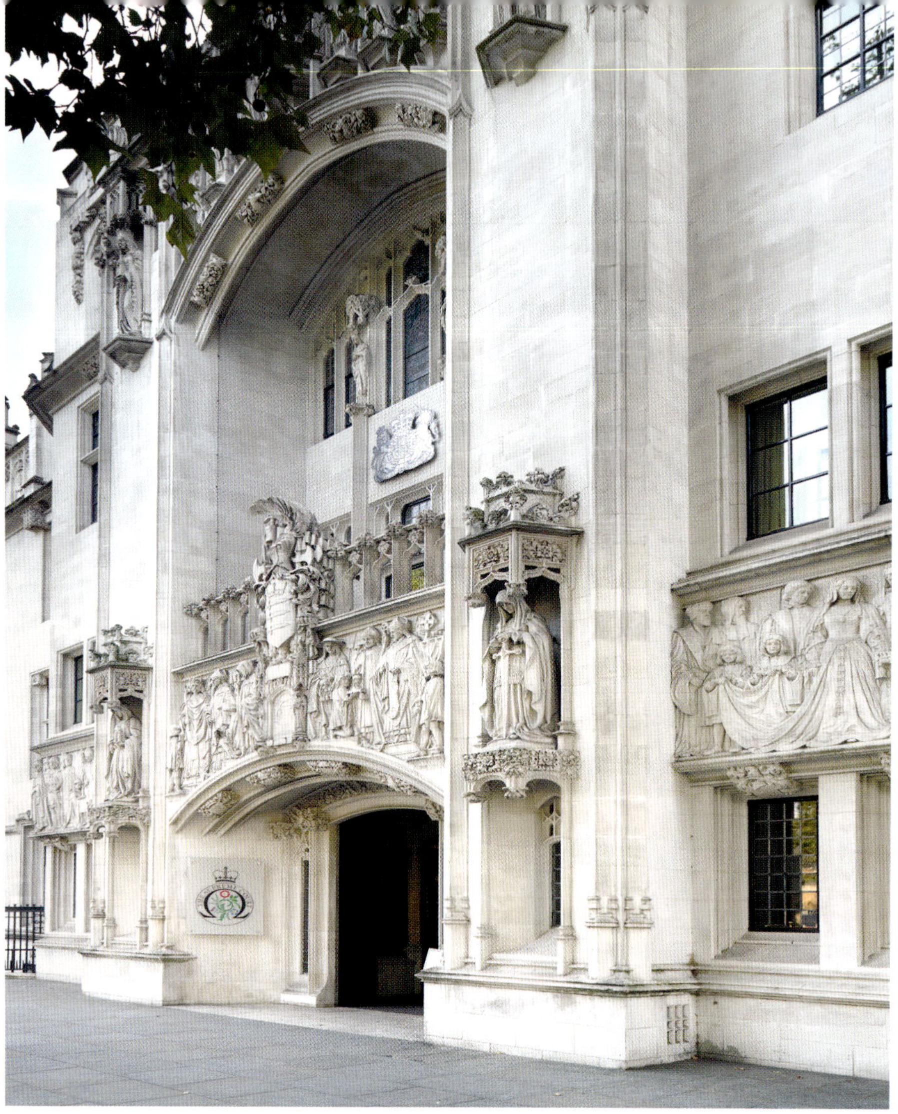

The Portland stone façade of the Supreme Court, with much statuary by Henry Charles Fehr; the central frieze depicts Henry III granting a charter to Westminster Abbey, flanked by King John with the Barons at Runnymede signing Magna Carta, and by Lady Jane Grey to the right.

CONTACT INFORMATION

Supreme Court of the the United Kingdom,
Parliament Square, SW1P 3BD
https://supremecourt.uk/
Royal Courts of Justice,
Strand, WC2A 2LL
https://www.nationaljusticemuseum.org.uk/

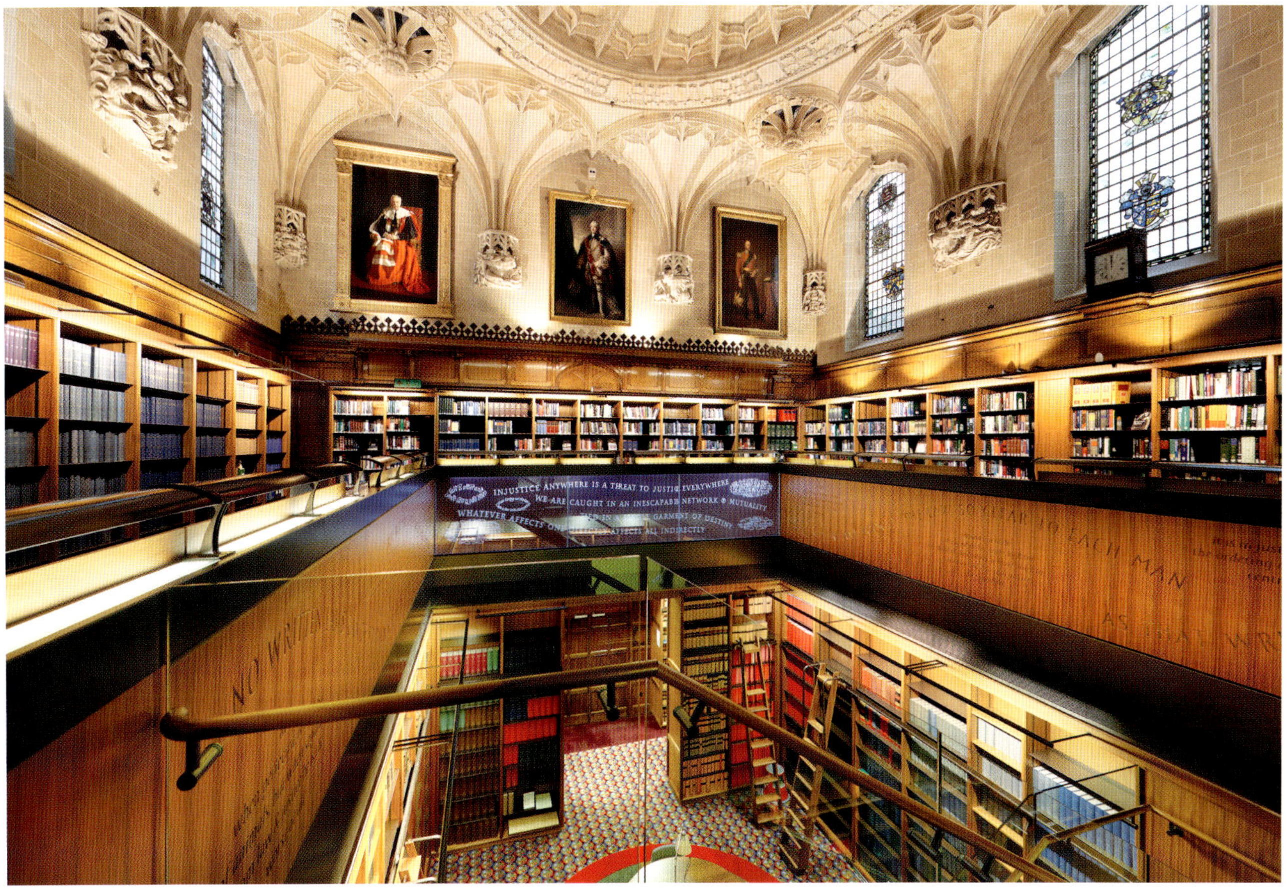

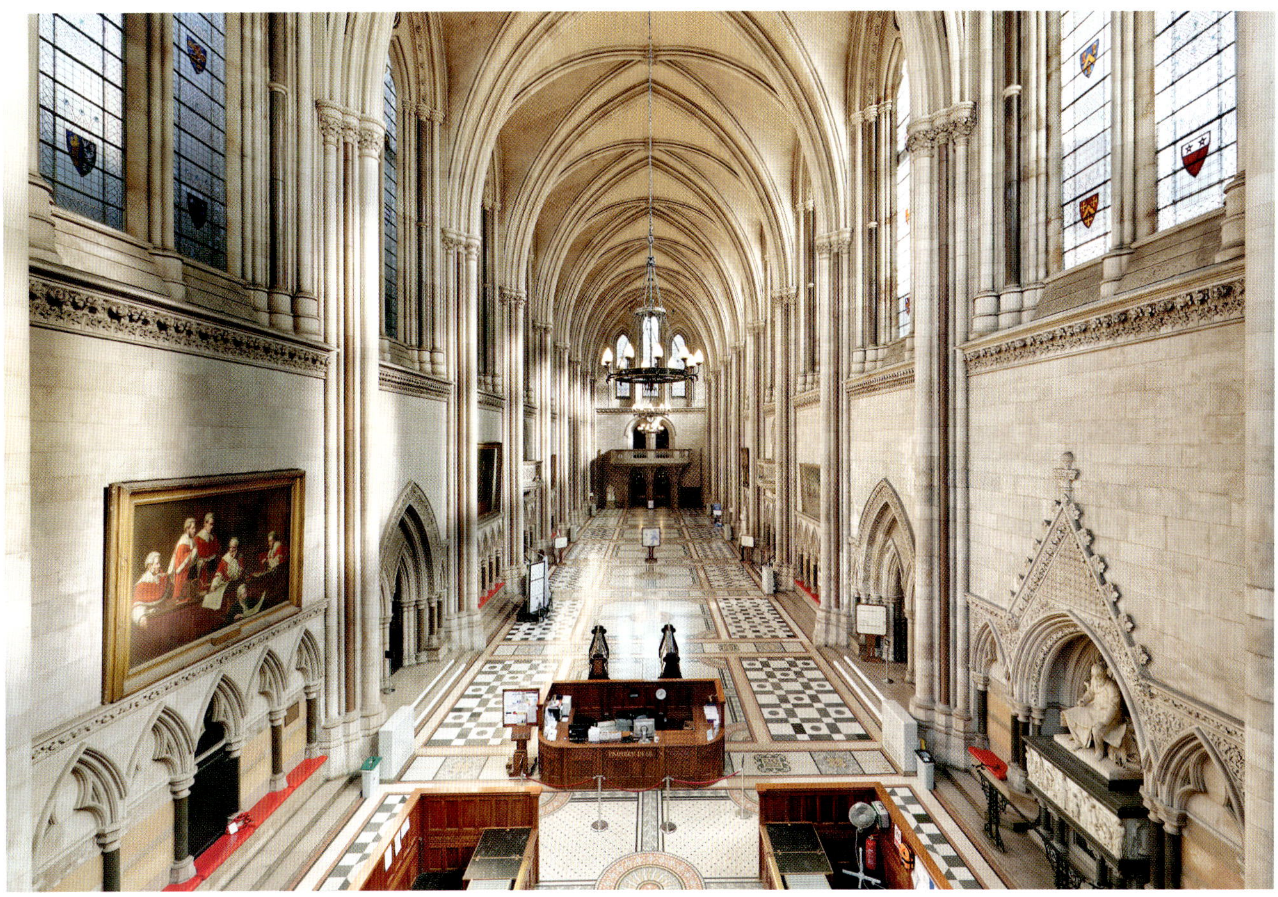

Right, above The Law Library in the Supreme Court is decorated with sayings from figures ranging from Ovid to Emerson, and on the glass balustrade here with quotations by Martin Luther King. The pop art carpet was designed by Sir Peter Blake.

Right The Main Hall of the Royal Courts of Justice was inspired by a thirteenth-century cathedral nave.

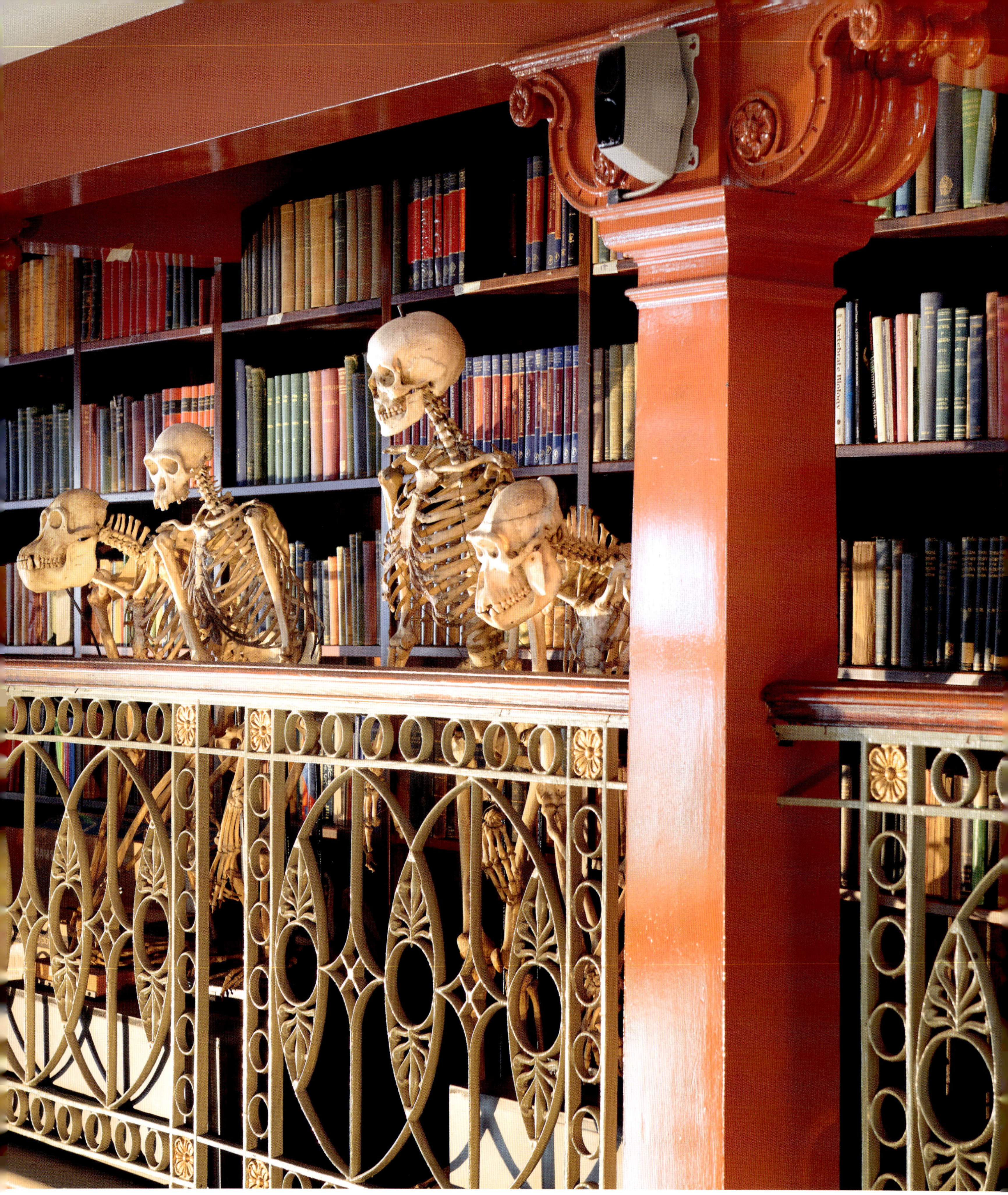

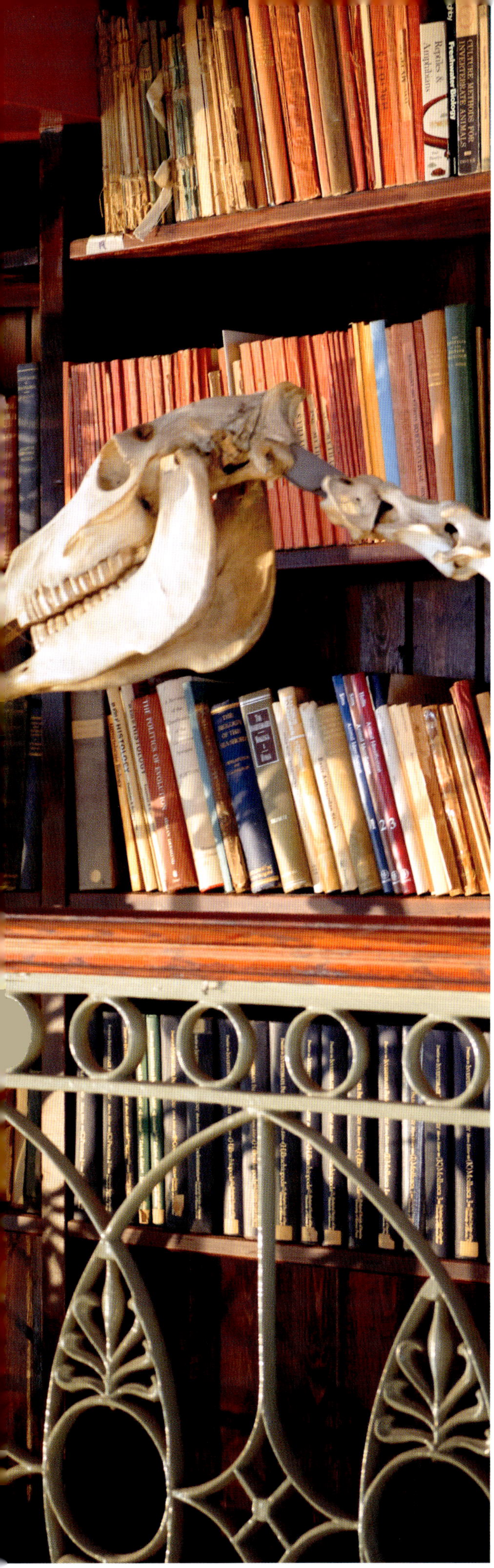

Grant Museum of Zoology

Looking down at visitors from the balcony are skeletons, from left to right, of an orangutan, chimpanzee, human, gorilla and donkey.

Visitors to the Grant Museum of Zoology are greeted by a line of skeletons seemingly looking down from the balcony, three simian and one human. They make a good introduction to a collection that contains 68,000 zoological specimens from the whole of the animal kingdom. The museum is packed with skeletons, mounted animals and specimens preserved in fluid. Some of the species represented are extinct, including a skeleton of a quagga and bones of the dodo and thylacine; others are endangered and extremely rare species such as the dugong. The museum is associated with University College London and is the last remaining university natural history collection in London.

The collection was started in the nineteenth century and is named after Robert Grant, who came to what was then called the University of London in 1827 to take the chair of zoology. His progressive scientific ideas were shaped late in the Scottish Enlightenment in Edinburgh, where one of his pupils was none other than Charles Darwin.

Grant was a natural choice for the newly founded English university, which set out to be secular, radical and liberal in thought. He taught zoology and comparative anatomy. Lacking any teaching materials with which to conduct his courses, he began to amass specimens, material for dissection, diagrams and lecture notes, and by the 1850s, the collection comprised 10,000 items. Comparative anatomy was just starting as a discipline and was seen as important for medical students.

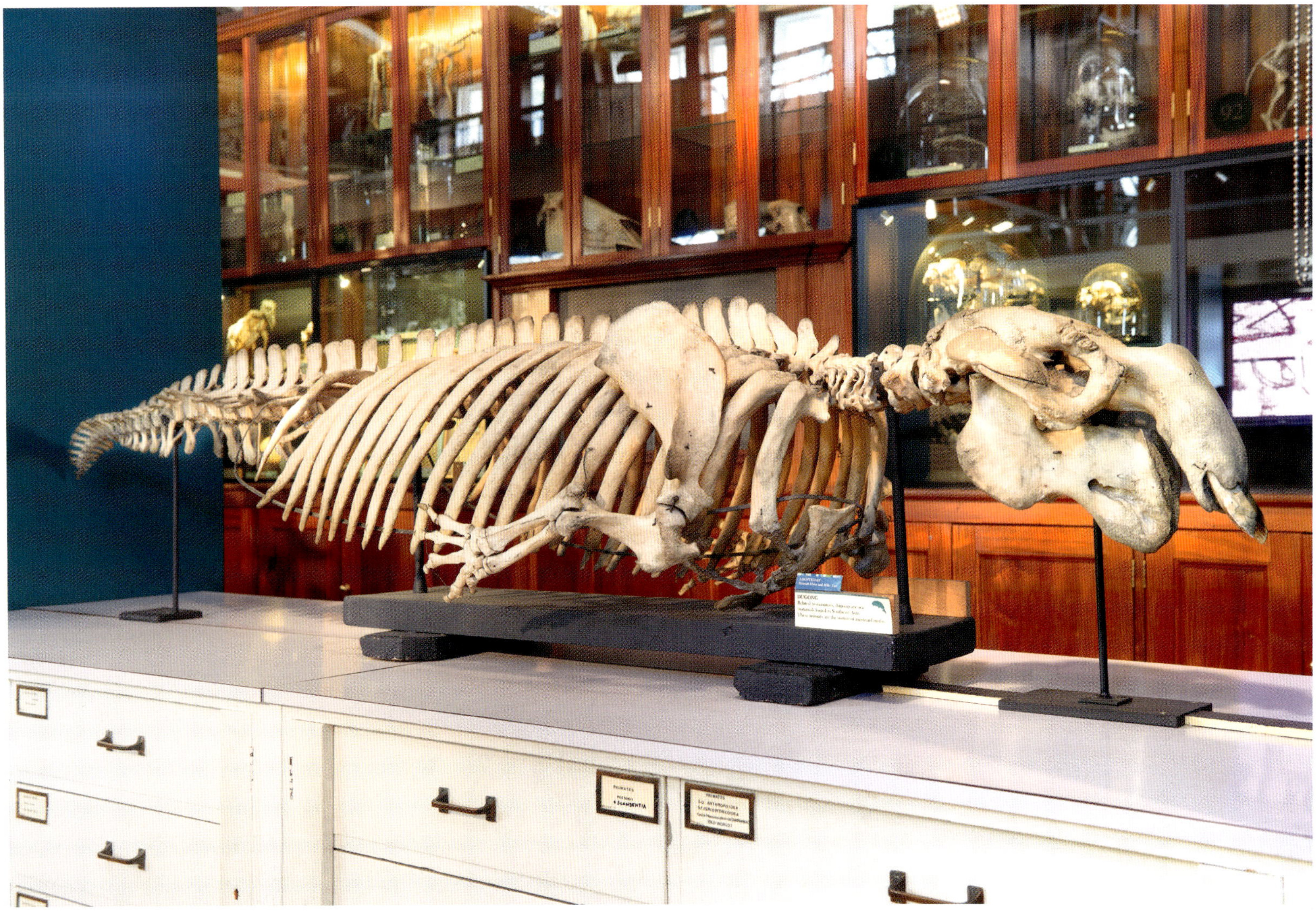

Grant's successors to the chair of zoology became, according to the precedent set by him, the curator of the comparative zoology collection and the museum continued to grow. It has become the foremost zoological museum in London as collections from other colleges, hospitals and societies were taken in.

The museum continues to be a resource and a teaching aid. Since first opening to the public in 1996, access has been extended and it has reached out further to visitors, schools, local communities and especially young people who are captivated by exhibits such as bisected heads, the brain collection, the walrus baculum, skulls of elephants (African and Asian), a complete wall formed of 4,000 mice specimens and a jar filled with moles, which generates a high level of fascination. There are the skull and antlers of the giant deer, also known as the Irish elk, found in a hotel in Country Kildare and bought to the museum in 1961. There is the Blaschka collection of models of jellyfish, sea anemones, sea cucumbers, gastropods and cephalopods. All the specimens in this collection were made from glass by Leopold Blaschka and his son Rudolph in the late 1800s. The soft bodies of marine invertebrates are particularly difficult to preserve, so the Blaschkas were commissioned to make anatomically accurate models from glass. The Blaschkas' skills died with them and their work has not been repeated.

The dugong skeleton in the Grant Museum is another valuable treasure. The specimen is 9 ft (2.7 m) long, which would indicate it was an adult. Unlike their sea cow relatives, which reside in estuaries and freshwater, dugongs are found only in coastal marine habitats. Adult dugongs usually grow to up to 10 ft (3 m) in length and weigh over one tonne. The closest living relative to the dugong is the elephant.

At the other end of the scale is the Micrarium, a small brightly backlit space constructed from more

Above The skeleton of a dugong, a relation of the manatee, which is a sea mammal found in South East Asia. These interesting creatures have long fuelled mermaid myths and legends across cultures.

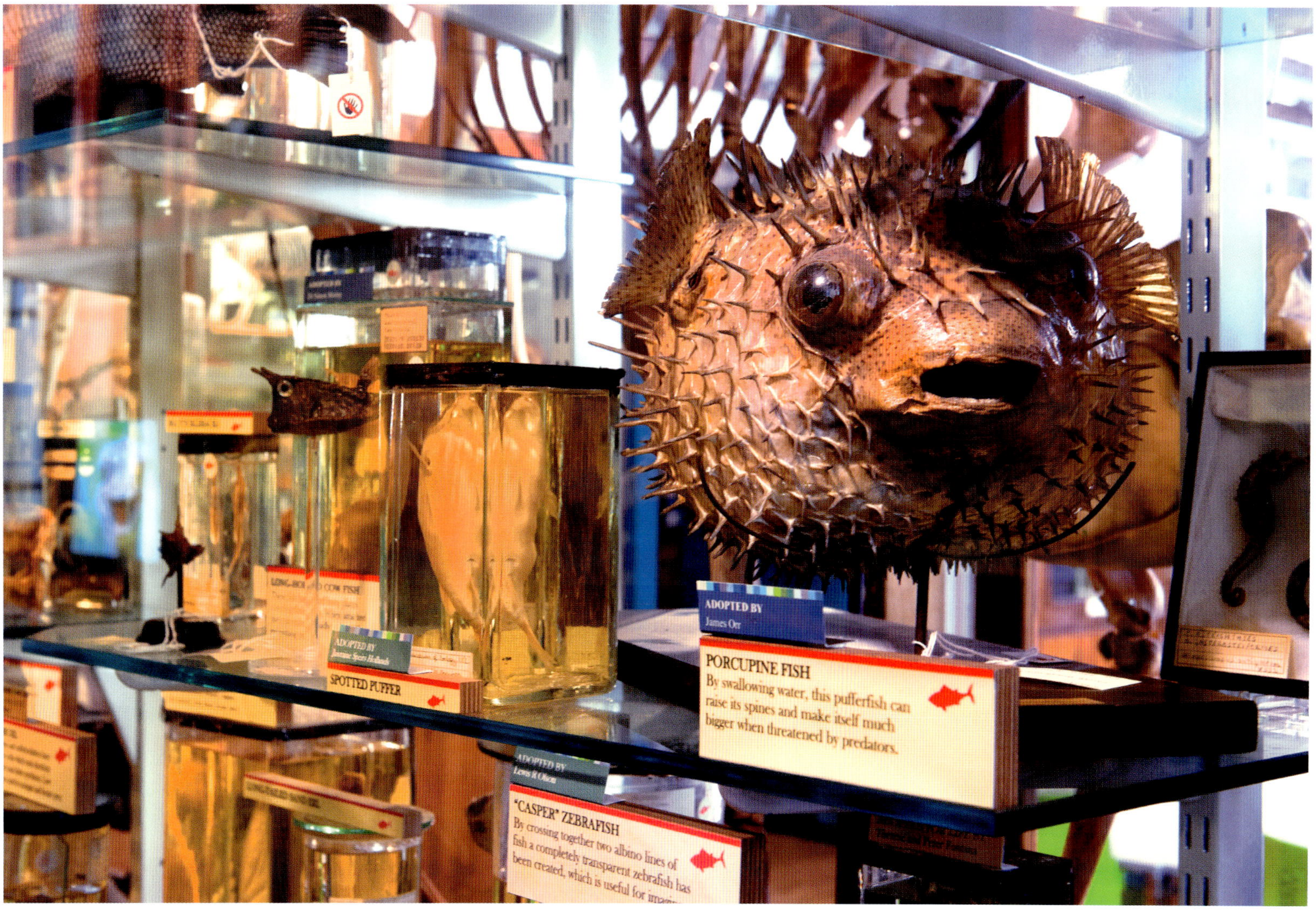

Above A porcupine fish or pufferfish, housed in the fish cabinet. These curious creatures raise their spines and puff themselves up when threatened by predators.

than 2,000 examples of microscope slides and magic lantern slides, mostly of invertebrates, although mammoth hair and giraffe horn can be found here. It was designed to overcome two problems with natural science collections: firstly, some 95 per cent of all known animal species are tiny, yet most of the specimens on display are large animals, with museum galleries therefore deeply unrepresentative of the natural world. Secondly, most natural history museums have extensive microscope slide collections, largely made obsolete by modern imaging techniques. The Micrarium is a single solution to both issues. The museum claims it is arguably the most beautiful 27 sq ft (2.5 m^2) in London.

A special characteristic throughout the Grant Museum is an authentically old-fashioned look to the room which, according to the curating team, causes visitors to say: 'This is what a museum should look like.' The distinctive decor is evident in the polished display cases, apparently Victorian, which carry a very large number of specimens densely displayed, and on the balcony with further exhibits and book-laden shelves. It seems as if the collection has been installed here for years, but in reality the museum has moved many times. This particular home was found in March 2011, in a room that was formerly the UCL Medical School library. The old-time ambience is tempered by some more advanced interactive displays where visitors can engage in dialogue about the evolutionary past via iPads and smartphones.

CONTACT INFORMATION

Grant Museum of Zoology,
Rockefeller Building, 21 University Street, WC1E 6DE

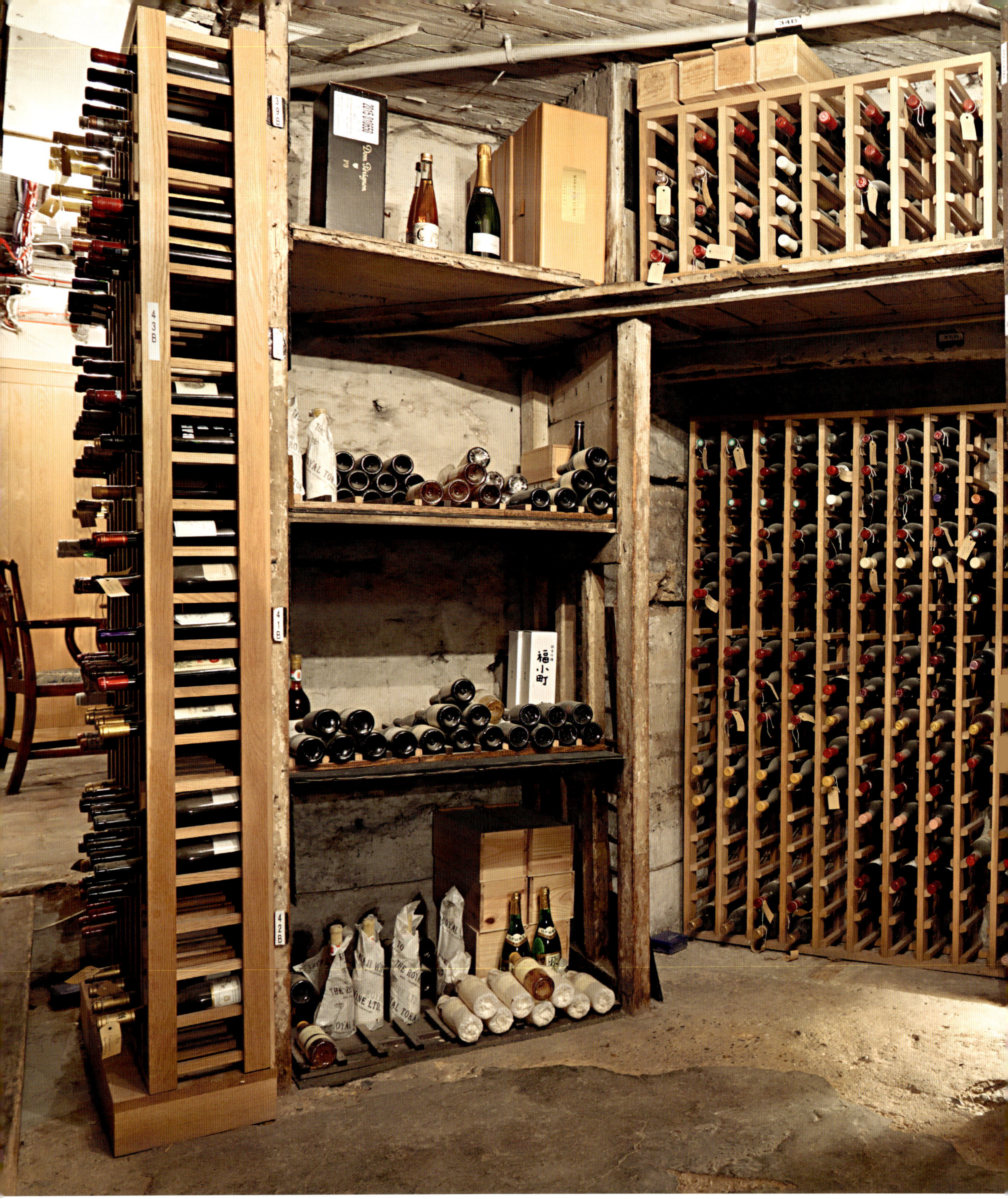

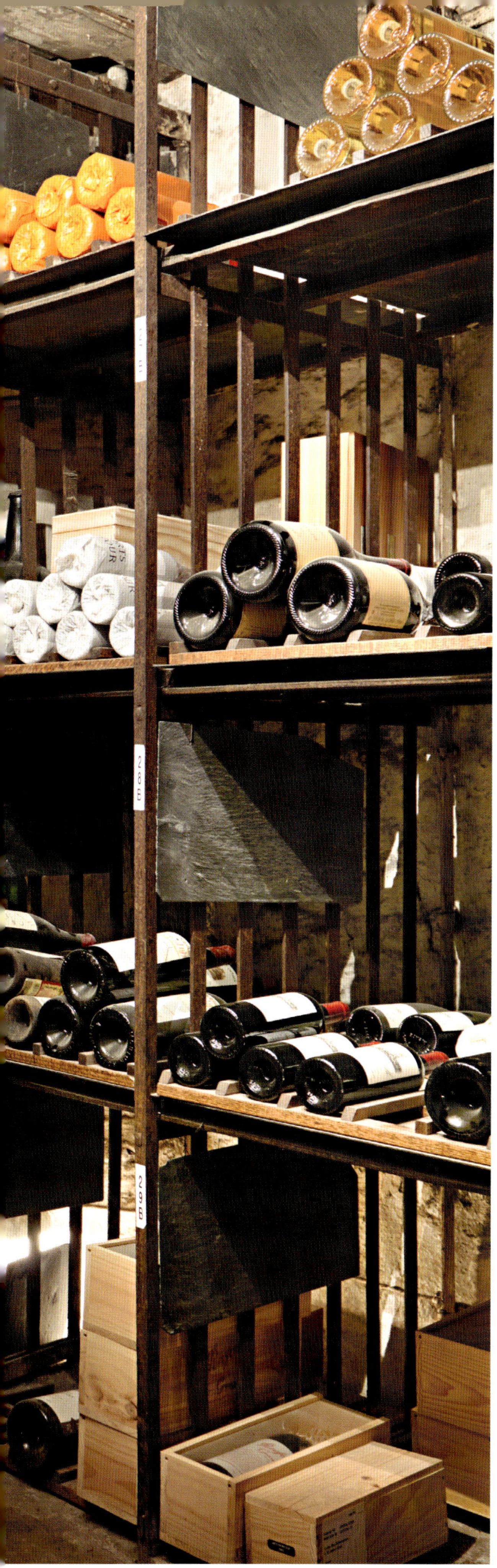

Berry Bros. & Rudd

One of a vast network of wine cellars belonging to Berry Bros. & Rudd.

At street level it is hard to guess the full extent of Berry Bros. & Rudd, Wine & Spirit Merchants, but there are clear signs of its antiquity. The windows of No. 3 St James's Street proclaim that it was established in the seventeenth century, and the paintwork on the frontage appears ancient, apparently black but in reality the darkest possible shade of green. Wine cellars below the shop extend for 2 acres to the back, front and side of the building.

A hanging sign outside shows a coffee mill, which was one of the shop's first lines of business, along with tea, snuff, sugar and spices, mostly imported from the New World. It was opened as a grocer's store in 1698 by a widow named Bourne, possibly Katherine Bourne, and served the increasingly fashionable area of St James's with its coffee and chocolate houses. Her descendants, including one George Berry, shifted the business emphasis to wine by the early nineteenth century.

Inside the panelled shop with its sloping wooden floor, hangs a large set of scales once used to weigh goods and, curiously, some of the customers. It used to be fashionable for men to have themselves weighed while they made their purchases, a set of scales being scarce domestic devices and knowledge of weight showing an awareness of health. At Berry Bros., the ledger has recorded since 1756 the results of some illustrious subjects, including the Regency dandy Beau Brummell, who was weighed here several times, Lord Byron, Lord Melbourne and Sir Robert Peel.

It used to be fashionable for men to have themselves weighed while they made their purchases.

In the time of Beau Brummell, wine was not regarded as a luxury item, for however expensive it was the bottle was always worth more. Wine was bought by the cask, and the servant whose job it was to put the cask wine into bottles was called the 'bottler', from which the word 'butler' derives. Bottling only became economical in the early twentieth century; any vessels dating from older times are now rare and expensive. Berry Bros. & Rudd displays an antique collection of these.

Berry Bros. & Rudd are Britain's oldest wine and spirit merchants, still operating under the ownership and management the Berry and Rudd families, now an international company with offices in China, Singapore and Japan, and buying and selling wines from around the world. As well as having long history, they claim to be the first wine merchants to open an online wine shop in 1994, and to establish an online wine broking exchange. The main warehouse in Basingstoke opened as recently as 1967, while No. 3 St James's Street continues as the flagship store and continues to expand its cellars.

One of these is Pickering Cellar, which extends under Pickering Place behind, dating from at least the seventeenth century. At the entrance is an alcove where Louis Napoleon, nephew to Napoleon Bonaparte, once took refuge in a dangerous moment during the Chartist Riots of the 1840s. He lived nearby on King Street, exiled following his second failed coup to become President of France. He and George Berry were friends and, together with the chef of The Athenaeum, had joined the militia to suppress the riots. When Louis Napoleon departed in 1848 he left his truncheon behind. It still hangs outside the cellar.

The space was once employed as a bottling cellar. Barrels were lowered on a hoist that is still sometimes used to take wine down from street level. The cellar is home to Berry Bros. & Rudd's wine school.

Another cellar is accessed through a discrete door in one of the houses in the courtyard behind. This is Sussex Cellar, built on two levels, in which thirty-six can dine. It is named after the Duke of Sussex, one of seven royal dukes who were customers of the company in the early nineteenth century. The cellar is a modernized space, influenced by Spanish bodegas, using tiles to create archways and columns through the mezzanine and the sub-basement level.

A walk through the alley to the side of Berry Bros. & Rudd leads to Pickering Place, claimed to be the oldest and the smallest public courtyard in London. This gas-lit enclave, with a sundial in the form of an astrolabe at the centre, is surrounded by five houses; over time it was home to a gambling den, bear-baiting, cockfighting, dog fighting and a number of duels, one of which was fought by Beau Brummell. It was once the site of Henry VIII's royal tennis court, with remnants of one wall remaining below ground. Prime Minister Lord Palmerston lived in the square, and later the novelist Graham Greene. No. 3 Pickering Place is the Berry Bros. & Rudd Townhouse, home to receptions in its Green Room and Long Room.

The most curious feature of the wainscoted alley leading to Pickering Place is described by a plaque just inside the entrance. A doorway here once led upstairs to the rooms used by the Texas Legation between 1836 and 1845. Effectively the Embassy of the Republic of Texas in Britain, it was established to support the international cause of the country, which was then a sovereign republic independent from the United States and Mexico. General Sam Houston, the Texan President, dispatched a diplomatic representative to London who worked in rooms leased from the wine merchants.

CONTACT INFORMATION

Berry Bros. & Rudd,
3 St James's Street, SW1A 1EG
https://www.bbr.com/

Opposite, top left
Berry Bros. & Rudd retains its original signage from the time when it was a coffee dealer.

Opposite, top right
An original set of scales for coffee, and occasionally people.

Opposite, below
Pickering Place, the smallest public square in London.

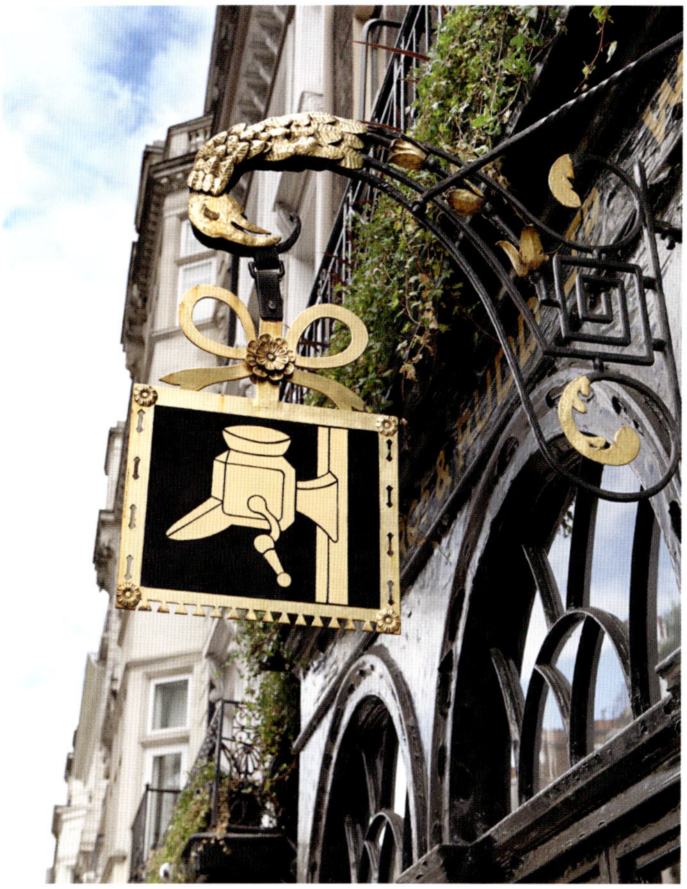

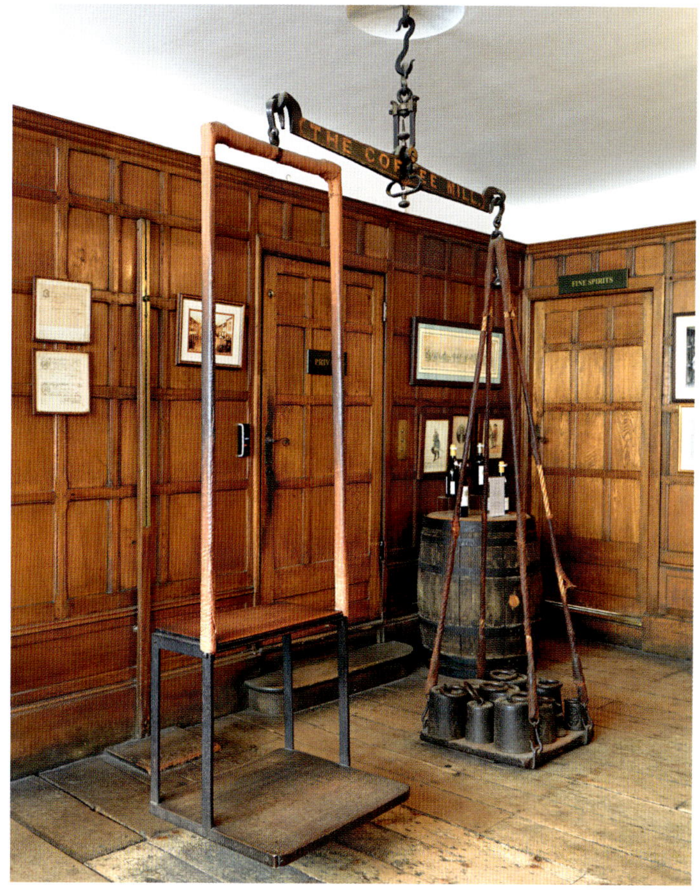

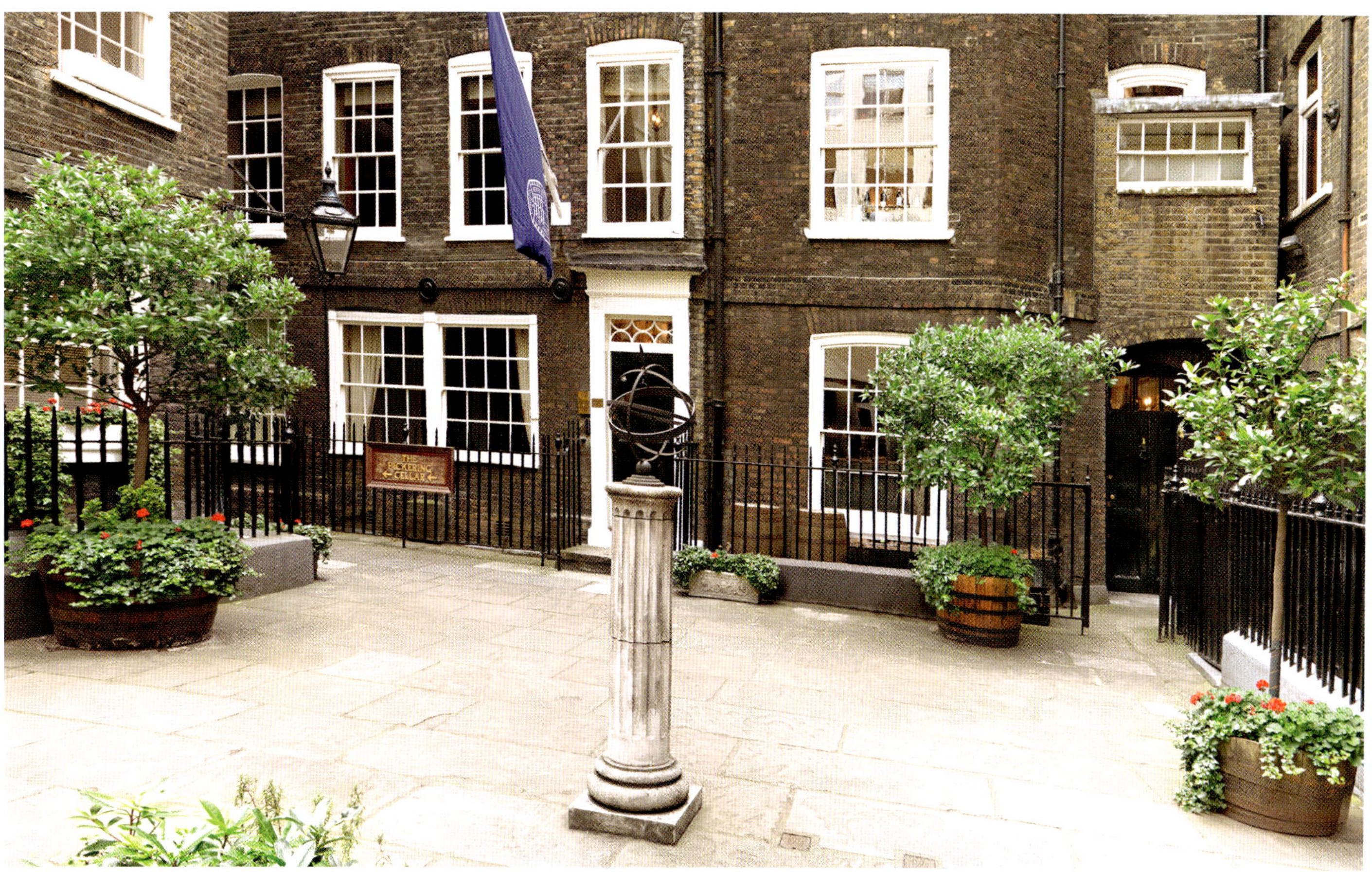

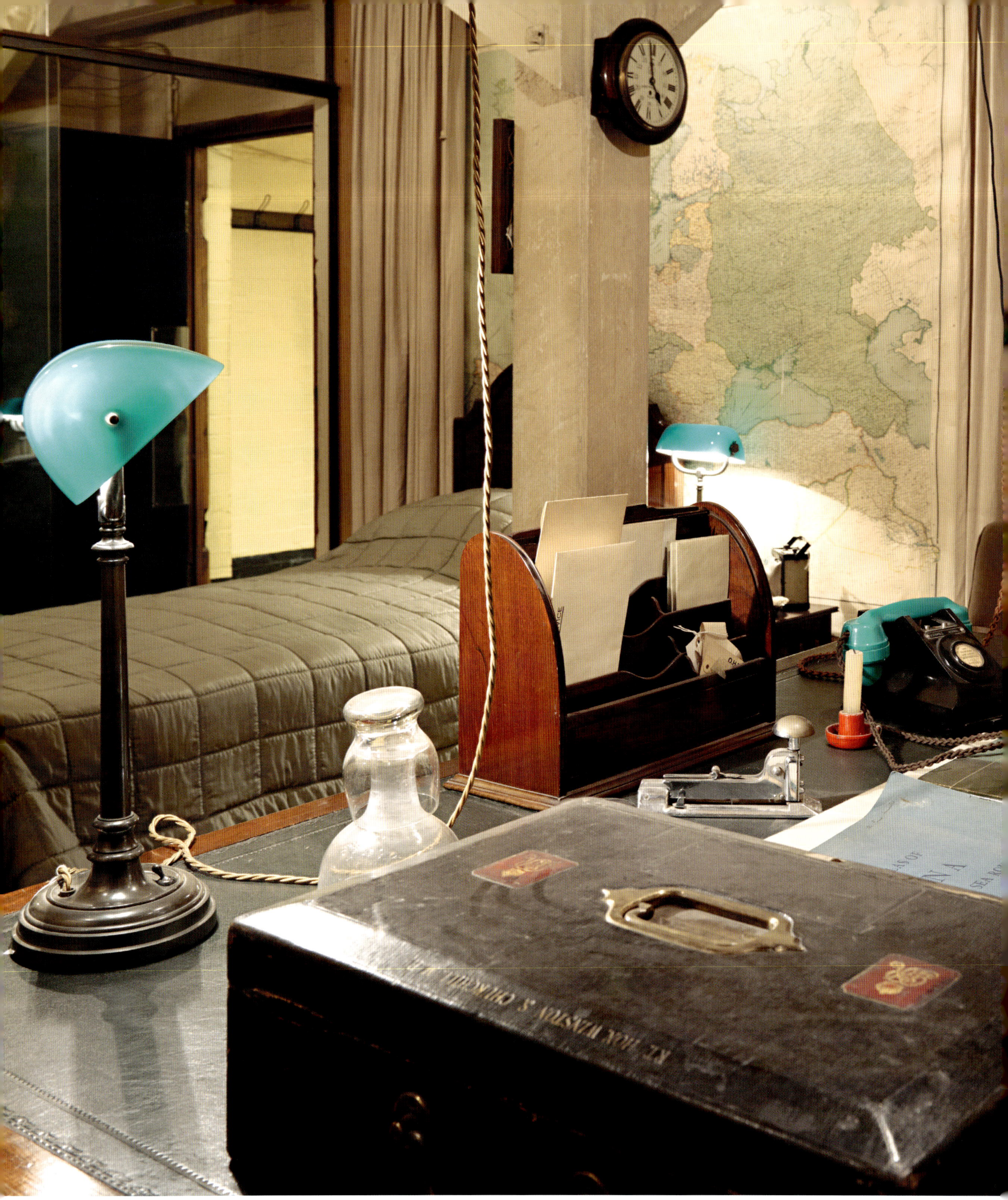

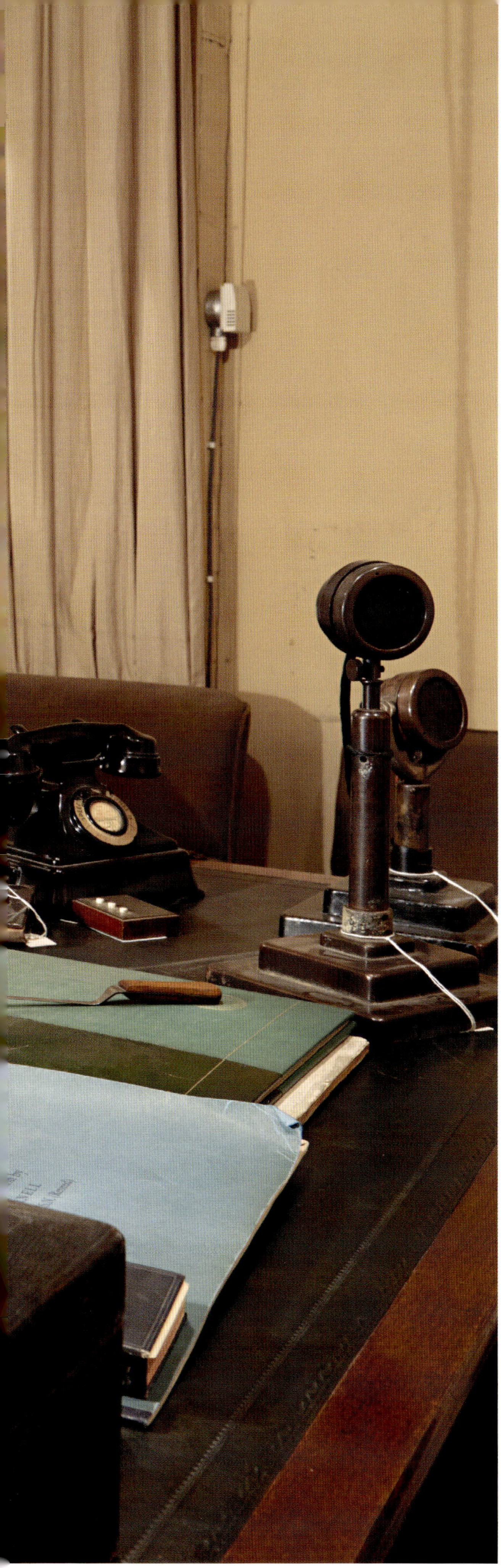

Churchill's bedroom and desk, with dispatch box.

Churchill War Rooms

Churchill War Rooms is the name of the museum which includes the underground Second World War command centre known as the Cabinet War Rooms and the intertwined Churchill Museum, which profiles the life of the statesman. Before entering the War Rooms through their bronze doorway in King Charles Street, some visitors stop to look at part of the Treasury building facing St James's Park, under which the War Rooms lie. A long concrete apron wall runs along the face at ground level, clearly a later addition to the frontage. It covers a feature of the War Rooms known as the Slab, a metre-thick layer of concrete with steel-rail reinforcement added in 1940, testimony to a time of great danger, and sign of desperate measures.

Authoritative studies reporting in the 1930s advised that the top level of government should be moved away from central London in case of war, and plans were drawn up for moves to fortified buildings located in the suburbs or dispersed across the countryside. This was considered imperative because of the threat of air attack on central London, but despite this, when war came, the best action that could be taken was to move the cabinet to converted rooms in a basement in the centre of Whitehall, close to Downing Street and the offices of state. Although the NPO housing the Treasury had the advantage of being partly of steel-framed construction, it was by no definition bomb-proof and the basement was shallow. In 1938 the roof had been reinforced with steel girders. The Slab was added in 1940 and later extended, but it was always understood that the Cabinet War

Rooms would not withstand a direct hit from a penetrating high-explosive weapon. Churchill nevertheless declared after becoming Prime Minister and visiting the underground Cabinet Room: 'This is the room from which I'll direct the war.'

He had no liking for underground quarters, and still favoured working and living at 10 Downing Street. This is where he was dining on 14 October 1940, when a bomb exploded on buildings only yards away across the road. Churchill was unhurt but Downing Street was badly damaged. As the war came dangerously close to Churchill, he came to rely more and more on the War Rooms, and his domestic accommodation was extended into a suite of rooms known as the Downing Street Annexe, both alongside the War Rooms in the basement and in more comfort upstairs on the ground and first floor in the Treasury building. He slept in his basement bedroom only a few times.

The rooms that can be seen today represent only part of what the Cabinet War Rooms once comprised. Over the course of the war the rooms were extended laterally under the Slab, above into the Treasury building annexe and downwards into a grim sub-basement known as the Dock. Besides the cabinet ministers and the Chiefs of Staff, who were supported by civilian aides and military officers, dozens of secretaries, telephonists and guards worked in the Cabinet War Rooms, which were permanently operational.

The Map Room and the Cabinet Room are the most important. Churchill's chair in the Cabinet Room carries an indelible link between the man and the place. On the wooden armrest can be seen the marks the Prime Minister made with his signet ring and fingernails.

There is a minimum of finish to any of the rooms, even in their restored state, which accurately represents the swift conversion from storage in 1938–9. Air-conditioning trunking hung on the ceiling comes from a warship supplier, the lighting is harsh and direct, pneumatically powered Lansom tubes deliver hard-copy messages in canisters and the only wall covering is maps. The little cubicle with vacant/engaged lavatory lock opposite the Map Room housed the Prime Minister's secure speech telephone link to President Roosevelt. In the Map Room, crowded ranks of colour-coded telephones linked the Cabinet War Rooms with operational commands.

After the Blitz, a further series of deep shocks was delivered to London across the span of the war, even as the tide turned in favour of the Allies. In early 1944, after a long comparative lull, bombers returned in what was called the Baby Blitz, and just after D-Day V-1 flying bombs started to fall on the city. As that threat was countered and controlled came the unstoppable V-2 missiles. The threat of more powerful secret weapons had been dimly glimpsed in 1943, and plans were drawn up to move to a secure citadel but not implemented. Churchill and his cabinet continued to work in the Cabinet War Rooms as flying bombs and rockets fell, through to the end of the war in Europe. The final duty officers in the Map Room signed out on 15 August 1945. The Cabinet War Rooms survived largely intact, opened only to a few selected visitors until adopted by the Imperial War Museum and opened as the Cabinet War Rooms in 1984, and developing into the Churchill Museum in 2005.

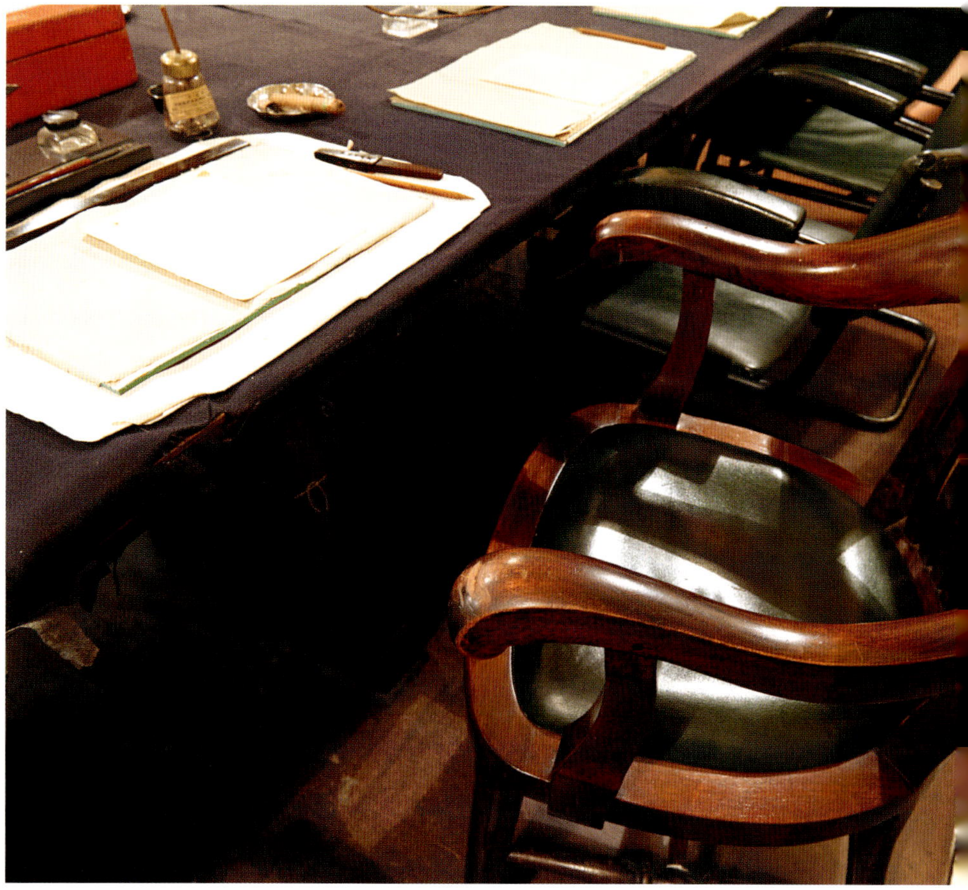

Above The scuff-marks of Churchill's signet ring are visible on the arm of his chair in the Cabinet Room.

Opposite, above The kitchen facilities serving the War Rooms were very simple.

Opposite, below Colour-coded telephones linked the Cabinet War Rooms to operational commands.

CONTACT INFORMATION

Churchill War Rooms,
Clive Steps, King Charles Street, SW1A 2AQ
https://www.iwm.org.uk/visits/churchill-war-rooms

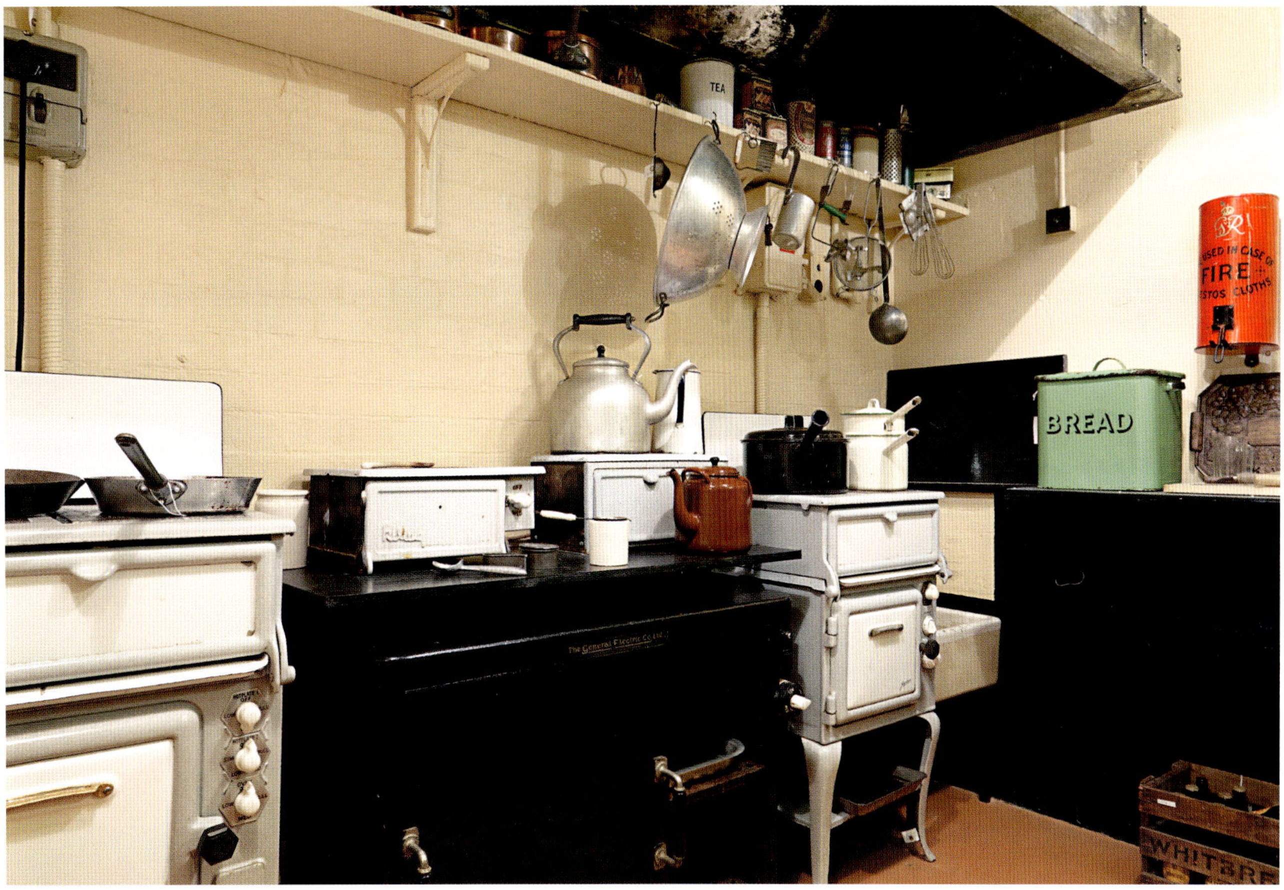
TEA
FIRE
BREAD

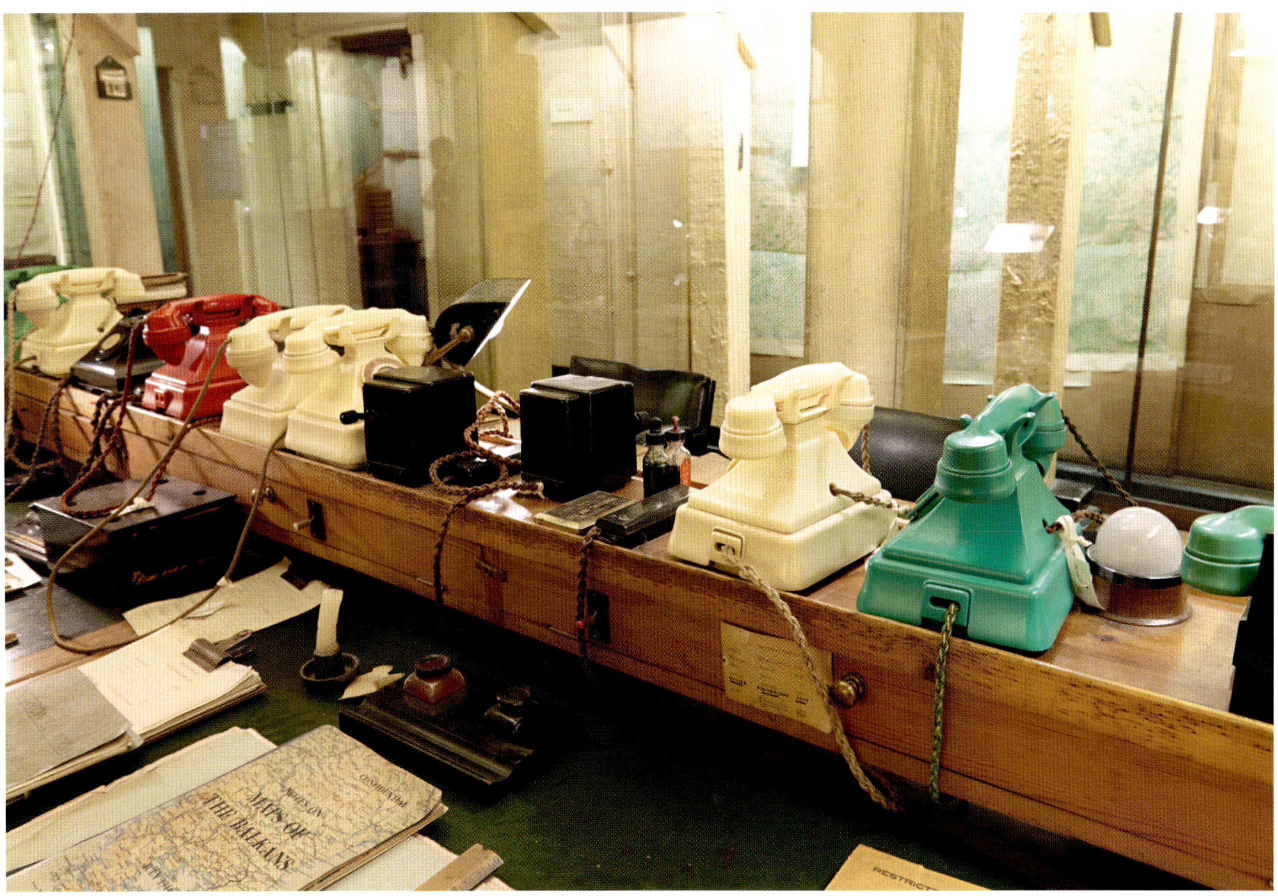
MAPS OF
THE BALKANS

Liberty London

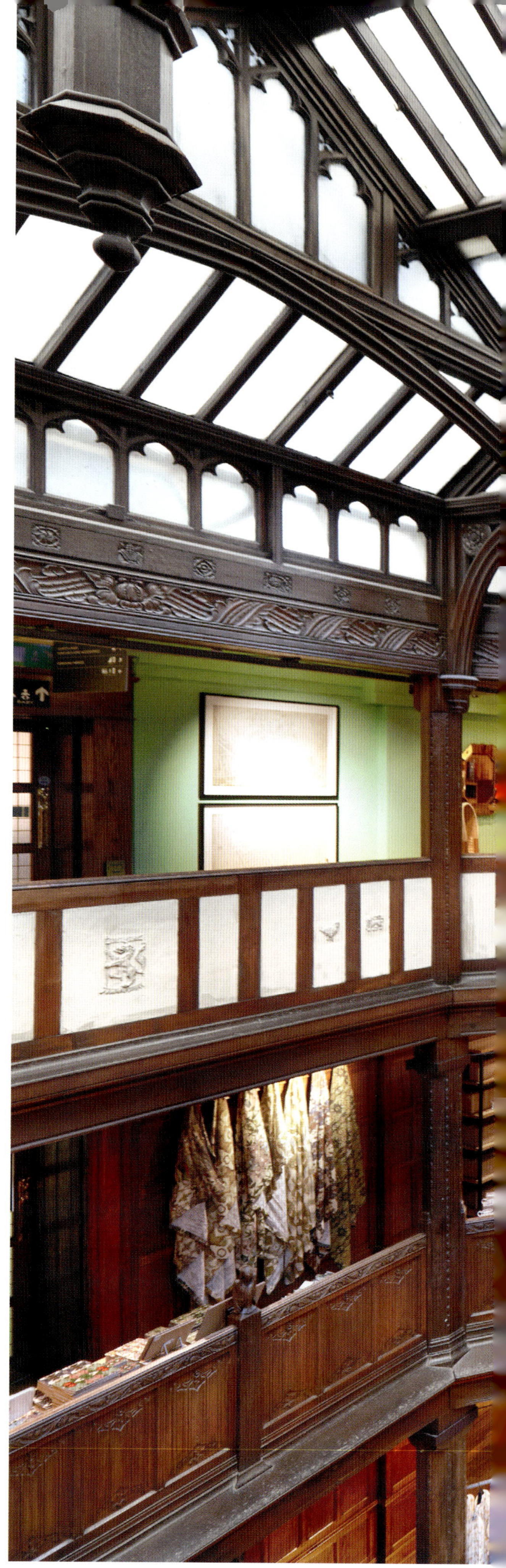

The hammerbeam roof under pitched glazing in the east gallery.

From the start of the Liberty business on Regent Street in 1875, the company set a distinctive style. First selling coloured silks and fans imported from Japan, it added silver, jewellery, wallpapers and carpets from across the Far East and Middle East. Taking inspiration from these designs, Liberty was soon printing and selling its own fabrics. Although the merchandise was an eclectic range, it came with an unmistakeable Liberty look that set the emporium apart from other department stores in London. When more floor space was required, a new half-timbered Tudor building emerged on Great Marlborough Street looking unlike anything else in the West End.

Sir Arthur Lasenby Liberty was by profession a retailer and fabric manufacturer rather than a designer, although he became a participant in the Arts & Crafts Society during the 1880s and developed a wider interest in the craft of printmaking. While still importing merchandise, the production of distinctive fabrics for dressmaking and furnishing increasingly occupied Liberty's business. More space was acquired alongside the original shop at 218a Regent Street, and round the corner into what was to become Great Marlborough Street. Architects Edwin Thomas Hall and Edwin Stanley Hall were commissioned to design the new buildings, which were built between 1922 and 1925. The site in Great Marlborough Street was freehold and therefore the conditions usually determining the design of buildings on the Crown Estate did not apply. Instead of creating another Nash-style classical building, the

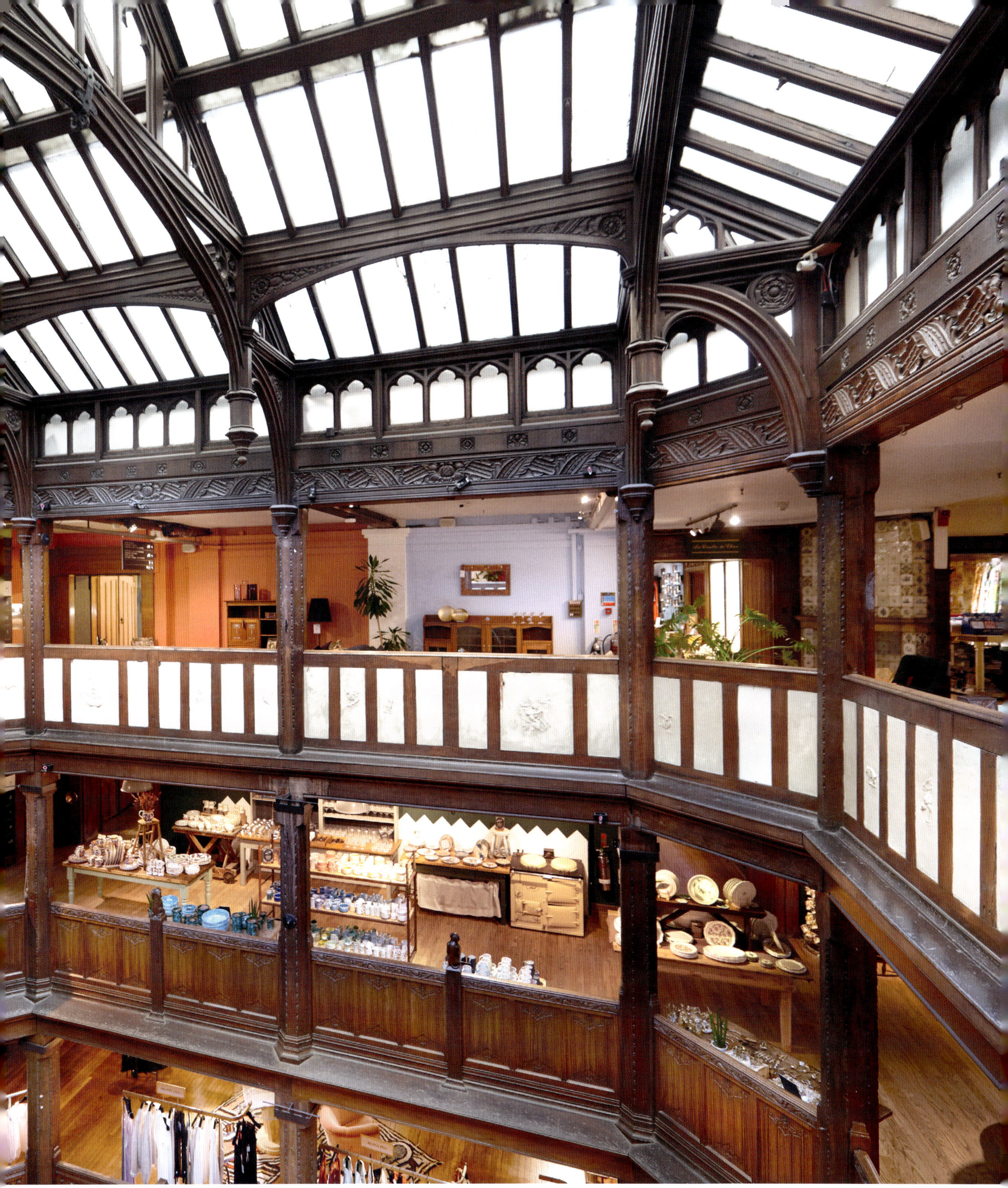

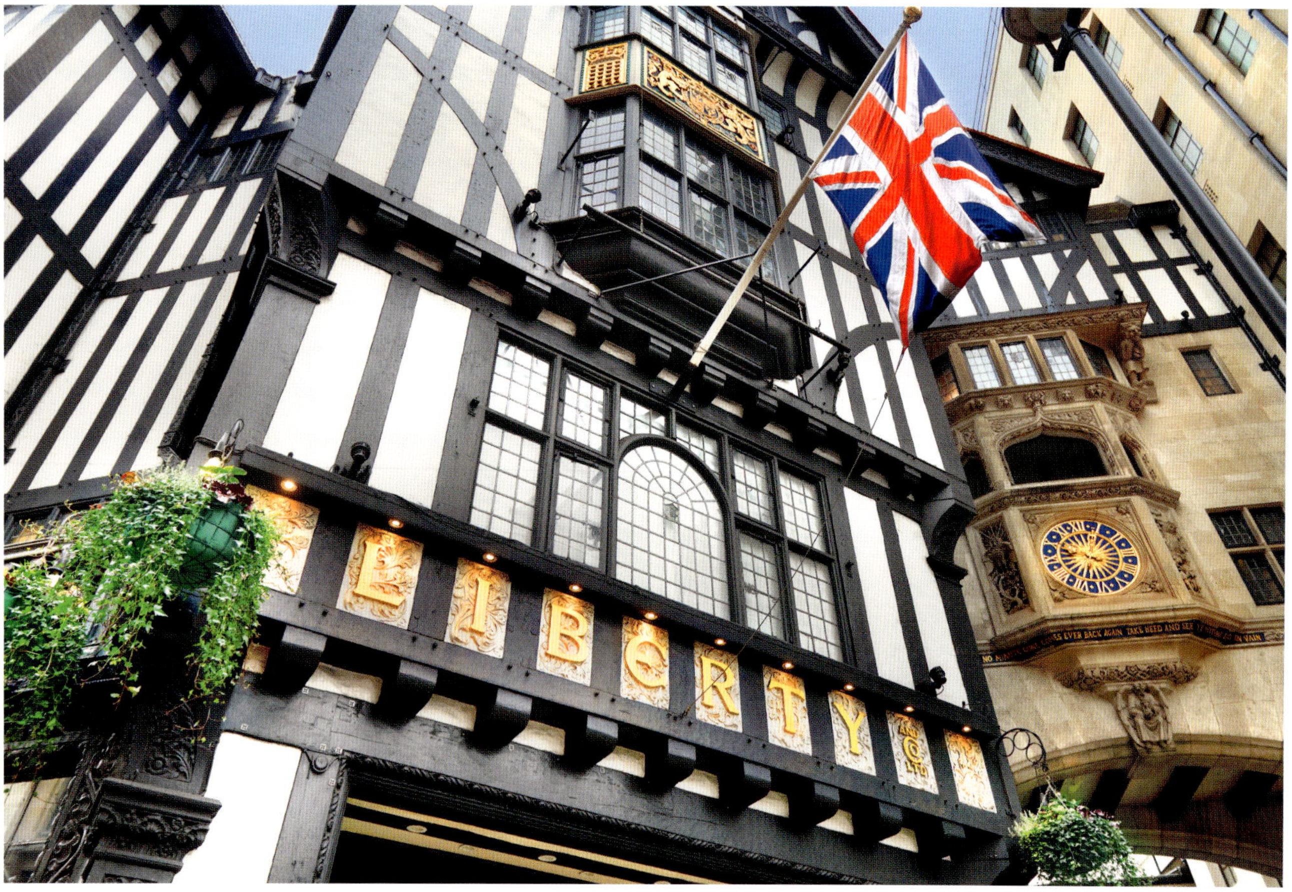
LIBERTY

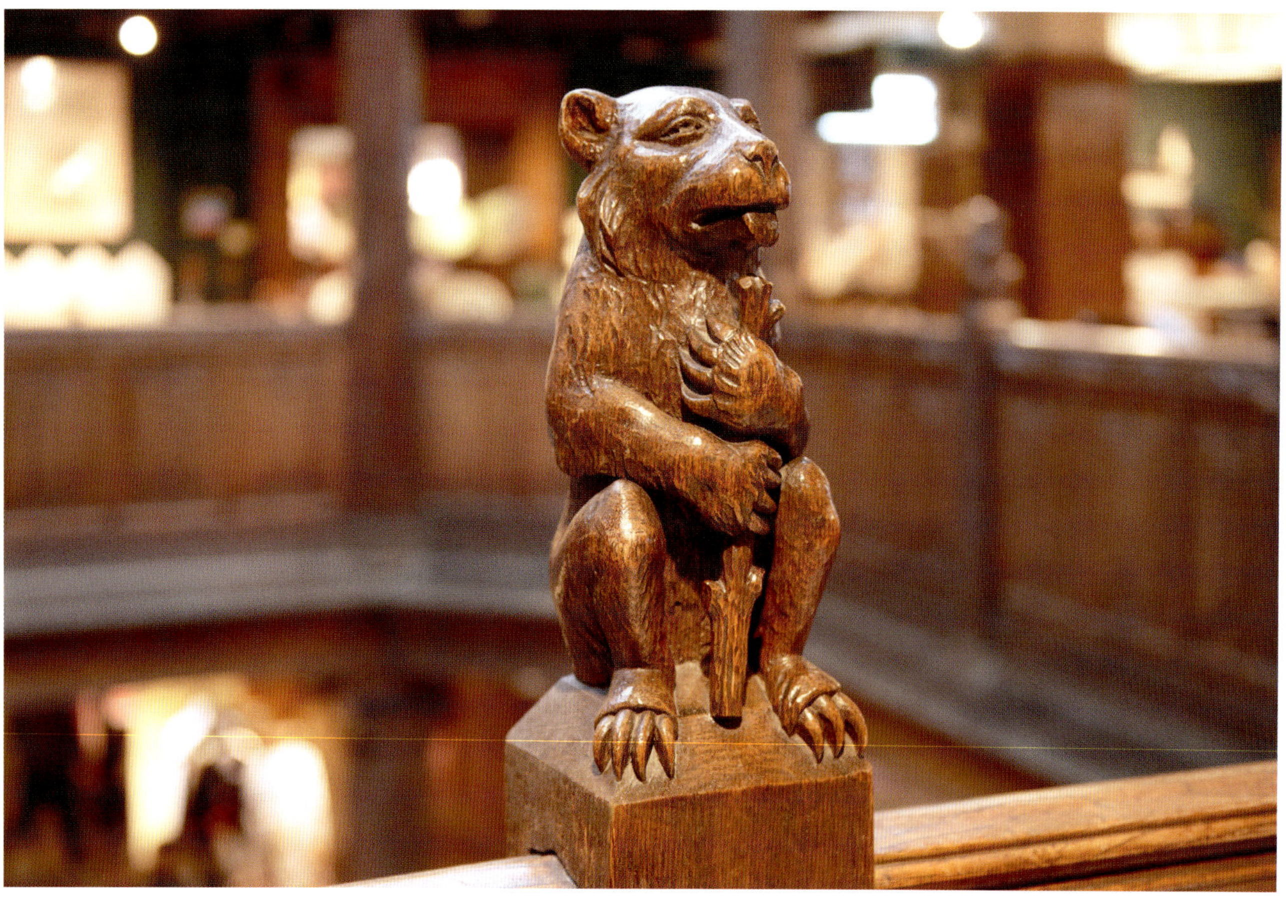

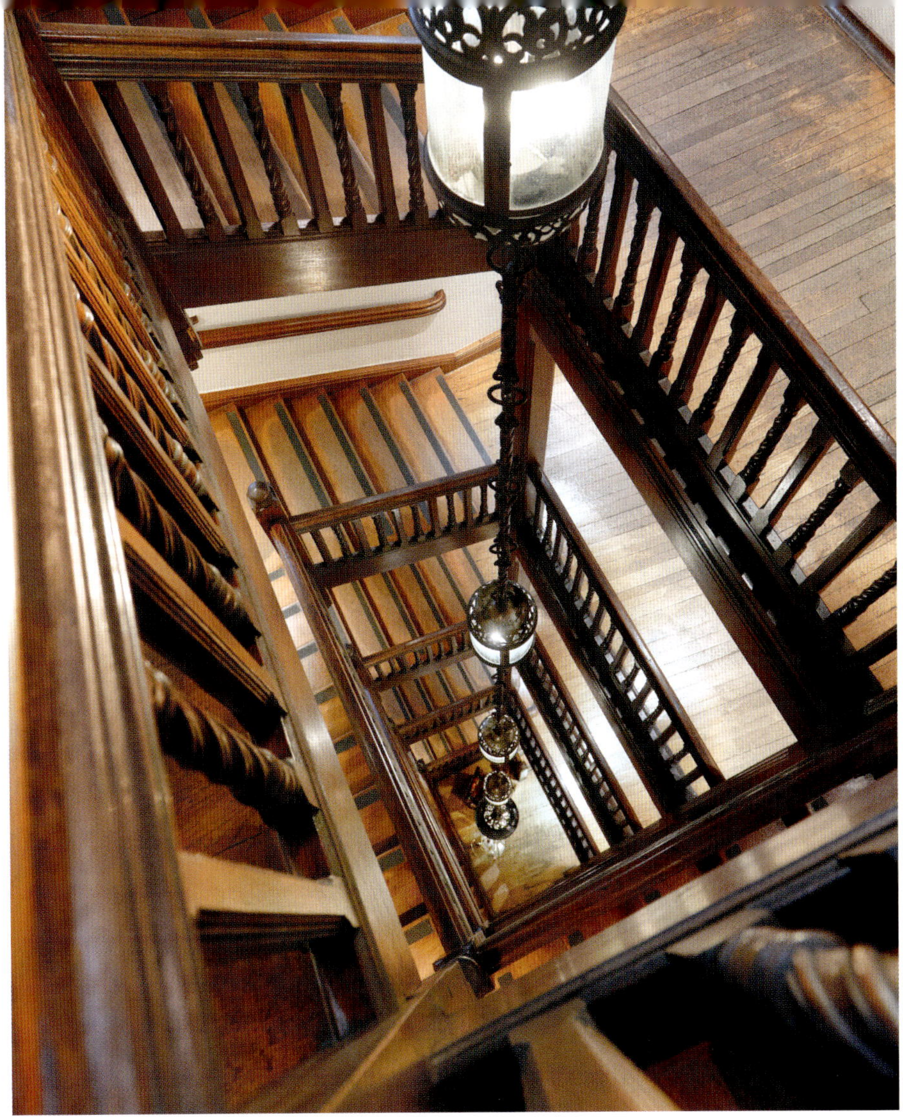

Opposite, above Liberty's entrance on Great Marlborough Street featuring the Liberty Clock. At each quarter of the hour St George chases the dragon around the clock and on the hour he slays the dragon.

Opposite, below A hand-carved hungry bear on the post of the third-floor east gallery is a product of Liberty's Arts & Crafts furniture workshop.

Above The suspended pendant lanterns on the back staircase are reputed to form the longest chandelier in Europe.

architects were free to adopt a different style and the chosen look was Tudor.

English Heritage research has suggested that the intention was to make the frontage on Great Marlborough Street resemble a group of shops rather than a continuous frontage, and the medieval buildings of the city of Chester may have been the inspiration for the design, particularly those in the Rows, where covered galleries enclose shops on the first floor. The Liberty building accordingly has gables and windows appearing to be at differing heights, all in black and white with an irregular style and topped with clusters of twisted chimneys. There is a large gilded copper weathervane in the shape of the *Mayflower*. Inside, the building was intended to evoke a feeling of luxury and spaciousness at the same time as having the intimacy of a comfortable country house – some of the spaces resemble rooms and even have fireplaces. Galleries rise in four storeys grouped around three wells, resembling the courtyard layout of old coaching inns. There are pendant hammerbeam roofs in different styles on each of the wells and seasoned oak doorcases and staircases throughout.

There is a great deal of wood because the architects and builders made particular efforts to design as much timber as possible into the construction. Two old wooden warships, HMS *Impregnable* and HMS *Hindustan*, which had lingered for years before being broken up at Woolwich in 1921, contributed their timbers to Liberty. The oak gun decks of the *Hindustan* became the floors and its ribs and stanchions were used in the galleries. Other wood from these two ships was used as cladding on the exterior of the building. The external frame was assembled in traditional style with morts, tenons and pegs and over 24,000 cubic ft (680 m^3) of timber was supplied. Some bricks are set between the timber framework and covered with Portland cement. The price of all this Tudor authenticity was high, requiring great craftsmanship, special materials and longer construction time, and it went against the trend of steel-frame construction that had been used at the new Selfridges store on Oxford Street.

The wooden detailing at Liberty was also to a high standard and can be seen particularly on the gallery posts on the third floor of the east atrium, where there are a series of intricately carved animals by Lawrence Turner, who ran Liberty's Arts & Crafts furniture workshop, which supplied decoration on panels and pillars in the store. More than twenty carvers worked on the interior fittings.

The nautical theme is continued in the back staircase, where a series of suspended pendant lamps descend from the roof almost to the lower basement, six lamps in all, evoking ships' lanterns in style. It is claimed by Liberty that this may be the longest chandelier in Europe.

The Tudor-styled Liberty store is so arresting that is easy to neglect the beaux arts classical building built one year later which lies alongside, connected to it by a bridge that transitions from one architectural style to the other. A fine clock, designed by the chairman of the British Horological Institute, is mounted over the archway. Under it lies the legend 'No minute gone comes ever back again take heed to see ye nothing do in vain'.

CONTACT INFORMATION

Liberty London,
Regent Street, W1B 5AH
https://www.libertylondon.com/

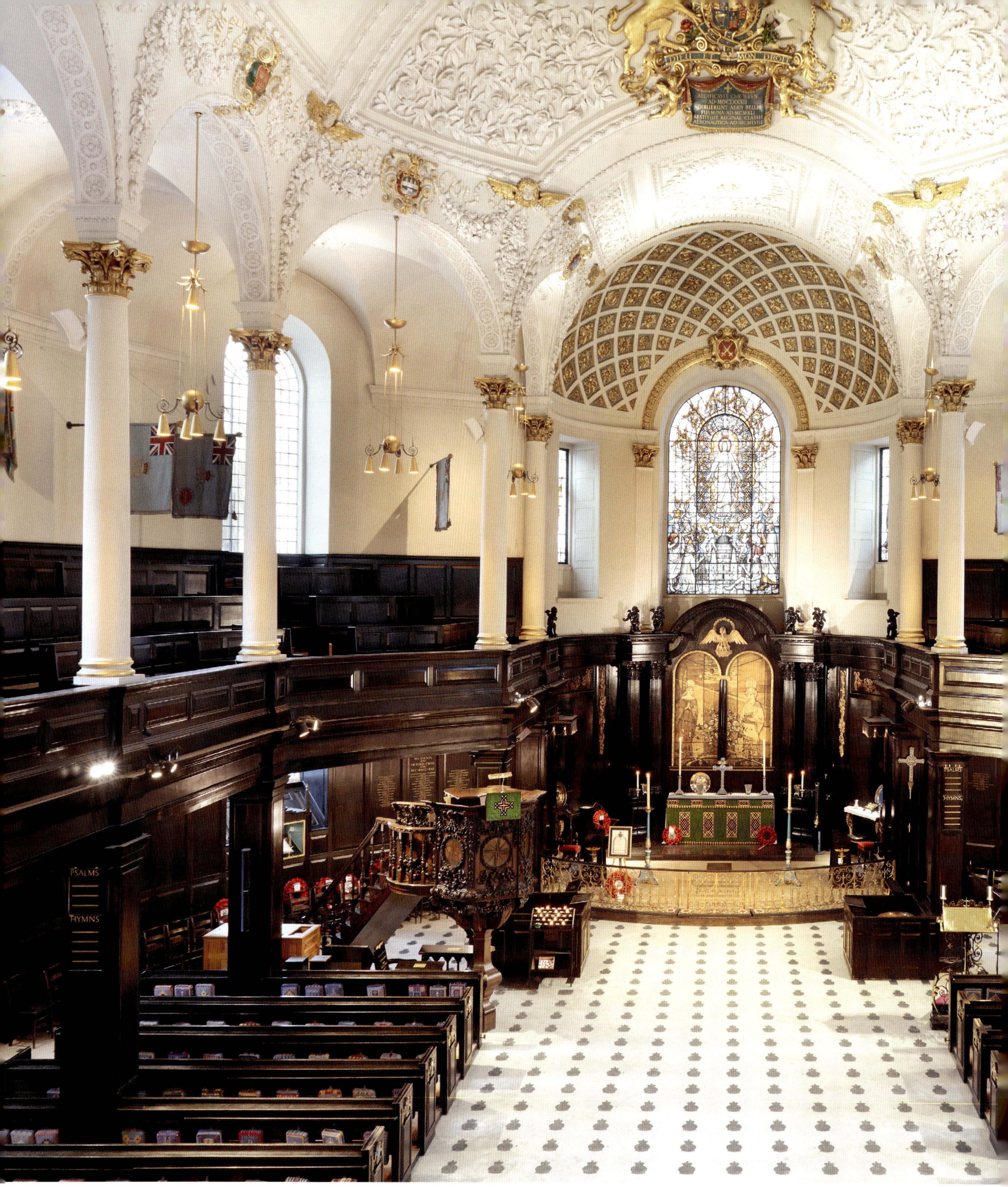
PSALMS
HYMNS

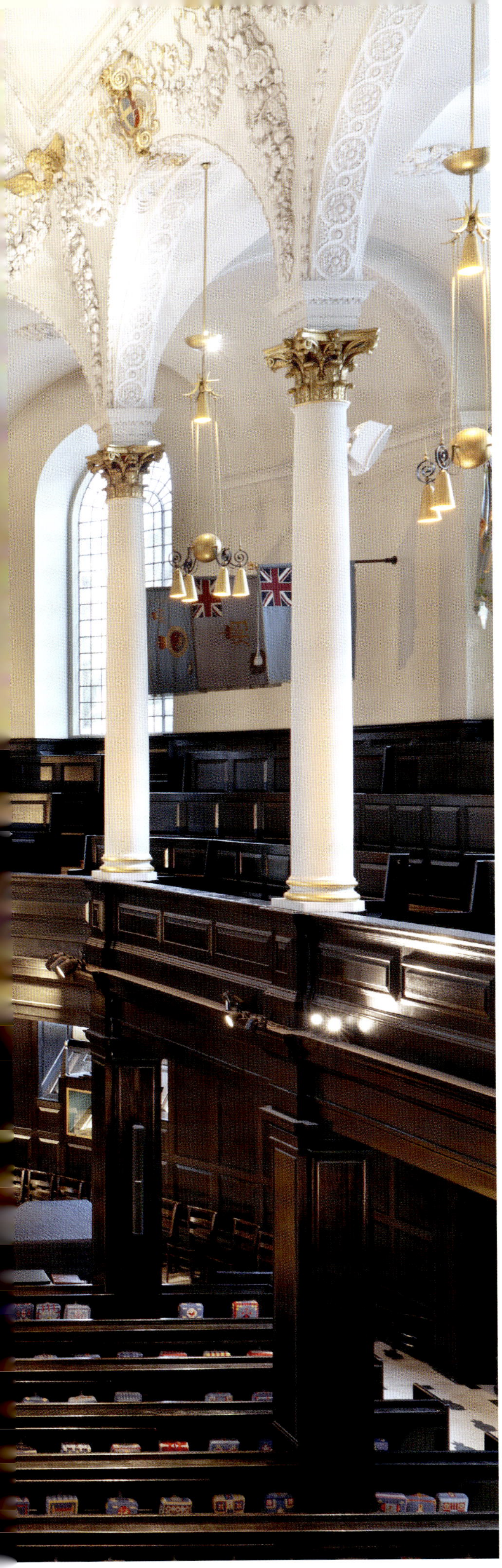

Main stained-glass window of the risen Christ; the pulpit by woodcarver Grinling Gibbons is an original feature of the Wren church.

St Clement Danes

St Clement Danes stands prominently on an island on the Strand at a spot where Christians first gathered more than a thousand years ago. It is the Central Church of the Royal Air Force and its history is steeped in layers of conflict, destruction and rebirth.

When the Romans abandoned Londinium in the fifth century, the Anglo-Saxon population drifted to the bustling marketplace of Lundenwic, a mile up the Thames. As this medieval port grew, it became a trading hub, and by the end of the eighth century it had attracted the attention of marauding Vikings from Denmark. The ferocity and frequency of their raids in the ninth century forced the Anglo-Saxons back inside the walls of Londinium, leaving the Danes free to establish their own town to replace Lundenwic. The Viking settlement became known as the old town or 'Ealdwic', now Aldwych.

Alfred the Great's victory over the Danes came in 878 and Danes with English wives were allowed to remain in Ealdwic. They converted to Christianity and it seems they adopted the Anglo-Saxon church already established there. In the eleventh century, a stone church was erected on the site of the wooden-framed building and dedicated to St Clement, patron saint of mariners, becoming St Clement-of-the-Danes. It was rebuilt to a Norman design following William I's conquest in 1066.

By the middle of the seventeenth century, the church, which had narrowly escaped the Great Fire of London, had become dilapidated and Sir Christopher Wren was commissioned to undertake not just a restoration but a radical rebuild. In designs for other churches Wren faced limitations posed by constricted ground plans, but here he had a freer hand and, with stonemason Edward Pearce, constructed a masterpiece incorporating the Saxon-Norman base of the tower into the new design. It was finished by the end of 1682 and shortly afterwards a pupil of Wren, James Gibbs, was commissioned to extend the tower with a three-tiered spire and a clock chamber. By the end of the eighteenth century, St Clement Danes became one of London's most fashionable churches, with worshippers including the theatre manager-actor David Garrick, writer Samuel Johnson and his biographer James Boswell.

As London's society moved westward during the nineteenth century, St Clement Danes declined, eventually requiring a major restoration. Inspired by the incumbent rector Septimus Pennington, the renovation saw bright stained-glass windows transform the church. A later rector, William Pennington-Bickford, inaugurated an annual service for primary school children, at which each child was given an orange and lemon, linking to the nursery rhyme with the line: 'Oranges and lemons say the bells of St Clement's'. The source of the rhyme and its meaning are obscure, but the connection became legend and a carillon machine in the tower was made to play the melody.

On 10–11 May 1941, the last night of the main Blitz, St Clement Danes was hit by incendiary bombs and its roof, wooden-framed and lead-covered, was set ablaze. The wooden interior quickly became a torch. All but the outer shell of the church and the tower were consumed. The Royal Air Force received the ruins from the Diocese of London in 1953. Using £250,000 of donations from a worldwide appeal and a trust, St Clement Danes was rebuilt between 1955 and 1958 as close as possible to the Wren design, and re-consecrated to remember all who have given their lives in service with the RAF. A new peal of bells was recast from the metal of the old at the Whitechapel Bell Foundry in 1955. Twelve bells are installed, including the Sanctus bell, which dated from 1558 and survived intact.

The timing of the church's adoption enabled a commemoration of the Royal Air Force at its most prominent and widely affiliated. Over 800 RAF and Commonwealth squadrons, units and stations are marked in the central aisle with badges of Welsh slate. The organ was donated by the US Air Force, and there is a shrine in the west gallery to the 16,000 members who died in the Second World War. Below is a simple crypt, the altar and sanctuary a gift from the Royal Netherlands Air Force, the font from the Royal Norwegian Air Force and the candelabrum from Belgium.

The wide central aisle is a divergence from the Wren layout and includes one of its several secrets: the flanking pews are telescopic and when extended provide extra seating and regain the original proportions of the church.

The focus of the church is the Book of Remembrance, containing the names of every airman and woman who has died in service in over a century of RAF operations. Encased in glass cabinets around the inner wall are ten volumes and the pages are turned each day.

CONTACT INFORMATION

St Clement Danes,
Strand, WC2R 1DH
https://www.stclementdanes.org.uk/

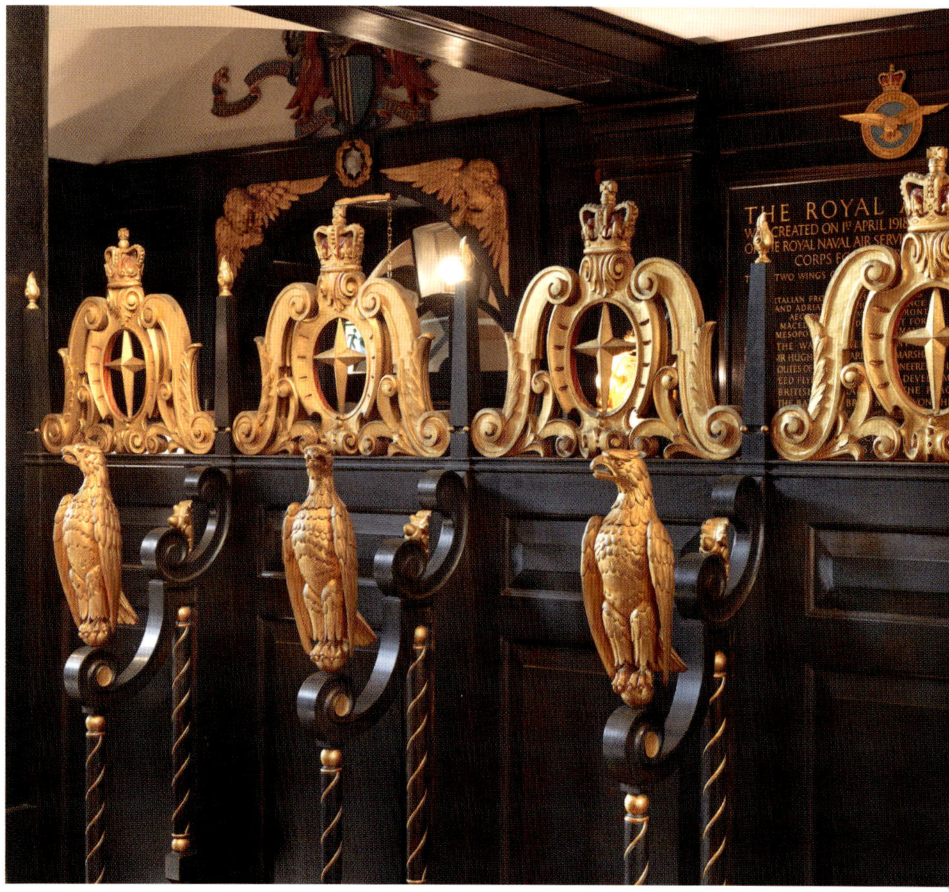

Above Monastic-style pew stalls at the west end of the nave, which are reserved for members of the Air Force Board, managers of the RAF.

Opposite, above
The upper tier of the belfry. Fixed to the beam are the Sanctus Bell, left, which dates from 1558, and at centre front, the flat fourth bell, tuned with the carillon to ring 'Oranges and Lemons'. Its inscription translates as 'I have outlived my troubles and give thanks to the stars'.

Opposite, below
The bell ringers' ropes.

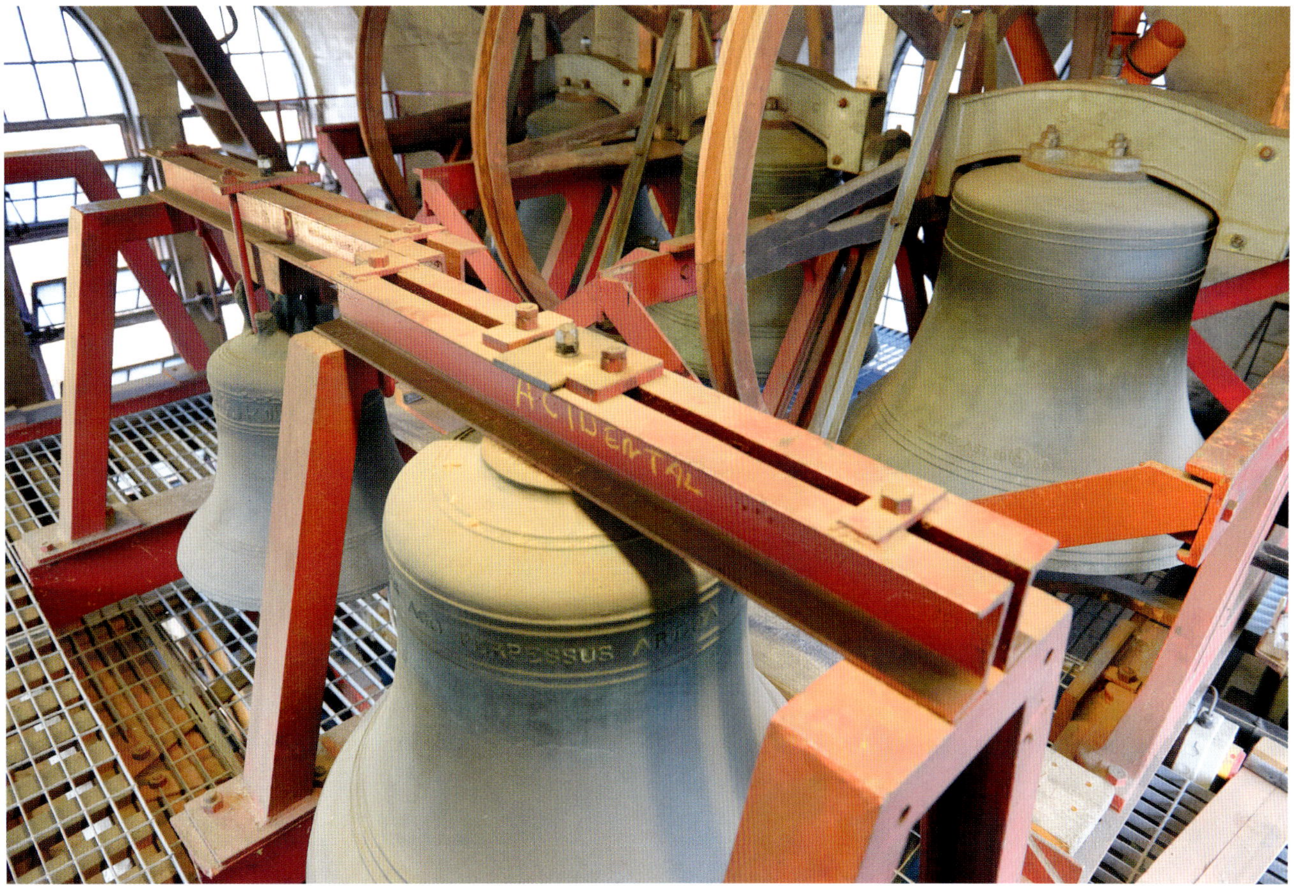

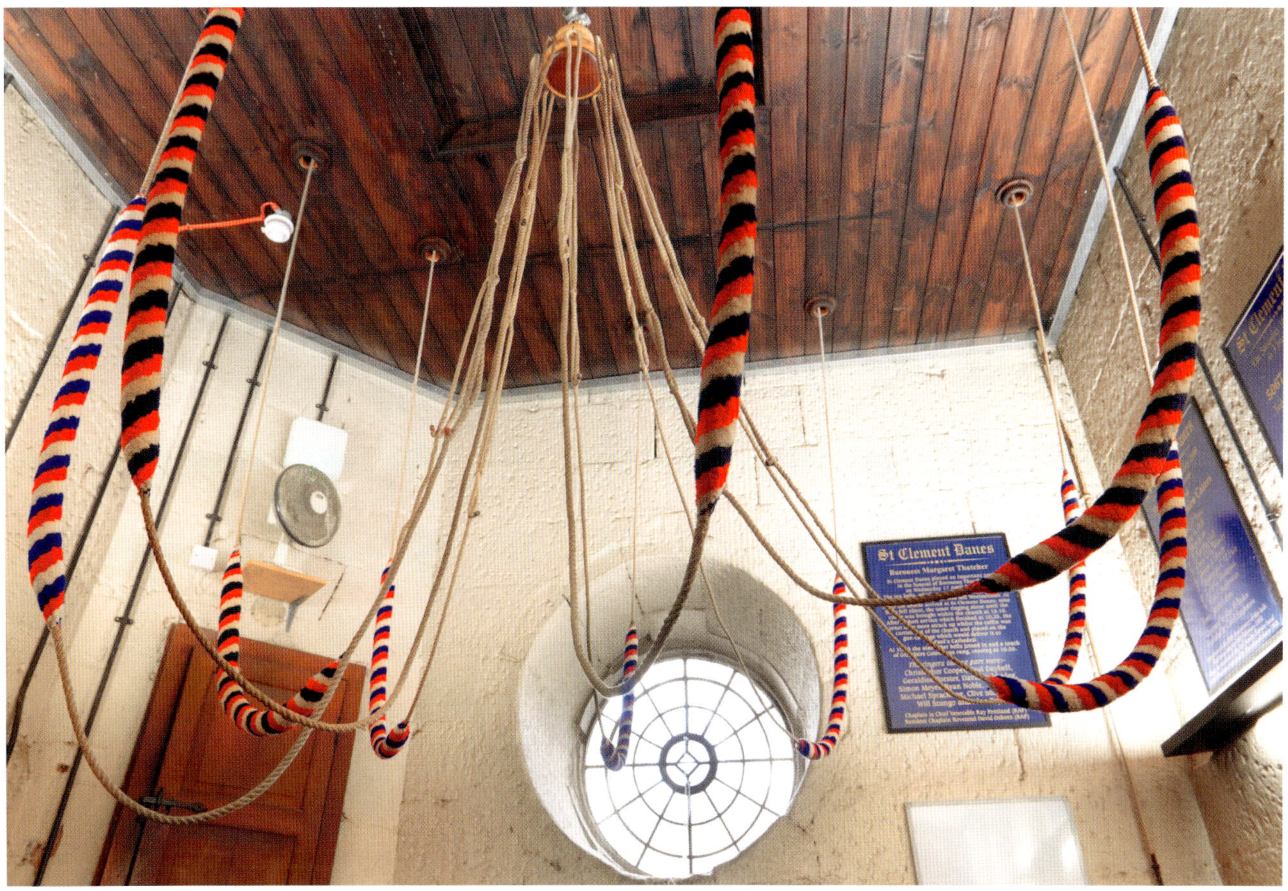
St Clement Danes

James Purdey & Sons Ltd

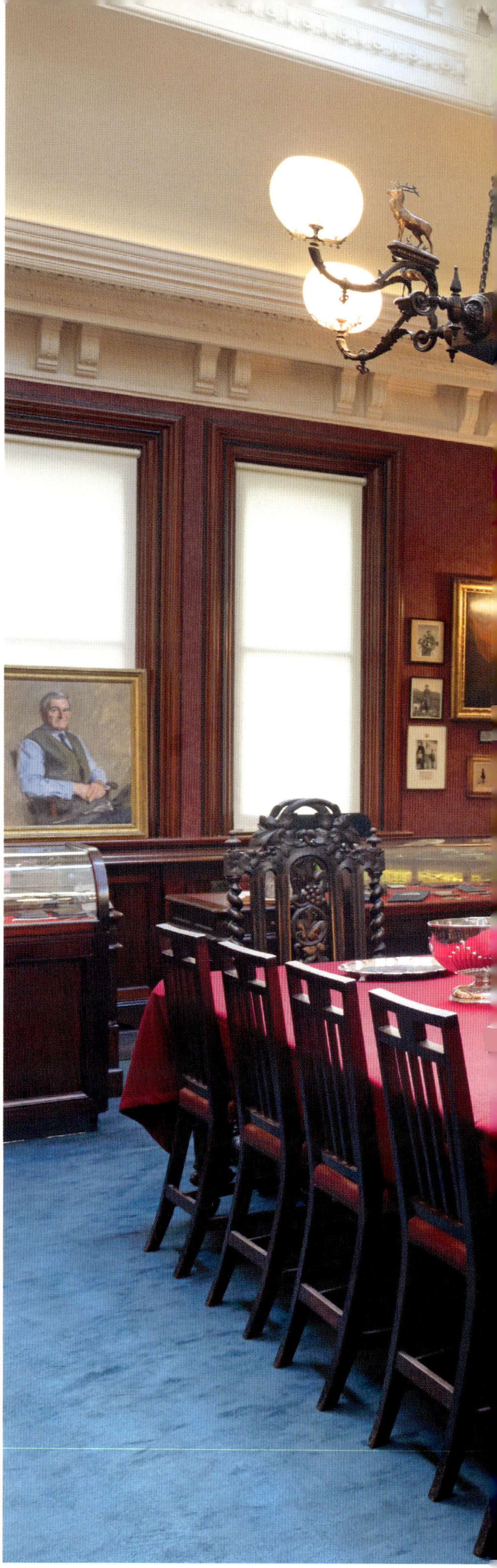

The historic Long Room at the Mayfair showroom, where Purdey portraits look down on a side-by-side 12-bore, a new trigger plate over-and-under and a Purdey best over-and-under with fine engraving; archive ledgers date back to 1818.

A fine sporting gun entirely made in London carries a special distinction and a high price. There are still a handful of great London makers, including Boss and Holland & Holland, but the most recognized name is Purdey, with its showroom in Mayfair and workshop in Hammersmith.

In the 2020s, a capable shotgun can be bought off the shelf for much less than a thousand pounds; a Purdey gun can cost a hundred times more than that. The smooth-bore shotgun with bead sight is one of the simplest types of firearm; Purdey take up to two years to produce a shotgun and make only about a hundred guns and rifles each year, all of them 97 per cent handmade.

The company's reputation was forged on making the best-handling guns of the Victorian period. A patent of 1870 provided an ingenious and simple design of bolt and top-lever mechanism. This innovation for aiding the opening and closing of drop-down guns did much to put the firm at the forefront during the golden age of gunmaking. Today, collectability is often the aim of the owner, who appreciates the high level of finish, and some guns are destined from the start to become what is known as a 'safe queen'. 'If you want to lock it away, it's the buyer's choice', says a spokesman for the company. Experienced sporting shots say the sheer functionality of any Purdey is undiminished: strong, reliable, neat, well-balanced and generally light. The firm makes side-by-side and over-and-under

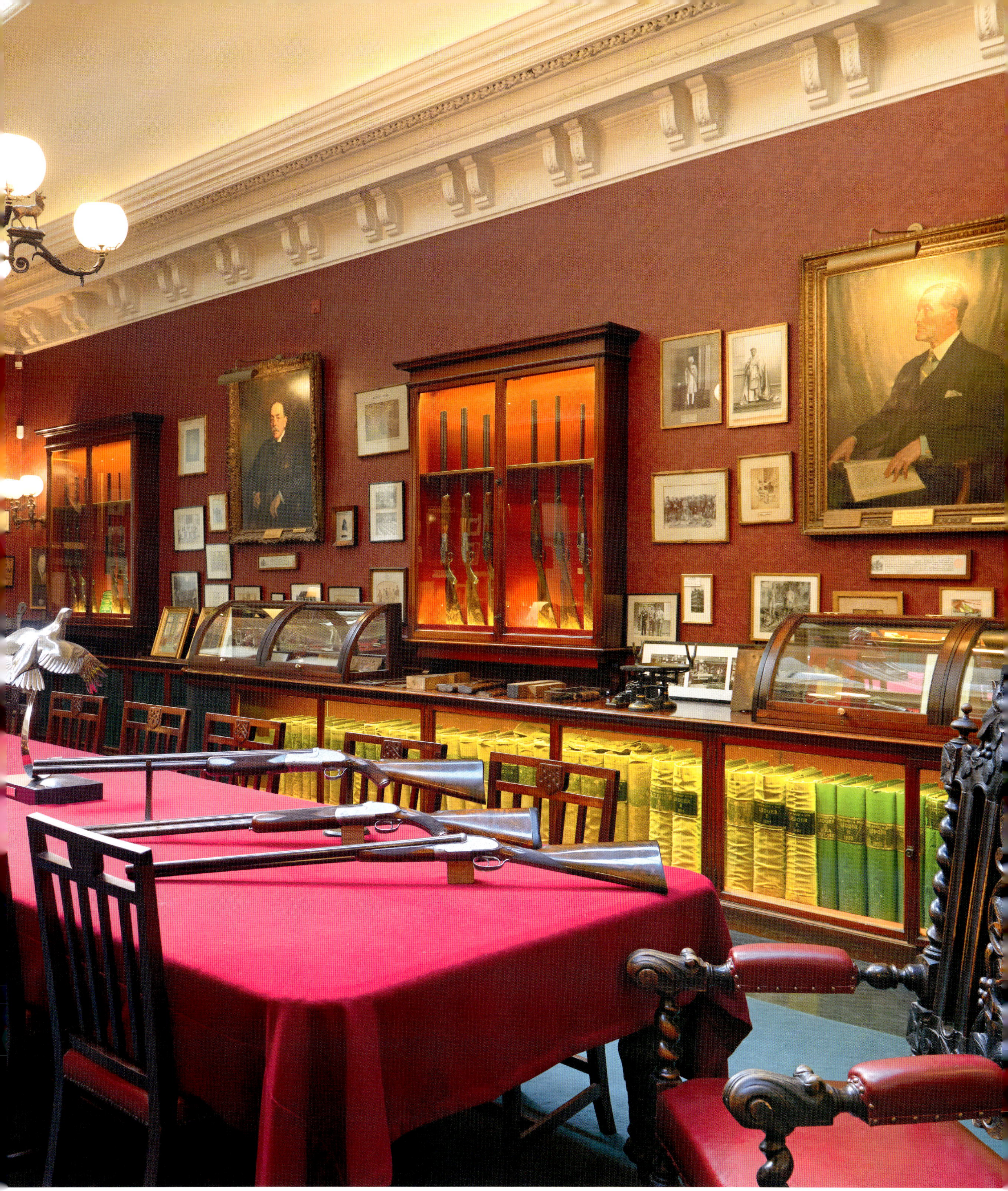

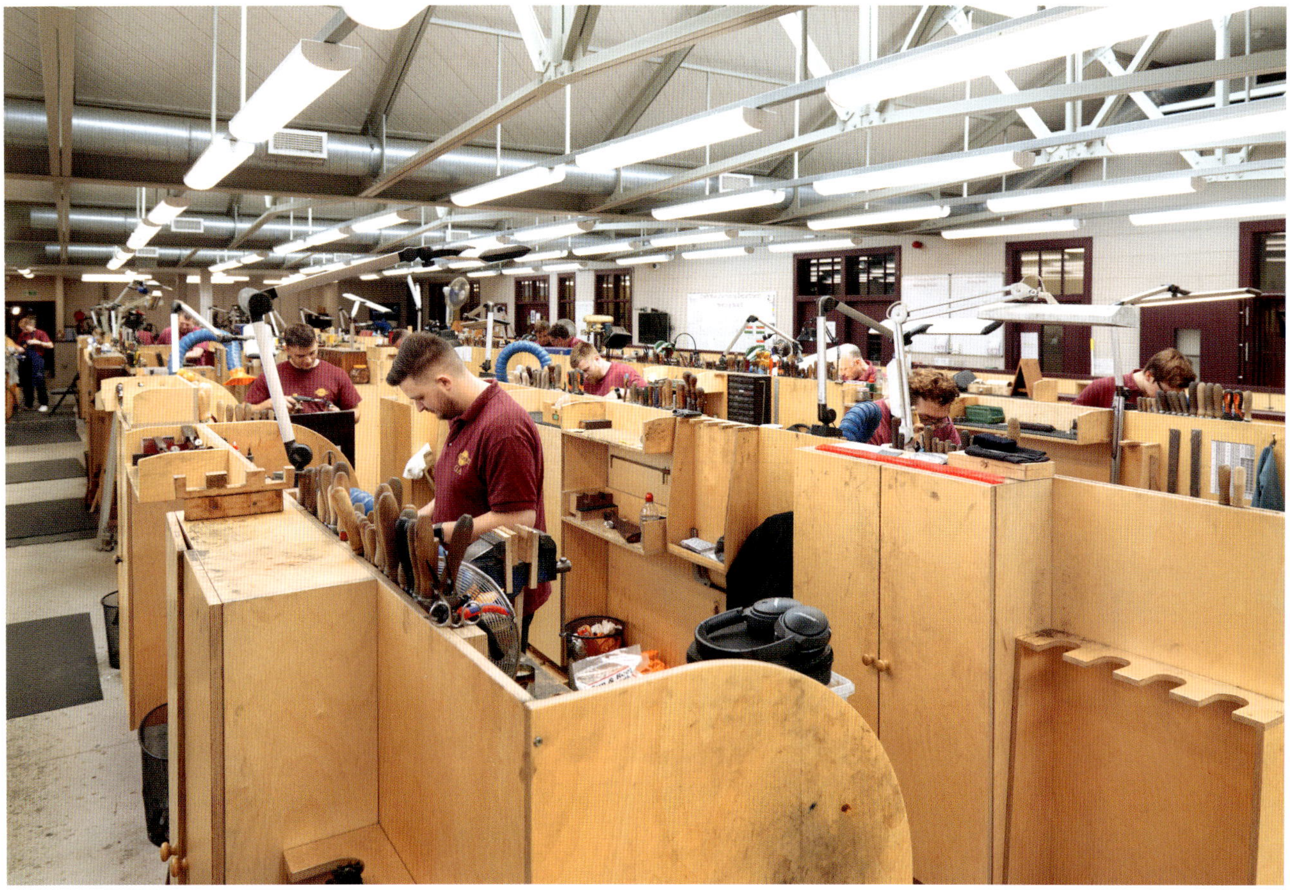

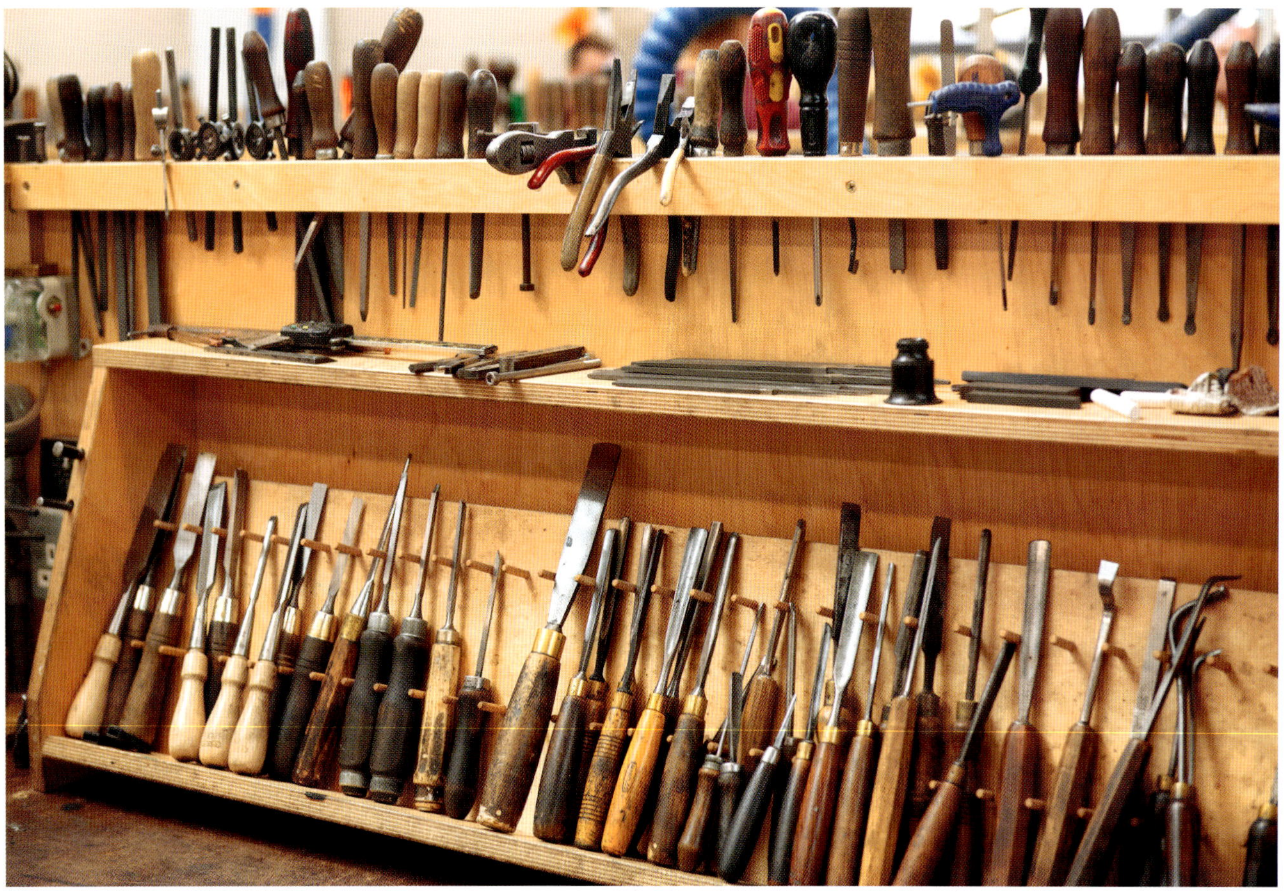

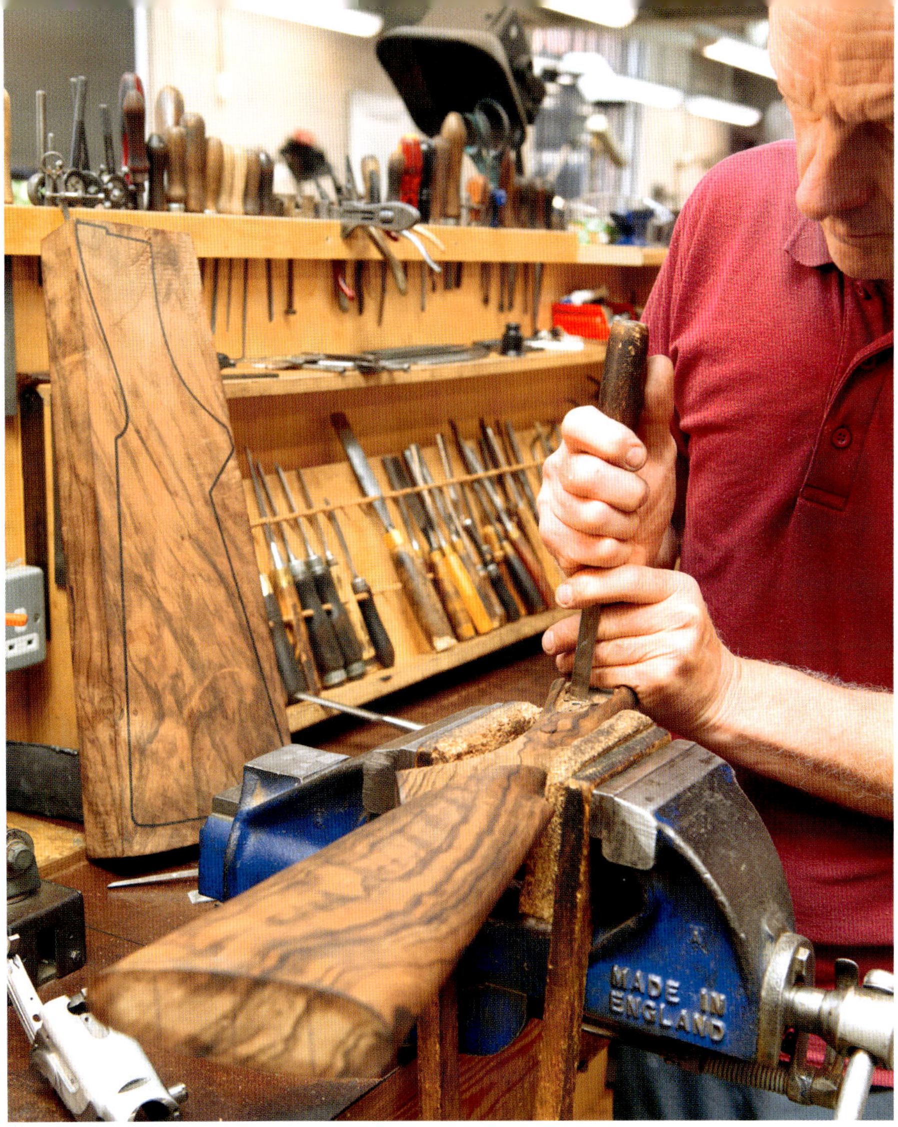

Opposite, above
The busy workshop, where gunsmiths take 600–700 craft hours to make each gun.

Opposite, below
Hand tools abound on a workshop bench. Each gun is an individual piece of art.

Above A craftsman preparing the walnut stock, held in a soft lead-lined vice.

shotguns, hammer-ejector guns, bolt-action rifles and double rifles.

The showroom is in Mayfair, centre of luxury retailing, but its location is rooted in history rather than prestige. The West End was once the home of diverse expert craftsmen, including gunmakers. From 1814 the first muzzle-loading flintlocks made by James Purdey came from a workroom in what is now Wardour Street, and later from a shop in Oxford Street. By 1883 the thriving James Purdey & Sons had moved to Audley House, a building which the firm had commissioned in Queen Anne-style red brick and red stone on the corner with Mount Street. The royal coat of arms over the entrance door is unsurprising. *Country Life* reported that by Edwardian times there was no crowned head of state in Europe without a Purdey.

On the top floor, thousands of cartridges were loaded by hand and originally guns were fitted with stocks and finished and engraved on the premises. On the ground floor is the Long Room, once an office, where James Purdey the Younger, the founder's son, would watch the craftsmen at work below through a well in the floor. In 1938 the well was closed over and a long table installed, which is still in place today. The space has been restored and has been described as resembling the gun room of an old country house combined with the smoking room of a London club. It is hung with portraits of the Purdey patriarchs, lined with memorabilia, and houses historic ledgers. The selection of wood for the stock by customers and the taking of measurements are still handled in the Long Room.

In 1949 Purdey acquired James Woodward & Sons, a London maker noted for an exceptionally good design of over-and-under guns. This became and remains the basis for Purdey 'best' over-and-unders. Over time, Purdey's factory for making actions and working on gun tubes for barrel-making has been located at various places in west London, eventually settling in Hammersmith in 1979, where all gunmaking is now concentrated. The factory was extensively reworked in 2015 to give a modernized environment and includes an indoor range for testing and regulating. Here, the traditional trades of the barrel-maker, actioner, stocker, engraver and finisher continue. Computer numerically controlled machines cut the outline of the action, which starts as a solid forged ingot. This goes to the actioner who uses smoke black from a paraffin lamp to deposit soot over the surfaces to reveal any unevenness. Locks, triggers and ejectors are made by hand. Racks of hand tools line the benches. While most of the materials, such as Turkish walnut and case-hardened EN36 steel are unmysterious, many of the processes certainly are. Application of a certain oil called slacum, devised by a legendary craftsman and factory manager early in the last century, takes up to six weeks. Numerous coats are applied to the stock. The deep glossiness of the blacking on Purdey barrels is widely admired and hard to copy. Assembly, known as 'putting together', is a two-part process, spread over three months.

In the Hammersmith workshop, a high volume of work is repair and servicing. Purdey guns from the 1890s, some with original barrels, are still supported.

CONTACT INFORMATION

James Purdey & Sons Ltd,
57–58 South Audley Street, W1K 2ED
https://www.purdey.com/

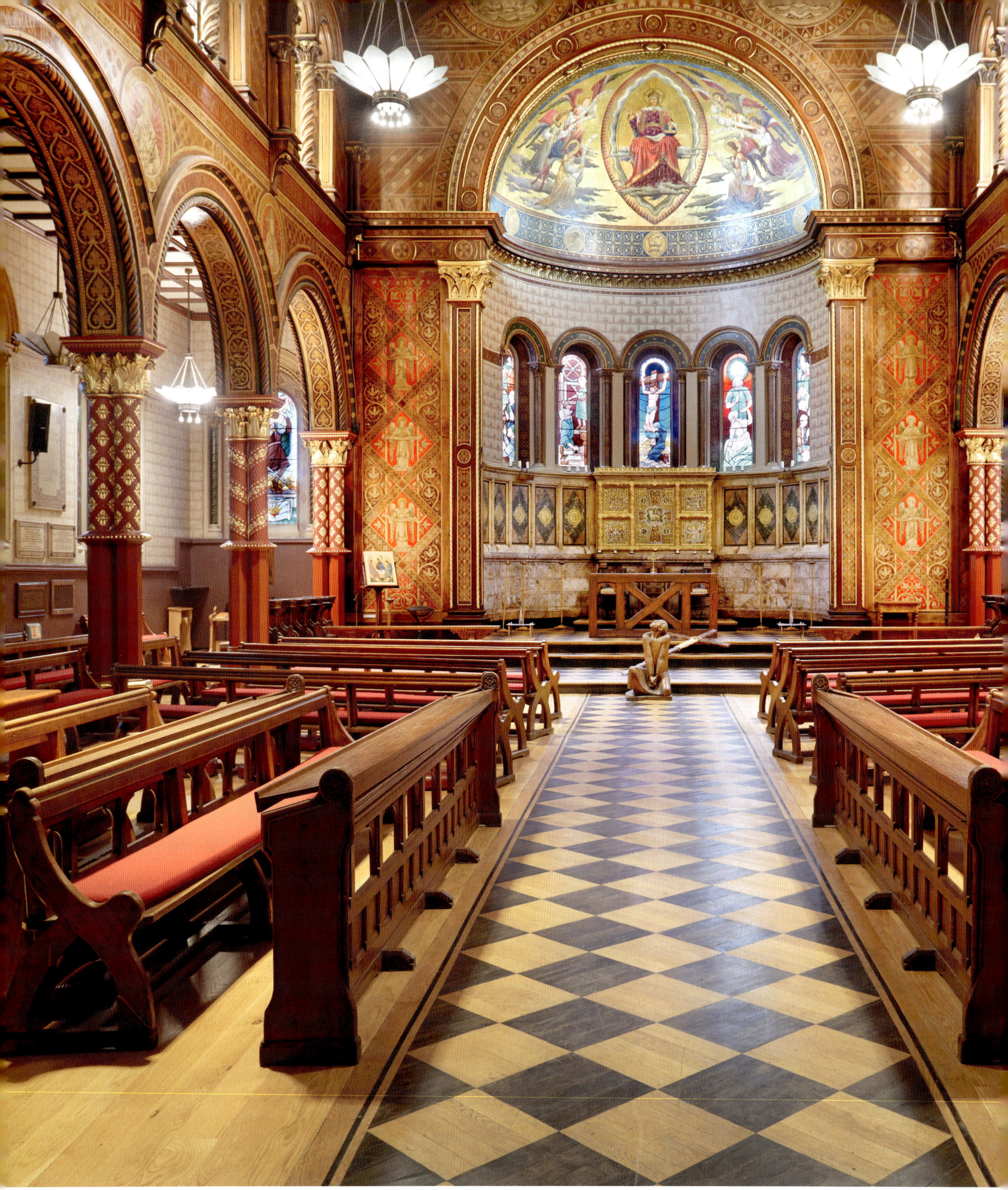

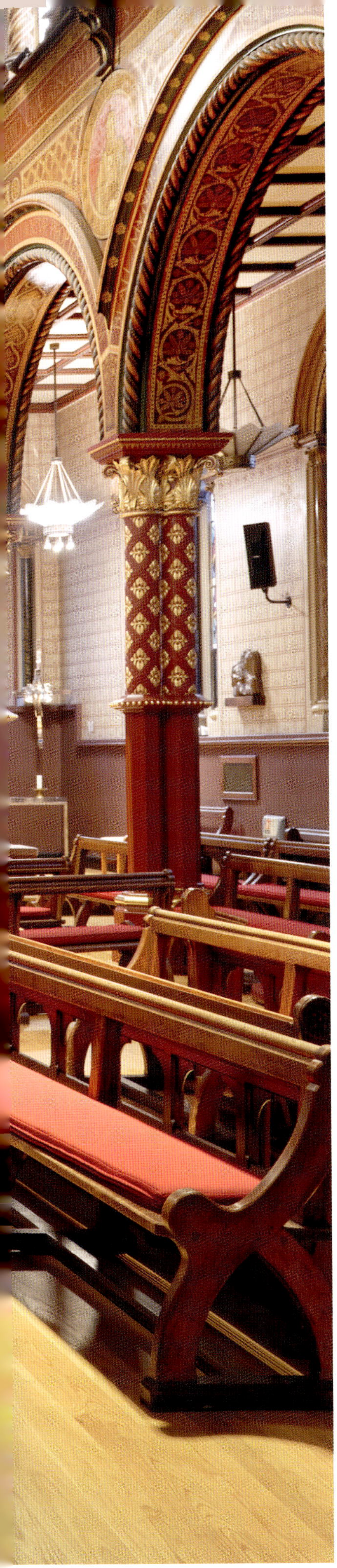

King's College Chapel

The double columns are cast iron decorated with brass.

King's College Chapel is located deep inside a university campus on the Strand. From a modern concrete entrance, it is reached by a double staircase and then via an academic corridor. Here, the spectacular chapel is revealed, variously described as Gothic-Byzantine, or Normano-Byzantine or simply Romanesque.

Its architect, Sir George Gilbert Scott, took inspiration from the ancient Christian churches of Rome, the classic basilica where a central nave is flanked by two aisles and an altar is housed under a semi-dome. The chapel itself was built upon in 1932 when the Hambleden Building of Anatomy was constructed above.

With the chapel embedded inside the King's College Building, visitors wonder how it manages to catch the sunlight that streams through its stained-glass windows. The answer is that the chapel has a secret street aspect. This can only be seen from the obscure passageway, Strand Lane. Some who explore this alley go in search of one of London's best-known curiosities, an ancient bath, supposedly Roman, found behind a window at pavement level. At this place it is necessary to look upwards to see how part of the nave and the apse of King's College Chapel project eastward from the jumbled assemblage of the main building.

King's College Chapel, with its decorations in parquetry, tile and paint, has been extensively restored to Scott's original design; modern stained-glass windows with characters from the Old and New Testaments are in the theme of the originals.

CONTACT INFORMATION

King's College Chapel,
Strand Lane, WC2R 2LS
https://www.kcl.ac.uk/visit/the-college-chapel

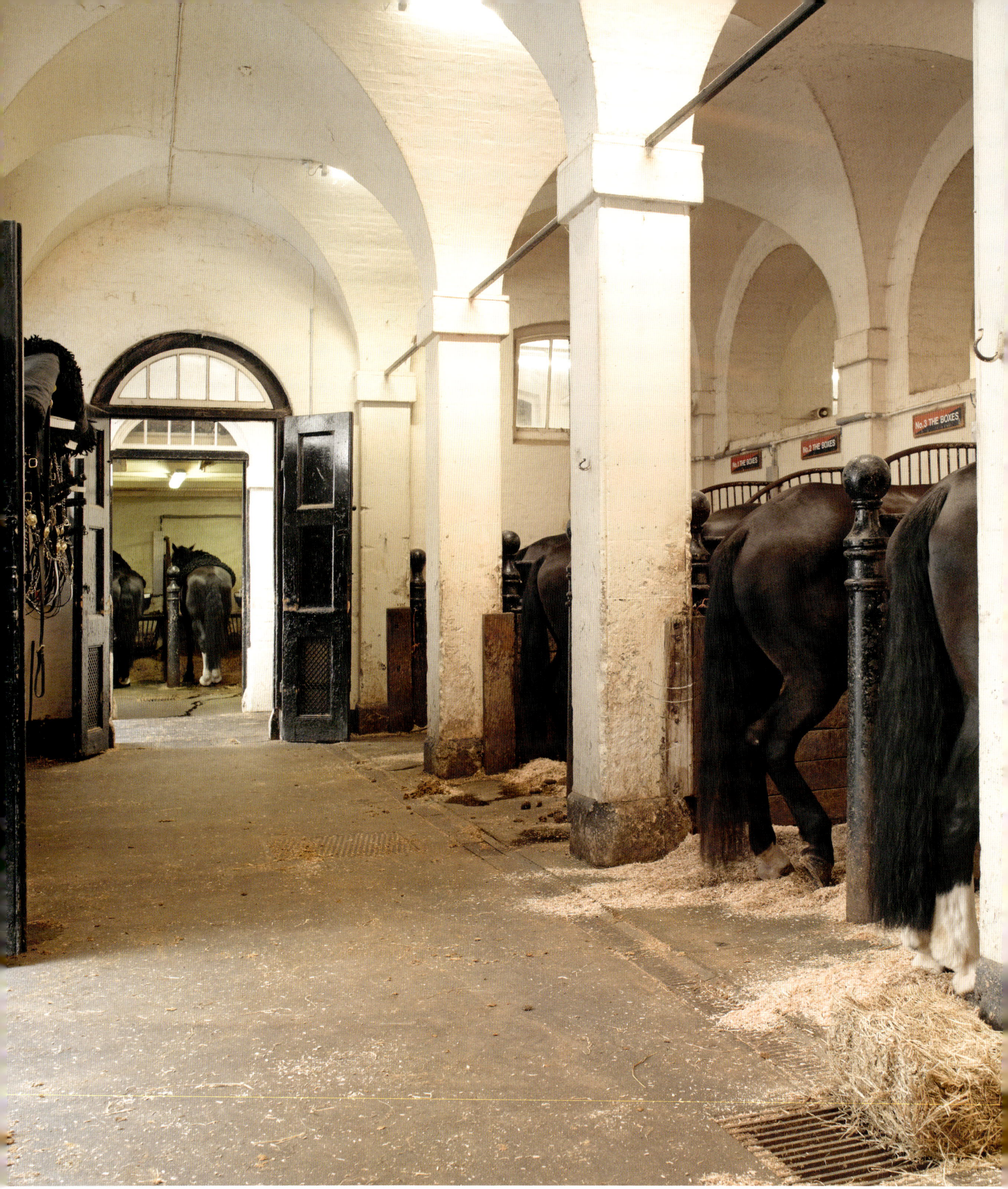
No.3 THE BOXES
No.2 THE BOXES

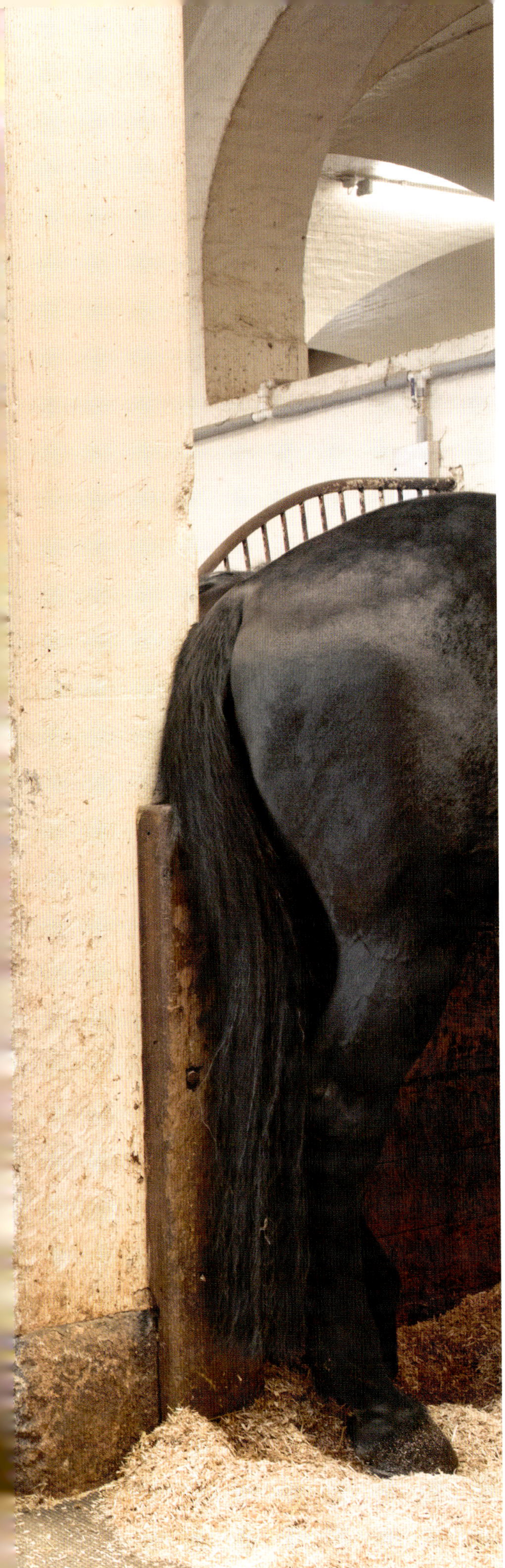

Horse Guards and Hyde Park Barracks

The stables of the Queen's Life Guard at Horse Guards.

The Household Cavalry Mounted Regiment, assigned to protect the Sovereign, can be seen at two places in London. Hyde Park Barracks are on the southern side of the park, about a mile from Buckingham Palace. The other location is Horse Guards, which is a building rather than an organization, facing Whitehall and closer to the Palace.

The bases and barracks of the British Army have always been easier to describe than its regiments and roles. In 1990, following the Army's endless tradition of amalgamation, the Life Guards (LG) and the Blues and Royals (RHG/D) became the Household Cavalry (HCav).

The Household Cavalry is itself made up of the Household Cavalry Regiment (HCR) and the Household Cavalry Mounted Regiment (HCMR).

Despite amalgamation, each regiment has been allowed to retain its separate identity, regimental headquarters, uniforms and accoutrements. The Life Guards, the senior regiment in the British Army, with a Royalist history, has amassed battle honours from Waterloo to Basra. The Blues and Royals, formed in 1969 by a merger of the Royal Horse Guards (Blues) and the Royal Dragoons (1st Dragoons), can trace their lineage back to the New Model Army; battle honours span the Peninsular War, Balaclava and the Falklands.

Horse Guards, where the permanent protection for the King is positioned, is a Palladian-style Grade I listed building between Whitehall and Horse Guards Parade. The current structure was built between 1751 and 1753 on the site of the former tiltyard (jousting courtyard) of the Palace of Westminster. A strange feature is the double-sided clock high over the archway, with two o'clock on its face marked with a black disc, said to commemorate the hour of execution of King Charles I in 1649 at the Banqueting House opposite.

Most of the ground floor here consists of stables that can accommodate 108 horses in restricted movement stalls, each with a feed-rack. The 'Cavalry Blacks' – traditional crossbreeds of the Irish draught and thoroughbred – are predominantly black touched with white markings. Other breeds include greys for trumpeters, all-black officers' chargers and drum horses. These are usually shires and Clydesdales, which can stand as high as nineteen hands, and are selected and trained to carry heavy solid silver kettledrums.

Guard is provided on alternate days by the Life Guards and the Blues and Royals. Two dismounted sentries are on duty until the gates are shut at 2000 hours, after which just one sentry remains until 0700 hours; once the gates are closed, no one, unless in possession of the password, can gain admission to Horse Guards. A guard changing ceremony – properly called Guard Mounting – is a daily event held at 1100 hours and 1000 hours on Sundays, lasting for thirty minutes.

The HCMR's main base is Hyde Park Barracks, formerly known as Knightsbridge Barracks, a name frequently still used. Barracks have existed on the site since 1795, but the current modern buildings were designed by architect Basil Spence and date from 1970. An accommodation tower block, called Peninsular Tower, controversial in its time, dominates. The barracks has its own a smithy and almost 300 horses are maintained in extensive stables on two levels, with ramps electrically wired to de-ice the surfaces.

The Dress Store at Hyde Park is filled with a range of military clothing. A drum major's state dress for the Sovereign's birthday parade (Trooping the Colour) includes a gold and embroidered tunic, the design of which dates from the Restoration, as do dark blue velvet jockey hats for musicians. Solid silver drums, weighing 66 lb (30 kg) apiece, are carried by the drum horses, traditionally named after Greek mythological heroes. Life Guards wear their chinstraps beneath the lower lip, while Blues and Royals wear straps beneath the chin. A holder on a helmet's pinnacle supports a faux horsehair plume: white plumes for Life Guards and scarlet for Blues and Royals. Tunic colours are red for the Life Guards and blue for the Blues and Royals. A polished steel breast and back plate called a cuirass is worn for mounted duty.

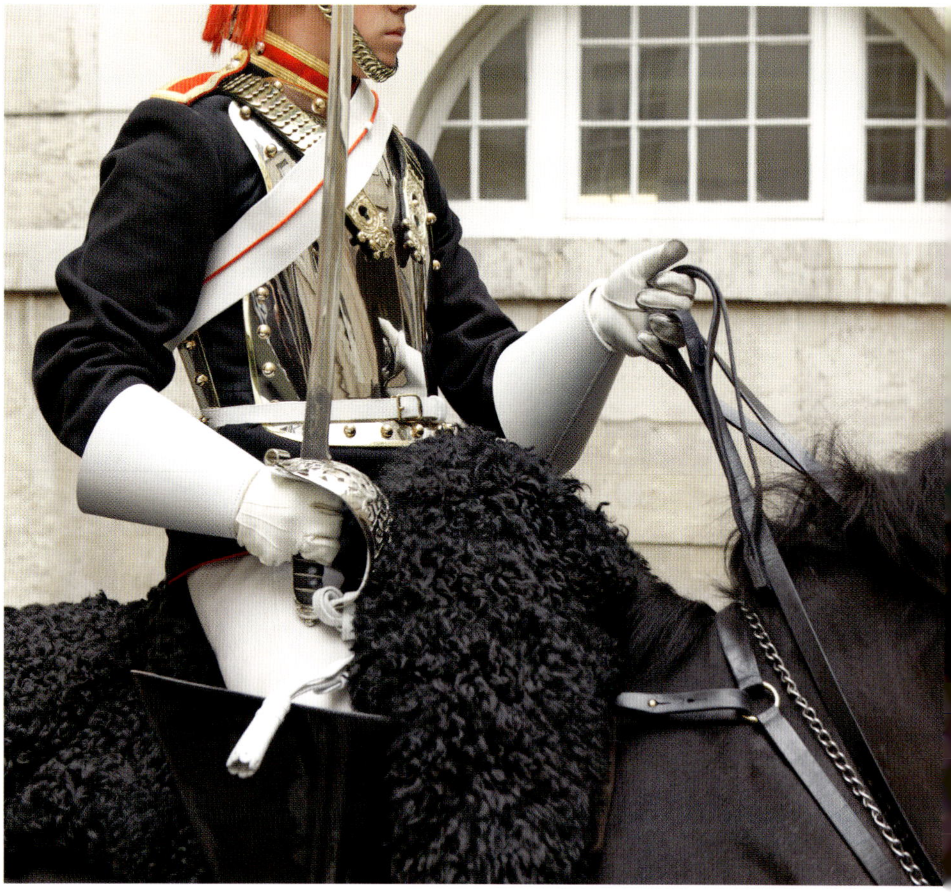

Above A Blues and Royals mounted guard at Horse Guards.

Opposite The forge at Hyde Park Barracks.

In July 1982, members of the Provisional IRA detonated a large nail bomb during a Changing of the Guard procession from Hyde Park Barracks to Buckingham Palace. Three Blues and Royals soldiers were killed outright, with a fourth dying within three days from his injuries. Other troopers sustained serious injuries, as did several spectators who were peppered with shrapnel, while seven horses were killed or subsequently put down because of injuries. When passing the site of the bombing, soldiers bring their swords down from slope to carry, combined with an eyes left or an eyes right, as a sign of respect.

CONTACT INFORMATION

Horse Guards,
Whitehall, SW1A 2AX
https://www.royalparks.org.uk/visit/parks/st-jamess-park/horse-guards-parade
Hyde Park Barracks,
20A Knightsbridge, SW7 1SE
https://www.army.mod.uk/learn-and-explore/about-the-army/corps-regiments-and-units/royal-armoured-corps/household-cavalry-regiment/

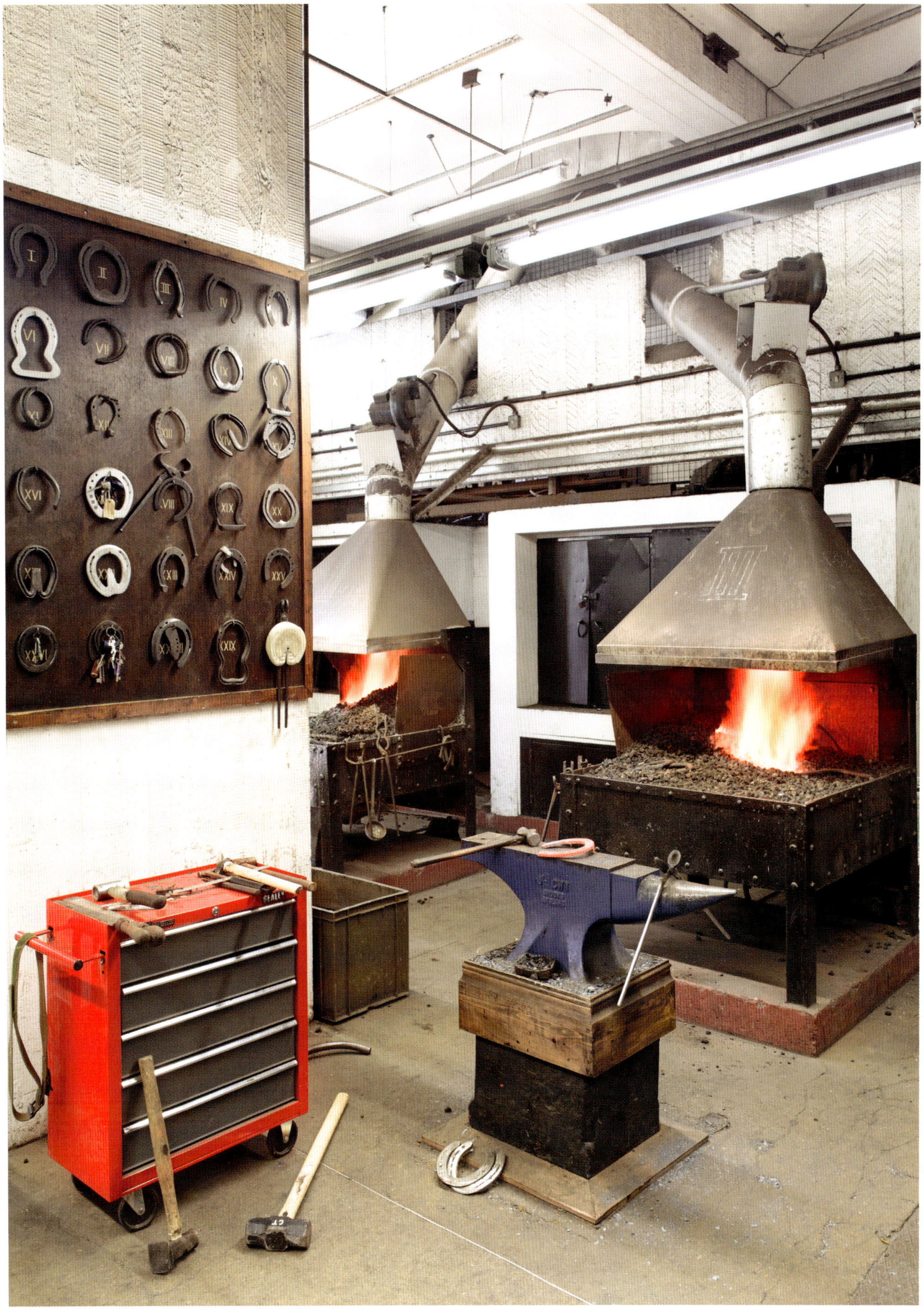

Westminster Cathedral

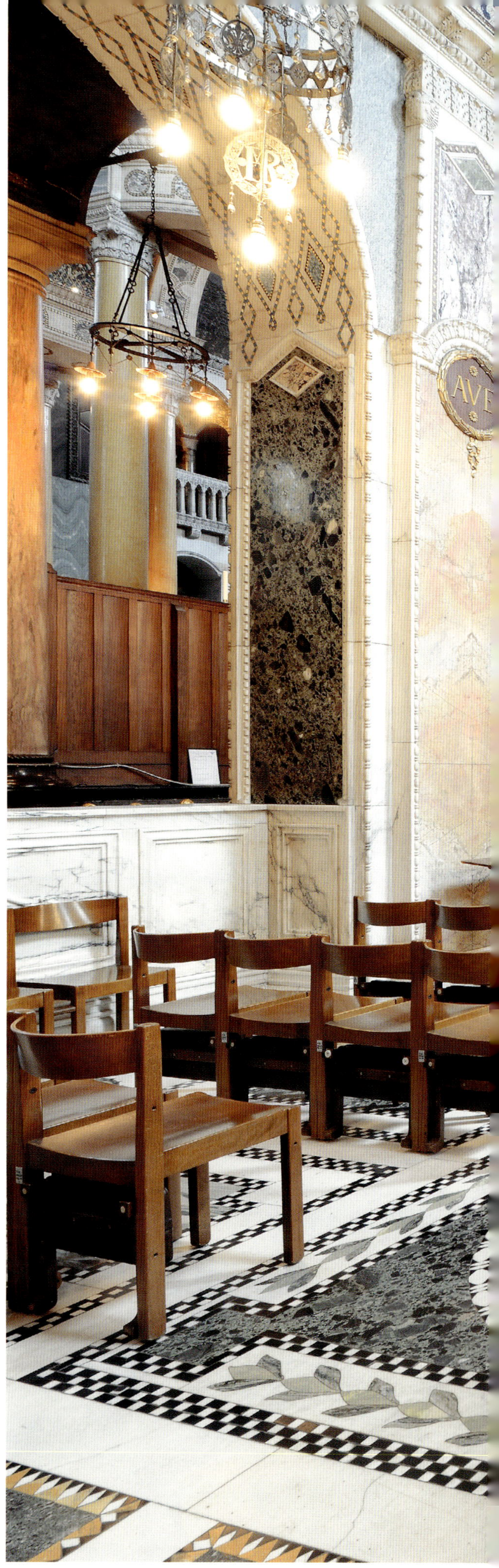

The Lady Chapel walls are clad in marble and the altar reredos is a mosaic of the Virgin and Child.

Westminster Cathedral's horizontal bands of red brick and white Portland stone are its visual signature and part of its neo-Byzantine architectural style. Its lofty campanile tower and long and tall continuous nave caused a great stir on completion in 1903.

The cathedral came to be built that way because of a particular set of requirements that emerged following the restoration of the Roman Catholic hierarchy in England and Wales in 1850. A cathedral was needed in London. Forty years of ambitious plans and ideas followed, and a massive gothic cathedral was schemed on a site close to Victoria station, but never started. In 1892, the third Archbishop of Westminster Cardinal Herbert Vaughan was installed, and he knew that a neo-gothic cathedral crafted from stone by masons would take decades to build. At the same time it was important that a new cathedral did not appear to rival Westminster Abbey in its appearance. There was also a need to build a proper congregational church, putting the sight and sound of the mass in front a large number of worshippers.

Cardinal Vaughan appointed architect John Francis Bentley and worked closely with him. There had been a revival in interest in Byzantine arts, and basilica churches in Italy were studied. The chosen design was a space without a crossing or transepts and – most importantly – it would be made in brick, like the great buildings of Constantinople. Practical

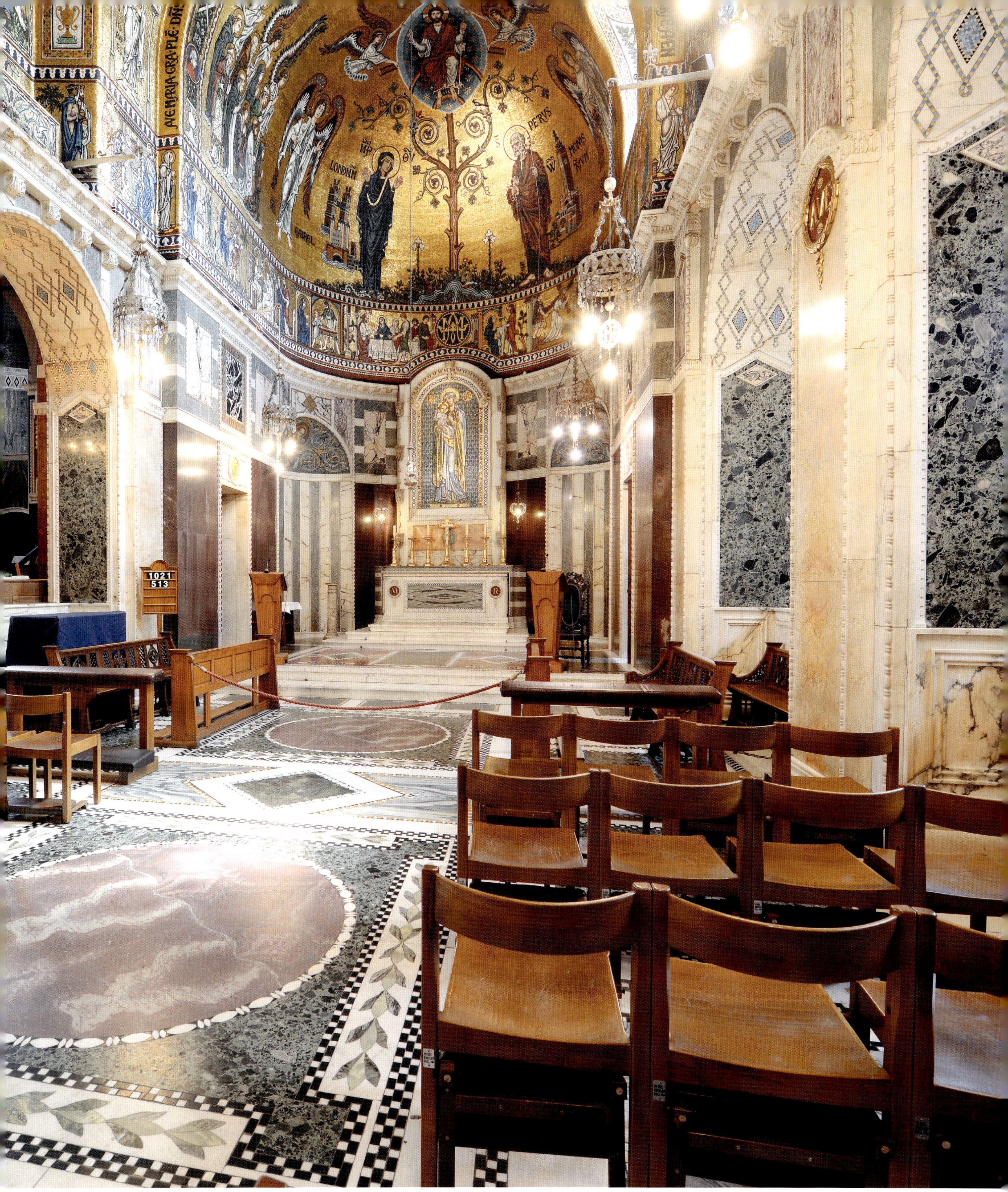

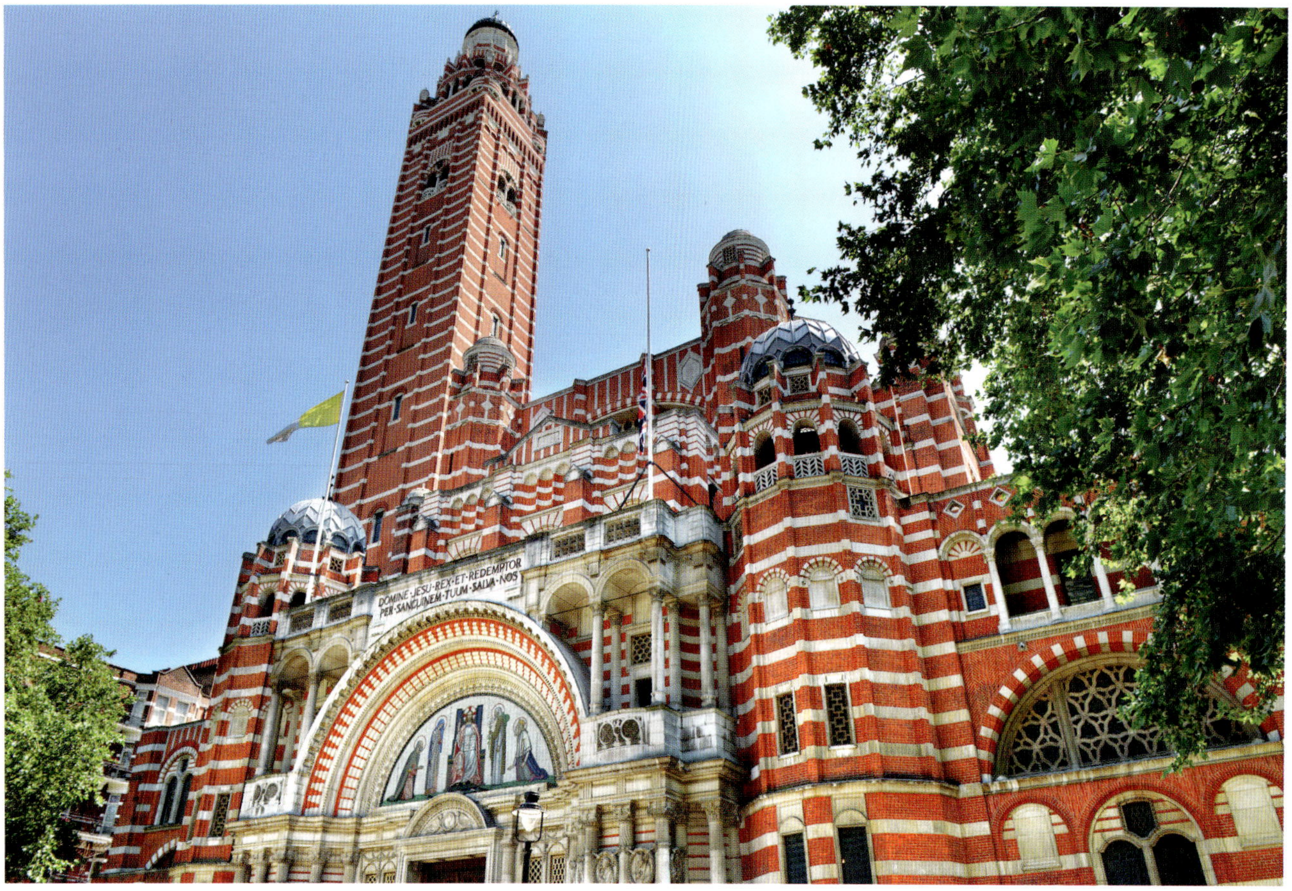
DOMINE·JESU·REX·ET·REDEMPTOR
PER·SANGUINEM·TUUM·SALVA·NOS

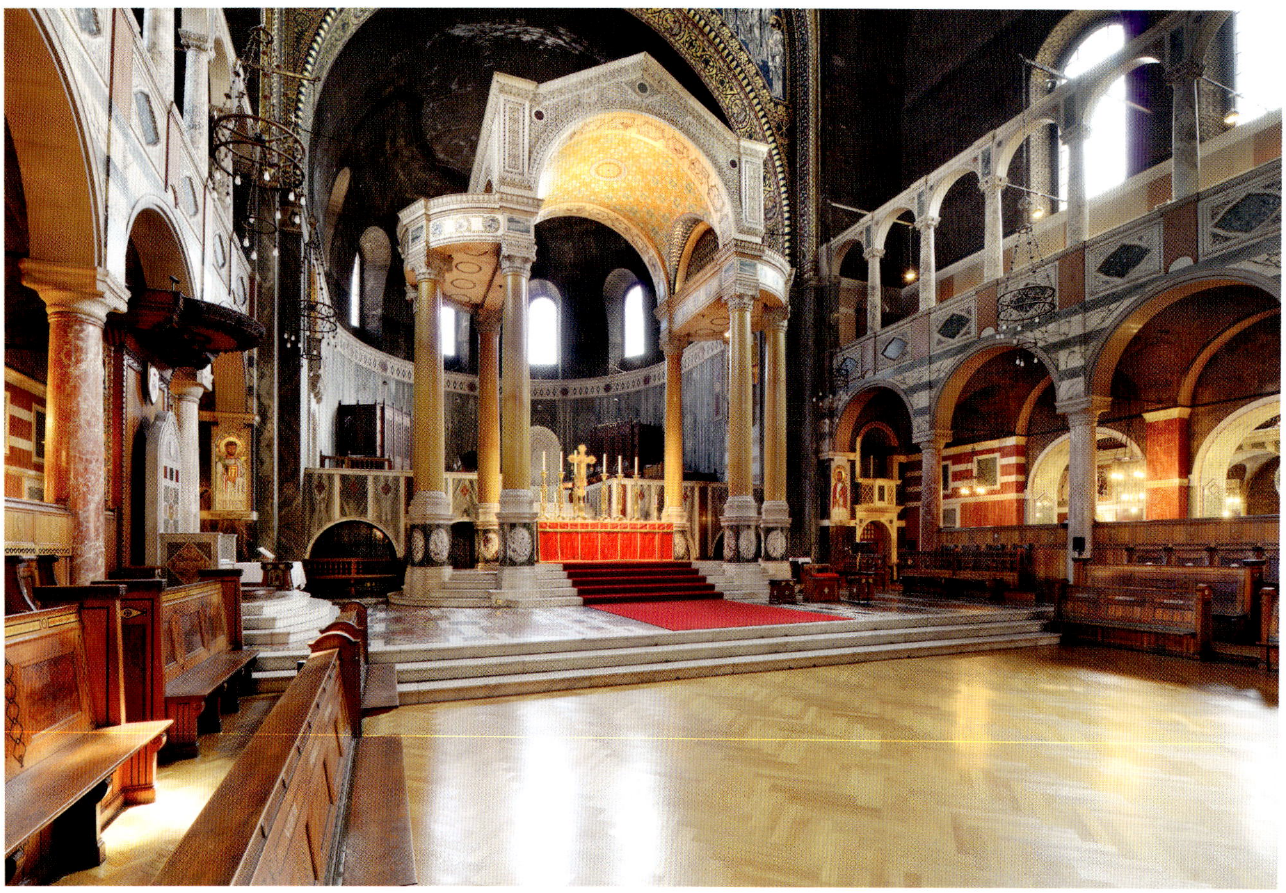

The chosen design was a space without a crossing or transepts and – most importantly – it would be made in brick.

Opposite, above
The Cathedral comprises almost twelve and a half million bricks from tower top to foundation.

Opposite, below
The high altar covered by its canopy. Rough brickwork remains visible in the vaulted ceiling above.

and spiritual, this design would enable swift construction and interior decoration could be completed later.

Building spanned the turn of the centuries, but was quickly accomplished between 1895 and 1903. Saucer domes of brick and concrete – three over the nave and one over the sanctuary – comprised the roof. Construction elsewhere was of non-reinforced load-bearing bricks throughout, with just a small number of iron ties. A little under twelve and a half million bricks were used in its construction, including Staffordshire blue engineering bricks, mostly hidden in the foundation, orange-red facing Bracknell bricks for the exterior and London Stock bricks for the internal lining of the building. It is the London stock that makes the deepest impression on many visitors today, because thousands of those bricks remain visible inside on the ceilings and arches, left rough for mosaics that have yet to be applied, testimony to the unfinished state of Westminster Cathedral. The gloomy brick-vaulted areas over lavish marble lower walls have become part of its character. The marble wall panelling is generally complete throughout.

There is no pictorial stained glass anywhere in the cathedral. A distinctive feature is the baldachin, which is the canopy over the altar: a massive structure supported by columns of yellow marble.

To the sides of the nave and sanctuary are eleven chapels, each different in character. An example is the Chapel of St George and the English Martyrs, with the floor bearing an English rose; and the rose motif is continued behind the altar and around the walls. On either side of the altar, the red cross of St George is displayed on marble shields. Panels list servicemen who gave their lives in battle. Above the altar is the last carving by Eric Gill, portraying Christ on the cross. To his left is St Thomas More, Lord Chancellor of England; to his right, St John Fisher, Bishop of Rochester, both executed for their refusal to deny the Supremacy of the Pope under Henry VIII. The marble floors and walls here were completed in 1931, and in recent years mosaics were applied to the upper walls and ceiling.

The Holy Souls Chapel is the only one to be completely designed by the cathedral architect John Francis Bentley himself. Every detail of the marblework and the grille was drawn by him and the mosaic decoration was executed by an artist before the cathedral was consecrated. Otherwise, the architect, who died in 1902, left no finished mosaics in the cathedral and very little in the way of drawings and designs. Subsequent architects and designers, supervised from 1936 by the Cathedral Art Committee, have decided on the mosaics and other areas of decoration, which have been the subject of controversy on several occasions, with work stopping and starting, generating letters to *The Times* about style and value and changes of plans.

The building is visually well-integrated with its surroundings, and several blocks of late Victorian and Edwardian mansion flats nearby have banded red brick and white stones façades in a style sometimes called Victorian Romanesque. These were built on land sold by the church when the cathedral was being developed.

Westminster Roman Catholic Cathedral is the mother church of that faith in England and Wales, and its largest place of worship.

CONTACT INFORMATION

Westminster Cathedral,
42 Francis Street, SW1P 1QW
https://westminstercathedral.org.uk/

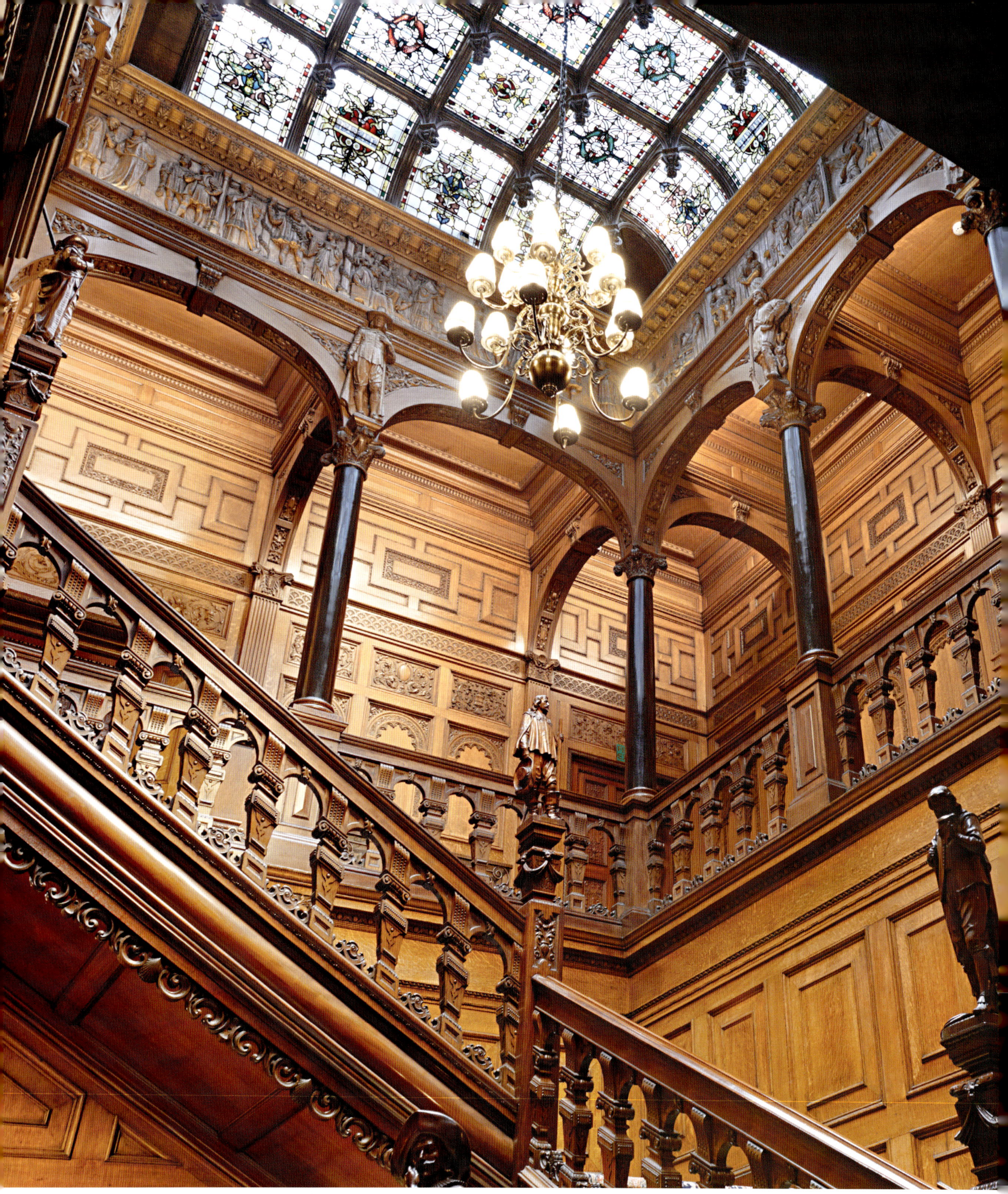

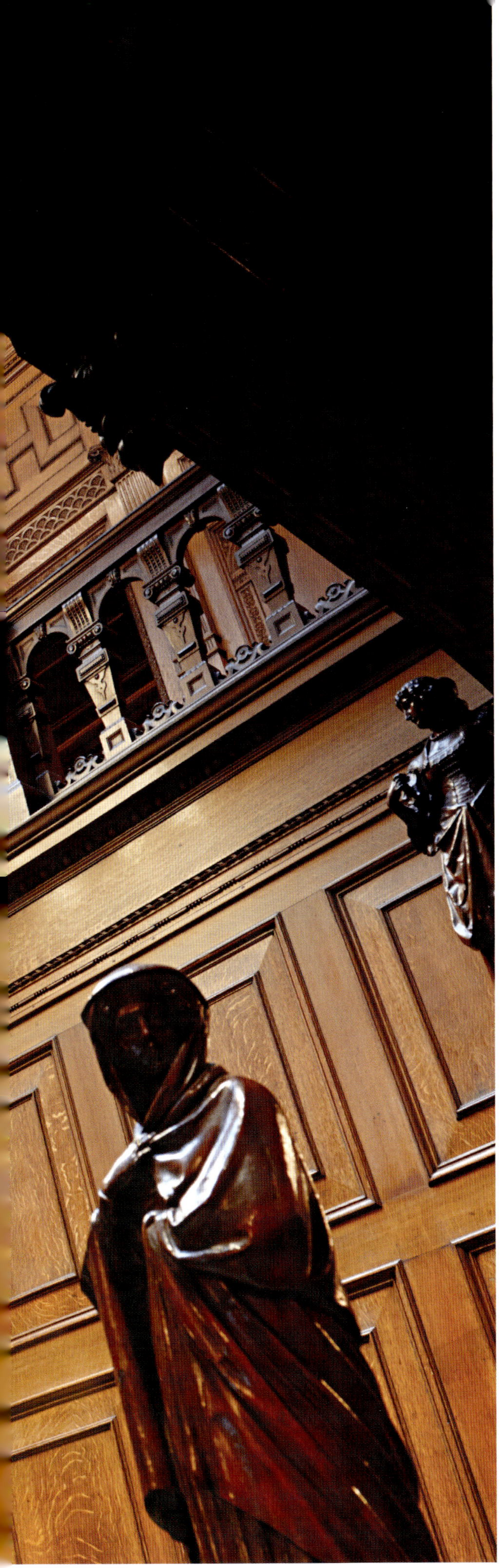

Two Temple Place

Staircase Hall, with its solid ebony columns, carved frieze and skylight. D'Artagnan looks across to Madame Constance Bonacieux, Milady de Winter, Aramis and Athos, with Porthos above.

For more than a hundred years the building at No. 2 Temple Place was noted only for what could be seen on the outside: on the roof, an elegant oversized copper weathervane in the shape of fifteenth-century ship and, flanking the entrance, lamp-pillars bearing statues of cherubs talking on a telephone.

The picturesque exterior always hinted the building was not an old historic artefact, and when this Tudor mansion in miniature was opened to visitors for the first time in 2011 an indulgent late-Victorian fantasy was revealed. Two Temple Place has an extraordinary interior. Its panelled rooms are embellished with romantic decorative details reflecting the interests and tastes of the man who commissioned it, William Waldorf Astor.

Astor had settled with his family in England in 1891, disenchanted with his native New York. The building was designed as the Astor Estate Office, the headquarters of a real estate and financial empire for the richest man in the world. It was completed between 1893 and 1895. Astor's other properties included a London home at Carlton House Terrace, the country house Cliveden in Buckinghamshire, and later Hever Castle in Kent, but the estate office was his most favoured home for much of his life. Although the Astor family did not live there, there was a small bedroom for William Waldorf's personal use.

It is impossible to identify a single theme or style to the interior, although characters from literature inform and inhabit much of the decorative detail. Astor's

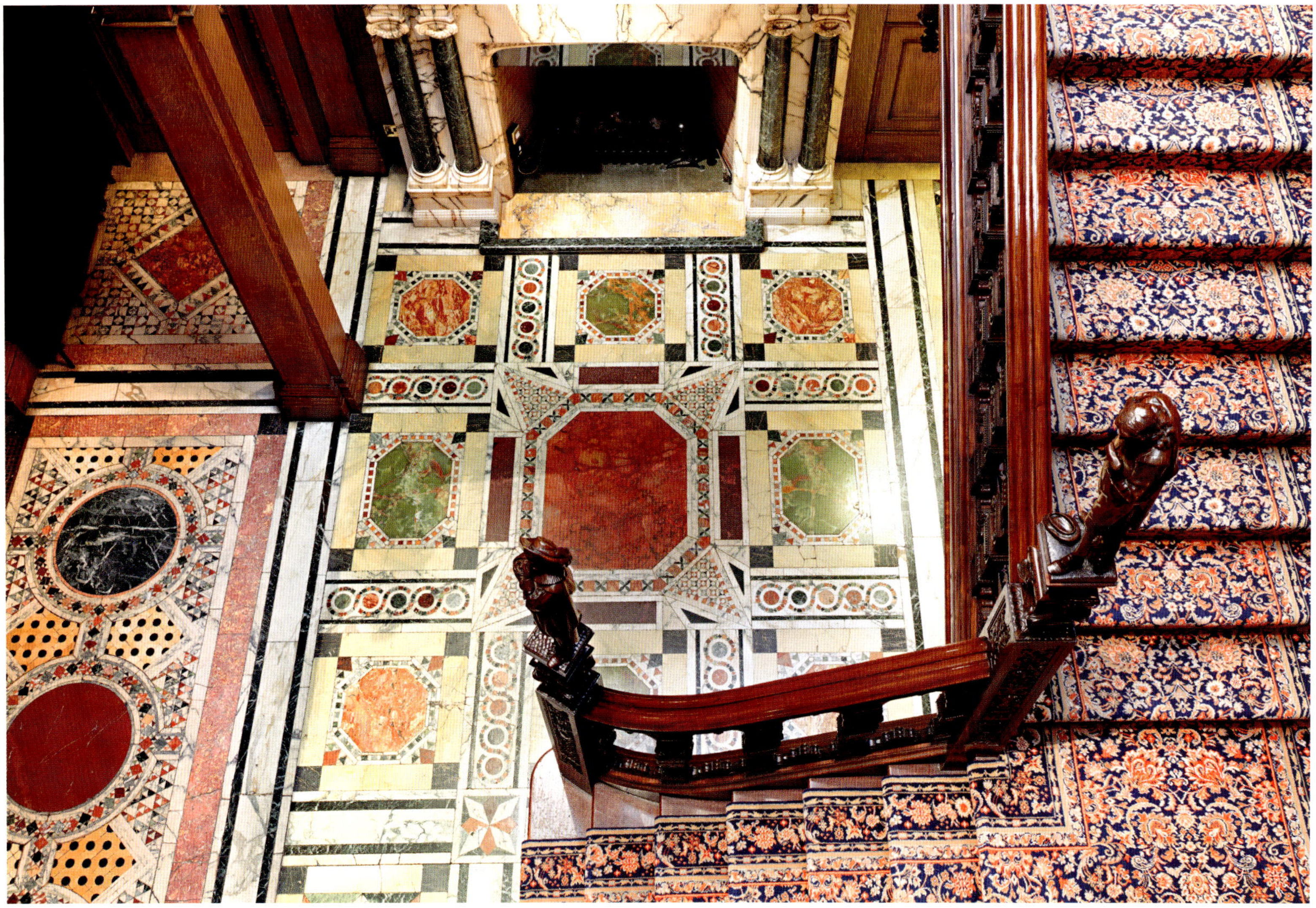

Characters from literature inform and inhabit much of the decorative detail.

favourite novel was *The Three Musketeers* by Alexandre Dumas and, inspired by this, the mahogany staircase carries statues of seven characters from the novel on the newel posts. Six further statuettes around the staircase gallery are of figures from American literature. Above these, ten solid ebony columns carry an oak frieze carved with eighty-two characters in scenes from Shakespeare's plays. Although the decorative subjects can be described as eccentric or illogical, the quality of materials and craftsmanship everywhere is to the highest standard.

The upper hall, with its hammer-beamed ceiling, was once Astor's office, and has a detailed frieze of fifty heads modelled in low relief, and figures from literature and history. The Lady of Shalott and Otto von Bismark are side by side, together with Voltaire, Machiavelli, Anne Boleyn and Christopher Columbus. The main doorway is panelled with bronzes of nine female figures from Arthurian legend. Stained-glass windows at each end depict sunrise and sunset, and seemingly a narrative from a nameless story.

Astor purchased a plot of land close to the recently established Victoria Embankment, once the factory of Gwynne & Co. pump makers, under the shadow of the towering Middle Temple library on the east side. There are only two floors and a basement, and most of the space was devoted to offices. Safety and security was a leading feature of the design, which included a large strongroom in the basement. The architect was John Loughborough

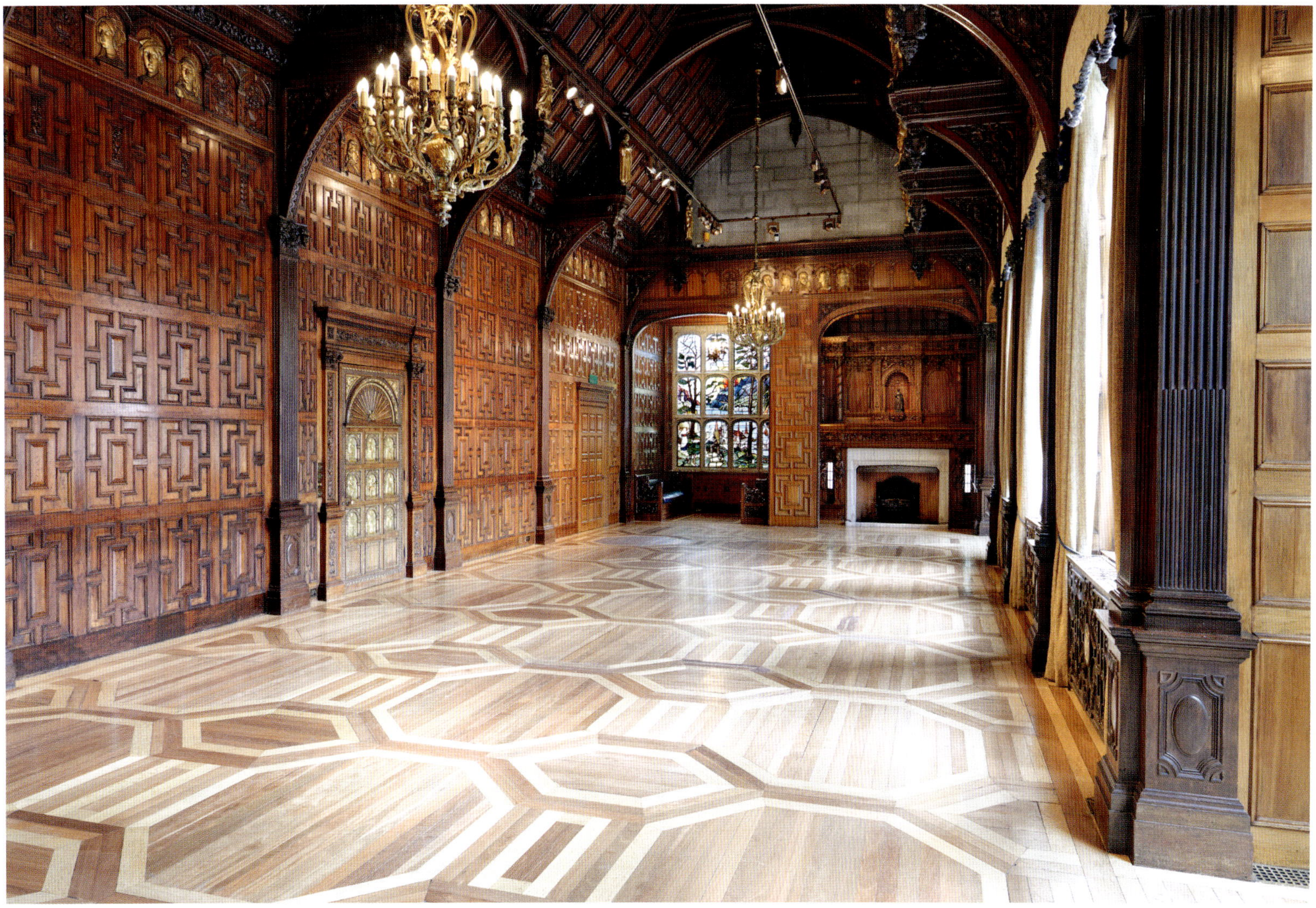

Opposite The floor is in inlaid multicoloured marble, in geometric patterns, inspired by Italian churches.

Above The Great Hall, once Astor's office, shows undecorated stonework at the ends and panelling in pencil cedar. The hammer-beam ceiling is Spanish mahogany.

Pearson, a leading Gothic Revivalist who had designed Truro Cathedral. The craftsmen and artists who worked on the decoration were selected by Pearson. Astor worked closely with Pearson, particularly on the detailing of the interior.

William Waldorf Astor was a cultured and complex man, at various times newspaper publisher, financier, real estate investor, hotelier, lawyer, diplomat and politician. After establishing the Astor family in England, and gaining a reputation as a benefactor and philanthropist, he sought honours and was made a peer in 1916.

The decoration of the Astor estate office is a celebration of the literature and history of the Old World, with a dash of the New World of the Americas, and a celebration of modern technology.

The building has changed hands only three times since the Astor family sold the property in 1922, each owner taking good care of the premises, although it was badly damaged in July 1944 by a flying bomb, which exploded on the neighbouring building to the west. The last commercial owner was the medical products company Smith & Nephew, who added a wing to the west, and gave it the name Two Temple Place. It was acquired by the charitable organization the Bulldog Trust in 1999. It operates as a headquarters and a gallery for the Bulldog Trust and is open to the public for annual winter exhibitions between January and April each year.

CONTACT INFORMATION

Two Temple Place, WC2R 3BD
https://twotempleplace.org/

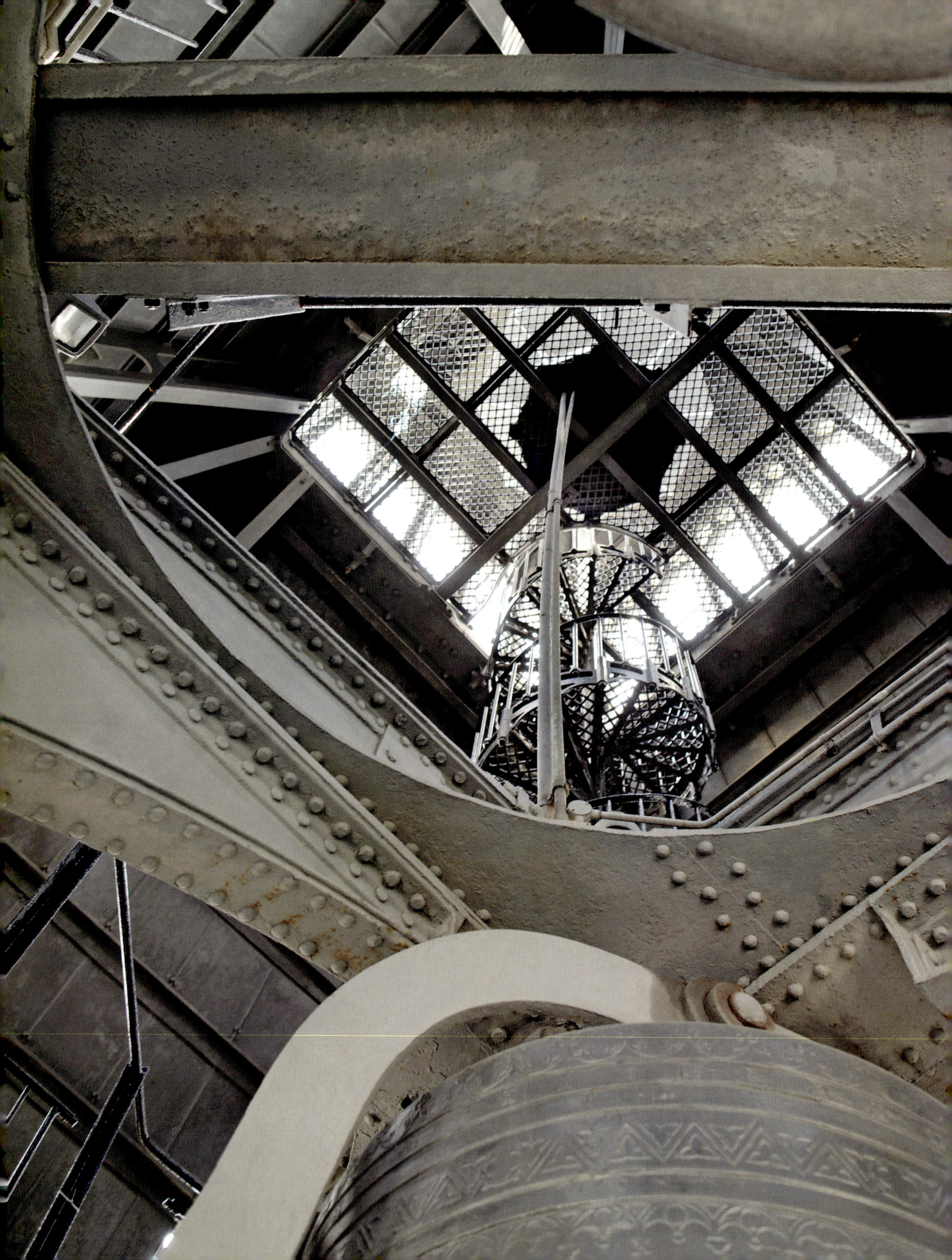

Big Ben

The top of the clock tower, housing the Ayrton Light, which is lit whenever Parliament meets after dark. The lantern is named after Thomas Ayrton, the first Commissioner of Works, who had the lamp installed.

Big Ben is probably the most photographed building in London. Almost all the tourists who come to the capital have the great clock tower of the Palace of Westminster firmly on their itinerary. This is partly because it is unique – there is really no other building in the world quite like it – but also because its huge clock and sonorous bells seem to embody the best of British engineering and accomplishment. Yet the story of the building suggests something different, and the familiar exterior conceals a complex and intriguing interior.

Big Ben is, strictly, not a building at all. The name refers not to the tower, but to the giant bell on which the clock strikes each hour, though the name long ago passed into common usage as a description of the whole structure – tower, clock and bells. It is thought to have acquired its sobriquet in reference to either Sir Benjamin Hall, the Chief Commissioner of Works in the 1850s, or Ben Caunt, a giant boxer of the period.

The tower of Big Ben stands 316 ft (96 m) high, and the staircase that winds up to the belfry has 334 steps, with a further fifty-nine to the lantern at the summit. The building, now officially known as the Elizabeth Tower, was begun in 1843, to designs by Sir Charles Barry, following a disastrous fire nine years earlier. Unusually for the period, the central core of the tower was erected first and the exterior added as the structure rose, but progress was slow and, when completed in 1859, the project was five years behind schedule. The centrepiece of the tower was to be a clock of unprecedented size and accuracy, and a competition was held for its design in 1846. The requirement was that the first strike of each hour should be accurate to within one second, and after five fruitless years a design was accepted from Edmund Beckett Denison, an MP with a strong amateur interest in horology, who was to become Lord Grimthorpe. The clock was constructed by E.J. Dent, a London firm more accustomed to manufacturing high-class pocket watches and chronometers for the Royal Navy. Grimthorpe's enormous clock has a pendulum 14 ft 5 in (4.4 m) in length and a mechanism 15½ ft (4.7 m) long, weighing around 5 tonnes. The clock was completed in 1854, but stood in Dent's workshops pending completion of the tower and was not installed until 1859.

The clock controls five bells, four to strike the quarter hours and mighty Big Ben itself. The current bell is the second, a replacement for the original which, to continue the theme of this troubled enterprise, cracked during testing in 1858. The 14-tonne monster was broken up and recast to a lighter, but slightly larger, specification. The new bell survived initial testing but proved too wide to be hauled directly up the tower. It was turned through 90 degrees and, over thirty torturous hours, winched into the belfry. Next, the hands on the four enormous dials proved too heavy and

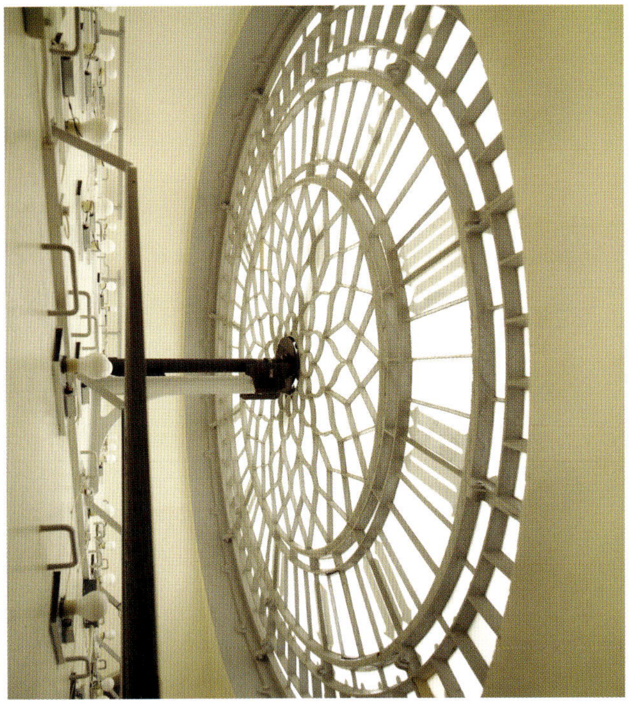

Left Inside the south clock face.

Right The winding mechanism that powers the clock, which uses old pennies as weights to regulate the time.

Far right The bell Big Ben, showing its crack and hole.

stopped the clock. The solution lay in hollow minute hands – which are 14 ft (4.2 m) long – made from copper. The clock was started in July 1859, but the drama continued two months later when Big Ben developed a crack, and was silent for four years. The crack was said to have been caused by the deployment of a hammer that was too heavy for the bell. It was repaired, but the crack is visible to this day, and audible in the bell's sonorous, slightly imperfect tone. The mechanism has belied its troubled gestation by performing with remarkable accuracy. It has undergone few modifications since 1859 and is still regulated by the use of old pre-decimal coinage, which is placed on the pendulum rod. The addition of a single old copper penny causes the clock to gain two-fifths of a second in twenty-four hours.

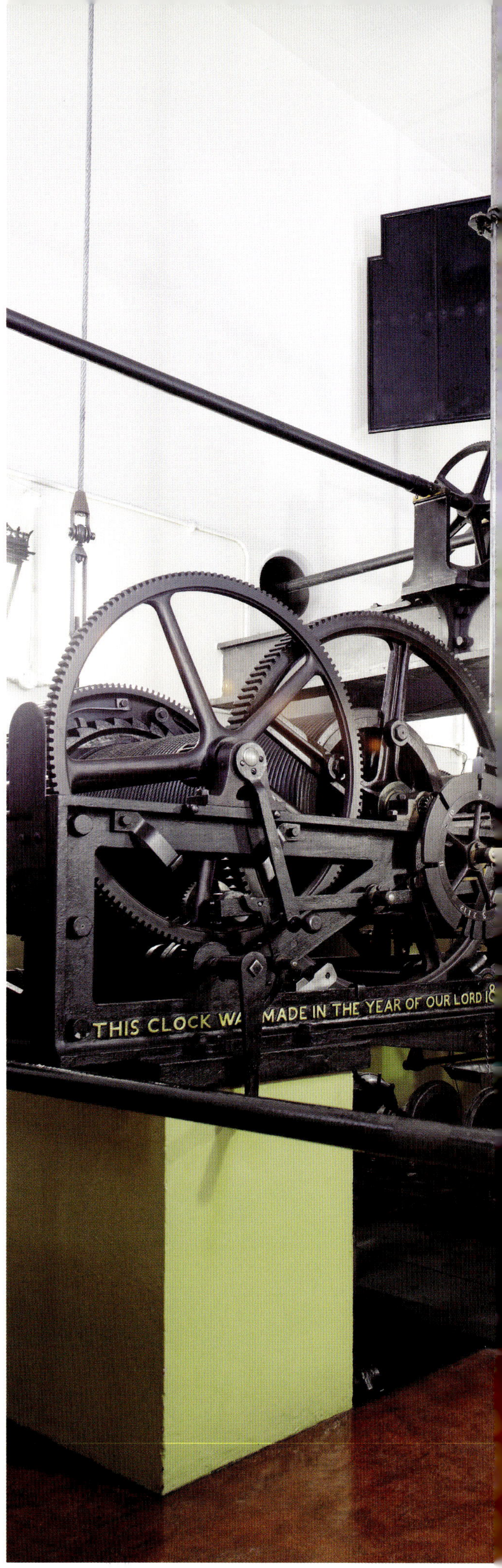

CONTACT INFORMATION

Big Ben,
Palace of Westminster, SW1A 0AA
https://www.parliament.uk/bigben/

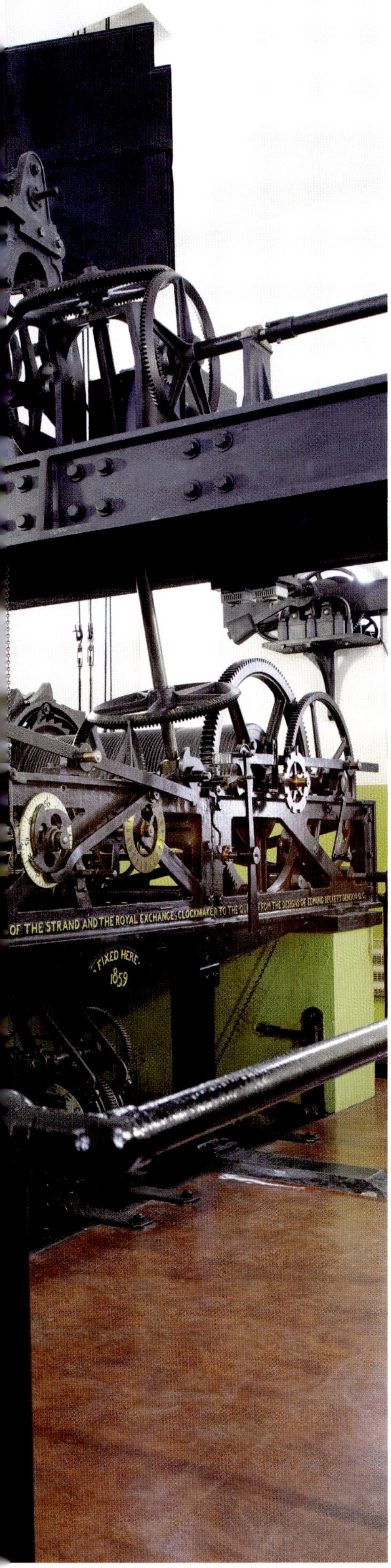
OF THE STRAND AND THE ROYAL EXCHANGE, CLOCKMAKER TO THE QU
FROM THE DESIGNS OF EDMUND BECKETT DENISON Q.C.
FIXED HERE 1859

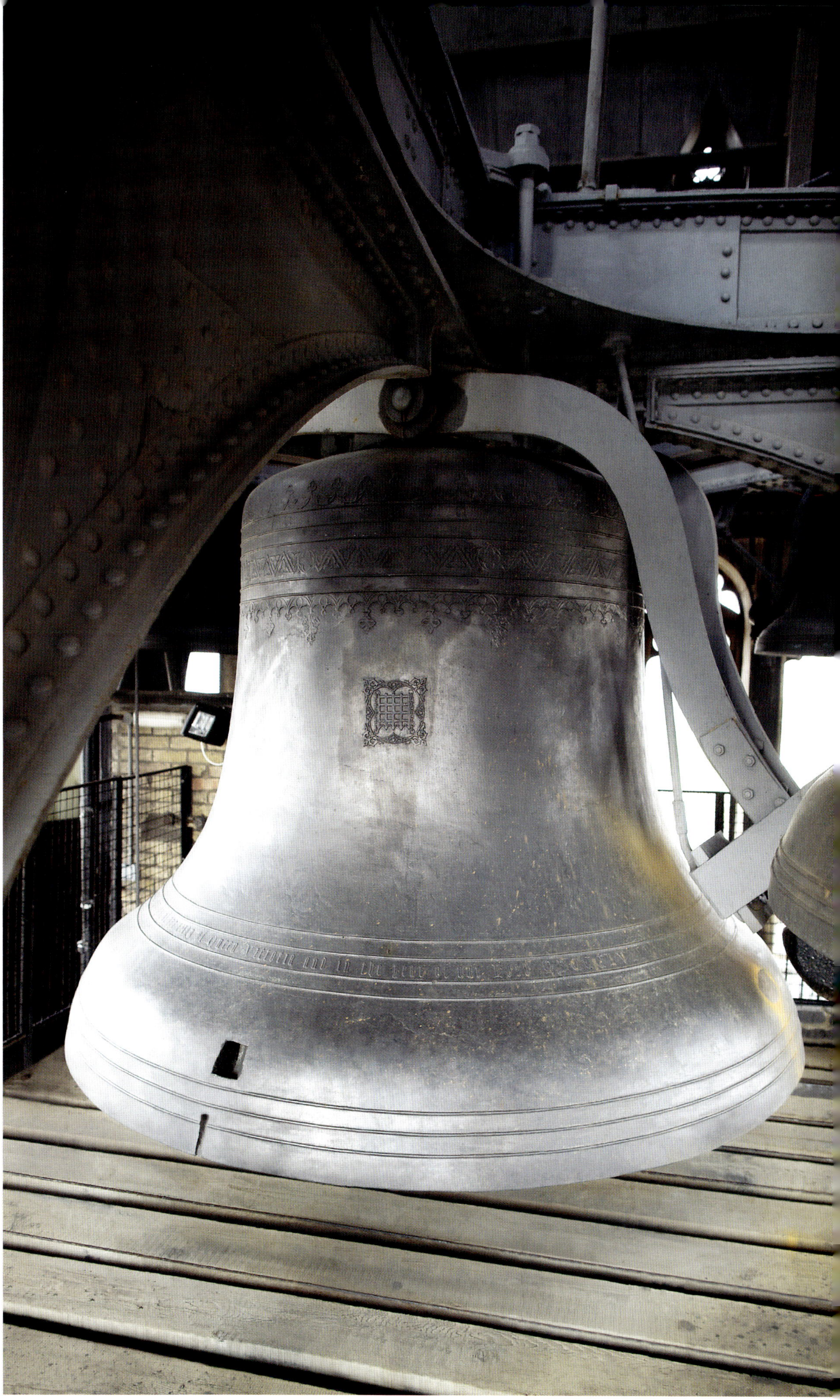

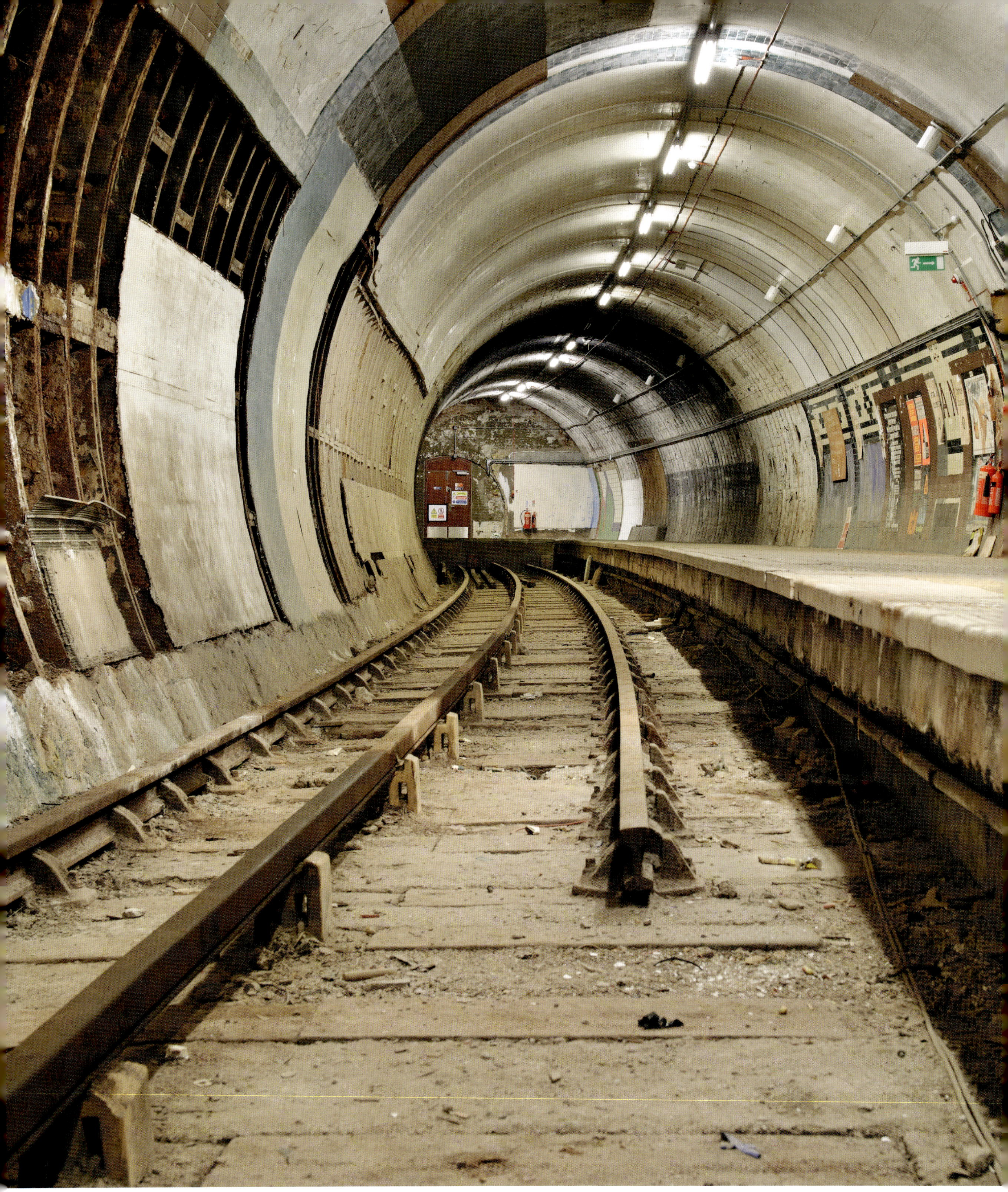

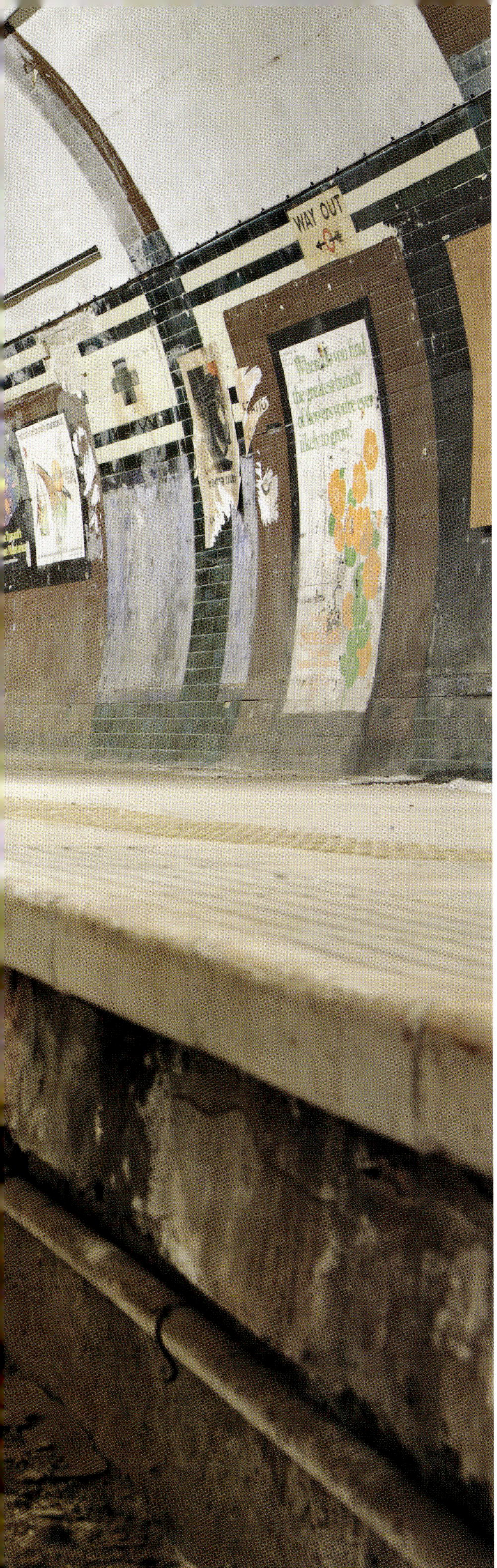

Aldwych Underground Station

Aldwych was always a dead-end, and part has been disused since 1917. Still intact, the lines on eastern Platform 2 run to a stop block, and the old Strand station name can still be detected on the wall, which has been used by London Transport for mock-ups of prospective designs. It is also used for terror attack drills and is the most popular Underground station for filming.

On one side of the station building the nameplate reads Aldwych and on the other side it says Strand, both denoting the same disused Underground station on a branch line going nowhere. Built on a route which once aimed at reaching Waterloo, Aldwych remained operational until as late as September 1994. As the most recent central London Tube station to be completely closed without replacement, Aldwych has not so far generated a great mythology, yet it is unique among the seventeen lost London Underground stations. It remains intact, with platforms and running rails in place and conductor rail electrified. Trains sometimes still run into and out of the station. Police officers, fire fighters and other unidentified gentlemen in civilian clothes frequently gather by the entrance in Surrey Street before moving discretely inside. Sometimes big trucks park close by, and heavy technical equipment is carried in. Aldwych station is closed, but clearly not dead.

Aldwych Tube occupies a peculiar position in every aspect, being a branch line terminus on a system that operationally favours through running from end to end, and sited fractionally off-centre for good business. It opened in 1907 on the south-eastern corner of London's Theatreland, at the time of a theatre-building boom. Across the road was the Gaiety Theatre, home of productions starring exotic Edwardian dancers, on the end of the newly built Aldwych crescent. When the station opened, the area was undergoing a massive improvement programme.

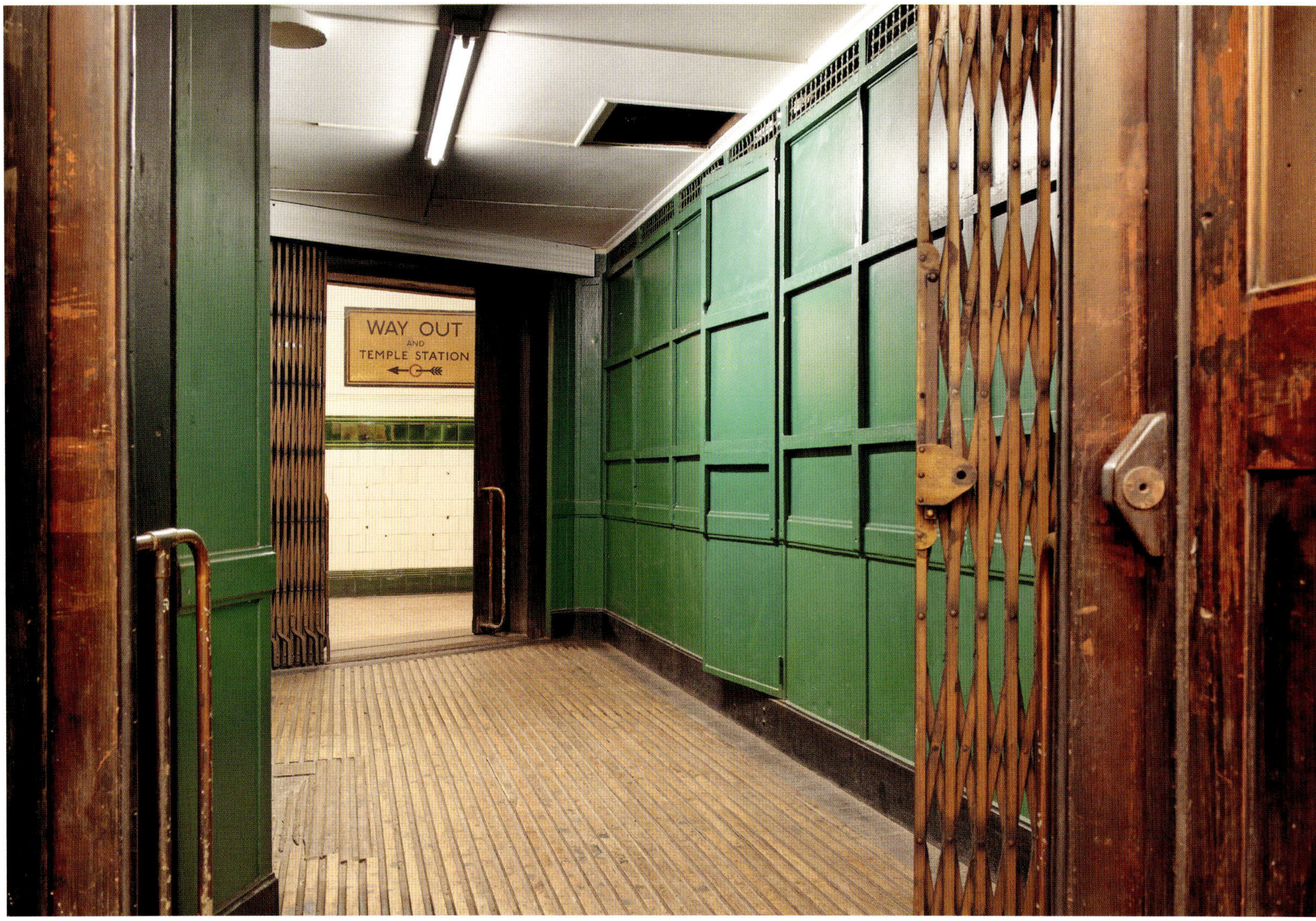

This was designed to relieve the hopeless congestion of horse-drawn, Victorian London, especially between St Mary-le-Strand and St Clement Danes churches. Widened roads, a tramway underpass at Kingsway and the station at Aldwych completed the modernization. The theatre boom lasted until the summer of 1914, the splendid high-water mark of Edwardian England.

Despite its position close to the heart of London, Aldwych station struggled to be viable from the start. While the West End teemed with office workers, tourists and theatre goers, the positioning of the station, then named Strand, was not ideal, and so long as it remained a spur it was always going to be tricky to operate trains back and forth to Holborn.

It was built at the end of an age when mass transit systems were still seen as potentially profitable businesses rather than merely a public service. American investment poured into many enterprises in Edwardian England, and the central sections of today's Bakerloo, Piccadilly and Northern lines remain as its legacy. Charles Tyson Yerkes, a buccaneering financier who had helped develop Chicago's streetcar system and was responsible for funding the Loop elevated railroad there, invested in a scheme to build an underground railway from Hammersmith to Finsbury Park.

This was the Great Northern, Piccadilly and Brompton Railway, and included in the plan was the possibility of an extension southwards from Holborn to Temple or under the Thames to Waterloo, but firstly to Aldwych. The company's corporate identity can be seen outside in the ruby-red glazed terracotta station exteriors, designed by architect Leslie Green, and in the Arts & Crafts tiling and detailing on the interiors. It is one of thirty stations designed by Green, most of which can be still seen, from Holloway Road to Gloucester Road, from Tufnell Park to Elephant &

Above One of the two surviving Otis electric lifts, non-operational, with access to the platforms now being by spiral staircase. At certain times tickets were issued from a booth in this lift.

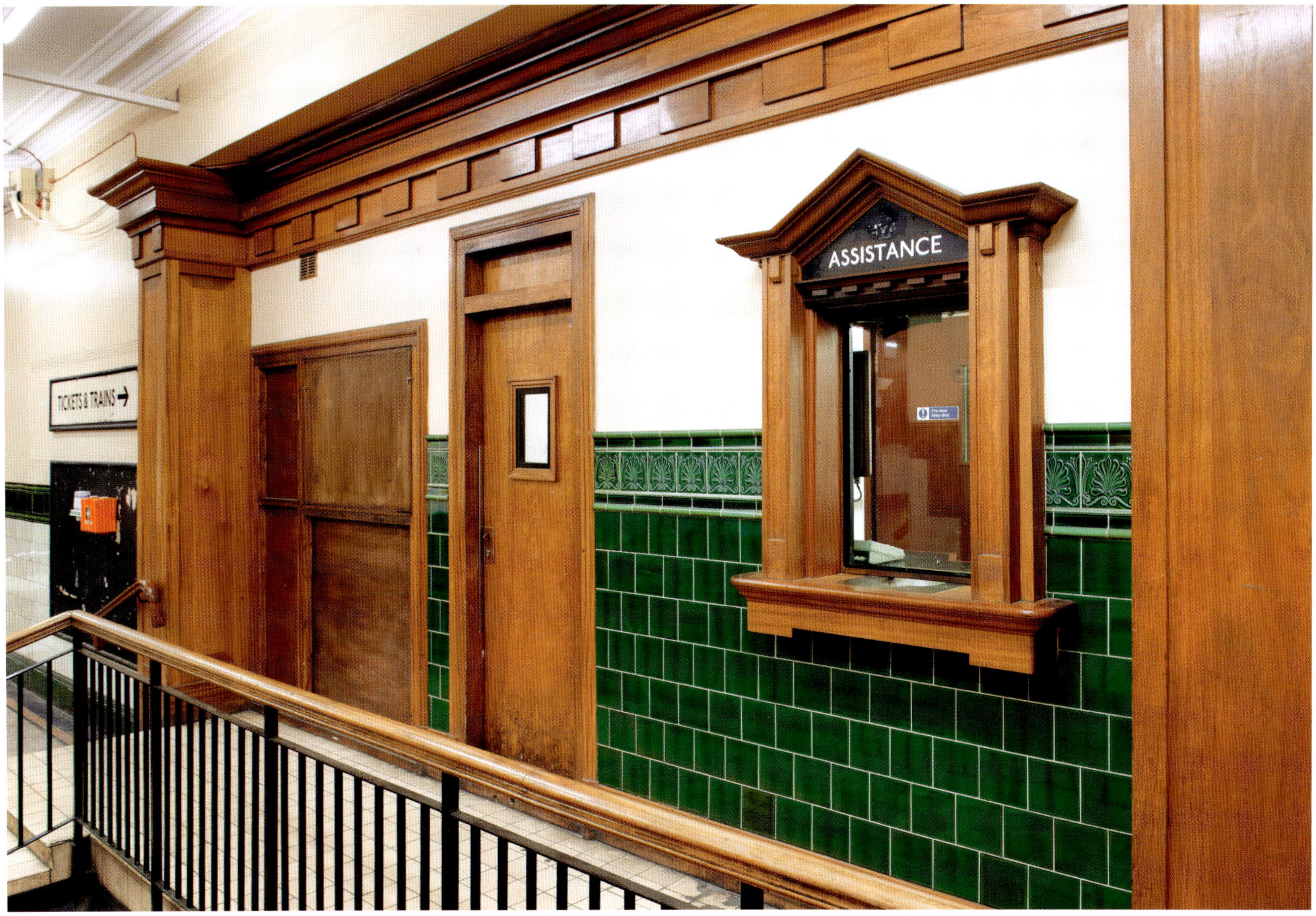

Above Cream interior decoration with green tiles was the house style of the Great Northern, Piccadilly and Brompton Railway.

Castle. The railway was soon amalgamated into the London Electric Railway, and came out of private ownership in 1933 with the formation of the London Passenger Transport Board. It was slated for closure in 1939, and did close during the war, when the station served as an air raid shelter, and one of its tunnels was used for housing national art treasures, including the 100 tons of the Parthenon Marbles. Reprieved and re-opened in 1946, a bid was made to extend the line to Waterloo in 1948 and again in 1965. But the station remained a lame duck in the transport system, and as few as 450 people a day were using the station during its last year of operation.

Today Aldwych station remains intact, with its two short platforms and two separate tunnels to Holborn, the eastern tunnel and platform having been disused since 1917. The booking office has been restored, and corporate events and theatrical productions have been staged in the station.

As for the equipment regularly seen shipped into Aldwych, it is one of London's most well used locations for television and feature films, which include *Atonement*, *The Krays* and *V for Vendetta*. The emergency services and other organizations regularly use the station for important training exercises. Trains are run in and out of the station for their benefit of emergency workers or filmmakers.

CONTACT INFORMATION

Aldwych Underground Station
Surrey Street, WC2R 2NE
https://www.ltmuseum.co.uk/whats-on/hidden-london/aldwych

St Christopher's Chapel

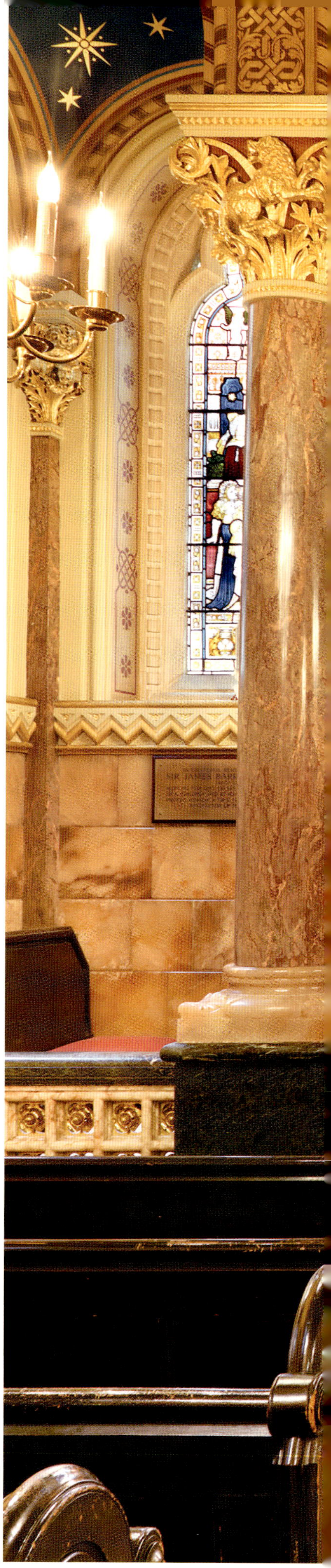

The small luminous chapel of St Christopher at Great Ormond Street Hospital is charming and poignant. The pews are scaled for children and themes of childhood can be traced throughout the chapel. There is a prayer tree where messages can be placed for sick children.

St Christopher's was built in 1875 in the popular neo-Byzantine style as Great Ormond Street gained a new central building by architect Edward Middleton Barry. The chapel was dedicated to the memory of his sister-in-law Caroline, whose husband made the donation which funded its construction. All the original decoration, not just the stained glass, is attributed to leading interior specialists Clayton & Bell.

When the chapel was restored, and reopened on 14 February 1994, it marked more than a revival of its alabaster, marble and glass. Following an operation that took two years to prepare and complete, the chapel was moved more than 60 ft (20 m) from where it had been built. Over time, Barry's monumental neo-gothic Victorian block presented increasing problems for the hospital, proving impossible to adapt for modern needs. There was a need to make a new clinical building on the spot. With the embedded chapel being Grade II* listed and a part of the Great Ormond Street legend, a radical solution was found. As the surrounding building was demolished, the chapel, then at first floor level, was cross-braced, underpinned by a concrete raft and enclosed in a sealed box. Lowered to the ground, it was moved by hydraulic rams on lubricated skates to its new position without harm.

The chapel is a very special place for patients, staff and families at the hospital and is therefore not open to the general public.

CONTACT INFORMATION

St Christopher's Chapel,
Great Ormond Street, WC1N 3JH
https://www.gosh.nhs.uk/patients-and-families/support-services/chaplaincy-and-spiritual-care/

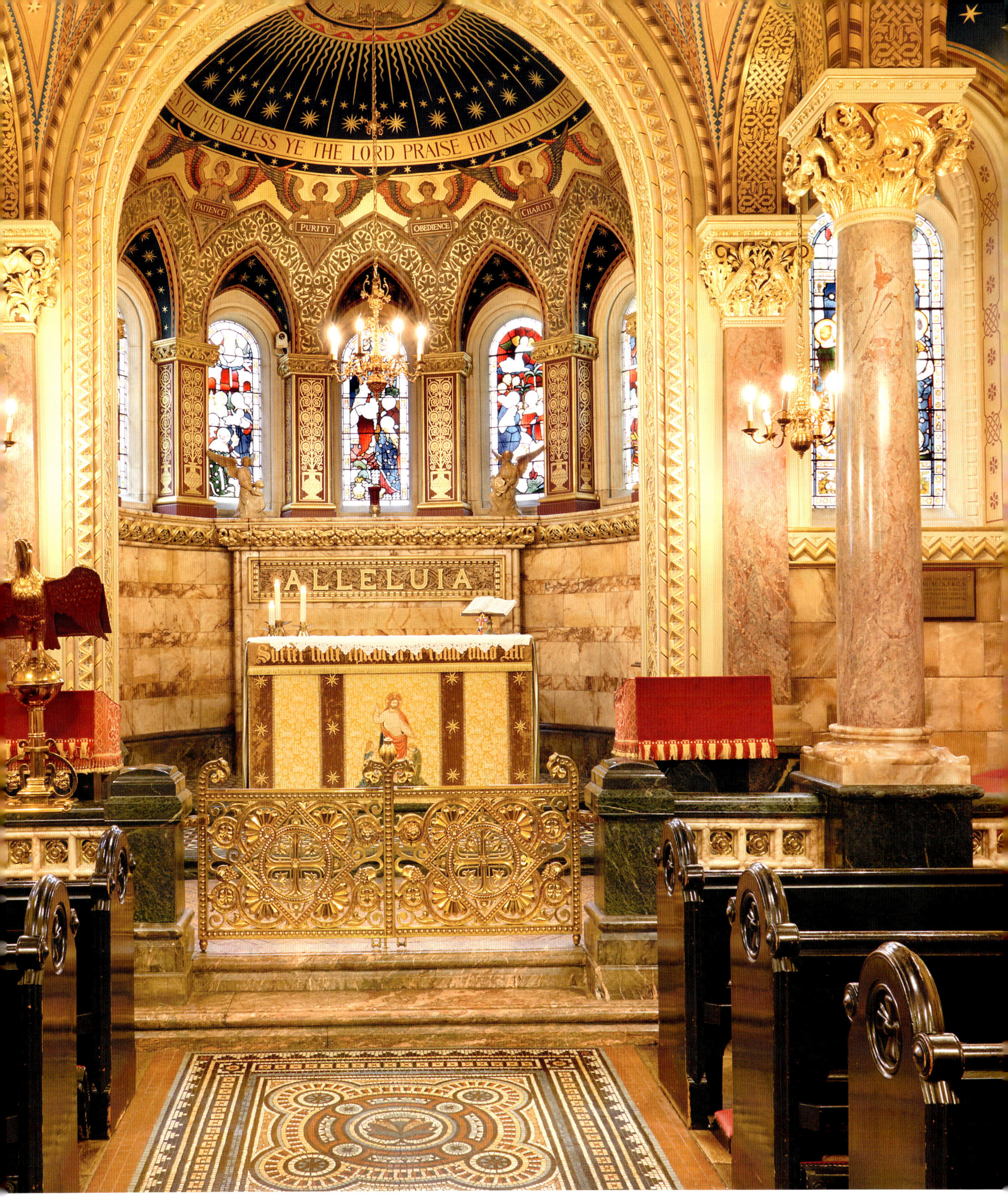
MEN BLESS YE THE LORD PRAISE HIM AND
PATIENCE
PURITY
OBEDIENCE
CHARITY
ALLELUIA

L. Cornelissen & Son

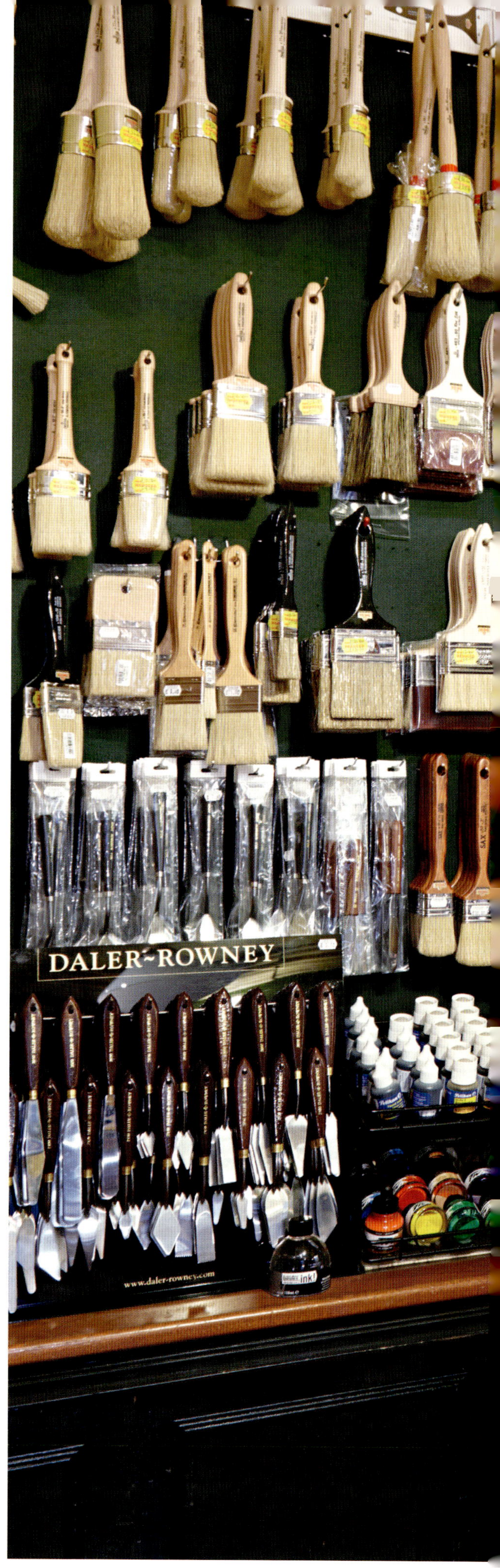

Sable, synthetic, signwriting... brushes of more than a hundred types are stocked.

L. Cornelissen & Son is a supplier of artists' materials on Great Russell Street, not far from the British Museum. The charm of the store is in the Victorian shop-fittings, which are exactly those created by the founders, and also in the range of specialist artists materials they contain; drawer after drawer is filled with pigments, brushes, prepared colour, gold leaf and printmaking equipment. It is possible to buy traditional quill pens made from goose and turkey feathers, cut by hand and cured in hot sand.

Cornelissen has been trading since 1855. The sign above the door states 'Artists' Colourmen', a description of those who blended pigments for painters from the eighteenth century onwards. Originally, the 'colourmen' bought pigments from an apothecary in order to grind and mix bespoke colours for individual artists. The colourmen developed into suppliers of ready-made colours off-the-shelf, firstly oil paints, then watercolours. By the middle of the eighteenth century many of the larger colourmen's shops offered a wider range of products, including brushes, paper and canvas.

Louis Cornelissen was a Belgian domiciled in Paris who, after the 1848 Revolution, left for England to set up shop in Covent Garden. His first line of business was supplying lithographic materials to printmakers and artists. Later, Cornelissen offered a full range of materials.

Coloumen marked their canvases and stretchers with individual stamps and labels, and it is possible

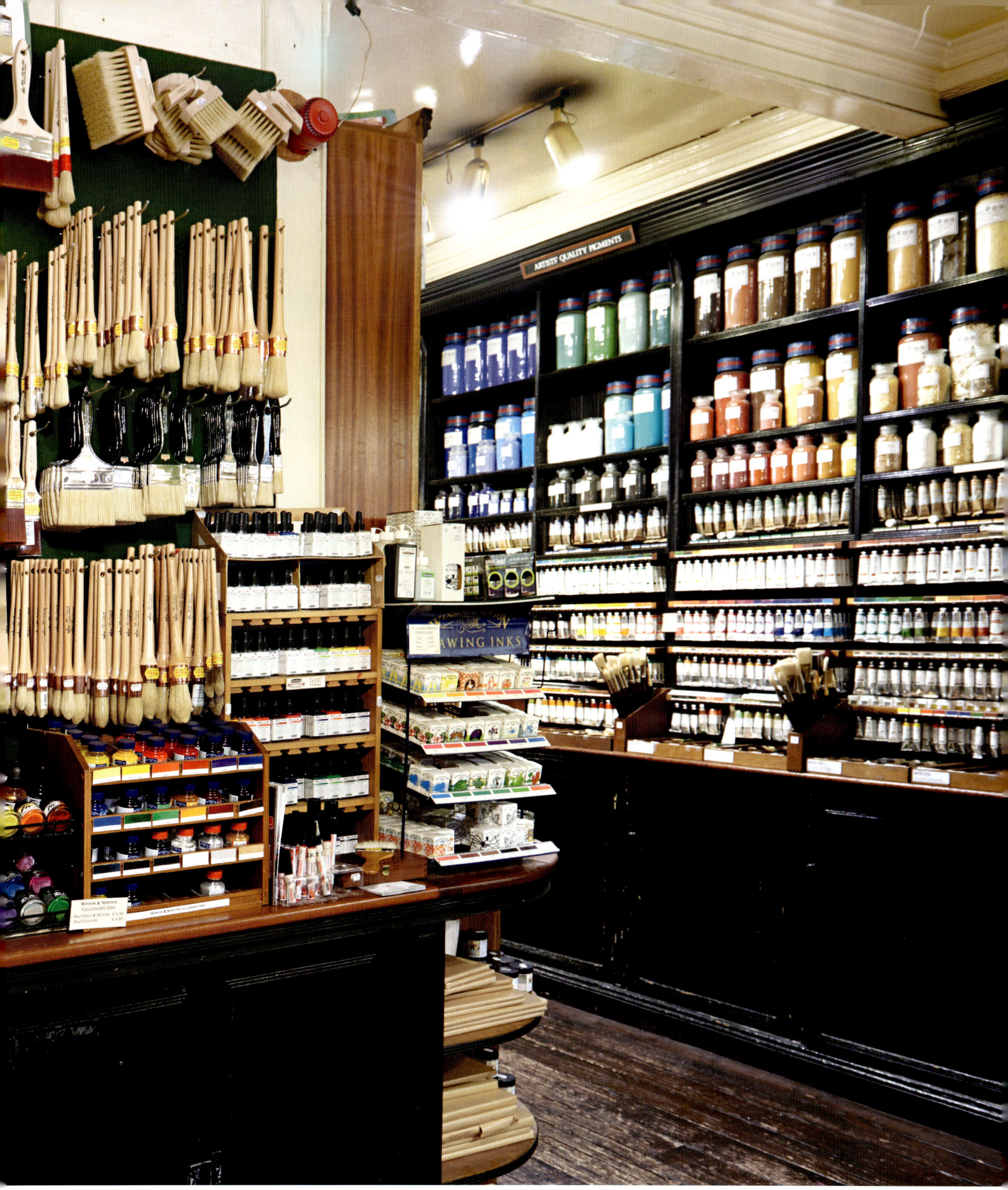
ARTISTS' QUALITY PIGMENTS
DRAWING INKS

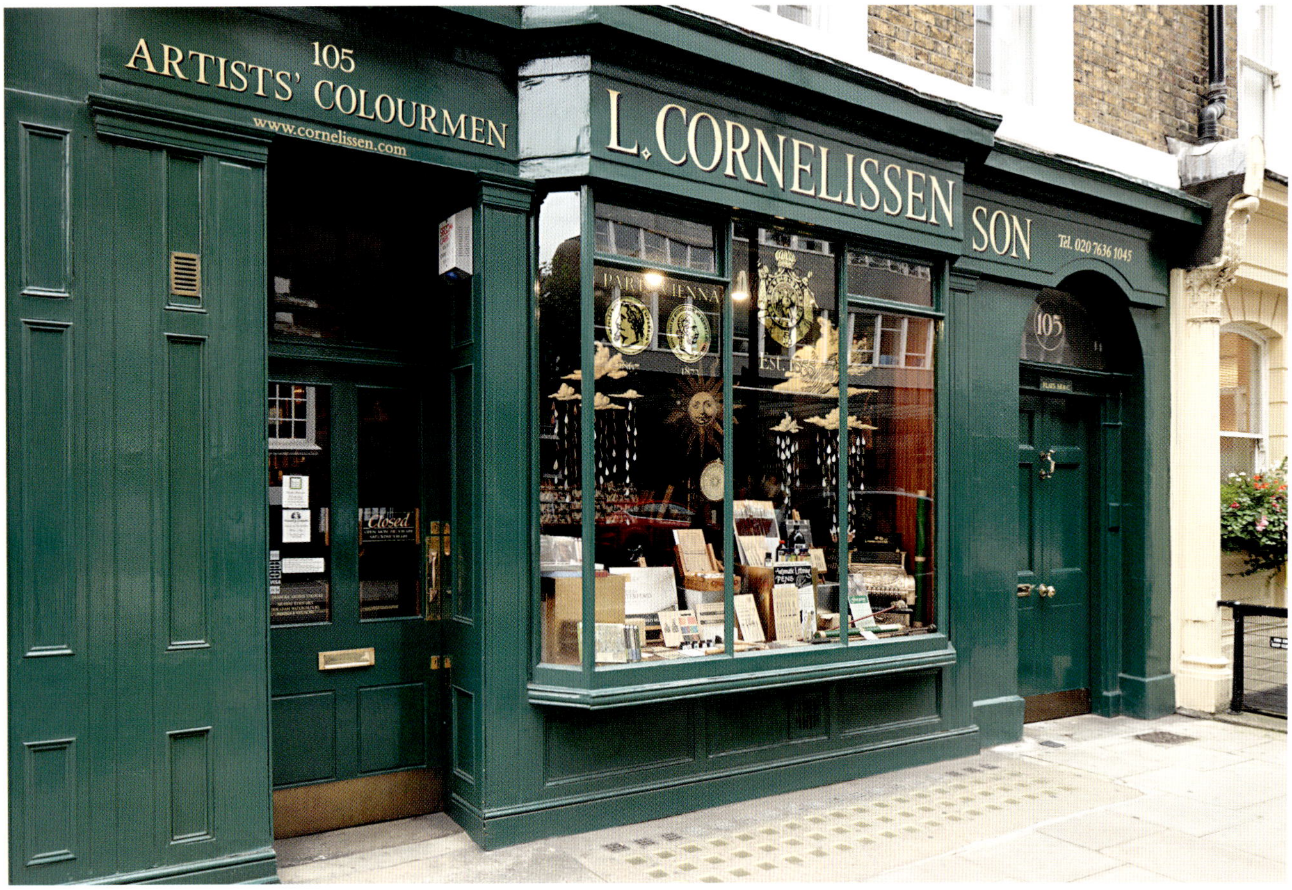
105
ARTISTS' COLOURMEN
www.cornelissen.com
L. CORNELISSEN
SON
Tel. 020 7636 1045

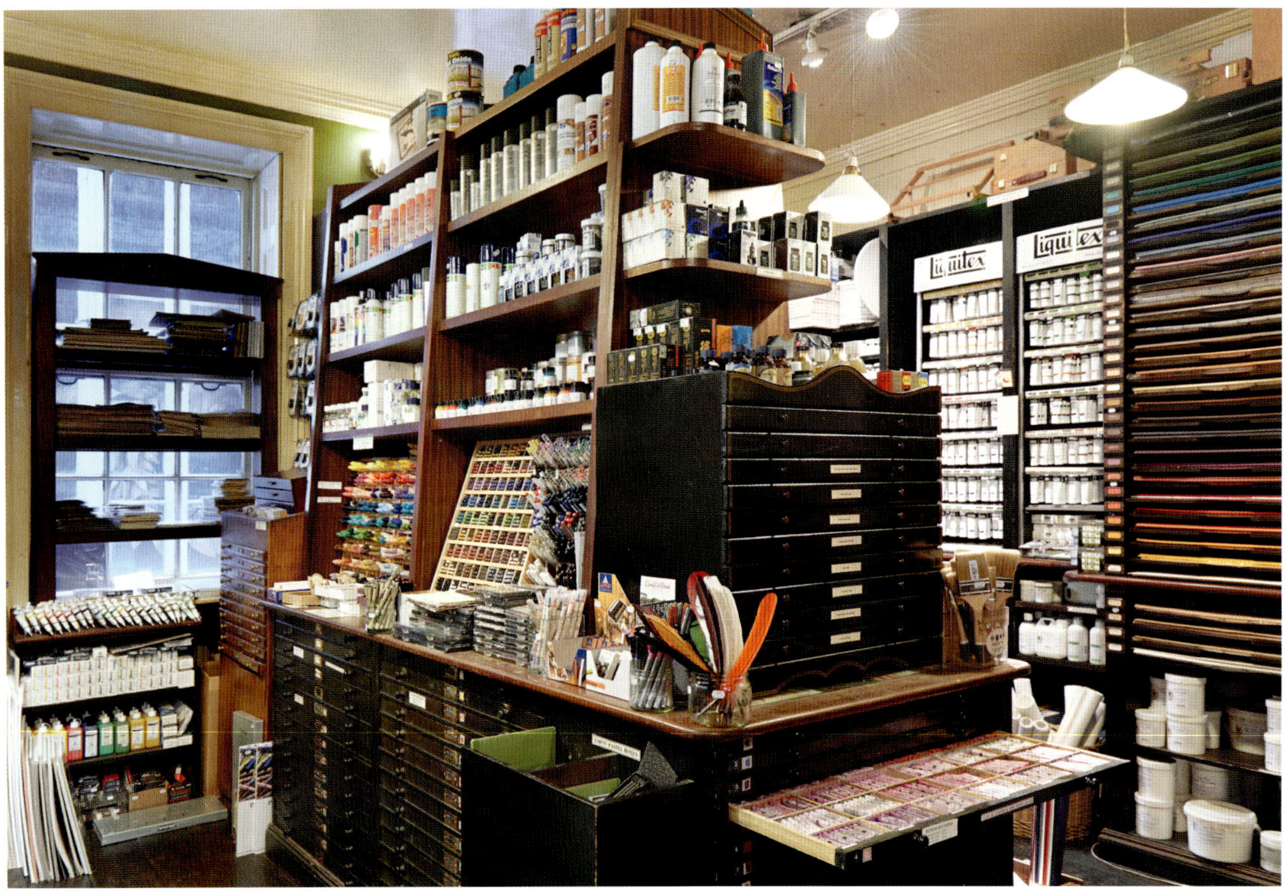
Liquitex
Liquitex

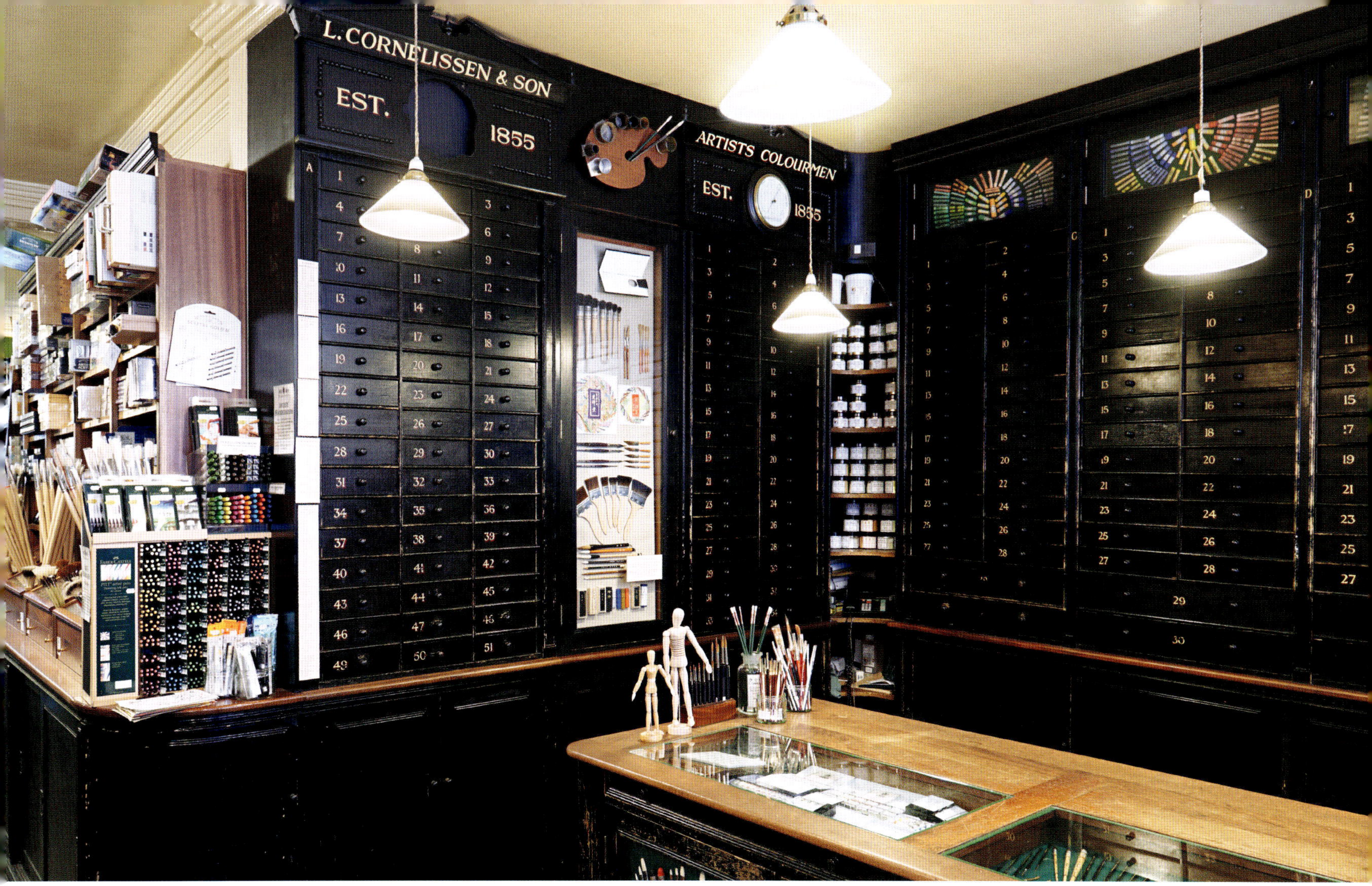

Opposite, above L. Cornelissen's green frontage has been its signature for more than a hundred years.

Opposite, below In the calligraphy section, four different types of quills are offered.

Above The drawers and cabinets for canvas, parchment and paper date from the 1860s.

to trace Cornelissen-supplied canvases used by painters such as Rex Whistler and Walter Sickert. These stencils give the company address as 22 Great Queen Street; this was L. Cornelissen's home from 1861 to 1987.

It remained a family-owned company until Leonard Cornelissen, grandson of the founder, died in 1977. The business was purchased by Nicholas Walt. It was compelled to move from Great Queen Street after the lease there expired in 1987. The shop in Great Russell Street, Bloomsbury, is a listed late-seventeenth-century building, with a nineteenth-century front that closely resembled the former premises. It was completed in the same distinctive sea-green finish. Everything was done to maintain continuity. All the original numbered drawers, cabinets, shelves and fittings were transferred and reinstalled. Cornelissen continues to look much like an apothecary where the early colourmen would have sourced their ingredients. It continues to stock several varieties of linseed oil, poppy oil, walnut oil and safflower oil. More than a hundred varieties of pigment are held; among the most specialized are obscure pigments known as 'early' colours, including genuine malachite, as used by the ancient Egyptians, and rose madder, in use since Roman times. Francis Bacon used Cornelissen's rose madder. Ford Madox Brown and Dante Gabriel Rossetti were past customers and Damien Hirst is a customer today. As a specialist supplier, the company keeps busy in unexpected ways. It receives regular orders for bulk artist-grade titanium white from a cosmetics manufacturer, from gilders restoring icons, and dozens of sword pinstriping brushes were recently supplied to a Californian bikers' club for the purpose of helmet decoration.

CONTACT INFORMATION

L. Cornelissen & Son,
105A Great Russell Street, WC1B 3RY
https://www.cornelissen.com/

Foreign, Commonwealth & Development Office

From 1806, Britain's first Secretary of State for Foreign Affairs, the rakish Charles James Fox, along with twenty of his successors, used a Westminster office situated in a ramshackle house in Downing Street. In 1852 one of its ceilings collapsed a fraction too close to the incumbent, Lord Malmesbury.

The incident came at a time of a growing British influence on the world stage, with the mid-Victorian period representing the peak of power. For a replacement building, a purpose-built bureau, rivalling the Quai d'Orsay in Paris or St Petersburg's General Staff Building, was planned. George Gilbert Scott, the project's architect, preferred the gothic style, but Lord Palmerston, the Prime Minister, favoured Palladian. The Italianate style prevailed. Construction commenced in 1861. Matthew Digby Wyatt, Scott's architectural partner, designed the India Office Council Chamber and the Durbar Court. English sculptors Henry Hugh Armstead and John Birnie Philip created relief portraits for the building's external stone façade, with subjects including Alfred the Great, Drake, Cook and Wilberforce, along with allegorical statues representing Law, Art, Commerce and the like. The building housed four different government departments: the Foreign Office and India Office initially, with the Colonial and Home Offices moving in by 1875. Its dignified exterior hardly rates a second glance by the thousands of tourists who pass through Whitehall, and the building is not highly ranked by enthusiasts of architecture. The interior is a different matter.

The India Office Council Chamber's importance in nineteenth-century foreign relations is emphasized by its height and size, and its elaborate use of gilt in a room used regularly by the Secretary of State for India and his council from 1868 to 1947. Dominating the room is the 1730 marble chimneypiece, the work of Flemish sculptor Jan Michael Rysbrack. Britannia is seen receiving gifts from the East. On either side of the fireplace, portraits of Robert Clive and Warren Hastings are testimony to erstwhile colonial glory, while furniture includes nineteenth-century mahogany chairs, and a newspaper stand brought from East India House. With the 1947 demise of the India Office its building was taken over by the Foreign Office, with the chamber hosting the 1948 London 6-Power Conference for discussions on Germany's future role by democratic and federal governance in the US, British and French sectors. Later, preliminary talks for early meetings of NATO officials were held in the chamber that in the twenty-first century is still used for daily meetings and conferences on international affairs.

At the nucleus of the Foreign and Commonwealth Office is the Durbar Court (a Persian word meaning Shah's Noble Court), based on designs for the courtyard of Rome's Renaissance Palazzo della Cancelleria. The London cortile's mosaic of tiles was influenced by Italian and Indian artistry, and the ascending levels of columns on all four sides are supported by ground floor Doric and first floor Ionic columns of polished, red Peterhead granite, and top floor Corinthian columns of

The Grand Staircase, Foreign and Commonwealth Office.

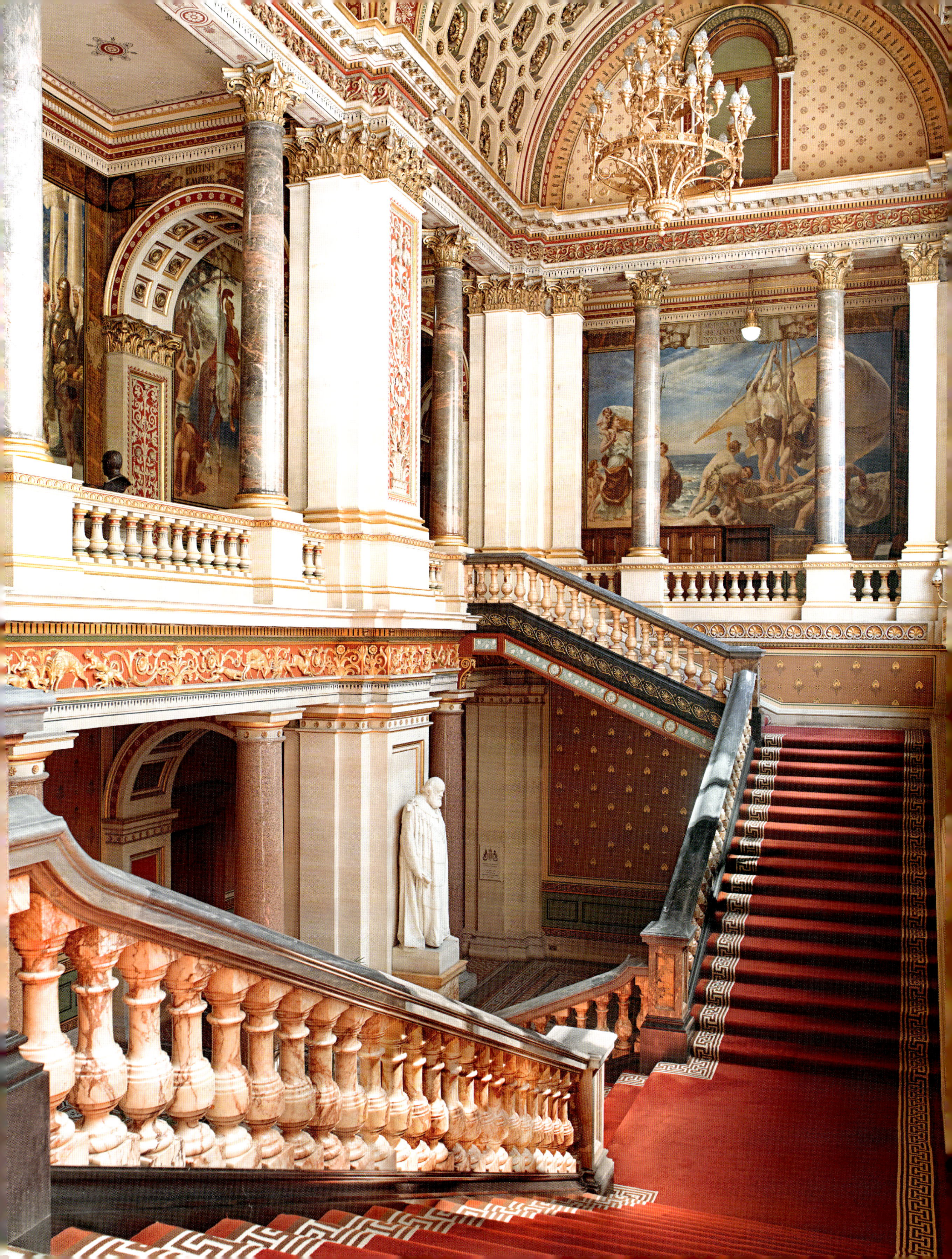

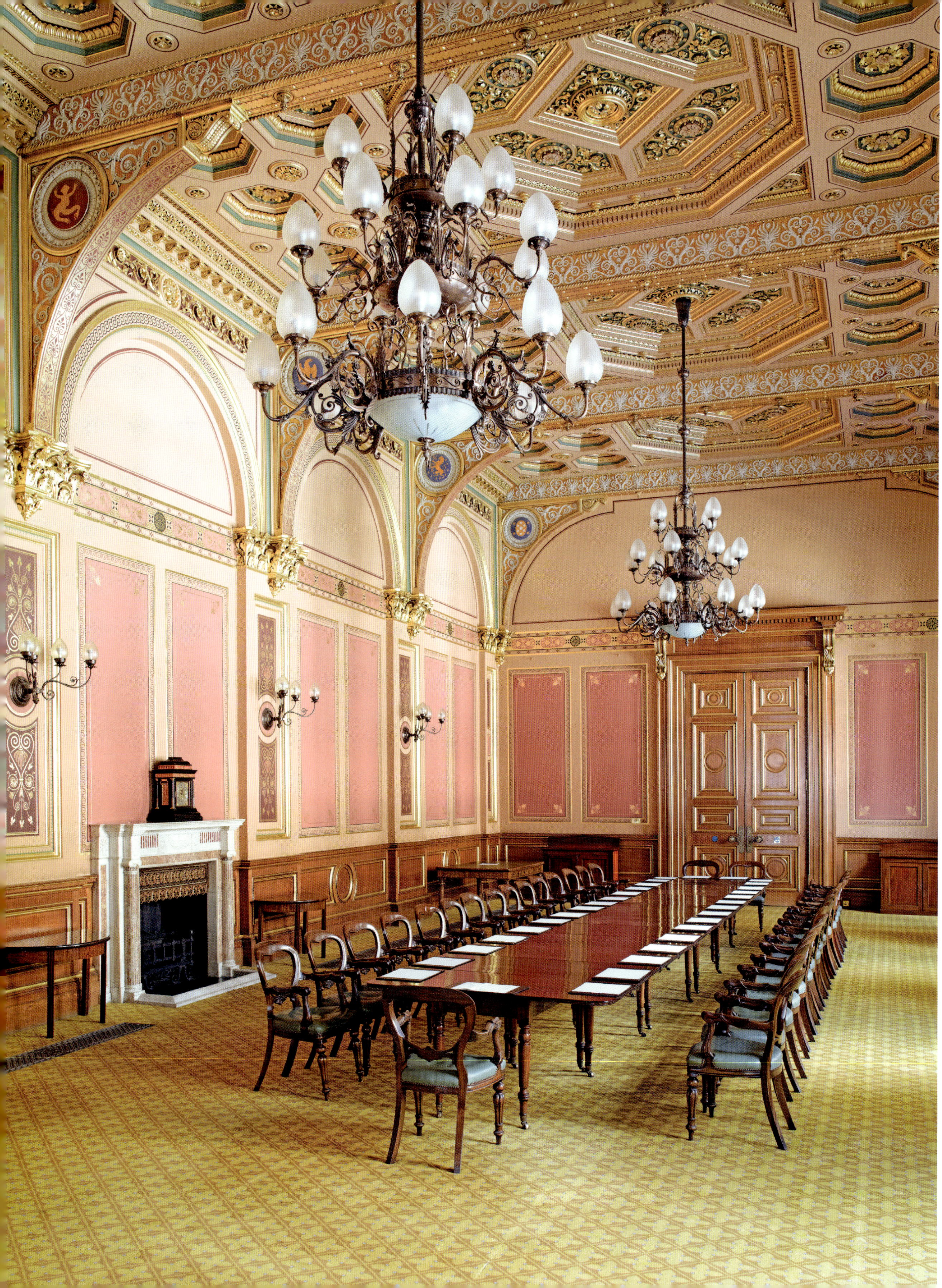

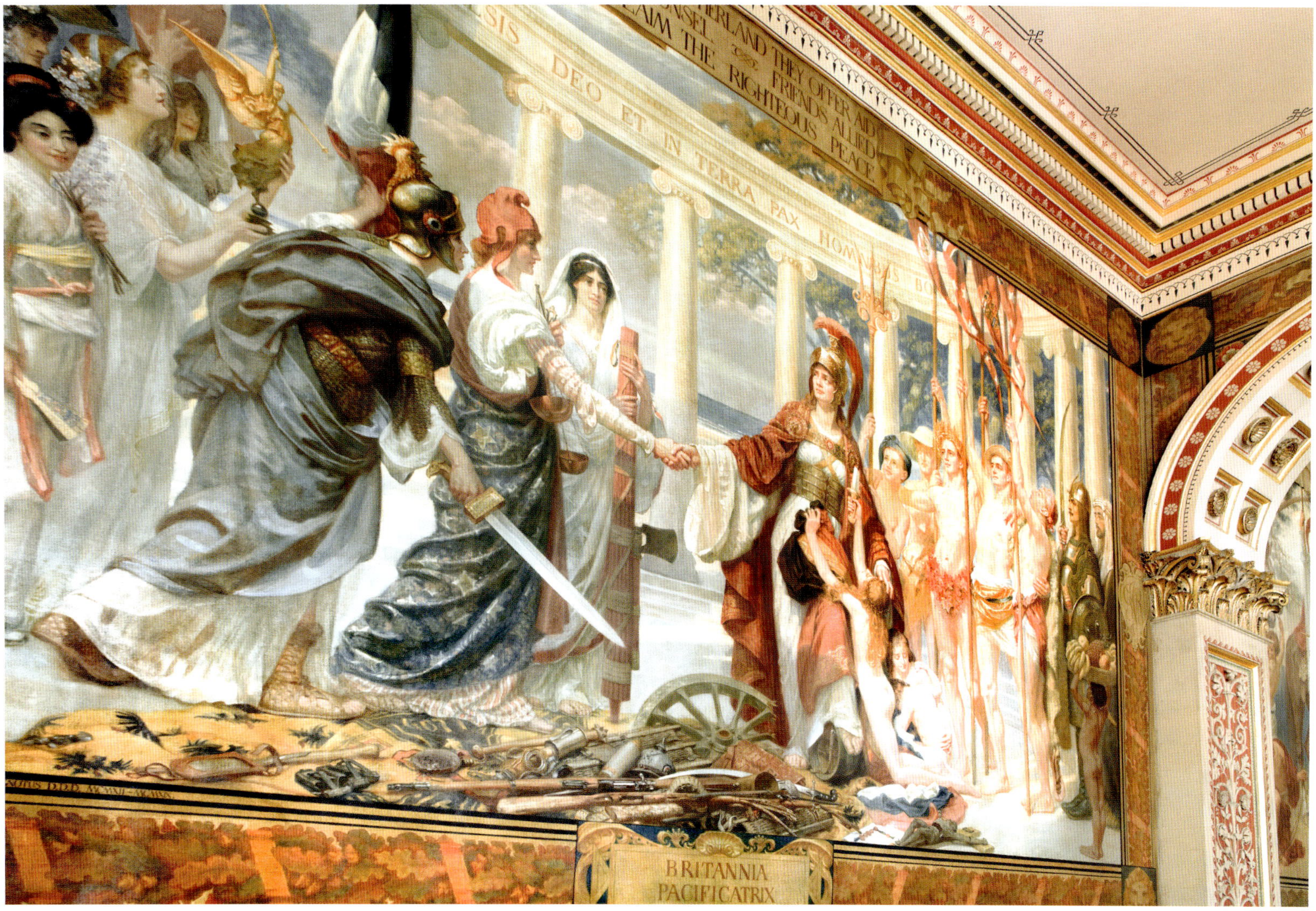

Opposite The Locarno Suite.

Above Sigismund Goetze's painting *Britannia Pacificatrix*, showing Britannia victorious after the First World War.

grey Aberdeen granite. The courtyard's pavement is Greek, Sicilian and Belgian marble. An open courtyard had been envisaged, but the addition of the glazed cast-iron roof, inspired by Wyatt's work at Crystal Palace for the Great Exhibition and Paddington station, allows flecked reflections of sunlight to seep into exotic surroundings. First used in 1867 for a reception honouring Ottoman Sultan Abdülaziz, the name Durbar Court only dates from 1902, when some of Edward VII's coronation celebrations were held there.

When designing what became known as the Locarno Suite, Scott envisioned an aura of grandeur by using space to create a 'Drawing-Room for the Nation' to host great occasions. The suite comprised three rooms – the 'Cabinet Room' (now known as the Grand Reception Room), the Conference Room and the smaller Square Dining Room – and guests entered via the left side of the grand staircase. The Dining Room, called the Cabinet or the Small Dining Room, was invariably used by the 3rd Marquess of Salisbury as his office, and his portrait hangs there. In 1925, the suite witnessed the signing of the Locarno Treaties to improve European diplomatic relations and, following some redecoration that same year, became known as the Locarno Suite. In 1935, the suite was chosen for the opening session of the International Naval Conference, and also hosted a dinner party for the state visit of President Lebrun of France in 1939. During redecoration in the 1990s, removal of plasterboard and grubby red silk hangings disclosed fading olive and gold decor with red and gold borders, enabling restorers to match the original colours to return the room to its former magnificence.

CONTACT INFORMATION

Foreign, Commonwealth & Development Office
King Charles Street, SW1A 2AH
https://www.gov.uk/government/history/king-charles-street

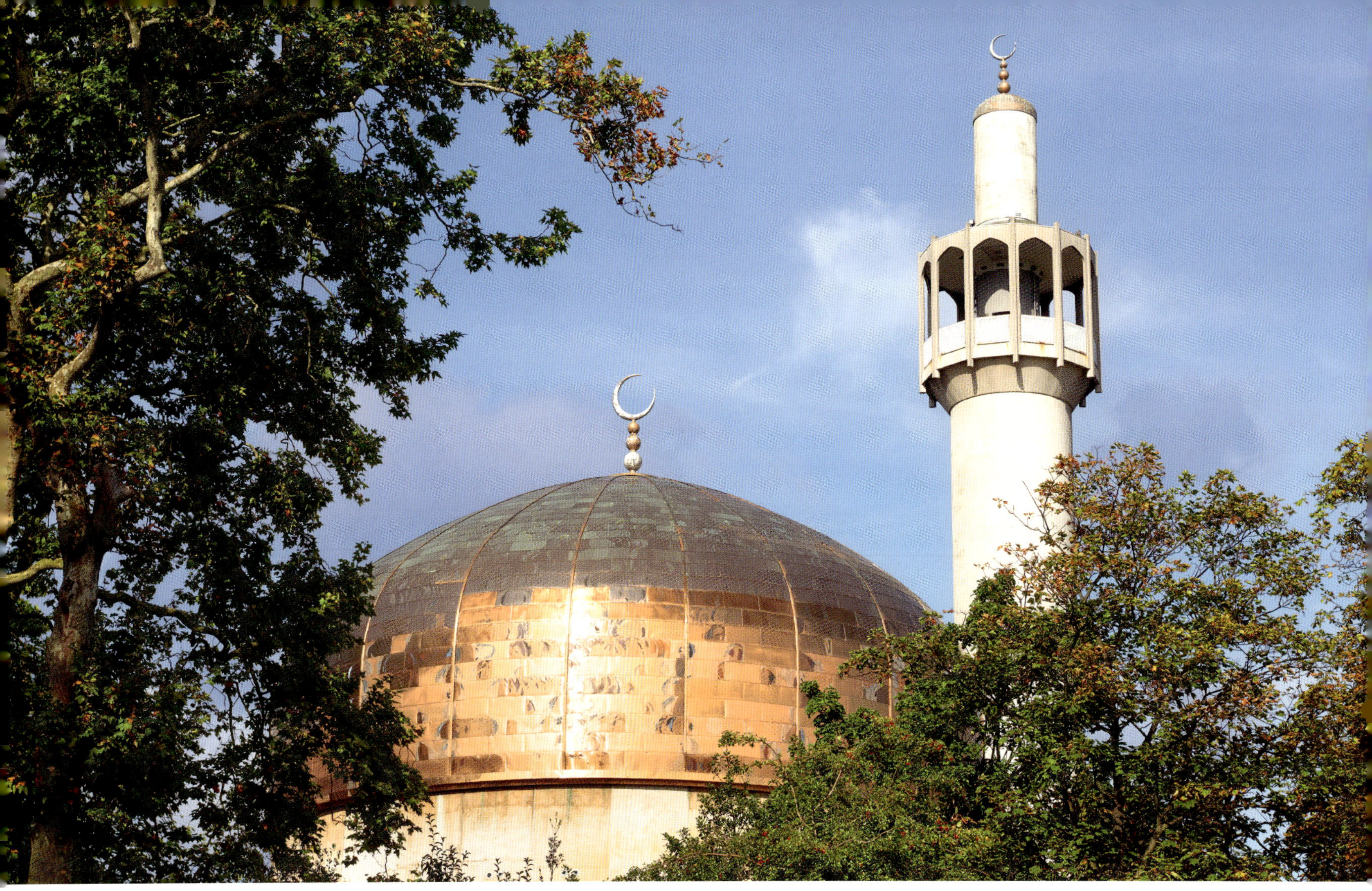

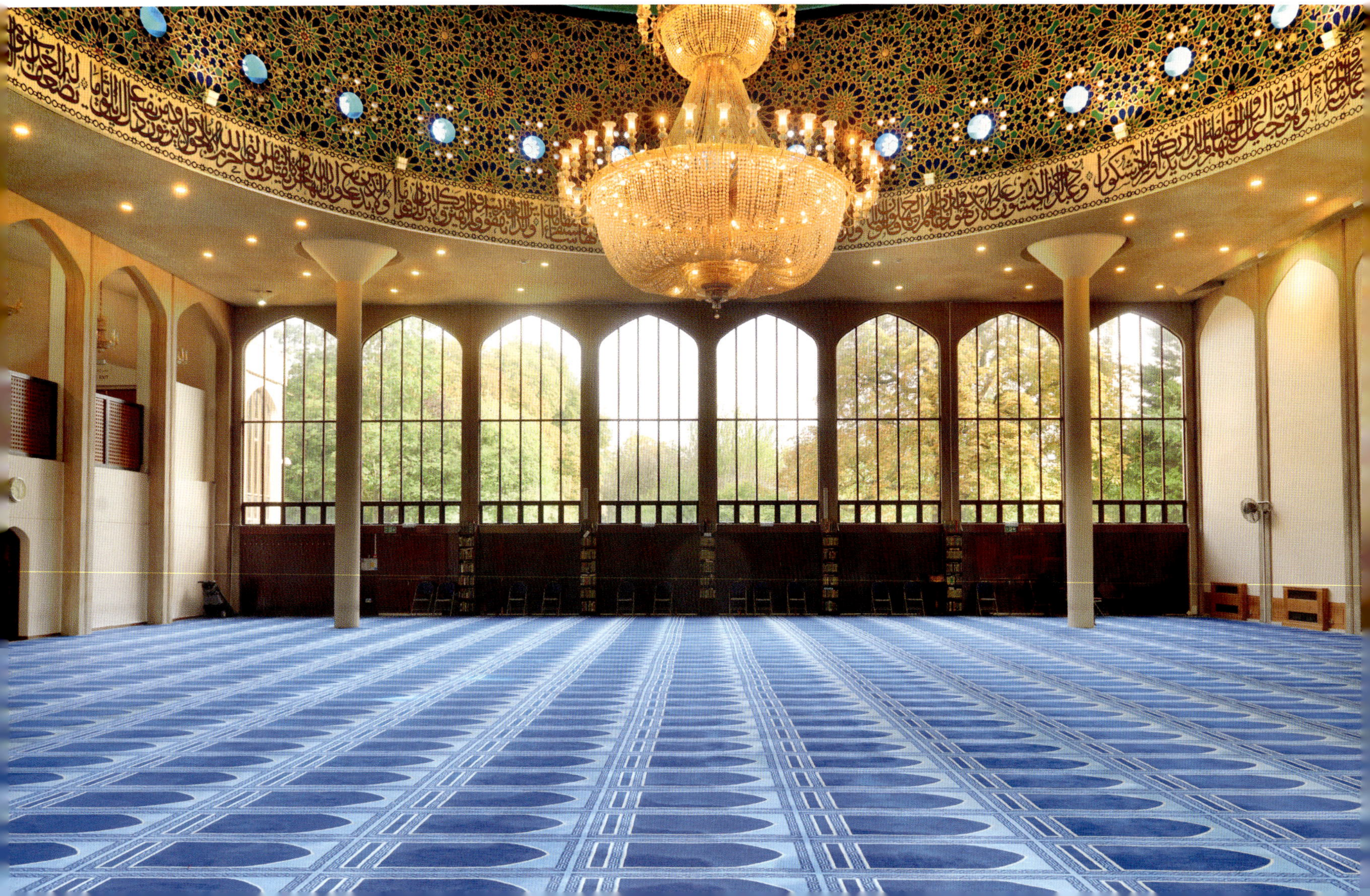

London Central Mosque & Islamic Cultural Centre

Opposite, above
The prominent golden dome and minaret in Regent's Park.

Opposite, below
The main prayer hall with two of the slender pillars supporting the dome.

The white minaret, golden copper dome and prayer hall of Regent's Park Mosque (properly known as the London Central Mosque and Islamic Cultural Centre) rose up between 1974 and 1977 near Hanover Gate alongside Nash Regency terrace townhouses. Plain in external decoration, its architect, Sir Frederick Gibberd, described it as a largely prefabricated building. All eighty-five façade units forming the walls were precast off-site. Some are glazed and some in-filled in a shape known as the four-centred arch, which is recognizably Islamic in architectural style. The prayer hall building is joined by a pair of three-storey wings containing administration offices, accommodation and the library, reading room and study areas.

Its emergence spanned seventy years, punctuated by delays, false starts and setbacks, and influenced by shifts in international relations and two world wars. With an Empire inhabited by more Muslims than Christians, an appeal was made to the British government towards the end of the First World War for a central place of worship to be created as recognition for the thousands of Muslims fighting for King and Country. When this did not develop, a separate trust fund was established by the Nizam of Hyderabad in 1928, and a foundation stone laid, but that development also stalled. It was after the start of the Second World War that Winston Churchill's war cabinet, mindful of need for support from Arab nations in the Middle East, approved £100,000 for purchase of a site. A substantial two-storey house known as Regent's Lodge, standing in a hectare of land on the Outer Circle of Regent's Park, was acquired. With the Islamic Cultural Centre and a temporary mosque established in Regent's Lodge, work on a grand new mosque seemed poised to start in the 1950s, but support from Muslim nations faded after the British military action at Suez in 1956.

After the project was revived, an architectural competition launched by the mosque trust in 1968 received fifty-two entries; the Gibberd design was selected, and construction was supported by a donation from King Faisal of Saudi Arabia and later by Kuwait, the UAE, Oman and Qatar. These added to the funds accumulated in trusts over the years by British Muslims. In 1994, with the addition of an administration wing, the forecourt alongside the prayer hall became an enclosed courtyard. At one time, inside and outside, as many as 6,000 worshippers can pray at the Regent's Park Mosque.

The mosque was far from the first to be established in Britain nor the first be awarded Grade II* status, that distinction belonging to Shah Janan Mosque in Woking, founded in 1889, listed in 1984, but London Central Mosque was long overdue for recognition. After more than forty years in the harsh London environment, the building is undergoing a significant renovation.

CONTACT INFORMATION

The London Central Mosque and Islamic Cultural Centre, 146 Park Road, NW8 7RG

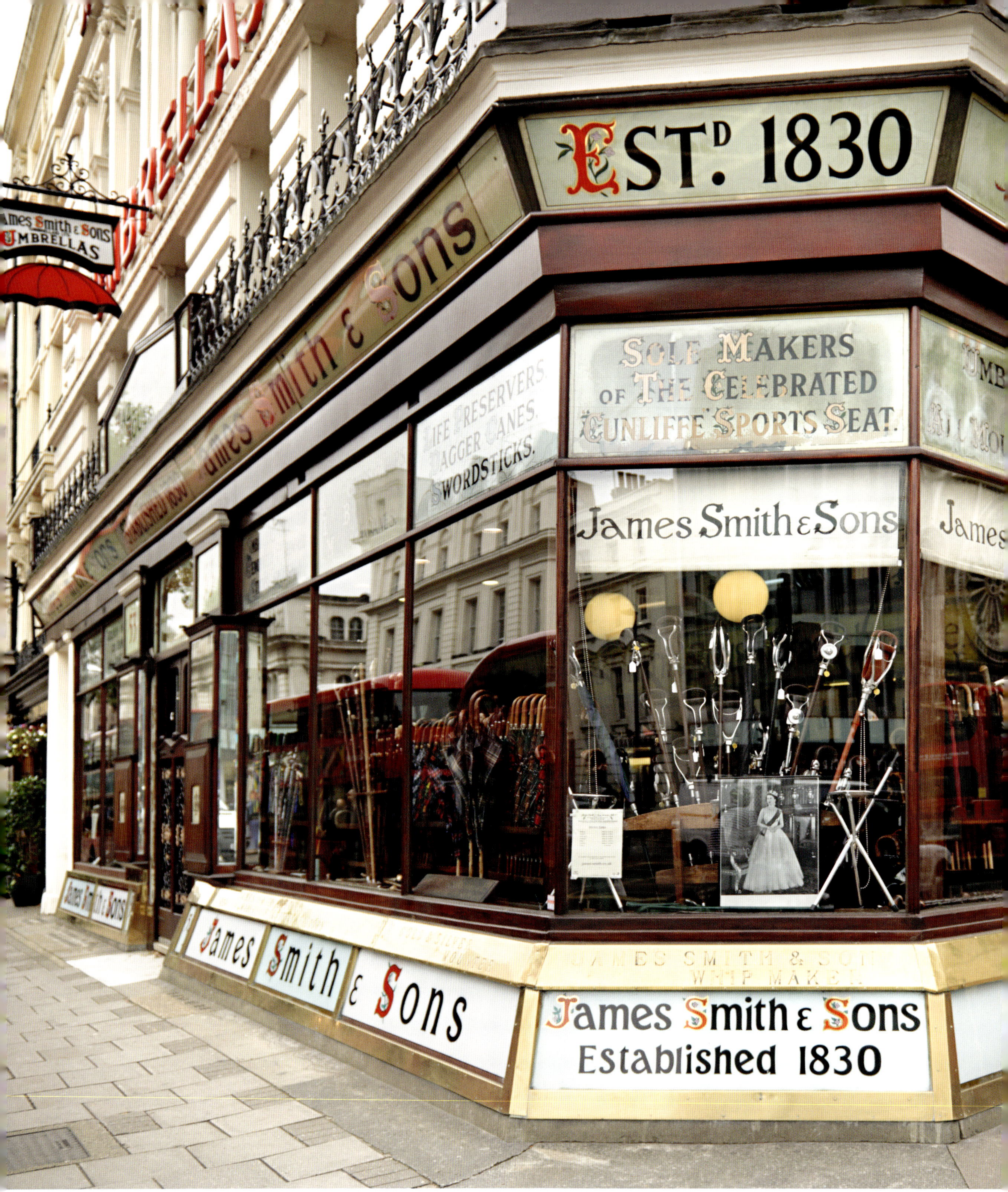
ESTD. 1830
SOLE MAKERS OF THE CELEBRATED CUNLIFFE SPORTS SEAT.
LIFE PRESERVERS. DAGGER CANES. SWORDSTICKS.
James Smith & Sons
James Smith & Sons
UMBRELLAS
James Smith & Sons
James Smith & Sons
Established 1830

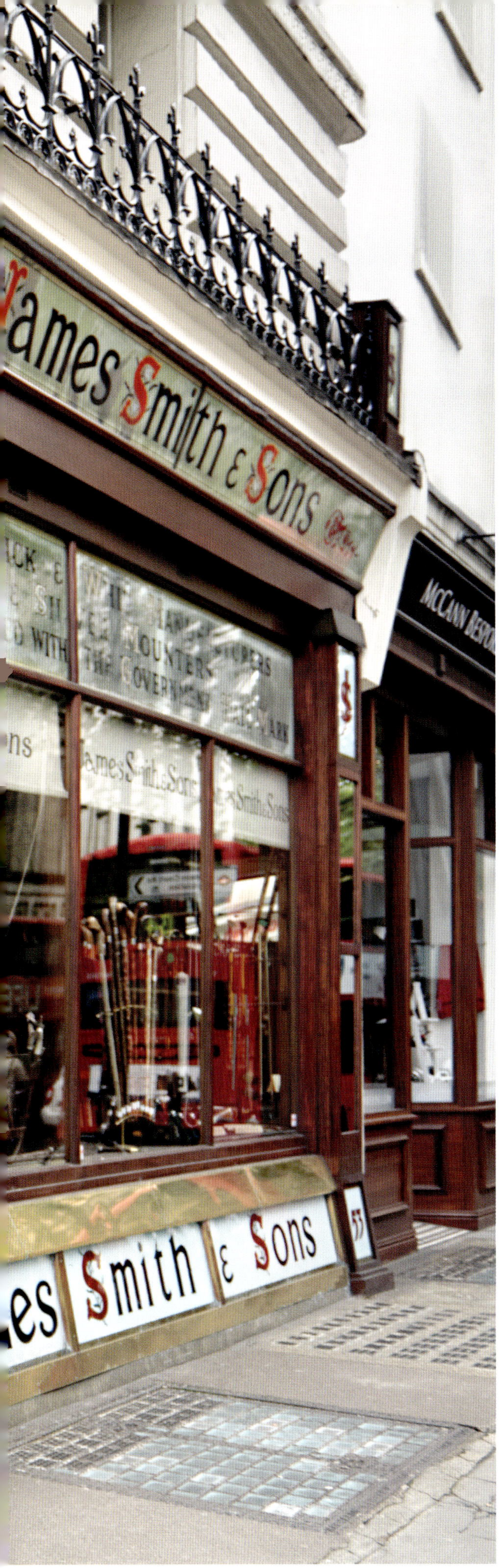

James Smith & Sons

Built on a tapered ground plan on the corner with Shaftesbury Avenue, James Smith & Sons is a distinctive shape and a monument to Victorian branding, with its extensive signage and packed window displays.

James Smith & Sons is one of the most distinctive shops in London, an unmistakeable landmark on New Oxford Street. Its brass, mahogany, wrought-iron and glass exterior is emblazoned with signage, which declares umbrellas and sticks for sale alongside tropical sunshades, sword sticks and dagger canes. Outside and in, the James Smith & Sons store has a patina that denotes character rather than neglect.

The shop has been sympathetically refurbished and attracts thousands of visitors. Part of the interior dates from the 1880s, when the business was already more than fifty years old. At that time, New Oxford Street was one of the most fashionable shopping streets in London and the shop design is a monument to the commercialism and branding of the era. The aim was to display as many products as possible and that is still the case, with hundreds of umbrellas and sticks in baskets and racks.

For the serious purchaser of a good umbrella, the main problem is one of choice. Given the number of styles, materials and colours available there is a strong chance of creating a unique item. A crooked handle of knurled bamboo, known as whangee, fitted with a silk cover, may be considered classic. An umbrella made from a one-piece solid stick is better to lean on. The stick is cut to length to suit the user. Smooth handles may be made from cherry, chestnut, hazel or hickory, and the handle can be covered in various leathers. A lighter city umbrella can be built around a steel tube. There are styles for town and country. There are travel umbrellas, which dismantle

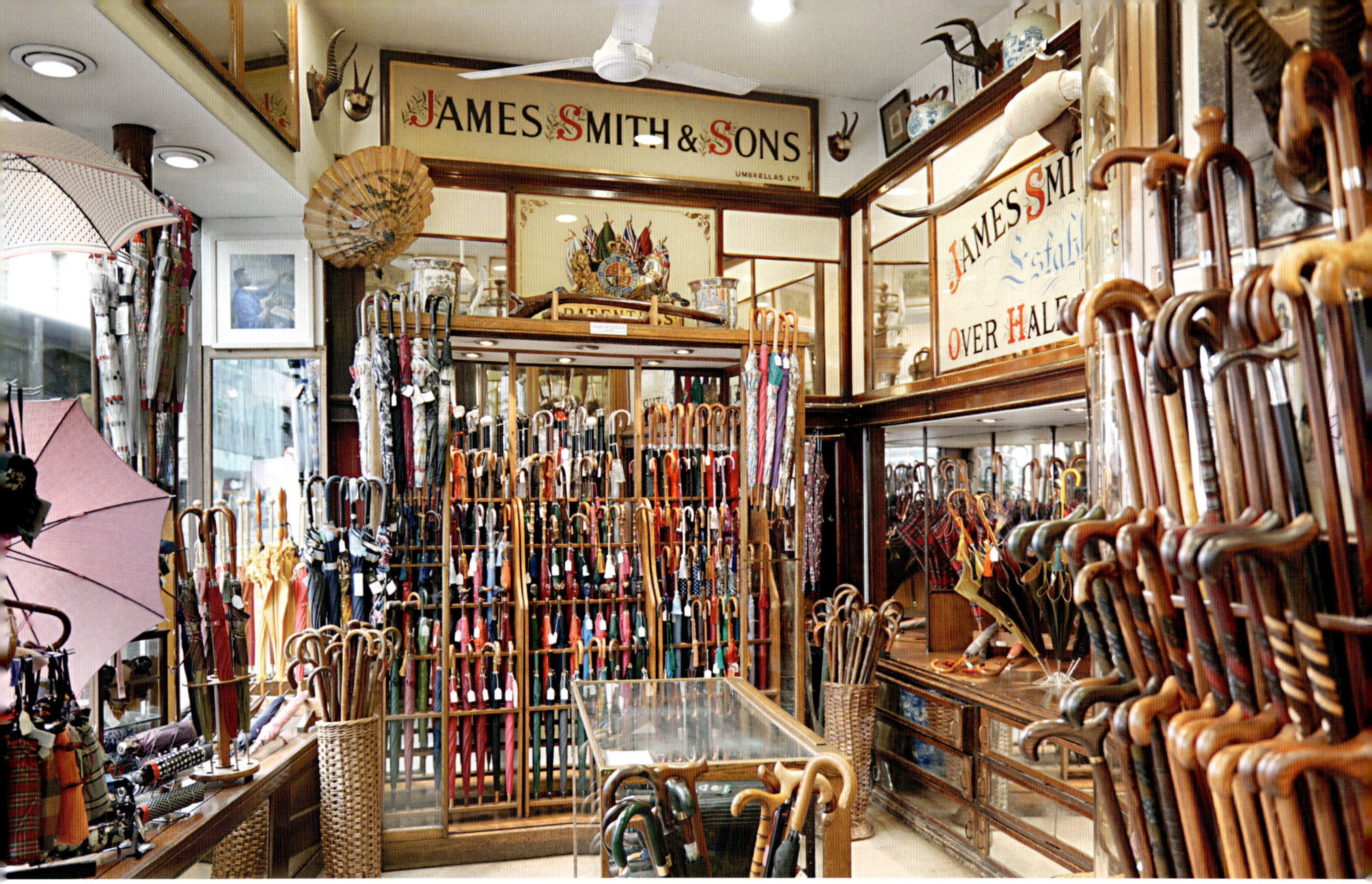

to fit a suitcase, folding umbrellas, sun umbrellas and umbrellas with animal-head handles in wood, nickel or resin. Styles of umbrellas for ladies come in walking length or pencil length. A choice almost as wide applies to walking sticks.

The company was one of the first to use the famous Fox umbrella frame invented by Samuel Fox, which replaced whalebone with lightweight u-section steel ribs. This type of frame was still being produced and fitted until recently. The company says there has been little change in the design and materials of the traditional umbrella over time, apart from the fact that most covers are now made from nylon rather than silk.

James Smith founded the firm in 1830 at Foubert Place, off Regent Street. There was once a James Smith branch shop just off Savile Row, which sold umbrellas to Prime Ministers Gladstone and Bonar Law. That branch moved to New Burlington Street, but was destroyed in the Second World War. The founder's son established the main shop in New Oxford Street in 1857.

Traditionally, umbrellas were made at the back of the shop and customers were served at the front. The tradition continues at New Oxford Street, where there are workshops in the basement. Some umbrellas and walking sticks are still made there, although sales are such that some production has to be outsourced to small family companies.

For years the company has made ceremonial umbrellas and it has produced maces for African tribal chieftains. During and after the First World War, many hundreds of thousands of military swagger sticks were sold to soldiers. James Smith once sold whips and crops. It can still supply the kind of stick known as a staff, which is associated with shepherds, and it also produces a wide range of seat sticks. One of the faded window signs even promotes 'life preservers': not a flotation device but a type of heavy stick suitable for use a club and no longer stocked.

CONTACT INFORMATION

James Smith & Sons Ltd, Hazelwood House,
53 New Oxford Street, WC1A 1BL
https://www.james-smith.co.uk/

Above Showcases and counters are original to the design of the Victorian craftsman working for Smiths.

Opposite Animal heads in nickel for canes or umbrellas; the straight style is called a derby, the rounded style is a crook.

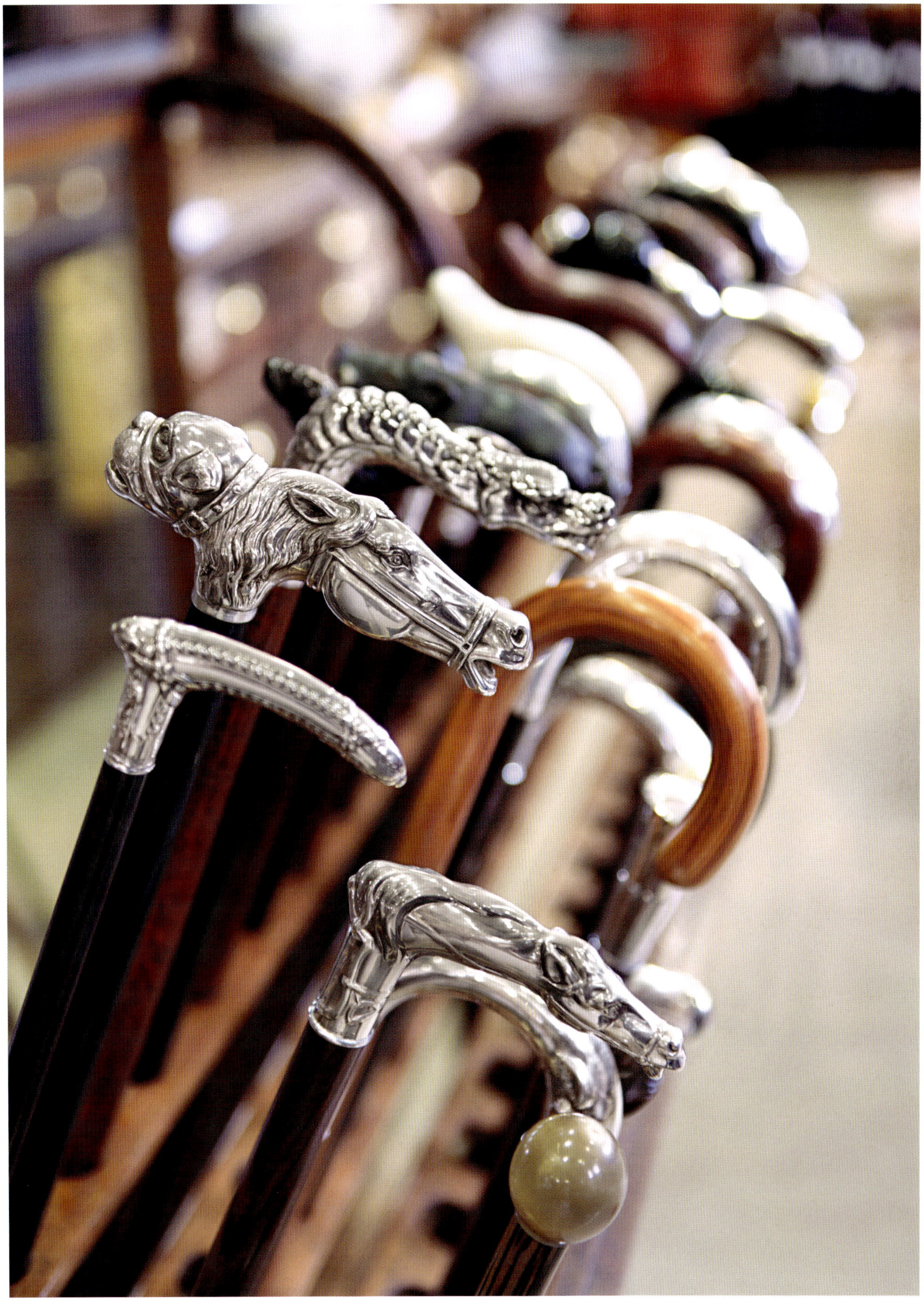

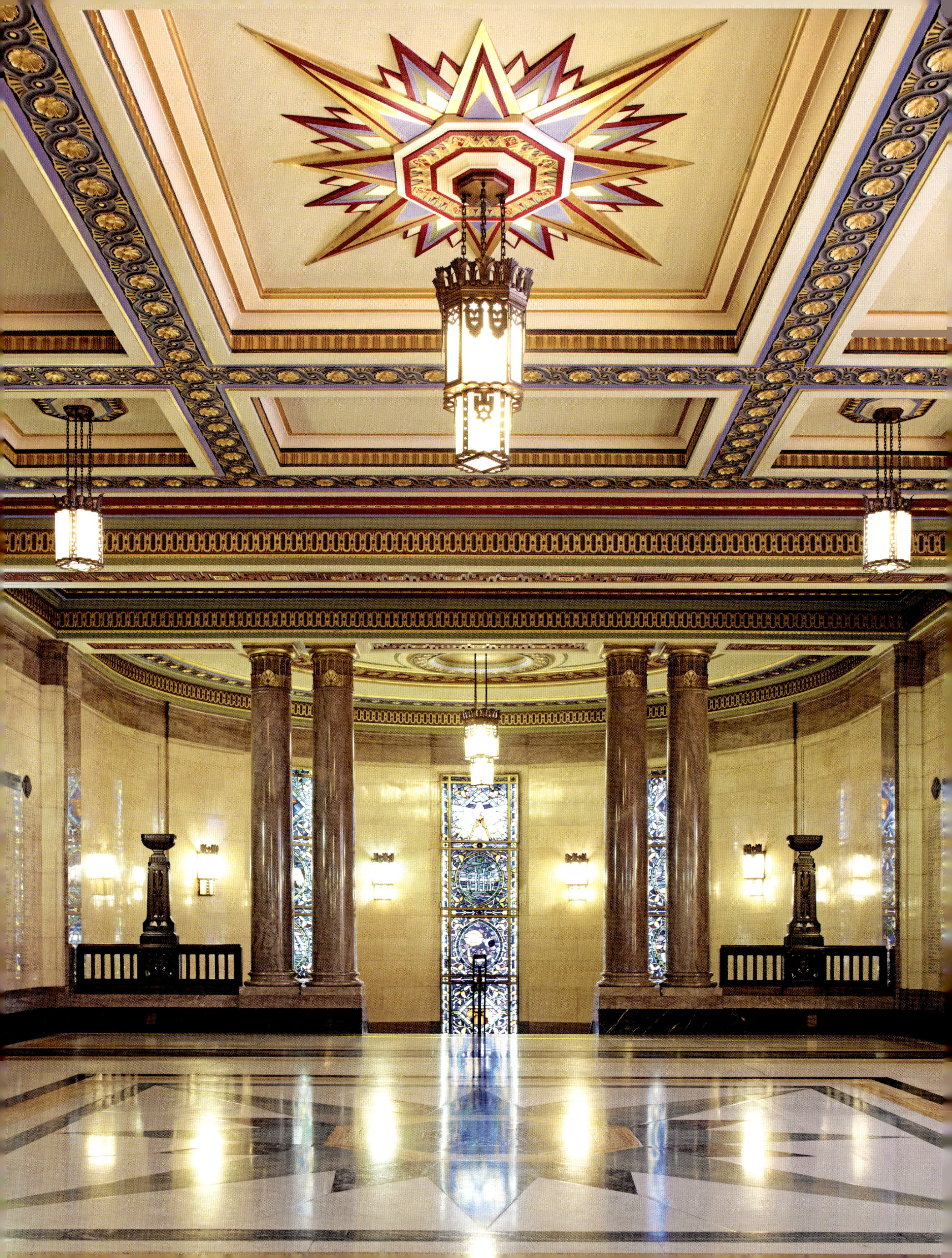

Freemasons' Hall

Marble-clad vestibule.

Freemasons' Hall, a monumental structure that overshadows Great Queen Street between Covent Garden and Holborn, is visibly laden with architectural gravitas, which may be appropriate for an organization inspired by the builders of medieval cathedrals and castles. In popular imagination, the building may also be endowed with great secret significance, representing concealed power dating back a thousand years.

But Freemasons' Hall is of recent construction, and Freemasons themselves emphasize that it is not a religious building. Freemasonry, they say, is secular and non-political, and is engaged in a multitude of charitable fundraising and volnteering activities. Free guided tours (available up to five times a day, six days a week) are one of London's lesser-known pleasures, but far from secret. Freemasons' Hall's remarkable interior only qualifies as secret or hidden for those unwilling to look inside. Those who do may find the application of symbolism overpowering. If the Hall itself is not riddled with secrets, its decoration is at least crying out for interpretation.

Freemasons' Hall is the third masonic building on this site since 1775. It was built between 1927 and 1933, and financed by a million-pound appeal, although the final cost was more than one third greater than that. Put out to competition, the winning design was by architects Henry Ashley and Francis Winton Newman, a partnership who specialized in functional designs for industry, commerce and public buildings. It is steel-framed and clad in Portland stone, and aligned diagonally to the local street plan.

The First World War and its aftermath exerted a profound influence on Freemasons' Hall, which was commissioned under the title The Masonic Peace Memorial Building. One of its main features is a bronze casket housing a roll of honour listing members who died in the 1914–18 conflict. The casket is typically elaborate. It rests on an ark lying in a reed bed, symbolizing a journey ended.

It is not clear if one overarching mind was responsible for the decoration of the interior, although much of the metalwork, including the roll of honour casket, is attributed to Walter Gilbert from H.H. Martyn & Co. of Cheltenham, which specialized in architectural woodwork, plasterwork and metal. Some of best work of this firm was for the staterooms of ocean liners, and it can also be found at the centre of Freemasons' Hall in the shape of the Grand Temple's massive bronze doors. These are set on balanced hinges and open at the merest pressure of a finger, although each weighs more than a ton. The design cast on the doors shows the building of the Temple of Solomon. Sword hilts lying flat on the surface are handles, the buried sword blades representing peace. The stylized, streamlined figures on the doors may have stepped off a mantelpiece from an apartment of the 1920s. In plain terms, Freemasons' Hall is an Art Deco building and the style and symbolism are well matched. The chequerboard black-and-white floor of the Grand Temple, which seems a

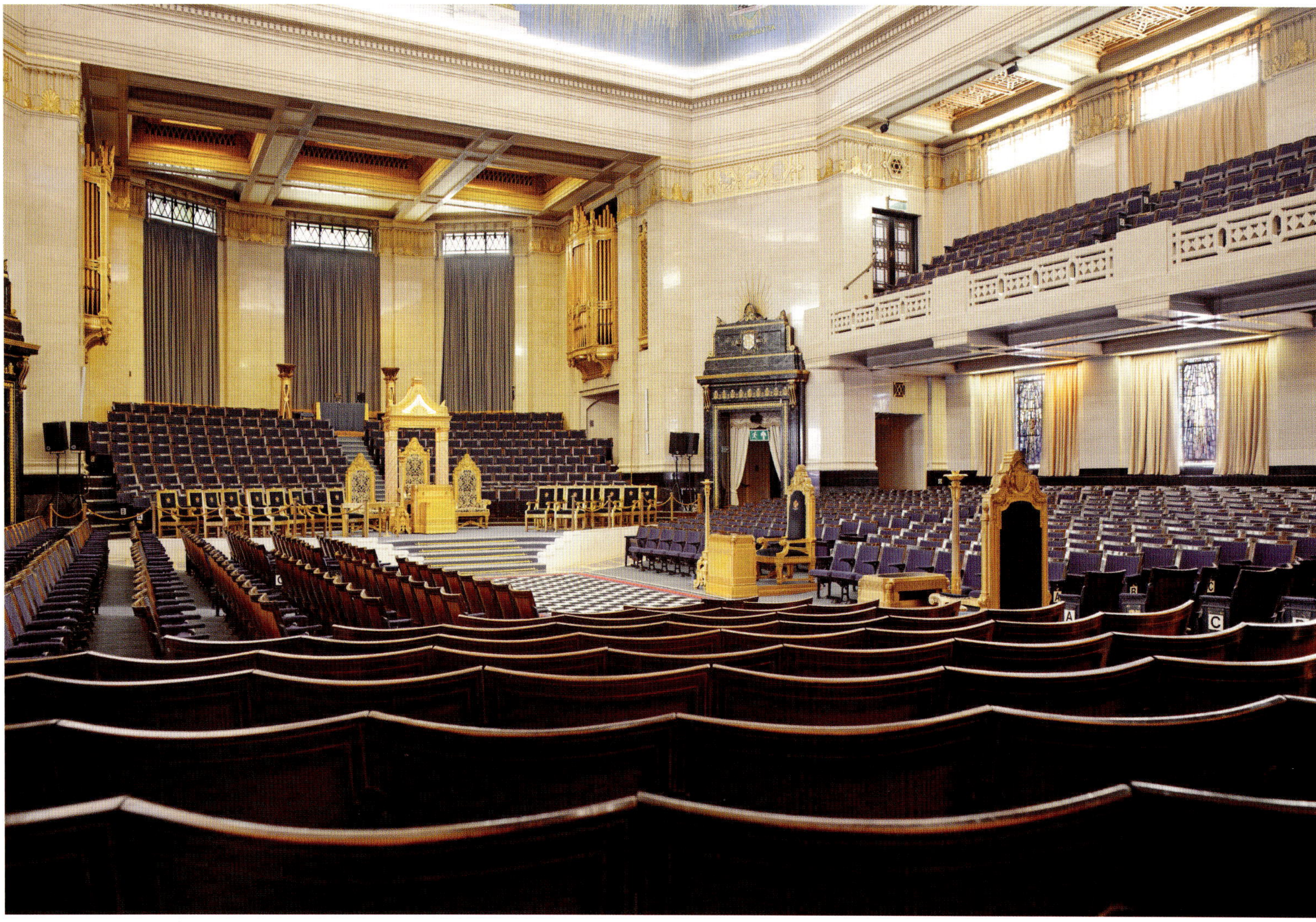

simple classic Modernist design, is in fact a symbol of diversity in Freemasonry. The Grand Temple is used sixty times a year. Lined with marble, galleried and high ceilinged, its main features are three huge gilded thrones for the officials, the central one being for the Grand Master. The ceiling comprises 1.5 million mosaic pieces set by Italian craftsmen.

On the first floor the processional corridor, 130 ft (40 m) long, is lined with Tasmanian blackwood, a form of mahogany said to be extinct, and is illuminated by a stained glass window with the figure of Justice shown blindfolded. Elsewhere are more than twenty lodge rooms, a library and a museum. The only strictly functional features visible are the internal courtyards glimpsed through the inner windows. These are made of white ceramic self-cleaning bricks. The courtyards do not seem to function as light wells, but Freemasons' Hall is not a gloomy place. It is a registered film and television location, and has masqueraded as MI5 headquarters in the television show *Spooks*.

A mosaic with an All-Seeing Eye at its centre, a frieze bearing signs of the zodiac, pentacles and compasses, ornamental blocks of stones both rough and finished: all the visual references in Freemasons' Hall seem profound. Yet despite the powerful symbolism, it seems that most visitors who take advantage of the tours, including *Da Vinci Code* enthusiasts, are quickly won over to the notion that Freemasonry is benign, and an effective charitable organization.

'That Dan Brown has got a lot to answer for,' says the guide ruefully to the visitors, 'but we have forgiven him.'

CONTACT INFORMATION

Freemasons' Hall,
60 Great Queen Street, WC2B 5AZ
https://museumfreemasonry.org.uk/

Above Grand Temple with Grand Master's throne flanked by deputies' chairs. The chequered floor design carries significance.

Opposite The bronze doors to the Grand Temple, with panels telling the story of the building of King Solomon's temple: Old Testament imagery in an Art Deco style.

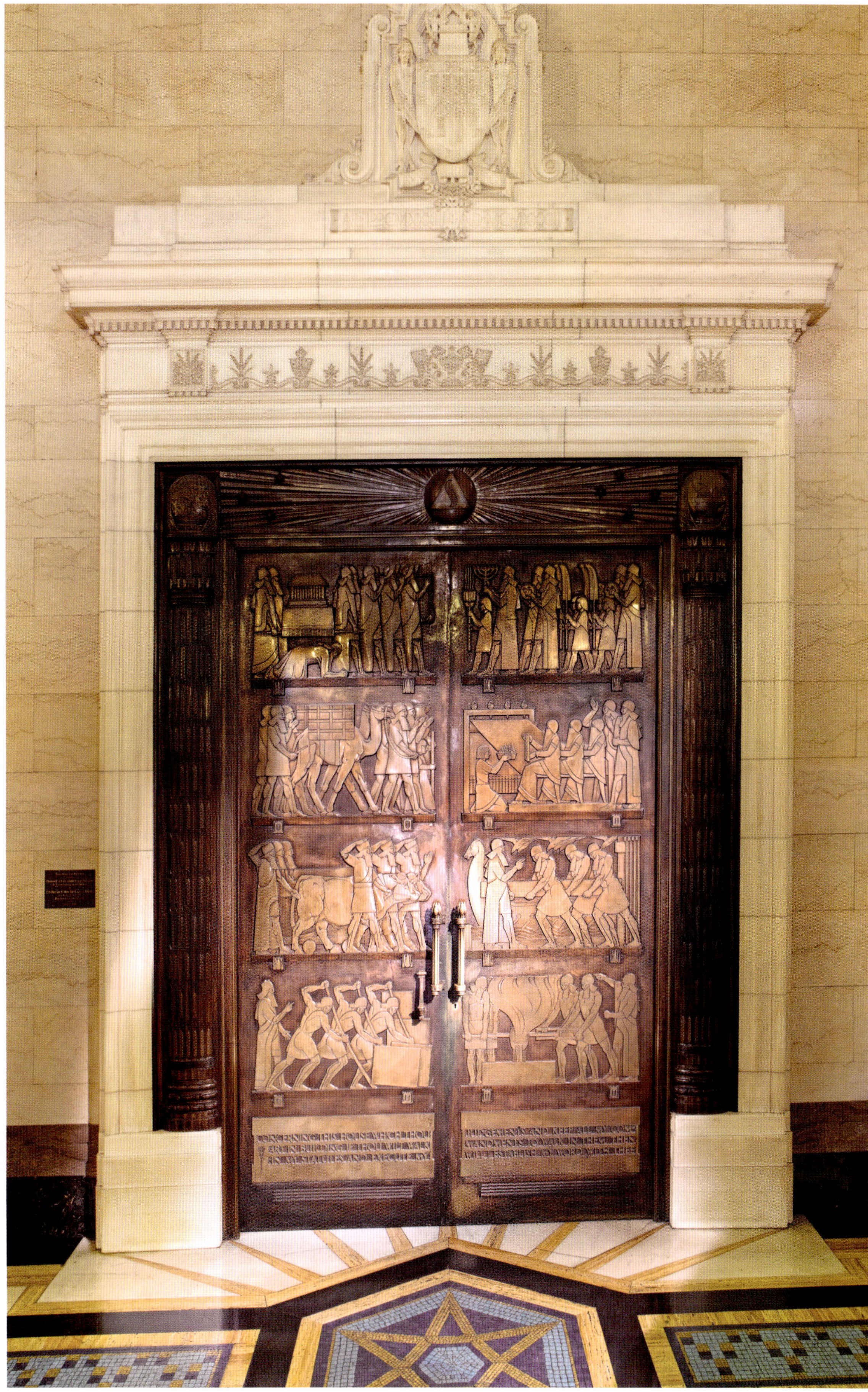
CONCERNING THIS HOUSE WHICH THOU
ART IN BUILDING IF THOU WILT WALK
IN MY STATUTES AND EXECUTE MY
JUDGEMENTS AND KEEP ALL MY COMM
ANDMENTS TO WALK IN THEM THEN
WILL I ESTABLISH MY WORD WITH THEE

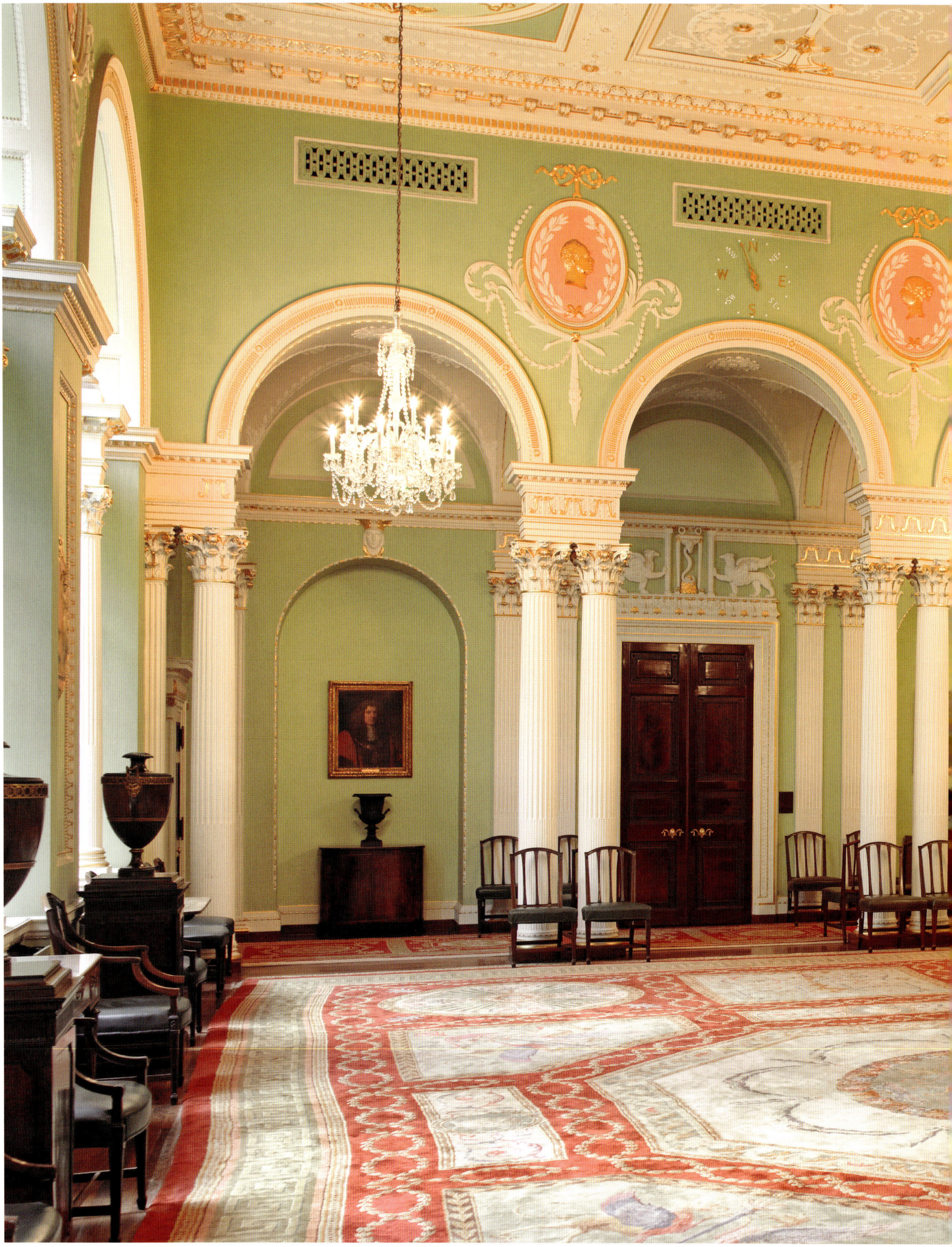

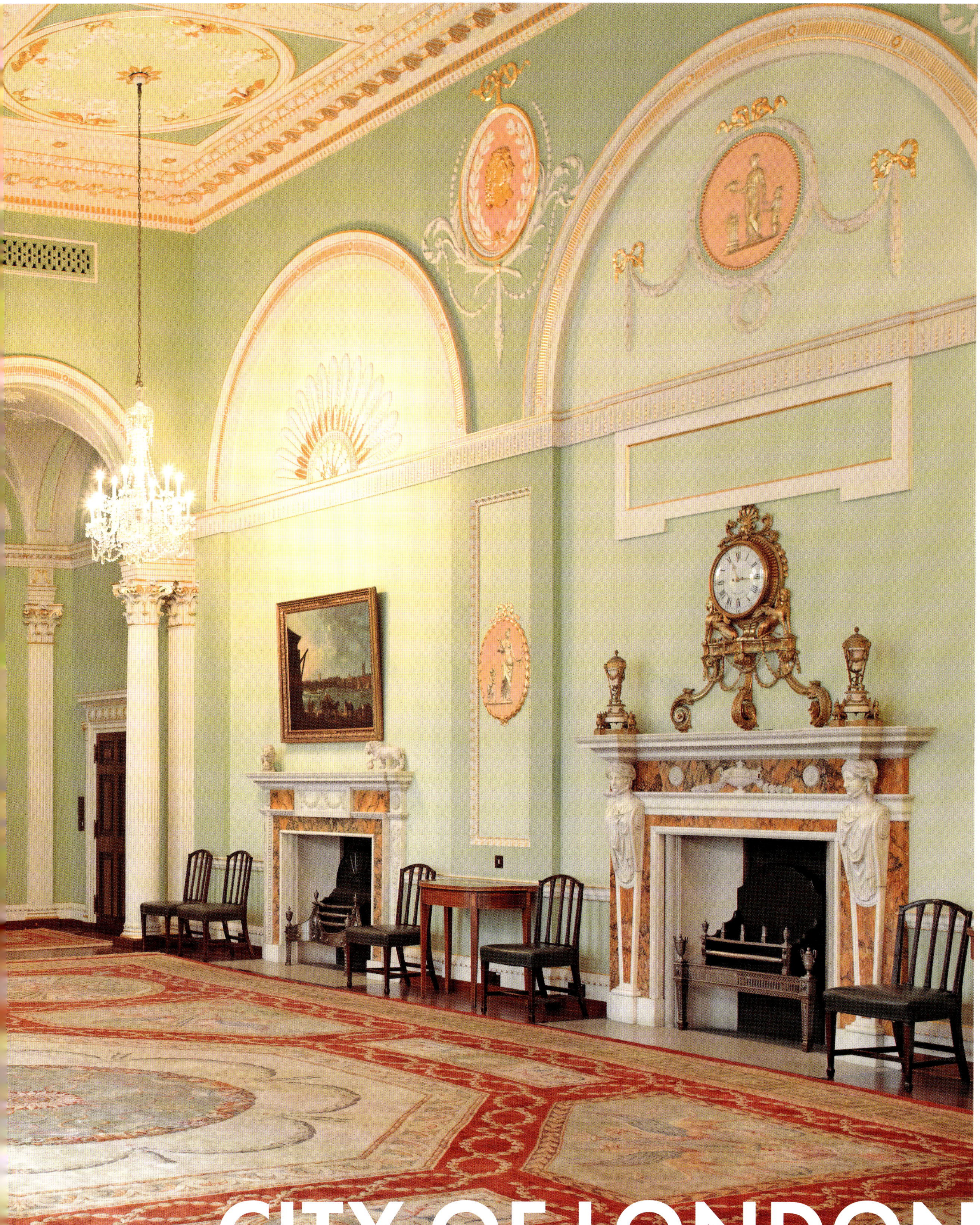

CITY OF LONDON

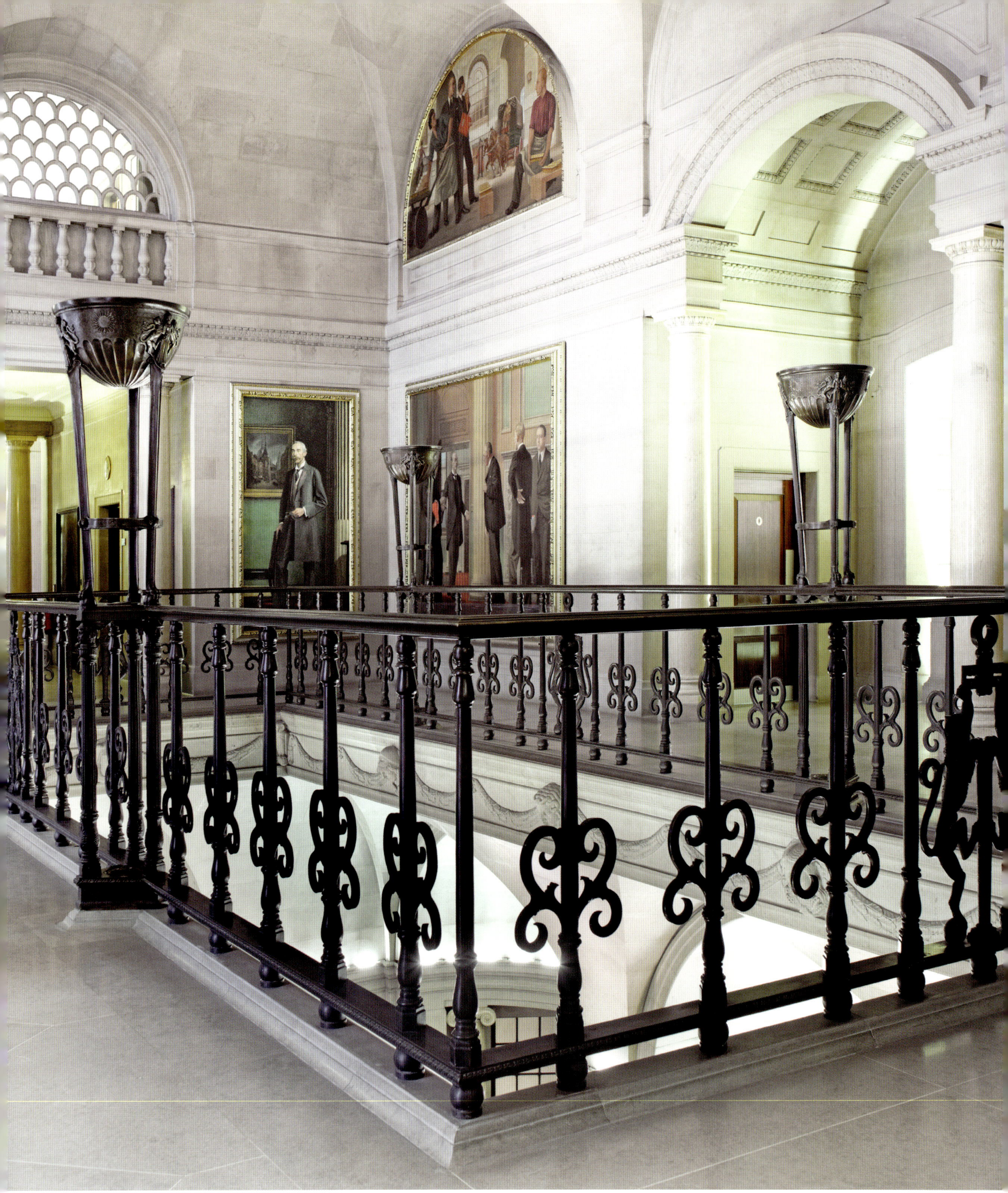

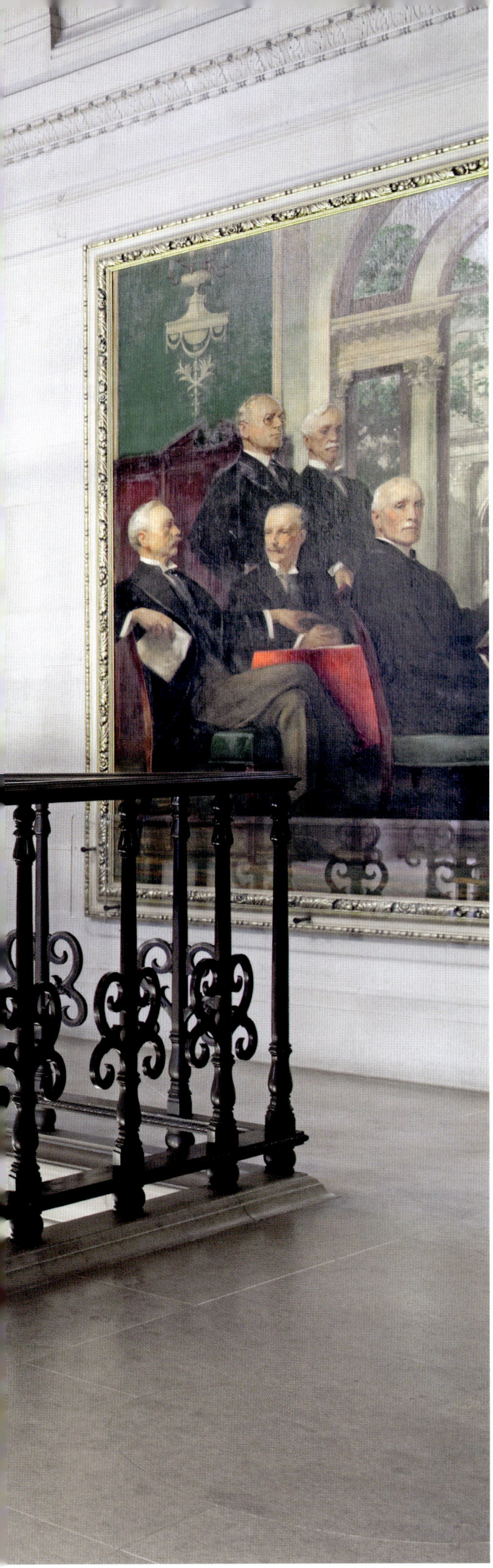

The Bank of England

Previous spread Court Room, including a wind direction indicator above the middle arch on the end wall, driven by a weather vane on the roof. A strong wind from the east indicated that ships were approaching London and that the Bank should prepare money for increased levels of trading in the City.

Opposite Entrance area on the first floor, with stone vaulted ceiling and wrought-iron balustrade carrying uplighters. The paintings are of former Governors and Directors, and the Committee of the Treasury.

The Bank of England building is an imperial neo-classical seven-storey structure of the early twentieth century looming over a long perimeter wall built a hundred years earlier. Taken together, these two elements once caused a great controversy. Many architectural studies dismiss the building, designed by Sir Herbert Baker in 1921, as dull, bombastic or unimaginative, and describe the wall as the greatest feature of the bank.

Eight architects have been associated with the building since its establishment in Threadneedle Street in 1734, but only Sir John Soane's work between 1788 to 1828 has been described as a masterpiece. Over forty years he created a series of offices, mostly no higher than three storeys, said to resemble a Roman basilica. Around this he designed a screening wall, devoid of windows, as it was designed as a fortified structure to resist attack. No lighting could come from the street side of the building, and many rooms are illuminated by a clever arrangement of top lighting. Only a single storey at the entrance portico projected above the wall. This building lasted for almost a century, and was being referred to as Soane's Bank or the Old Bank when the time to change it came after the First World War.

There was a compelling need to enlarge the bank as its responsibilities grew, and much of Soane's bank was demolished in four stages between 1925 and 1939 and replaced by the new building, seven storeys above ground and three below. Destruction of Soane's bank

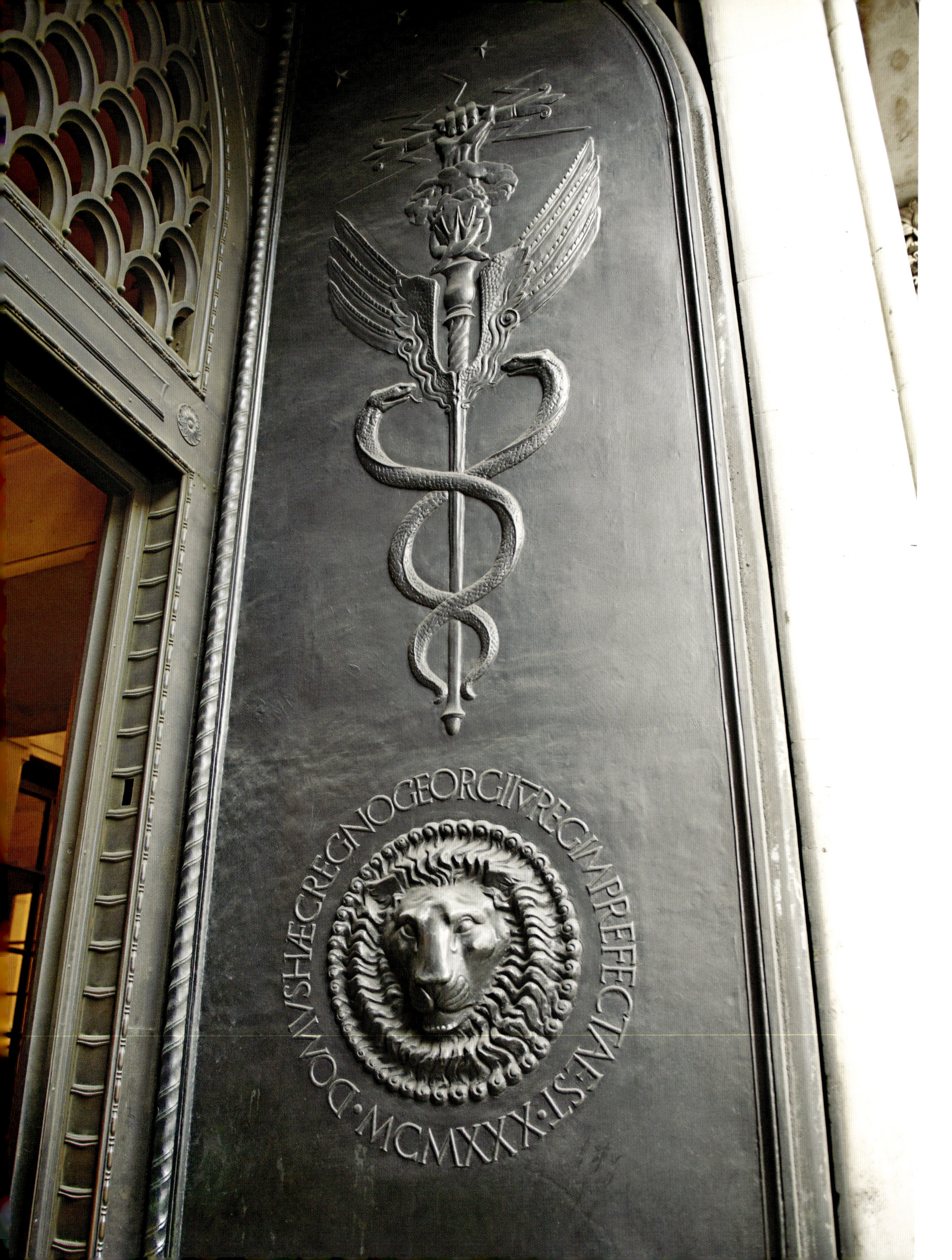
DOMVSHÆCREGNOGEORGIIVREGIMPREFECTA·EST·
MCMXXX·

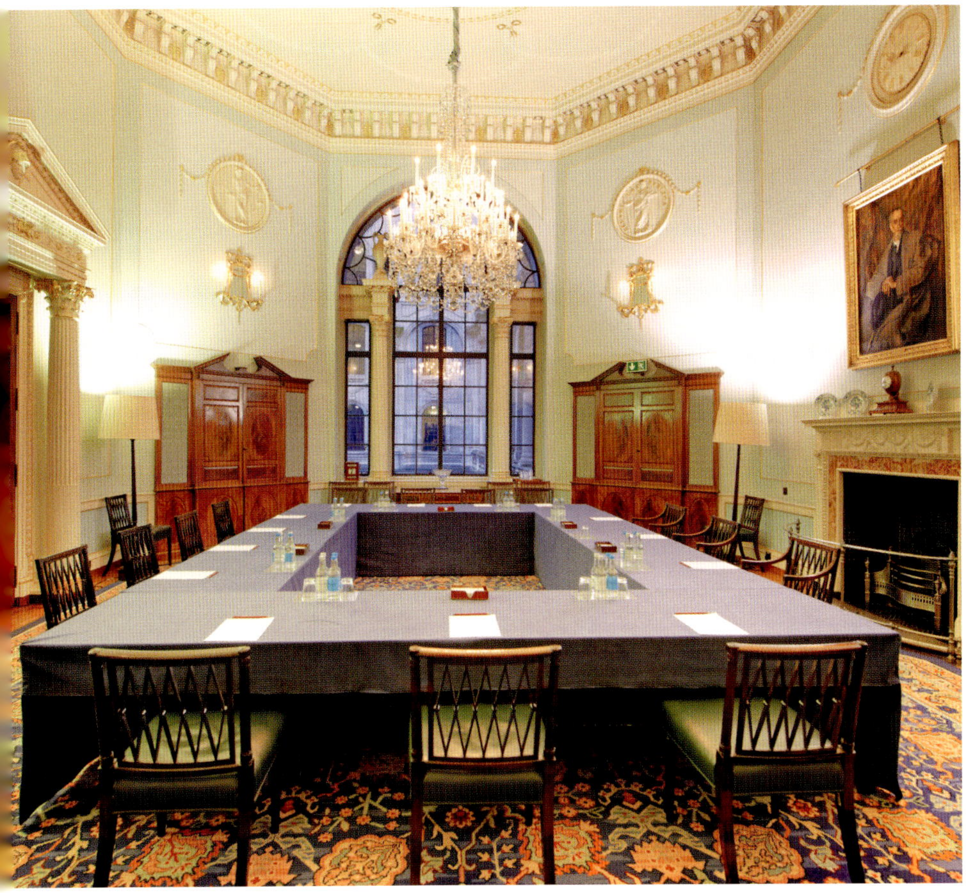

Opposite Bronze door on the Threadneedle Street entrance, with a caduceus design by Sir Charles Wheeler dating from 1930. The hand of Zeus grasps a bolt of lightning, symbolizing the electrical force powering modern banking.

Above The first-floor Committee Room, in an eighteenth-century style, where monthly meetings of the Monetary Policy Committee set the interest rate.

building generated great criticism at the time and since then the trend has been to increasingly venerate Soane's work and deride Baker's, although some sensitivity was shown both by the bank and the architect in the decision to preserve the wall and rebuild the bank. There had been calls by the City of London authorities for street widening, which would have required the demolition of at least one side of the Soane wall, and also pressure to modify the shape of the site, which is an awkward trapezium. Those proposals were resisted, the groundplan preserved and the result was a compromise of aesthetics, function and conservation, even if the building overpowers the wall.

Except for the eight gold bullion vaults spreading over two of the floors below ground, most of the functional working spaces of the Bank of England are unremarkable, but the formal rooms are stunning. Some rooms do survive from Soane's time, and from an earlier architect, Sir Robert Taylor, from 1765–70, although rooms and furnishings have been relocated in some cases, or recreated. The octagonal Committee Room, where interest rates are set by the Governor and the Monetary Policy Committee, retains its original ceiling design and marble chimney piece. The Court Room, in green, pink and gilt, represents Taylor's design and has fine plaster decoration and three marble chimneypieces. On a wall in this room is a replica wind direction indicator of 1805, driven by a shaft from a weathervane on the roof, which once helped inform the directors of the shipping arrivals. Soane's top-lit Bank Stock Office of 1792–3 was reconstructed by historic architecture specialists Higgins Gardner & Partners in 1986–8.

Today, an appreciation of Soane's wall at street level requires a walk of half a kilometre and some imagination. Made of channelled Portland stone, it lines Threadneedle Street, Prince's Street, Lothbury, and Bartholomew Lane, punctuated by fifty Corinthian columns and a number of pilaster low relief false columns, blind recesses and a single statue, which is of Soane himself. There are still no windows. A decorated frieze relieves the forbidding masonry on three sides. The colonnade which forms the north-west corner, or Tivoli Corner, was based on the Temple of Vesta, which the architect sketched during a visit to Italy in 1779. Along the length of the wall, Soane's classic symmetry and symbolically empty niches can be hard to appreciate from the narrow streets. All the original door openings remain now filled with modern bronze doors decorated by sculptor Sir Charles Wheeler.

There is public access to the Bank of England Museum on the east side from Bartholomew Lane. The first room of the museum is a reconstruction of Soane's Bank Stock Office of 1793.

The Bank once contained a barracks housing a detachment of thirty soldiers, and a printing office where banknotes were produced. The Bank of England was founded in 1694 to raise money during a time of war and it spent the first forty years of its life in rented premises. It long functioned as a commercial bank as well as for raising money for the government and was still owned by private stockholders past the middle of the last century, but by then was acting effectively as a national central bank. It was nationalized in 1946, and became fully independent in 1998.

CONTACT INFORMATION

The Bank of England,
Threadneedle Street, EC2R 8AH
https://www.bankofengland.co.uk/

Bevis Marks Synagogue

Bevis Marks Synagogue is the oldest Jewish house of worship in London, and the only synagogue in Europe to have held regular services continuously for over 300 years. It stands in a quiet courtyard behind a gated stone archway in the City of London. The inscription in Hebrew above the entrance reads: 'Sanctified to the Lord, Holy Congregation, Gate of Heaven, New Year 5462', which represents the year 1702. The synagogue is virtually unchanged from that date.

Portuguese and Spanish Sephardic Jews were permitted to re-establish and practice their religion in England after 1656 when Oliver Cromwell relaxed the exclusion laws, and a small synagogue was established in London. As more Jews arrived fleeing the Inquisition, a larger synagogue was commissioned. When the building contract was signed in February 1699, Jews were still not permitted to build on the public thoroughfare, and the synagogue was sited in a discreet yard just off what is now Bevis Marks Street. The exterior style of the building was much like other City of London churches of the time. The builder was Joseph Avis, a Quaker Merchant Taylor liveryman and carpenter, who had worked for Sir Christopher Wren on St Bride's Fleet Street and on St James's in Piccadilly.

There are two legends about the construction of Bevis Marks that cannot be verified, but are said to reflect shifting political attitudes of the time. One

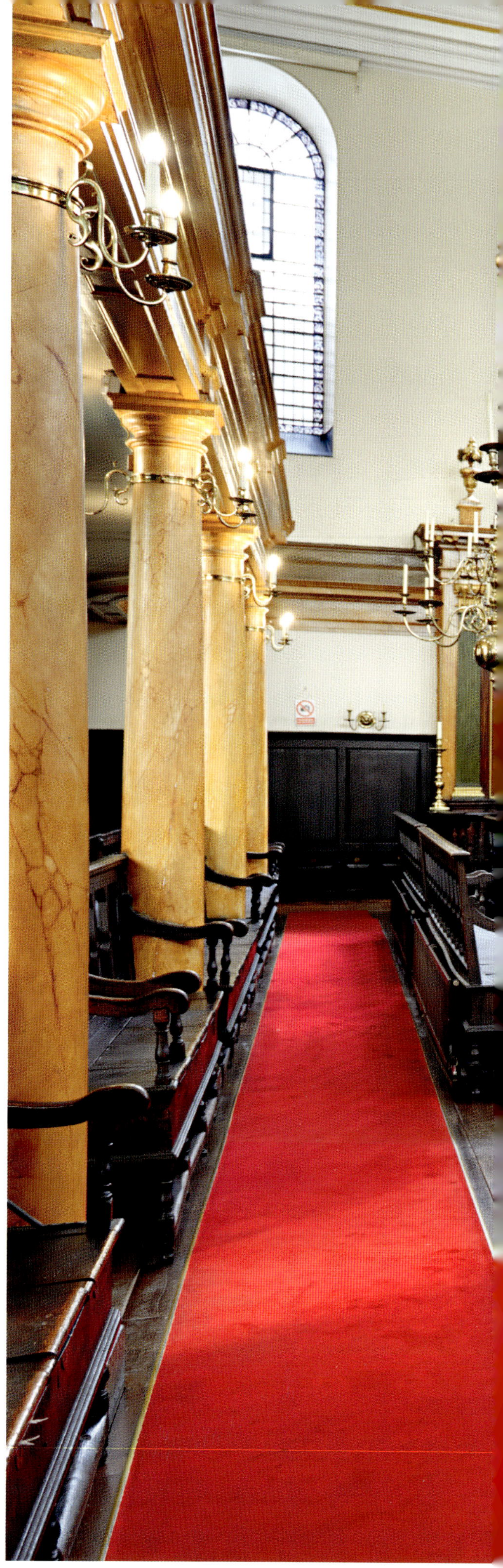

All the furniture and decoration date back to the opening in 1702.

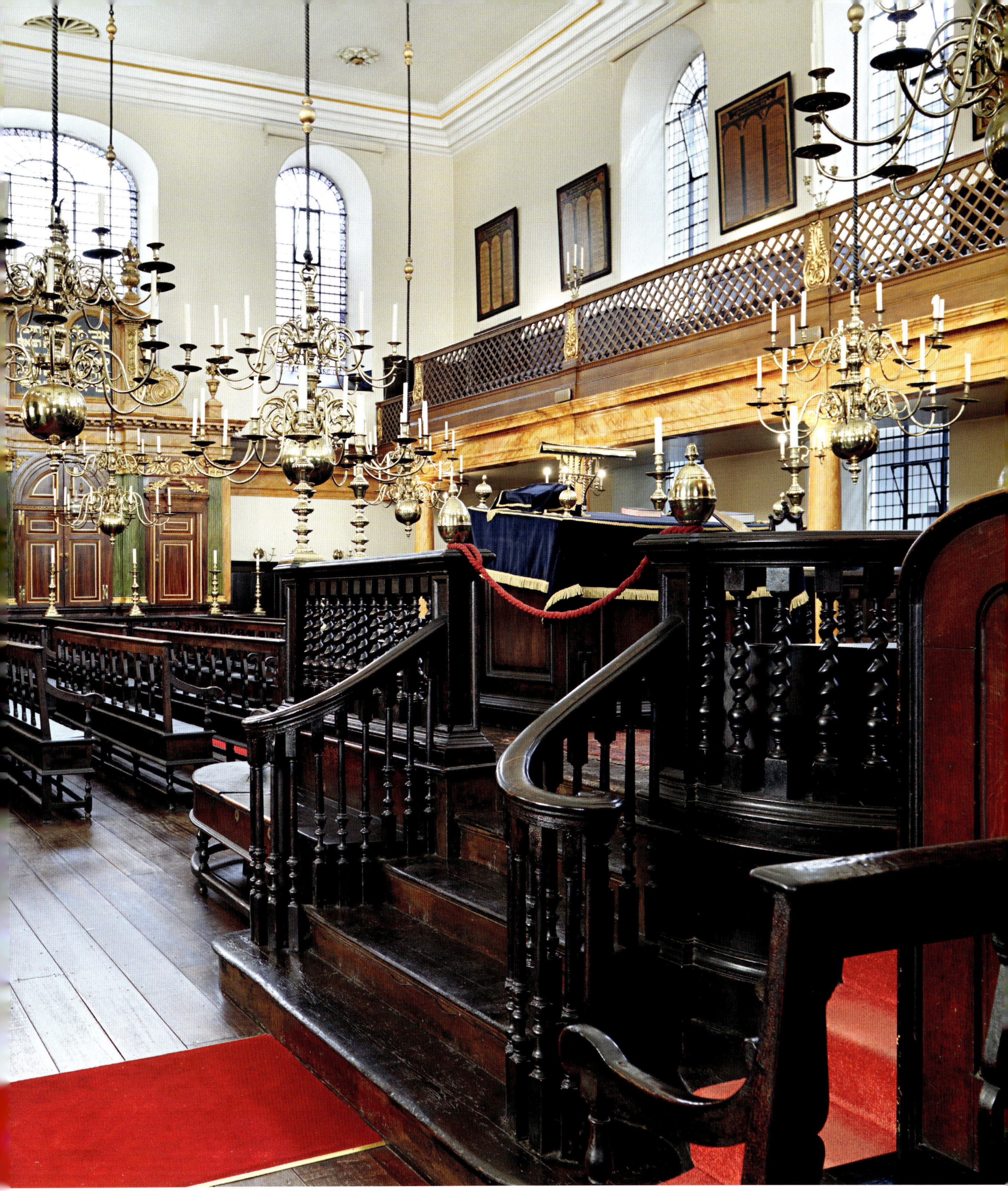

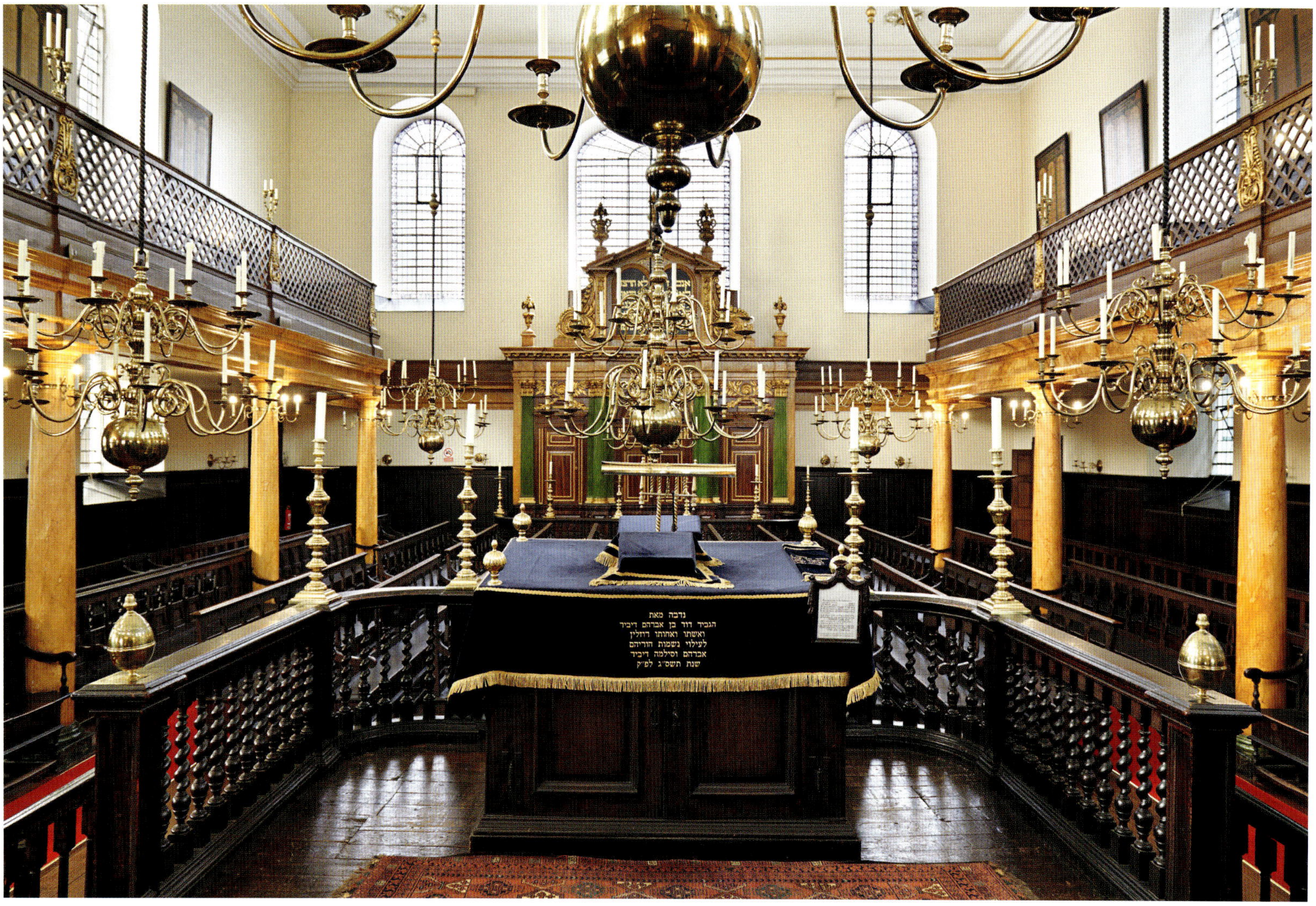

Above The reader's desk inside the *bimah*, covered by a blue throw with gold embroidery and fringe. The women's gallery is behind wrought-iron grilles above to the left and right.

is that Princess Anne, later Queen Anne, presented an oak beam from a Royal Navy warship for incorporation in the roof, showing royal support from the House of Stuart. The other claims that Joseph Avis returned the profit he had made on the contract, saying he would not profit by building a House of God, showing friendship from the Puritan side.

The main inspiration for the layout and decoration of the interior was the Amsterdam Synagogue, influential because it represented a rare enclave for Jewish worshippers of the age. Twelve Doric columns, representing the twelve tribes of Israel, support the upper women's gallery. In front of the Ark and around the reading desk are ten large candlesticks, emblematic of the Commandments. The seven suspended brass candelabra represent the days of the week; the largest central lamp for the Shabbat was a gift from the Amsterdam Synagogue. Candles are still lit for festivals and weddings. The heavy dark doors with original iron locks and massive keys are still in use.

The Ark containing the Torah scrolls appears to be made of coloured marble, but is painted oak and the interior is lined with Spanish gilded leather. Benches are positioned on the east–west axis and face inwards around two aisles for the procession of the Torah. Some of the benches in the back rows may be the oldest items in the building, the original seats brought from the preceding Creechurch Lane synagogue of 1657. The end-of-bench seat once occupied by Sir Moses Montefiore, Victorian financier and banker, activist, philanthropist and Sheriff of London, who was a leading worshipper at Bevis Marks, is roped off and reserved for important visitors, such as when Prince Charles and Prince Philip came for the 300th and 250th anniversaries respectively.

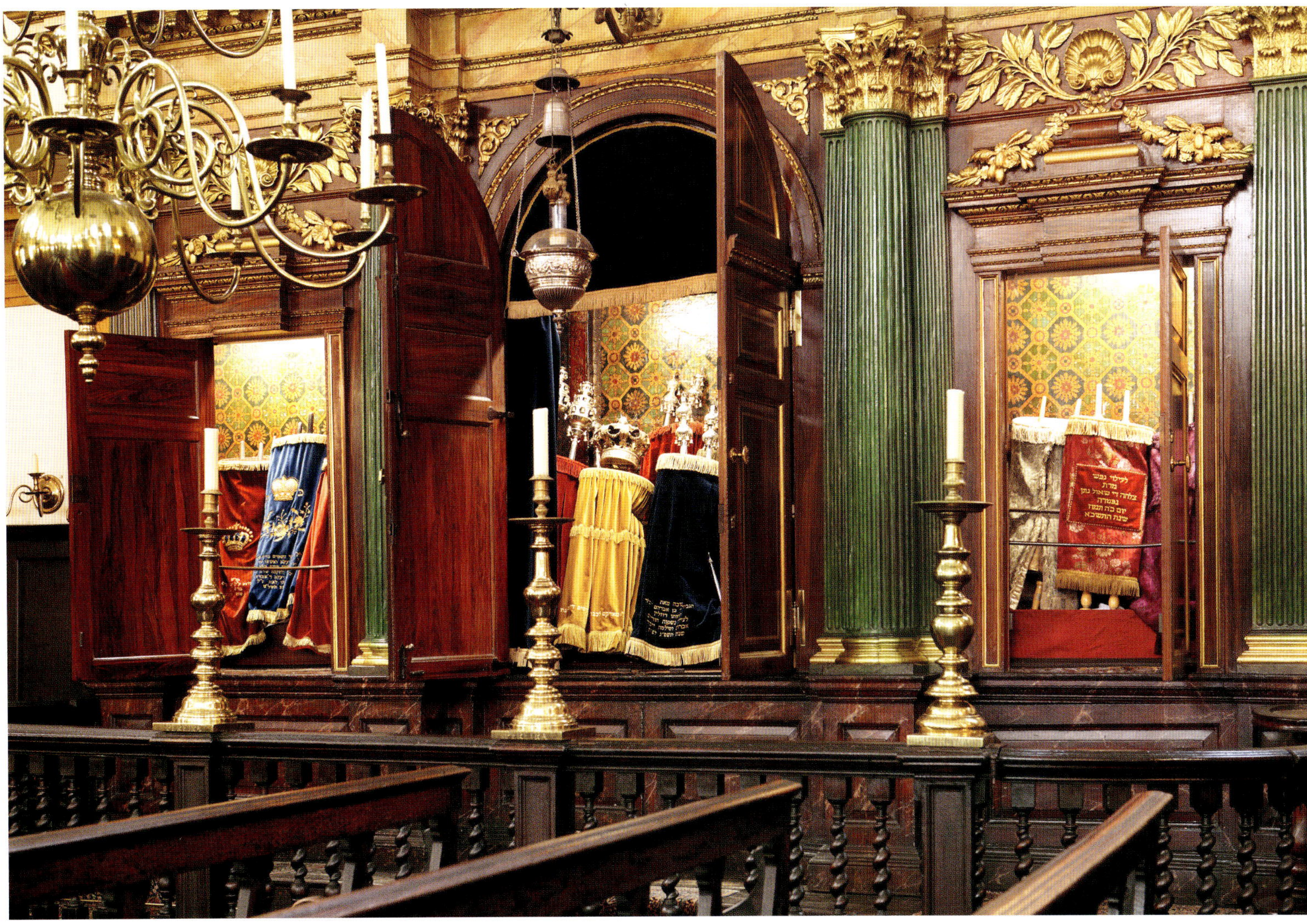

Above The Torah scrolls and the Ark, which is hand-carved from oak, with the doors grained to imitate mahogany. The columns and base are painted to resemble coloured marble.

A fire destroyed the roof in 1738; it was replaced in 1749, but for many years the synagogue escaped much of the destruction that London experienced. It was located in the area of densest bombing of London during the air attacks of 1940–5, and was surrounded by areas of widespread devastation, but no bomb fell directly on Bevis Marks Street, and it escaped with only minor damage. It was the Baltic Exchange and Bishopgate bombs of 1992 and 1993 that caused more considerable damage to the synagogue, requiring new ceiling joists and floorboards. The work was completed in 1995.

At first, the synagogue was built on a leased plot of land, but in 1747 Benjamin Mendes da Costa bought the leasehold of the ground and presented it to the congregation. For Sephardic believers, Bevis Marks was the leading centre of the Anglo-Jewish world for 150 years, until the shifting of the community from the City changed the balance across London. The traditional Sephardic Spanish-Portuguese service is still celebrated. Today, Bevis Marks is the synagogue of the Square Mile, and also an important place for explorers of the City, nominated by Jewish Heritage for the European Routes of Jewish Culture.

CONTACT INFORMATION

Bevis Marks Synagogue,
4 Heneage Lane, EC3A 5DQ
http://www.sephardi.org.uk/bevis-marks

Ironmongers' Hall

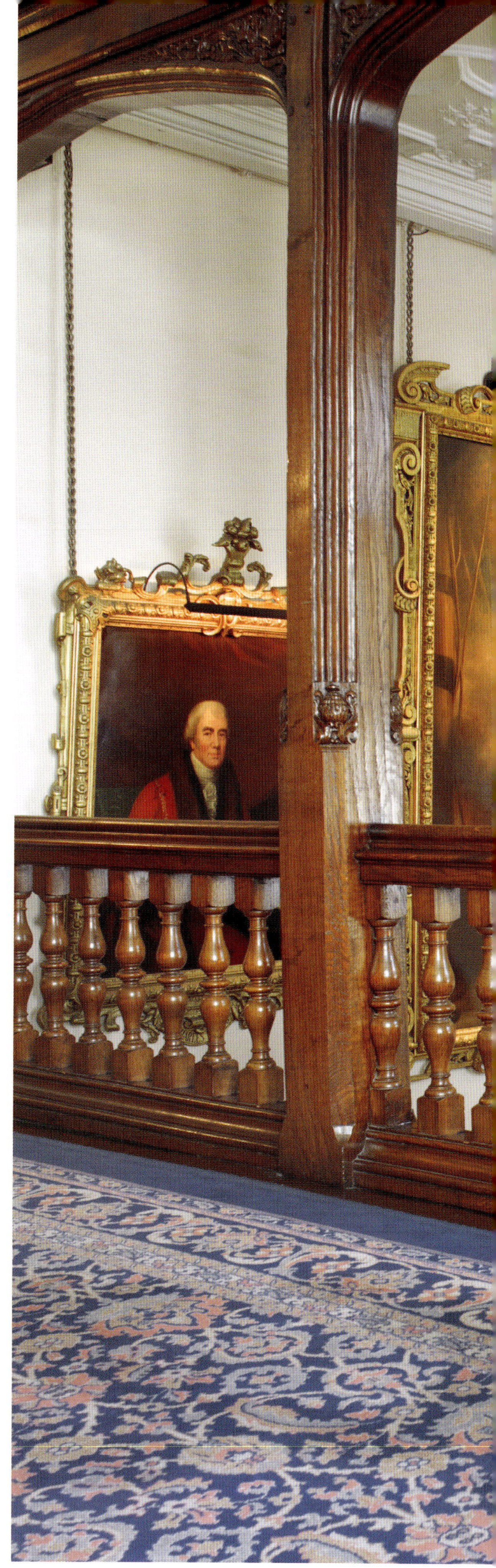

The staircase and landing, featuring a portrait from 1685 of Sir Robert Geffrye, Lord Mayor of London.

The Worshipful Company of Ironmongers ranks tenth among the livery companies of the City of London, traditionally described as the Great Twelve in order of precedence. The company acted as a fraternity of professionals operating as a society for the mutual benefit of its members but the association with its namesake trade faded long ago as the iron industry shifted northwards away from Kent. The Ironmongers' Company moved to philanthropy and education. Its work now is the administration of charitable trusts and participation in the pageantry of the City.

Ironmongers are believed to have created a body to protect and regulate their trade as early as 1300 and within thirty years they were participating in the elections of City officials and choosing four of their members to work with the mayors and sheriffs of the capital. The Ironmongers received a grant of arms in 1455. The charter of incorporation from Edward IV followed in the 1460s. It lost its charter and suffered extortion under Henry VIII and later monarchs. It was obliged to pay a fine to the notorious Judge Jeffreys in 1668 to redeem the charter.

The guild's first home was in Fenchurch Street, at a property purchased in 1457. The building was converted into a hall for the fraternity, and later enlarged, before being rebuilt by 1587. The Ironmongers' Hall was not destroyed in the Great Fire of 1666, but was again rebuilt in 1745. This structure was damaged in an air raid in July 1917 and later demolished. The present building, designed by architect Sydney Tatchell, in

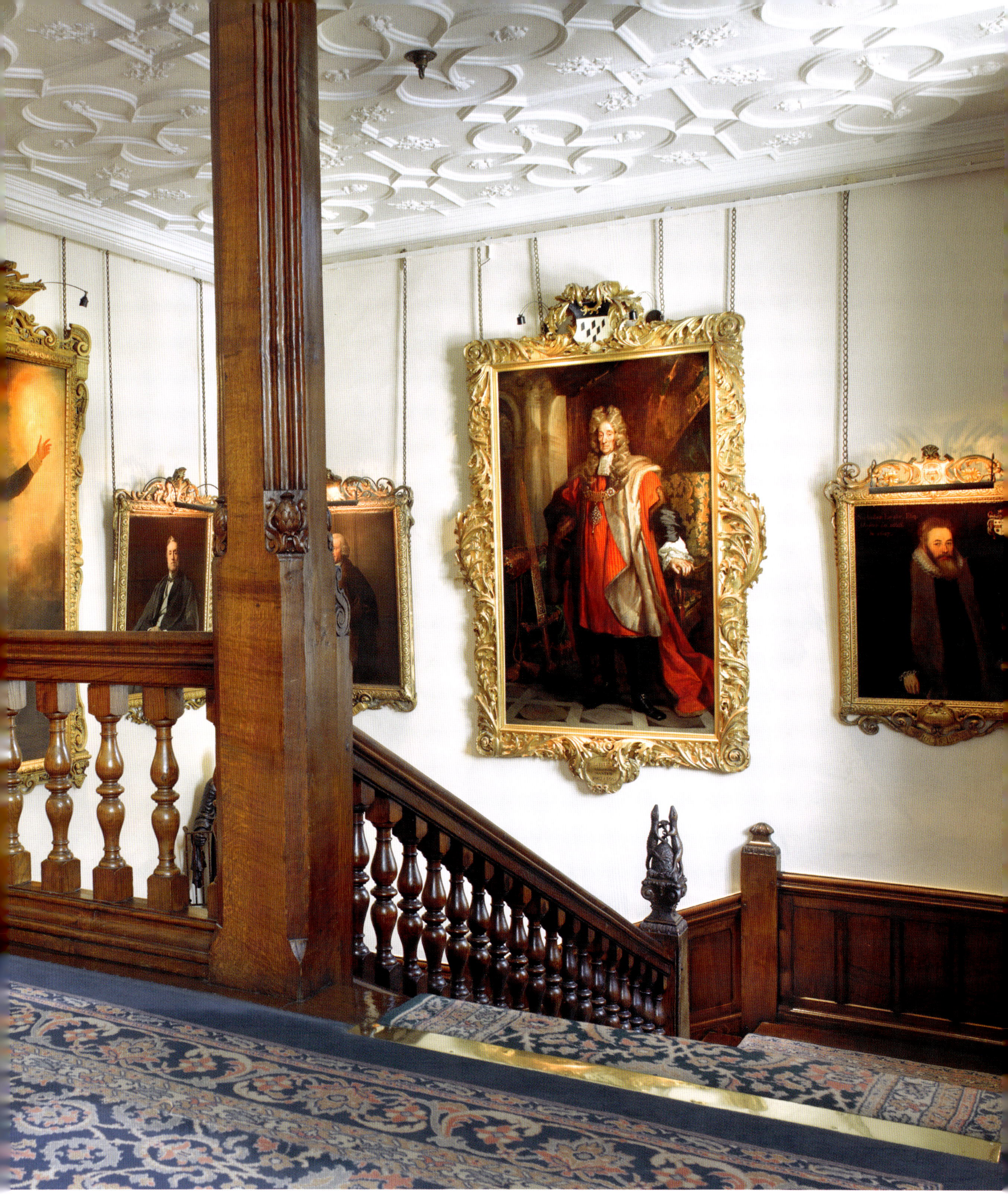

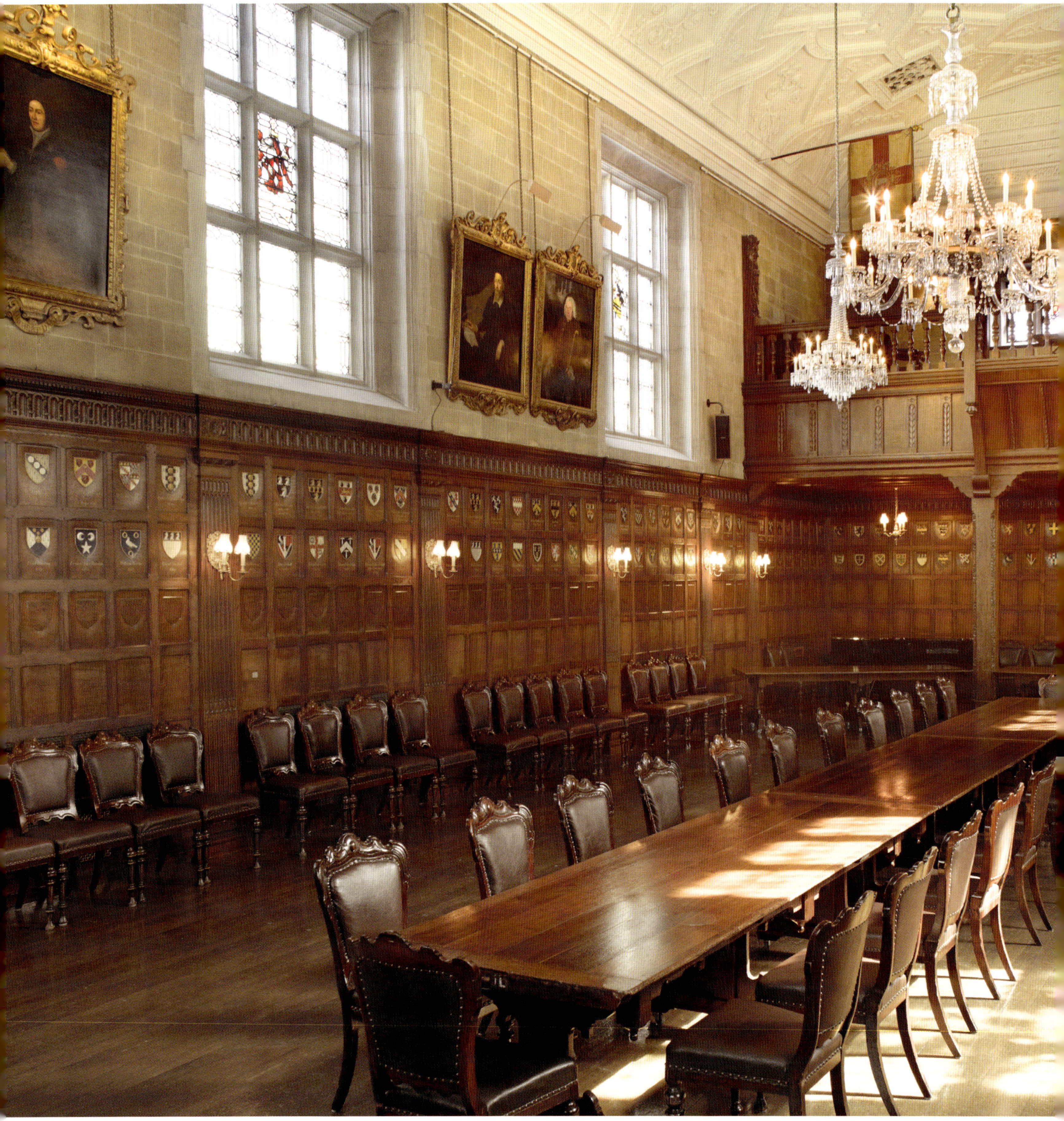

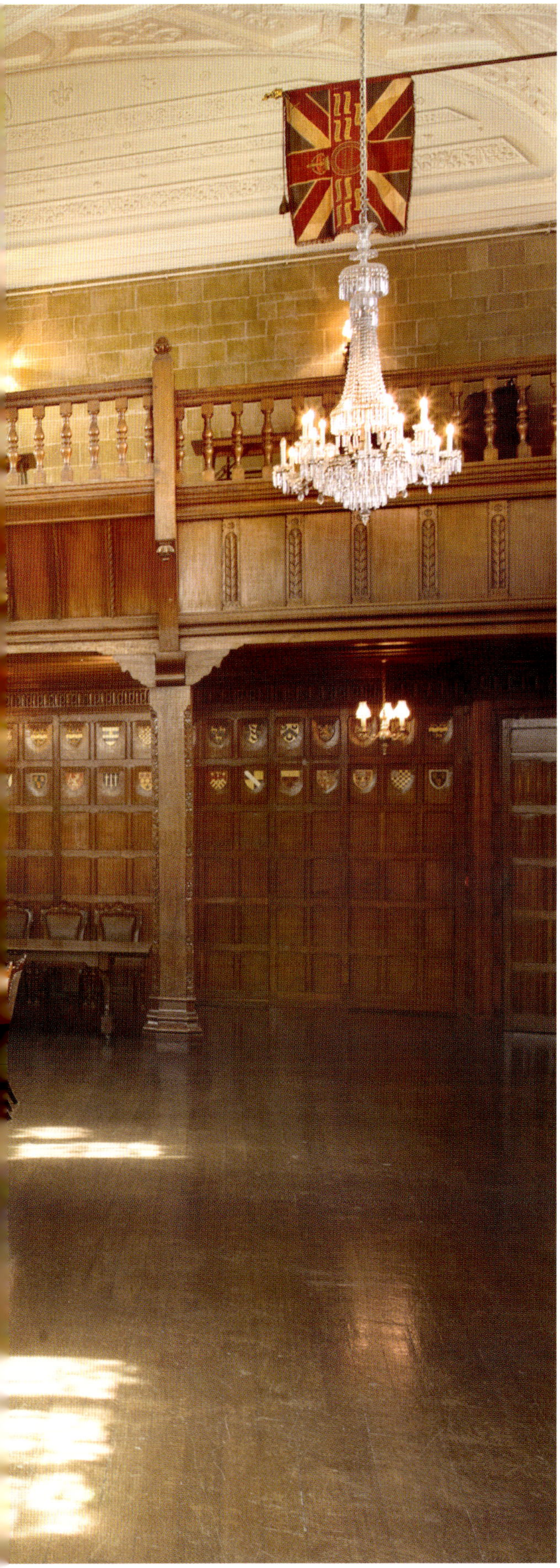

The banqueting hall, where the decoration conjures up heraldic imagery and connections with the monarchy and lord mayors of London.

Shaftesbury Place, in a cobbled courtyard behind Aldersgate, was formally opened in 1925.

The L-shaped hall is built in the neo-Tudor style to reflect the company's long and distinguished history, although it was built around a modern steel frame. It now strikes a great contrast in architectural style with the brutalist Barbican estate close by. It escaped serious damage during the Second World War, in an area of great devastation. The ground and first floor storeys are of handmade red brick, the second upper floor storey half-timbered. There is a cloister and fountain in the outer angle of the ground plan.

Above the front porch, which is approached through a courtyard, is a carving of the Ironmongers' Company's coat of arms, incorporating two salamanders. Salamanders, like iron, were reputed to be able to survive fire. Inside the porch is the entrance hall, its walls of the wood panelling that continues as a main feature of the building, together with a fireplace in antique style and, leading off it, a wide staircase.

The luncheon room on the ground floor also features the traditional oak panelling, with Regency furniture, a Turkish carpet and an impressive stained-glass window at one end of the chamber. Along from the luncheon room, the court room includes high settees from the previous hall along the walls and a statue of Edward IV, who gave the company its royal charter in 1463, while the chamber is overlooked by a magnificent stained-glass window that incorporates glass from the company's first hall dating back to 1457.

Upstairs is the drawing room, where a huge William Morris tapestry is hung in place of wallpaper. It is claimed to be the largest William Morris tapestry in England. The room also features a massive fireplace and elegant windows, along with a large bookcase. Among the many paintings is a portrait of Izaac Walton, author of *The Compleat Angler*.

On the first floor is the double-height banqueting hall, the centrepiece of the Ironmongers' Hall. The oak panelling and Waterford chandeliers, which hang from the elliptical ceiling, were salvaged from the previous hall in Fenchurch Street.

CONTACT INFORMATION

Ironmongers' Hall,
Shaftesbury Place, EC2Y 8AA
https://www.ironmongers.org/

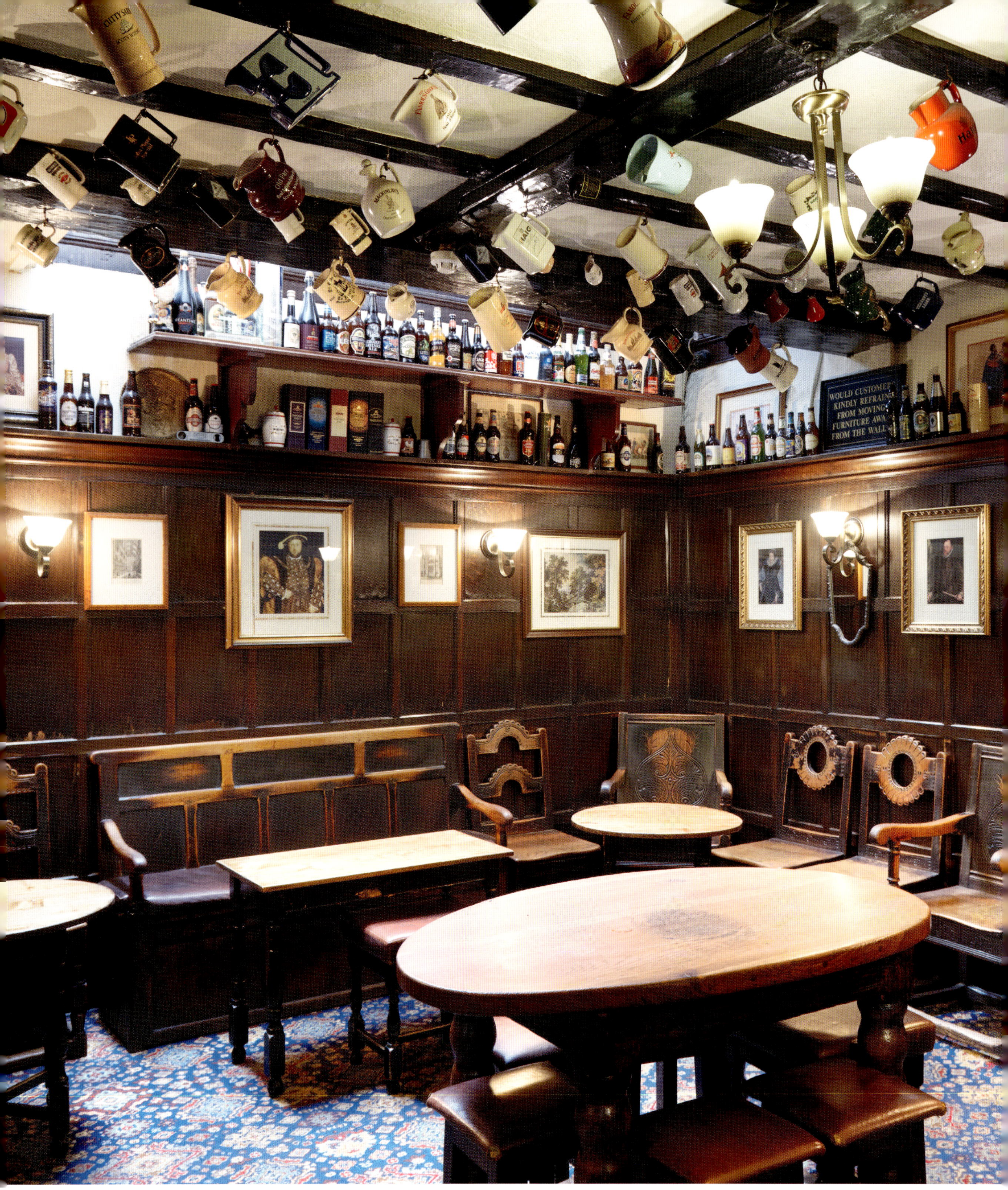
WOULD CUSTOMER
KINDLY REFRAIN
FROM MOVING
FURNITURE AWA
FROM THE WALL

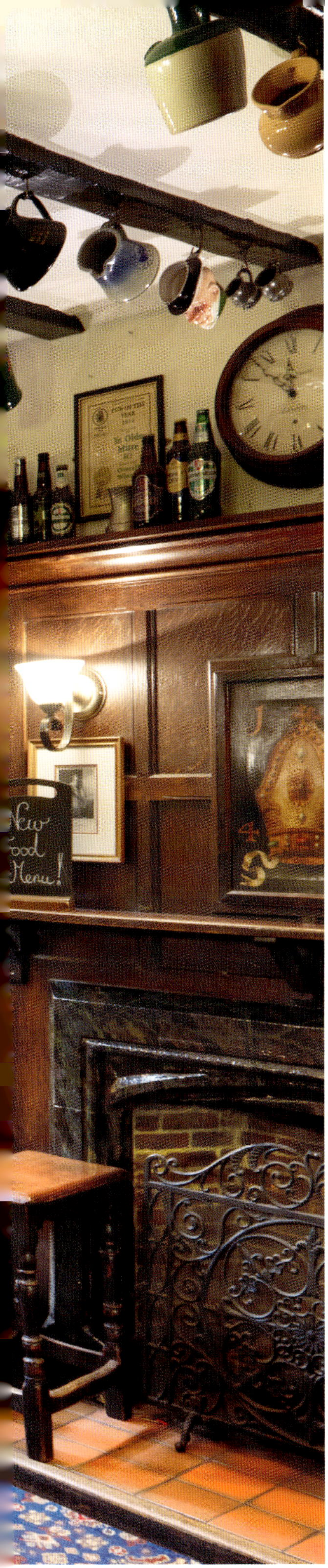

Ye Olde Mitre

A cosy bar with legends attached.

Ye Olde Mitre is hidden in a narrow alleyway between Hatton Garden and Ely Place. There are two cosy wood panelled bars with old fireplaces, a snug, an upstairs dining room – and large slice of history and legend.

It was built in 1546 for the Bishop Goodrich of Ely, Cambridgeshire, in the grounds of the bishop's palace, Ely House, to cater for servants. Goodrich had sided with Henry VIII in his conflict with the established church. But as lines of power and influence shifted, a later Bishop of Ely in the time of Elizabeth I was forced to lease part of the estate to Christopher Hatton, her most favoured Chancellor. This became Hatton Garden. Today near the entrance of the bar in a glazed cabinet the trunk of an old cherry tree is said to mark the boundary between properties held by the Bishop of Ely and Sir Christopher. Harder to prove is the claim this was the tree around which a young Elizabeth danced with her future Chancellor. The rumour that Elizabeth and courtier Hatton were secret lovers is impossible to verify, although history nails this as a claim specifically made by Mary Queen of Scots in 1584.

Ely House and the bishop's estate were swept away when the Crown took over the area in 1772 and the pub was rebuilt at that time. The oldest parts are the wooden staircase walls and a stone mitre set in the walls which comes from the gatehouse of the old palace. For many years the legacy of the pub lying in the jurisdiction of Cambridgeshire meant the landlord had to apply to that county to renew the licence.

CONTACT INFORMATION

Ye Olde Mitre,
Ely Court, Ely Place, EC1N 6SJ
https://www.yeoldemitreholborn.co.uk/

Daily Express Building

The Daily Express Building at 120 Fleet Street caused a sensation at its opening in 1932 with its curvaceous black glass skin and its stunning Art Deco lobby. Fleet Street up until then had been lined with bland buildings resembling banks, and the Express building stood out marvellously. Sir Owen Williams was praised as the creator of the design, but the credit for the building should be shared. The design of the lobby was handled by another architect, Robert Atkinson, who had created several super-cinemas with lavish interiors, and here he emulated the style of the most extravagant skyscraper entrances of the time. A starburst ceiling is moulded into a lantern. Serpent handrails flank the approach to an oval stairwell. Rosewood veneers, smooth marbles and reflective metallic surfaces abound, bracketed by two relief murals.

Even some of the most high-minded architectural critics of the time liked the building, although the Modernist principle that interiors should be integral to the building does not seem to have been applied in this case. The building was not for architectural purists, although the public loved it. Insiders admired the structure by Sir Owen Williams, who was a civil engineer for years before he became an architect, and a specialist in concrete structures, spending much of the 1920s working as structural engineer on a succession of bridges.

His expertise solved a problem for Beaverbrook Associated Newspapers, who had started to extend

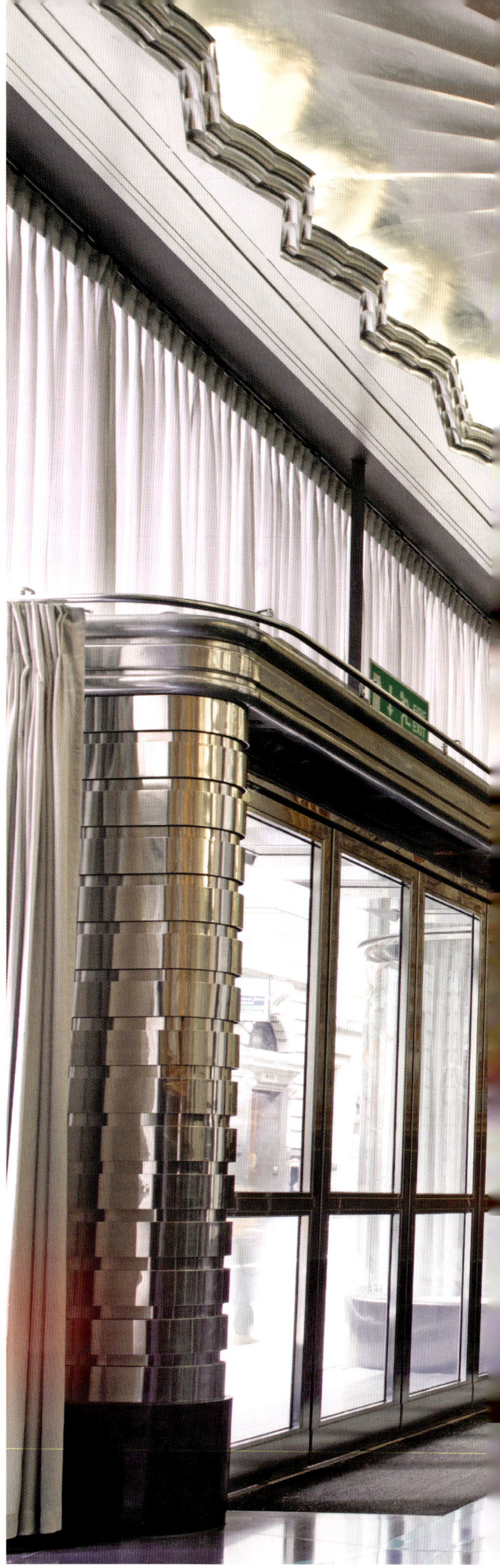

A relief sculpture entitled Britain by Eric Aumonier looks down on the marble, rosewood and metallic surfaces in the entrance lobby with Fleet Street to the left.

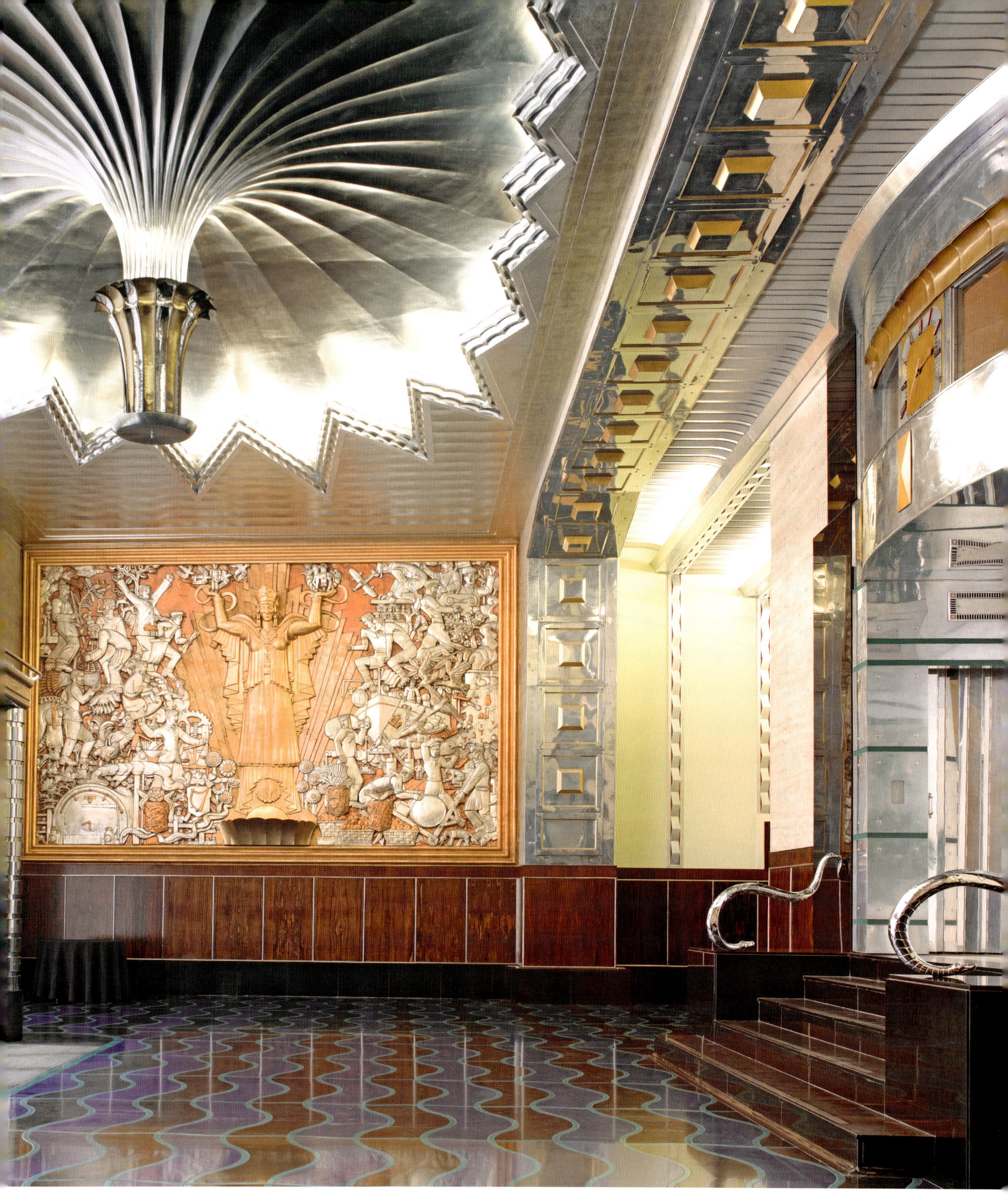

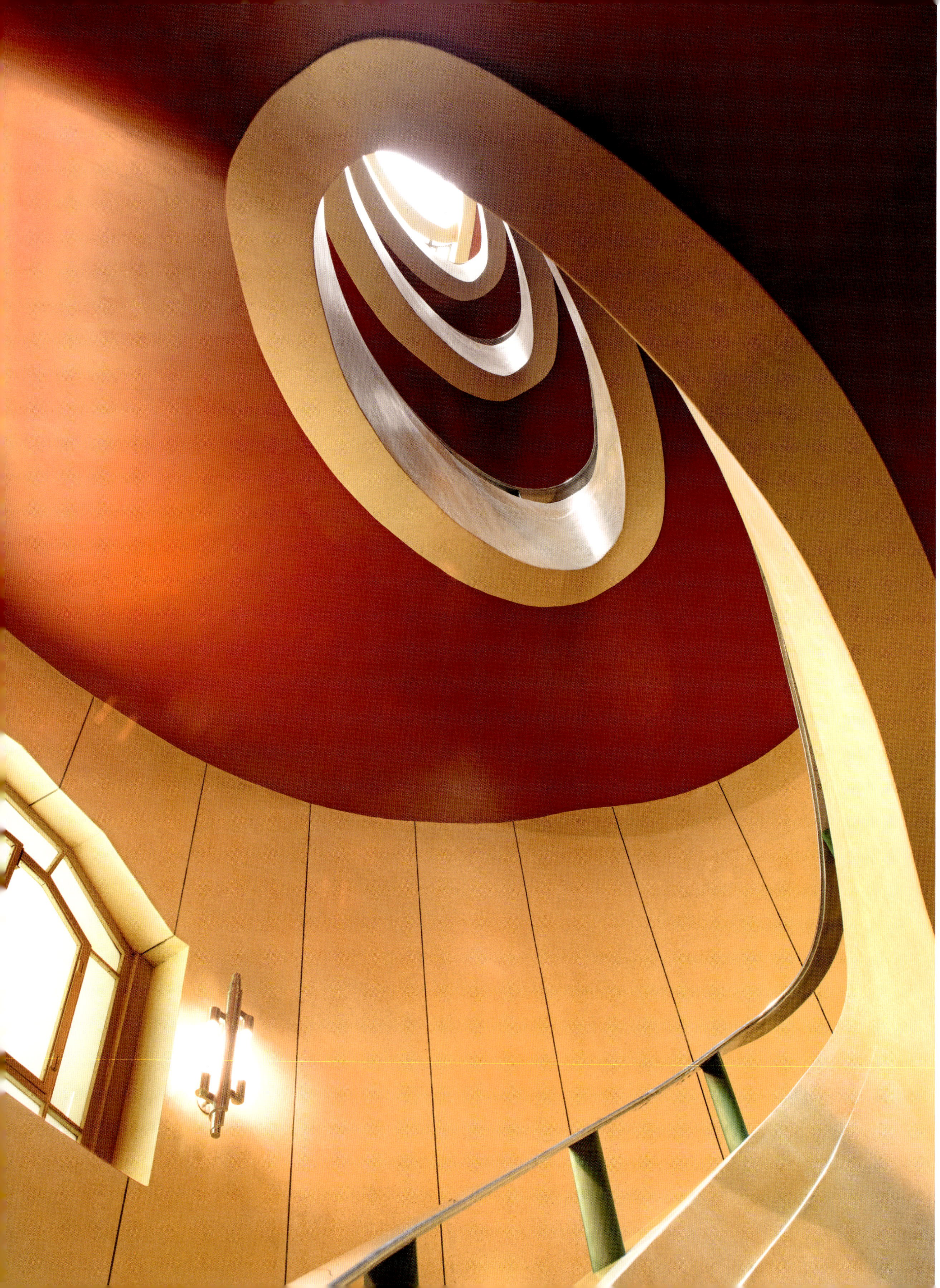

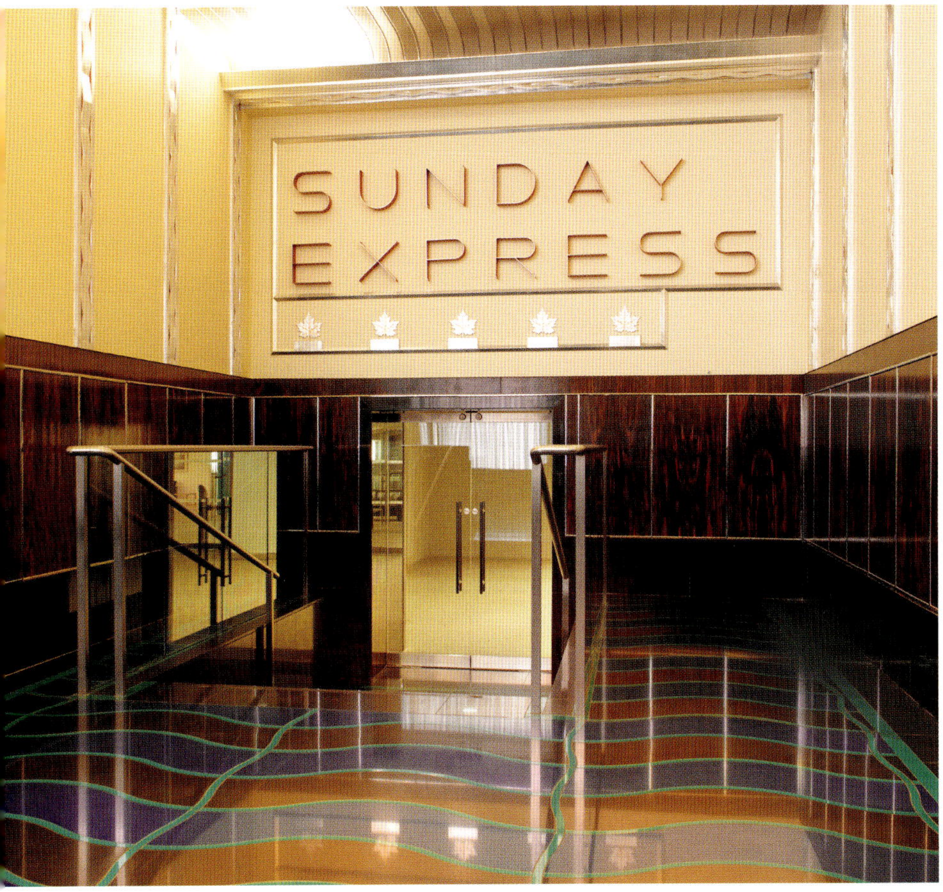

Opposite Beaverbrook Associated Newspapers included the *Sunday Express*; the decorations below the Art Deco sign are maple leaves, denoting the Canadian ancestry of the ownership.

Above The oval-plan stairwell, in lavish cinema style, has been extended during the restoration.

its Fleet Street headquarters with a steel-framed design, but found the grid would be too intrusive, robbing them of space. Space was critical in the basement, where three huge presses were to be positioned. The engineering solution was to build a reinforced concrete eight-legged table straddling the basement with a mezzanine floor as the top. Over this, a series of single-span frames were stacked upwards. On the outside of the ribbed floors were mounted panels of black Vitrolite glass supplied by Pilkington, with clear window glazing hung between. The joints were covered by sills made of a newly developed alloy called Birmabright, which shined in sunlight. At night, the Express Building exuded activity, with the windows, divided by the alternate opaque layers, always brightly lit up. The black glass building set a house style for Express Newspapers, and very similar premises for the company followed in Glasgow and Manchester (which improved on 120 Fleet Street by surrounding the street-level print hall with glass).

A mystery remains over exactly who was inspired to apply the black glass to the structure. Some architectural historians have said it may not have been the bridge builder Sir Owen Williams, who disliked adornment and had said 'architects do little more than decorate what the structural engineer has achieved'. His contemporaneous factory building for Boots at Nottingham has strictly functional glass. Robert Atkinson does not seem to have contributed to the exterior. The original architects for the steel frame design, Ellis & Clarke, had been retained, and may have contributed the Vitrolite panels, but their first submission had used Portland stone cladding.

Another possibility is that the Lord Beaverbrook himself exerted a strong personal influence on the finish, as the North American-born press baron craved a building of self-confident modernity to set it ahead of its staid rivals. In 1932 the *Daily Express* was just getting into its stride, soon to break the 4 million daily sales barrier to become the world's best-selling newspaper. If anything, 120 Fleet Street is a monument to what was the greatest popular newspaper of its time.

What can be seen today in the building, which is occupied by Goldman Sachs, is much more than a restoration. Between 1998 and 2000 Hurley Robertson & Associates re-engineered and improved on what had existed in the later days of newspaper ownership. An extension called Aitken House had grown flush on the east side, which even when clad in Vitrolite was a clumsy addition. Aitken House was demolished without a murmur, and a smoothly curved pavilion added on the east side to make the building symmetrical for the first time. The building had stood empty for years after the newspaper left in 1989, and much had been lost in the way of fixtures, which had to be recreated, including the metal snake handrails.

The fabulous entrance lobby lives on, cleaned and upgraded as a tribute to Atkinson, much of whose other work has been demolished with the demise of cinemas. The plaster ceiling has been strengthened and the original wave patterned floor design recreated in terrazzo ceramics. Two stylized patriotic relief sculptures by Eric Aumonier depicting Britain and Empire continue to look down.

CONTACT INFORMATION

Daily Express Building,
120–129 Fleet Street, EC4A 2BE

London Stone

First recorded in c.1100, London Stone is an historic landmark of oolitic limestone.

The few facts known about London Stone are so outnumbered by myths that most accounts are compelled to describe it in legendary terms. The idea exists from early folklore that if the stone was moved, damaged or destroyed, the future of London itself would be jeopardized. Another legend is that it is part of a Druid altar, as described by visionary poet-painter William Blake.

The London Stone is oolitic limestone, serving as a Roman milestone or monument. A recent study by Museum of London Archaeology (MOLA) suggests it was quarried in the Cotswolds. The stone is shown on medieval maps located on the south side of Candlewick Street (afterwards Cannon Street), opposite St Swithin's church.

In 1450, when Jack Cade, leader of the Kentish rebellion, entered London, he is said to have struck the stone with his sword and declared himself lord of the city. This is dramatized in Shakespeare's *Henry VI, Part 2.*

In 1742, it became a traffic hazard and was moved north of the street against the new Wren church of St Swithin. There seems to have been a compelling need to preserve the stone and it was moved twice more in 1798 and in the 1820s and placed in the church's south wall. St Swithin's was bombed, but the stone remained in the ruined wall until 1960 when it was moved to the Guildhall Museum for safekeeping and then returned to Cannon Street in 2018. Officially listed (Grade II*) as a structure of special historic interest in 1972, its origin and the true purpose remain unknown.

CONTACT INFORMATION

London Stone,
111 Cannon Street, EC4N 5AR
https://londonstone.org.uk/

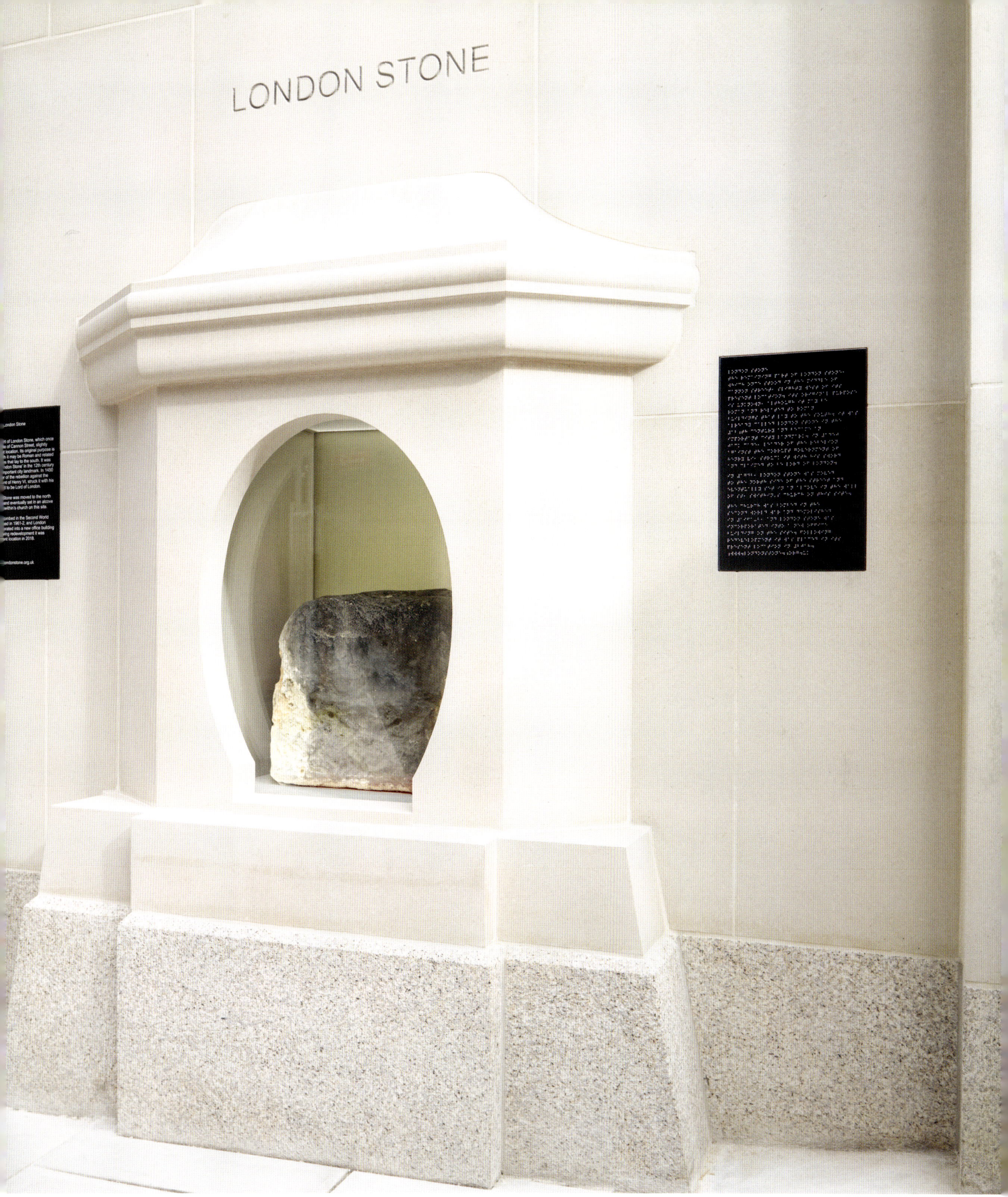
LONDON STONE

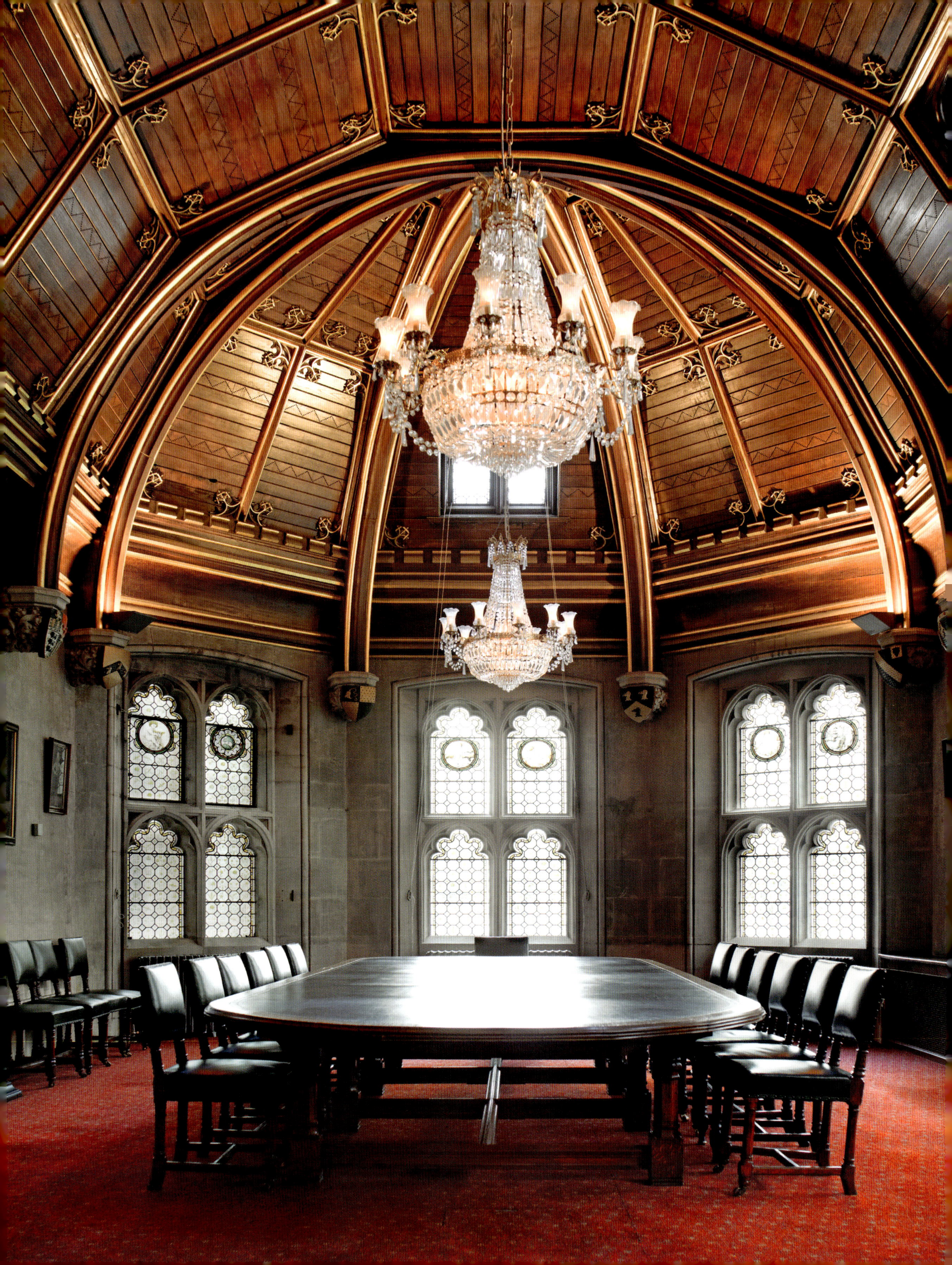

Guildhall

The chief commoner's parlour room, with vaulted ceiling in Elizabethan style.

Guildhall, which is the Town Hall of the City of London, was completed in about 1440. Earlier buildings existed on the site serving the similar purposes since about 1128 or earlier, although no historian or archaeologist has ever pinned down exactly when London's first Guildhall was built.

It is arguable that Guildhall is the oldest surviving secular building in the City, and it can also be claimed that it possesses the greatest historical interest after the Tower of London. Guildhall is laden with layers of history and legend, a medieval building with Saxon and possibly Roman antecedents.

Oldest of the legends is that Brutus of Troy, who was the mythical first king of ancient Albion, had his palace on the site of Guildhall, with giants Gog and Magog chained to the gates. Fearsome effigies of Gog and Magog have consequently watched over the building's Great Hall for centuries. More feasible is that Dick Whittington financed the building of Guildhall. Richard Whittington (1354–1423) certainly served several terms as Lord Mayor, and was known as a wealthy trader who loaned money and left charitable bequests to benefit London.

Firmly rooted in history are ten notable state trials that were held in Guildhall in the turbulent years between 1546 and 1615, which are listed on a memorial tablet. Most famous were those of Lady Jane Grey, briefly Queen of England, and of Archbishop Thomas Cranmer, both tried for High Treason. Guildhall survived the Great Fire of London in 1666, although it was damaged and its roof burned off.

The Great Hall is an impressively high vaulted space attributed to a master mason named John Croxton. Its scale and proportion are impressive today, and must have been overwhelming to those who saw it in the 1440s. Each successive century bought extensive changes. George Dance the Younger added a porch in 1789, and the Victorians inevitably made an extensive external renovation, which changed many details and added a minstrel's gallery inside and a display of standards of measurements. The moment of greatest danger came on the night of 29–30 December 1940, when a heavy air raid started a series of fires across the City which began to join up, forming a fire storm that nearly overwhelmed parts of London as fire fighters struggled to keep the flames away.

Guildhall was saved, but again suffered severe damage. The roof and windows were mostly destroyed but the four walls still stood, and much of statuary inside remained intact, although the figures of Gog and Magog were again destroyed. These were replaced in 1954 and the next year the restoration was complete, with a new roof on steel cantilevers designed by Sir Giles Gilbert Scott, the fifth to be applied to date. A statue of Churchill was unveiled, joining those of Nelson and Wellington, Apollo, Mercury, Neptune and Britannia.

Guildhall is laden with layers of history and legend, a medieval building with Saxon and possibly Roman antecedents.

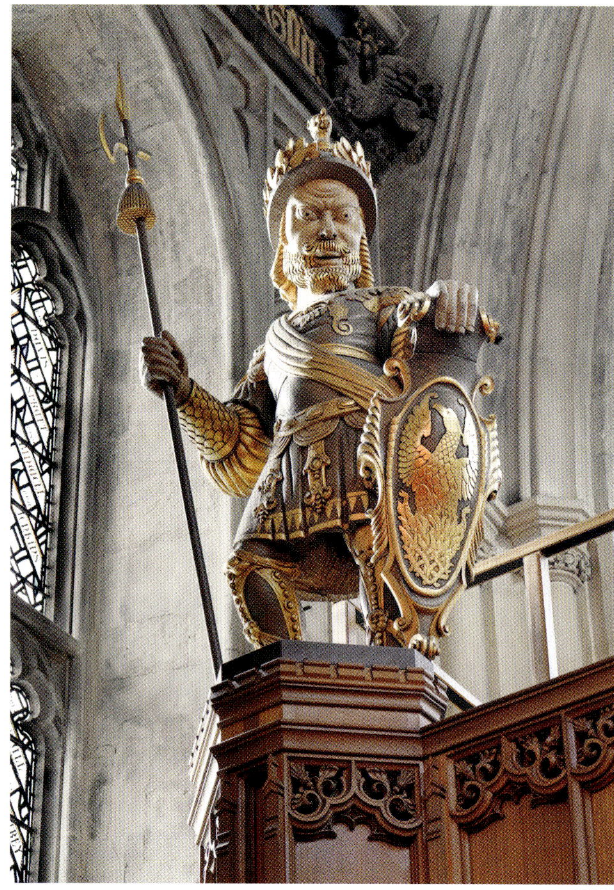

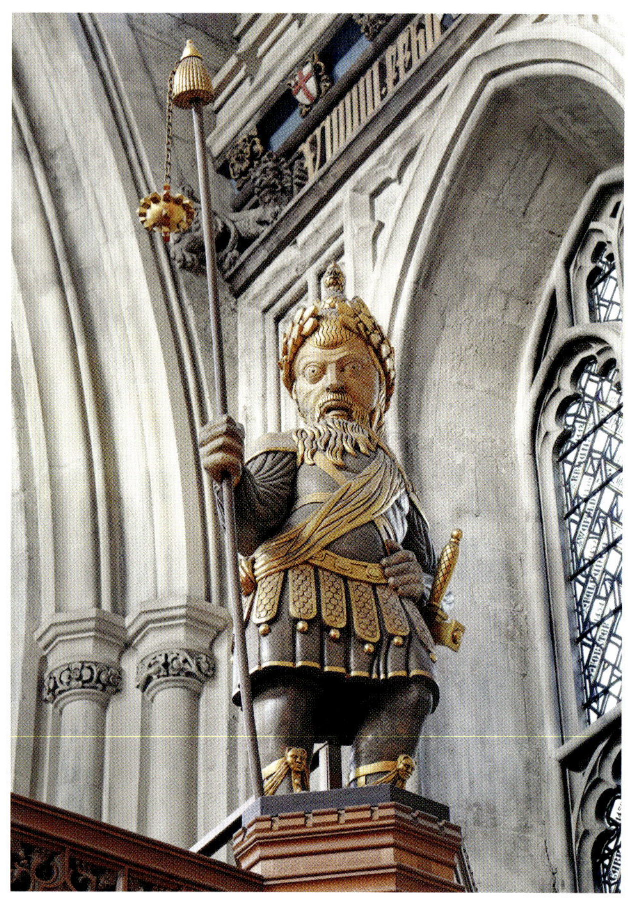

Right Giants Magog (above) and Gog (below) oversee the Great Hall.

Opposite, above Guildhall Standards of Length.

Opposite, below The Great Hall.

High on the walls are displayed pennants of the twelve leading livery companies of the City of London. Other rooms to the side of the Great Hall include the print room, the chief commoner's parlour and the old library.

With the rebuilding of Guildhall, work was also completed to the west side on new offices for the Corporation of London and on the eastern side was built the Guildhall Art Gallery, designed by Richard Gilbert Scott in 1999. During work on the foundations, remains of a Roman amphitheatre were found 20 ft (6 m) below ground level. The amphitheatre was partially excavated and can now be accessed from Guildhall Art Gallery. On the surface of yard the internal dimensions of the amphitheatre have been outlined by a large circle. The discovery of the amphitheatre was a surprise to historians of Guildhall, who have revised assessments of the early buildings on site, estimating that the siting of an earlier Saxon Guildhall was influenced by the amphitheatre's position. Remains have also been found of a thirteenth-century gatehouse built directly over the southern entrance to the Roman amphitheatre. The current hall's west crypt may be part of another thirteenth-century building.

Today Guildhall – never expressed as 'The Guildhall' – is used for official functions, entertaining visiting heads of state and for the official installation of the Lord Mayor, and is the scene of an annual keynote speech by the Prime Minister.

CONTACT INFORMATION

Guildhall,
71 Basinghall Street, EC2V 7HH
https://www.thecityofldn.com/directory/guildhall-great-hall/

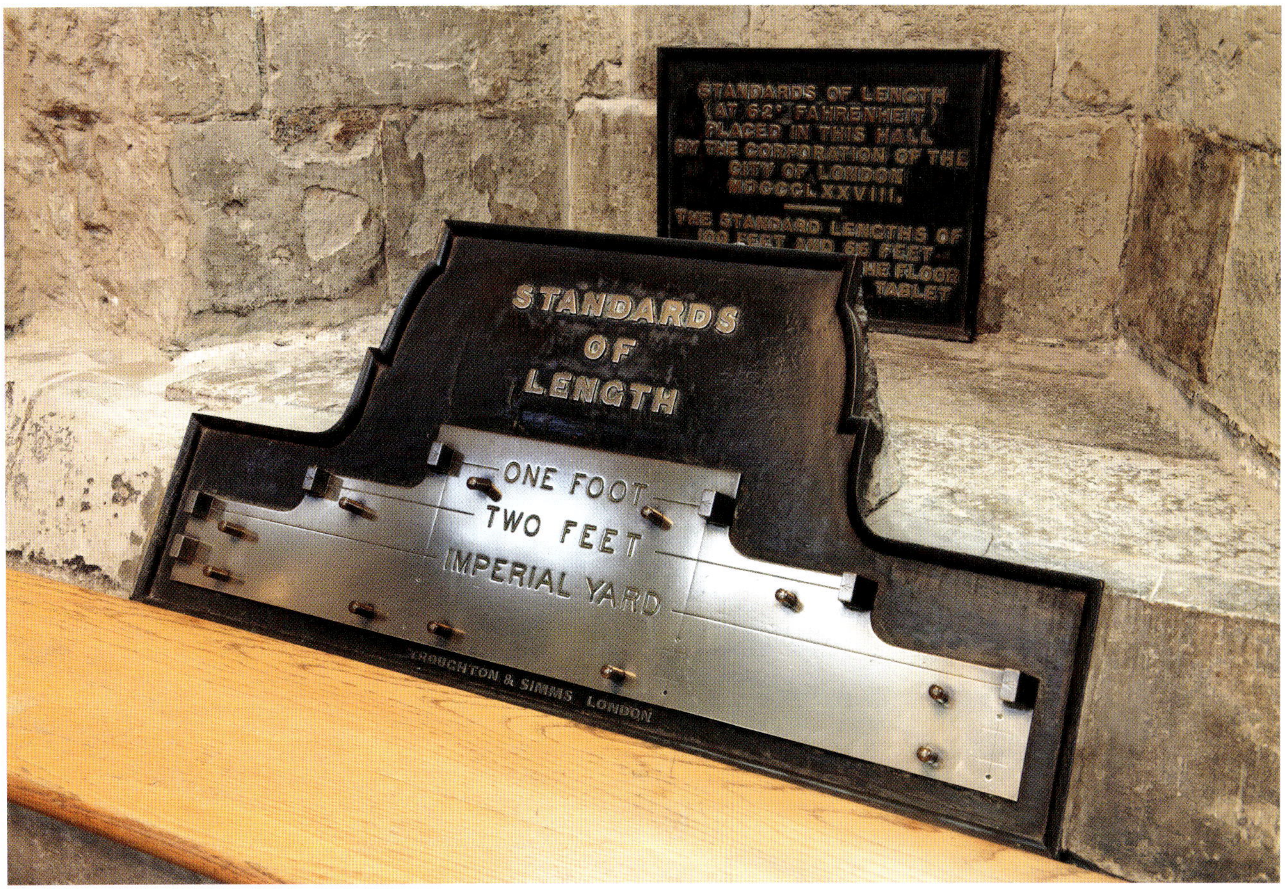

STANDARDS OF LENGTH
(AT 62° FAHRENHEIT)
PLACED IN THIS HALL
BY THE CORPORATION OF THE
CITY OF LONDON
MDCCCLXXVIII.
THE STANDARD LENGTHS OF
HE FLOOR
TABLET
STANDARDS
OF
LENGTH
ONE FOOT
TWO FEET
IMPERIAL YARD
TROUGHTON & SIMMS LONDON

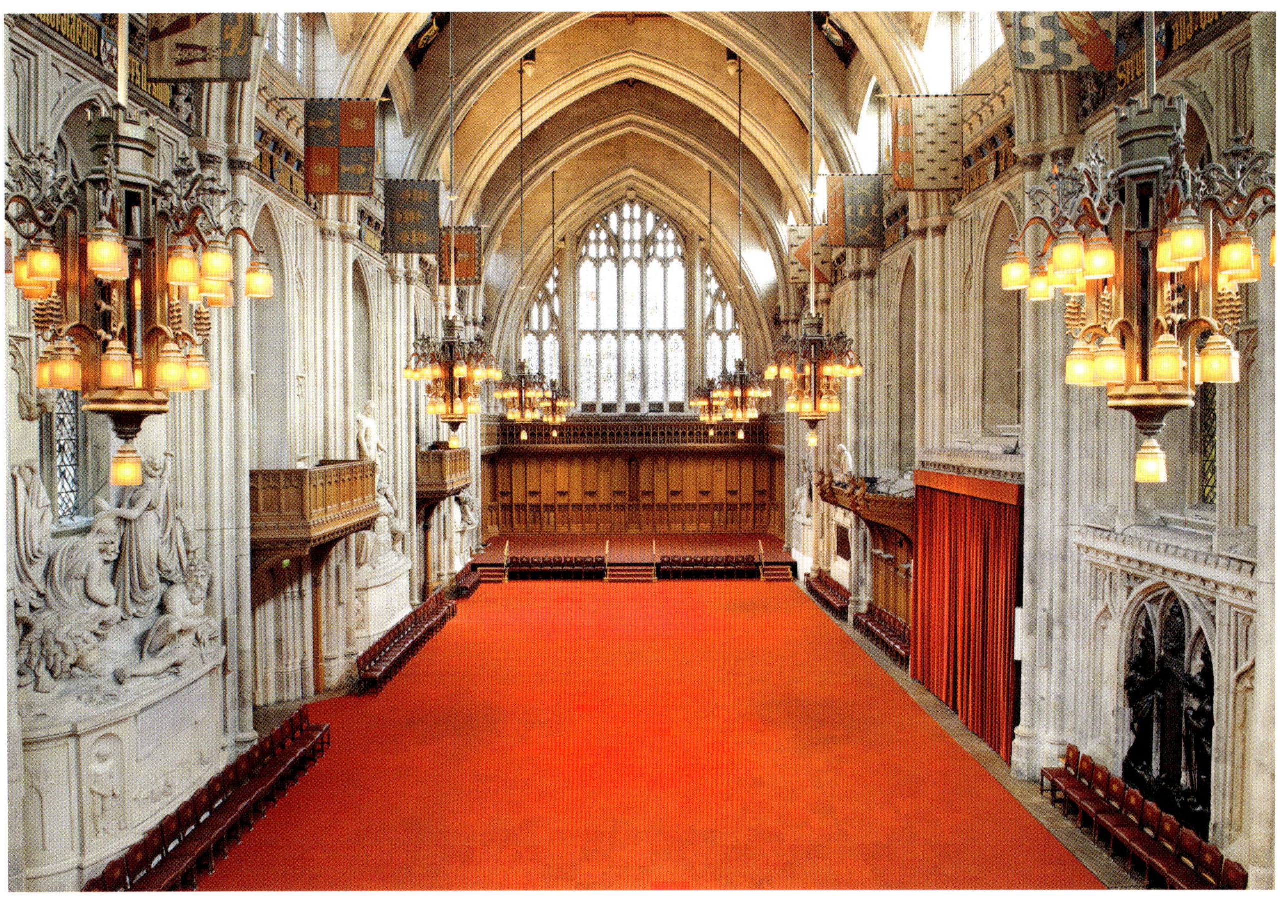

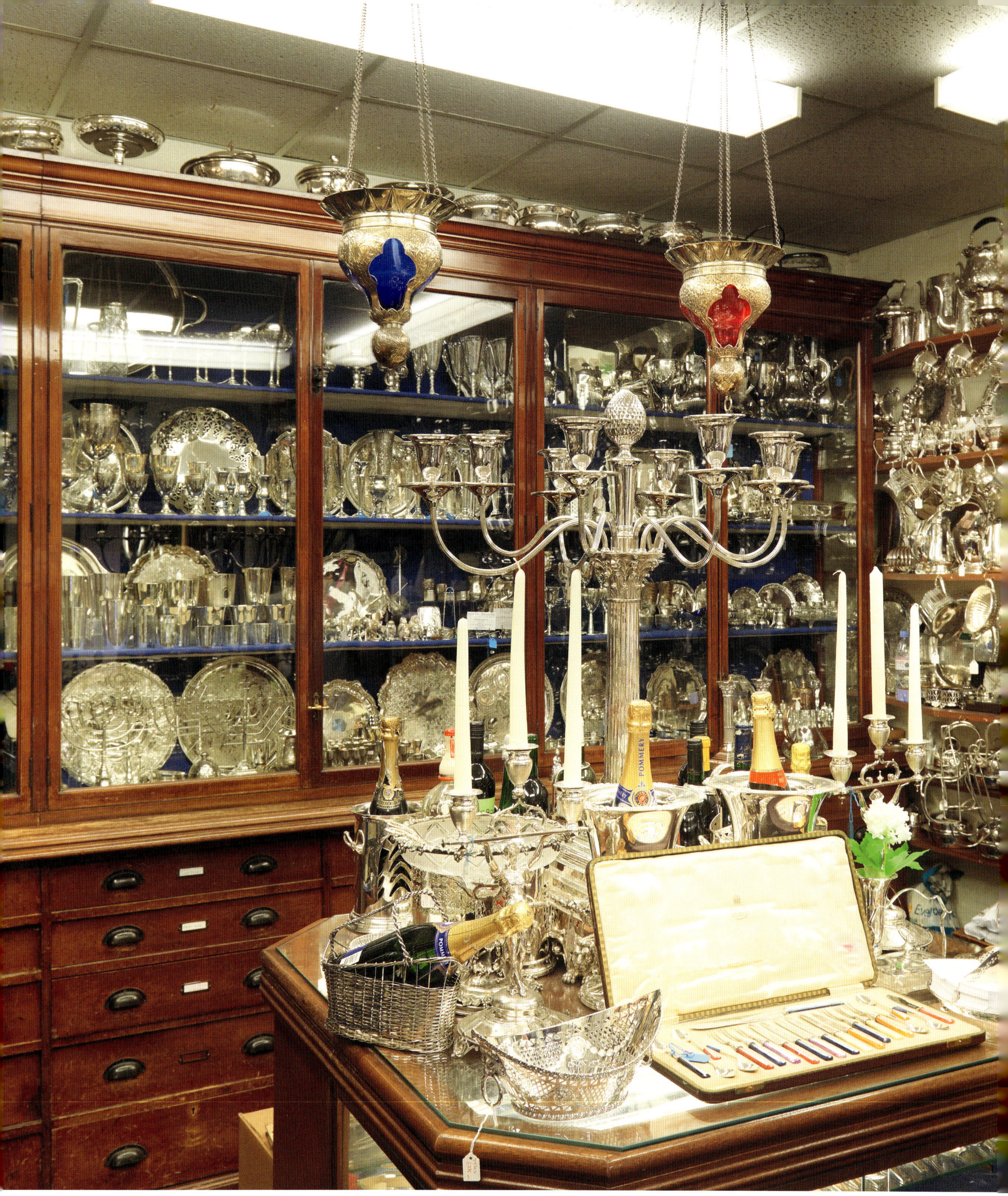
POMMERY

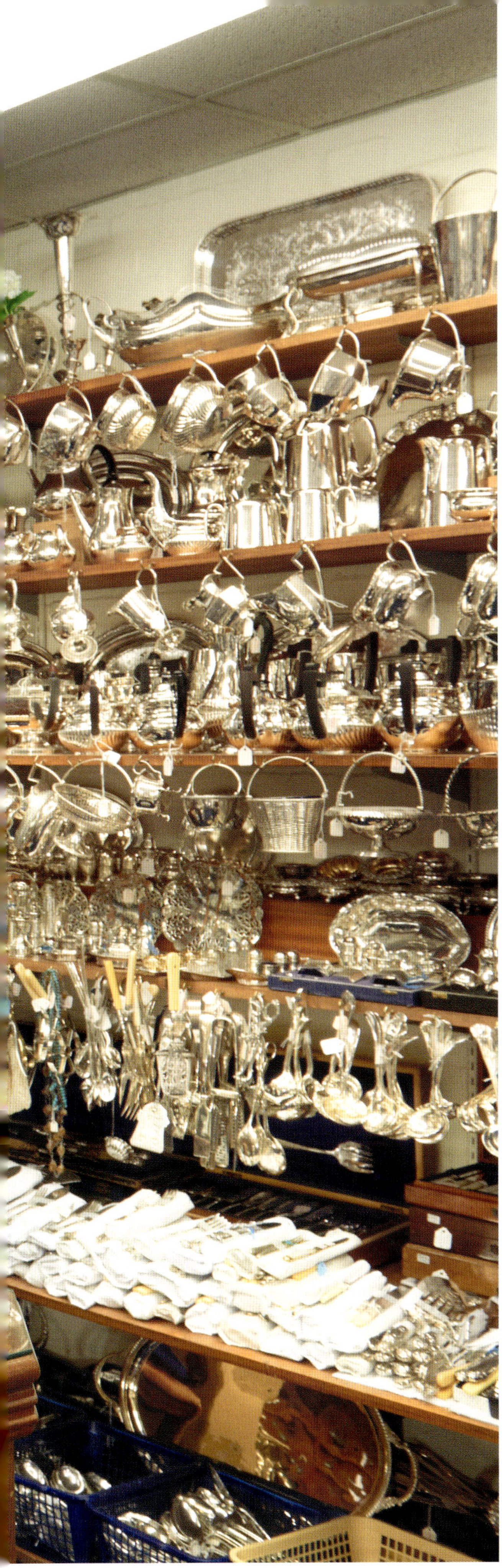

London Silver Vaults

Candelabrum, champagne and collectibles shown by a specialist in early silver and vintage silver plate.

London Silver Vaults is a treasure trove for visitors in search of precious objects. Its own publicity describes it as a hidden gem. In plain terms the Vaults are an underground retail arcade populated with retailers dealing in vintage silver, modern silver cutlery and silverware. There is also gold and jewellery, antique costumes, rare stamps and crystal, but silver dominates. The Vaults claim to offer the largest collection of silverware for sale anywhere in the world, ranging from the highest value museum-quality treasures to small affordable pieces.

It opened as Chancery Lane Safe Deposit about 1885 under an ornate wrought-iron arch and an armoured portcullis at 61 and 62 Chancery Lane. Steps descended two levels to vaults equipped with the latest technology in the form of fire-proof doors, strongrooms and safes. It boasted 'the magnificent of a palace, security of a fortress, convenience of a club' all illuminated by new-fangled electric light and protected by night guards armed with revolvers. There was a waiting space and writing room, and a separate room for ladies. By 1887 the company had expanded to 5,000 operational safes for a range of customers, many of them wealthy London residents safeguarding documents and treasures whenever they departed for the country. Others were jewellery merchants from nearby Hatton Garden renting strongrooms and safes for overnight storage of gems and precious metals.

Over time business shifted from private customers towards dealers who began operating directly from

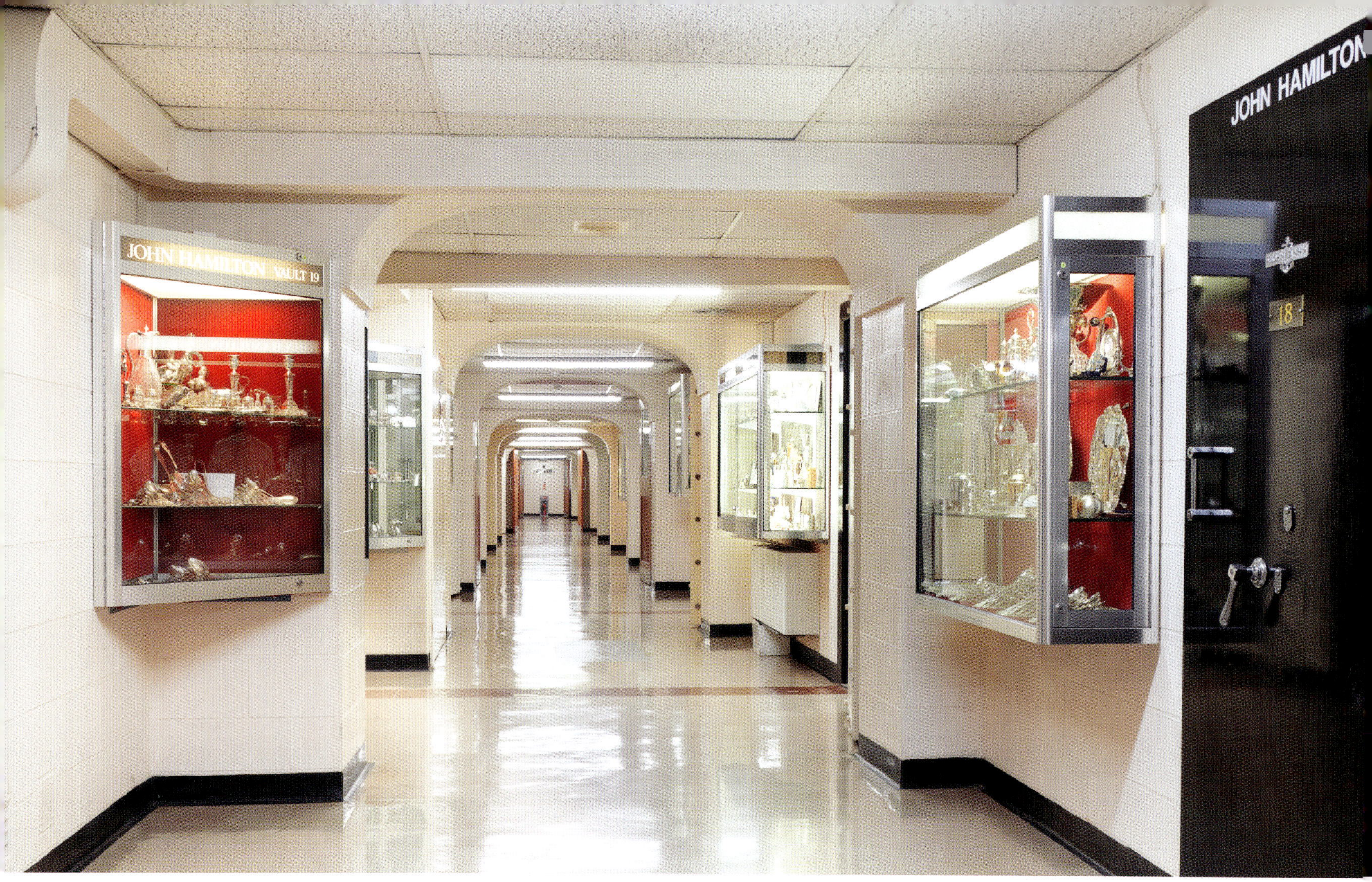

the vaults in the 1930s. In the Blitz of September 1940, the buildings on the surface at Chancery Lane were blasted by high explosives and set ablaze by incendiaries. Later V1 flying bomb strikes scorched the area and the official wartime bomb damage map compiled by London County Council charts the total destruction of the buildings at street level. Yet the Safe Deposit vaults survived unscathed, except for some water ingress from firefighting. Business continued and in 1953 after extensive remodelling of the Safe Deposit, the London Silver Vaults emerged. The old elaborate surface entrance arch had been swept away after the bombing and the Silver Vaults address modified to 63–64 Chancery Lane, although the entrance is intriguingly around the corner in Southhampton Buildings. Today the nameplate John Tann – the inventor and pioneer of the modern safe – can be seen on the armoured entrance door and on the doors of more than seventy rooms housing the silver dealers. Some of these are multi-generational family businesses, which have been operating in its corridors for decades.

Close alongside, and under the Silver Vaults at a level three times deeper, lies a colossal once-secret tunnel system. The Blitz, which had in 1940 failed to dent the Chancery Lane Safe Deposit, did inspire construction of a lengthy underground shelter complex at 100 ft (30 m) to accommodate 8,000. This was completed by 1942, but never operated as a shelter, eventually becoming a strategic nuclear-hardened telephone switching station known as Kingsway Deep Level Exchange, operated by British Telecom until offered for sale in 2008. It is poised to reopen in the late 2020s. The exact thematic purpose has not been announced but modern developer London Tunnels promises 'a unique underground immersive experience coupling history or science or nature and the arts' deploying large-scale curved screens, harnessing interactive structures, scent-emitting technology and hundreds of acoustic pinpoint speakers for a multi-sensory experience. Subterranean secret Holborn is a subject in itself.

CONTACT INFORMATION

London Silver Vaults,
53–64 Chancery Lane, WC2A 1QS
https://silvervaultslondon.com/

Above The Vaults retain the long corridors of the former safe deposit, with doors by the Tann company, makers of the first modern safes, now protecting dealers' rooms.

Opposite, above Inside lies the display of a leading silver cutlery specialist.

Opposite, below A glimpse of the selection of one of the founding members of the Vaults, Langfords, which operated from the Chancery Lane Safe Deposit in 1937 and became a founding member of the London Silver Vaults in 1953.

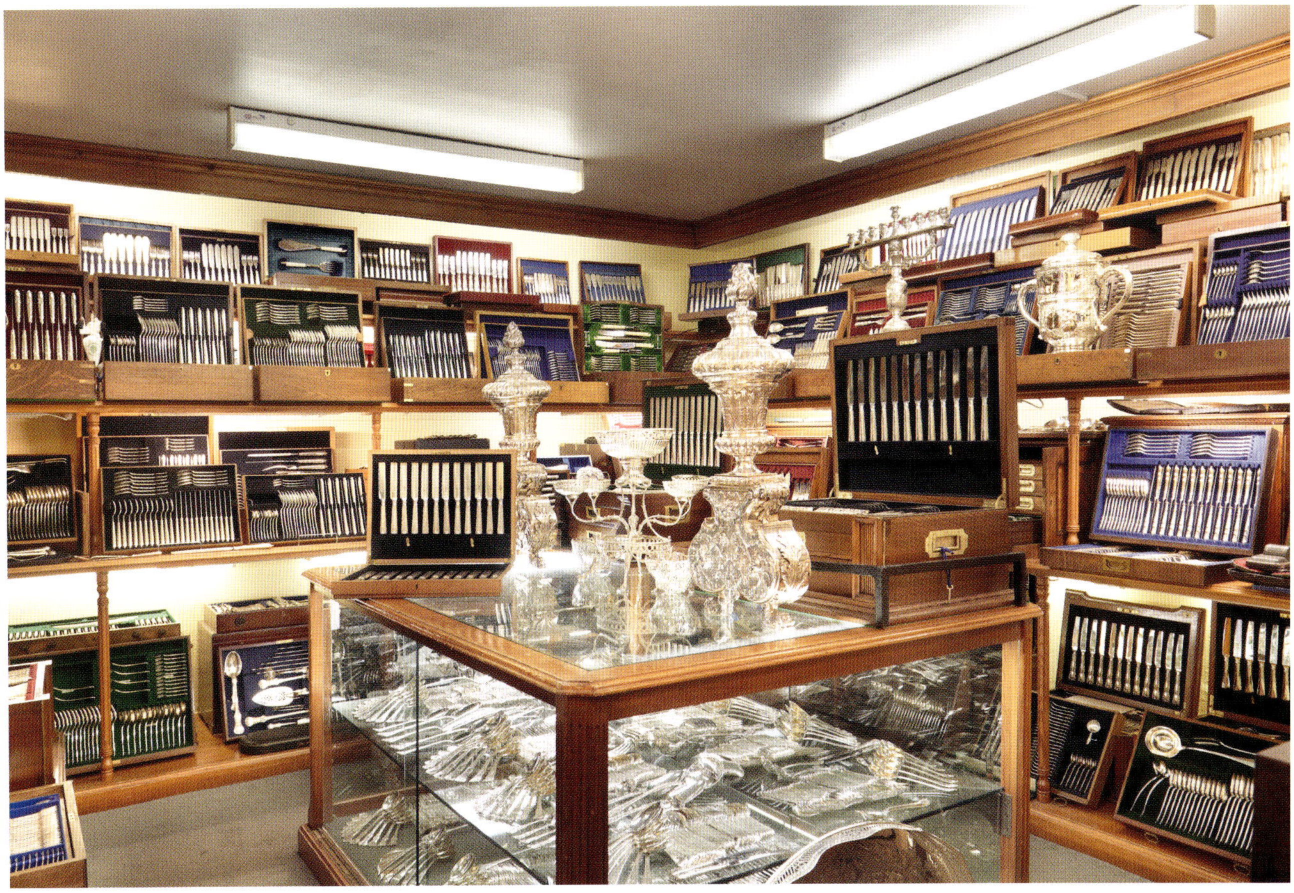

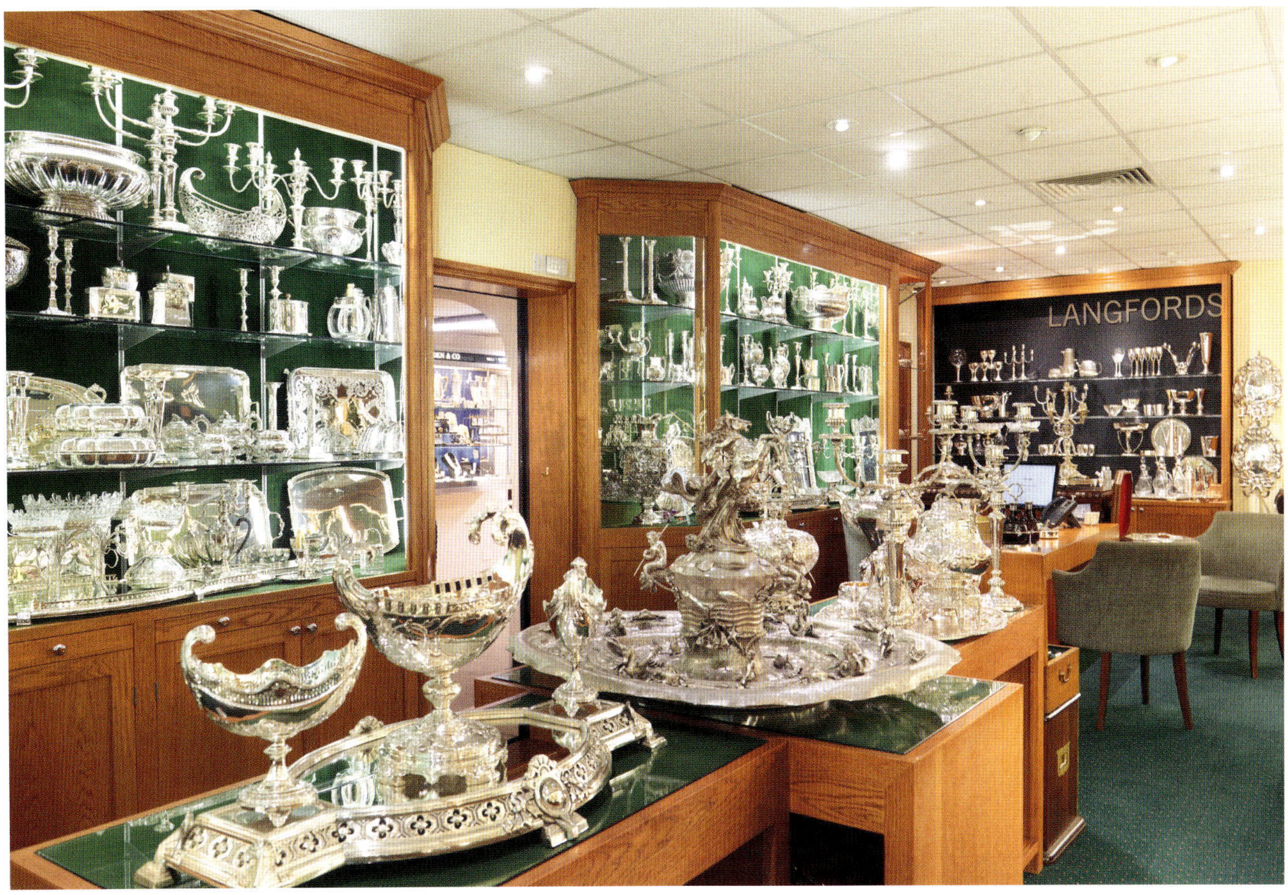
LANGFORDS

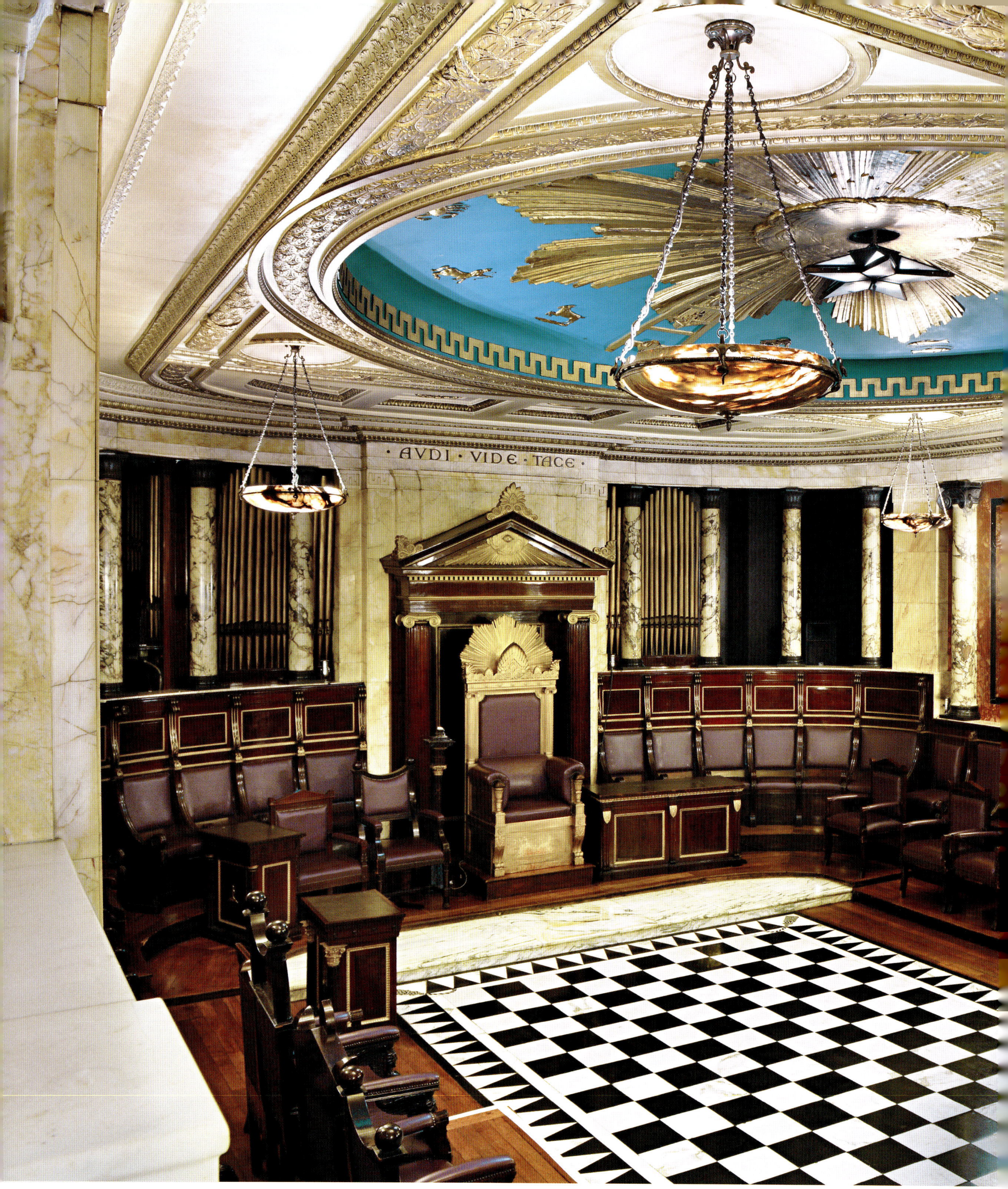
AVDI · VIDE · TACE

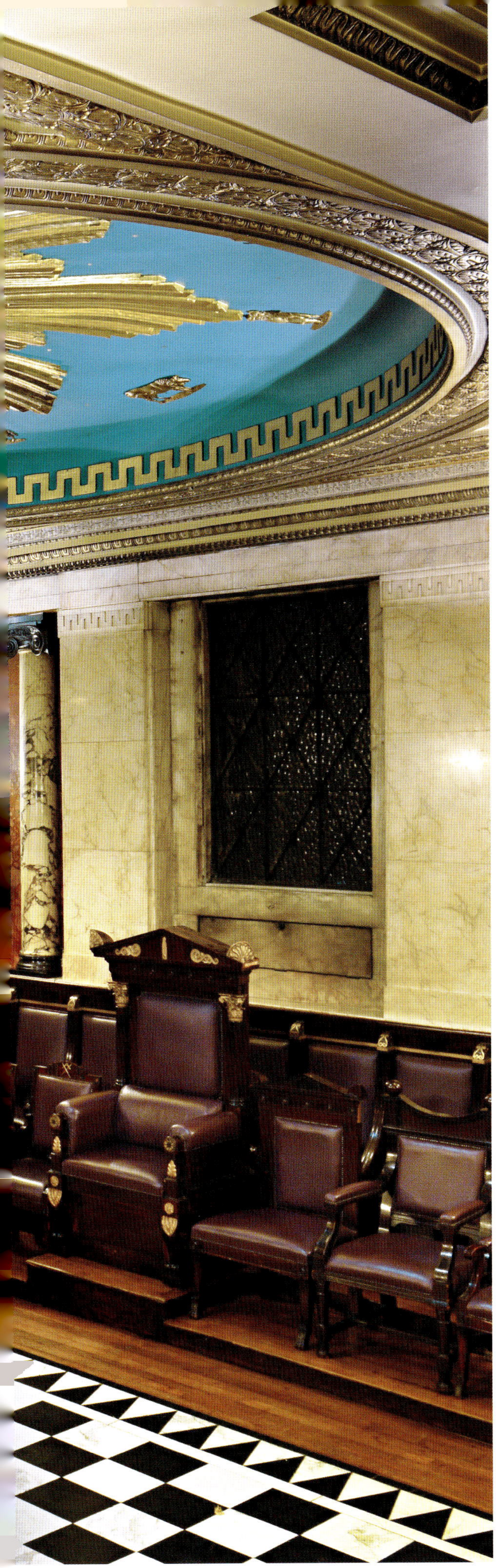

Masonic Temple at Andaz London

The pipe organ, by Norman and Beard of London, was integrated into the original design of the Temple in 1912. The black-and-white checkerboard flooring is symbolic of diversity and duality.

It is strange that a railway hotel at a major London terminus should include an elaborate masonic temple. That hotel is today known as the Andaz London Liverpool Street, and the temple remains on the first floor. It is in regular use for fashion shows, product launches, wedding receptions and cabaret dinners, and has even hosted a festival of horror mystery films. Stranger still, when the hotel was known as the Great Eastern, it until quite recently housed not one, but two masonic temples.

The Great Eastern Hotel was opened in 1884 at the front of Liverpool Street station, serving as the new terminus for railway routes from East Anglia. Designed by father and son Charles and Charles Edward Barry, it had a vast number of bedrooms but only a few bathrooms, in the late Victorian style. In response to growing demand for hotel accommodation, the ground plan of the hotel was doubled between 1898 and 1901 and a masonic temple constructed in the basement.

It was a time of growth for Freemasonry, and several hotels built across England by the main railway companies at that time were to include a lodge room. Far larger and more lavish than any of them was the second masonic temple at the Great Eastern, consecrated in November 1912. Lord Claud Hamilton, Chairman of the Great Eastern Railway, together with family members and other railway company directors who were also Freemasons, commissioned the temple and paid for it out of their own pockets. The architects

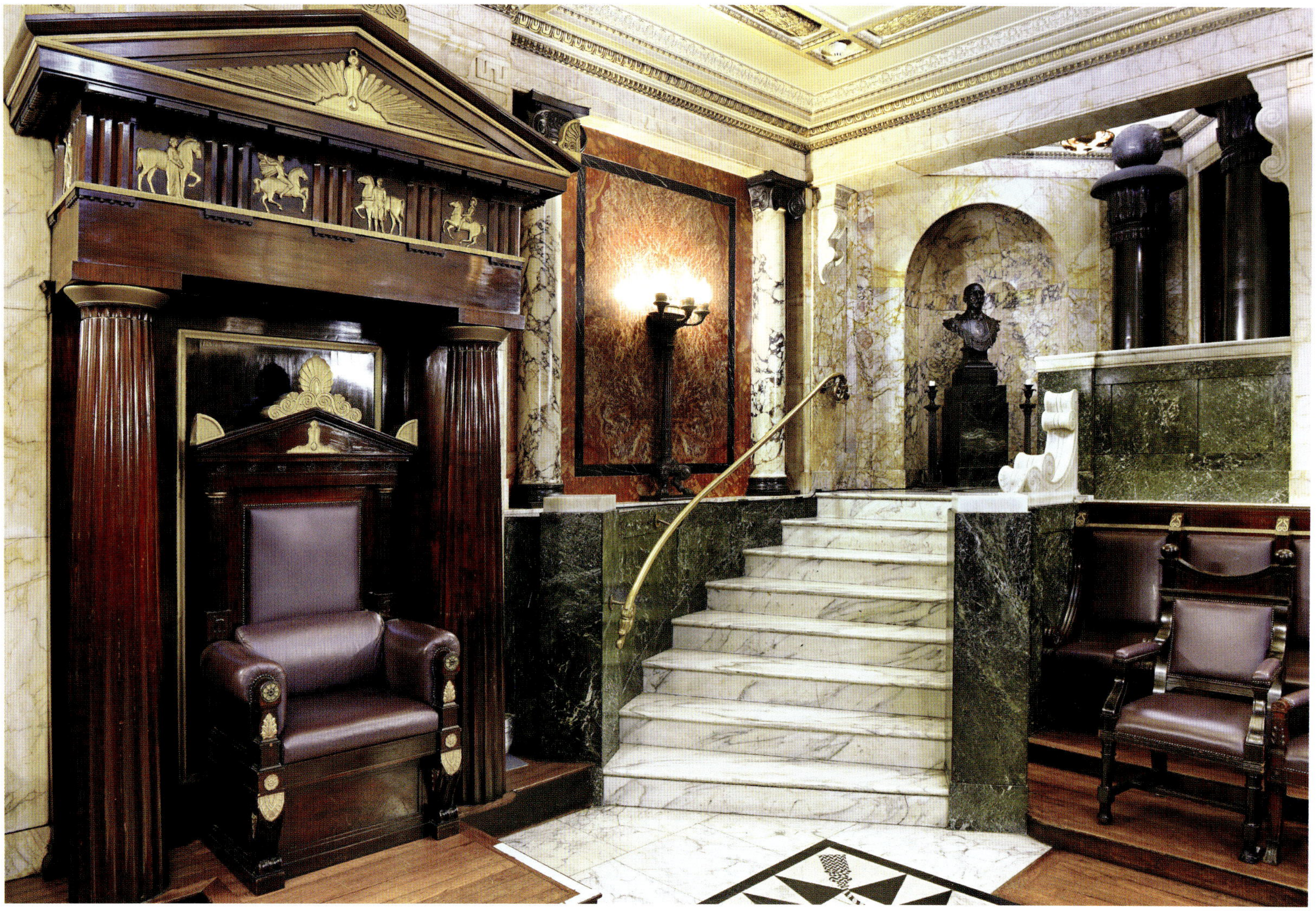

The black-and-white chequered marble floor is a classic masonic feature.

were Brown & Barrow, Alexander Brown being the Grand Superintendent of Works for the United Grand Lodge of England. It was in some ways a corporate statement for the railway company, costing £50,000 at the time, more than £4 million by today's standards. This did not include the cost of structural alterations needed to strengthen the building because of the decision to place the temple on the first floor, and the sheer weight of the materials used. Italian craftsmen were bought over to supervise the marble work. This room was called the Grecian Masonic Temple, and the previous one the Egyptian Temple.

It is the Grecian Temple which exists unchanged today, accessed by twenty-seven steps up a winding staircase through a mahogany-panelled anteroom. The visitor must then descend more marble steps to the sunken floor of the temple. Above is a sunburst ceiling, painted with signs of the zodiac and a ladder to heaven bearing the virtues Faith, Hope and Charity. There are hand-carved mahogany chairs for the Worshipful Master and the Senior and Junior Wardens.

The space features rare marbles of three different types, offset by Doric columns around the doorway at one end and Ionic at the other. There is even a pipe organ integrated into the wall. The black-and-white chequered marble floor is a classic masonic feature.

The hotel eventually closed in 1996 and was sold. In spring 2000, the Great Eastern Hotel reopened its doors to reveal an extensive restoration. At the start of 2006, the property changed ownership again.

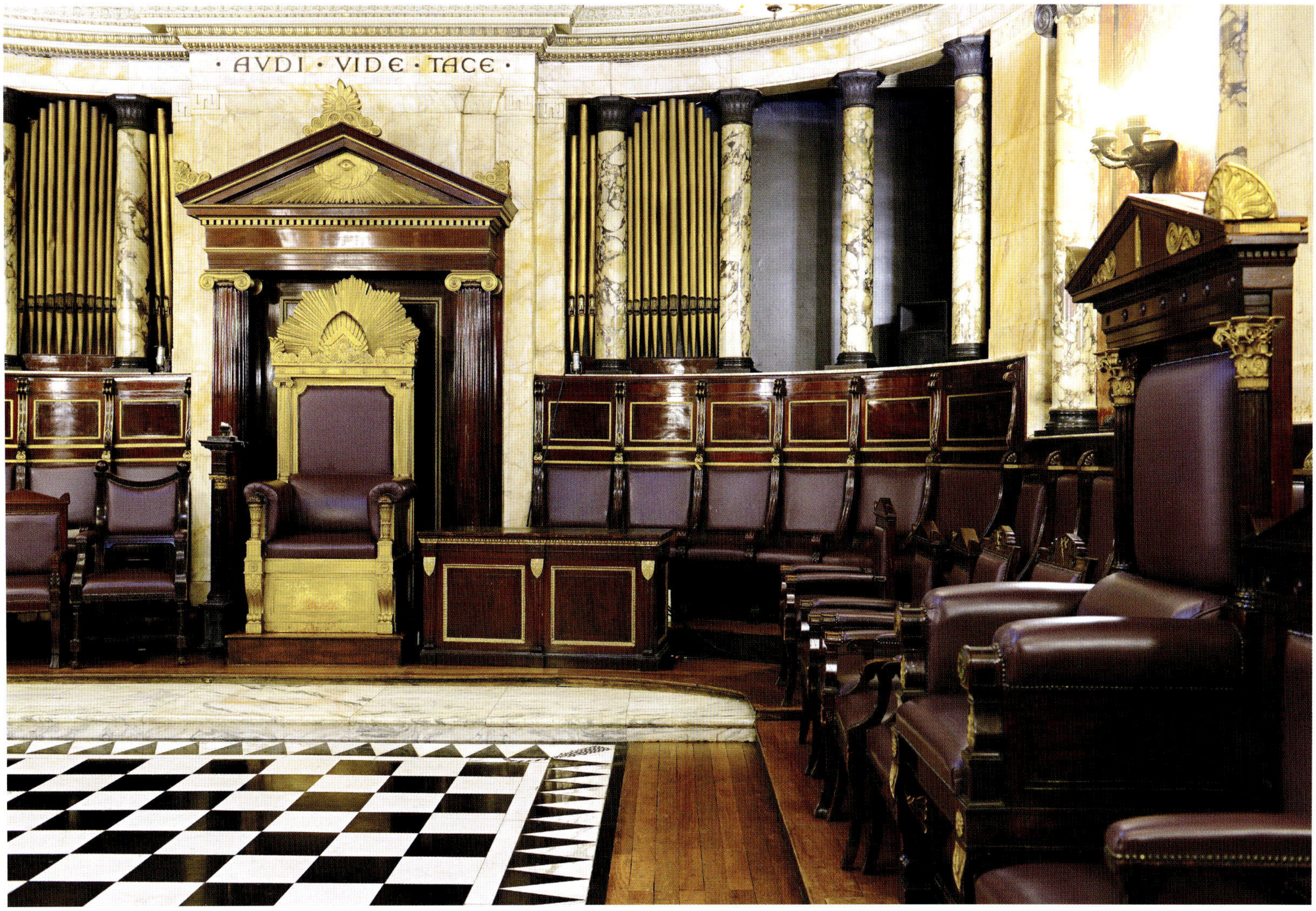

Opposite The Senior Warden's throne. The bust to the right is of the Duke of Connaught, Queen Victoria's son, Grand Master of the United Grand Lodge of England.

Above The Worshipful Master's gilded chair, under the motto *Audi, Vide, Tace* ('Hear, See, Be Silent'), overlooks the Grecian Temple.

Hyatt Hotels & Resorts now operates it the under the Andaz brand, a five-star boutique hotel with 267 rooms, all of them different.

It was inevitable, given the temple's mysterious imagery and windowless secrecy, that a strange story should develop and attach itself to the room. This bears repeating, if only because it is included in the hotel company's official profile of the space. For decades it is said that staff at the Great Eastern Hotel regularly walked past an inconspicuous looking wall, unaware of what lay behind it. During reconstruction, someone examining the drawings for the building noticed there was an additional room that had long been kept a secret. The wall was demolished, and the temple was rediscovered in the 1990s after years of disuse. For the temple to slip from corporate memory and be sealed up in disuse must be closer to myth than fact. Others suggest that the Grecian Temple was always in regular use until the hotel closed for refurbishment, and it is still occasionally used for Masonic purposes today.

Meanwhile, the Egyptian Temple was transformed into a gym and fitness centre during the hotel remodelling, but not entirely obliterated. Some of the guests working the cardio machines in the basement gym may look and wonder about the origin of the splendid doorway, the painted Egyptian lotus buds on the red-and-gold pilasters, and the traces remaining of a splendid ceiling.

CONTACT INFORMATION

Andaz London Liverpool Street,
40 Liverpool Steet, EC2M 7QN
https://www.hyatt.com/andaz/en-US/longe-andaz-london-liverpool-street/weddings/the-masonic-temple

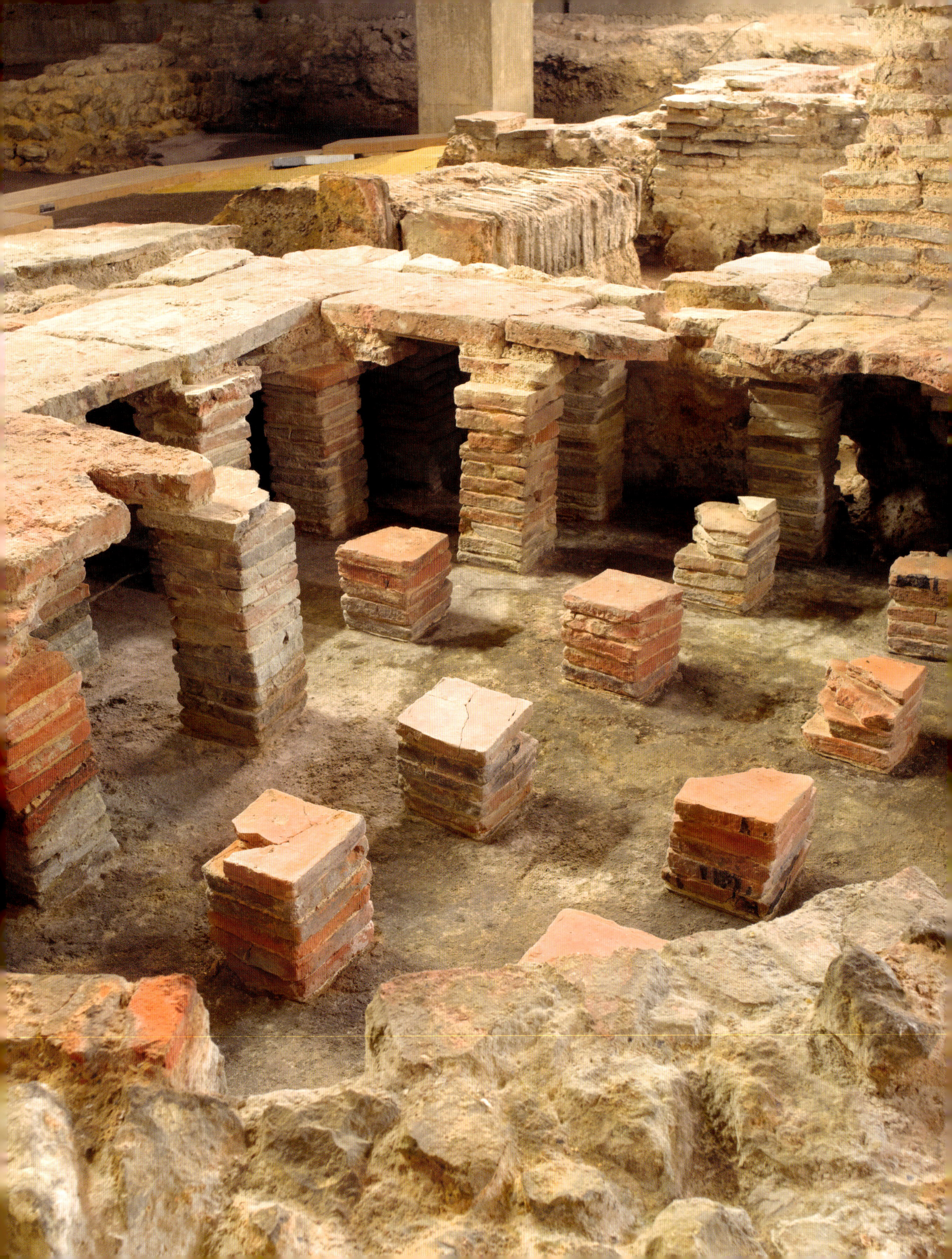

Billingsgate Roman House and Bath

Third-century bathhouse with *pilae* stacks, which are tiles built up into pillars supporting the floor as part of heating system.

One of the most spectacular set of Roman remains in London – a house and bath at Billingsgate – is rarely open to visitors. Victorian workmen found them while digging the foundations for the New Coal Exchange in January 1848 across the road from where the first Billingsgate market building was about to be constructed. Below the ruined old Dog Tavern, at a depth of 12 ft (3.5 m), they uncovered the ground plan of a Roman house, with walls remaining up to 3 ft (90 cm) high in places. At the centre was a small chamber mounted on pillars: a hypocaust, which was an ancient heating system. The remains were protected and arched over when the Coal Exchange was completed.

From the start the ruins benefited from a newly enlightened attitude by the City of London authorities. They were immediately recognized as a valuable find, and ranked as a major news story, generating a full page of coverage in the *Illustrated London News*. The first attempt to further excavate the area came as early as 1859. Under the Monuments Act of 1882, the Roman house and bath became one of the first scheduled monuments in London.

It has taken more than a century to develop a fuller picture of what the site represents. Archaeologists have calculated that it is a riverside house built in the second century, with a bathhouse added in its central yard during the following century. The house seems to have comprised two wings. It is not clear whether it was an expansive private villa or some kind of lodging establishment. The house would not have survived long after the end of Roman occupation, which came in 409–410 CE. In the east part of the house a hoard of copper coins was found that included the image of Emperor Honorius, indicating a date later than 395 for continued Roman habitation. A Saxon brooch found in debris was disposed in a way that suggests that the tiled roofs of both buildings had collapsed by the middle of the fifth century.

Further excavations were made in 1967–70 when Lower Thames Street was being widened to become a dual carriageway. It became a main thoroughfare, a forbiddingly busy road. A new office building was being built and the Roman site ended up being hidden, but preserved, in a sub-basement under 100 Lower Thames Street. The concrete foundation piers of the modern building reach down into the ground alongside the delicate stacks of Roman tiles supporting the floor of the bathhouse. In the 1970s some cement capping was applied to the remains, which was found to be suffering from decay; later this work was removed and improved conservation methods applied.

CONTACT INFORMATION

Billingsgate Roman House and Baths
101 Lower Thames Street, EC3R 6DL
https://www.thecityofldn.com/event/guided-tours-of-billingsgate-roman-house-and-baths/

Temple Church

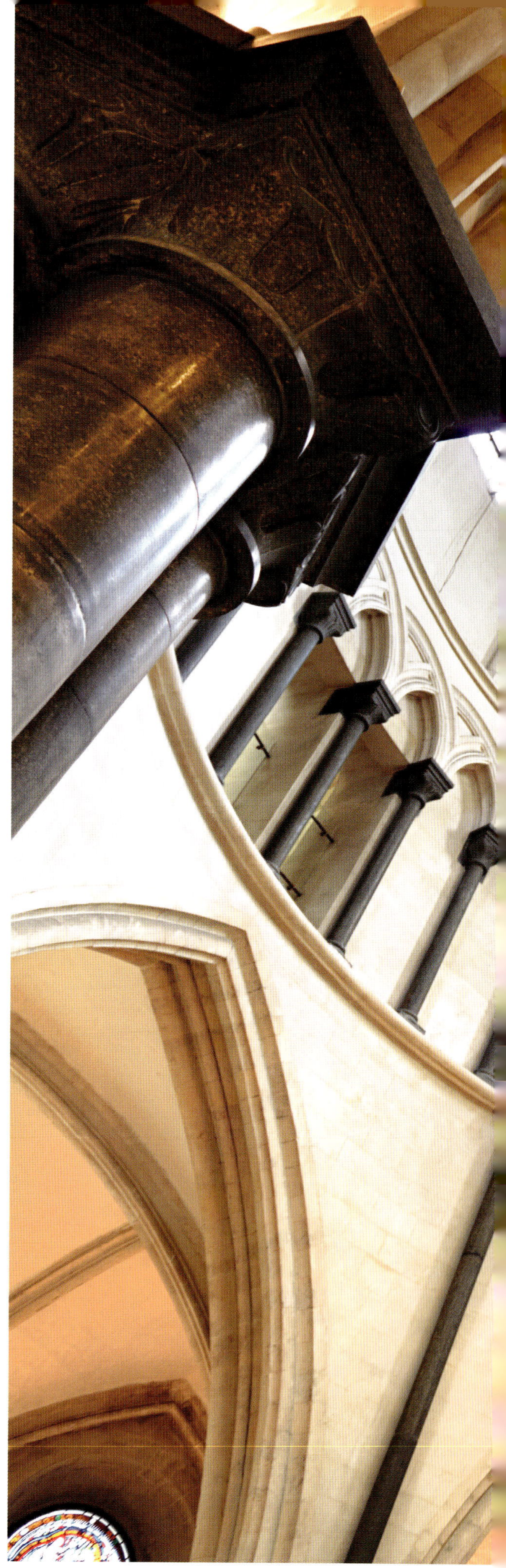

'The round' is the oldest part of the Temple Church.

The Temple Church, with all its facets of history, symbolism and myth, surprises visitors today with its well-lit simplicity. It was built to the round design of Jerusalem's sixth-century domed Byzantine Church of the Holy Sepulchre, faithful to the tradition of the Order of the Knights Templar. Circular-naved churches are rare in the British Isles, although not all round churches are associated with military orders. The Temple Church was consecrated in 1185 in the presence of Henry II, England's first Angevin king. It comprises two distinct parts: the original circular building, known as 'the round', which is now the nave, and the rectangular addition on its eastern side, now the chancel, built half a century later, in 1240. The round church, some 55 ft (17 m) in diameter, accommodates a circle of Purbeck marble columns. It is likely both Temple Church's walls and gargoyles were initially painted in bright colours.

Temple and its Church were commandeered between 1214–15 by King John – who was then in conflict with both the Pope and the Barons of England – for use as a government office. It was here that he was confronted by the Barons and compelled to ride to Runnymede, where he signed the Magna Carta. William Marshal, 1st Earl of Pembroke, re-issued Magna Carta after John's death to ensure its survival, before being laid to rest here in Temple Church.

During the era of Templar initiation ceremonies, new recruits entered the west door of the round church at dawn, and swore vows of piety, chastity, poverty and obedience to the order. Some of the strangeness and

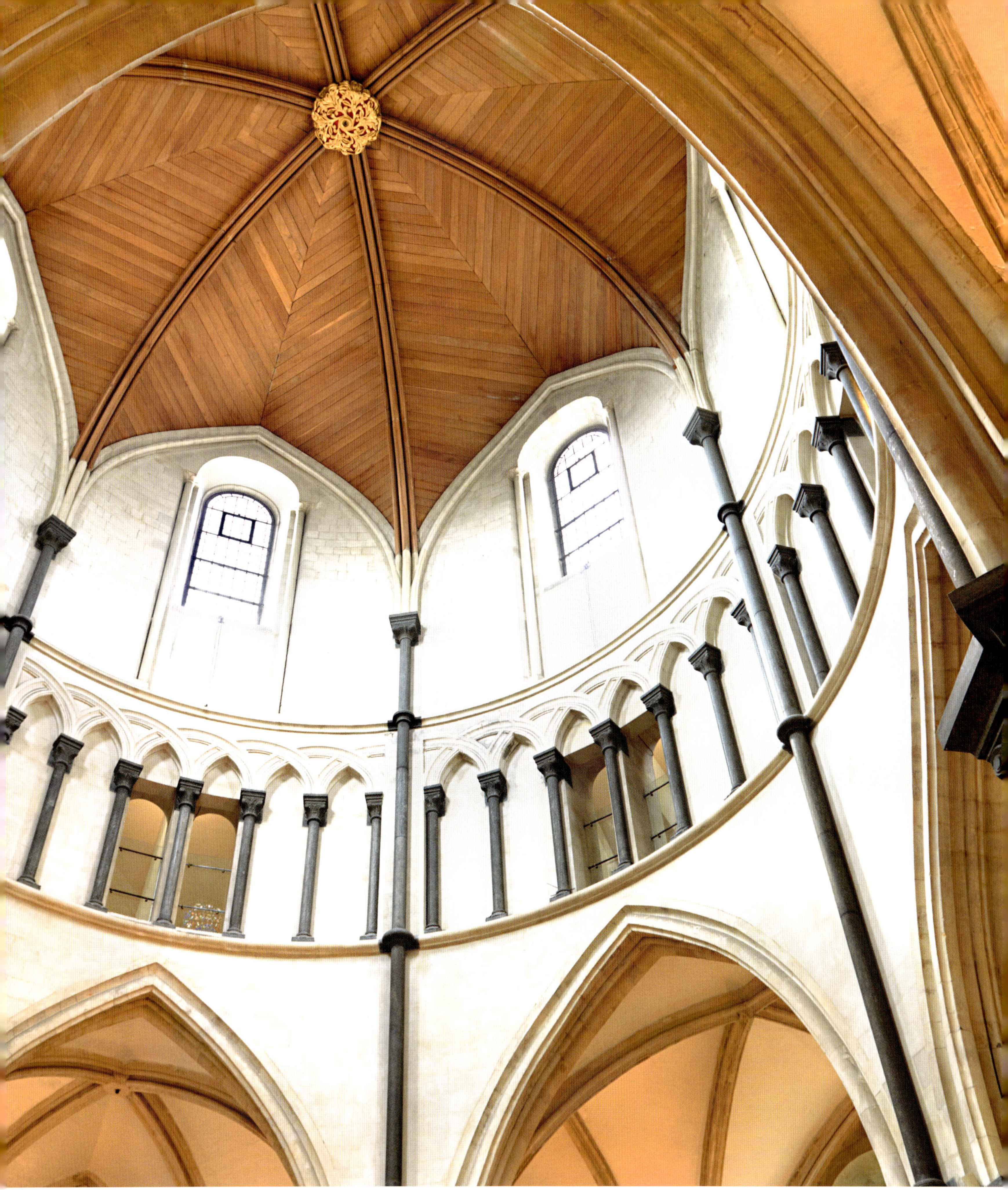

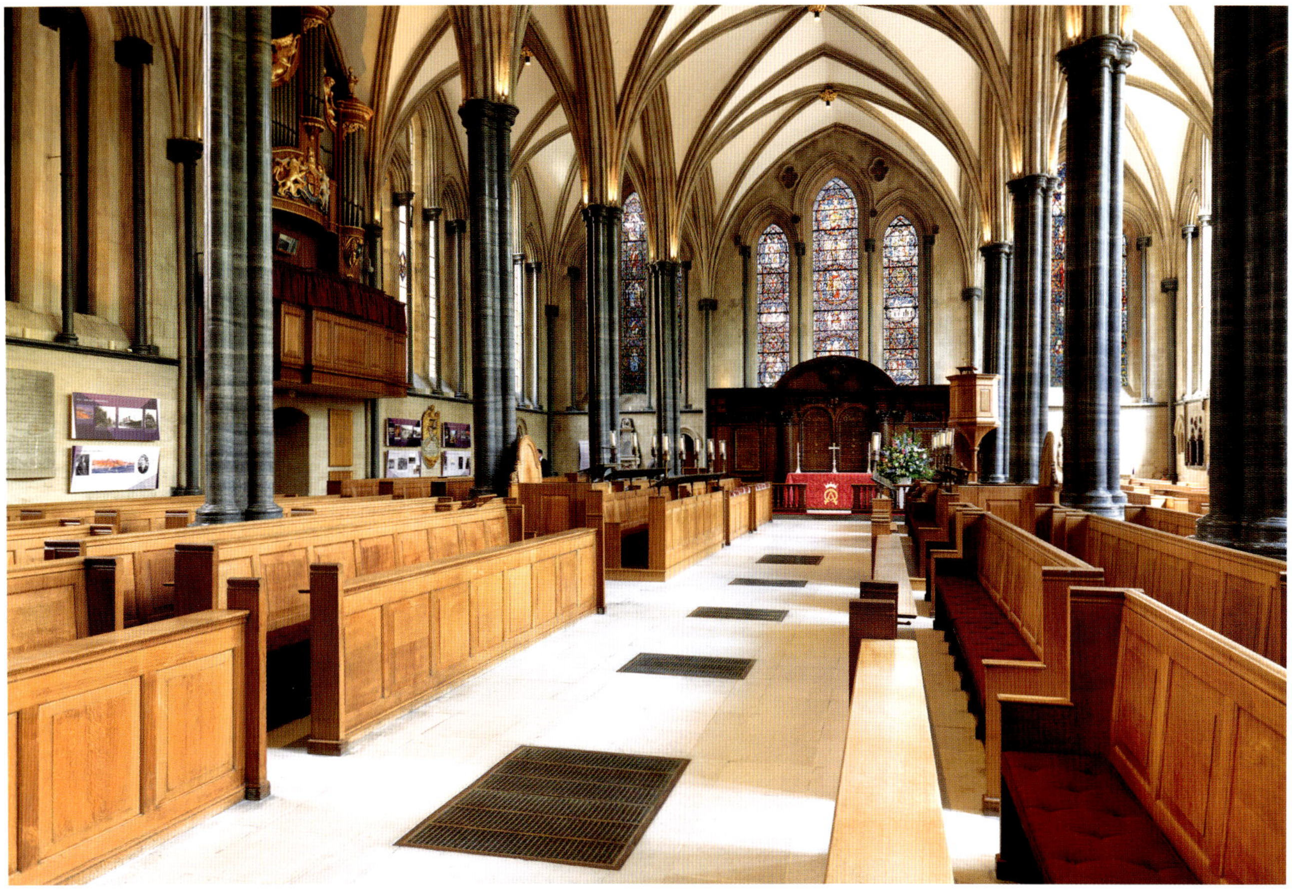

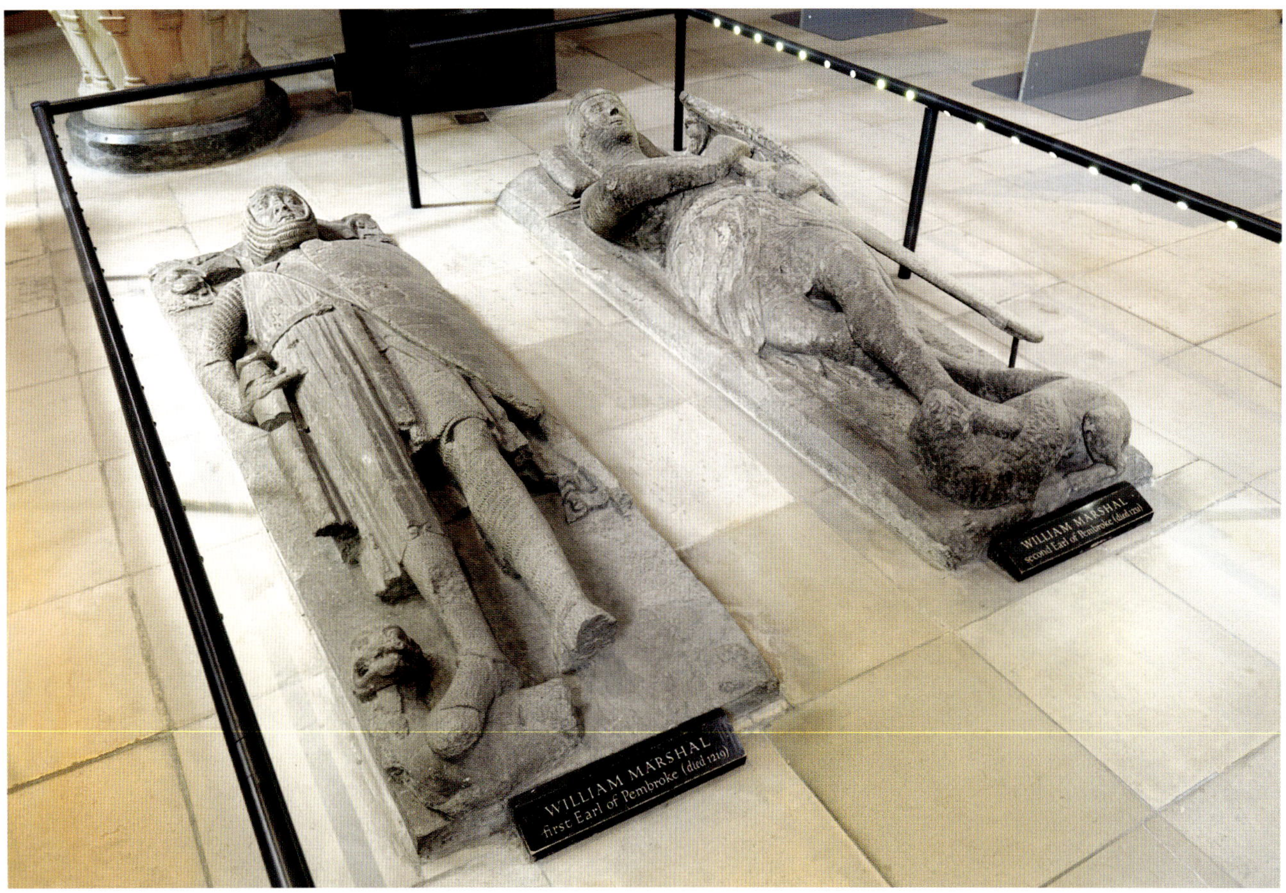
WILLIAM MARSHAL
second Earl of Pembroke (died 1231)
WILLIAM MARSHAL
first Earl of Pembroke (died 1219)

The Temple Church, with all its facets of history, symbolism and myth, surprises visitors today with its well-lit simplicity.

Opposite, above
The chancel is a later addition to 'the round' nave, dating from the early thirteenth century.

Opposite, below
The monument to William Marshall, 1st Earl of Pembroke (left), and the 2nd Earl (right).

secrecy attached to these Templar ceremonies became the source of interest when an inquisition was launched, contributing in part to its downfall. In 1307, Pope Clement V ordered Christian monarchs to arrest the Templars across Europe and to seize their assets, leading to Edward II's control of Temple Church before its transfer to the rival organization the Knights Hospitaller, and then reversion to the Crown in 1540.

In the 1580s, Temple Church played out the stresses within the Church during what was called the 'Battle of the Pulpits'. Master Richard Hooker preached his Gospel interpretation, a moderate fusion of Anglican/Catholic tenets, whereas Reader Walter Travers took up the austere ideals of Calvin, causing one observer to comment: 'If Canterbury was preached in the morning, come afternoon it was contradicted by Geneva [the headquarters of Protestant reformation].'

Although it was spared serious damage in the Great Fire of 1666 – the maximum westerly spread of the blaze just touched Temple Church – it did receive some revisions by Christopher Wren, including a fine carved altar screen. There were plans to introduce an organ for the first time, but the two Inns of Court could not agree which design of organ to install, and two trial instruments were built. Many organists, including George Frederic Handel, played on them.

The controversy resulted in deadlock and it was decided the choice should be made by the Lord Chancellor, the notorious Judge Jeffreys. Jeffreys, a member of Inner Temple, diplomatically chose the organ designed by Father Smith, favoured by the Middle Temple. Even if honour was satisfied, each of the Inns continued to appoint their own organist for nearly a hundred years until 1814.

The church underwent further restoration in 1841, under direction of architects Sydney Smirke and Decimus Burton, who decorated the walls and ceiling in high Victorian gothic style. Exactly one hundred years later, incendiary bombs set the round church's roof ablaze, with the organ and internal wooden sections destroyed, and the Purbeck marble columns in the chancel cracked in the searing heat.

The church was rededicated in 1958. Much has been changed or restored over 830 years, but the title of the chief priest remains the Reverend and Valiant Master of the Temple. At Temple Church, the distinctive ground plan has endured and much of the porch of the Norman west door is original stone.

An exceptional stroke of luck enabled the architects of the 1945–58 restoration, Walter and Emil Godfrey, to use the carved reredos designed by Wren (and executed by carver William Emmett). Removed by the Victorian restorers and salvaged, the screen had spent over one hundred years in a museum in County Durham, and it was possible to recover it and refit it in its original position. The marble columns in the round were replaced to their original shape after 1945; their authenticity includes a curious outward lean.

A visitor entering through the south door sees nine marble effigies of martial figures lying on the floor of the round; these include William Marshal, Geoffrey de Mandeville and Robert de Ros, dating from 1227. With the extensive reworking over centuries, these effigies are best understood as monuments rather than as marking tombs, although the men represented were interred nearby. The visible damage to the figures mostly dates from the Blitz, relatively recently restored.

The east window, a gift from the Glaziers' Company in 1954 to replace glass destroyed in the war, shows Christ's connection with the Temple at Jerusalem. In one panel he talks with the learned teachers, in another he ejects the money-changers. The window also pictures some of the people associated with Temple Church over the centuries, including Henry II, Henry III and several of the medieval Masters.

CONTACT INFORMATION

Temple Church,
Temple, EC4Y 7BB
https://www.templechurch.com/

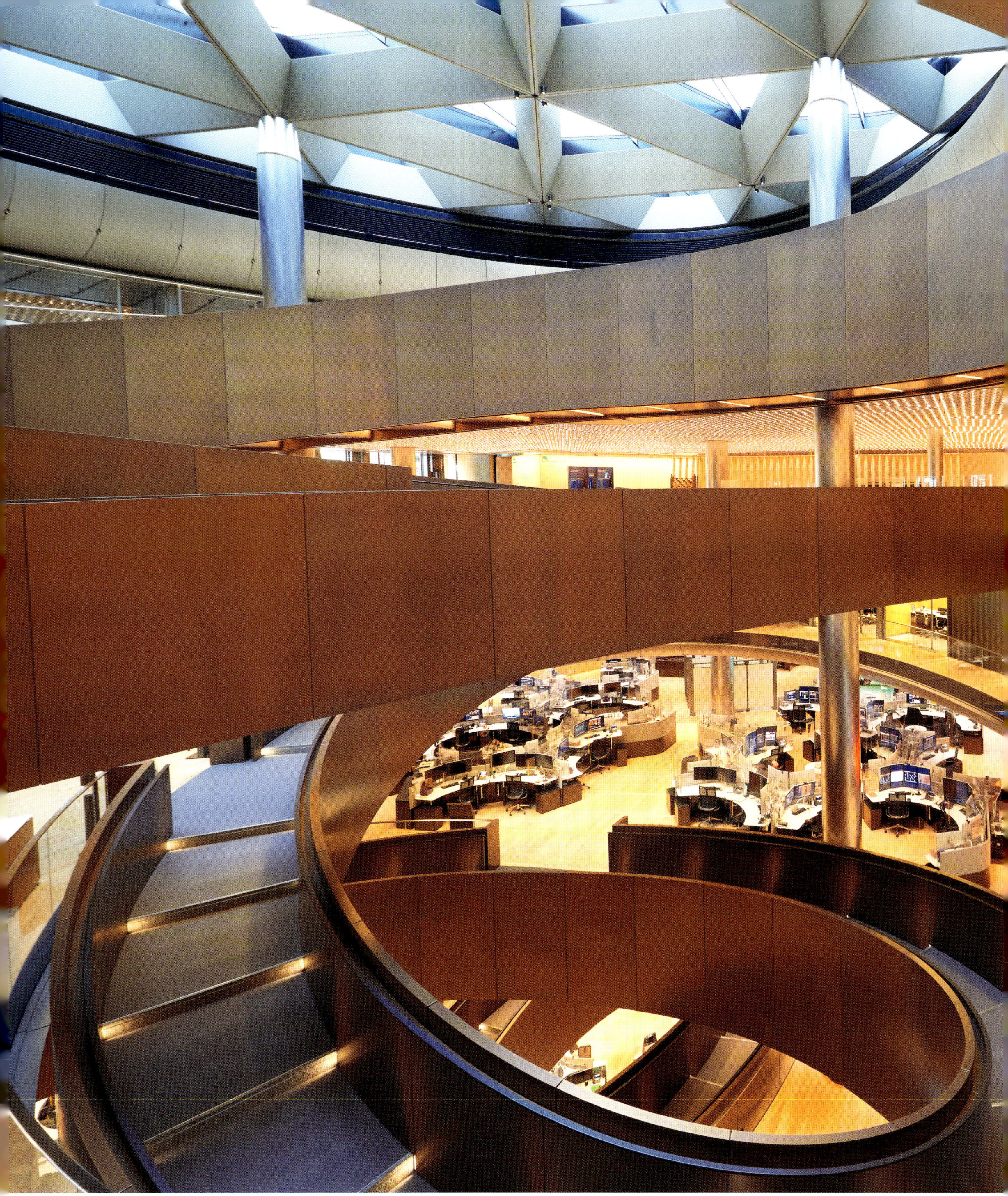

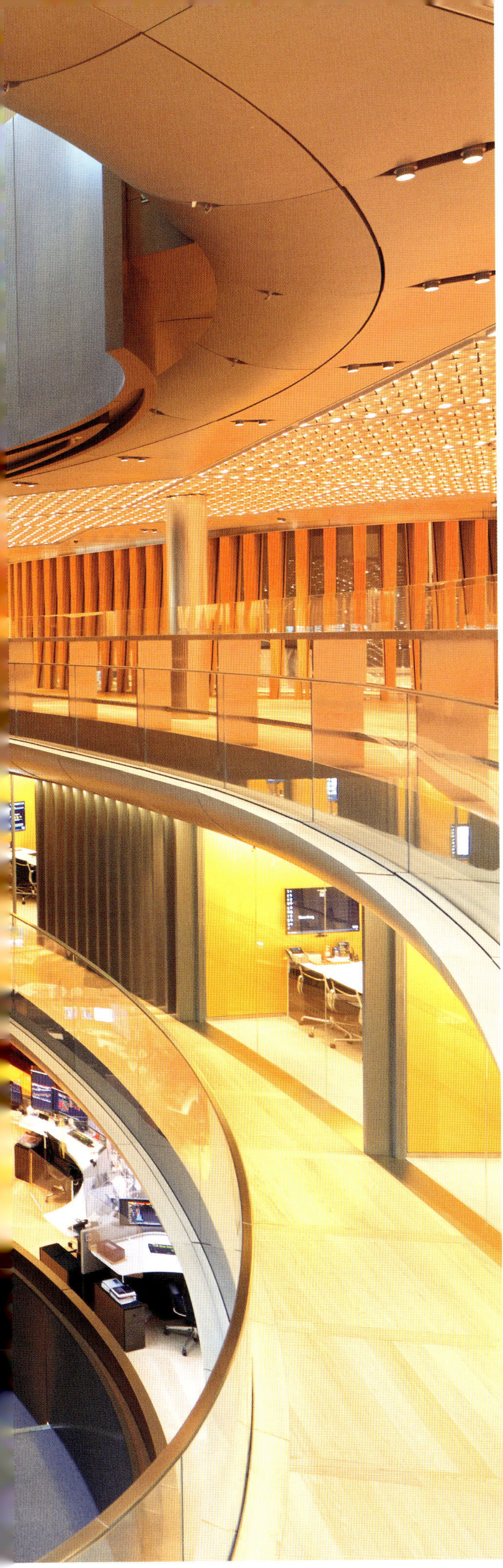

Bloomberg London

The central ramp, part of a triple helix spiralling over six floors.

The Bloomberg headquarters 'does not impose itself on the City or the historic buildings that surround it' says its declaration of architectural principles. It eschewed any prestige or status gained through tallness. It emerged just eight floors and 130 ft (40 m) high near skyscrapers soaring to forty, fifty and sixty storeys. Its technical sustainability credentials are impeccable, claimed to be the best anywhere, 35 per cent more energy-efficient and 70 per cent more water-efficient than a typical office. From its upper windows, St Paul's Cathedral is seen at a nicely respectful eyeline level to the west.

Nevertheless, the footprint of the Bloomberg headquarters is mighty, comprising two buildings joined by bridges and covering a whole block of the City. The façades flow around Cannon Street, Walbrook, Bucklersbury and Queen Victoria Street, making it hard to number its different elevations. There is a distinct warmth to the colouring, with cladding in Derbyshire sandstone. All the tinted windows are flanked by vertical bronze fins resembling half-open shutters which enable natural ventilation and control solar exposure.

This European headquarters of the Bloomberg financial business news data company was opened in 2017, a cutting-edge creation aiming to be the most advanced commercial space in the City. One of its most notable features was enabling the proper location of the remains of the Temple of Mithras, a Roman ruin that had been unearthed in the 1950s. It

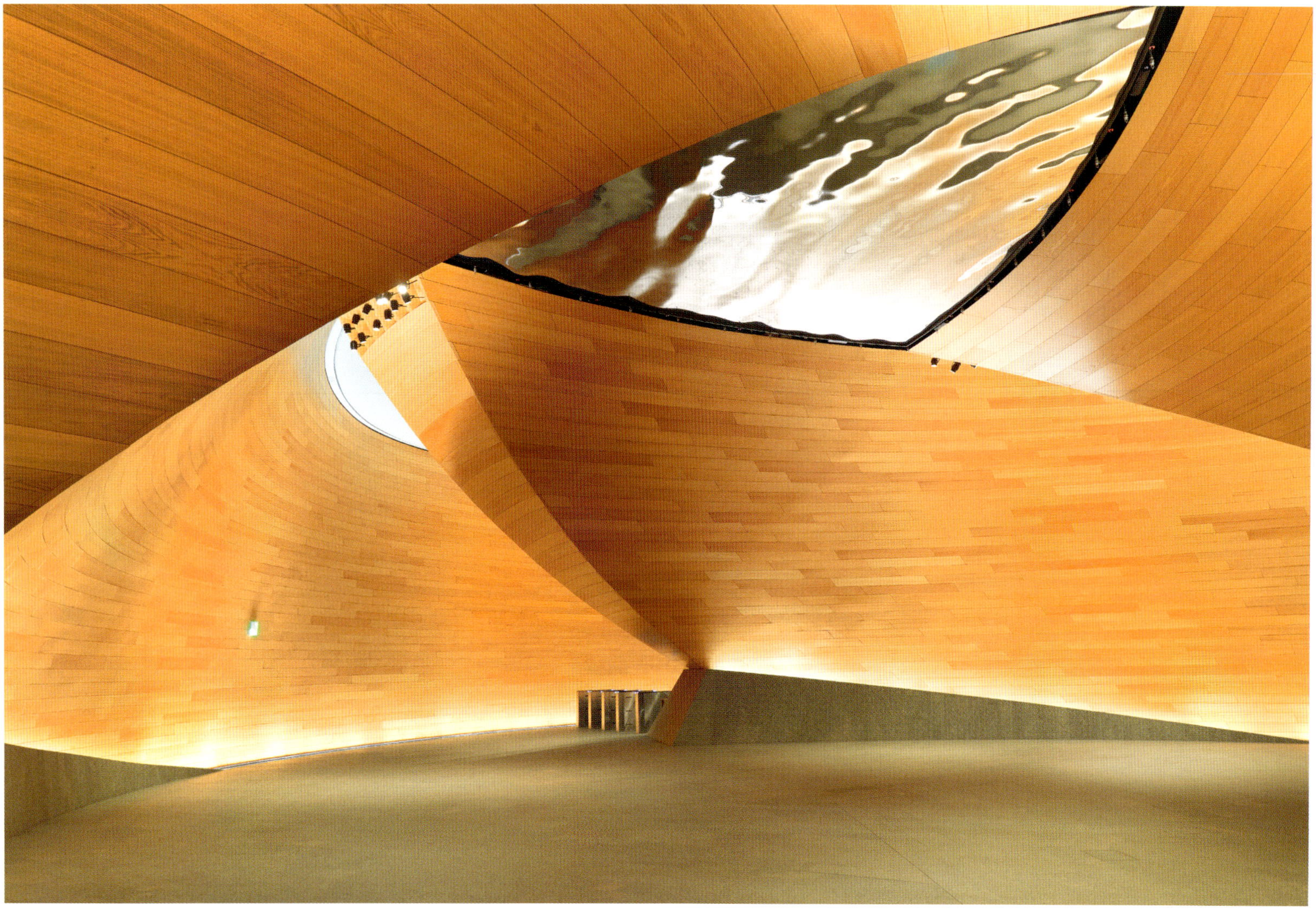

In the centre is spiral ramp which rises in a triple helix to span six floors.

now lives under the Bloomberg building as the London Mithraeum, part light-show and audio environment and open for visitors. Also on display are Roman artefacts discovered in 2012–14 during the construction of the new headquarters.

Another scrupulous action was recreation of a portion of the lost Roman road Watling Street that linked Dover with St Albans. It forms Bloomberg Arcade in the space between the north and south buildings, with a number of restaurants, open to everyone. Somewhere below lies a lost river of London, the Walbrook. A cast-bronze sculpture-installation recreates these waters at pavement level.

The interiors at Bloomberg are perhaps its most spectacular feature. The reception lobby is a three-walled hallway called The Vortex, a leaning, twisted wood-panelled structure. In the centre is spiral ramp that rises in a triple helix to span six floors. The 4,500 workplace desks that are in the north building are said to be exemplary when measured in terms of equality and layout. On the fifth floor is the broadcast studio.

Above The Vortex lobby, part hallway, part work of art in wood and polished aluminium.

CONTACT INFORMATION

Bloomberg London,
3 Queen Victoria Street, EC4N 4TQ
https://www.bloomberg.com/city-of-london

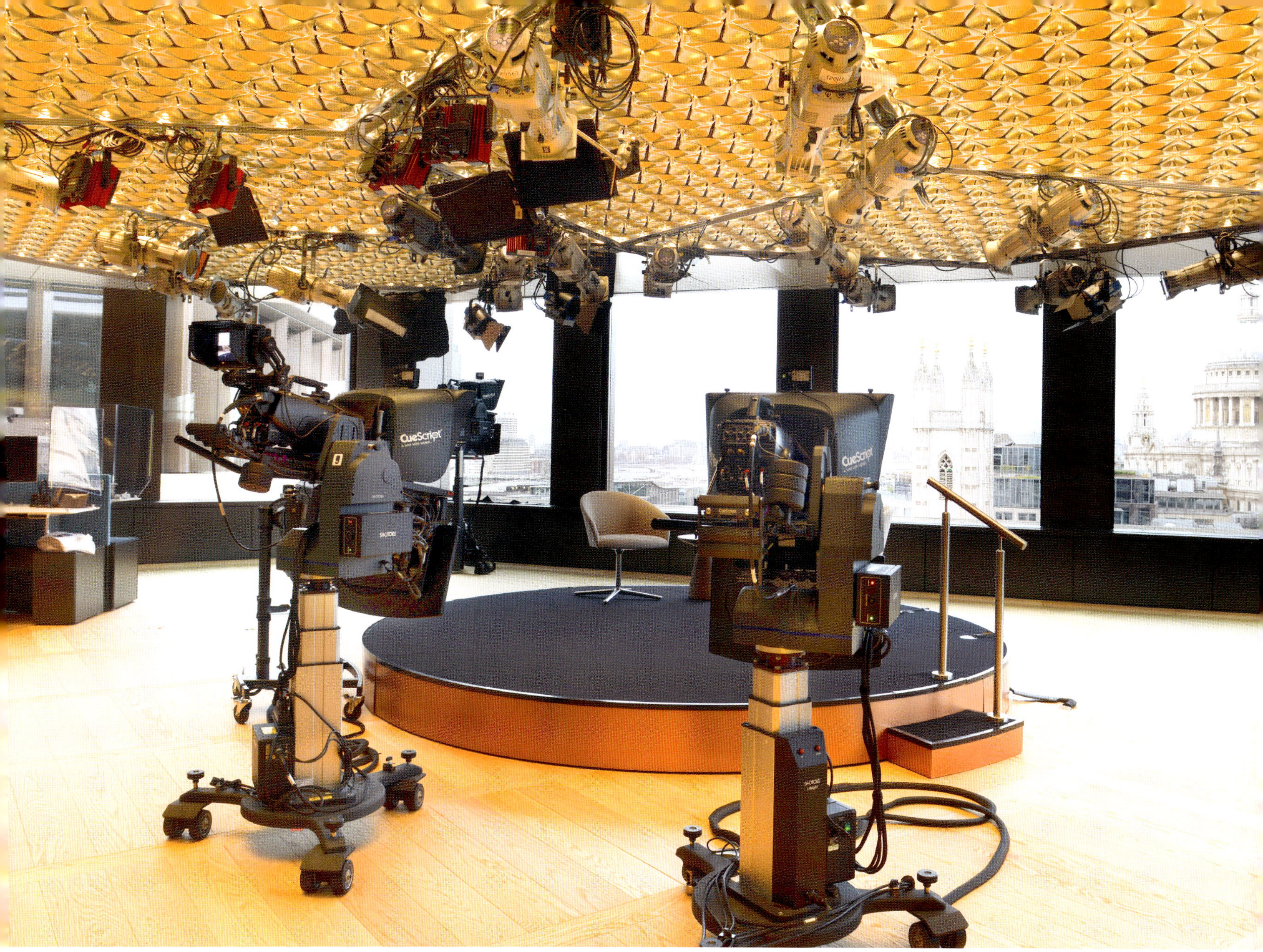

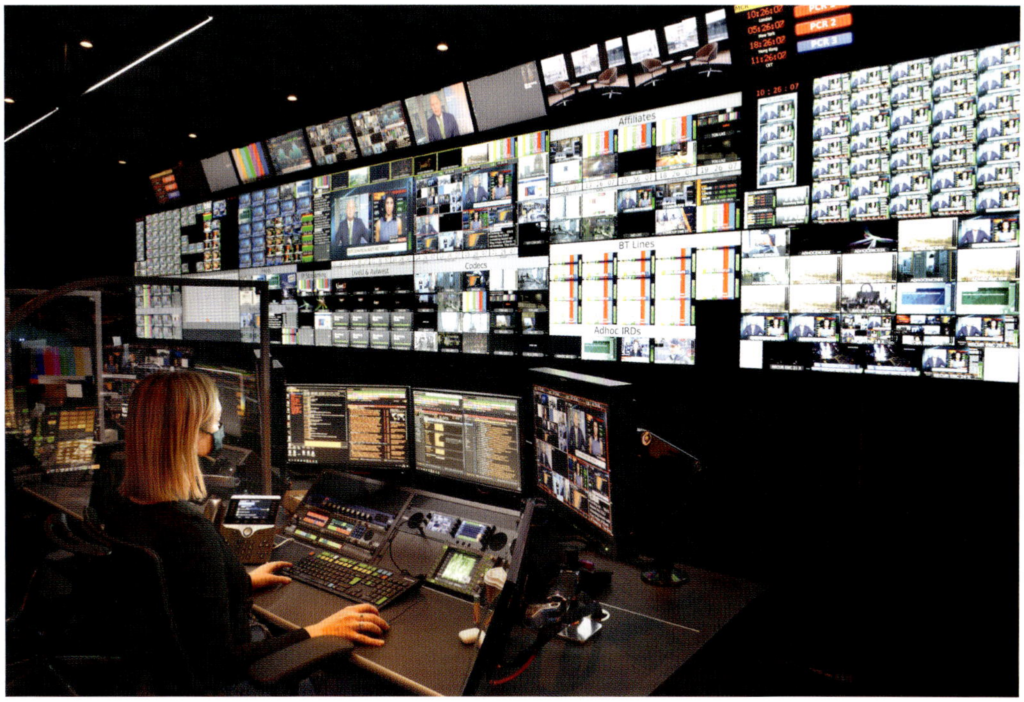

Above The broadcast studio on the fifth floor. Note the view of St Paul's Cathedral to the west.

Left State-of-the-art workstations for news data handling are at the operational centre of the building and at the core of the Bloomberg business.

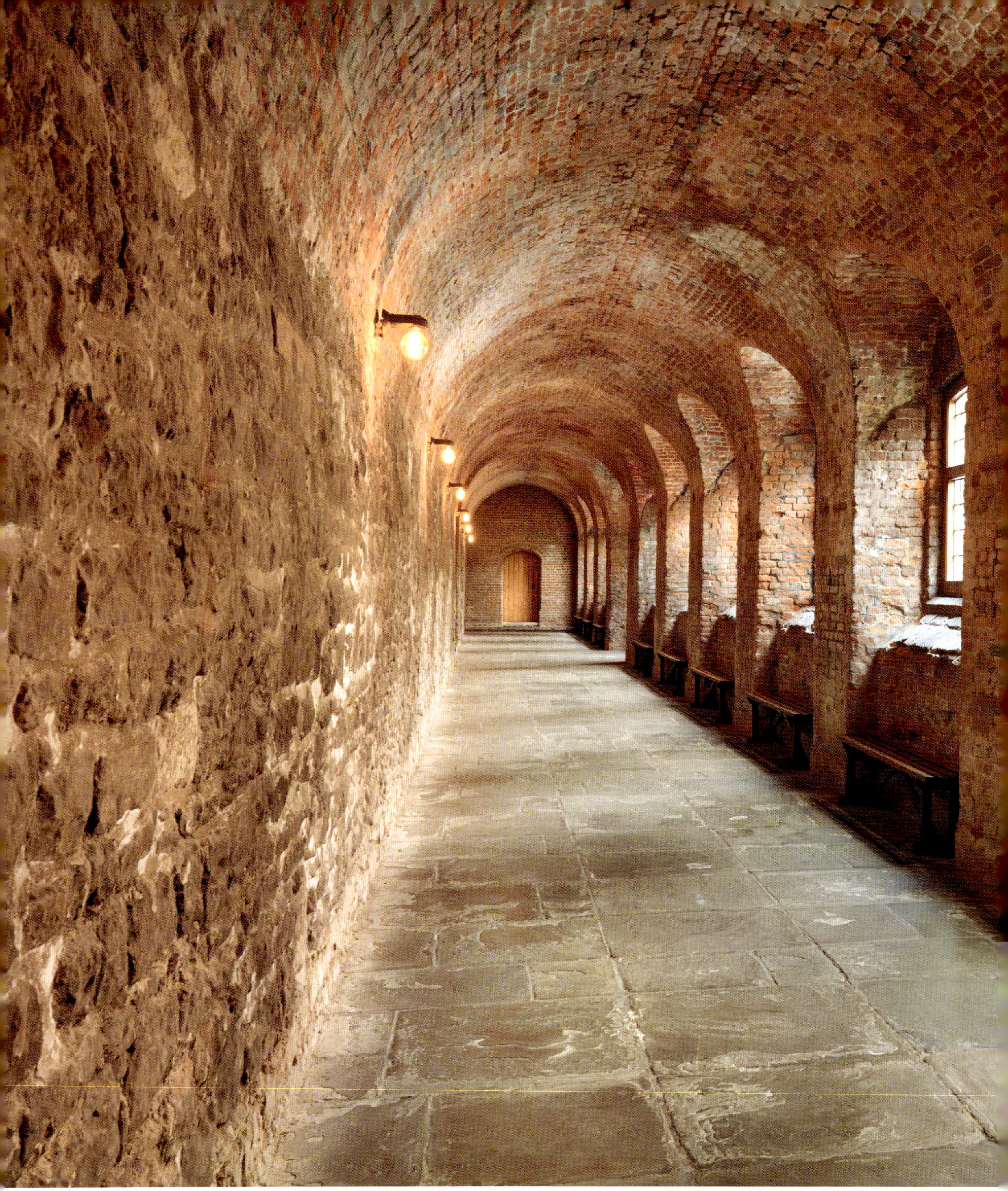

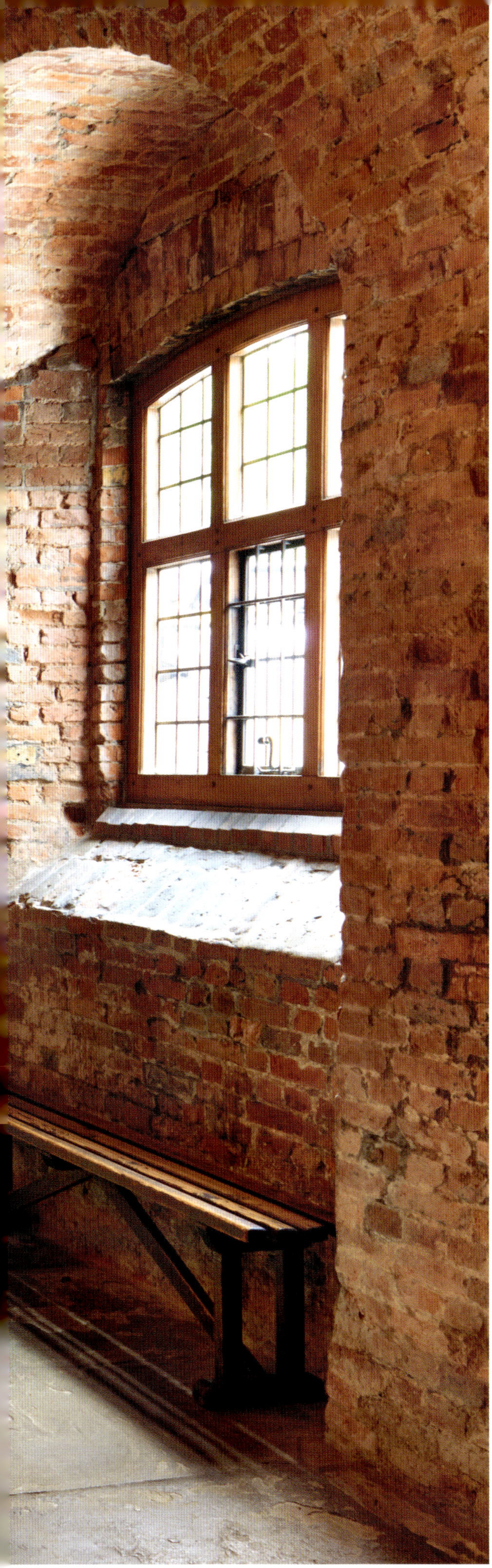

The Charterhouse

The Norfolk Cloister, where the rules for the 'throw in' and 'offside' in football were conceived.

The Charterhouse lies just to the north of the City of London boundary, a collection of fine buildings hidden beyond the arch of a fifteenth-century gateway off a cobbled square. It was originally a Carthusian monastery dating from the late 1300s, which subsequently underwent several distinct changes of identity and purpose. During Tudor times it operated as a mansion house in the ownership of powerful noblemen. It once a housed a notable public school. Today, it serves as a modern almshouse and a secluded retirement home, retaining some of the fabric from the fourteenth century and some architecture from the twenty-first. The latest addition is a museum with exhibition space and a learning centre opened in 2017 in collaboration with the Museum of London.

A burial ground was established on land in West Smithfield about 1350 during the Black Death, and a chapel was built alongside. The hermitage of a priory built to a square ground plan was started in 1372 under the sponsorship of Baron Walter de Mauny, a soldier much favoured by Edward III, to whom he acted as an adviser. The order of monks came from La Grande Chartreuse near Grenoble in France. They belonged to the Carthusian Order and the anglicizing of this gave the name Charterhouse. A chapter house and a series of small houses for a complement of twenty-four monks were built, with surrounding cloisters. Thomas More sometimes worshipped here and possibly lived here as a young law student. The monastery was politically favoured and thrived for almost a hundred years, but the devout Carthusians would not accept Henry VIII's Act of Supremacy over the English Church, and many of the Charterhouse monks died in the turmoil of the Dissolution, brutally executed at Tyburn or starved to death during imprisonment. Prior John Houghton was hanged, drawn and quartered. One quarter of his body, including an arm, was afterwards suspended above the gateway of the London Charterhouse.

Seized by the Crown, Charterhouse was acquired by Lord North, who demolished the church and cloisters, built new courtyards and added the Great Hall to develop an expansive mansion. Lord North was close to the highest level of the establishment and Elizabeth I arrived at Charterhouse from Hatfield on the fifth day of her reign in November 1558 and stayed for five days before proceeding to the Tower of London on the way to her coronation in Westminster Abbey. The mansion complex was sold to Thomas Howard, 4th Duke of Norfolk, who further added to it. Norfolk later became caught up in the Ridolfi plot to overthrow Elizabeth, and he was executed in 1572.

It was under the brief ownership of Thomas Sutton, a commoner made wealthy by coal mines and speculation, that in 1614 Charterhouse began its journey to becoming an almshouse and school. Sutton had long held the wish to create a benevolent institution, and under a foundation established by him endowments were bestowed for a school for forty boys between nine and fourteen years. There was also an almshouse for eighty men over fifty years of age, unmarried, army or naval officers or businessmen who had become disabled or disadvantaged in some way. These were to be called Brothers, and the institution known as Sutton's Hospital in Charterhouse. Although the charter had stipulated that the scholars were to be the children of poor parents, it did not intend that they were paupers, but rather those descended from the professional rather than landed classes. Fee-paying day boys and boarders were also admitted.

Some new buildings were commissioned, others enlarged or adapted and Charterhouse School was active at this site until 1872, when it moved to Godalming. Part of the site was then employed by Merchant Taylor's School, which operated here until the site was sold in 1933 to St Bartholomew's Hospital, which established a medical college there. Today this is Barts and The London School of Medicine and Dentistry.

Charterhouse continues as a community of over forty single elderly men of limited financial means, some of whom are former military officers; others teachers, clergymen and artists. Modern Charterhouse includes the Admiral Ashmore building, completed in 2000, and the Queen Elizabeth II infirmary, converted from existing buildings in 2004.

With changes of purpose, and building programmes spanning more than 500 years, with serious bomb damage in 1941, demolitions and modern additions, the architecture and history of Charterhouse is varied and layered. When work was under way to restore the bomb-damaged buildings in 1947, the foundations of the original chapel from the time of the Black Death were unearthed, and the grave and remains of Baron de Mauny discovered. Today's chapel incorporates part of the old chapter house. The Great Hall and the Great Chamber are splendid rooms from Lord North's day, both expanded and extensively rebuilt in recent years. Wash House Court is an authentic quadrangle of modest brick and stone Tudor outbuildings. There was once a range of buildings erected to Sir Christopher Wren's design in 1672 and demolished in the 1820s.

There is even a persistent claim that the cloisters of Charterhouse contributed to the formulation of the rules of Association Football. Students at Charterhouse played football inside the cloisters, and when the ball was kicked outside beyond arm's reach, a player was allowed to leave and return it to play into by a throw-in, an action which was incorporated into the rules of the game. Players who tried to gain an advantage by jumping out of the cloisters and running in front of the ball were penalized: the first application of the off-side rule.

CONTACT INFORMATION

The Charterhouse,
Charterhouse Square, EC1M 6AN
https://thecharterhouse.org/

Opposite, above
The Great Hall with its hammer-beam roof. The chimneypiece from 1614 bears the arms of Thomas Sutton.

Opposite, below
The chapel was once the Carthusian chapter house of the early fifteenth century. The pew ends are Jacobean.

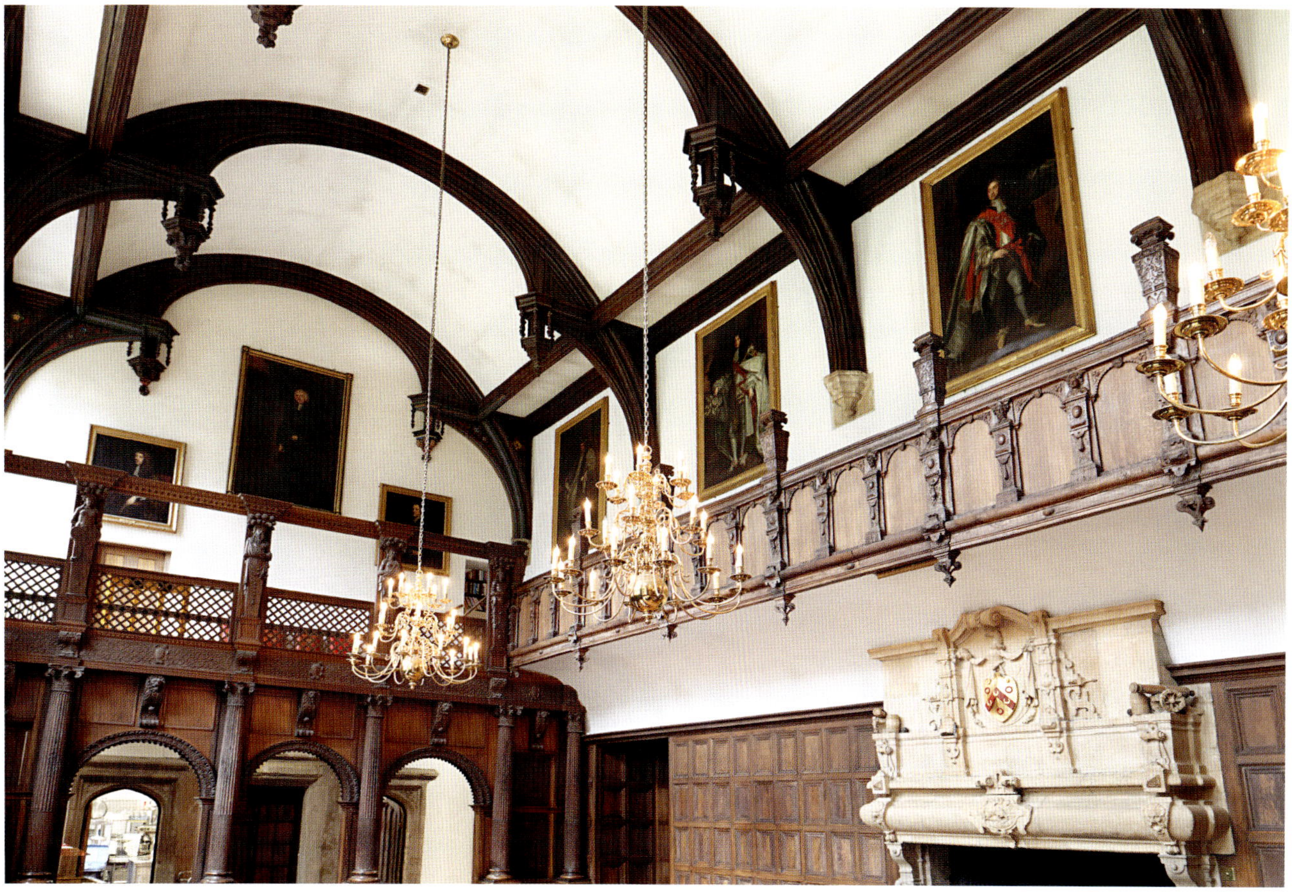

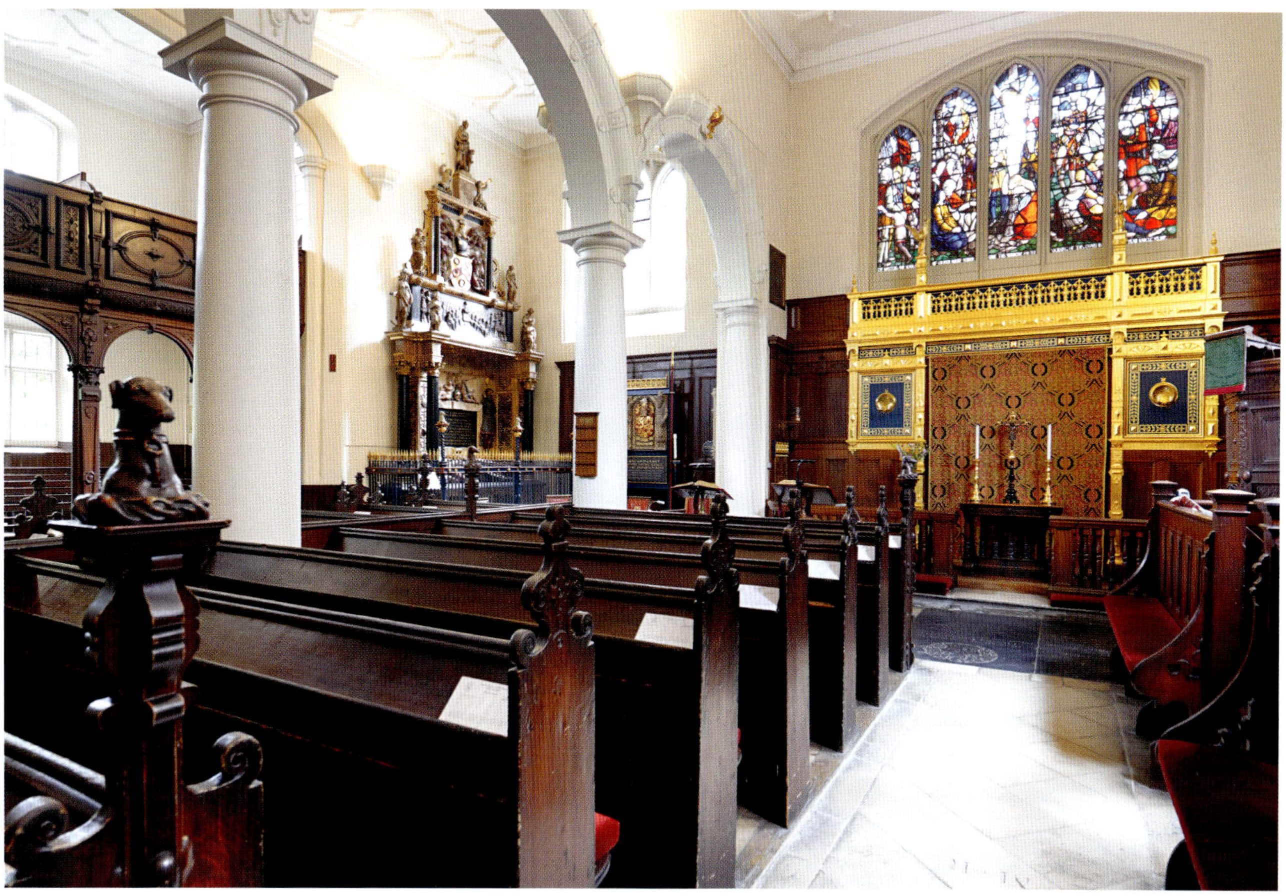

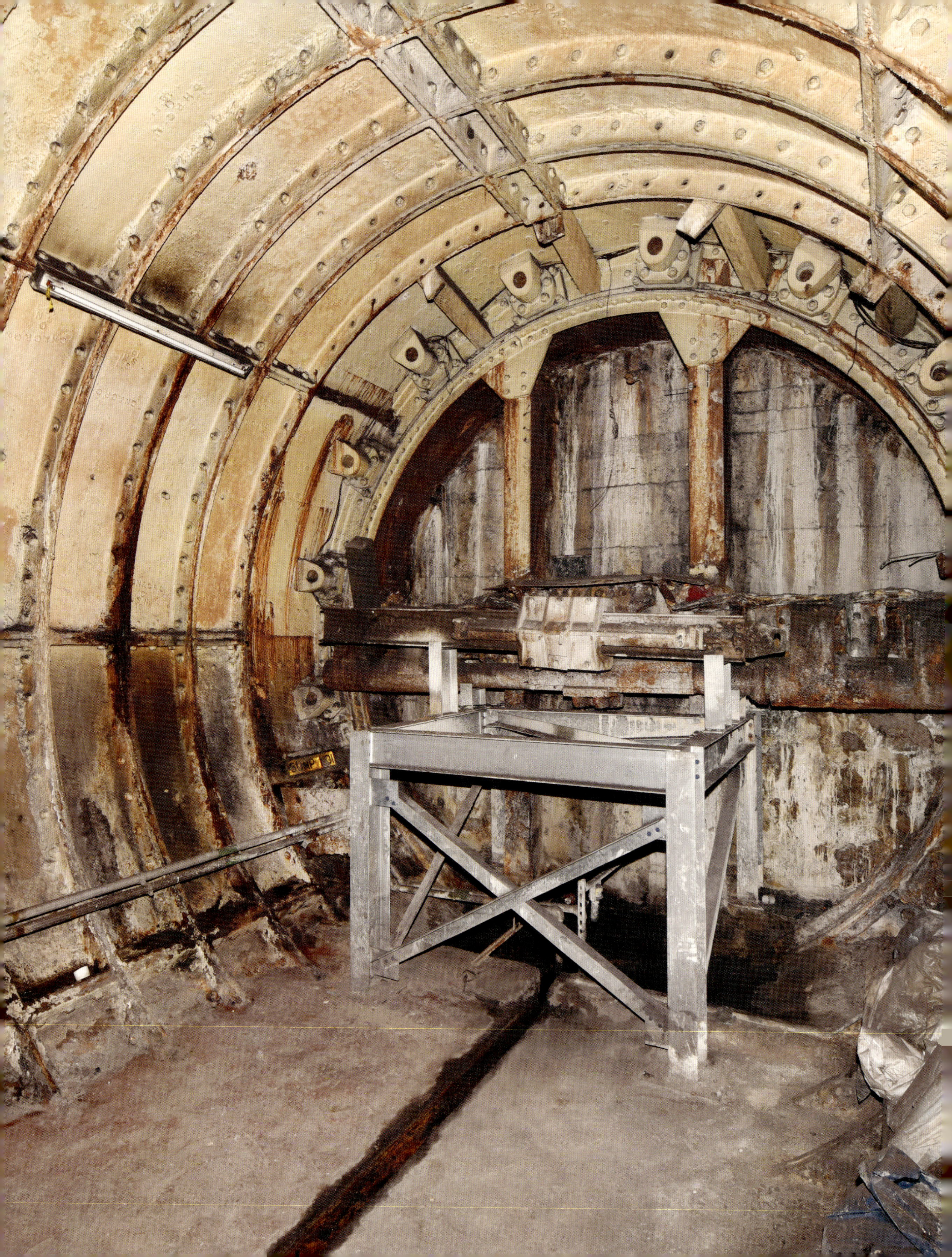

Greathead Shield

At the end of a short tunnel by Moorgate's platform 10, lies a Greathead Shield with its ring of hydraulic rams, positioned for work but destined to be abandoned.

Marooned at Moorgate station for almost 120 years is a rare example of the Greathead Shield, the technology that dug tunnels for much of the London Underground system. While the earliest tunnels, for the Metropolitan, Hammersmith & City, Inner Circle and District lines, were made by digging up the streets – a process known as cut-and-cover – later routes were bored by the Greathead Shield at deeper levels.

James Henry Greathead's device improved on an invention used by Marc Brunel for London's first deep tunnel: the Wapping–Rotherhithe of 1843. Here, a massive tunnelling cylinder housing a honeycomb of thirty-four cells worked by miners had slowly inched forward. Greathead's smaller shield had fewer cells and the advantage of hydraulically powered rams pressing against the completed tunnel segments to advance the cutting face. Circular tunnels cut by this method were smaller and the expression 'Tube' began to be used to describe them and the trains that ran inside.

The shield lying at Moorgate is unique. The Great Northern & City Railway planned a route for main-line suburban trains from the north right into the centre of the City, and a Greathead Shield was designed to bore twin tunnels 16 ft (5 m) in diameter for full-sized rolling stock. It opened between Finsbury Park and Moorgate in 1904, but the track connections intended at the northern end for through trains were barred by the main-line surface operator. The line, destined to be known as the Big Tube, was worked back-and-forth in isolation for years.

A southward extension to Lothbury, close to the Bank at the heart of the City, was authorized but progressed only a few yards before the GN&CR were forced to pause and park the shield at Moorgate. There was a chance it would be revived when fortunes improved, but the boom years of developing London's underground system were ending and the GN&CR disappeared in a round of takeovers and amalgamation.

In 1976, following a reshuffle of transport responsibilities, the Big Tube was connected to the British Rail surface network between Finsbury Park and Drayton Park, enabling trains from the far north, or at least Hertfordshire, to run into Moorgate, fulfilling the original vision of the GN&CR promoters after seventy years.

CONTACT INFORMATION

Greathead Shield,
Moorgate station,
Finsbury, EC2M 6TX

Lloyd's of London

In the City, the application of facetious names to new buildings has flourished: the Gherkin, the Cheesegrater, the Walkie-Talkie and the Scalpel. One particular building was once dubbed the Oil Rig, the Coffee Percolator and the Motorcycle Engine, but these names did not stick. Lloyd's of London on 1 Lime Street brushed them off to be celebrated as one of the outstanding British architectural achievements. It became the youngest structure to be awarded Grade I listing, receiving the recognition in 2011, just twenty-five years after it was completed. The Historic England listing describes it as 'an awe-inspiring futuristic design with essential elements that survive remarkably well' and 'form a wonderfully incongruous backdrop' to many neighbouring listed buildings in the City.

It was also once described as 'a building on life support', a reference to the way the pipes, ducts, lifts, staircases and toilet pods are hung outside the supporting structure. The architecture was by the Richard Rogers Partnership. Richard Rogers had collaborated on the Centre Pompidou in Paris, a trail-blazing design of the 1970s, which had externalized air conditioning, electricity and water supplies in order to free up usable space inside. In the Lloyd's building the idea was taken further, but unlike at the Pompidou, the building does not depend on a steel frame. Although from most outside aspects the Lloyd's building appears dominated by six gleaming stainless-steel towers, the heart of the structure is a

The Lloyd's building is designed 'inside out' – all of the service functions are removed from the interior and placed at the exterior of the building. This frees up the interior to create an open and flexible plan that allows for uninterrupted activity on each level.

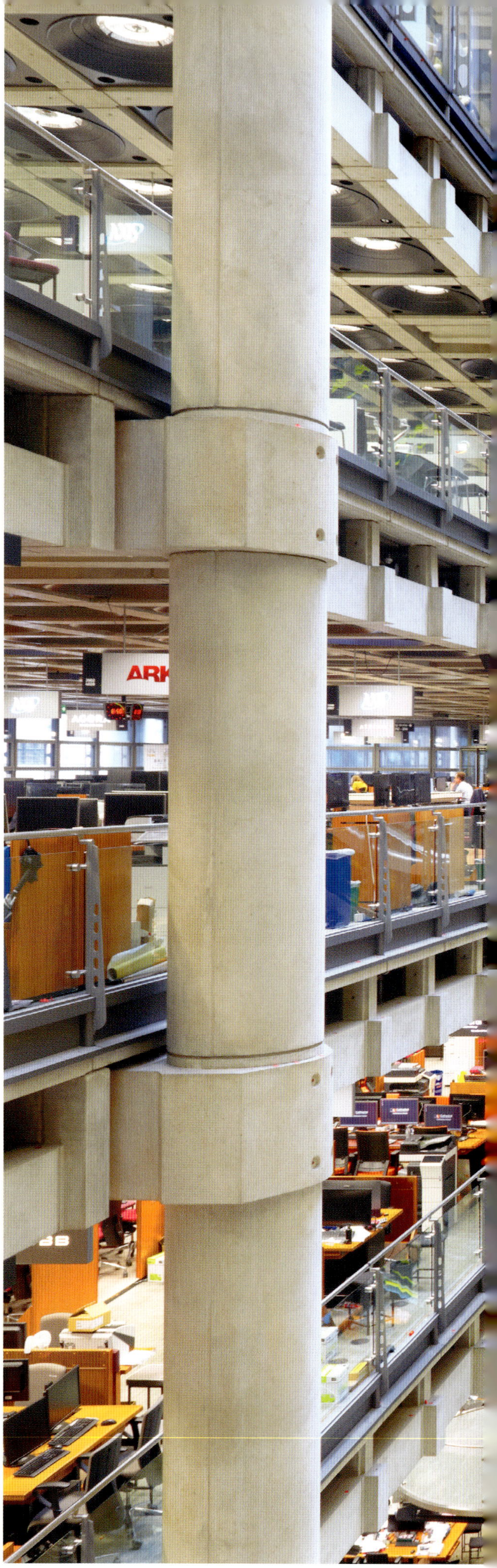

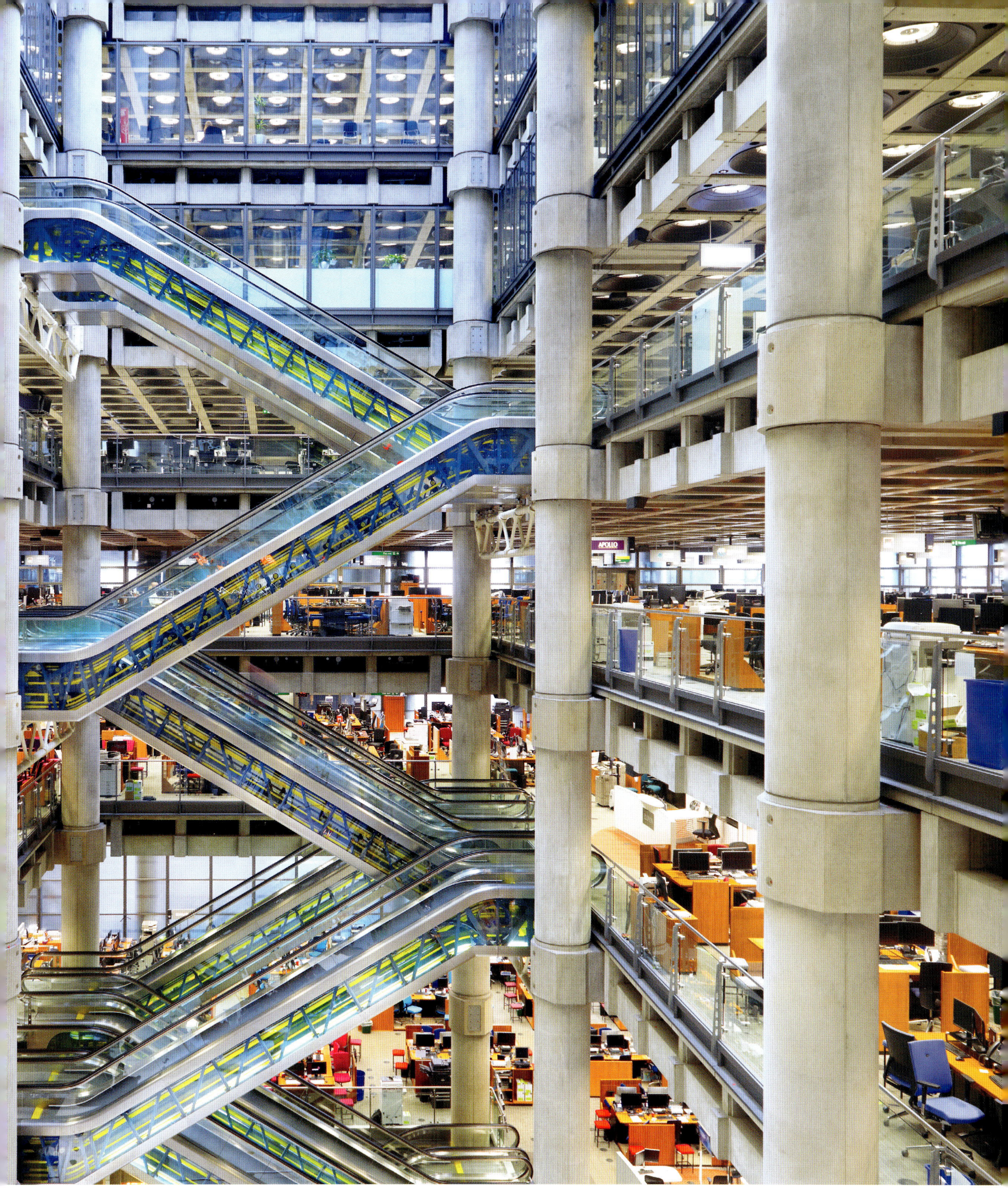

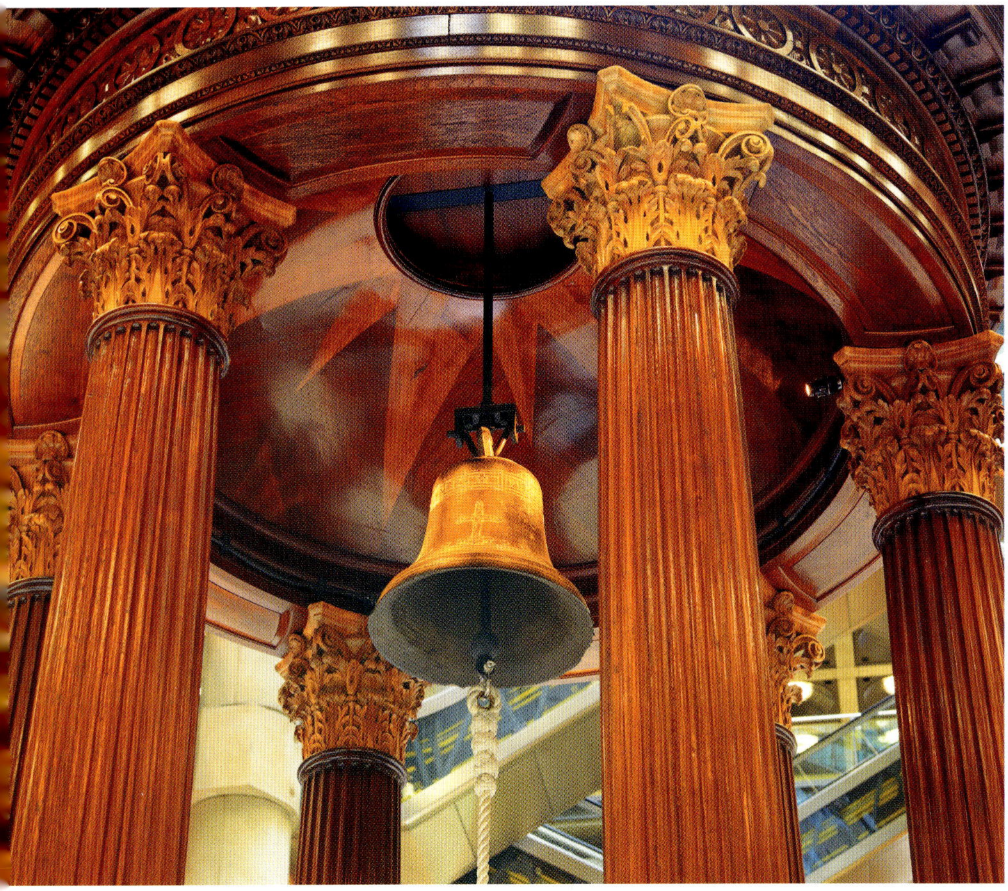

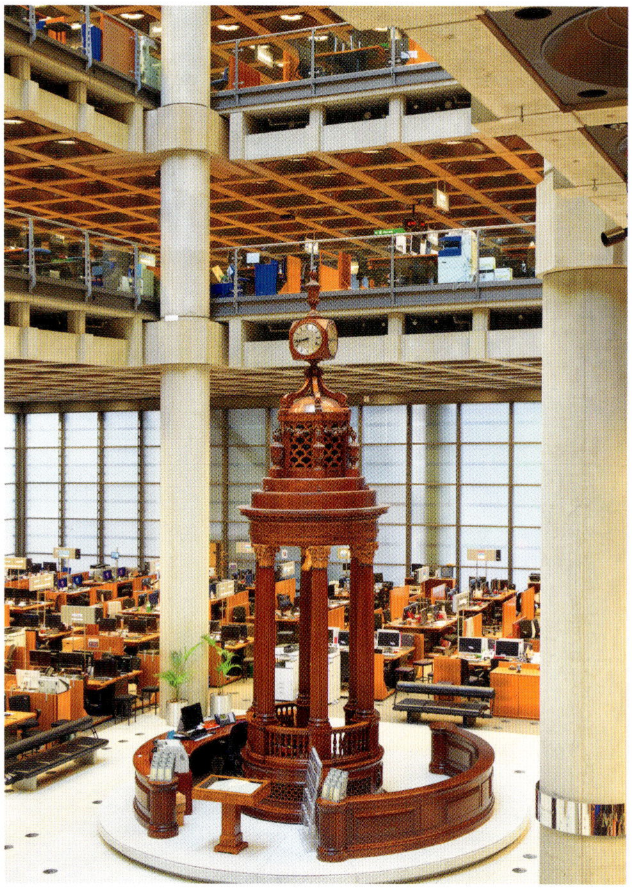

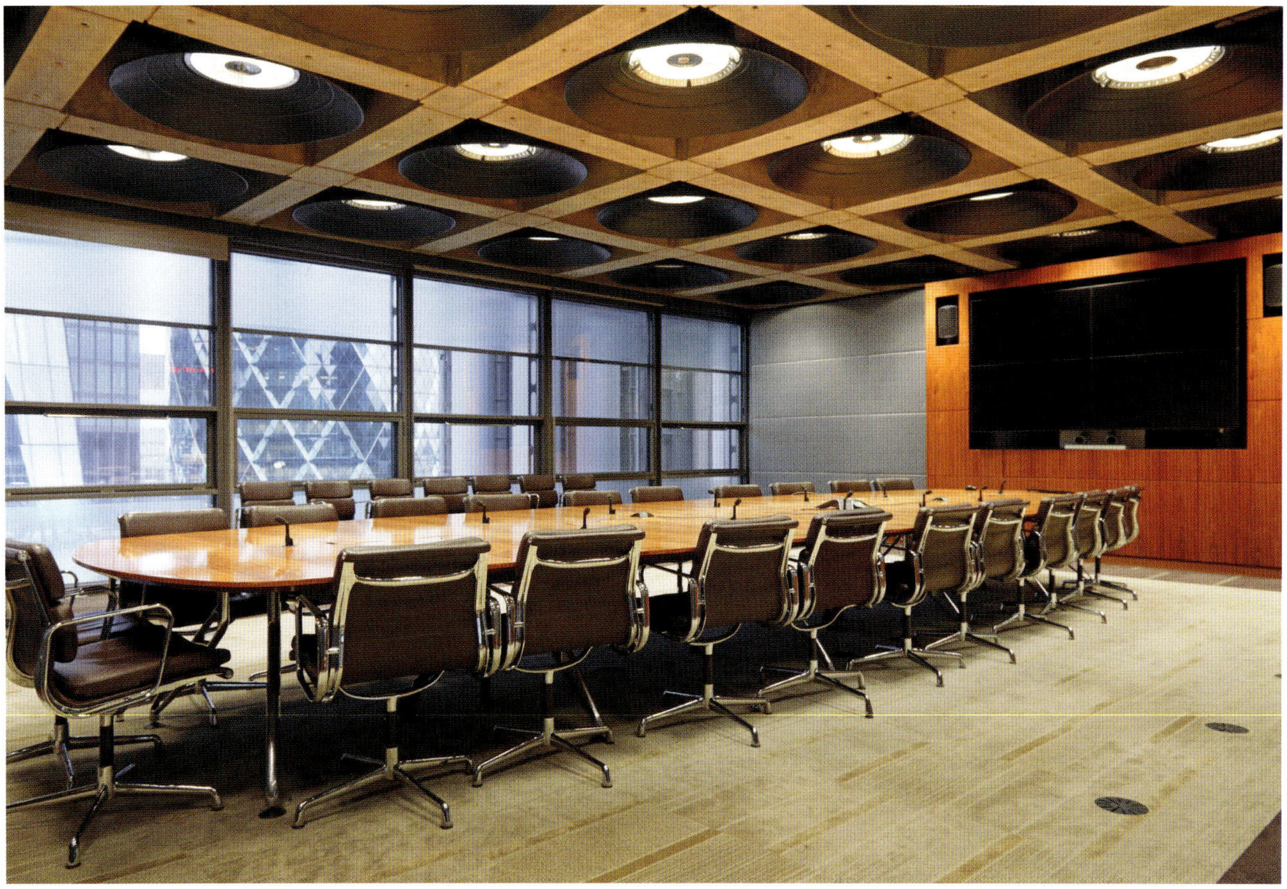

Above A close-up of Lutine Bell, which is rung before announcements of ships overdue or lost at sea.

Right above The Lutine Bell on the ground floor.

Right The Lloyd's of London boardroom.

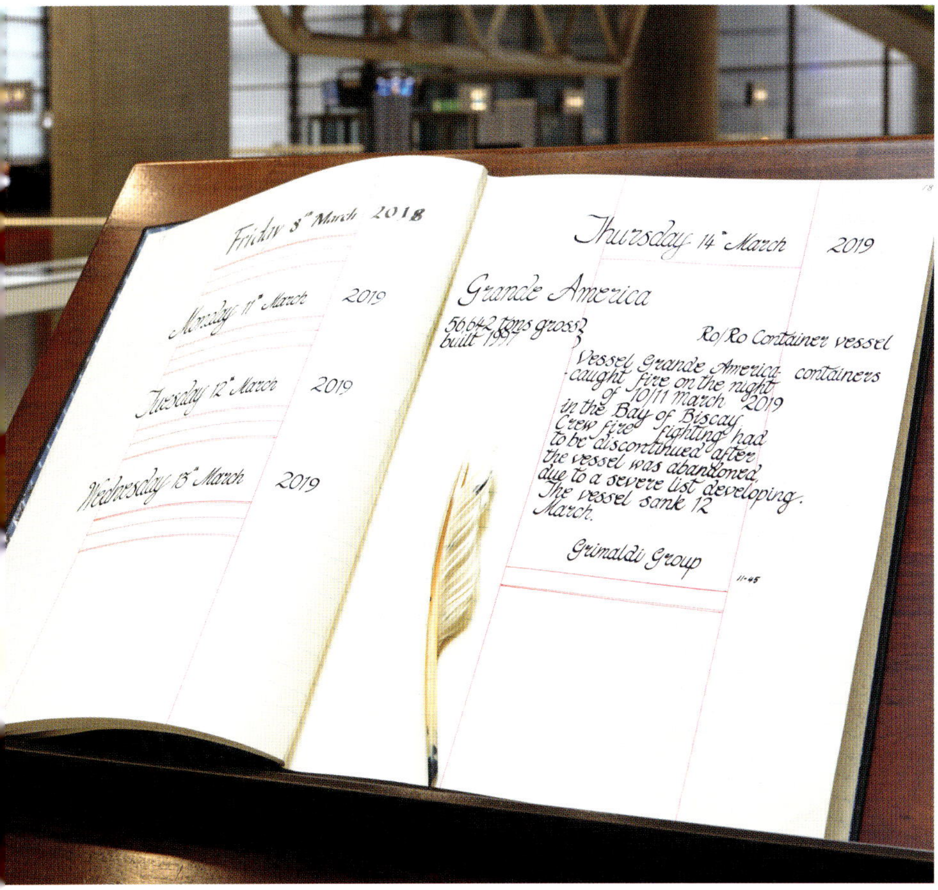

The logbook of lost ships.

The Lutine Bell is struck to mark occasions of ceremony and mourning. Lost ships are still recorded in logbooks at Lloyd's, handwritten in ink and cursive script.

series of twenty-eight concrete columns, which carry the fourteen floors by pre-cast brackets. The atrium rises 200 ft (60 m) to a steel-and-glass, barrel-vaulted roof. The principal business of Lloyd's is conducted in the main underwriting room – the first four levels of the atrium connected by banks of escalators. This is known simply as the Room and the desks where the underwriters work are known as boxes, a back reference to the tables in the corners of Edward Lloyd's Tower Street Coffee Shop of 1688. It was here that merchants with foreign interests and shipowners first did insurance business for ships and cargoes. Lloyd's has lived in eight buildings across the City over its 300-year history, while developing marine insurance underwriting into all fields of insurance. Insurance companies still pay a fee to have a box and a small percentage on every policy written goes to Lloyd's. Lloyd's provides the building and regulates how the underwriters work.

On the ground floor of the Room is the Lutine Bell, first hung in Lloyd's Royal Exchange headquarters in 1859. It was salvaged from the wreck of HMS *Lutine*, which sank carrying £1 million of gold and silver bullion insured by Lloyd's. The bell became part of Lloyd's tradition, rung twice when overdue ships came in safely, or once to signify if a ship was lost. It is mounted in the rostrum, a mahogany temple designed for the 1928 Lloyd's building based on the monument of Lysicrates in Athens. Now the Lutine Bell is struck to mark occasions of ceremony and mourning. Lost ships are still recorded in logbooks at Lloyd's, handwritten in ink and cursive script.

Lloyd's legacy and tradition are embedded in other parts of the building. A display of artefacts and memorabilia associated with Lord Nelson and Trafalgar includes his collar of the Order of the Bath, the logbook of HMS *Euryalus* active at Trafalgar, recording receipt of the signal 'England expects every man to do his duty' and a fragment of a piece sail from HMS *Victory*. The uniformed assistants at Lloyd's wearing red or blue livery who call out the names of brokers are still known as waiters, a legacy of the coffee shop origins. The Robert Adam Room on level 11 is a 1770s interior salvaged from Bowood House in Wiltshire and first intended for the committee room of the Lime Street headquarters of 1958. The façade on the Leadenhall Street side of the building working as the entrance to Tower 5 is the stone frontage of the Lloyd's premises of 1928.

CONTACT INFORMATION

Lloyd's of London,
1 Lime Street, EC3M 7HA
https://www.lloyds.com/

Honourable Artillery Company

An active regiment of the British Territorial Army, now properly known as the Army Reserve, occupies a remarkable patch of hidden green territory close to the City of London. The Honourable Artillery Company (HAC) carries a fine array of regimental traditions, layers of history, and several armorial-heraldic distinctions. Its Army Reserve troopers are dedicated to the modern military arts of surveillance and target acquisition, using imaging equipment and weapons-locating radar. The sharp end of the HAC is represented by three patrol squadrons of trained reconnaissance soldiers, equipped to operate and survive behind enemy lines if required, and the selection process for the patrols is notably tough.

Attached to this function is a charitable institution, akin to a City livery company, sometimes known as the Company or House. This supports the active units and has its own civilian ceremonial organizations. Together, the active side (the Regiment) and the Company share a fine building, Armoury House, and the stretch of land in front known as the Artillery Garden. All this exists in E1, close to the noisy concrete roundabout at the end of Old Street, just off City Road, and enclosed to the north by Bunhill Fields Burial Grounds. Few who pass are aware of its existence. This is the London Estate, home of the HAC since 1641. Armoury House itself dates from 1735.

The first surprise for visitors to the HAC is the expanse of Artillery Garden. Once used for archery practice, it is now a huge sports field overlooked by office buildings on the edge of the City. It has enough space for soccer, rugby and hockey pitches. There is a cricket square close to the spot where one of the oldest cricket pitches was laid in 1725.

The HAC was incorporated by Royal Charter in 1537. Within the infinitely baffling byways of British Army precedence, the HAC can claim to be the oldest regiment in the Army, while at the same time being the second most senior unit of the Territorial Army. It is also the second oldest military organization in the world (after the Vatican's Pontifical Swiss Guard). The word artillery is now misleading, for although the HAC has operated field guns, and still does for saluting purposes, across the centuries it has encompassed archers, grenadiers and infantry rifle companies. Today its active side includes a detachment of Special Constabulary to the City of London Police.

The Company of Pikemen and Musketeers are a purely ceremonial unit of the HAC, made up of veteran active members, and it serves as the bodyguard of the Lord Mayor of London on ceremonial occasions, primarily at Guildhall and Mansion House. It is armed and uniformed in the style of 1640, and the armoury houses their gleaming equipment, together with the instruments of the Corps of Drums. There is also a ceremonial HAC light cavalry troop, which acts as escort to the Lady Mayoress.

The windows of the Great Stairs.

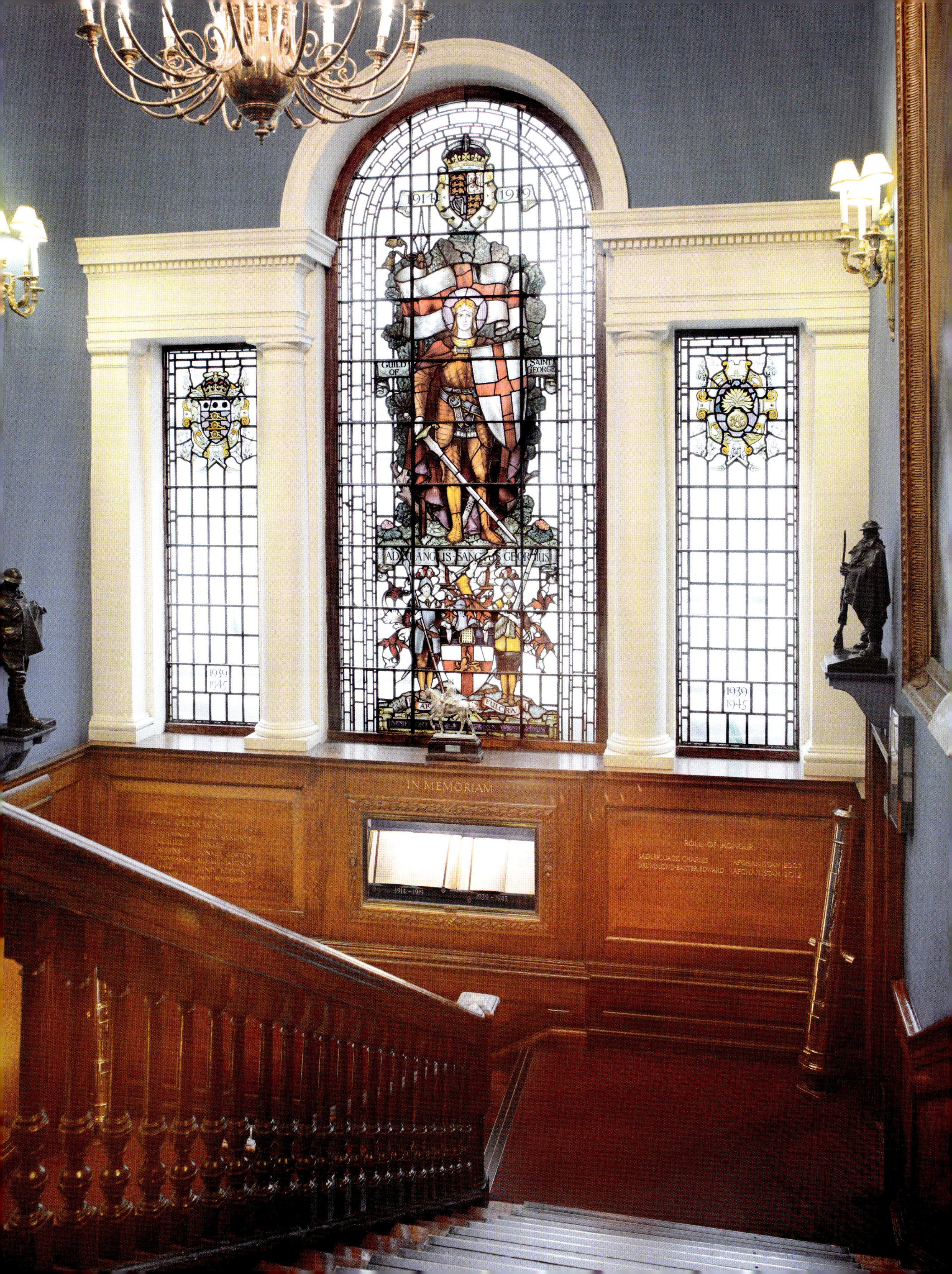

1914
1919
GUILD OF
SAINT GEORGE
1939
1945
IN MEMORIAM
ROLL OF HONOUR
1914 - 1919
1939 - 1945

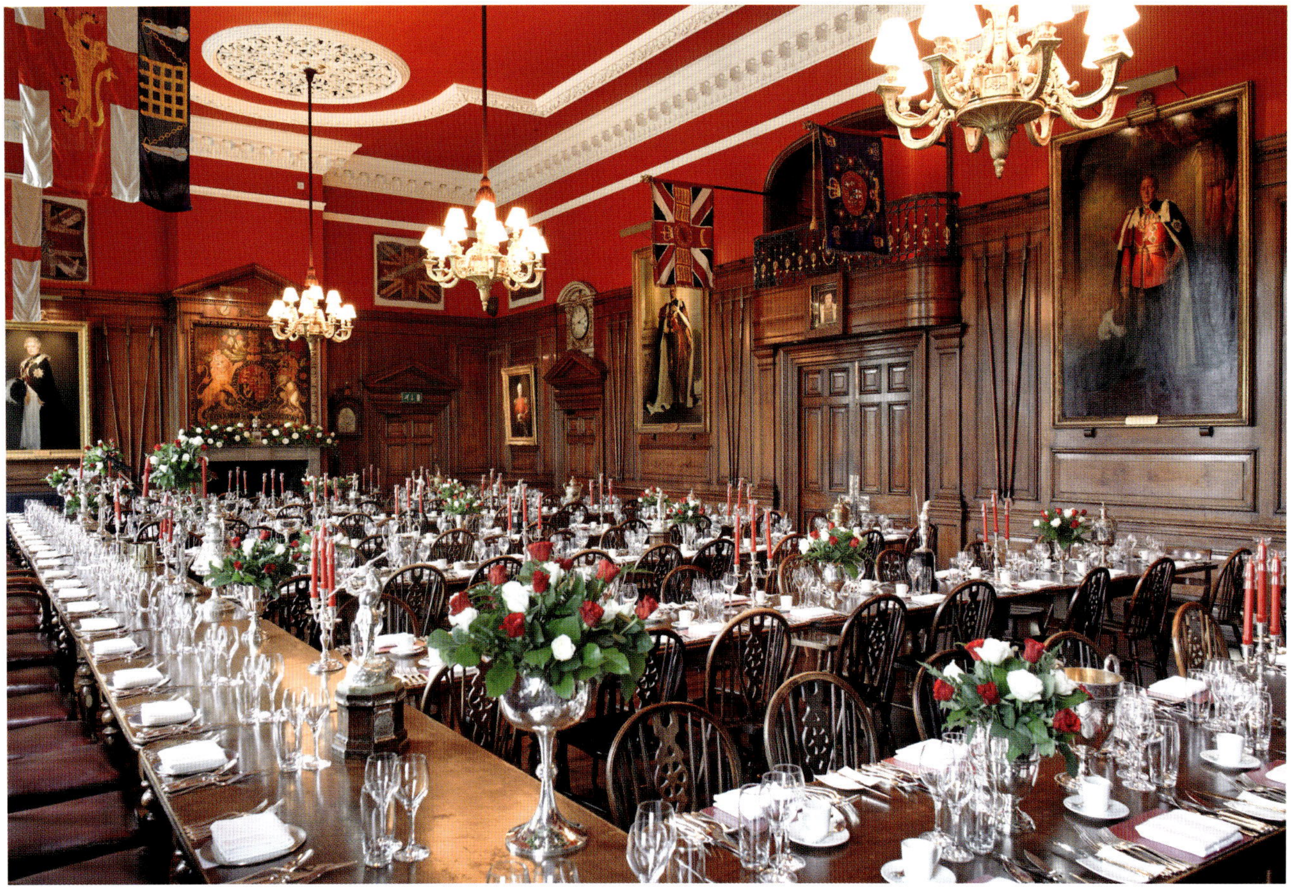

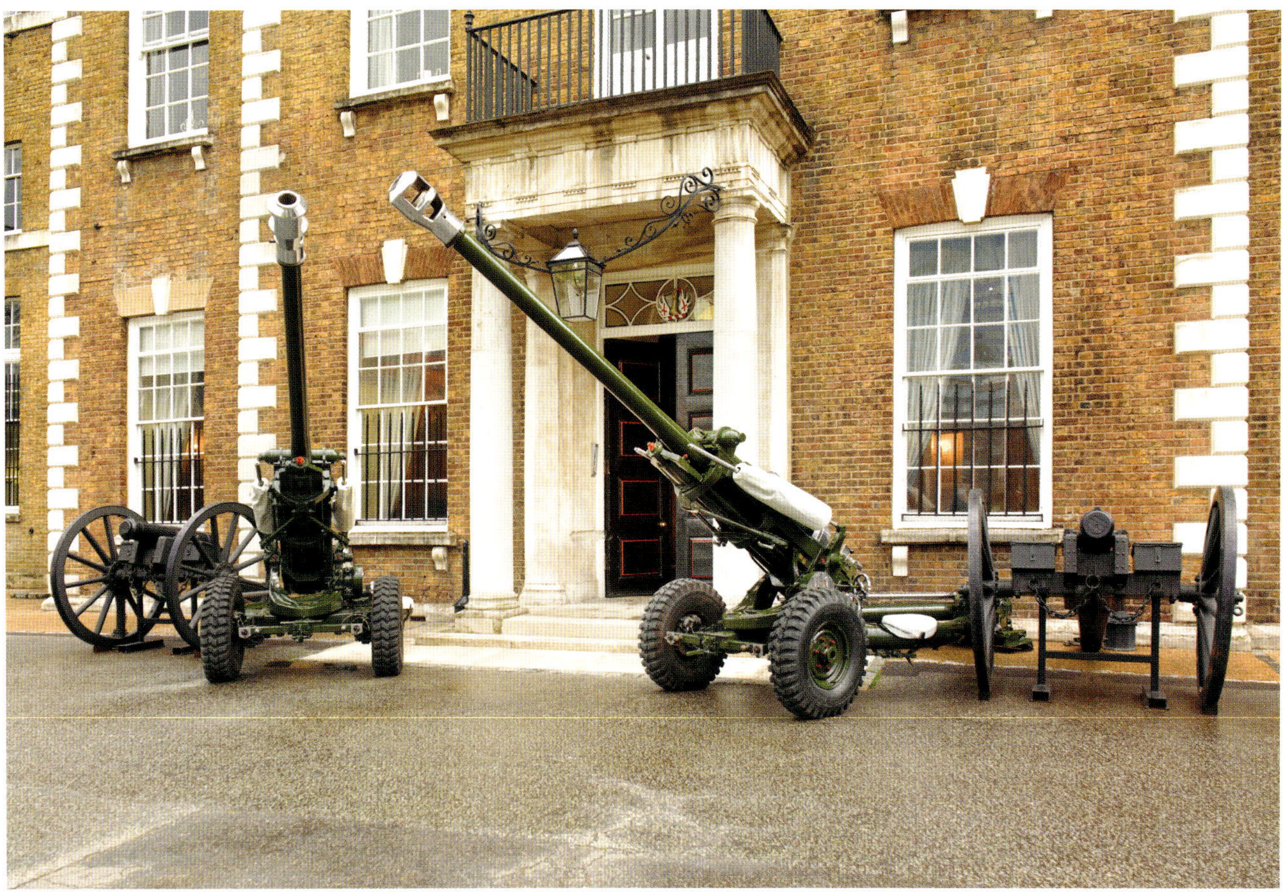

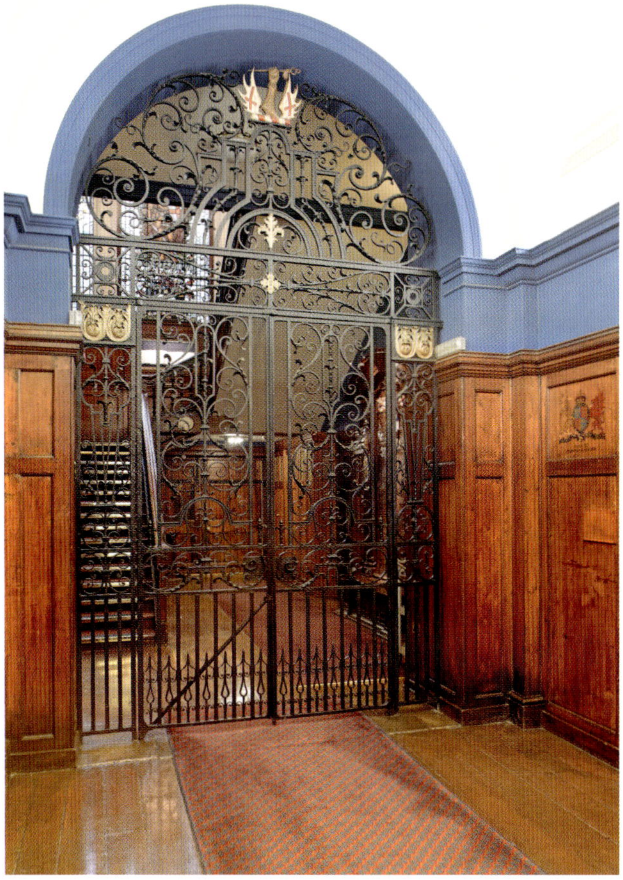

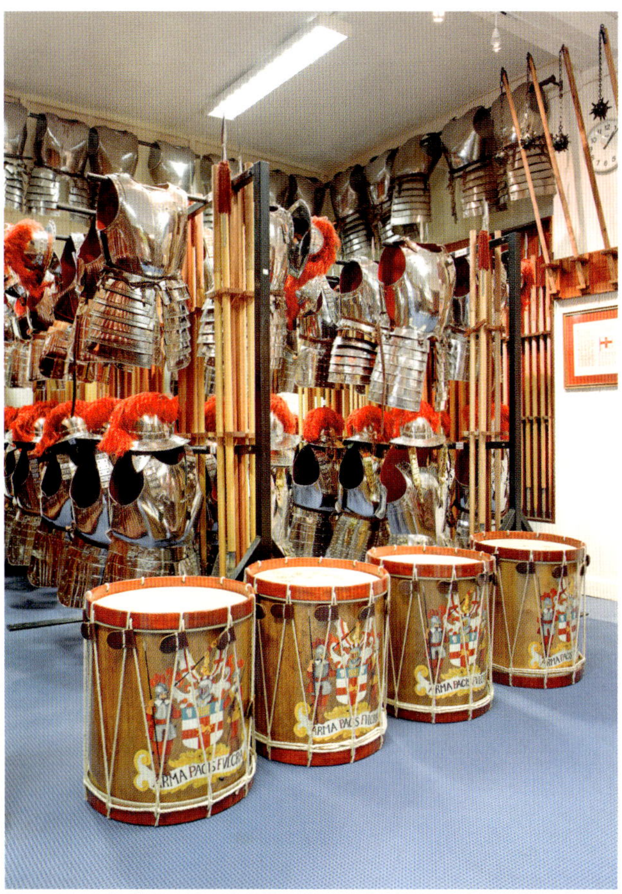

Opposite, above The Long Room laid out for the annual St George's Dinner, the Company's principal dinner of the year, held every April close to St George's Day.

Opposite, below Ceremony and function: saluting guns ancient and modern at the door of the Honourable Artillery Company.

Left, above A pair of wrought iron gates, installed in 1746, in the entrance hall at Armoury House

Left, below The armoury.

The HAC can claim to be the oldest regiment in the Army.

Armoury House retains many of its eighteenth-century features and is bristling with hardware and history. At the top of its Great Stairs, which are illuminated by a stained glass window, there is a battered stone pillar, known as a rover. This is an ancient archery target mark, reputed to be the only surviving example anywhere. It was removed in 1881 from a wall near a bridge over the Regent's Canal nearby. A ship's bell from the vessel that carried the 1st Battalion HAC to France in 1914 is preserved here. The panelled Long Room is lined with portraits of former captain generals and colonel commandants. In the Court Room sits the Court of Assistants, the board of governors for the HAC, who share the room with a rare example of sixteenth-century jousting amour.

Adjoining Armoury House is Finsbury Barracks. The two buildings are linked by a modern extension faced in striped stone and granite dating from 1994. Owned by the HAC, Finsbury Barracks is now administered by the Reserve Forces' and Cadets' Association. It was built in 1857 as the headquarters of the Royal London Militia, and from 1907 was the base of the Auxiliary Forces of the City of London. It dates from an age when the role of reservists and territorials was being developed, and drill halls were being built all across Britain. Finsbury Barracks remains a functional operational building leased back to the Army, and one of the memorable features of the HAC is seeing where pageantry ends and function begins.

CONTACT INFORMATION

Honourable Artillery Company,
Armoury House, City Road, EC1Y 2BQ
https://hac.org.uk/

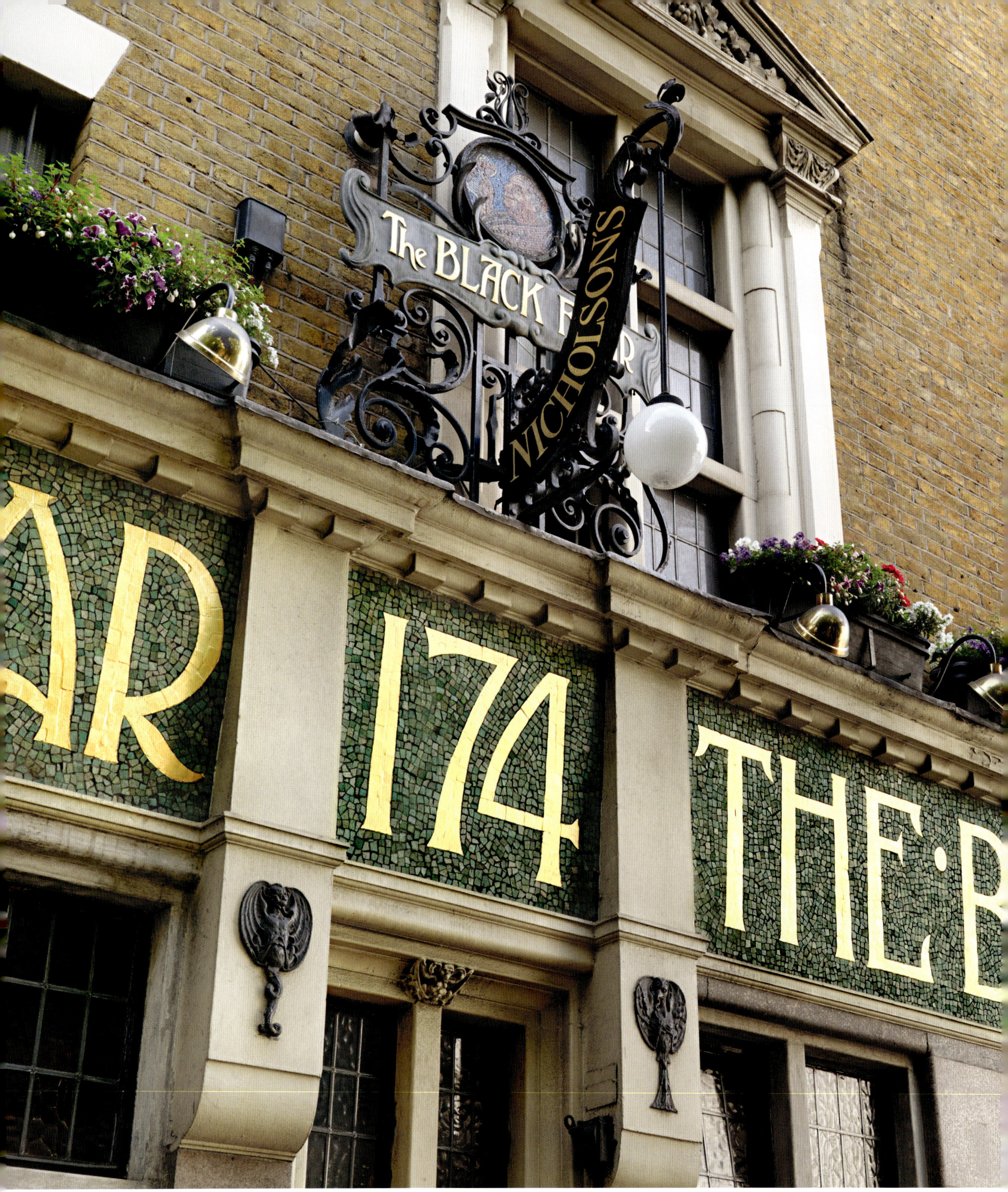

The BLACK F R
NICHOLSON'S
AR 174 THE·B

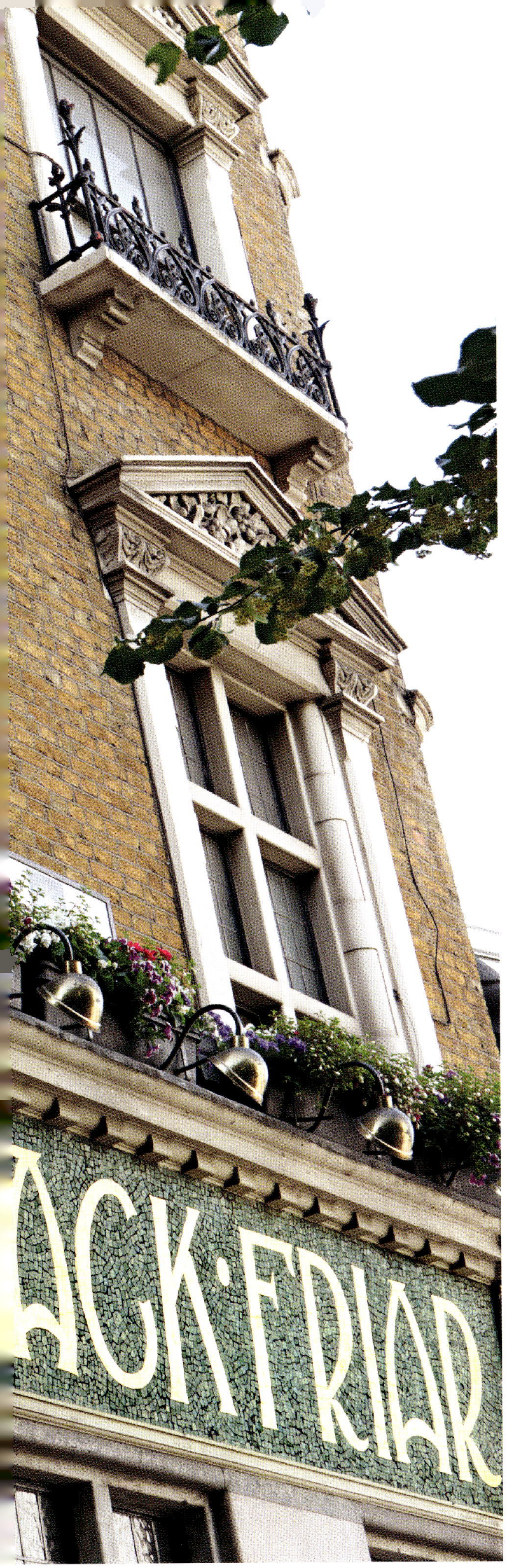

The Blackfriar

The striking signage in green-and-gold mosaic dates from the 1903 remodelling.

The Blackfriar pub on Queen Victoria Street stands like half-opened book, with the stone figure of a friar embedded on its spine. Inside lies an Arts & Crafts-styled fantasy world unlike any pub in London.

The multi-coloured marble-faced walls are adorned with pictorial panels and friezes. The decorative theme is based on monks and good spirits, with happy friars living jolly lives. Monks are depicted fishing, gardening, washing and pushing a wheelbarrow carrying a trussed pig. Everywhere there are mosaics, copper reliefs, scripts bearing axioms, stained glass, brass, mahogany and mirrors. A light-hearted design touch is applied with high-quality materials used throughout. Outside, the style continues: the clock on the spine has a mosaic face and even the strictly commercial signage for 'Worthington Ales in a Bottle' and 'Booths Gin' is rendered in copper relief with Arts & Crafts fonts, flanked by figures of friars. All of this was inspired by the Dominican monastery that existed close to site between 1221 and 1538, and gave its name to the Blackfriars area.

A late addition to the pub, beyond the original bars, was the Grotto, a barrel-ceilinged room lined with alabaster and marble, built out into a vault under the neighbouring railway, separated from the saloon by three arches. There are no windows, but mirrors are used to good effect. Despite the apparent constraints of its shape, The Blackfriar is deceptively roomy.

The pub was built in 1875, but did not gain its special interior until it was remodelled in 1903.

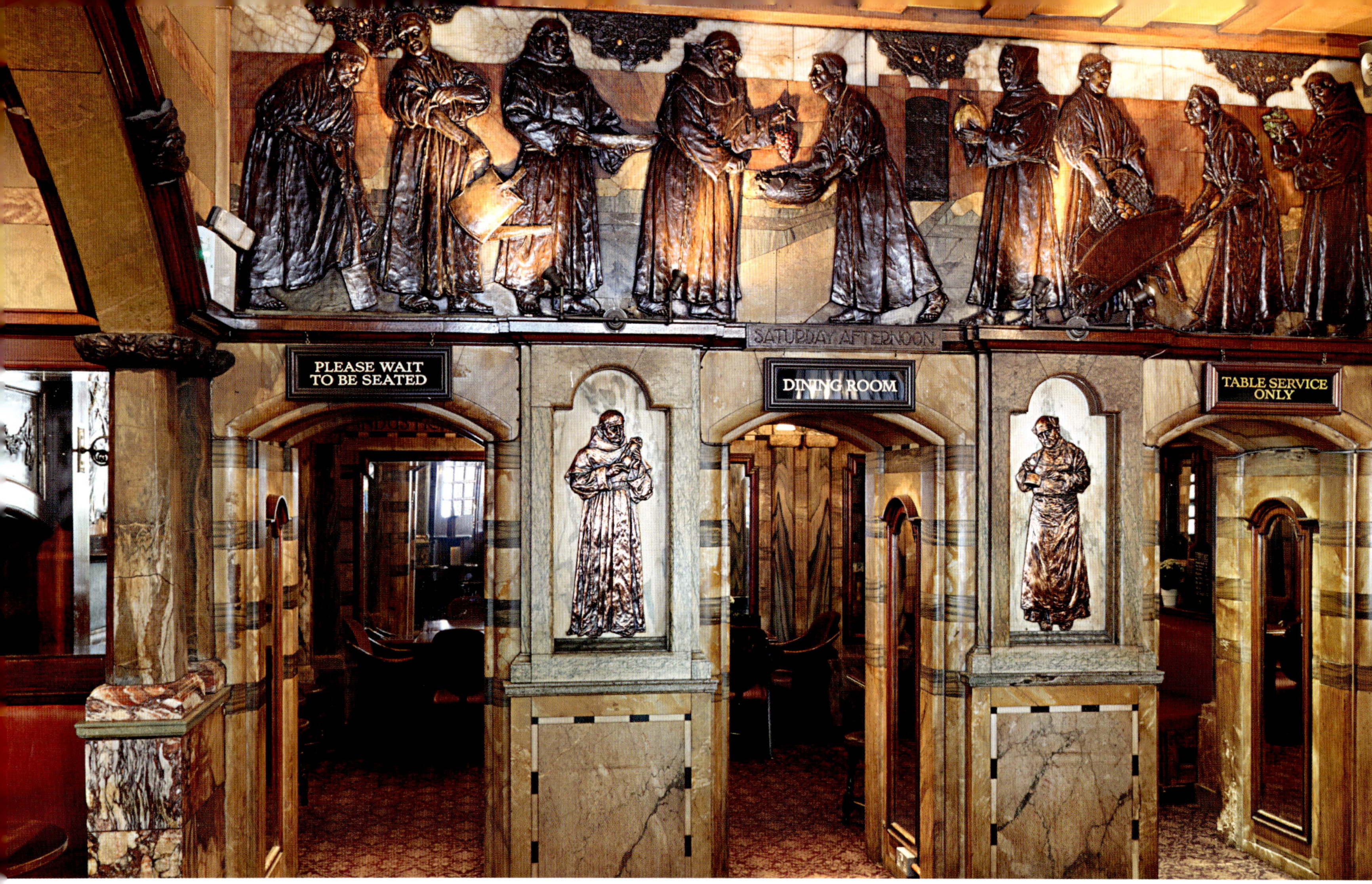

Herbert Fuller-Clark was the architect, and sculptors Henry Poole, Frederick Callcott and carver Nathaniel Hitch were employed to create the decorative features. The curious shape of The Blackfriar can be understood by its position next to the old London, Chatham and Dover Railway line running alongside, which existed before the pub was built. The back wall of the pub was built right against both the railway and a signal box that straddled several tracks at this point. Back then, the railway bridge over Queen Victoria Street was tight against the pub because it was more than twice as wide as the bridge in place today. It was the reduction of tracks and the narrowing of the bridge that cast The Blackfriar adrift. The pointed end of The Blackfriar was generated by the need to fit into the irregular ground plan of streets existing at the time.

The Blackfriar was under threat in 1964, when the area around it was slated for redevelopment and the pub marked down for demolition. The preservation movement was at that time gathering support, after early setbacks in London, and a campaign by the Victorian Society, led by poet Sir John Betjeman and Lady Dartmouth, saved it.

In a pub bristling with interesting features, there is a plaque outside making a possibly tenuous claim: 'It is believed that Emperor Charles V, the Papal Magistrate and Henry VIII's court sat on this very site during the dissolution of Henry VIII's marriage to Catherine of Aragon in 1532.' Elsewhere, it has been recorded that during the proceedings King Henry detested the stink of the River Fleet, which flowed into the Thames at this place.

London's lost River Fleet certainly now flows underground a few feet from The Blackfriar, and nearby it is possible to find fragments of stonework from the lost abbey of Blackfriars, and the theatres and courtyards that supplanted it in Shakespeare's time. There is a true whiff of history at this spot and a maze of streets to explore just a few steps away.

CONTACT INFORMATION

The Blackfriar,
174 Queen Victoria Street, EC4V 4EG
www.nicholsonspubs.co.uk
Open 9am–11pm Monday–Saturday,
12pm–10.30pm Sundays.

Above 'Merrie England' scenes of frolicking friars are displayed in copper relief.

Opposite Standing alone, The Blackfriar fitted tightly into its previous surroundings.

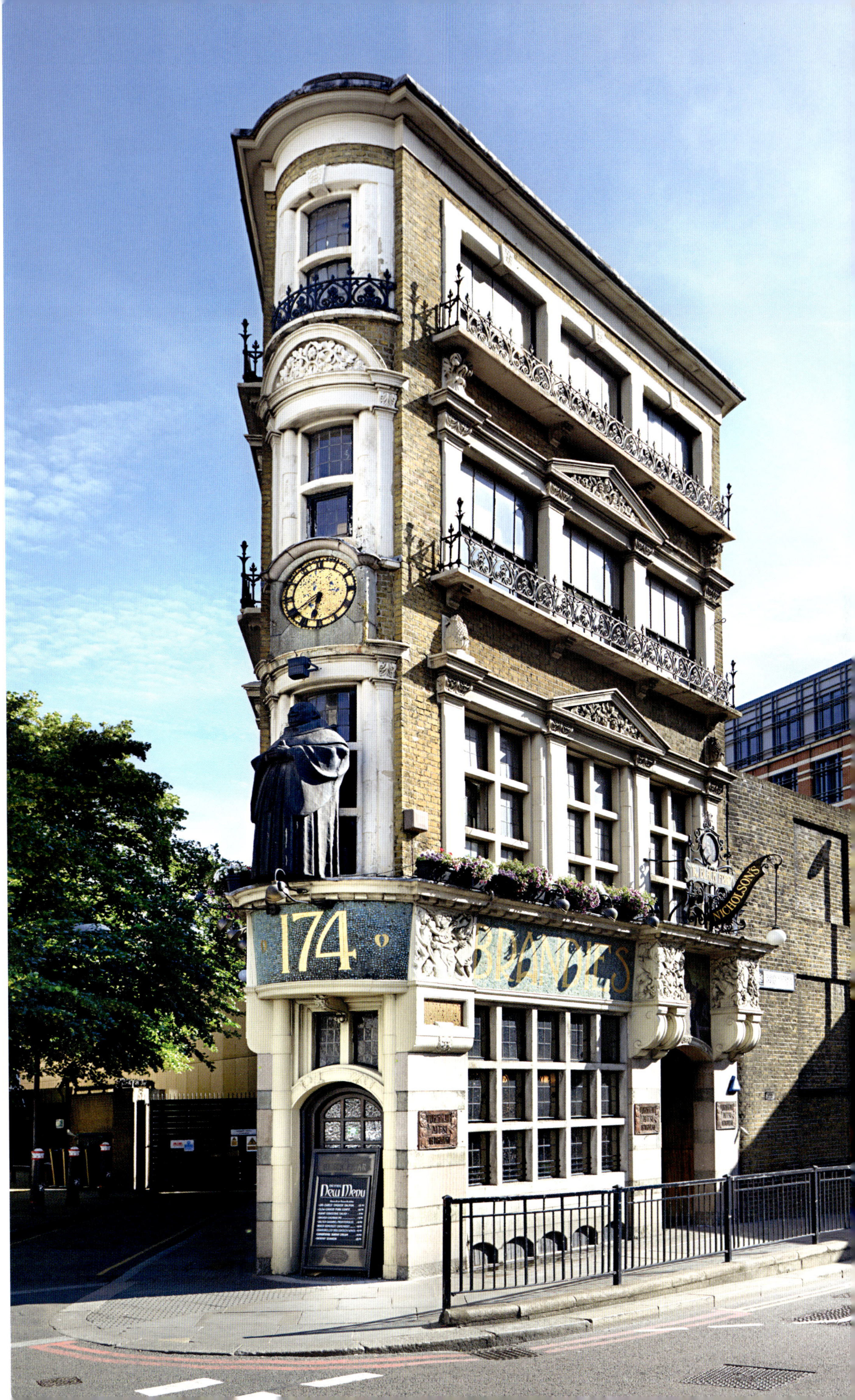
174
BRANDIES
NICHOLSONS
New Menu

Tower Bridge

The jagged profile of Tower Bridge is the very symbol of London and the least secret location in the city. Its neo-gothic façades of Cornish granite and Portland stone evoke a Scottish castle, but are built on a steel frame. Much of the original operating system for Tower Bridge still exists – some of it concealed, some on show, all of it solid, advanced Victorian engineering.

Tower Bridge was intended to improve road transportation to serve developments to the north and south, while allowing ships access to the many wharfs and warehouses that lined the River Thames as far as the arches of London Bridge – which for most vessels was the practical limit for upstream navigation.

A road crossing to the east of the City was needed to ease London's truly awful traffic problems, particularly on London Bridge. The new bridge had to be suitable for horse-drawn traffic and pedestrians, so could not be steeply graded. After years of debate and a competition, a design by architects Sir Horace Jones and engineer Sir John Wolfe Barry was selected. And after eight years in the building, Tower Bridge was completed in 1894.

What was needed was a way of instantly generating a smooth, linear action for raising the spans of the bridge. Steam was king in Victorian Britain, but steam did not provide the complete answer. It might have been feasible to lift the road decks directly, using engines to drive a train of gears through a clutch. That would have been slow and extremely cumbersome. Steam engines were best

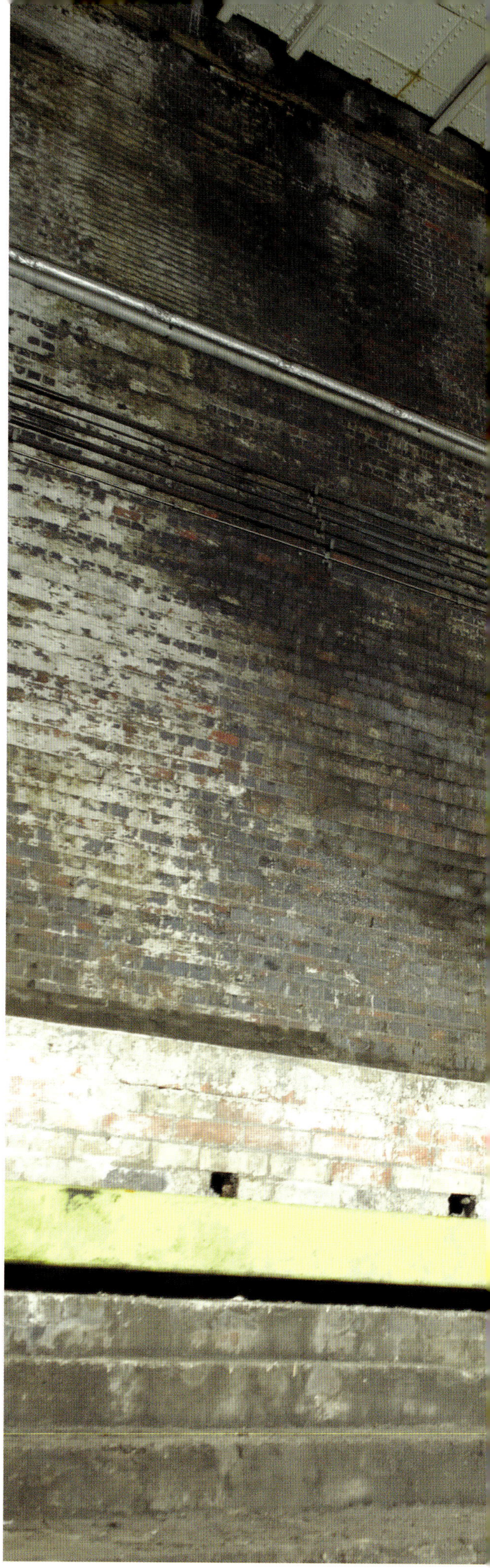

Bascule chamber under the south pier of the bridge. Below this chamber lie the steel caissons, which made the digging of the foundations possible, and above the operating machinery, including two accumulators.

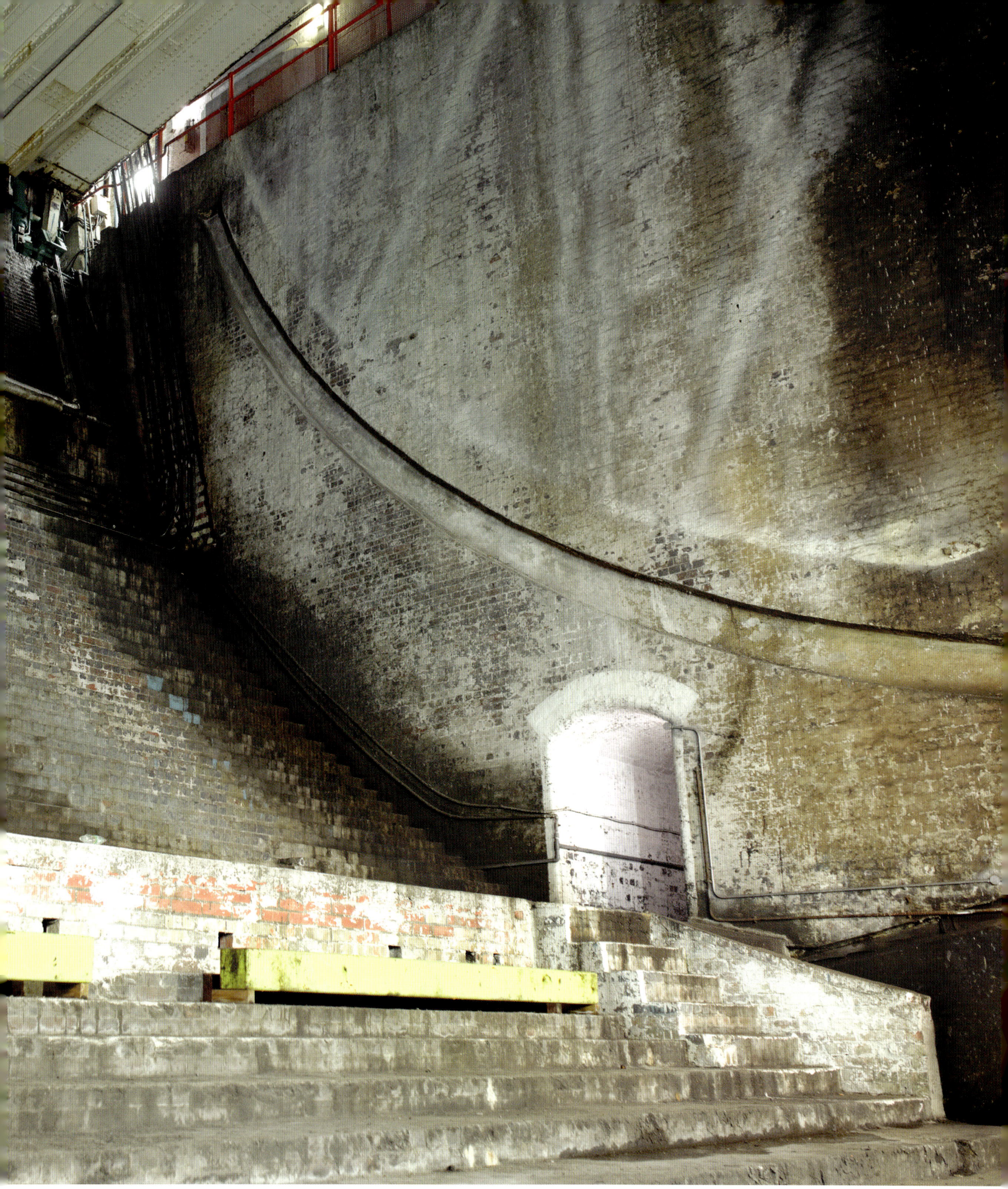

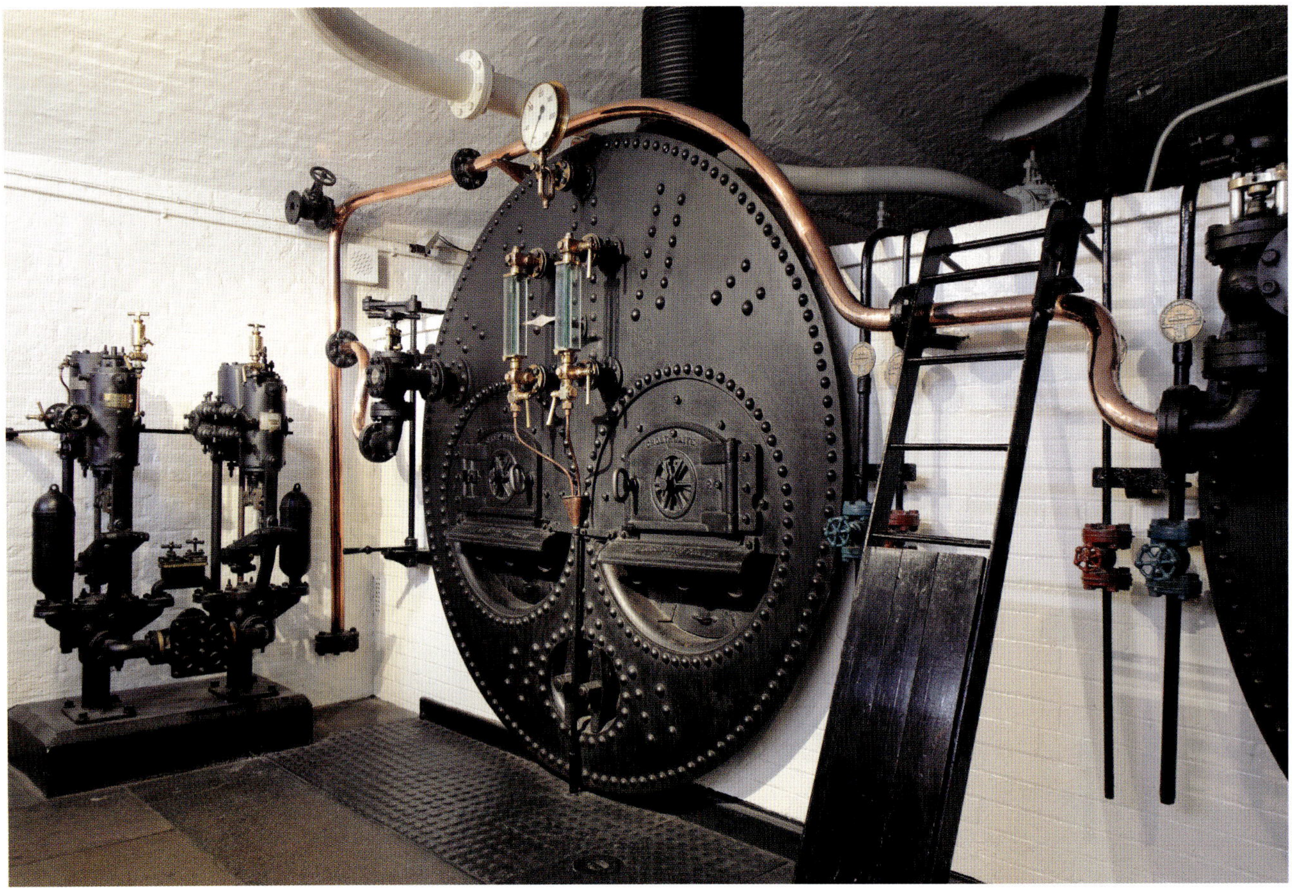

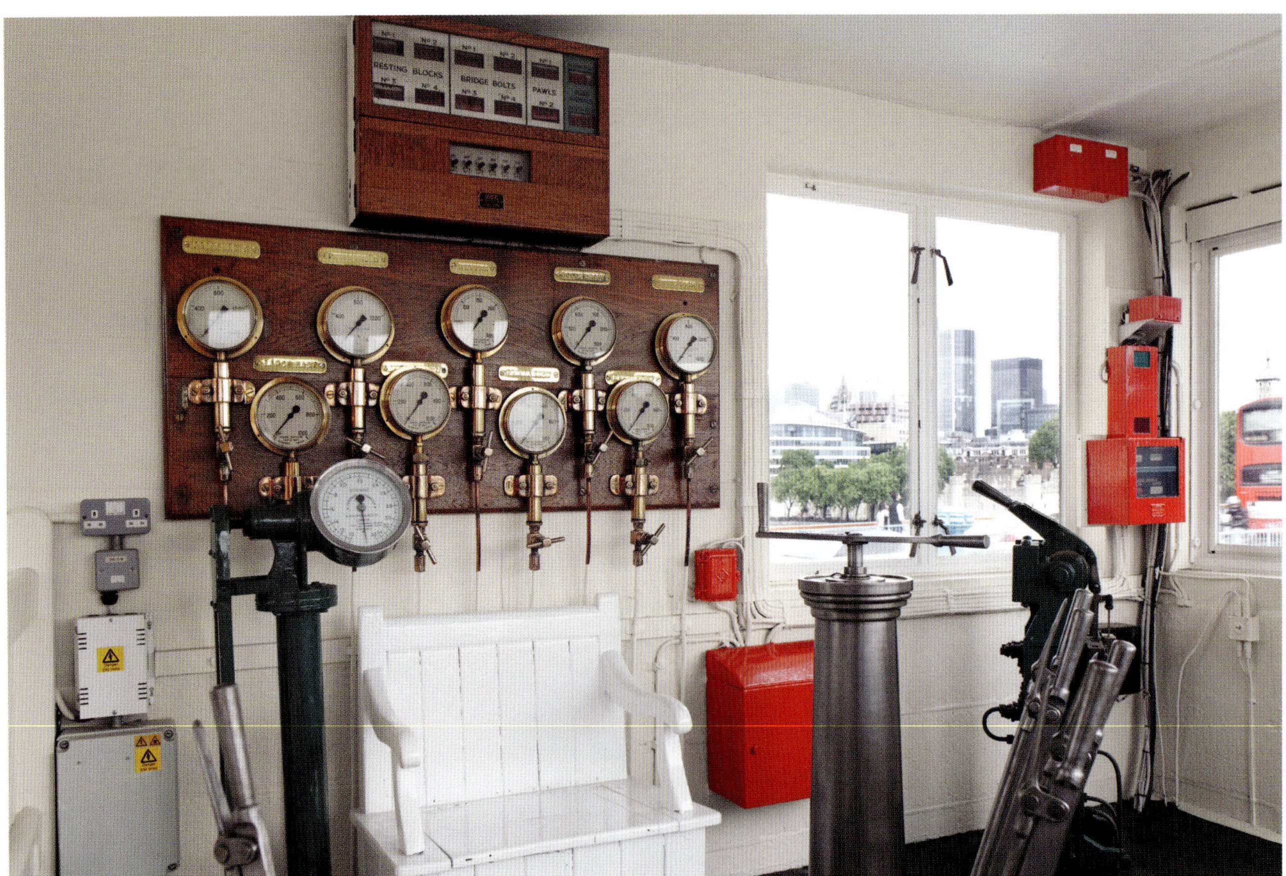
RESTING BLOCKS
BRIDGE BOLTS
PAWLS

Tower Bridge opened fifty times a day during its first year of operation.

Opposite, above
Lancashire boiler – one of four originals. The bridge depended on steam power until 1976.

Opposite, below
Steam age mechanical levers for opening the bridge, together with position indicators, and a panel for instruments displaying water and steam pressure.

able to produce reciprocating or circular motion, and such power could not be stored.

Electrical power held great promise in the 1880s, but at that time the crucial breakthrough needed to enable alternating current (AC) for municipal systems had not been achieved. The direct current (DC) system of the time was feeble and inefficient; the largest dynamo anywhere in 1888 produced just 500 horsepower.

The solution selected was state-of-the-art, being the application of hydraulic power, using water under pressure. This had been first developed by Sir William Armstrong for dockside cranes in the north-east of England. It was ideally suited to power cranes, lifts, presses and lock gates – and perfect for opening a bridge.

Disused elements of the original system remain in place, as a testimony to the ingenuity of the architect and engineer. Four classic Lancashire boilers housed on the south side of the bridge provided steam for relatively small two-cylinder tandem compound steam engines and pumps under the south approach road, generating water pressure of 750 pounds per square inch. Pipes took the high pressure water to six hydraulic ram systems called accumulators, two in each pier and two on the south side of the bridge. Heavy weights were lifted by water pumped into each accumulator shaft, and held at top of the travel with the inlet valves closed. With the weight held poised, power was stored, and it could be unleashed at the turn of a handle.

In each pier four lifting engines – water-powered three-cylinder motors – received water under pressure and turned gears to the bascules, opening the span. The bascules themselves carry heavy counterweights to the order of 400 tons, and raising them to 86 degrees could be completed in a minute.

The multiple engines, boilers and accumulators provided what modern engineers call 'high redundancy' – in that everything was duplicated and twice the required power was always available.

The pedestrian lifts to the elevated footways were also hydraulically powered, as was the crane mounted on the south side to unload coal from barges.

This system was entirely self-contained and dedicated solely to Tower Bridge, but, as a further back-up reserve, water could be drawn from the public power supply mains of the London Hydraulic Power Company, which had stations at Rotherhithe, Bankside and Wapping, providing a hidden system of liquid muscle across London for nearly 100 years. For many years it was common to see 10,000-ton merchant ships alongside just west of the Bridge. Hay's Wharf took over most of the facilities on the south side, where a forest of cranes worked.

On the north side, New Fresh Wharf accommodated particularly big vessels. All of this was dependent on the opening of Tower Bridge.

In 1965 the cranes upstream of Tower Bridge dipped their jibs to salute the passing of the funeral launch bearing Winston Churchill's coffin. These cranes were all finished with by 1969. The decline and death of London's working wharfs and docks, from its peak capacity in 1961, was swift. Tower Bridge opened fifty times a day during the first year of operation, but eventually road tunnels under the Thames, and the development of new enclosed docks downstream eased some of the traffic burden. The overhead walkways were out of use by 1910.

The quietly functional Tower Bridge was the furthest downstream crossing until the opening of the Queen Elizabeth II Bridge at Dartford in 1991. Tower Bridge still opens fifteen times each week on average, given twenty-four hours' notice, and the spans lift in the same way, with astonishing speed, smoothness, quietness and ceremony, now powered by electric motors driving an oil hydraulic system.

CONTACT INFORMATION

Tower Bridge,
Tower Bridge Road, SE1 2UP
https://www.towerbridge.org.uk/

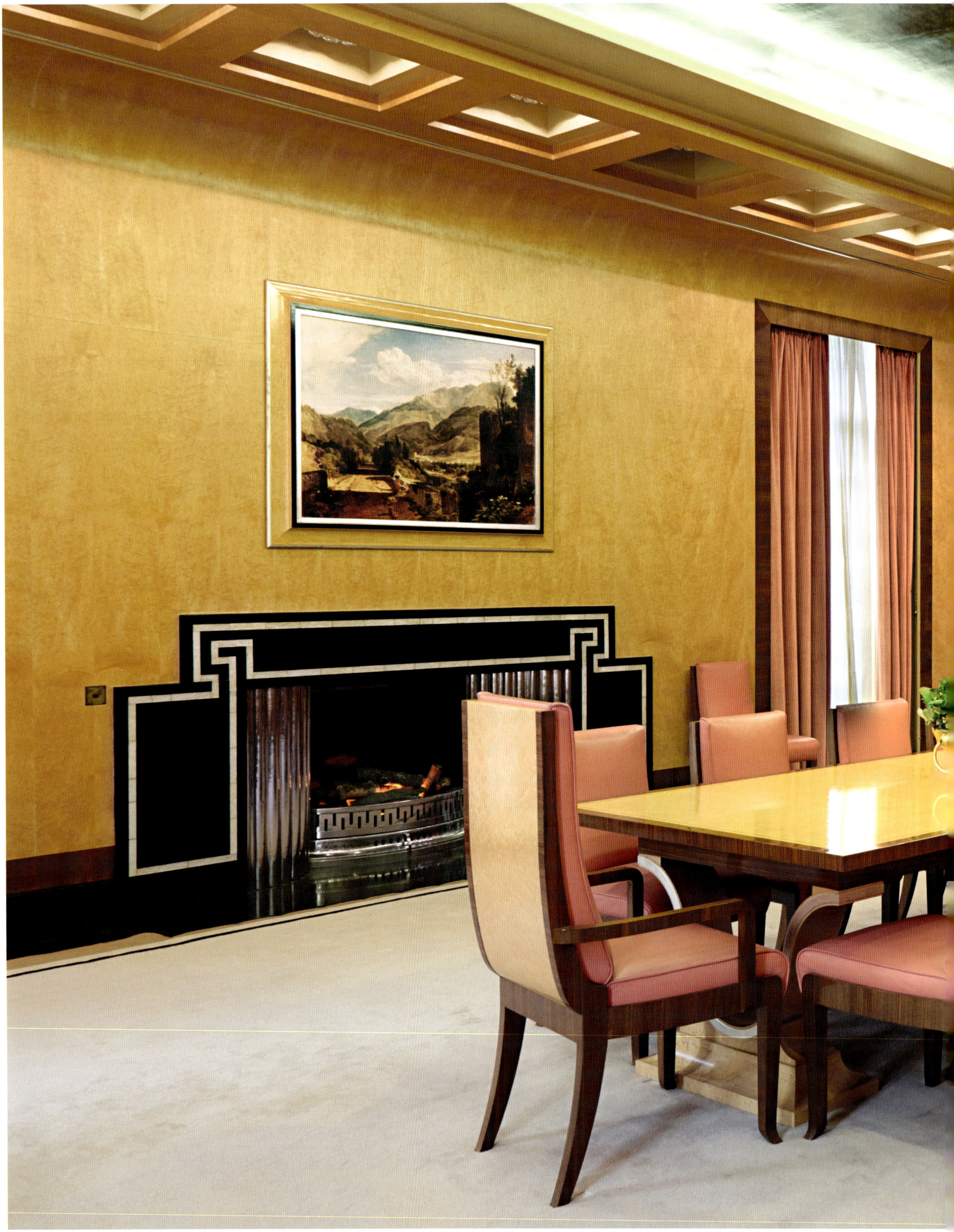

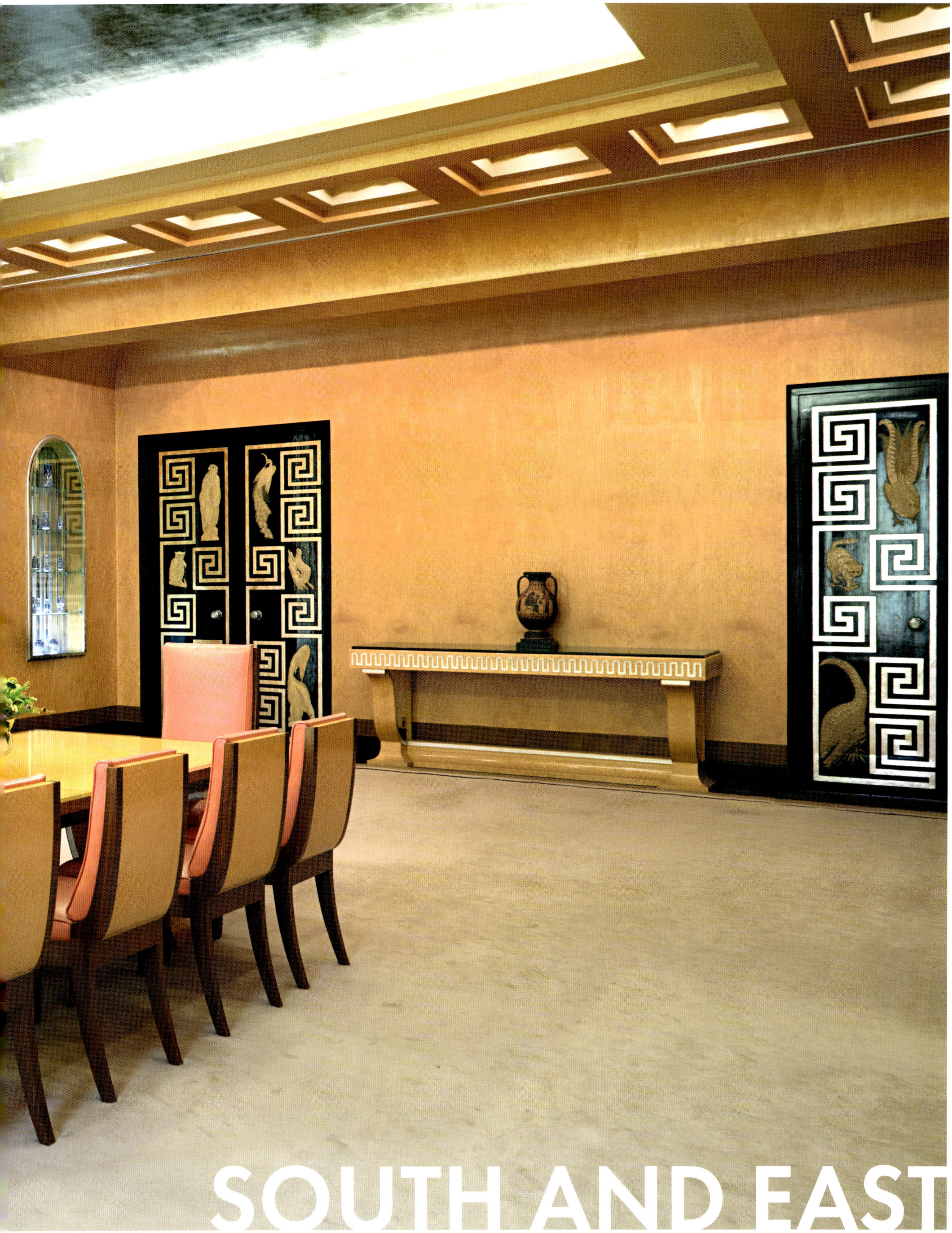

SOUTH AND EAST

Eltham Palace

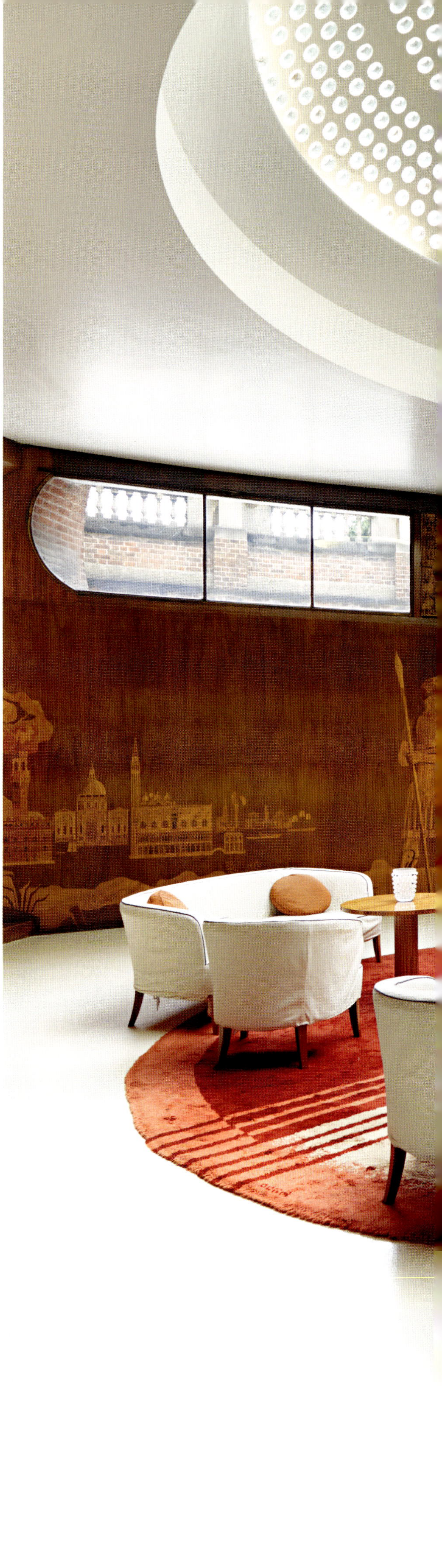

In the early 1930s, wealthy couple Stephen and Virginia Courtauld were looking for a semi-rural retreat near London for entertaining and displaying their art collection. On the edge of south-east London lay the remains of Eltham Palace, disused as a royal house since the 1600s, comprising mostly the Great Hall. This had narrowly been saved from dereliction by the Office of Works. It is not clear whether the idea came from the Courtaulds themselves, or from their architects John Seeley and Paul Paget, but it took a measure of vision and imagination to see that a house could be created there. A leasehold and building permission were obtained from the Crown, and a new house was designed and built between 1933 and 1936. One wing directly joined the Great Hall, and a semi-circular colonnade linked it to another new wing beyond. Outside, a high degree of visual harmonization between old and new was achieved by using red brick and stone dressing.

Inside, the Courtaulds then had a free hand to develop some spectacularly modern rooms and spaces, deploying leading designers and craftsmen and the highest-quality woods from around the world. Swedish artist Jerk Werkmäster, architect and designer Rolf Engströmer and Italian interior designer Peter Malacredia were tasked with producing a series of interiors in varying styles.

Eltham Place has a triangular entrance hall with walls lined with Australian blackbean veneer and decorated with marquetry that includes background

Previous spread
The dining room.

Opposite
The entrance hall.

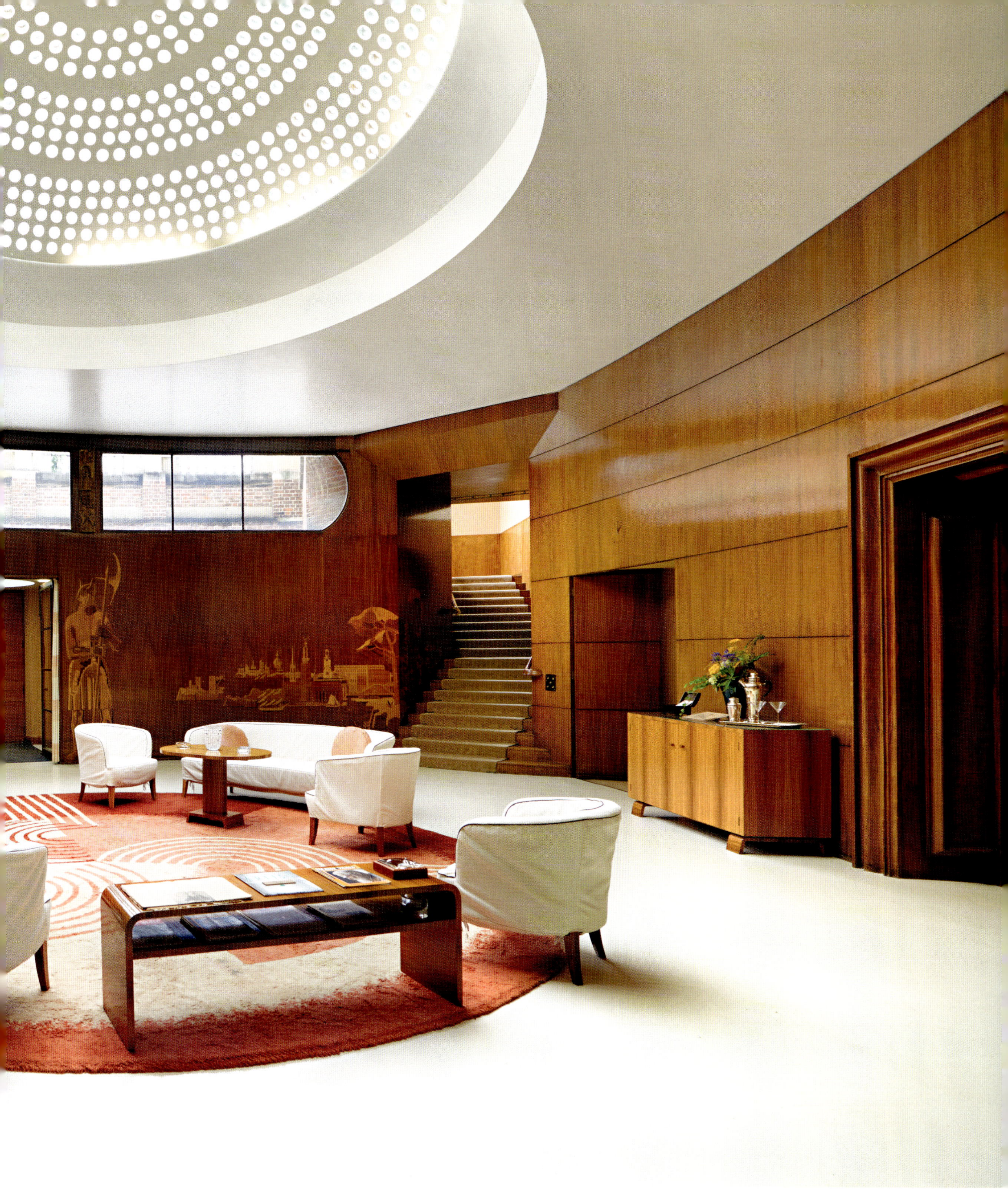

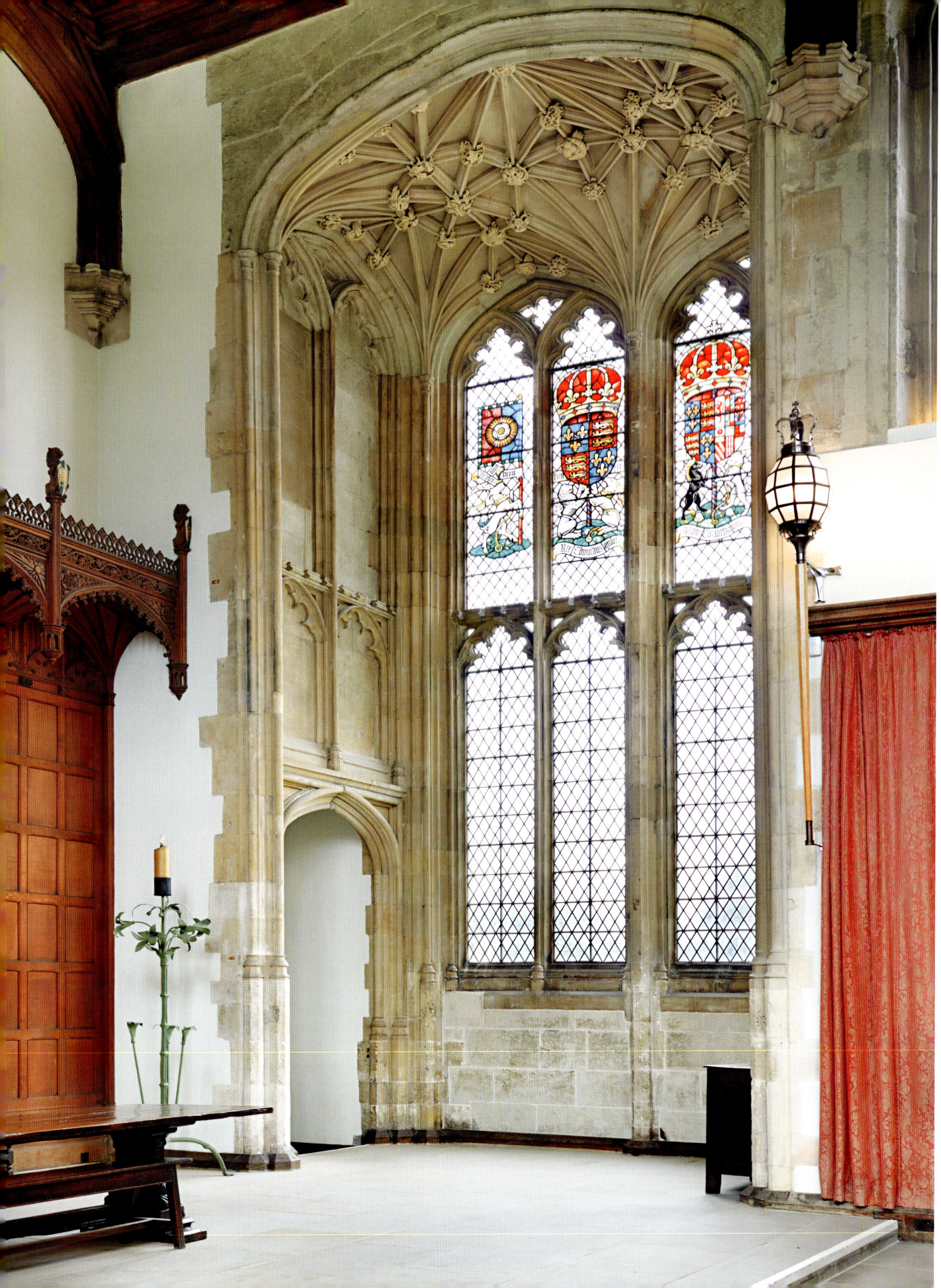

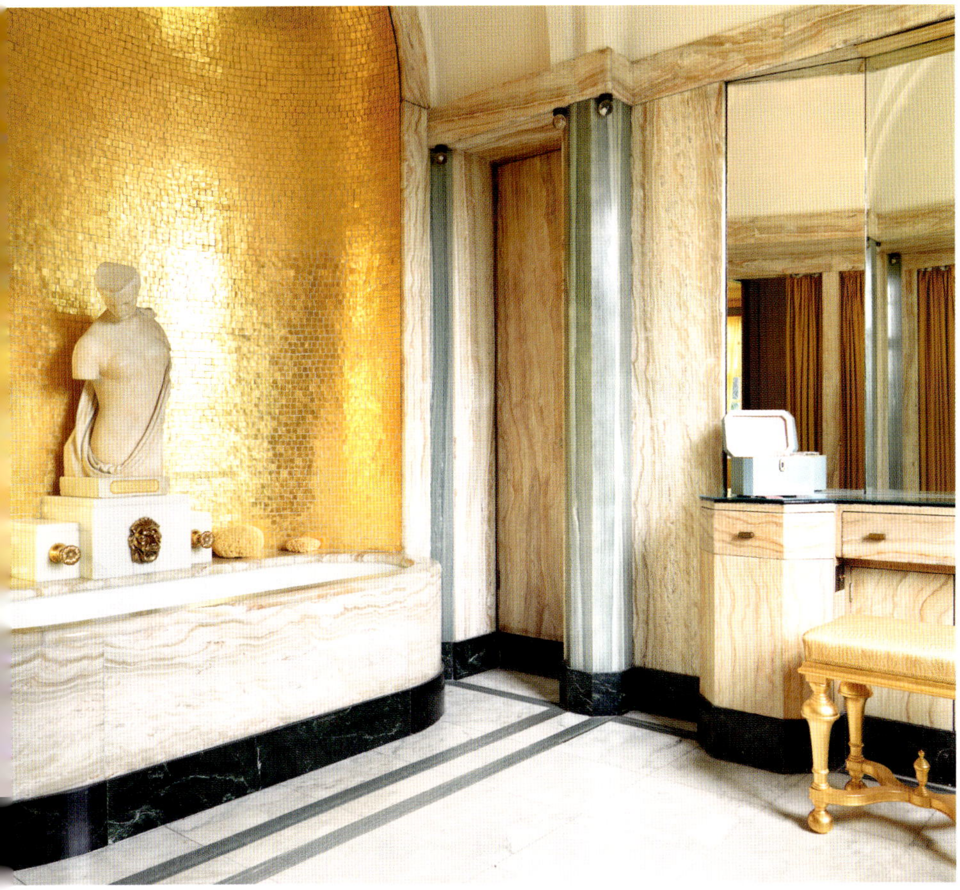

Opposite The Great Hall.

Above Virginia Courtauld's bathroom.

scenes from Italy and Scandinavia. Light streams in from a glass dome. The dining room carries contrasting tones and textures on its surfaces with bird's-eye maple veneer walls and an aluminium-leaf ceiling. Animals and birds, drawn from life at London Zoo, decorate black-and-silver doors. False beams are decorated with Hungarian folk art.

On the first floor, the overall look has been described as Cunard Style, reflecting the influence of the luxurious ocean-liner cabins and staterooms of the age, featuring built-in furniture and smooth veneered surfaces, often with curved ends. The most exotic room is Virginia Courtauld's vaulted Art Deco bathroom, with gold mosaic and onyx, complete with gold-plated bath taps and a statue of the goddess Psyche. Stephen Courtauld's suite is an aspen-panelled bedroom with a vitreous-blue mosaic bathroom.

There is also modern technology in the form of electric fires, built-in audio and, more doubtfully, a centralized vacuum cleaner system, with pipes and sockets built into the skirting of each room. The Courtaulds also created an impressionist garden around the remains of the palace's old moat and bridges. Stephen Courtauld was financial director of Ealing Studios and a trustee of the Royal Opera House. In the late 1930s the parties at Eltham Palace were filled with celebrity guests.

In recent years, several other rooms at Eltham have been opened to visitors, including Virginia Courtauld's recreated walk-in wardrobe, and a map room, where the family's secretary planned their extensive worldwide travels by liner, yacht and aircraft. Conservators uncovered large maps of areas to which the Courtaulds travelled pasted to the walls. Vignettes were painted onto the walls around the maps, depicting scenes and characters from around the world. A billiards room, photographic dark room and a luxurious underground air-raid shelter have also been opened.

The preserved Great Hall is of false hammer-beam construction, with the short vertical posts morticed into the ends of the arch-braced horizontal hammer-beams, with curved wind-braces to strengthen the roof trusses. Intending the Great Hall to be used as a music room, the Courtaulds had a minstrels' gallery added at one end. Much of the 1930s work represents the owners' and architects' concept of what a medieval great hall should look like. Stephen Courtauld's collection of Jacobean furniture remains here.

It was the nation's need to preserve the Great Hall, and the Courtaulds' agreement to do that as part of building their house, that unlocked the project in the first place. English Heritage suggests that particular support from the former Ministry of Works Ancient Monument Inspector Sir Charles Peers, who had overseen previous preservation work on the Hall, played a crucial role. The prevailing official attitude to preservation favoured fencing a site off, introducing information placards and surrounding it with lawns – essentially converting it into an archaeological site. At Eltham, we see a novel, possibly unique, response to the problem of conserving a historic building.

The tenure of the Courtaulds at Eltham ended in 1944, and the house became the headquarters of the Royal Army Education Corps until 1992. English Heritage adopted Eltham Palace in 1995.

CONTACT INFORMATION

Eltham Palace,
Court Yard, Greenwich, SE9 5QE
https://www.elthampalace.org.uk/

British Vintage Wireless and Television Museum

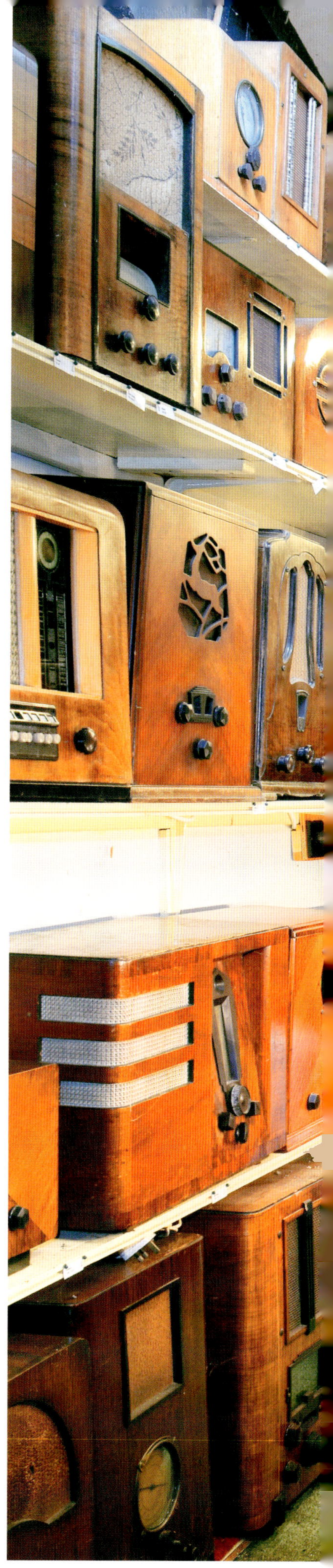

The British Vintage Wireless and Television Museum is a strongly nostalgia-driven experience for enthusiasts, as a comprehensive social history of broadcast receiver hardware in 1,500 objects. It always aims to use working equipment. The collection s tarts with crystal sets and advances through the introduction of VHF transmission to DAB Digital Audio Broadcast. Most radios here are British-made, together with some American sets. As it tracks development of the transistor radio, an increasing number are from Japan. There are table-top types, floor-standing consoles, portable, hand-bag style, some radiograms and a few gram-only, otherwise known as record-players.

Television broadcasts started on 2 November 1936 with the start of the first BBC 405-line image resolution high-definition service, and from there the museum has the whole line of TV development closely pegged. The museum repairs TV receivers rather than rebuilding, claiming that around 95 per cent of the original manufacturers components are still be in working even when 70 years old or older. This ability to see televisions operating now as when new is a unique feature. For instance, improved image came with 625-line broadcast in the 1960s. In the museum televisions run from an extensive radio frequency distribution system using what are called Aurora standards converters, allowing conversion of later 625-line back to the original 405-line for an authentic lower-resolution glimpse of the past.

This horned monster is the centrepiece of the first-generation television sets on view.

CONTACT INFORMATION

British Vintage Wireless and Television Museum
23 Rosendale Road, SE21 8DS
Open by appointment only: call 020 8670 3667
https://bvwtm.org.uk/

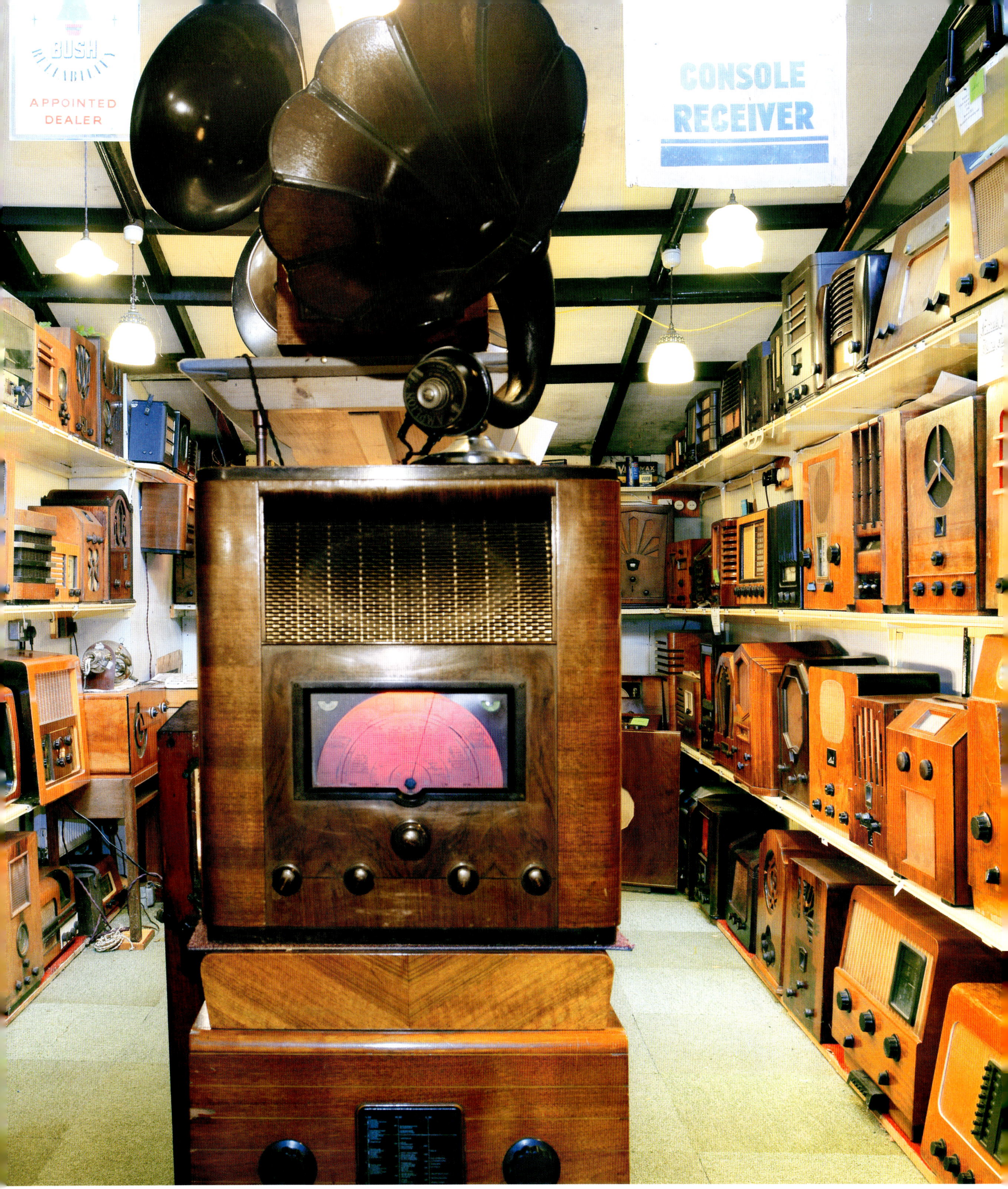
BUSH
APPOINTED DEALER
CONSOLE RECEIVER

Clapham South Deep Level Shelter

Clapham South Deep Level Shelter, built for air-raid protection, has been repurposed several times in pursuit of the needs of a changing world.

The use of Tube stations as Blitz shelters had at first been barred by the authorities, who were made to reconsider when thousands forced their way into Liverpool Street Underground station during air raids in September 1940. Within days, many operational Tube stations were officially sanctioned as shelters and in November plans were issued for purpose-built deep shelters. London Transport, with its experience in underground construction, was commissioned to manage the making of these by the Ministry of Home Security. Eight locations were eventually worked below existing Tube stations, four of them south of the Thames: Stockwell, Clapham North, Clapham Common and Clapham South.

The design was for twin tunnels 100 ft (30 m) below street level, each ¼ mile (400 m) long and divided into two decks, with sleeping accommodation for 8,000 people, washing facilities and chemical toilets, medical rooms, canteens and recreation areas.

Clapham South was fitted out in June 1942; the intensive phase of the Blitz had ended in May 1941. This relative lull in bombing persuaded the Ministry to keep the deep shelters on standby, a wary response partly based on the expense of opening and supervising the tunnels, and also on the unpredictable nature of the menace. Instead, areas of the south London shelters were made to accommodate soldiers on leave, and part

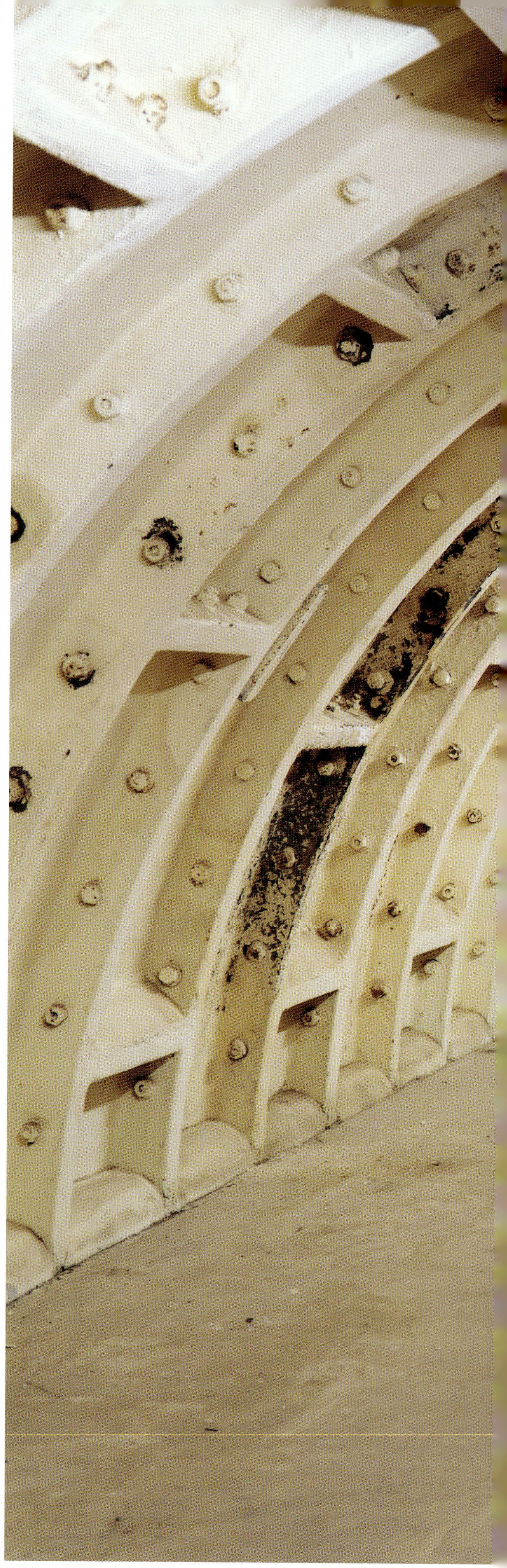

The Hardy shelter, at one of the secret wartime tunnels.

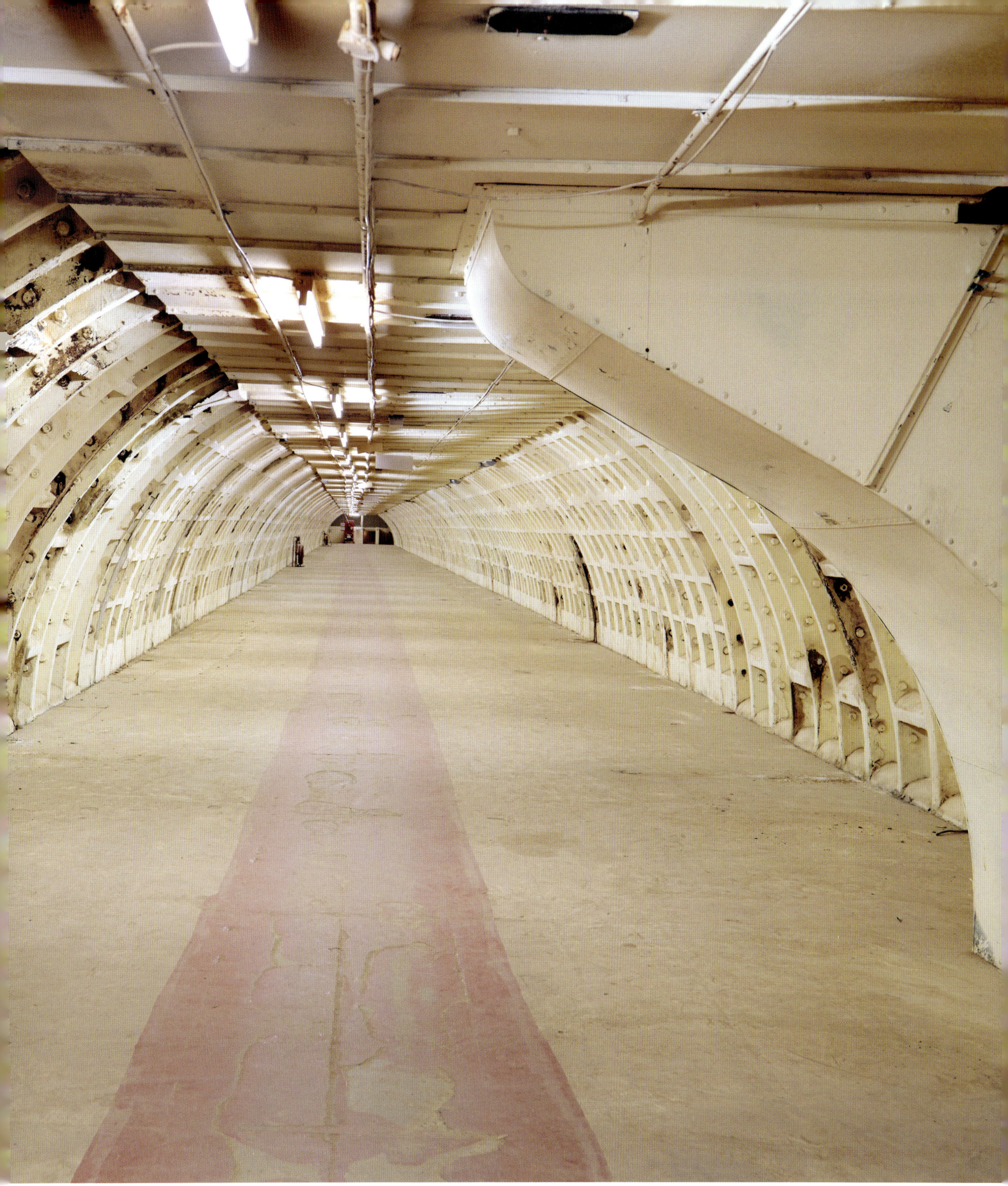

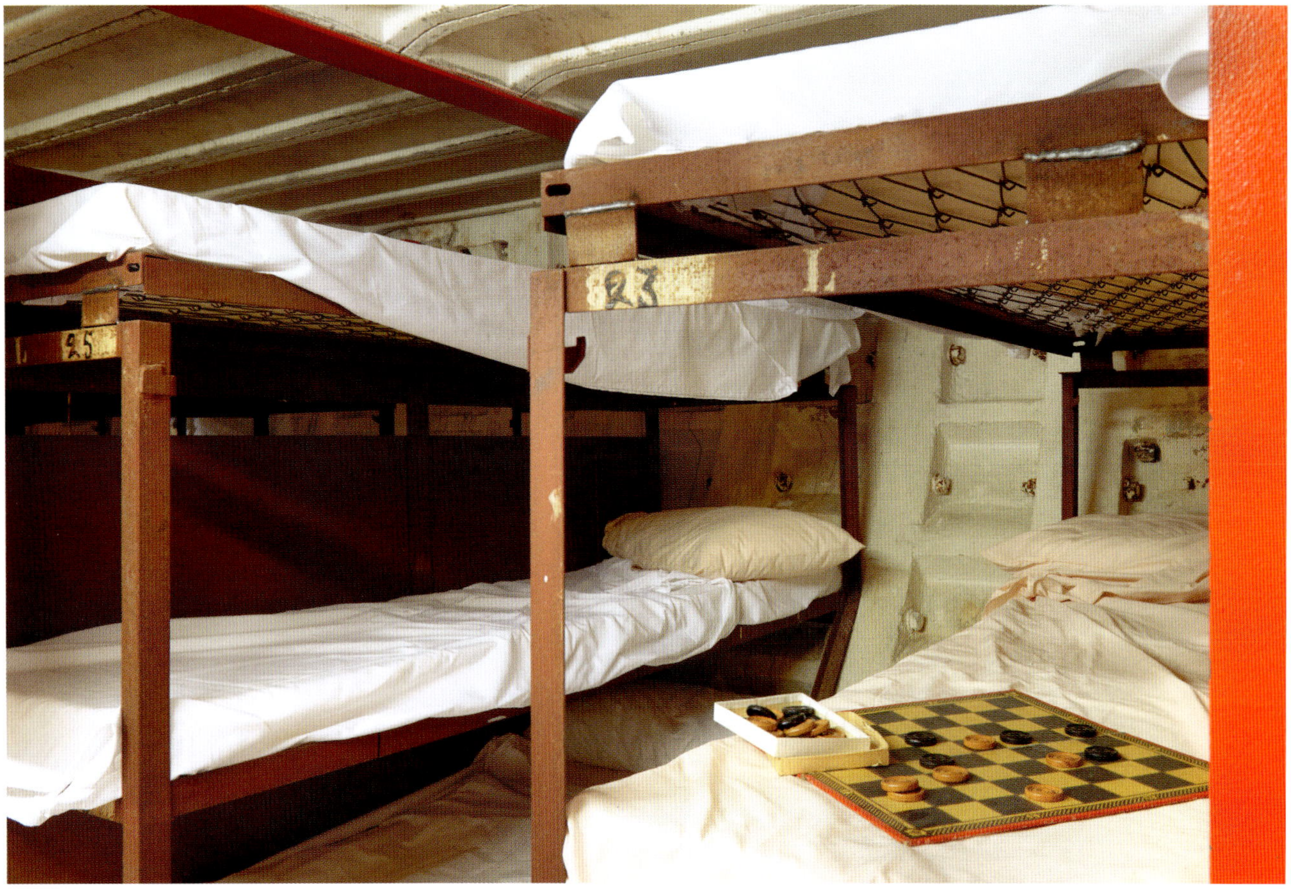

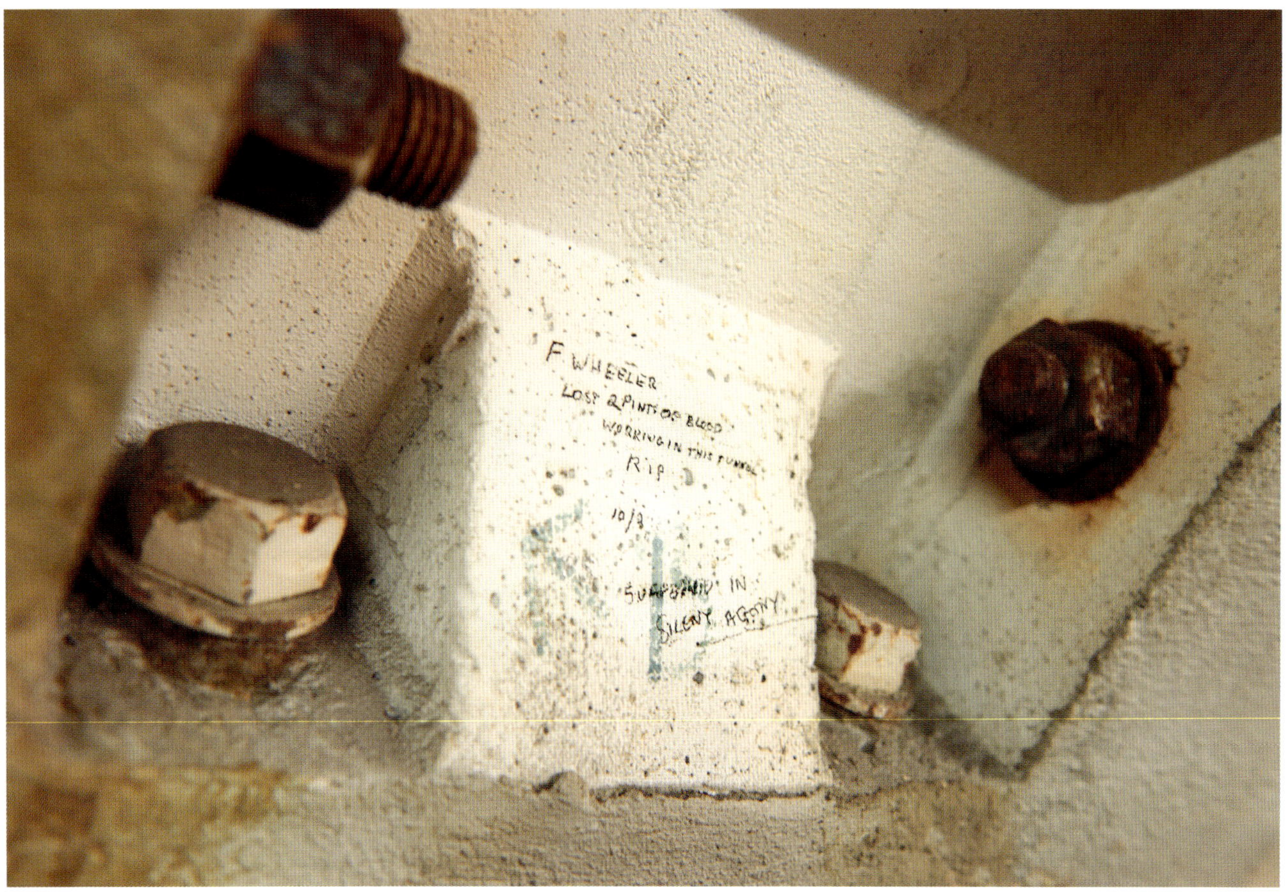

Left above Many bunks remain in place in Ley shelter, which is triple tiered in places. After the Second World War in 1948, these were used to house Caribbean migrants from the Empire Windrush, when the lack of housing meant even temporary accommodation was in short supply. For six shillings and sixpence a week, inhabitants received food and a bed in a shelter underneath Clapham South Tube station.

Left Graffiti on the wall in Grenville shelter. More graffiti can be found on the tunnel segments made by those sheltering, soldiers and, in this case, a workman.

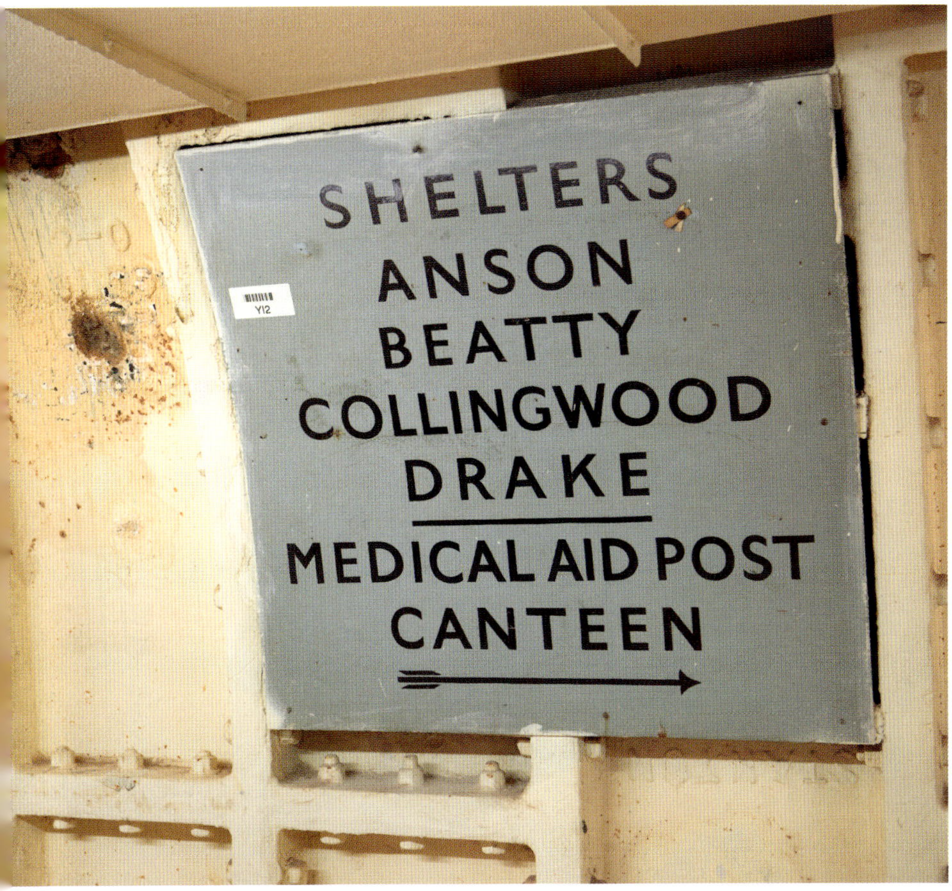

A cross-passage sign at the Balham end of the secret wartime tunnels. Upper-level tunnels were divided into sub-shelters named after alphabetically listed admirals of the Royal Navy, with the intention of helping shelterers to remember their locations.

of the new deep shelter at Goodge Street was given over to General Eisenhower's headquarters. Only those at the highest level of wartime government could dimly glimpse a forthcoming danger posed by enemy missile technology.

Raids on London resumed with the so-called Little Blitz starting in early 1944; even these attacks did not cause the authorities to open up, but a new threat came with the first V-1 flying bomb to hit London in June 1944. As these attacks intensified, Clapham South was opened on 19 July. The borough of Wandsworth recorded the greatest density of V-1 impacts of any London district, with 122 hits up to September 1944, and as that threat abated, V-2 ballistic rockets started to fall on the city. The last air-raid warning came in March 1945. The highest occupation of the deep shelters on a single night was 12,297 people, full capacity was never approached.

Post-war purchase of the shelters by London Transport was an option coupled to its participation in the programme, with an eye on conversion to an express Tube route. This influenced the engineering of the shelters and at Clapham South the tunnels were built in a long curve aligning with the other deep shelters at Clapham Common and Stockwell. The diameter of all the main tunnels was more than 16 ft (5 m), possibly capable of taking full-sized rolling stock but not big enough to provide any deep platforms for passengers at Clapham South. Although there was, and is, a connecting stairway to the existing Tube station, the intention was to develop non-stop or limited stop services from central London to the end of the Northern line at Morden and beyond. This had been mooted pre-war, again in 1940 and in the London Transport annual report of 1945, but the tunnels were never destined to be joined and several historians and chroniclers of the Tube doubt if the fast-track idea was realistic or desirable. As the plan melted away and the option lapsed, there were other uses.

The shelter became a leave hostel for military personnel and, in 1948, temporary home to over 200 migrants from Jamaica arriving on the HMT *Empire Windrush*. The nearest labour exchange was in Brixton, and the location of Clapham South can claim to have shaped the future influence of West Indians on south London. The Festival of Britain of 1951 brought thousands to London, and the shelter became a low-cost Festival Hotel for visitors. The following year, troops were accommodated for ceremonial duties during the funeral of King George VI, and visitors for Queen Elizabeth II's coronation were housed here in 1953. A fire at Goodge Street in 1956 highlighted the vulnerability of shelter habitation, and further use for accommodation was barred. A long twilight spell under mothballing and use as a storage facility followed.

Remaining in the ownership of the Ministry of Works and its successors, the property arm of the government eventually sold seven deep shelters to Transport for London in the late 1990s. It may have seemed like a delayed fulfilment of destiny, but the focus was now on property management rather than rail transport, the shelters now mostly serving as commercial secure archives and, in one case, a salad farm. Clapham South has been leased to the London Transport Museum and is open to visitors at certain times.

CONTACT INFORMATION

Clapham South Deep Level Shelter,
Clapham Common, SW12 9DU
https://www.ltmuseum.co.uk/whats-on/hidden-london/clapham-south

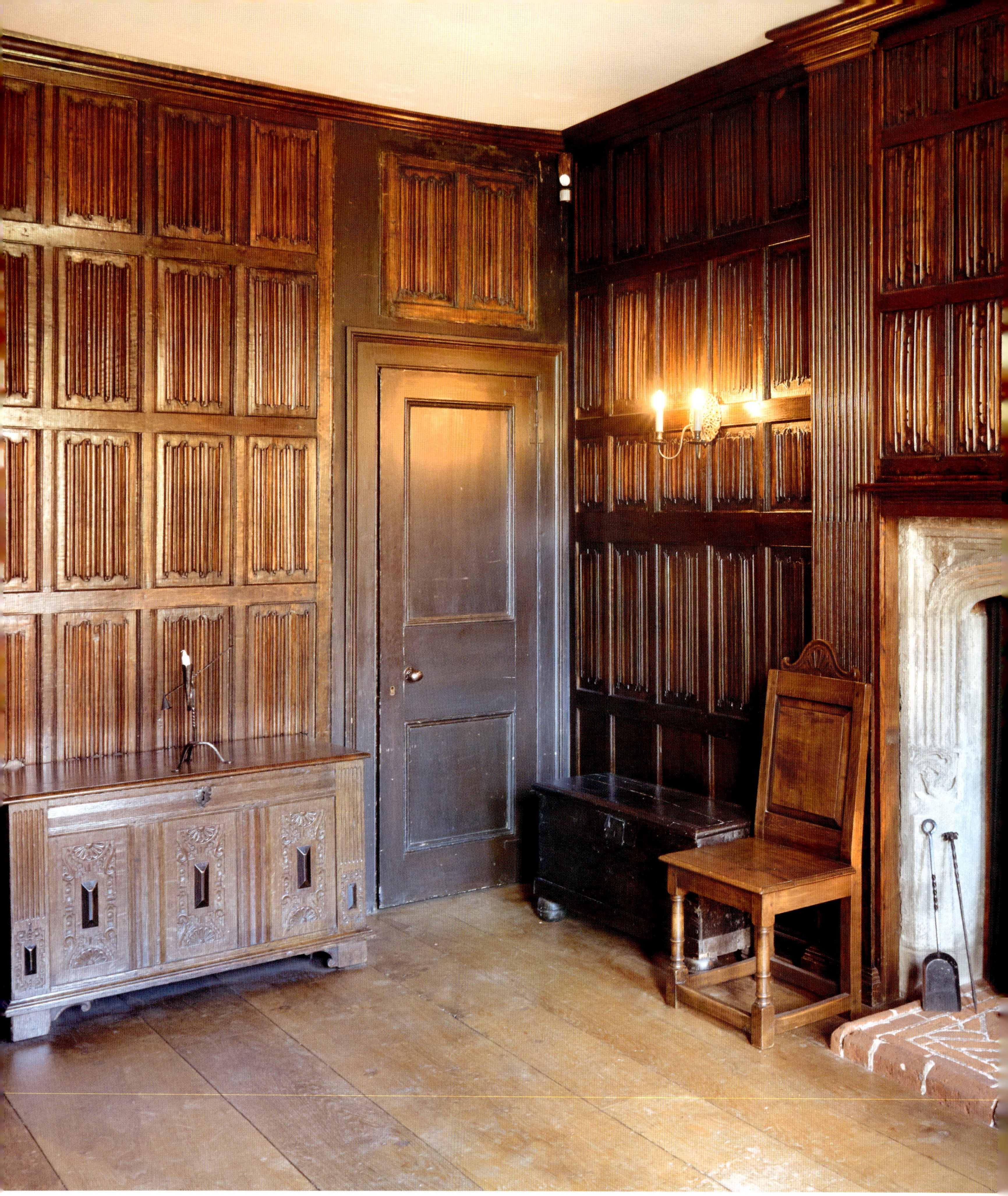

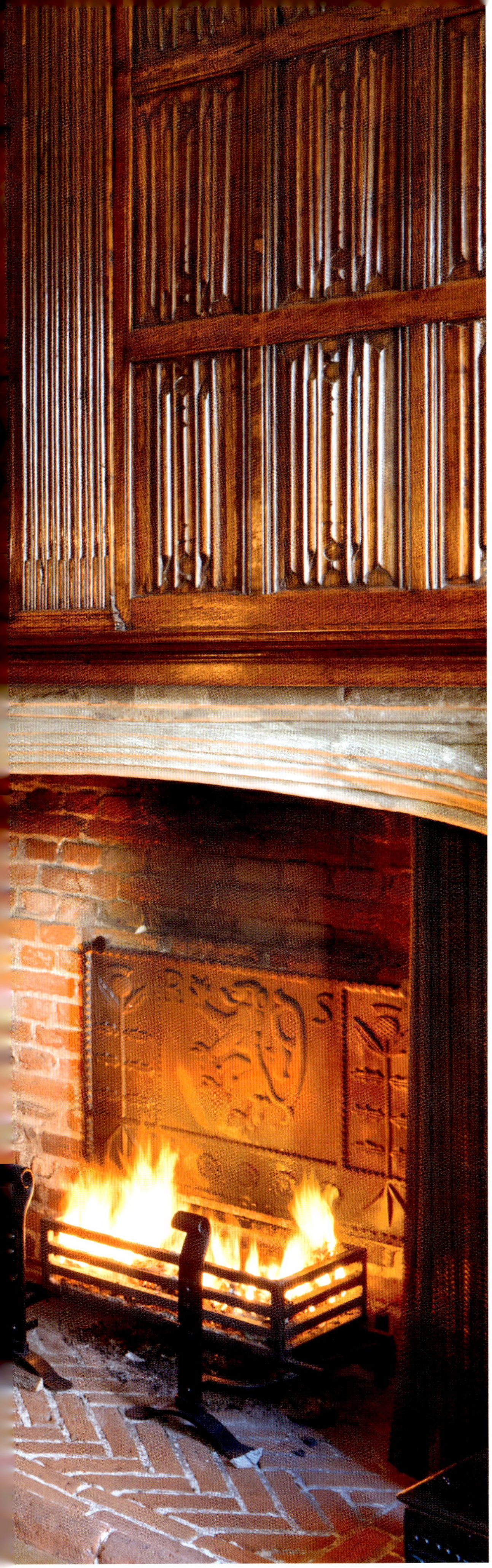

Rare oak-panelling in the linenfold parlour.

Sutton House

Sutton House in Hackney is one of London's oldest houses. A National Trust guide has claimed it to be the oldest domestic building in the East End. That is partly a product of geographical and historical definition, as relatively few London houses survive from before 1666 and rural Hackney village came slowly into the embrace of the city after the Great Fire. When the process of urban absorption was complete by around 1870, Sutton House was already almost 340 years old. Dendrochronology, the science of wood dating, places its construction at 1534–5.

The house was built for a Tudor courtier, Ralph Sadleir, who worked closely with the statesman Thomas Cromwell, serving as his secretary. Cromwell had been gifted one hundred oak trees from the royal forest at Enfield by Henry VIII, and some of these may have been used in construction of the house. However, it was the use of brick as the principal material that was unusual, found only in the grandest houses of the time, when wattle and daub construction around a timber frame prevailed; its original name, Bryk Place, reflected its notable status. It was not a palace, but a substantial three-storey house built on an H-shaped ground plan, with two wings joined by a central hall. One of the outstanding rooms was the linenfold parlour, the name describing the resemblance of the carved oak panelling to gathered fabric. On the top floor were rooms for servants, under the wings two cellars for storing ale and wine and, in between, a great chamber and great hall, also finely panelled.

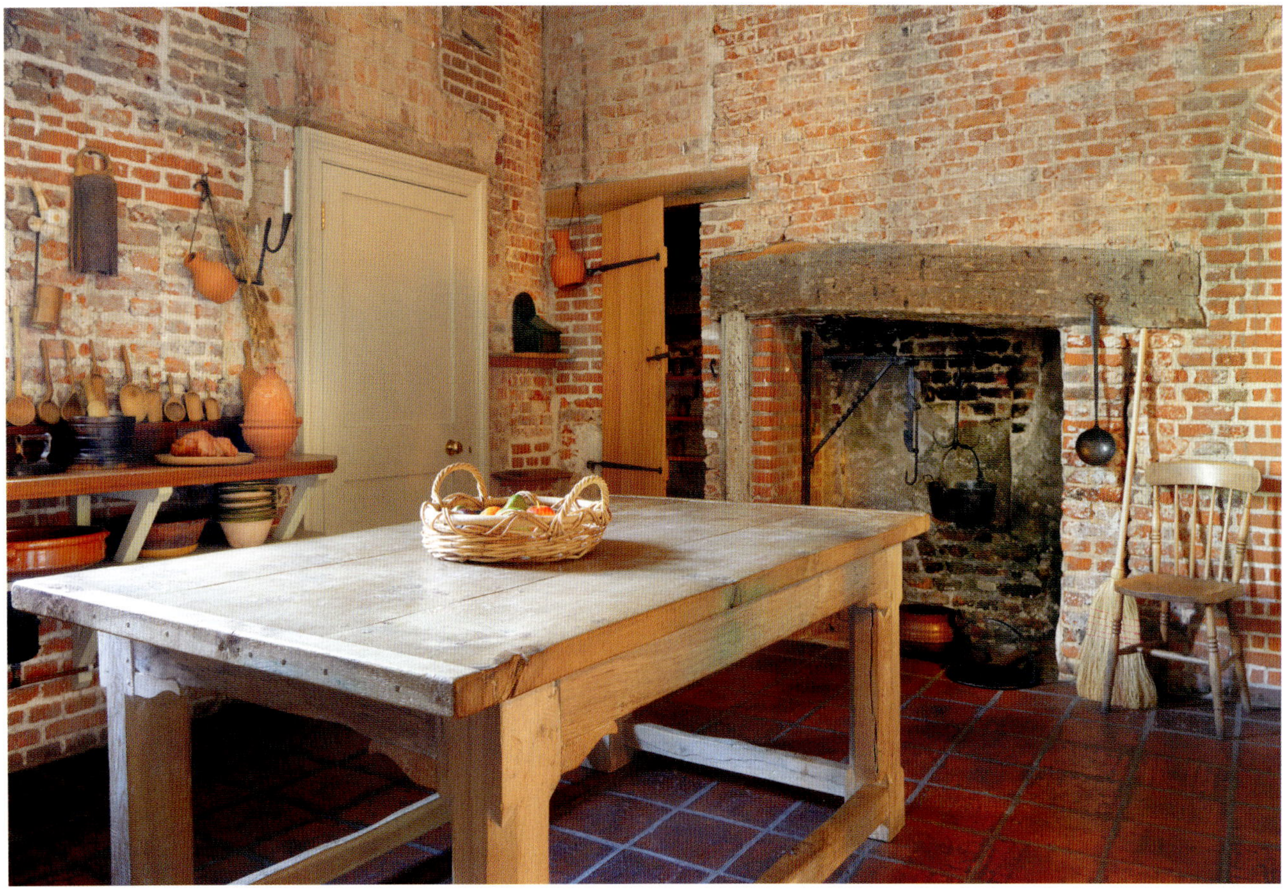

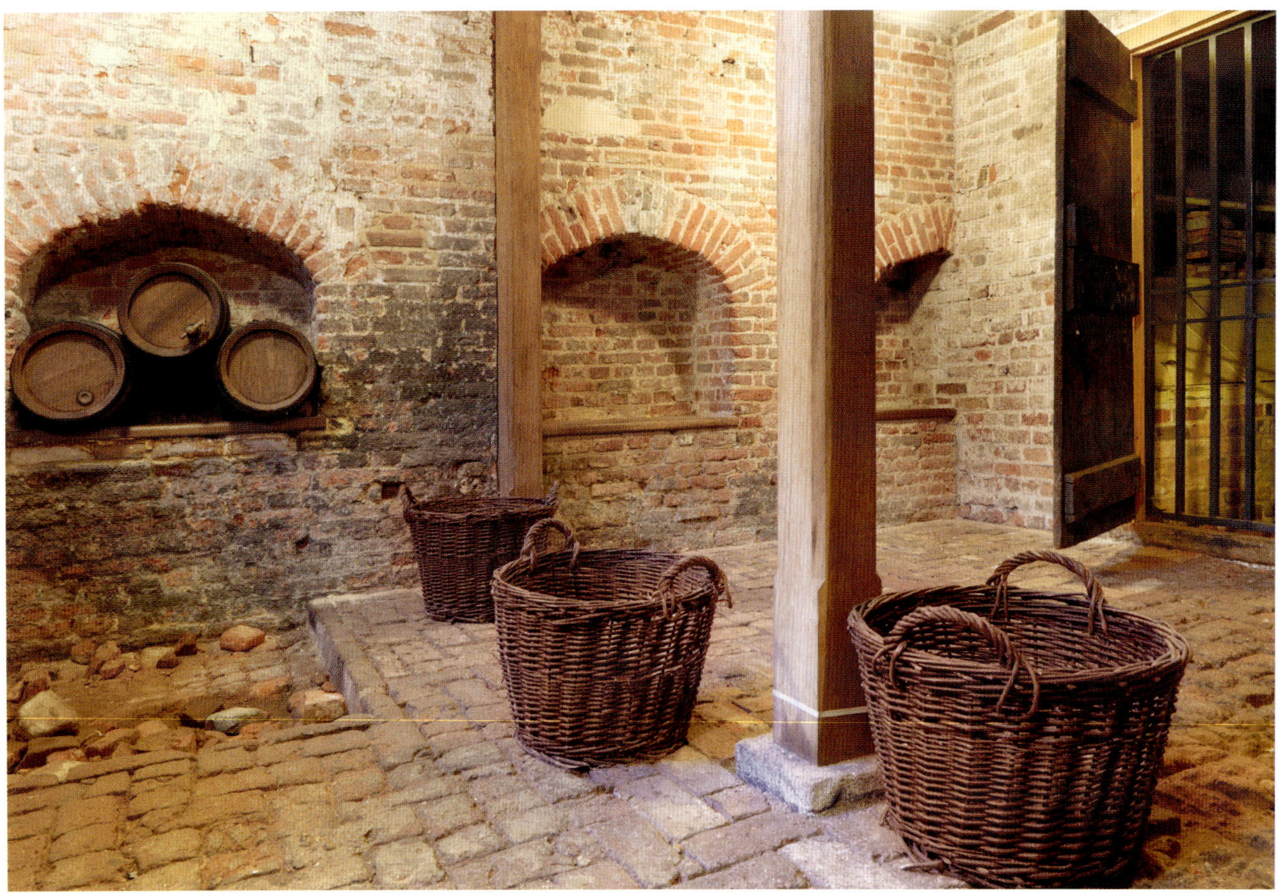

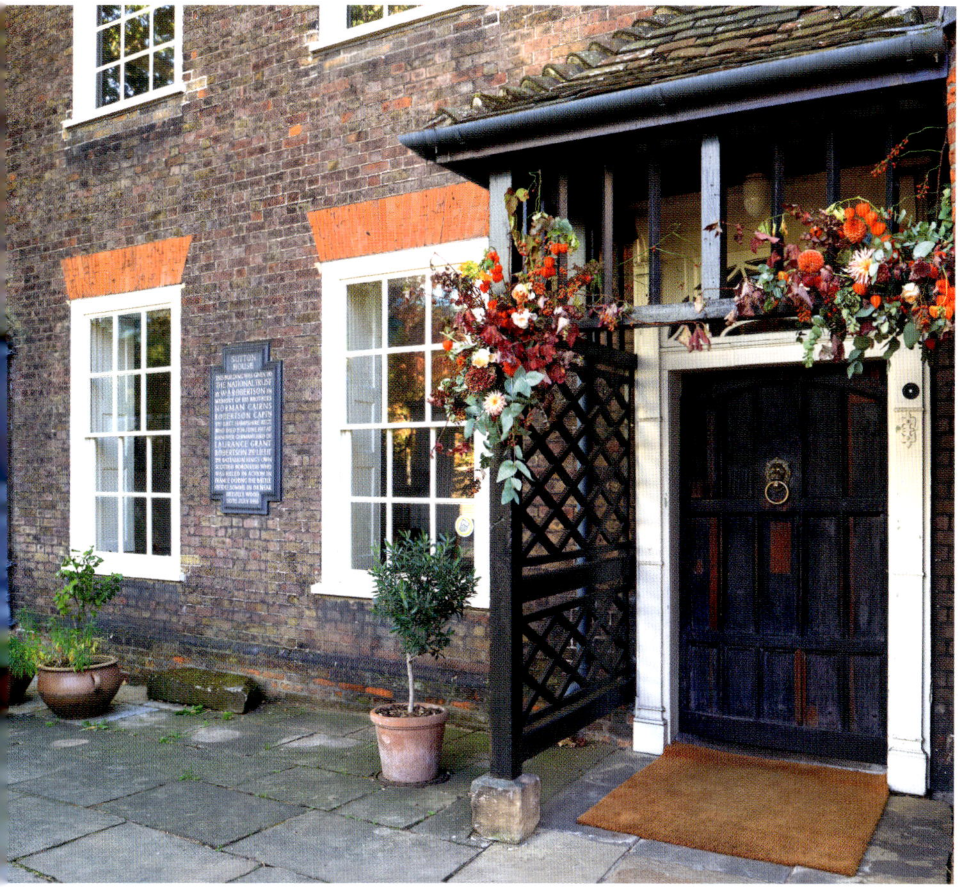

Opposite The Tudor kitchen (above) and the cellar (below).

Above The entrance to one of London's last remaining Tudor houses, Sutton House, which was originally built in 1535 by Sir Ralph Sadleir, Secretary of State to Henry VIII, as his family home.

Sadleir gained a knighthood and became principal secretary to King Henry, and by 1546 had built a grander mansion in Hertfordshire. Bryk Place was sold to a wool merchant, then to a silk merchant, and it was leased to become a girls' school between 1657 and 1741. At this point, the house came into the possession of a builder, who updated it with larger sash windows and covered up many of the Tudor features. Its next occupiers were of Huguenot descent, when French Protestant merchants came to England to escape persecution and typically settled in places on the north-eastern side of London. The house was much altered and divided into two self-contained residences, known as Milford House and Picton House, with one side occupied by a solicitor who was Hackney's chief clerk and the other part becoming a school again.

In the late nineteenth century, the house was influenced by change as the village merged into London and became more occupied with workshops and factories. As the more prosperous families moved outwards, many larger houses were further divided and multi-occupied, some becoming industrial places. Against the trend, Milford House and Picton House were reunited under the possession of the rector of St John at Hackney as the St John's Institute, a social and recreation centre, but by this time the building was in a state of disrepair, having lost some of its outbuildings and gardens. After an appeal, the St John's Institute was re-opened with a grand ceremony in 1904, with some of the Tudor features restored, including the panelling and two fireplaces, and with a new annexe called the Wenlock Barn in Arts & Crafts style in the courtyard behind.

When the church relinquished the Institute, it came into the possession of the National Trust. It was not opened to the public but leased to organizations, including charities and public services. Surviving the Blitz undamaged, it become the headquarters of Hackney Social Services until the tenancy passed to the trade union, which stayed until 1982. It had continued to be called the Institute until 1953 when it was mistakenly named Sutton House in the belief that it was once the home of Thomas Sutton, a wealthy Hackney-based businessman who had founded Charterhouse Hospital and School in the 1600s; this ownership was disproved by subsequent research but the name has remained.

The house continued to mirror the changing character of Hackney, which by the 1980s was a cosmopolitan inner-city suburb with little industry and a distinctly alternative subculture developing at street level. After the union left, the National Trust struggled to find tenants, and the house was occupied by squatters and became known as the Blue House, a home for some, and also a social centre. The barn was a music venue for a few years. A car breaker's yard squeezed alongside in a garden. When the squatters were evicted, thieves and vandals came to steal the panelling and fireplaces, which were recovered. A group of Hackney residents formed the Sutton House Society, which worked with the National Trust to restore the house. It was opened by the National Trust in 1994 as a house-museum and a focus for cultural and social events. All its archetypal timeline has been celebrated, from Tudor to punk. There is a restored squatter's bedroom in the attic, with a graffiti mural, and the space where the breaker's yard operated is now a garden.

CONTACT INFORMATION

Sutton House,
2/4 Homerton High Street, E9 6JQ

London Sewing Machine Museum

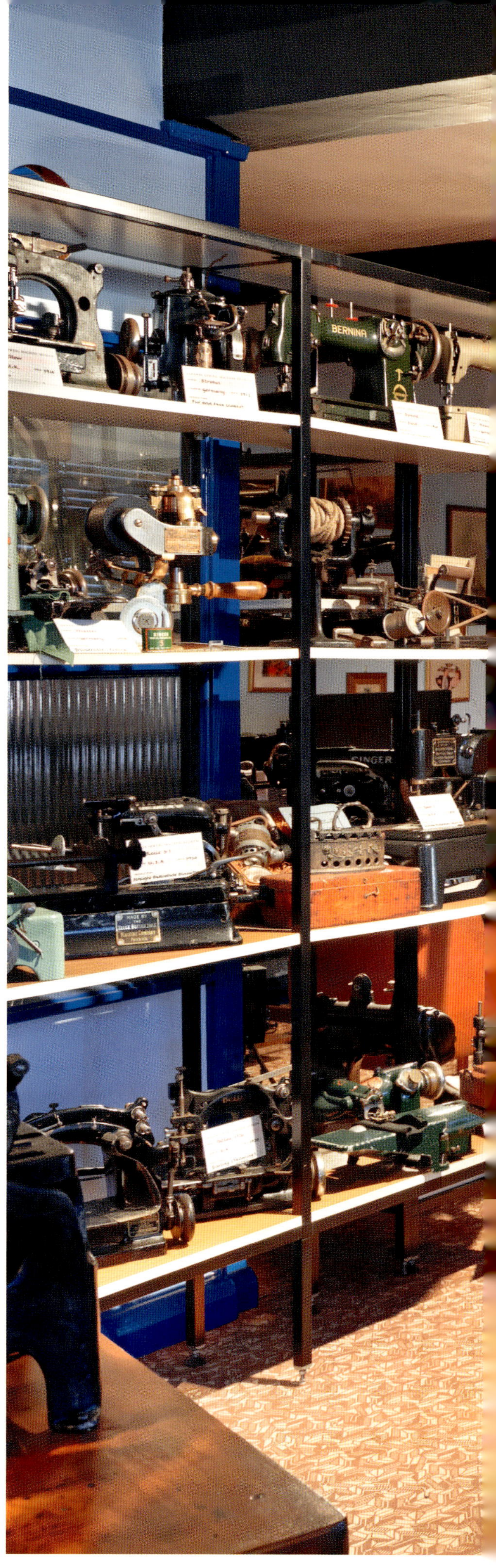

A range of industrial sewing machines on display.

The first sewing machines started operations at a workshop in Paris in 1830 and weeks later the factory was torched by a furious band of tailors. They could not tolerate the idea that any device could replace stitching by hand. The inventor, Barthélemy Thimonnier, fled Paris with a machine he managed to salvage and tried to establish a factory to make more and better machines, but he did not prosper. Soon an eruption of sewing machine activity started in the US with improved designs emerging working on differing principles. An argument raged over patents and marketing between inventors Elias Howe and Isaac Singer and many feared that the machines would force jobless seamstresses and dressmakers on to the streets. The sewing machine underwent a turbulent evolution, yet by the end of the century, there were more than 600 makers worldwide and it could be claimed that the machine had changed the world and gained universal acceptance. It became hard to dislike the sewing machine, especially in the home.

Much of this history is found in hardware at the London Sewing Machine Museum in Tooting, a treasure house telling the story of the sewing machine from 1830 to 1950. It is located at the site of a modern sewing-machine sales company and has restricted opening hours, generally allowing visitors only for a few hours on the first Saturday each month. There are more than 600 sewing machines exhibited, one room for domestic types and another for industrial machines.

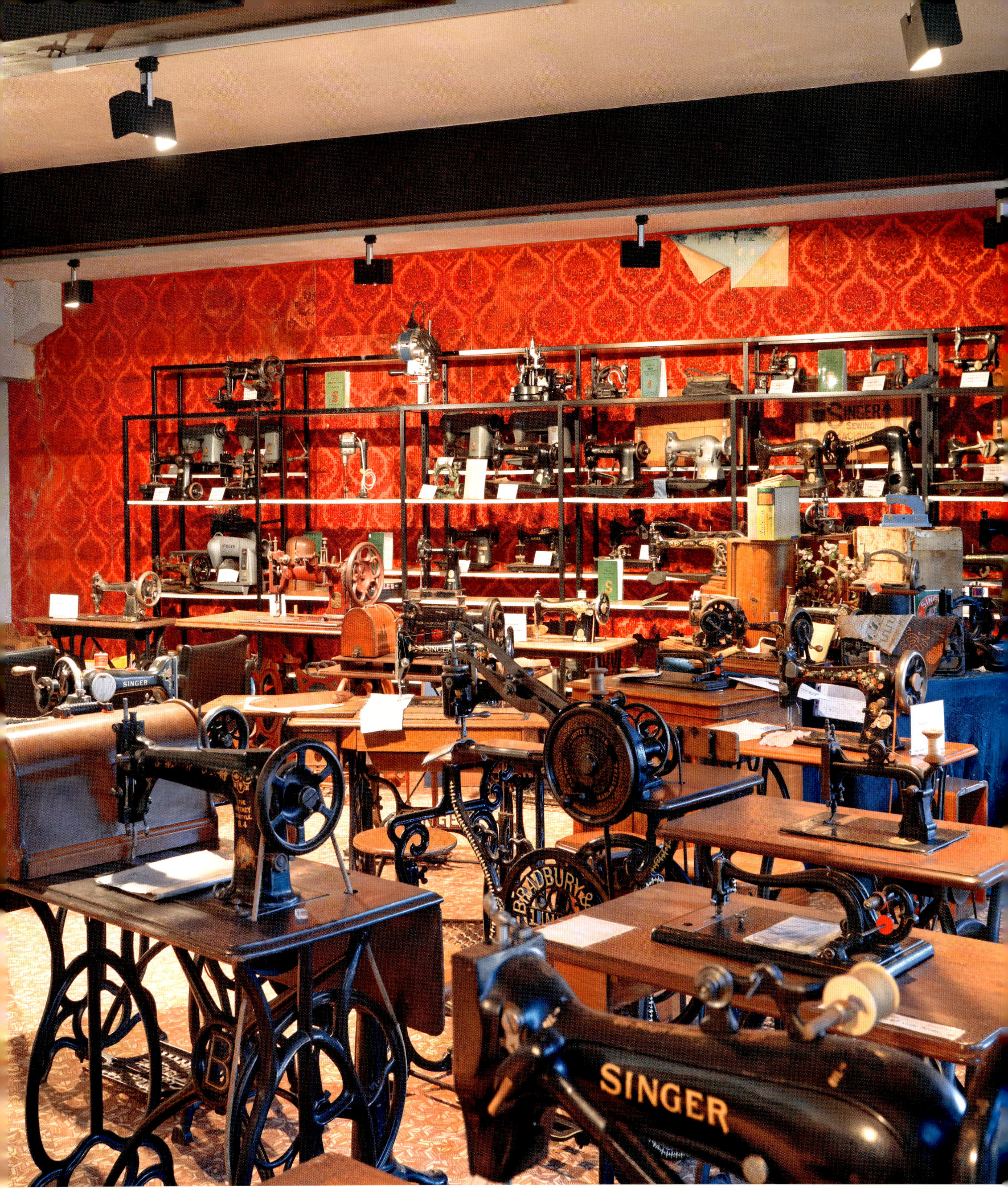
SINGER

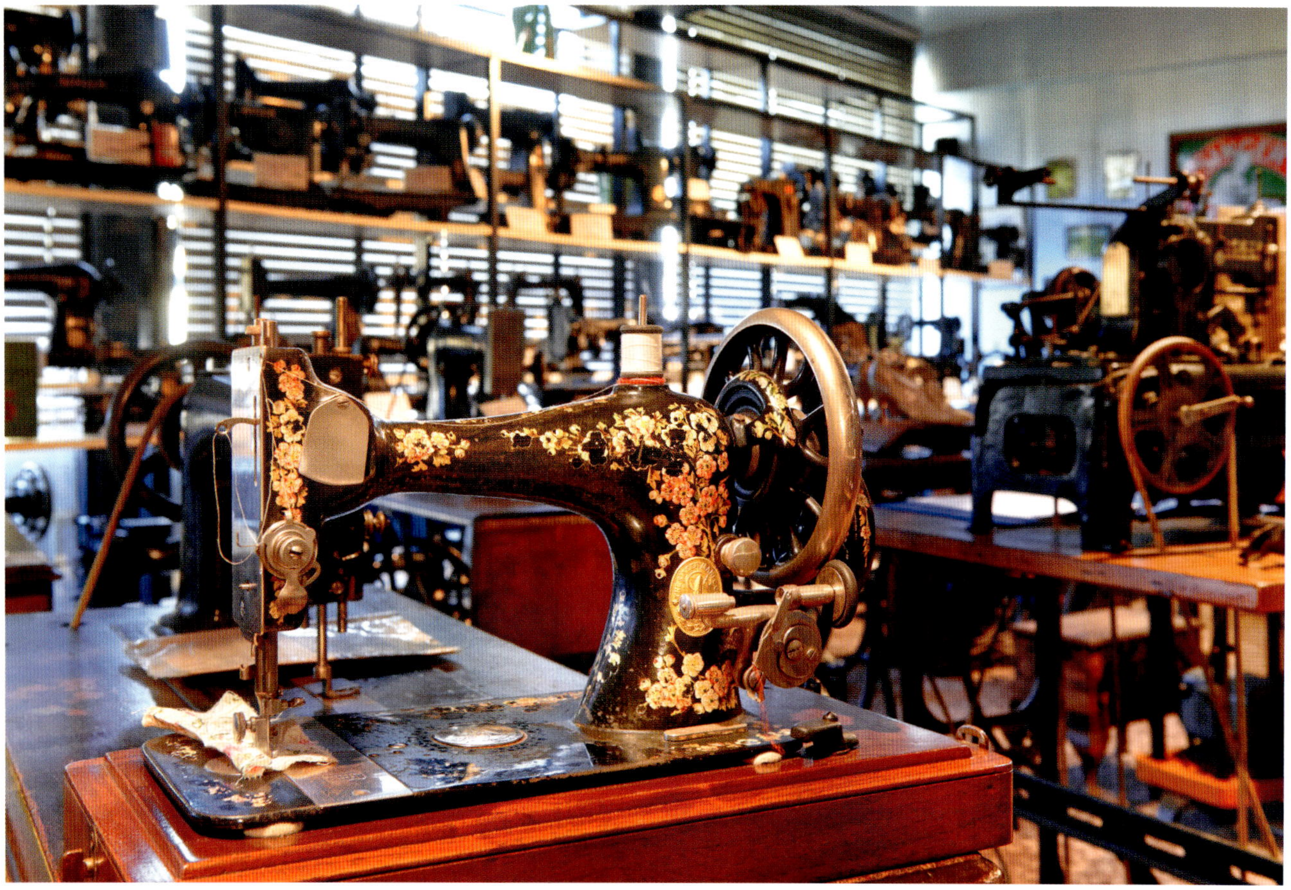

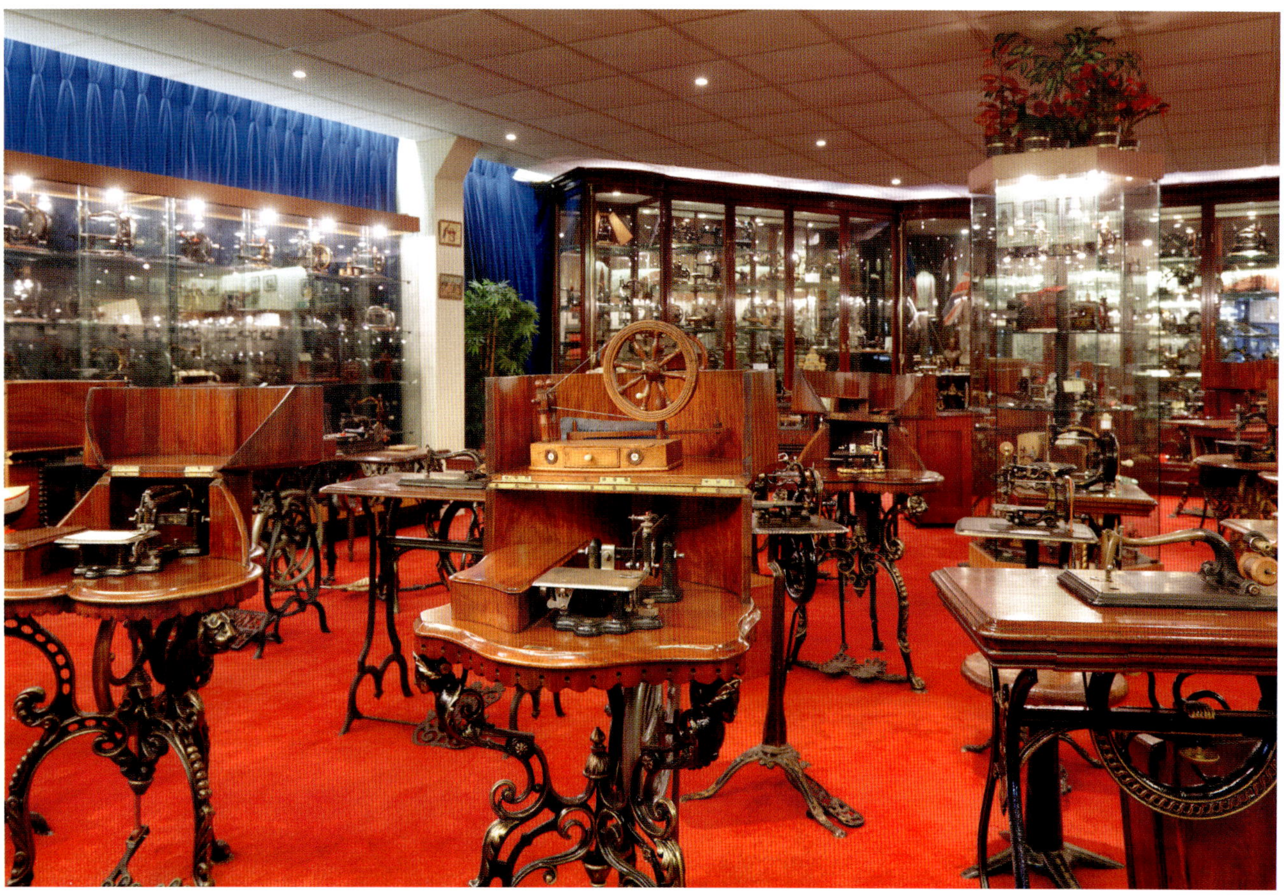

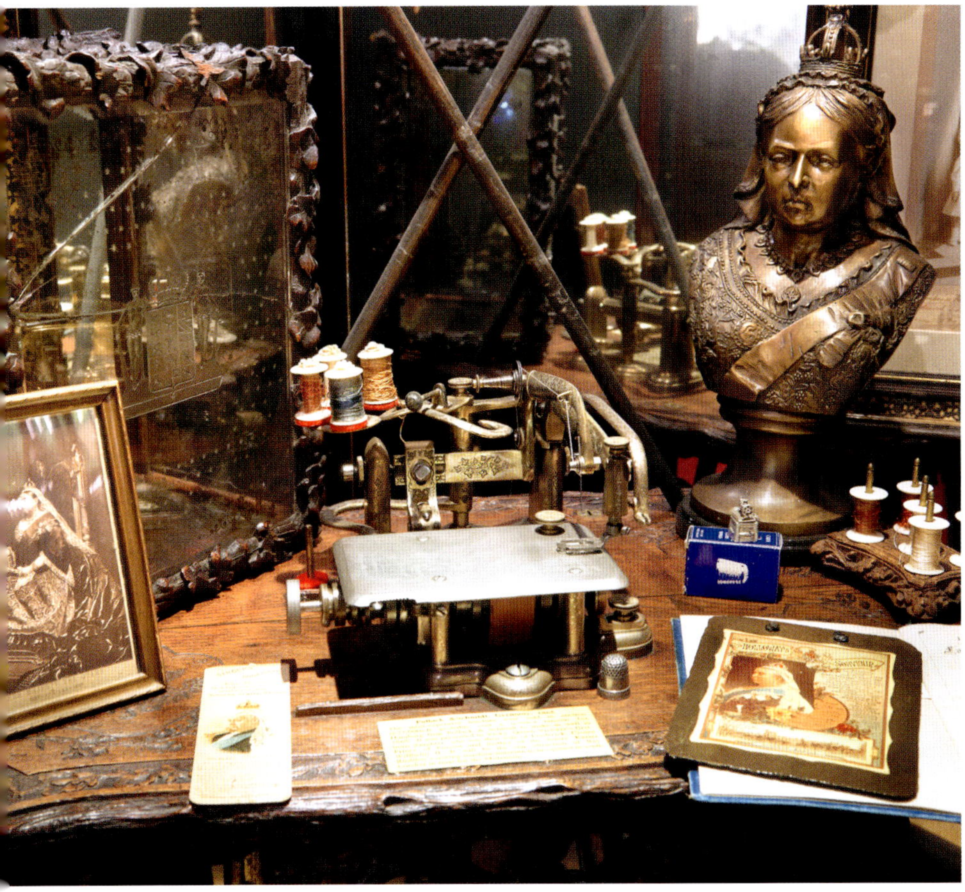

There are more than 600 sewing machines exhibited, one room for domestic types and another for industrial machines.

Opposite, above A Singer sewing machine, Model No. 28.

Opposite, below A collection of domestic sewing machines.

Above Queen Victoria's daughter Vicky's sewing machine, which was made in 1865 by Pollack & Schmidt of Hamburg.

The collection was assembled by the managing director of the Wimbledon Sewing Machine Co Ltd, Ray Rushton, and has roots in south London going back over seventy years. After the war, Ray's father, Thomas Ruston, started a business repairing and selling second-hand machines, first from home and then from the T.A. Ruston shop in Merton Road, South Wimbledon, at a time when the average wait for a new machine from the factory was six months. A replica shopfront is an exhibit in the museum. Over time the business developed into the Wimbledon Sewing Machine Company, eventually dispatching machines across the world and marketing its own Wimsew machines. At the same time, a collection of old machines was accumulating, including special types for embroidery and for sewing gloves, shoes, handbags, curtains, leather and fur, for patching boots and for making buttonholes. Knowledgeable enthusiasts recognize four-needle machines for sewing corsets. There are machines for sewing sails, tarpaulins and parachutes. There is a unique machine from a Scottish maker dated 1904 with the head cast in the shape of a lion. Rushton family history says it was bought from a rag-and-bone merchant for £7 in the late 1940s. There are machines with personal history attached, one of which was owned by Charlie Chaplin's mother Hannah, a seamstress, and another owned by the mother of Boy George, who used it to make his stage costumes.

One of the most prized exhibits is the sewing machine given as a present to Queen Victoria's oldest daughter, Victoria Adelaide Mary Louisa, on her wedding to Frederick, Crown Prince of Prussia, in 1858. The machine has ornamental engraving under a silver gilt finish. The stitch plate is engraved with a view of Windsor Castle and a cut-glass cover carries Prussian and British coats of arms. Accessory boxes and instruction manual are bound in blue velvet with gilt brass monograms. The ivory cotton reels are carved with a crown motif. The machine was bought at auction for £23,500 in 1997, but it is not the most expensive machine in the collection. That is an historic machine made by Barthélemy Thimonnier, the French inventor who had fled Paris in 1831 after attacks by rioters, and dating from that time. The machine, which is treadle operated and made largely of wood, was discovered in the basement of an abandoned sewing factory in Argentina and purchased by the Rushton family for £50,000 and may be one of only two or three survivors.

The London Sewing Machine Museum regularly supplies film-makers with authentic props, and its machines can be seen in *Downton Abbey*, *Call the Midwife* and *Made in Dagenham*.

CONTACT INFORMATION

London Sewing Machine Museum,
292–312 Balham High Road, SW17 7AA

Southbank Skate Space

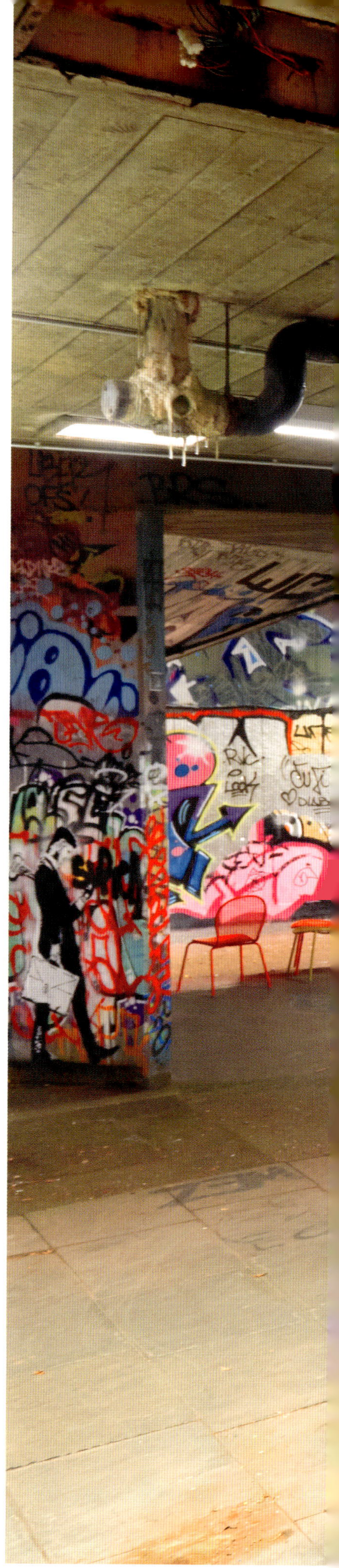

The graffiti that decorates the Southbank Skate Place is constantly changing.

Recognized as the birthplace of British skateboarding, the undercroft at the Southbank Centre has been home to boarders, bike riders and taggers for more than fifty years. Threatened with extinction when redevelopment of the area loomed, a fierce campaign was started in 2014 by skaters and local enthusiasts. They worked with the Southbank Centre to promote the renovation of the space in a project that from 2019 provided new lighting, repaired sections of the floor and reopened another section.

Concrete is the universal material of the Southbank Centre. Much of the foundation structure consists of mushroom-headed octagonal columns set at varying levels, as seen in the picture. Ramps and ledges and steps occurred where levels changed. There was headroom. Building work finished in 1967 and it was always intended in this form as an open pedestrian area. A part of the Brutalist architectural aesthetic was that the exposed concrete surfaces were left to carry the grain marks of the wooden shuttering used to hold the concrete poured in the construction process. Those traces might be harder to see in the undercroft now. Graffiti artists are constantly at work. It is a funky environment by any measure.

Skateboarding swiftly translated from its homeland of Venice Beach LA to London sometime close to 1973 and the first skaters discovered an arena of slopes and ledges which freakishly suited their sport. BMX bikers came too, and later street performers and musicians.

It is public space and there are no set opening times.

CONTACT INFORMATION

Southbank Skate Space,
337–8 Belvedere Road, SE1 8XT
https://www.southbankcentre.co.uk/venues/outdoor-spaces/undercroft-skate-space/

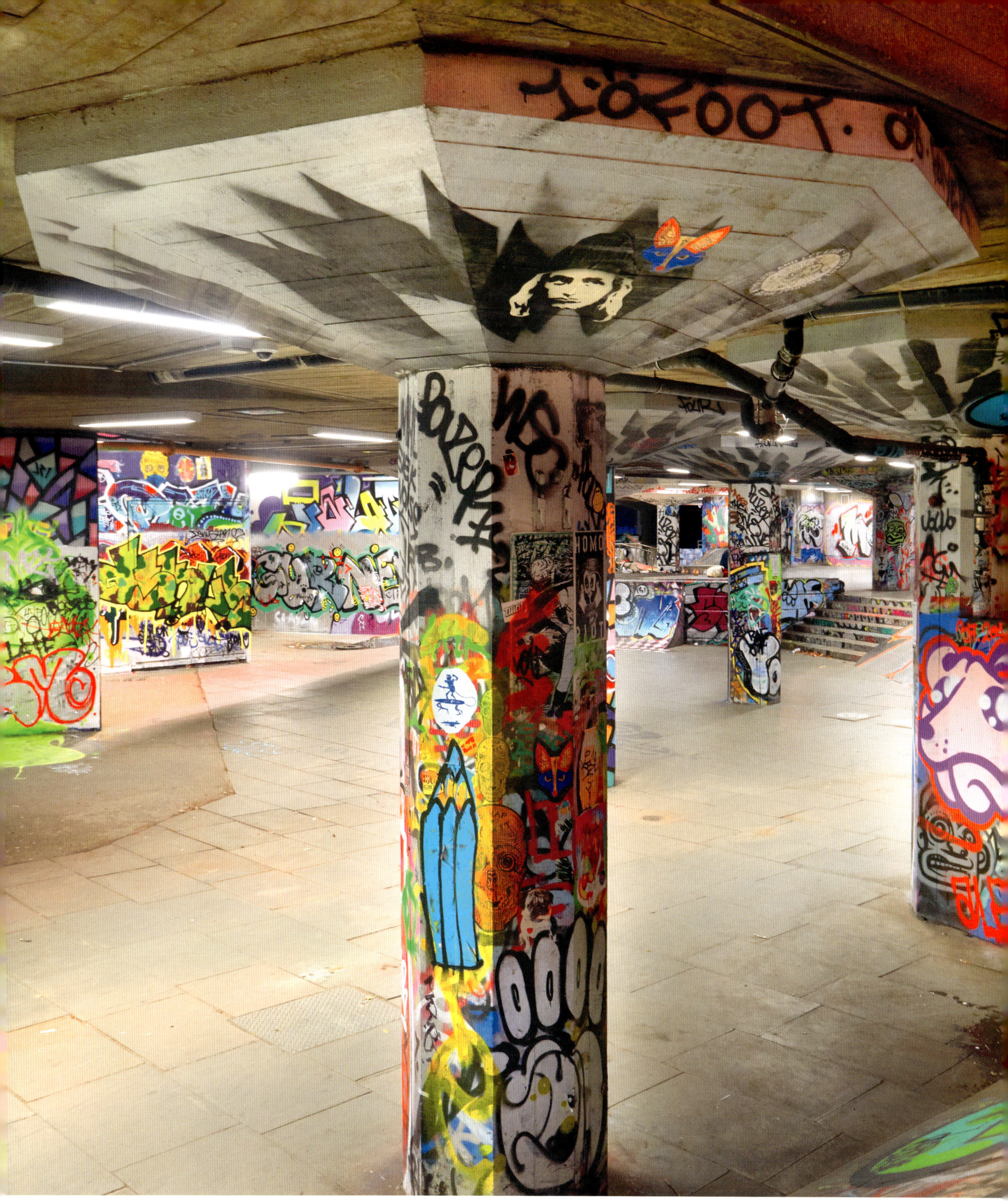

Wimbledon Windmill Museum

One of the first industrial buildings in Britain to undergo preservation, conversion and restoration was the windmill on Wimbledon Common, and that happened as long ago as 1893. Wimbledon windmill had a short working life spanning 1817 to 1864 and was quickly converted into housing. Today it is a museum and an enduring curiosity, preserving its functional and residential elements.

While windmills were built from commonplace materials, they were never entirely primitive machines. Like the steam engines that superceded them, windmills appear to work on the simplest of principles, but some features of their operation, such as the aerodynamic interaction of the subtly twisted sails with the wind, are more complex than is first apparent. The mysteries of the shutters, fantail, striking gear and the cap at the top of the windmill are explained by displays in the Wimbledon museum, together with the technology of the milling machinery below.

Today there are so many trees around Wimbledon Common that the mill is blanketed from the wind on most days. Although the fantail continues to turn the cap into the wind, there is seldom an effective wind available strong enough to turn the sails. It was originally built as a hollow post mill, a type common in Holland but rare in Britain, and Wimbledon is the only remaining example in this country. It is driven by William Cubitt patent sails, where the shutters are centrally controlled by pushrods and levers. The

The sails have a subtle twist to them; the fantail turns the cap and the sails into the wind.

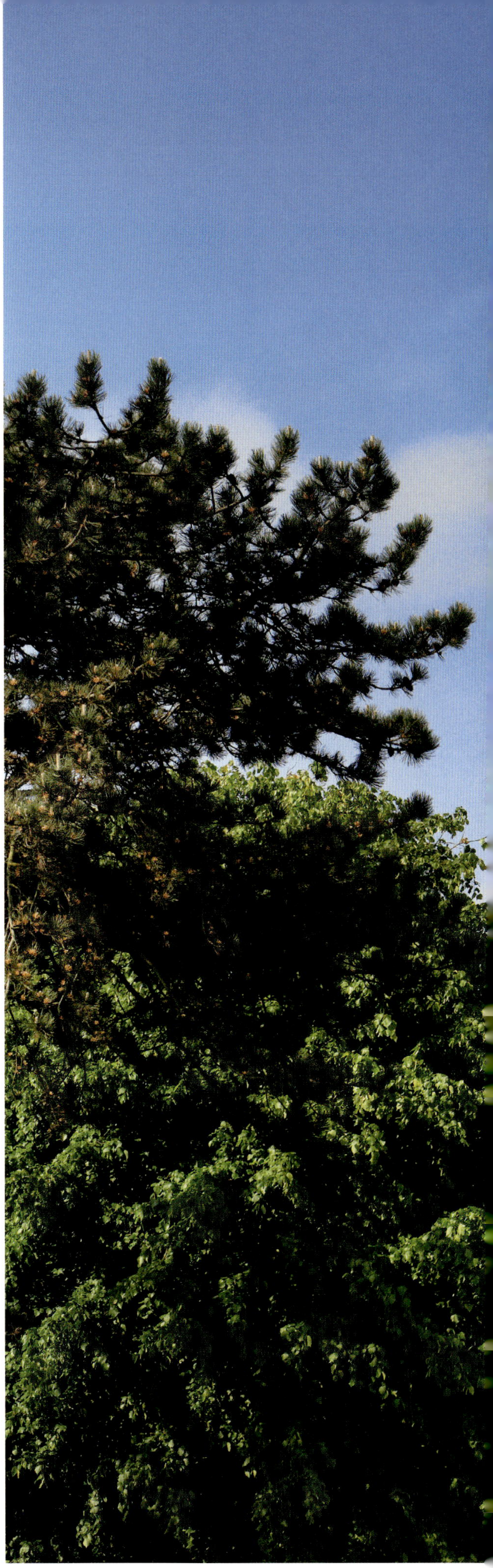

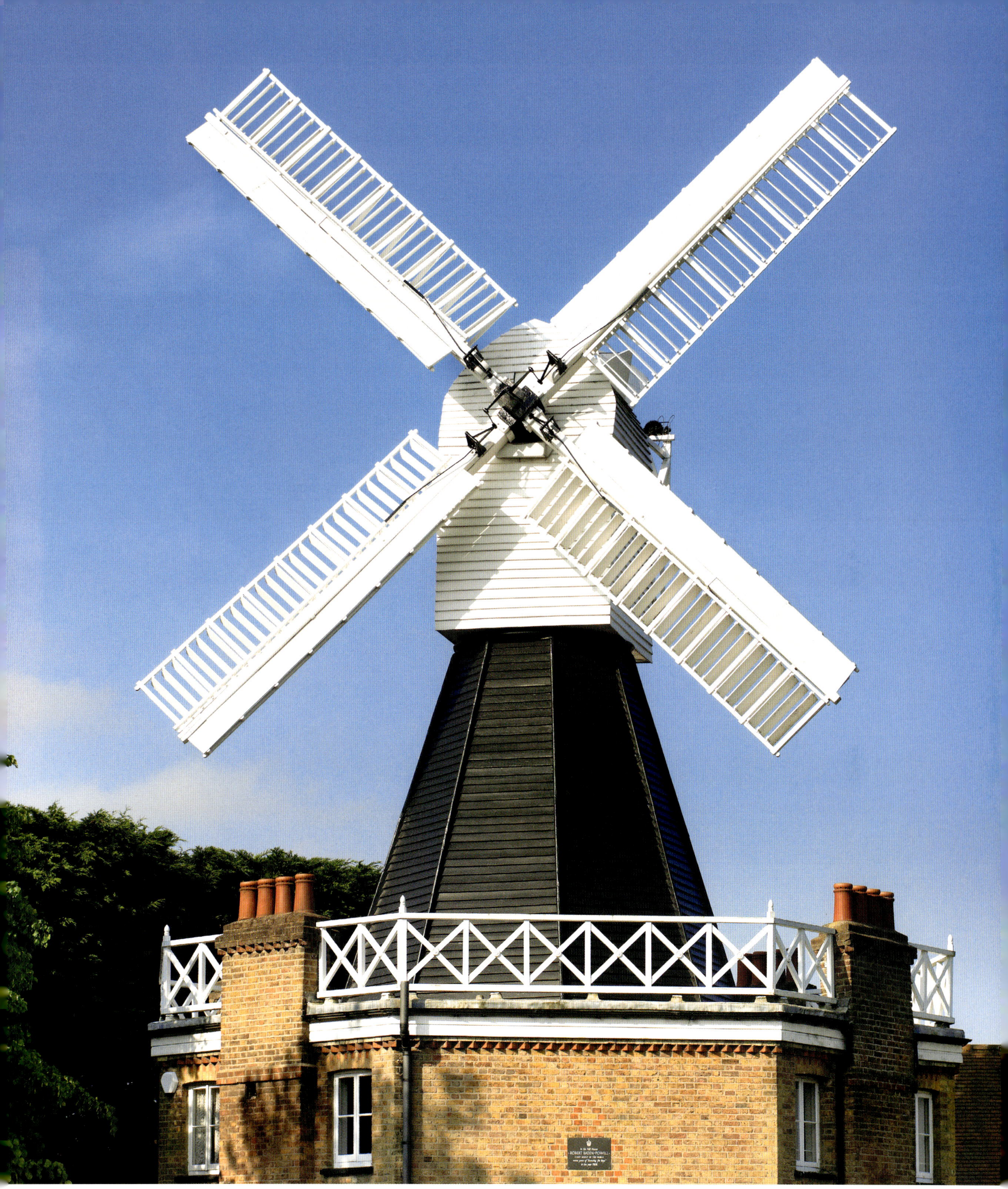

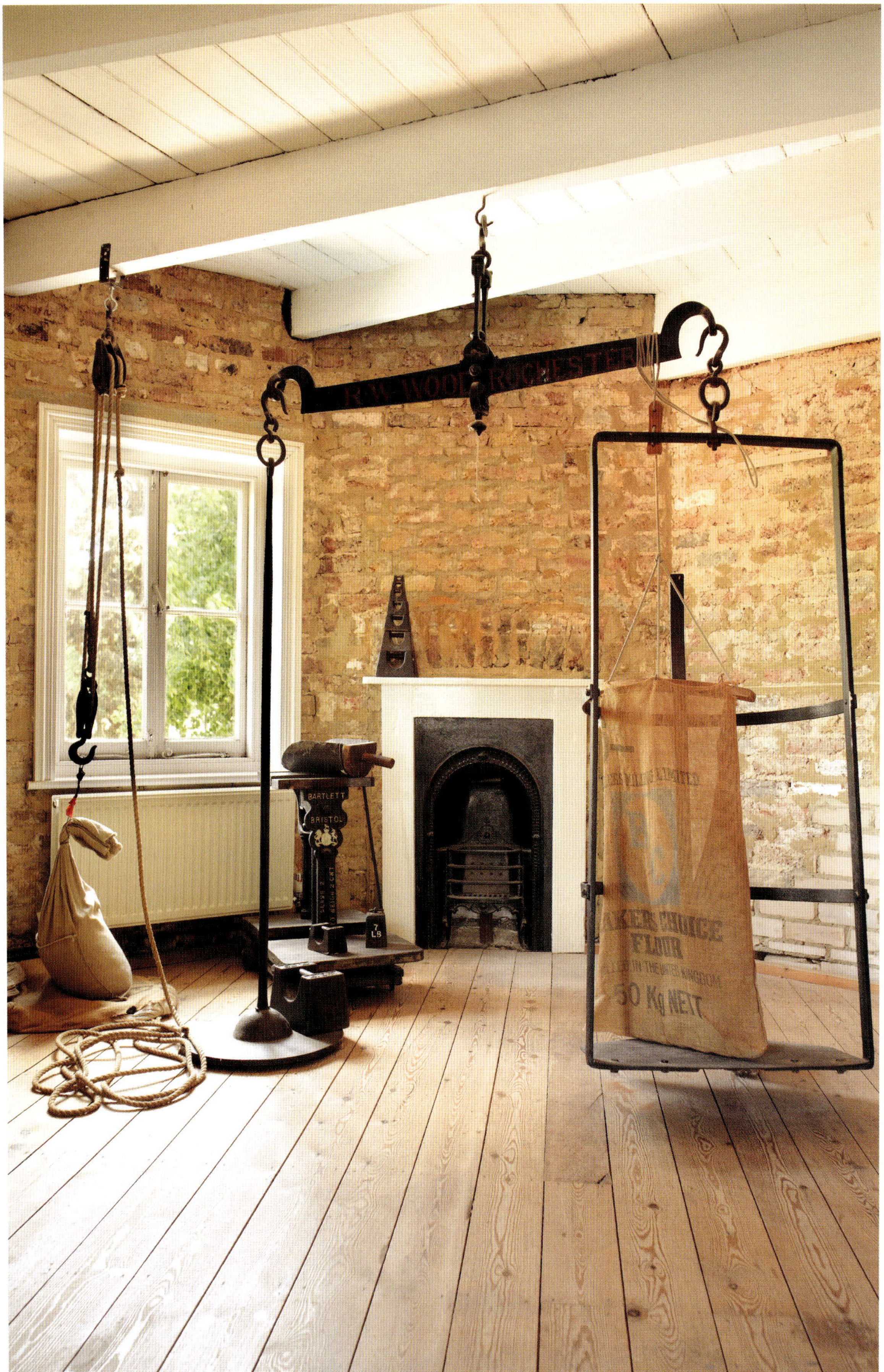
R.W. WOOD ROCHESTER
BARTLETT
BRISTOL
FLOUR
50 Kg NETT

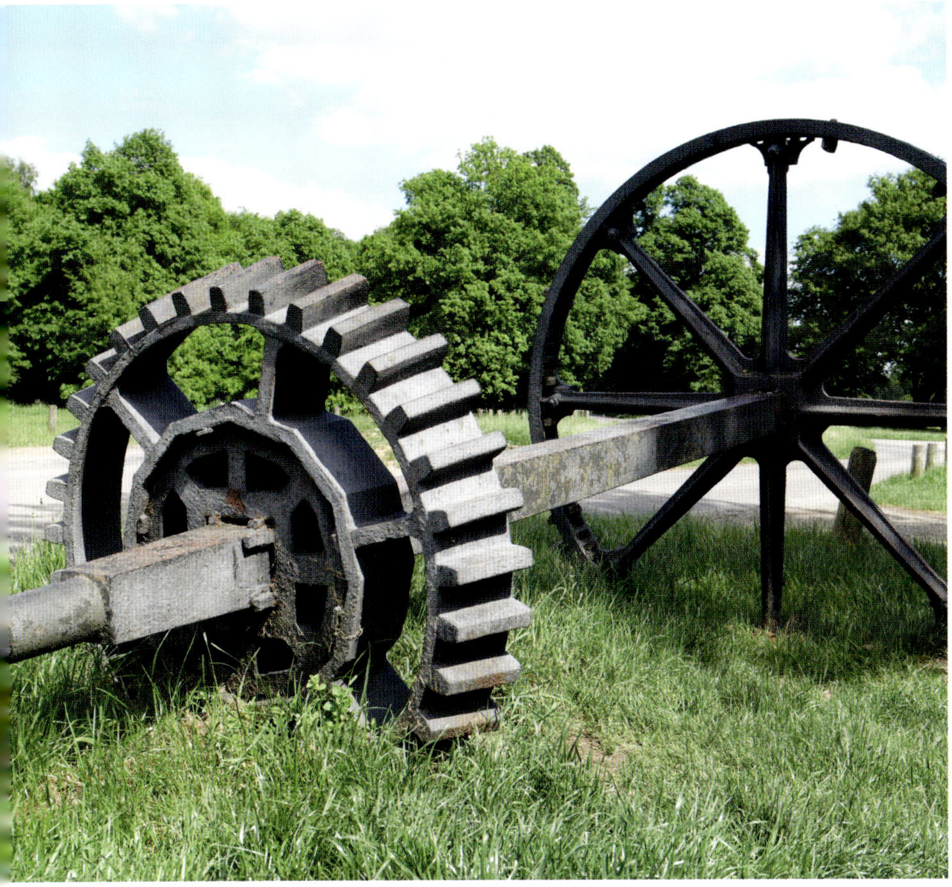

The mechanism is self-adjusting, able to handle sudden gusts, and the shutters can be opened or closed by chain and gears while the sails were turning.

Opposite The fireplace was installed when the windmill was converted to house families in about 1870. The scales, balance, and pulley are operational relics.

Above An example of a great spur wheel (from Canterbury). The large gear carries wooden teeth, some of which remain in place.

mechanism is self-adjusting, able to handle sudden gusts, and the shutters can be opened or closed by chain and gears while the sails were turning.

The land on Wimbledon Common for the siting of the windmill was granted on a 99-year lease from the Spencer family, the lords of the manor of Wimbledon. The 5th Earl Spencer repurchased the lease when milling ceased, and announced plans to enclose the Common for a new manor house, garden and park which he intended to develop and to sell off the remaining acreage as building land. This move was blocked by Parliament and after litigation the Wimbledon and Putney Commons Act in 1871 assigned care of the Commons and the windmill to a Board of Commons Conservators.

The last millers to work the mill had removed the grinding stones and some of the machinery. Earl Spencer had converted the mill into housing for six families, extending the brickwork to enclose the timber of the first floor. The roundhouse – which is octagonal – acquired doors and windows and four chimney stacks. By 1890, when the windmill was under the care of the conservators, the timberwork was found to be consumed by dry rot; much of this had been caused by enclosure of the old timber by bricks. When demolition was threatened, a public appeal raised £400. A restoration in 1893 restored the roof of the roundhouse, replaced timberwork, and rebuilt some of the gearing. This first restoration is claimed as a pioneering preservation action of industrial archaeology. The mill continued to be used as accommodation, in later days for the Commons Ranger. In 1949 the building gained Grade II* listing and was restored again in the 1960s and 1970s. A new set of sails was fitted in 1967. Over time the windmill has required a great deal of maintenance, alteration and restoration work. It opened as a museum of windmills in 1976, eventually occupying the two floors of the roundhouse. Before the windmill reached its bicentenary year of 2017, more work was required after one of the sails broke away.

From the 1818 a miller's cottage stood behind the windmill and it remains today, greatly enlarged. In 1905, the Honourable Mrs Maria Fetherstonhaugh acquired the house to use as a retreat. She was an admirer of Robert Baden-Powell and offered it to him as a quiet place where he could write his new book, *Scouting for Boys*, which he completed at the mill house in the winter of 1908.

CONTACT INFORMATION

Wimbledon Windmill Museum,
Windmill Road, SW19 5NR
https://www.wimbledonwindmill.org.uk/

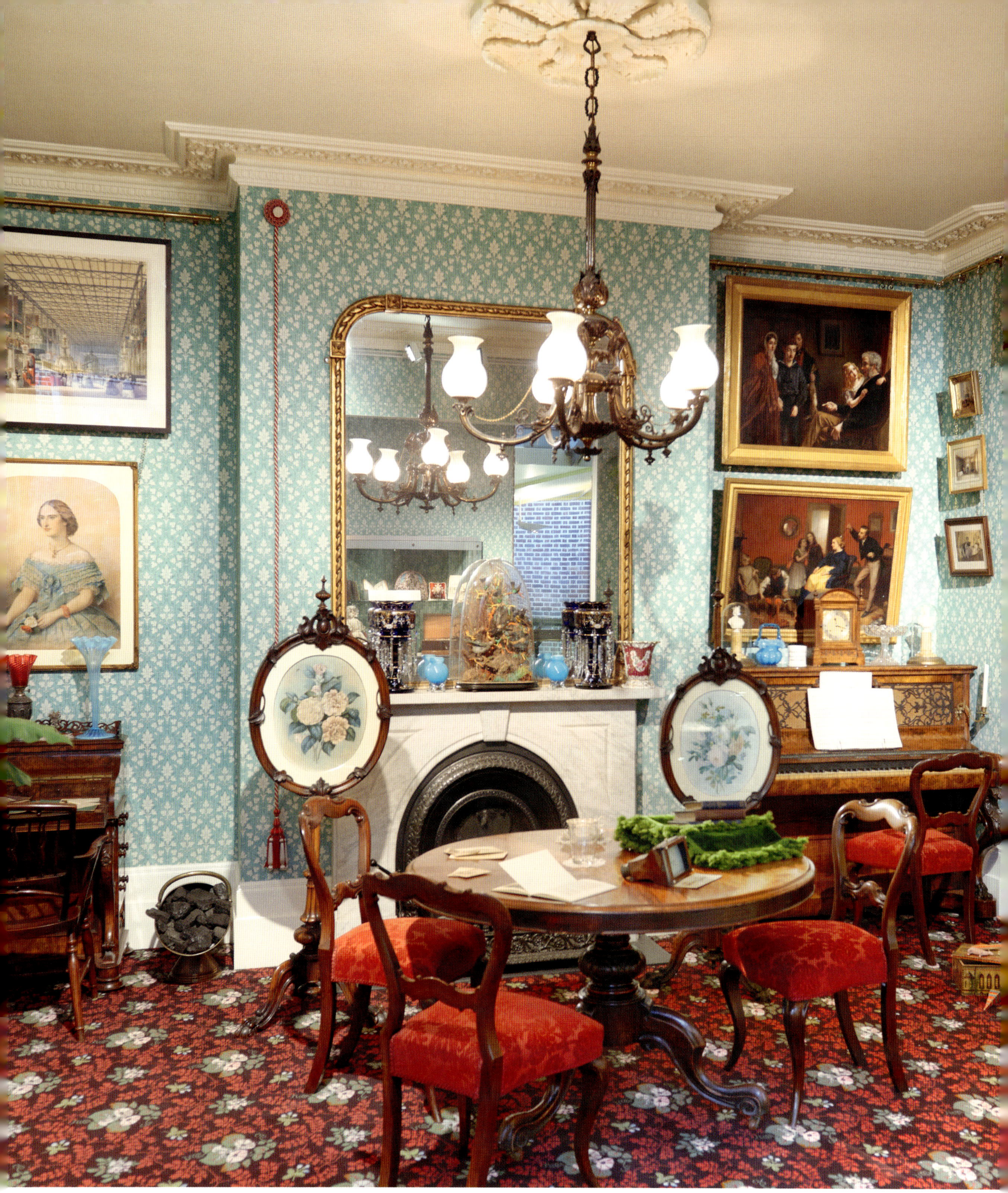

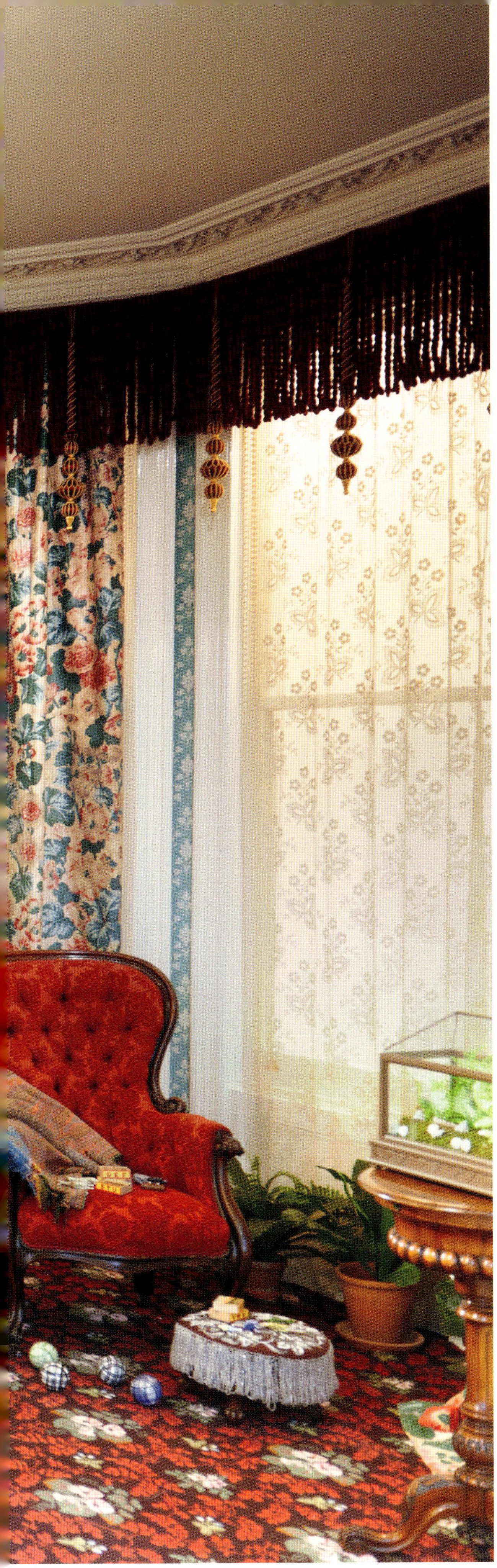

Museum of the Home

Recreated drawing room of 1830 based on several first-floor spaces of the period.

Many generations of Londoners who grew up in the east and north of the capital remember this museum from school visits, being a special outpost of culture and education in the London Borough of Hackney for more than 100 years. It is the Museum of the Home, once known as the Geffrye Museum, and at its centre are a series of room interiors from 1630 to the present and beyond.

It lies far from main tourist routes in a terrace of Queen Anne buildings set back from the Kingsland Road in Shoreditch. The terrace was originally almshouses built 1714 in a quiet place out of town by the Ironmongers' Company to accommodate pensioners connected to the livery company. This was a controlled gated community with a chapel at its centre which the residents were required to attend each week. The chapel remains in place today.

Changes in the 1800s saw the area translate from agricultural to industrial as local manufacturing developed, particularly furniture making. The livery company moved its almshouse accommodation to Kent and after the last resident moved out in 1912 London County Council took it over as the Geffrye Museum to reflect the local industry. First acquisitions were furniture making tools, furnishings and architectural fittings. In the 1930s period rooms were created, spanning 1630 to 1800. Contemporary furniture was added from 1950 and the room-sets advanced through time.

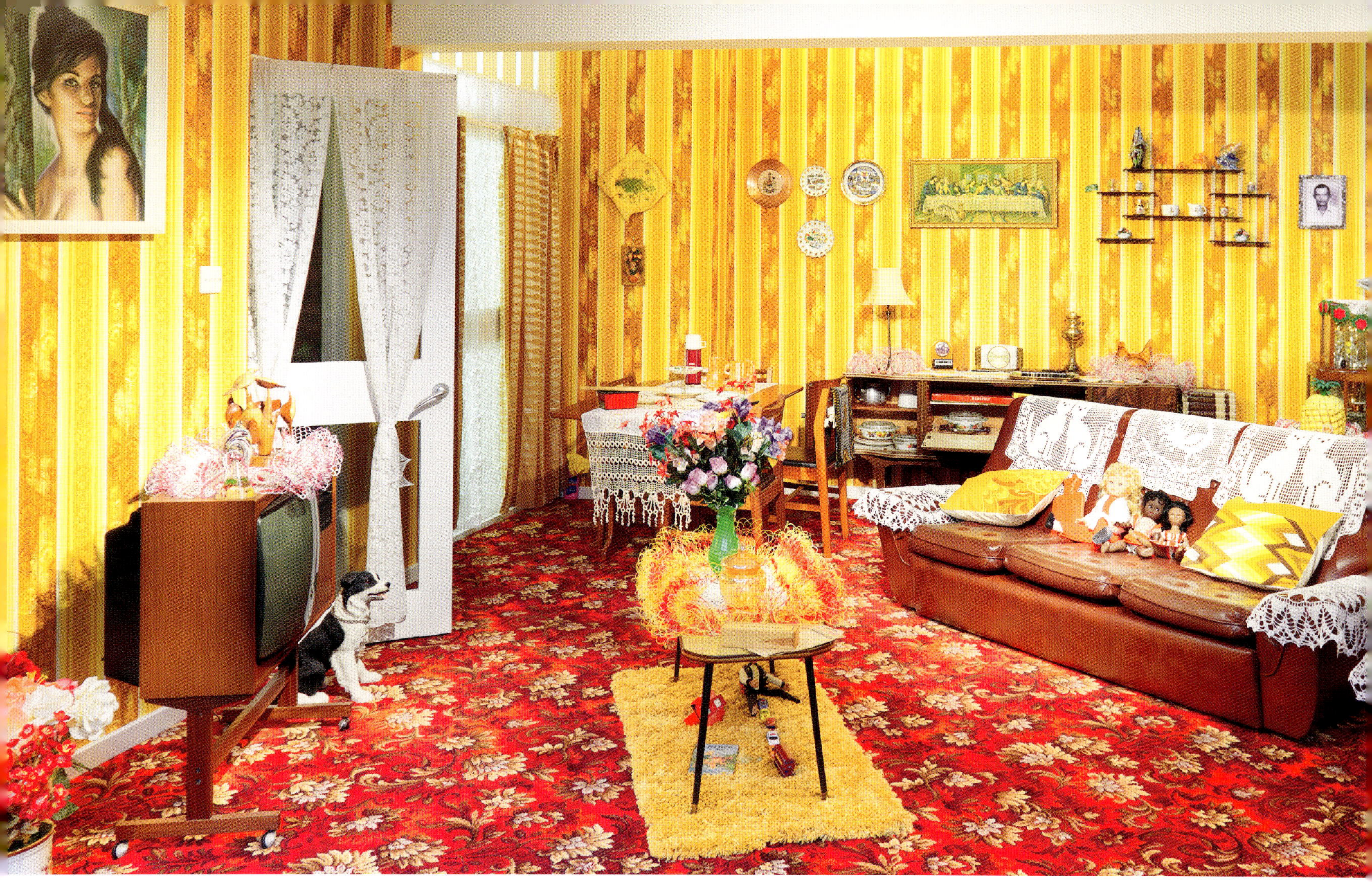

There was significant change to the museum when it re-opened in 2021 after three years of closure. The name Museum of the Home, which had always been applied to the collection of domestic interiors, now became its over-arching title. The name Geffyre was banished. It was Sir Robert Geffrye, twice master of the Ironmakers Company and a former Mayor of London, whose legacy had led to the establishment of the almshouses. Geffrye was proved to have part-owned a ship chartered to transport enslaved Africans to Barbados and Jamaica. The fact is scrupulously recorded on a legend board in the museum.

There was more careful adjustment. The museum had tended to represent the material culture of the homes of the urban middle classes. On reopening there was a switch to a broader range of homes from a variety of cultures and backgrounds. Objects which had origins abroad and could be the product of colonialism, cultural appropriation and exploitation were given close attention. Missing voices, based on local community mapping, were added, African-Caribbean, Vietnamese and Bangladeshi.

Rooms through time continue: a hall in 1630; townhouse in Chelsea 1878; a tenement flat 1913; upstairs 1956; a high rise flat in 2005, each with a narrative attached. These change as new stories and objects are collected. Most acclaimed on reopening was front room of a terraced council house on the nearby De Beauvoir estate in 1979 belonging to a British Caribbean family, packed with detail.

Outside lie gardens in seven different period styles to show the change in English town gardens. Alongside is one of the almshouses, restored with rooms in the style of the 1780s and 1880s. It is where it all began.

CONTACT INFORMATION

Museum of the Home,
36 Kingsland Road, EC2 8AE
https://museumofthehome.org.uk/

Above Front room family home 1979 Hackney terraced council house British Caribbean family, famous classic print left of glamorous Tina.

Opposite, above Hall house room in 1630, oak draw-leaf table, oak court cupboard, Bible dated 1616.

Opposite, below Changing spaces: a previous room arrangement showed cosy Modernism in early-twentieth-century style.

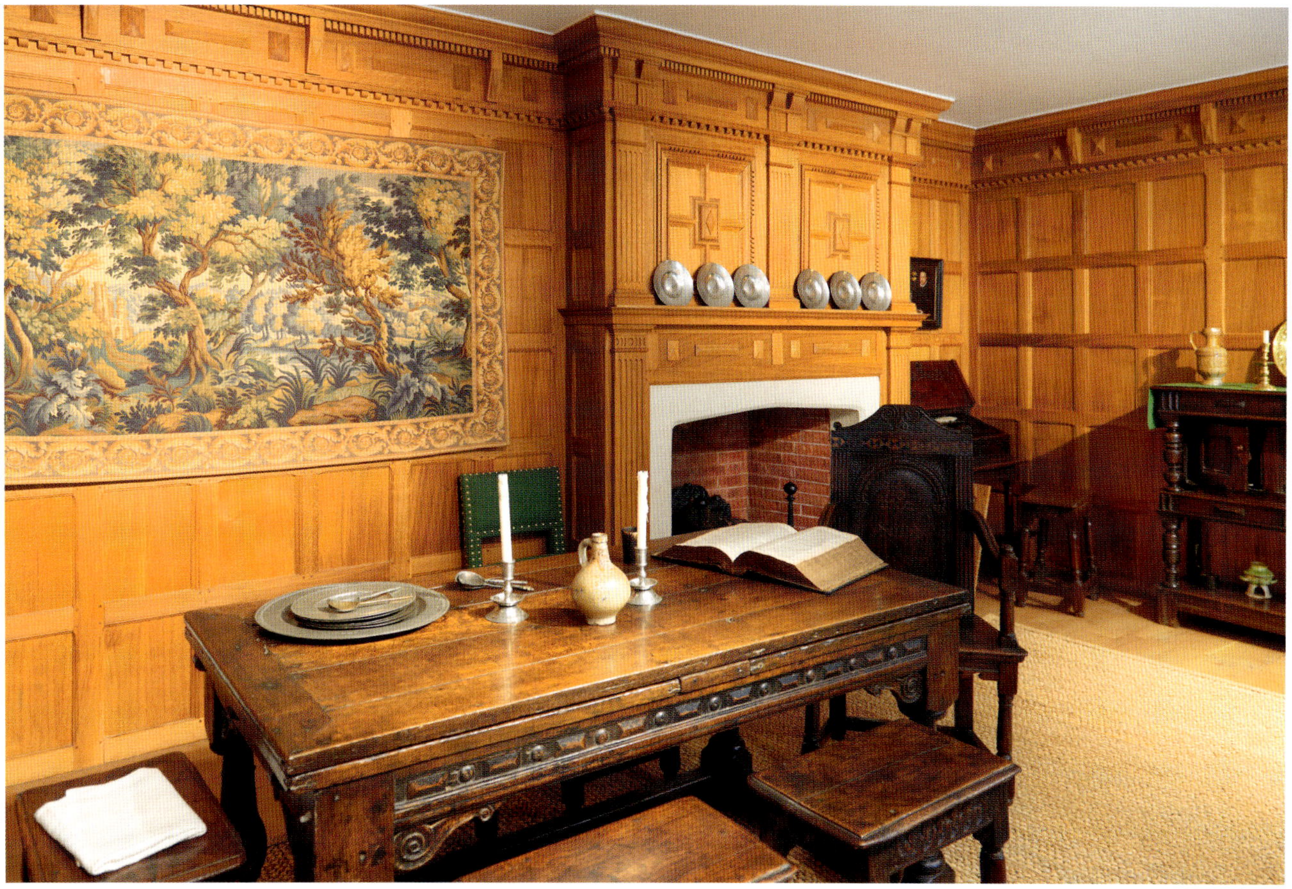

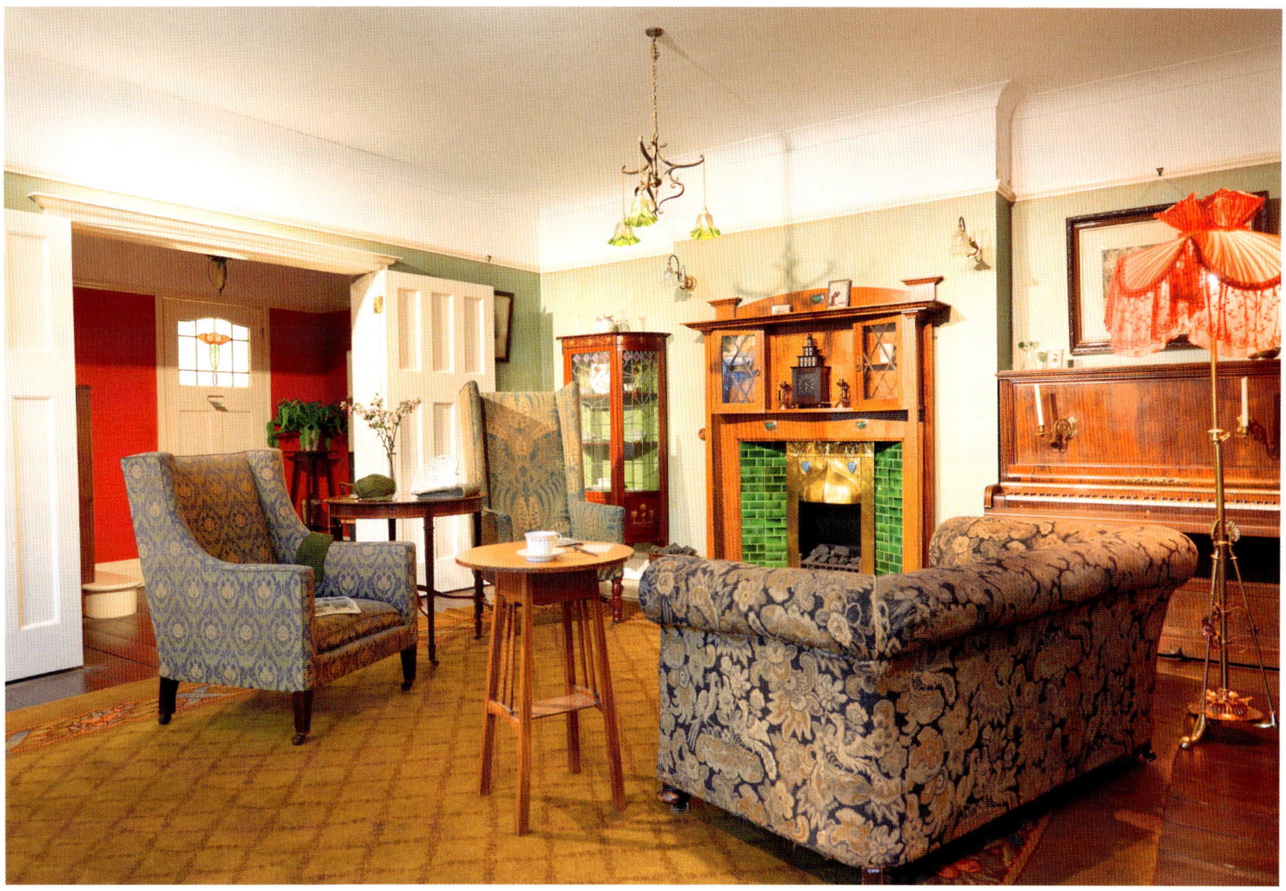

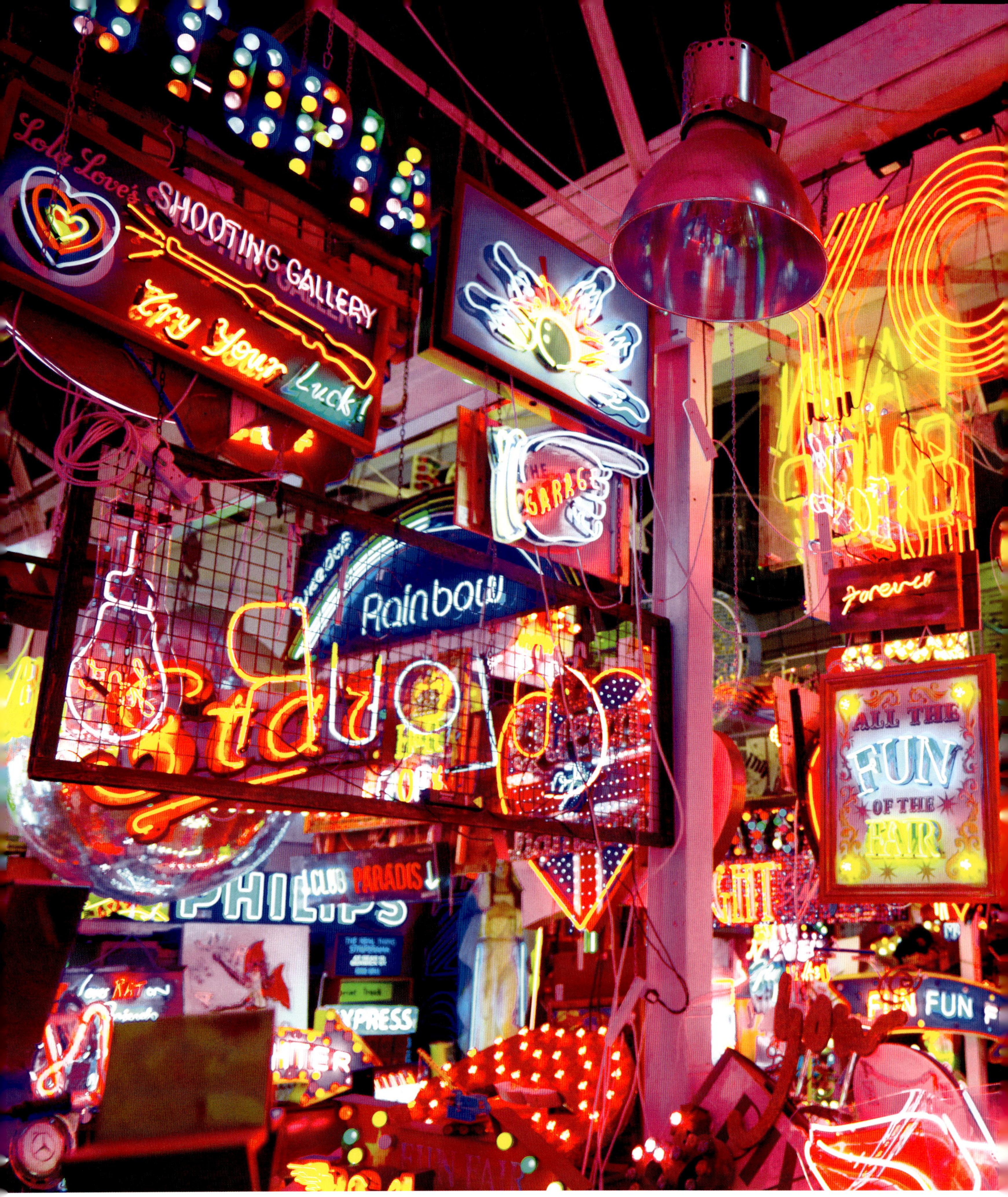
Lola Love's
SHOOTING GALLERY
Try Your Luck!
Rainbow
forever
ALL THE FUN OF THE FAIR
PHILIPS
CLUB PARADIS
FUN FUN

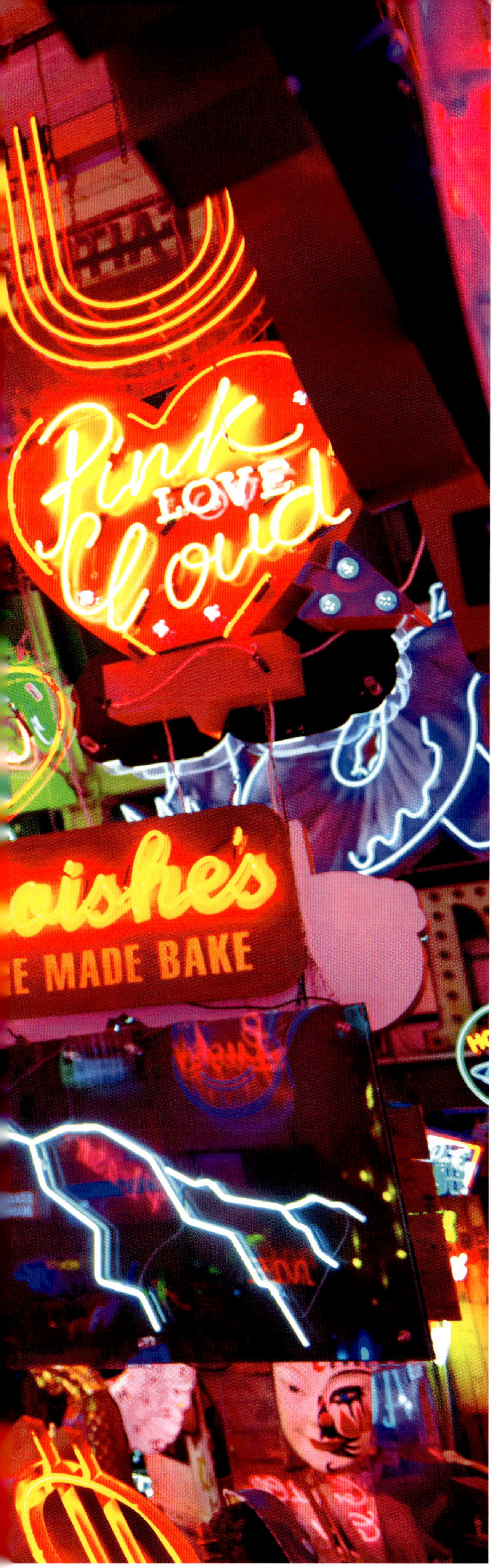

God's Own Junkyard

This neon wonderland contains an enormous collection of vintage signs.

God's Own Junkyard is a gallery-museum and showroom operated by the Bracey family, which can be described as a neon dynasty. The family-owned company Electro Signs is based nearby and is a major supplier and manufacturer of neon signs, LEDs and bulb signs, electro props, architectural signs, awnings and banners. God's Own Junkyard is believed to be the largest collection anywhere of illuminated graphic systems of all types, some sculptures, mirror balls and the like, but mostly hundreds of neon signs, many of them salvaged, of which 80 per cent are offered for sale at any time.

Neon happened first in London. 'The blaze of crimson light from the tube told its own story and was a sight to dwell on and never forget,' said University College London chemist Morris Travers when the gas was first isolated by him and Sir William Ramsay in a UCL laboratory in Bloomsbury in 1898. Its first application was advertising signage, celebrated in God's Own Junkyard in Walthamstow today.

Signage started with Richard Bracey, a Welsh coal miner who came to London after the Second World War, trained as an electrician and started work with a company called Power Neon, an established maker of neon signs. He lived in the East End and worked on installations across London, including helping to maintain the array of neon at Piccadilly Circus. In 1952 he started Electro Signs, a workshop supplying neon to circuses, entertainment arcades and funfairs around London, in the south-east and at seaside

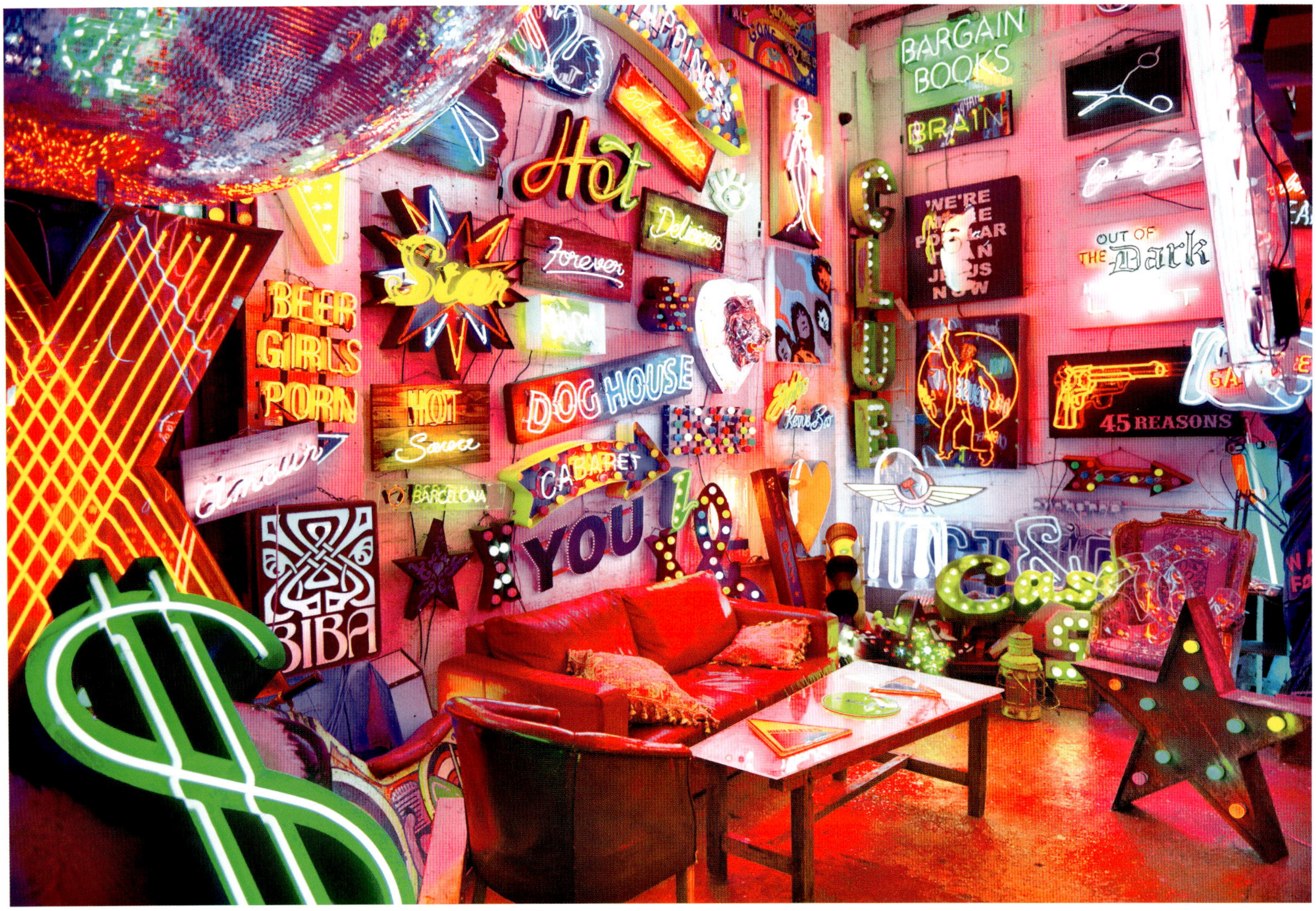

The neon signs are mostly available for sale or for hire.

towns along the east coast. One of the early Bracey signs was for Bar Italia on Frith Street, its neon incorporating a clock with the glowing words Caffe Espresso and Universal, a classic sign of its time that survives today. It was an early example of the company's work in Soho, which was soon to become a dominant market. In 1958 the famous Paul Raymond Revuebar opened at 11 Walkers Court, highlighting its striptease with a towering Richard Bracey designed and constructed sign. Soho, a colourful place in every respect, continued to be a rewarding but sometimes tough environment for Electro Signs through the 1960s and 1970s.

From 1972 Richard's son Chris Bracey, knowledgeable in graphics and design, increasingly guided the company. He was to become a creator of fluorescent tube artworks and a collector of signs. A turning point came in 1986 when a film art-department assistant asked for Chris Bracey's help in gaining access to a Soho club location for a forthcoming feature. The film was *Mona Lisa* with Neil Jordan directing and Bob Hoskins starring. It required authentic London backdrops and also some neon signs to dress the set. A deal was done. More neon work for film followed with *Batman*, *Eyes Wide Shut*, *Charlie and the Chocolate Factory*, *Judge Dredd*, *Tomb Raider* and *Mission Impossible*. On Chris Bracey's death in 2014, his son Matthew came to head the company with his mother and brothers.

The film connection and TV connections continue with either custom pieces or examples drawn from GOJ, and Matthew Bracey is an established neon-light artist. The company has traditionally created a Christmas exhibition for Selfridges' windows.

Neon has largely been displaced by liquid crystal displays and LEDs for mainstream advertising purposes. For example, the last big sign at Piccadilly Circus illuminated by neon, owned by Sanyo, was

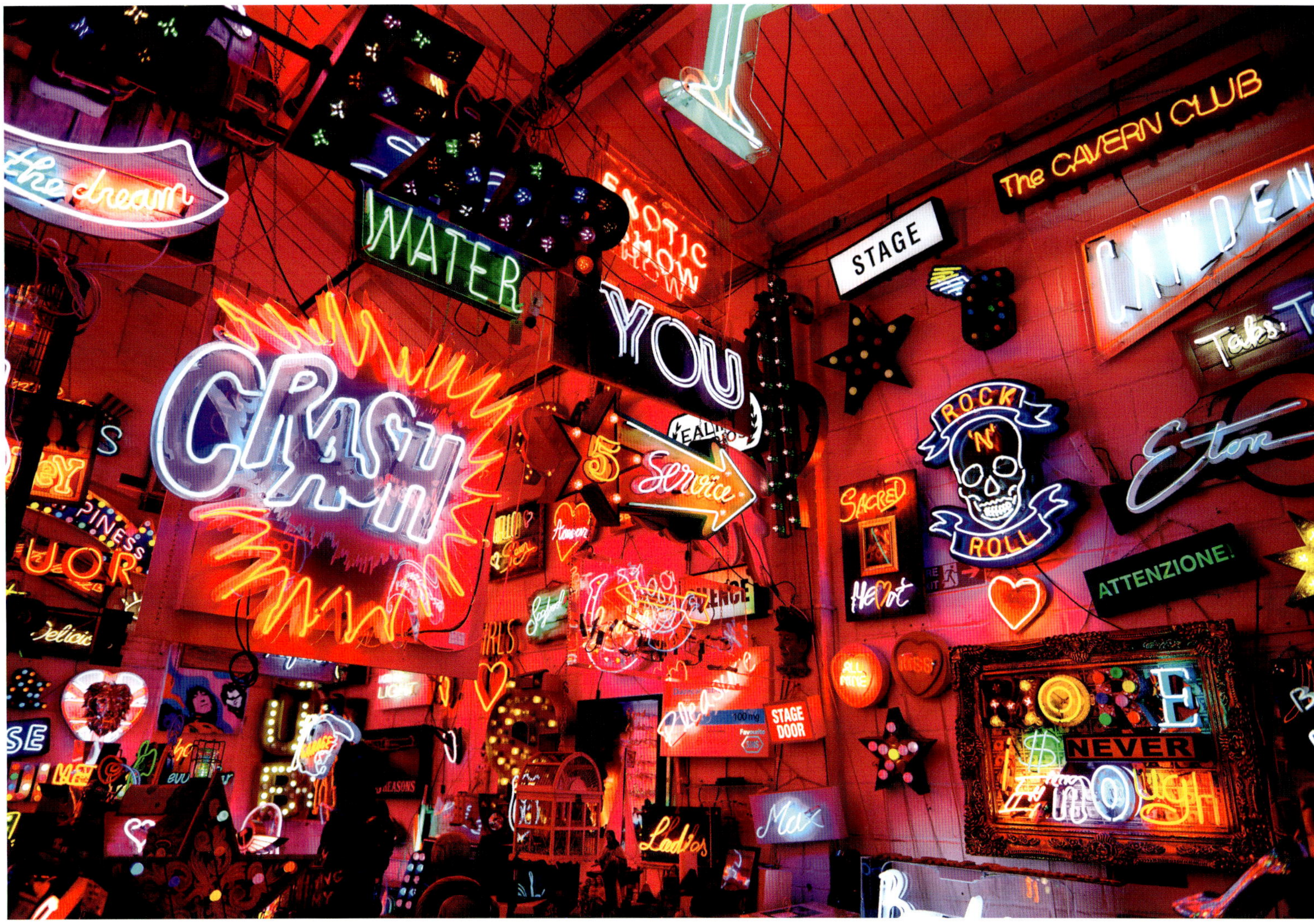

The collection includes both new and used – some are salvaged signs, reclaimed neon signs, old movie props and retro displays.

shut down and removed in 2011, while at the same time there is a growing appreciation of neon as an artform. GOJ has sold pieces to Grayson Perry, Kate Moss, Damien Hirst, Vivienne Westwood and Lady Gaga. Eighty per cent of commissioned works are for display in homes.

Soho changed. The Raymond Revuebar sign was restored, rehabilitated and reinstalled in 2014. It reads 'personal appearances of the world's greatest names in striptease – lavish revue – licenced bars', but the show has long gone. Fawn and India James, granddaughters of Paul Raymond, commissioned it as a tribute to their grandfather and as a piece of public art for Soho. The sign was remade by the Braceys.

Regarding the name of the collection, Chris Bracey, who had been actively collecting neon signs from the 1970s, may have been stirred by a visit to the Neon Boneyard in Las Vegas, a storage facility for old signs, or inspired by the words God's Own Junkyard from architectural writer Peter Blake's 1963 book about the visual ruination of America. That may be ironic, because Blake identified the proliferation of signs and billboards as a major damaging force. In any case, GOJ at Walthamstow is informed throughout by a kind of rock 'n' roll sensibility; the words hip, funky and retro apply, it is high in kitsch, sometimes lower in tone and always exciting.

CONTACT INFORMATION

God's Own Junkyard,
Unit 12, Ravenswood Industrial Estate,
Shernhall Street, E17 9HQ
https://www.godsownjunkyard.co.uk/

The Old Operating Theatre Museum & Herb Garret

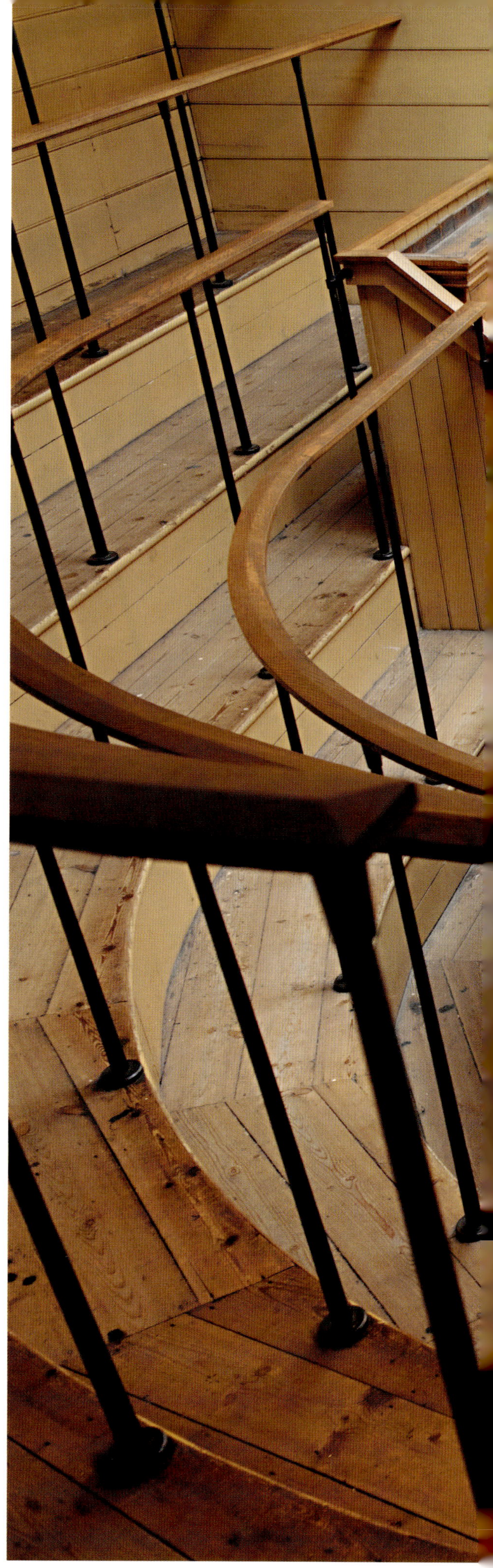

The five levels of terraced standings are where medical students packed the theatre to observe surgery between 1822 and 1862.

The Old Operating Theatre in St Thomas Street occupies a curiously offset and concealed location in the roof of an old church, a position which caused it to be sealed up and disappear from sight for almost a century. Today it is simple for any visitor able to climb a short spiral staircase to see the once-forgotten operating theatre and the herb garret beside it.

It was diligent work by an antiquarian that led to its rediscovery. Raymond Russell, a historian researching the old St Thomas' Hospital site and the life of an eminent Victorian surgeon, found scholarly references linking an abandoned operating theatre to St Thomas' Church. These suggested that the structure of an old theatre building could be seen from the street, which did not seem to be true. The accounts said that the theatre had been on located on the church roof. One morning early in 1956 Raymond Russell climbed the church tower up to the first floor level and, using a ladder, investigated an opening high on the side of the tower chamber. A space inside, dark because the skylight glass above had long been covered with slates, contained the recognizable shell of the operating theatre. The theatre was to be found not *on* the roof, but *inside* the end of the roof space.

The operating theatre had opened in 1822 in part of the roof once completely occupied by a herb garret used by apothecaries to dry, cure and store medicinal plants. The 1703 church and its predecessor were the

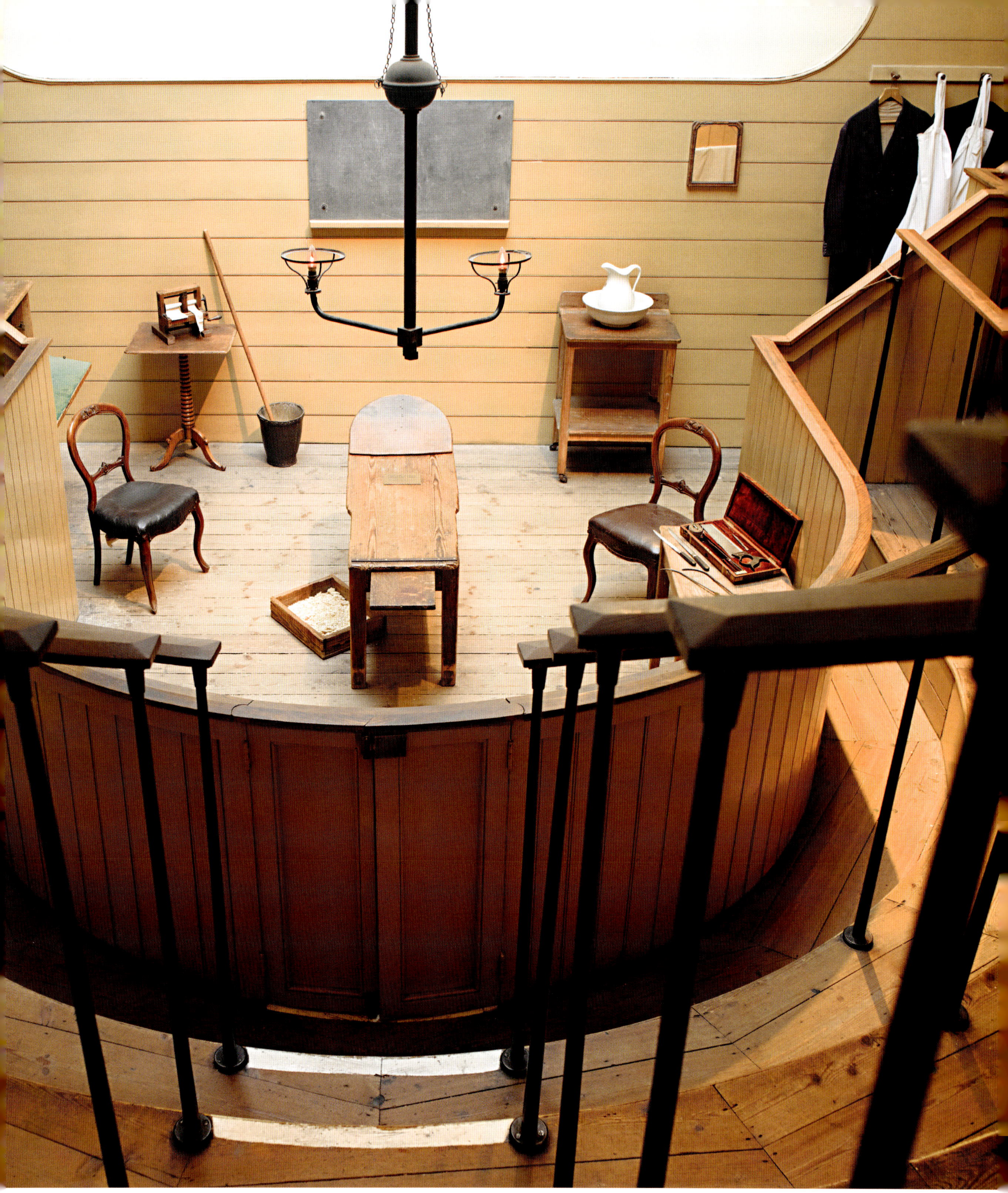

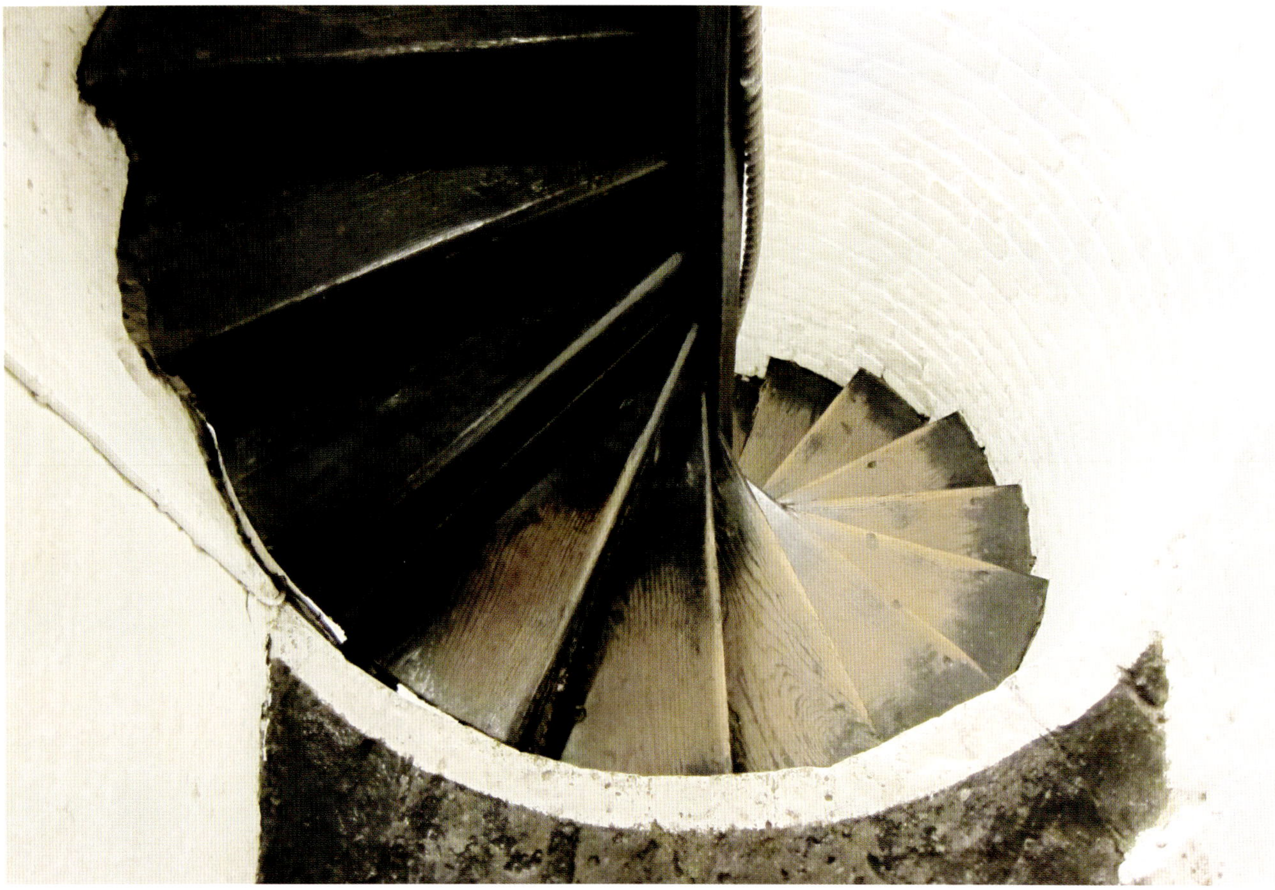

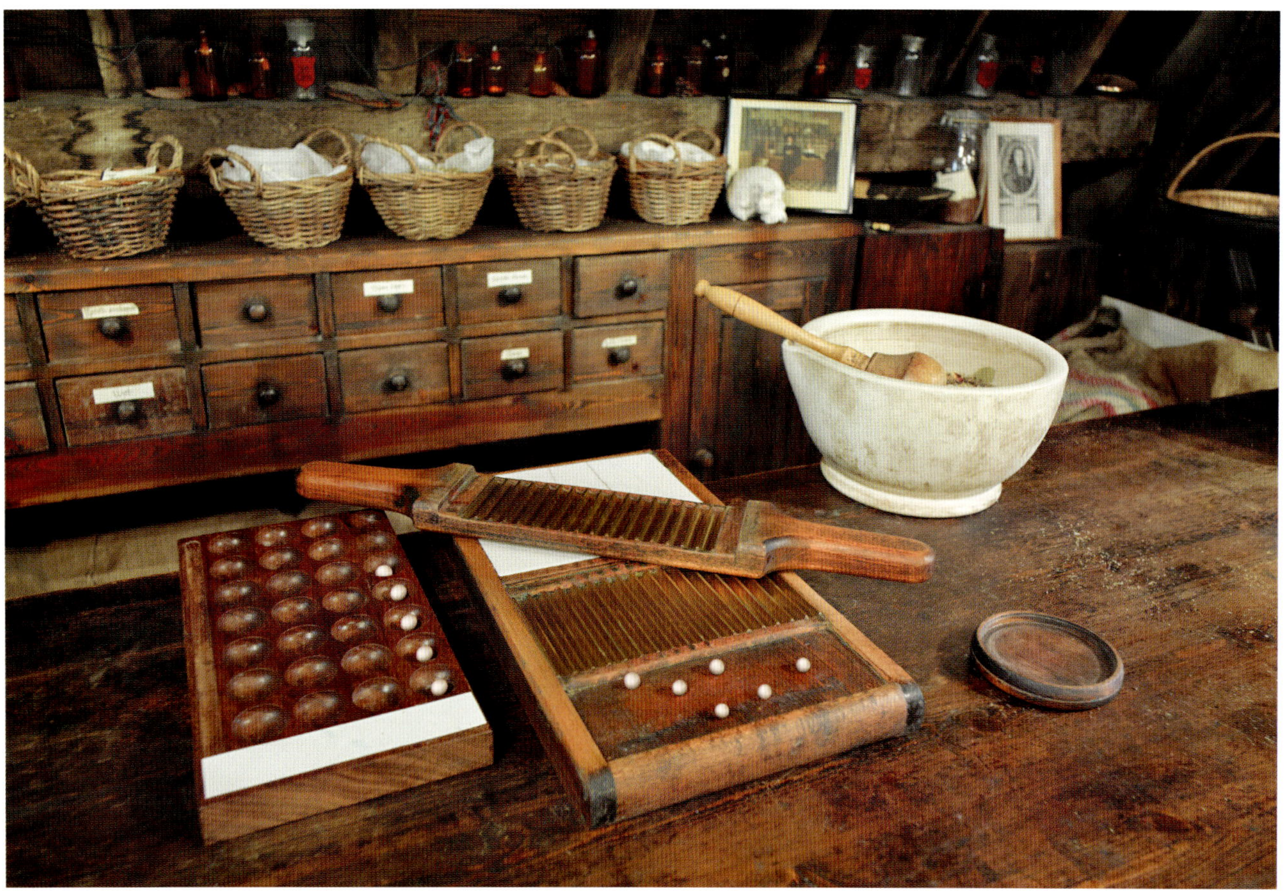

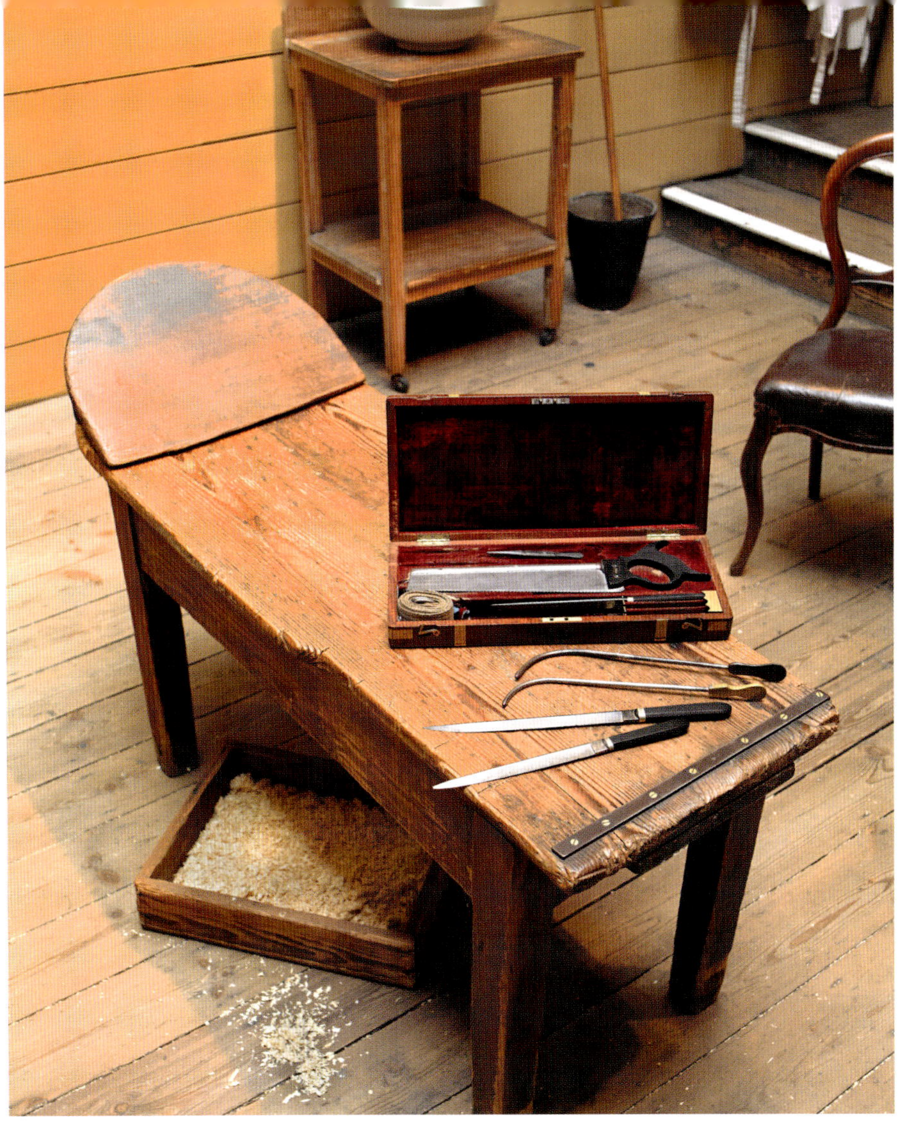

Opposite, above A spiral staircase in the church tower is the only entry route, leading first to the herb garret.

Opposite, below A pill-making tablet mould, displayed in the herb garret.

Above In the operating theatre, an amputation set stands poised, and a drip-tray filled with sawdust is in position under the table.

chapel of St Thomas' Hospital, the institutions having been interlinked from medieval times until the hospital was squeezed out of its Southwark location by the expansion of London Bridge station in 1862. The hospital moved to a new site at Lambeth, and the church closed as a place of worship. Much of the old hospital was demolished. A surviving building, once housing the women's ward, which had been connected to the operating theatre through linking doors, was taken over by the post office. Links were severed, and the doors bricked up.

After rediscovery, the Old Operating Theatre was painstakingly reconstructed between 1957 and 1962, based on the outlines of structures remaining on the walls and from a dusty ground plan on the floor. The floor itself was found to be a false level, packed with sawdust to soak up water when the theatre was scrubbed. An inventory of the fixtures and fittings of the old hospital had been made by the railway company in 1862, which included the operating theatre. This described its layout of steeply raked semi-circular steps, with no seating, separated with rails on iron supports. These were the five levels of 'standings' which were occupied with medical students observing operations.

A wooden operating table dating from around 1830, which was taken from University College Hospital, now occupies centre stage. The theatre was illuminated by skylight and gas light and was altogether an advanced facility by the standards of the age, but it was not until late 1840s that anaesthesia is likely to have been introduced. Traces of ether were found under the floorboards, and the antiseptics being developed by Joseph Lister came too late to be employed here. Conditions would have been primitive; the wooden drip-tray filled with sawdust positioned under the operating table is a reminder. This is claimed to be the oldest operating theatre anywhere in Europe, built when medicine was barely entering the age of science.

In 1962, the garret and operating theatre were opened to the public, and during the 1990s the herb garret was built up as a major display area. When the theatre was made, the herb garret seems to have been reroofed and dormer windows inserted at the rear, but these were long-covered with dirt. During restoration of the herb garret, opium poppy-heads were found in the rafters. A dark, dry and ventilated place remote from the vermin found at lower levels, the garret handled a wide variety of preparations, not all of them herbs, including snail-water, laudanum and leeches. The apothecary was at one time the chief resident medical officer of the hospital and responsible for prescriptions for surgical cases.

In recent times, the St Thomas' Church building has served as a chapter house meeting room for Southwark Cathedral, as an office for insurance brokers, then a property developer's headquarters. Hidden above in the roof space, the old operating theatre is still something of a mystery venue, undetectable from street level, although its skylight may be now glimpsed from The Shard, which towers over the area.

CONTACT INFORMATION

The Old Operating Theatre & Herb Garret,
9a St Thomas Street, SE1 9RY
https://oldoperatingtheatre.com/

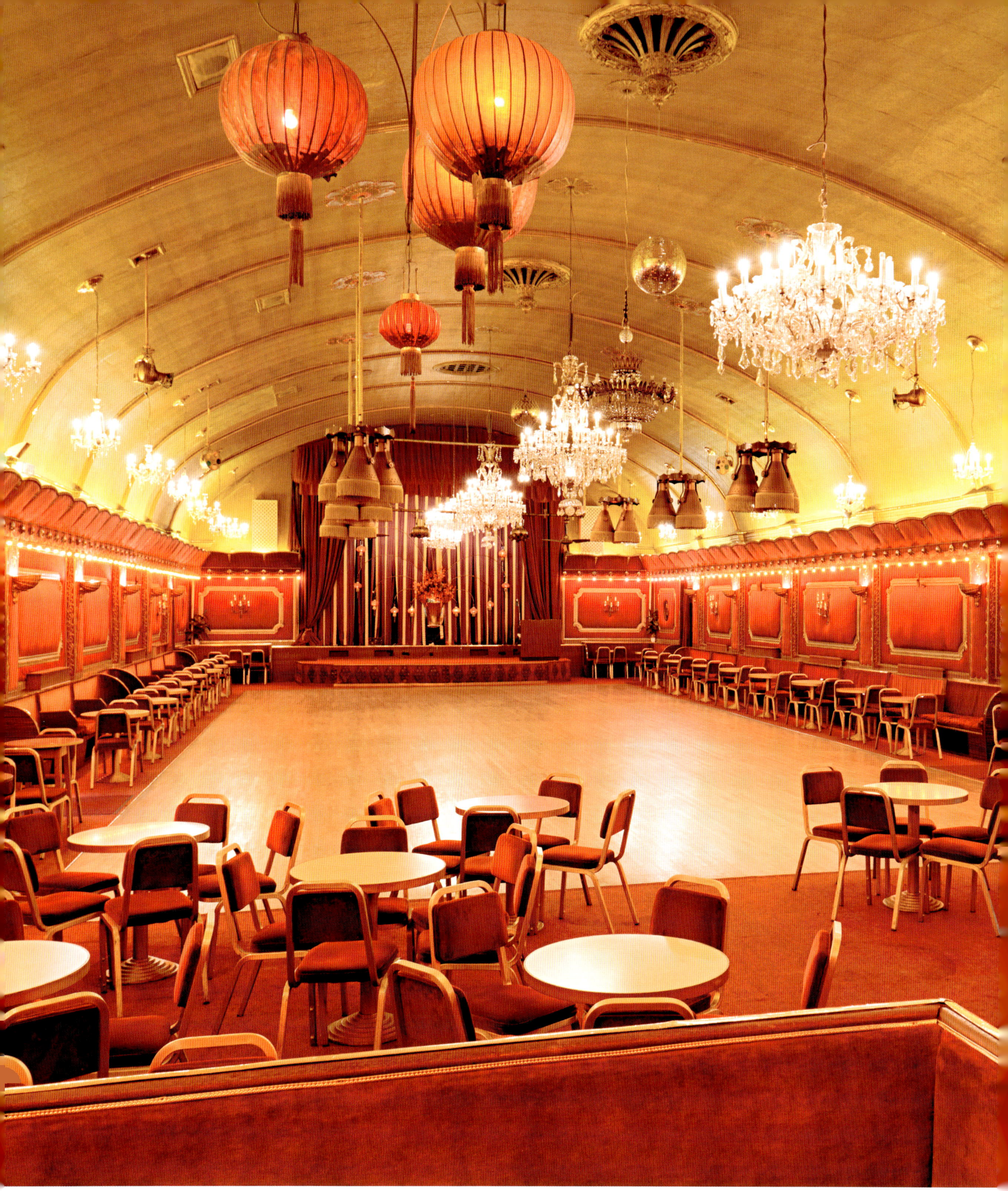

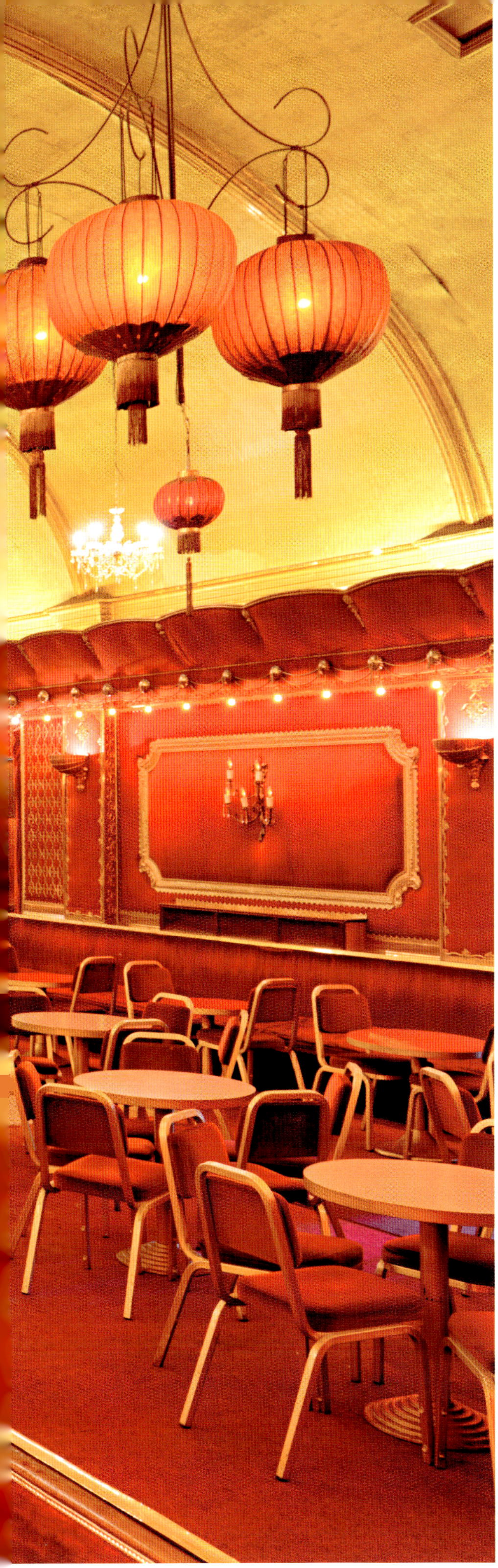

The vaulted ceiling in the ballroom is the only visible legacy of Rivoli's cinema ancestry.

The Rivoli Ballroom

The Rivoli Ballroom is a wonderful anachronism, unveiled at the dawn of the 1960s to evoke the style of an age just passed, and as years have passed its charm has increased.

In the scarlet-and-gilt ballroom there is a riot of influences at work. Illumination is by Chinese lanterns, French chandeliers, glitterballs, candelabra and scallop sconce uplighters. Wall decorations consist of padded red velour panels with pelmets and gilt framing. At the end is a proscenium with a red plush curtain and raised stage for the band; at the opposite side, a raised viewing dais. Banquettes, fixed tables and paired chairs run along each side for couples. The most important feature is the sprung Canadian maple dance floor.

The building started out as the Crofton Park Picture Palace in 1913, a modest cinema typical of its time, built without a balcony and seating 525. In 1931, it was re-named the Rivoli Cinema, a café was installed, and outside a façade was added in Art Deco style, including pilasters topped with plasterwork urns and a raised parapet. The seating capacity was increased to 700 in an extended auditorium.

It remained an independently operated cinema into the 1950s, squeezed by the growth of television and the grip on film distribution held by the ABC and Rank chains, which controlled the latest Hollywood releases. The last picture show for the Rivoli Cinema was an incongruous double bill of *Reach for the Sky* and *The Nat 'King' Cole Musical Story*, shown on 2 March 1957, after which the building was closed for more than two

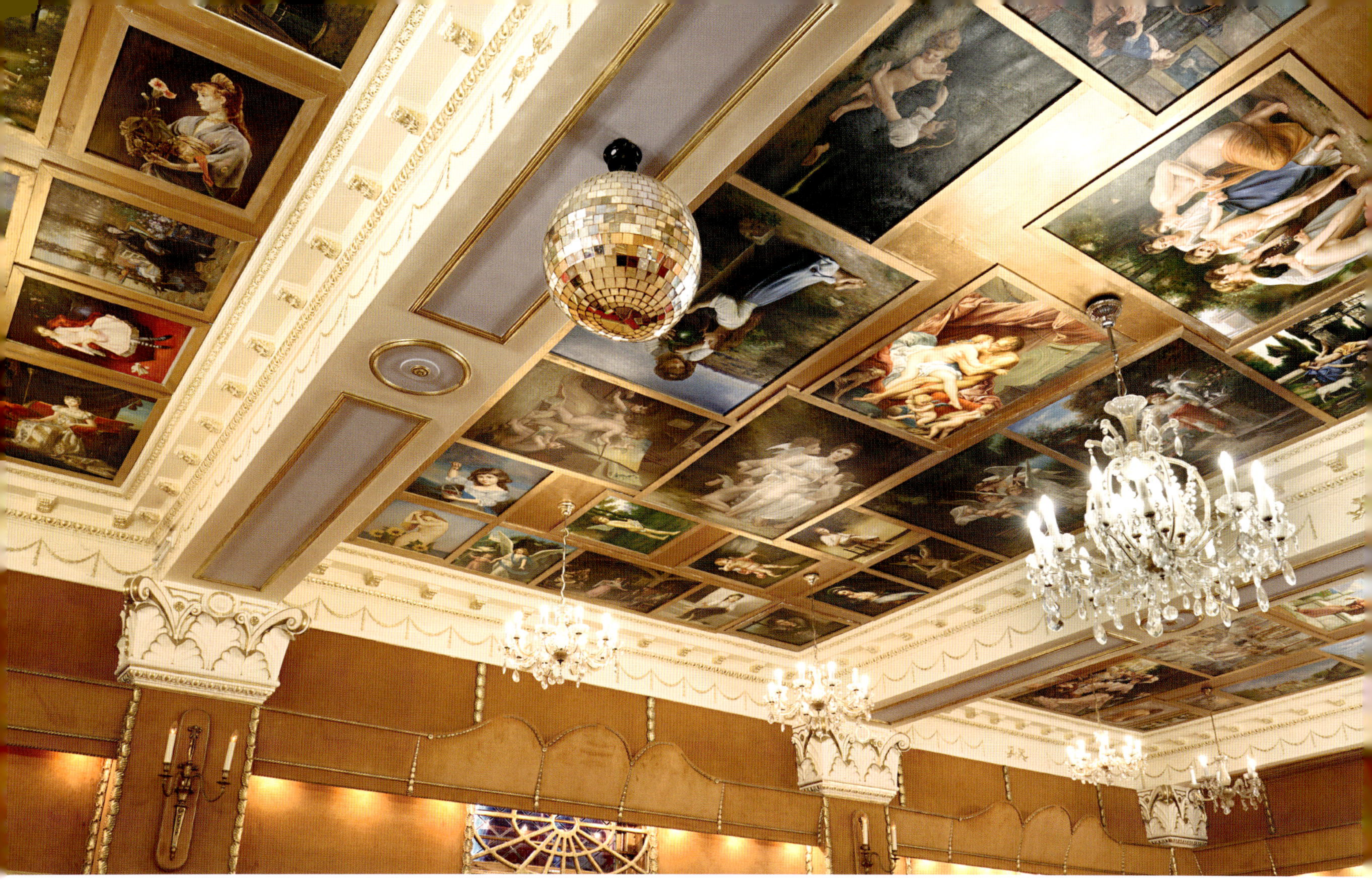

and half years. A local businessman and dance enthusiast named Leonard Tomlin applied to have the cinema converted into a dance hall, and plans were approved by the local authority in September 1958. It opened on Boxing Day 1959.

As revealed then, the Rivoli Ballroom did not conform to one particular style or period, although it certainly harked back to before the Second World War, possibly aiming for the 1920s. It is self-consciously retrospective, and there is signage for the 'Ladies' Powder Room' and the 'Gentlemen's Cloakroom'. The foyer has marquetry panelling with decorated doors. Bars were added on each side of the dance floor, and a second function room seems to date from this time: a neo-classical gold-walled room in Adam style. The ceiling is covered with reproductions of old romantic rococo-style oil paintings.

Producers of music videos have discovered the Rivoli as an atmospheric location. Elton John's 'I Guess That's Why They Call It The Blues' was filmed there in 1983, and the following year part of Tina Turner's *Private Dancer*, setting a trend for more to follow, and also for television commercials and trailers. Scenes for at least six feature films have been shot here, including *Spy Game*, where its bar masquerades as an East Berlin location for Brad Pitt and Robert Redford. It has also been a nightclub for crime film *Legend*, a restaurant in *Muppets Most Wanted* and in *Avengers: Age of Ultron* it appears in a flashback sequence where dancers perform the lindy hop.

In January 2008, the building was Grade II listed by English Heritage, which cited its 'highly unusual interior', the total effect of which is 'luxuriant, exotic and deeply theatrical'.

It served a live music venue for smaller bands through the 1960s and, more recently, for numerous fashion shoots. Ballroom, Latin, salsa and jive dancing continue at the Rivoli. It is tempting to see it as a romantic survivor sustained over time by the elegant art of ballroom. The sign outside the Rivoli still declares 'Dancing Tonight'.

CONTACT INFORMATION

Rivoli Ballroom,
350 Brockley Road, SE4 2BY
https://www.rivoliballroom.com/

Above Chandeliers, disco balls and reproduction oil paintings on the ceiling of the Gold Ballroom.

Opposite, above Red plush continues in the Ladies' Powder Room. The design of intersecting curves seen in the marquetry on the door is continued from the foyer.

Opposite, below The side bar buffet with booths was added during the Rivoli's conversion to a ballroom.

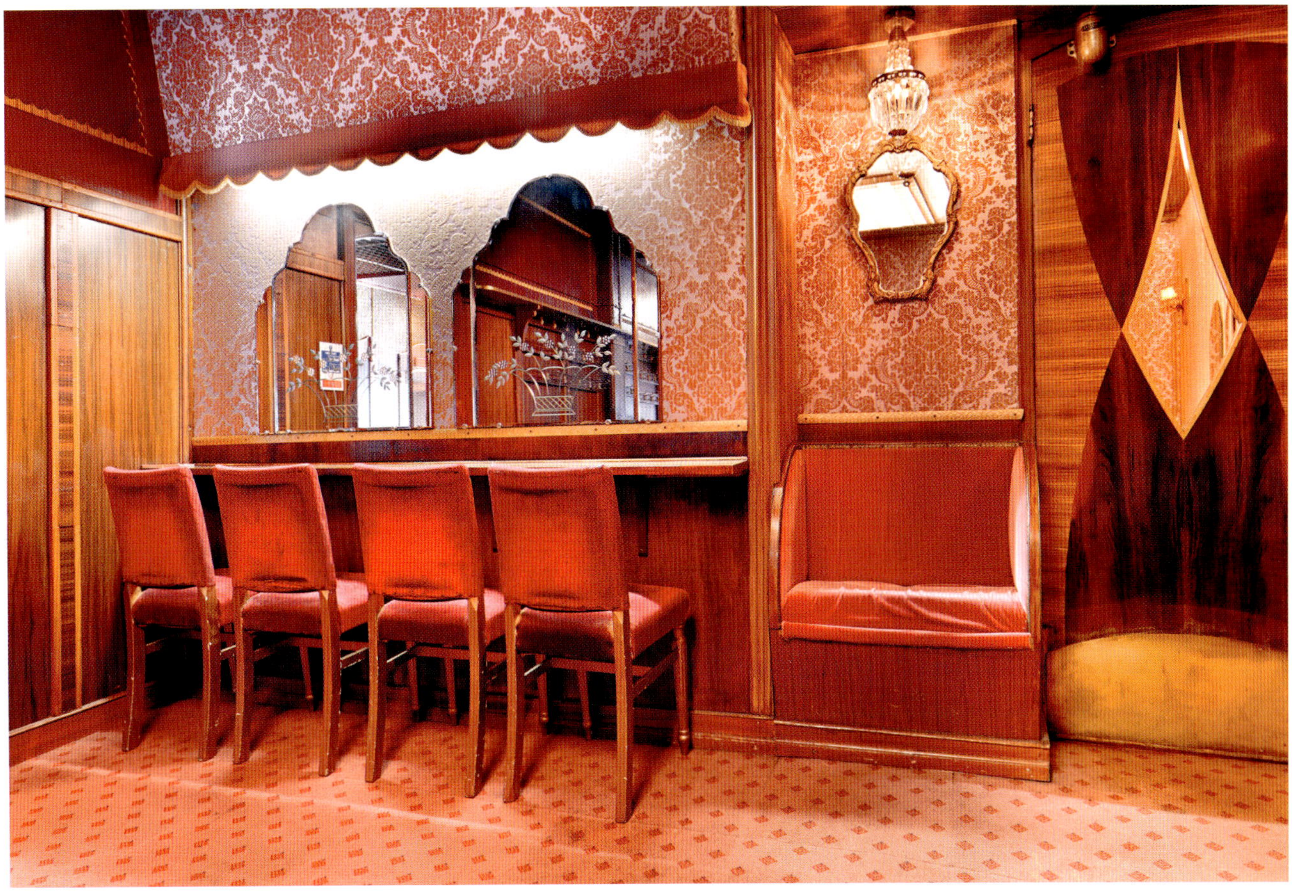

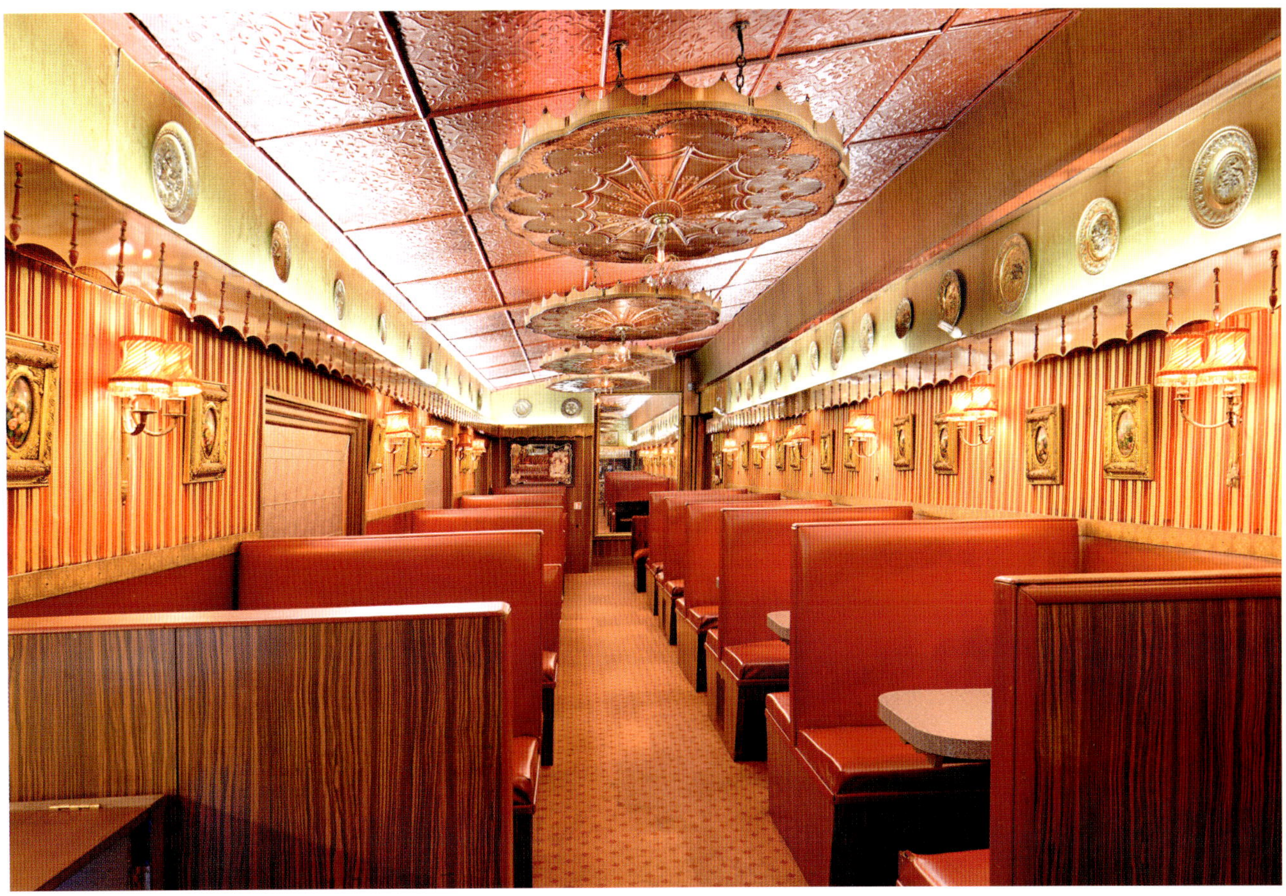

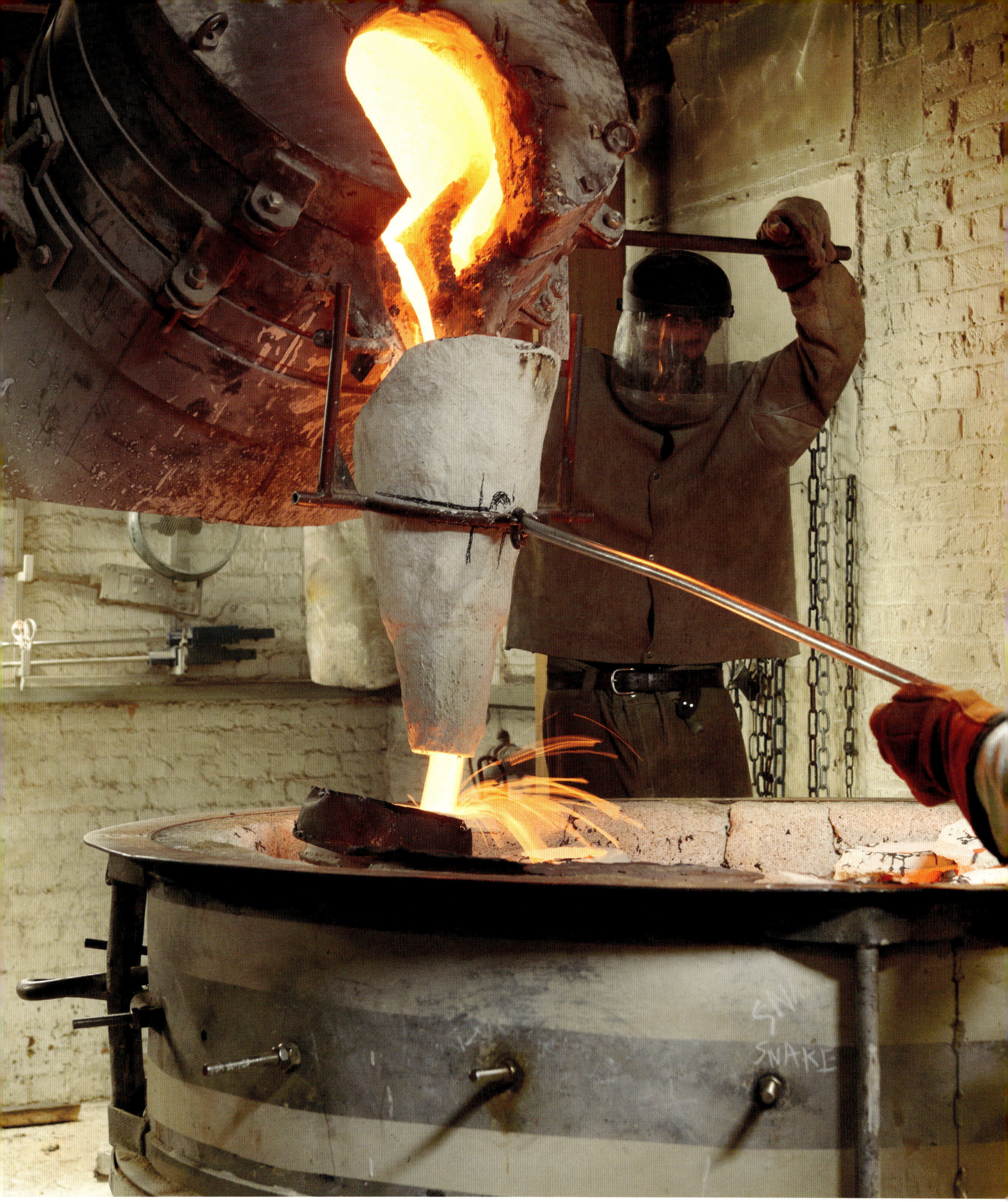
SNAKE

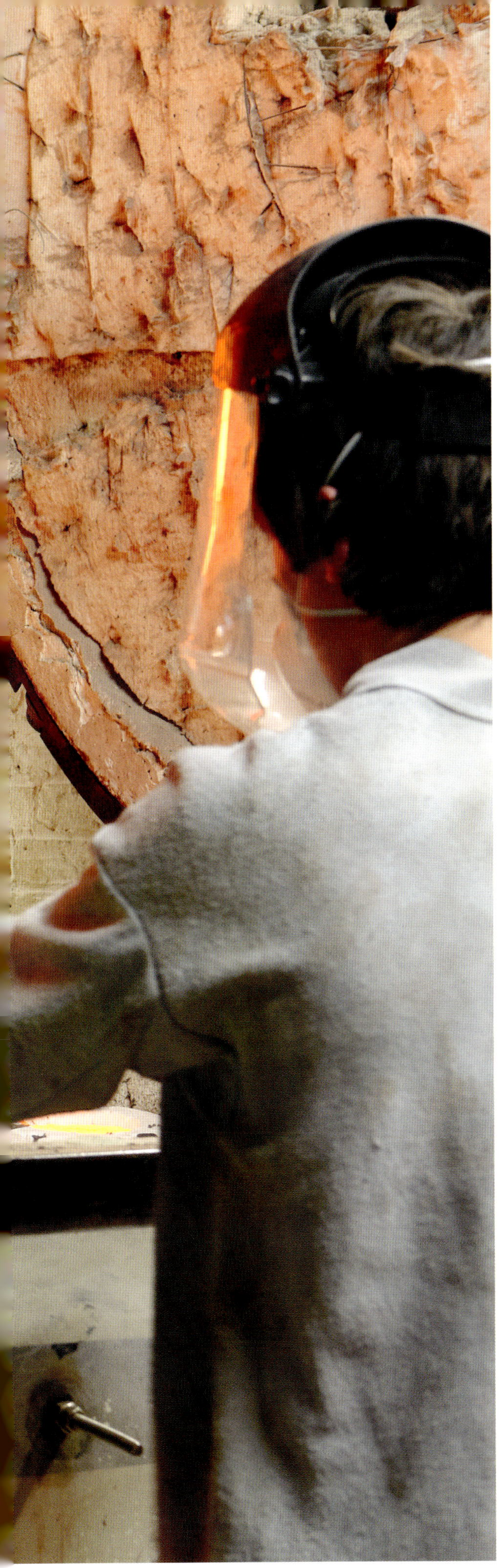

Bronze Age London

The crew pouring molten bronze of 1,170 degrees centigrade into the ceramic shells.

The process of translating statuary into bronze is a specialized craft limited to a handful of practitioners in London, one of the largest and busiest being the Bronze Age sculpture casting foundry in Limehouse. This art foundry set up by the sculptor Mark Kennedy to cast his own work was steadily expanded to offer casting services in bronze and aluminium to other artists and companies for public and private sculptures. It specializes in lost-wax casting of bronze and aluminium and has the capacity to pour and cast a half-tonne of bronze at a time for monumental large sculptures, with separate techniques for pouring small and detailed sculptures and medals. The foundry is in East London's Docklands, close to Canary Wharf.

Bronze Age has worked with over 1,500 artists and statues cast at Limehouse can be seen all over London. A figurative public sculpture in the City – a wall depicting students from Christ's Hospital School – by Andrew Brown is one of the latest from the Bronze Age foundry. At Kings Cross railway station is the bronze statue of Sir Nigel Gresley by Hazel Reeves. At Royal Victoria Dock, outside the ExCel, the three figures comprising the massive *Dockers* statue by Les Johnson is one of the largest sculptures handled by the foundry. Close by, at Canada Square, are two lion sculptures standing at the HSBC headquarters building, which are replicas of two original sculptures at the office in Hong Kong, China. The originals were moulded on site by Bronze

Age and reproduced at Limehouse. More delicate is *The Tree of Life* frieze on the façade of the Whitechapel Gallery by Rachel Whiteread, her first permanent public commission – clusters of leaves cast in bronze and finished in gold leaf. Further afield in Britain are Nigel Boonham's statue of Martin Luther King Jr at Newcastle University, unveiled in 2019, as well as Hazel Reeves' statue of Emmeline Pankhurst, the political activist and leader of the Suffragette movement, in St Peter's Square, Manchester.

In Britain, the method of casting sculpture and statuary in bronze started to develop in early Victorian times. In the 1880s, bronze was coupled to the revival of lost-wax casting, a technique that dated back thousands of years for smaller statues, but was this time being applied to large statues. Lost-wax casting can reproduce intricate detail and make a strong, long-lasting work, although this is achieved by an arduous and time-consuming process. The processes used by Bronze Age have evolved with the introduction of some more modern materials but are based on the following long-established rituals. The first stage is mould-making, which requires the entire surface of the original sculpture to be coated with silicone rubber before resin and fibreglass are added. Detail as fine as a fingerprint can be picked up. The mould is used to make a wax positive, which is hollow, as the final bronze must be. A ceramic shell is made in layers surrounding the wax, incorporating channels for the bronze to flow. The inside cavity of the hollow wax is filled with a plaster-based mixture called Core. When the wax is melted away by a propane burner, the hollow ceramic shell remains. This is placed in a supporting bed of sand, with a cup mounted to receive the molten bronze. Next comes the pour. Bronze ingots are heated to 1,170 degrees centigrade in a crucible and poured through the cup into the void. After cooling overnight, the ceramic shell and feeder system is removed by high-power water-blasting. All that was once wax is now bronze.

For large sculptures cast in sections, fabrication by welding follows. The welds are chased back before a surface finish is applied. The finishing of bronzes by applying a patina is mostly achieved using various combinations of different layers of chemicals with heat. Bronze Age say this is a crucial stage, transforming the casting, enhancing and enriching the sculpture and bringing the sculpture to life.

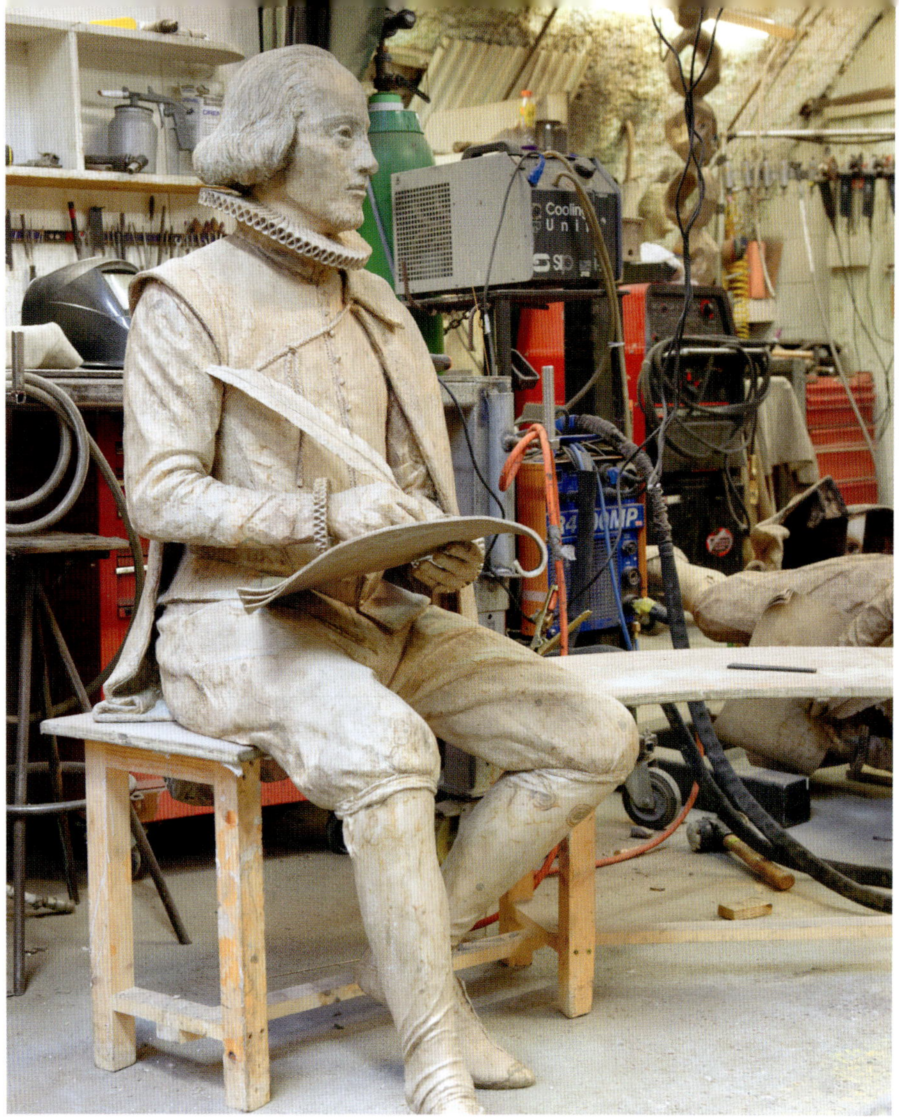

The bronze of William Shakespeare pictured here in the metal workshop at the foundry is a collaboration between Raphael Maklouf and Hayley Gibbs for a new building and exhibition space on an historic site at Shoreditch, where a theatre dating from 1576 existed. Another noted literary figure memorialized in bronze is Agatha Christie by Ben Twiston-Davies in Covent Garden.

Tours of the Bronze Age foundry can be made by booking in advance.

Above This completed bronze of Shakespeare, pictured here in the metal workshop, is courtesy of Raphael Maklouf, Hayley Gibbs and the Belvedere Trust.

Opposite Moulds being cleaned and prepared for use in the wax room (above); the ceramic shell department (below).

CONTACT INFORMATION

Bronze Age London,
Gallery Building, Basin Approach, Limehouse, E14 7JG
https://www.bronzeage.co.uk/

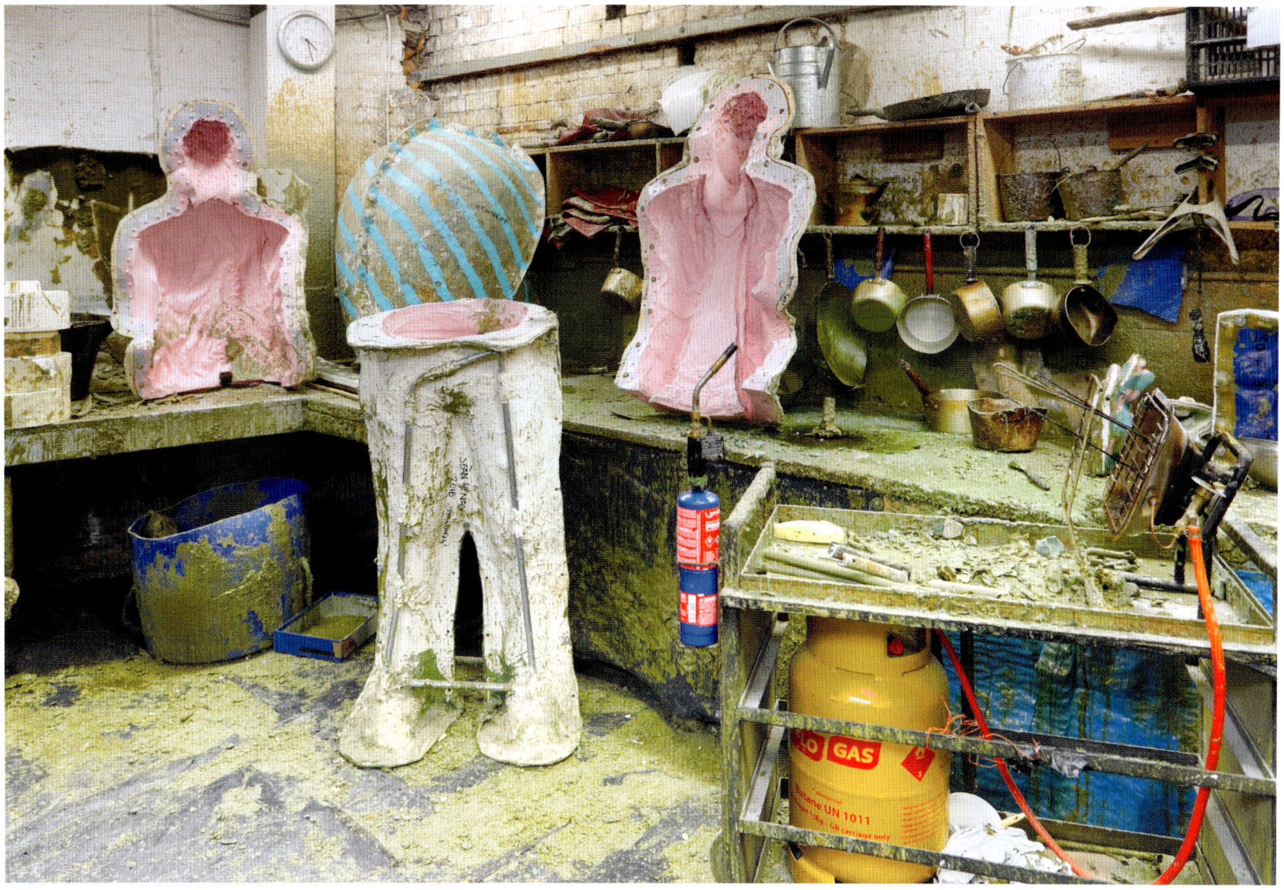
GAS
Butane UN 1011

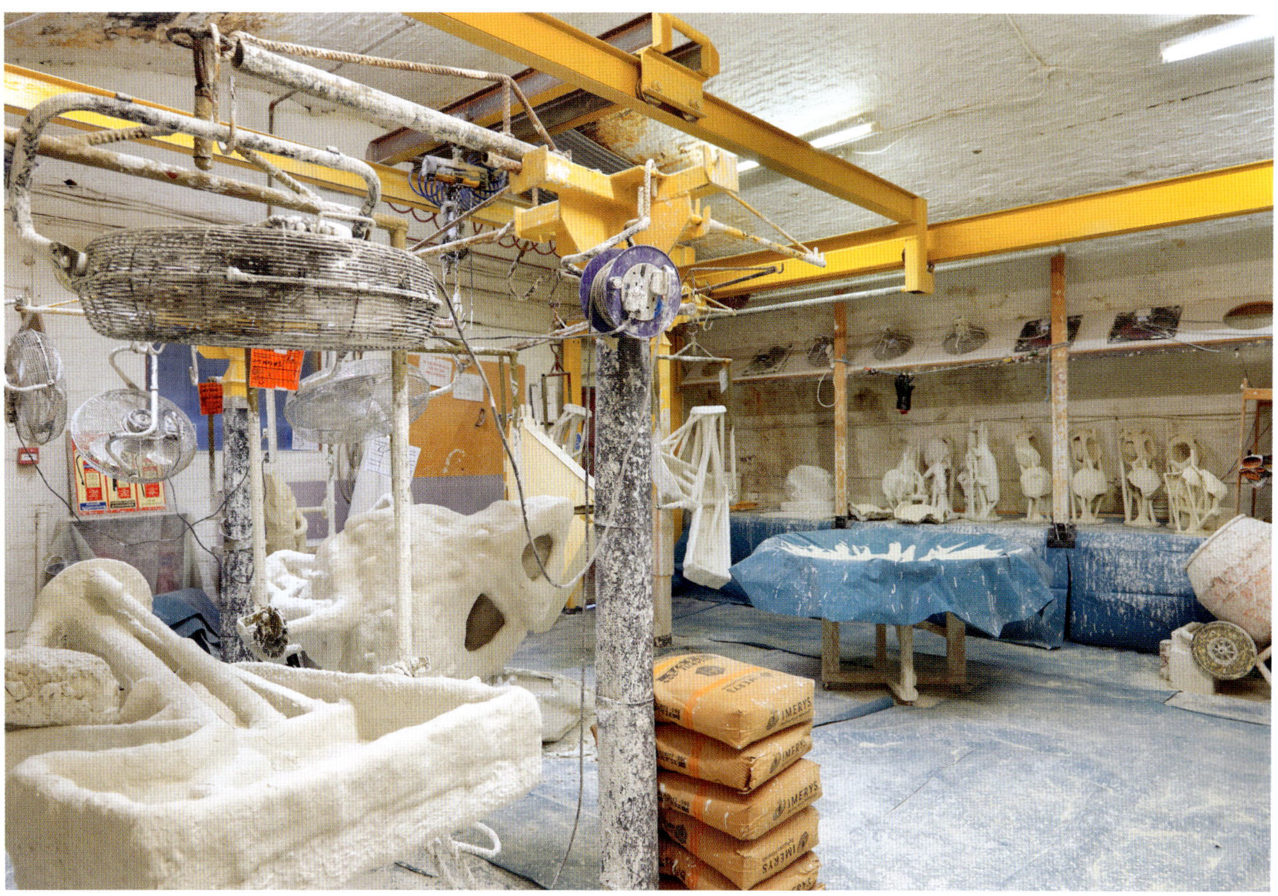
IMERYS

Southside House

Eccentric, enchanting and charming are the words most often used to describe Southside House, an old, much-reworked Tudor-Georgian residence on a corner of Wimbledon Common. Its rooms house whimsical collections and its garden carries a series of curiosities.

The origins of the house are obscure, possibly based on the amalgamation of a country manor house and a Tudor farmhouse lodge by Robert Pennington, a legal clerk of the Court of Chancery, who wanted to escape the London plague epidemics in the 1600s. The building was further developed in the 1750s with the addition of a wing and a combining frontage of brick façade. The result is a house that has a unified front with a central doorway under a clock tower and a rear aspect that resembles two or three houses joined together. Inside is a collection of family possessions reflecting the history of the house, and possibly some legends.

A descendant of Pennington, Hilda Pennington Mellor, married the Swedish-born writer Dr Axel Munthe, author of *The Story of San Michele*, the sometimes fanciful biography, which became a bestseller in the 1930s. Their youngest son was Malcolm Munthe, who as a British Army liaison officer and Special Operations Executive representative, served during the Second World War in Finland, Norway and Sweden and later in Italy. Major Malcolm Munthe resolved to restore the bomb-damaged Southside House, incorporating his family history. The highly personal result has been described by a curator of Southside House as a 'psychological landscape'.

The entrance hall.

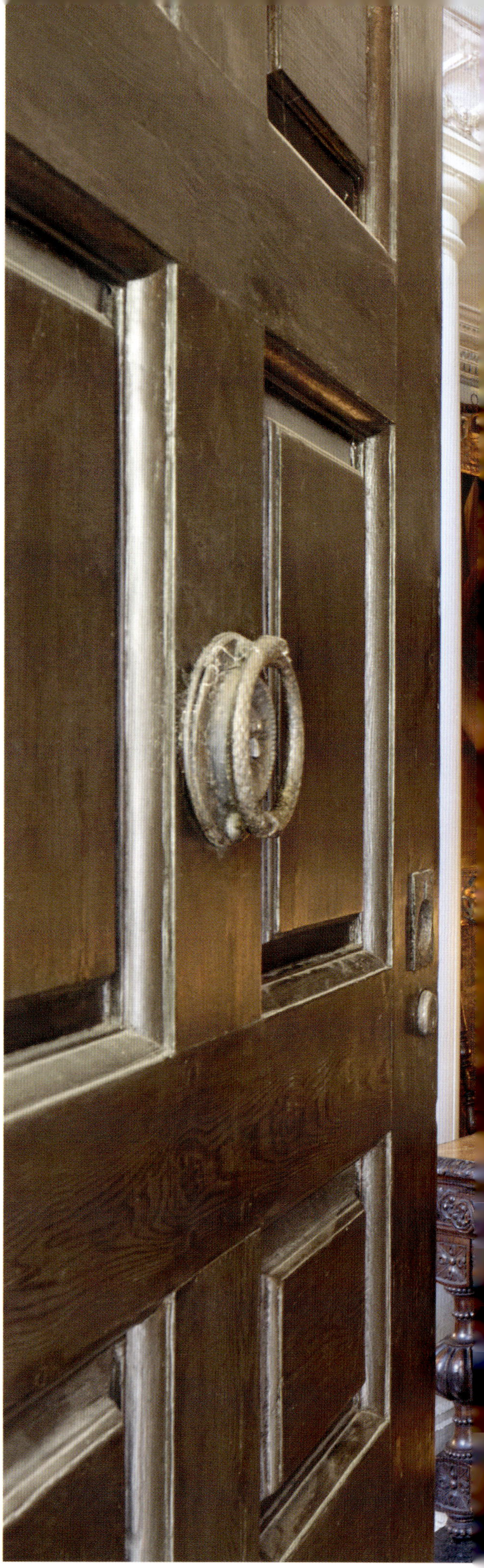

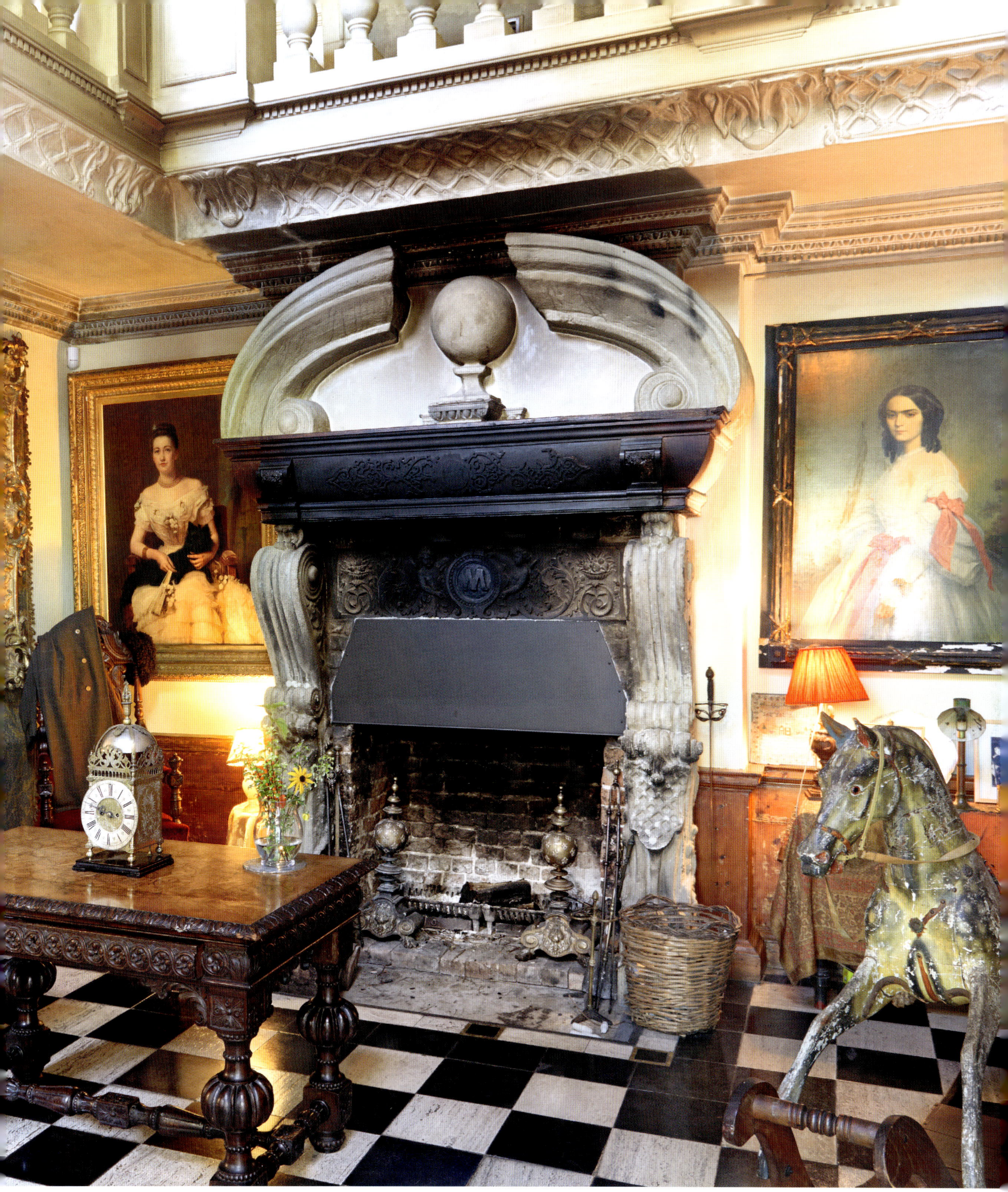

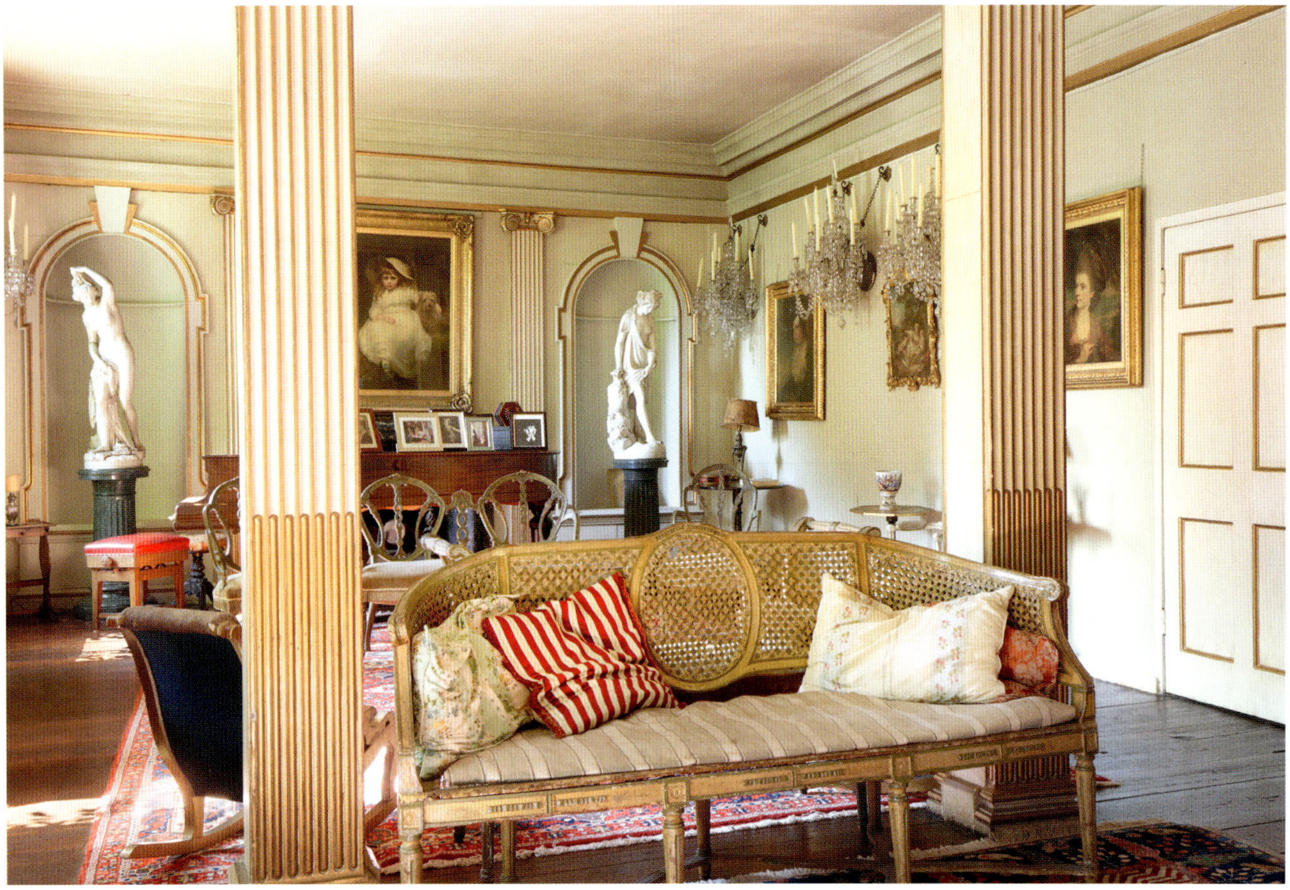

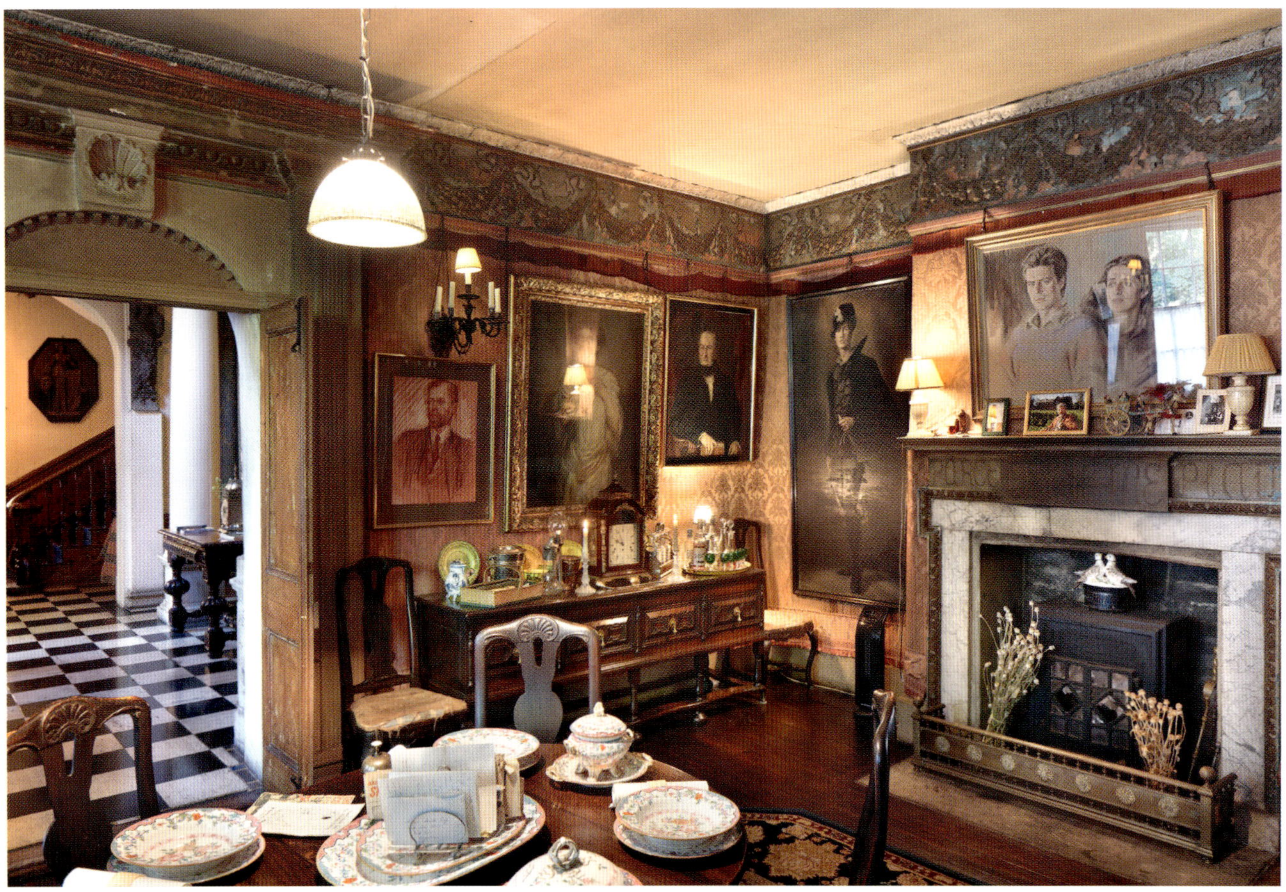

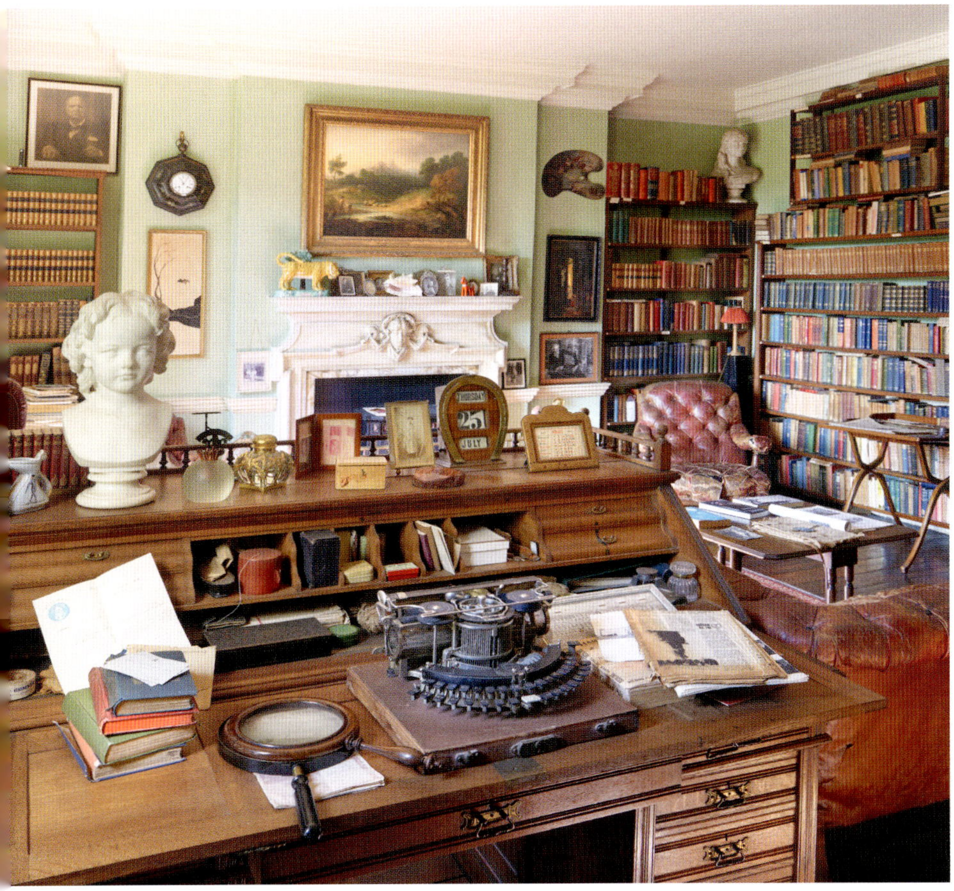

Opposite, above The atmospheric music room is still used for a variety of musical events.

Opposite, below The ornately decorated breakfast room.

Above The library, which houses a writing desk and a rare circular Hammond typewriter.

The scope of the post-war refurbishment was limited by the money available and the result is not a shining example of restored surfaces, but a collection of pictures, mementos and furnishings making associations with history. Some of the pieces come from the family's home in Biarritz, south of France, including paintings, chandeliers and some statuary. Southside House was first opened to visitors in 1982.

A visitor enters Southside House from the rear through the garden hall, which has traces of faux windows in the technique called *trompe l'oeil* and walls hung with family portraits. The old rocking horse which stands here once belonged to Horatia, daughter of Lord Nelson and Lady Hamilton. Lord Nelson, Sir William Hamilton and Lady Hamilton were guests of John Pennington at Southside when they were living at nearby Merton Place. Lady Emma Hamilton, it is claimed, performed attitudes – choreographed poses in imitation of shapes in classical artworks - in the music room. The room has a portrait of Emma Hamilton and the table where they all played cards.

Earlier, Frederick, Prince of Wales, is said to have stayed at Southside House after attending a military review on the Common in 1750. The recreated room is decorated with yellow silk wallhangings and a bed with scarlet headboard and embroidered Prince of Wales' feathers in silver thread. Some accounts say this bedhead refers to a later Prince of Wales, Edward VII, who visited the Pennington home in Biarritz. A display case contains what is reputed to be a string of pearls worn by Marie Antoinette on the day of her execution, presented to a member of the Pennington family by Empress Joséphine. There are other precious objects including an emerald and gold ring, gifted to Hilda Pennington by the former Queen Natalie of Serbia. Hilda had been courted as a teenager by Alexander I of Serbia, and his mother Natalie, hearing of her impending marriage to Axel Munthe, presented her with some of her then late son's heirlooms.

The library is furnished in a later style with items including busts, books, a rare circular Hammond typewriter from the nineteenth century and somewhere there is said to be a painter's palette belonging to Sir Joshua Reynolds.

One of the strangest legacies of Southside House is not on display – a stash of weapons discovered under the dining room in 2011. After a fire the previous year, clean-up work uncovered steps under the hearthstone to a room containing a chest. Inside were found a Sten submachine gun and .45 automatic Colt pistol, magazines for the M1 Garand rifle and some rounds of ammunition. The weapons, which were removed by police officers, were believed to have been hidden by Malcolm Munthe, who died in 1995. The arms cache has never been explained.

Behind the house, the garden is spread over almost 2 acres (a hectare) and was once occupied by wartime allotments. Restored, again by Malcolm Munthe, there are few flowers but a shell grotto, an orchard, grassy pathways, box hedges, a stream enclosing an island and two classical temples, all in a landscape that is rather wild in places.

Southside House has served as a backdrop in several films, including *Mr Turner*, *The Invisible Woman* and *Gormenghast*. It is run by the Pennington-Mellor-Munthe Charity Trust and hosts tours during part of the year.

CONTACT INFORMATION

Southside House,
3–4 Woodhayes Road, Wimbledon, SW19 4RJ

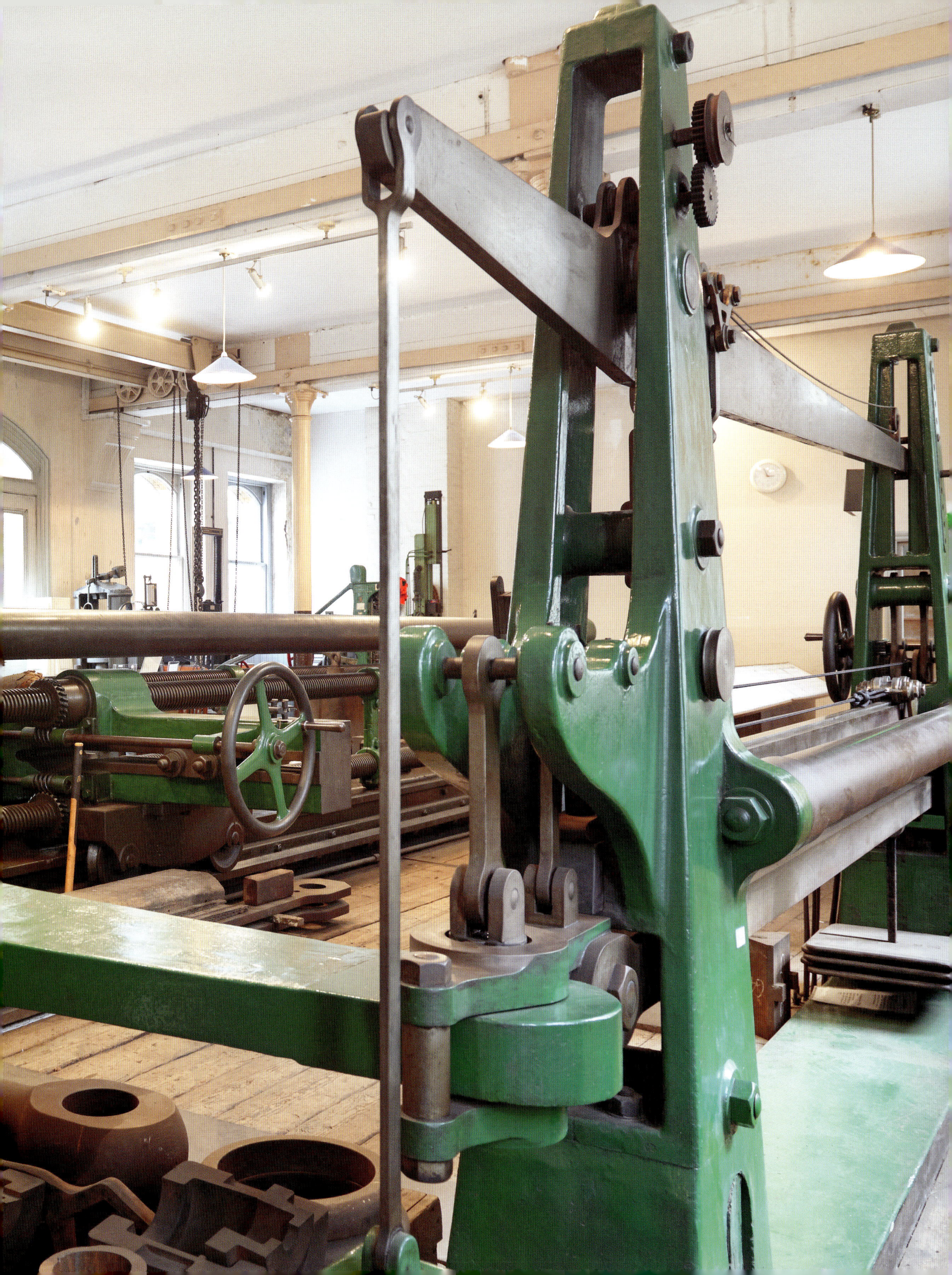

Kirkaldy's Testing Works

Most of the ground floor in the Kirkaldy Testing Works is filled by the Universal Testing machine.

Over the doorway of 99 Southwark Street, the legend 'Facts Not Opinions' is carved in stone, the rigorous motto of Scottish engineer David Kirkaldy. Inside is a colossal machine, which is a monument to the first age of scientific materials testing. In full working order, the Kirkaldy Universal Testing machine is a unique technological survivor.

David Kirkaldy gained expertise in the design and testing of boilers and other marine machinery as chief draughtsman at Glasgow engineers Robert Napier & Sons. In 1861, he left the company and devoted the next two years to the design and patenting of a large-scale testing machine. Greenwood & Batley of Leeds were commissioned to construct it. More than 47 ft (14 m) long and weighing 118 tonnes, it was delivered by rail to London in 1865.

The machine is a fixed hydraulic cylinder housing a ram, which drives a carriage exerting load on the test specimens. It was described as capable of pulling, thrusting, twisting, shearing, punching and bulging. Power came from the high-pressure water main of the London Hydraulic Power Company, with the addition of a booster installed inside the works. Kirkaldy claimed that the machine could exert forces up to 450 tonnes.

In the first Industrial Revolution, engineering had swiftly shifted from the era of wood, stone and rope to cast- and wrought-iron and then steel.

With this came an often-imperfect understanding of the qualities of the materials. Kirkaldy established the first independent commercial testing house. The machine tested many samples salvaged from the Tay Bridge disaster, and the strengthening links for Albert Bridge and for Hammersmith Bridge, when more than 150 pieces were tested to failure. The world's first major steel bridge, constructed at St Louis in 1874, depended on Kirkaldy testing. German steelmaker Alfred Krupp was a customer, and later components for Wembley Stadium and parts of the framework for Sydney Harbour Bridge were tested. A machine for testing marine chains was installed in the basement, and another for concrete testing by crushing.

The precise occasion when the mighty machine made its last operational commercial test has not been recorded, although Kirkaldy tested the suspension cables for the Skylon sculpture created for the Festival of Britain in 1951 and the works operated until 1974. Preservationists established a museum in 1983. Now the Kirkaldy museum houses a wide collection of testing machines.

CONTACT INFORMATION

Kirkaldy's Testing Works,
99 Southwark Street, SE1 0JF
https://www.testingworks.org.uk/

The Kia Oval

Many visitors to this historic ground approach from the Oval tube station and enter through the tall black gates which are a reminder that this is both a test match venue and the home of Surrey County Cricket Club (Surrey CCC).

The gate posts are topped with urns, commemorating the 'death of English cricket' when England was defeated by Australia in a test match played here in August 1882, the first time England had lost at home. These are the Hobbs Gates, which commemorate the great Surrey batsman, Sir John Hobbs, better known as Jack Hobbs, who scored more than 60,000 runs and 199 first-class centuries in first-class cricket, more than any other cricketer of any era.

Beyond the gates is the impressive Micky Stewart Members' Pavilion. This imposing structure also incorporates the urn design as well as giant pictures of Surrey greats – in 2020, it was Surrey and England opener Rory Burns and Surrey Women and England all-rounder Natalie Sciver-Brunt.

The Oval is loaded with references to Surrey CCC players of today and of the past. Micky Stewart is a Surrey legend, as is his son, Alec, both gifted batsmen who played many tests for England as well as their county. The ground's stands and gates bear the names of other Surrey legends – such as the Bedser Stand, the Peter May Stand and the John Edrich Gate.

Also much in evidence around the ground are the Prince of Wales Feathers, important because the land

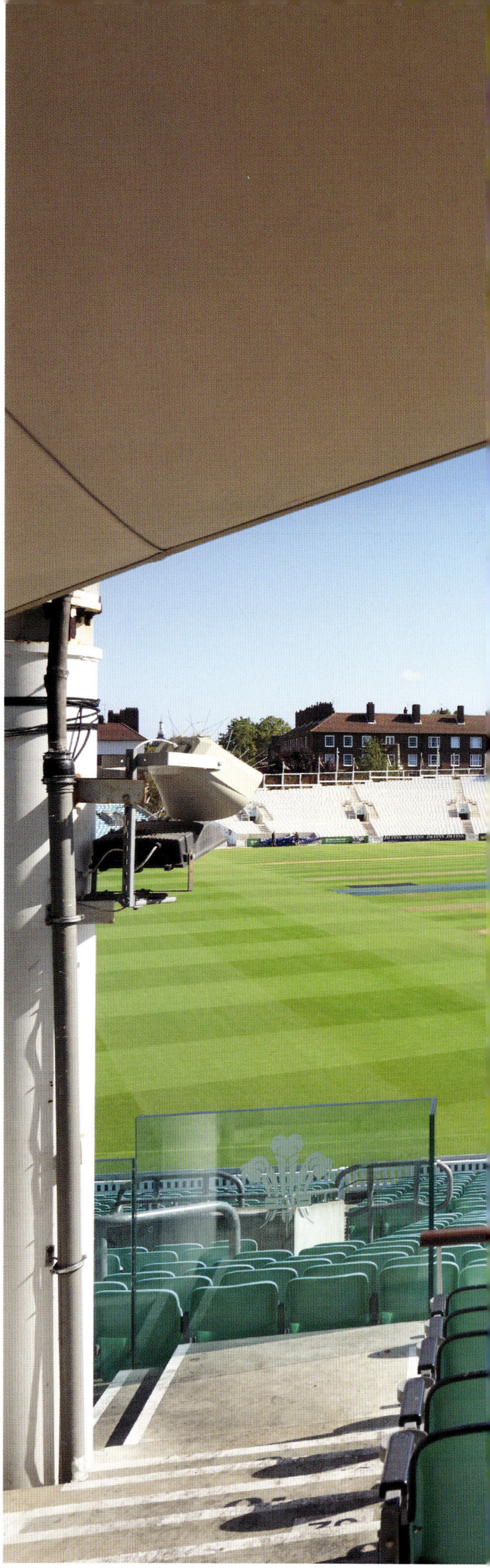

A view of the Pavilion from the stands.

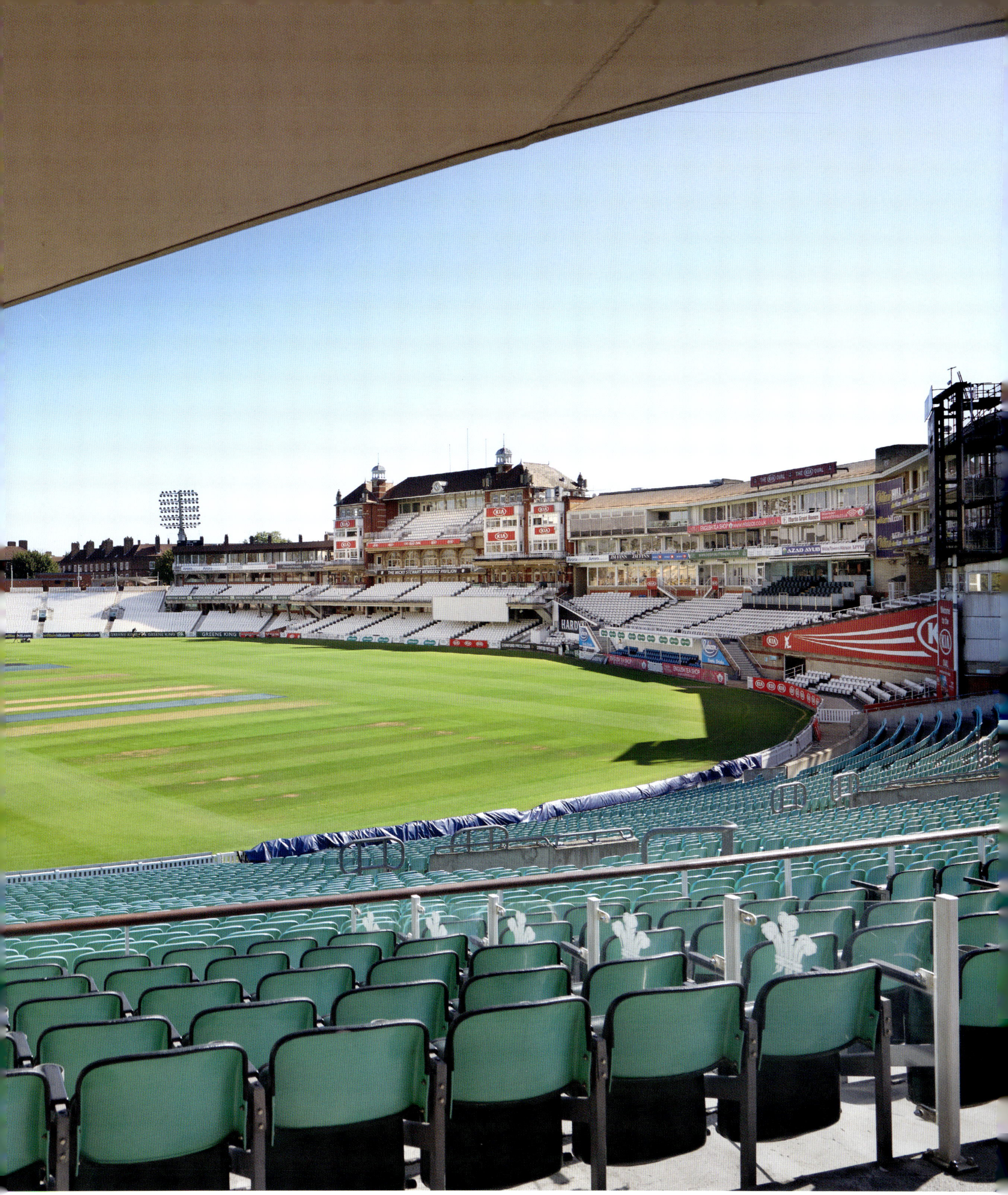

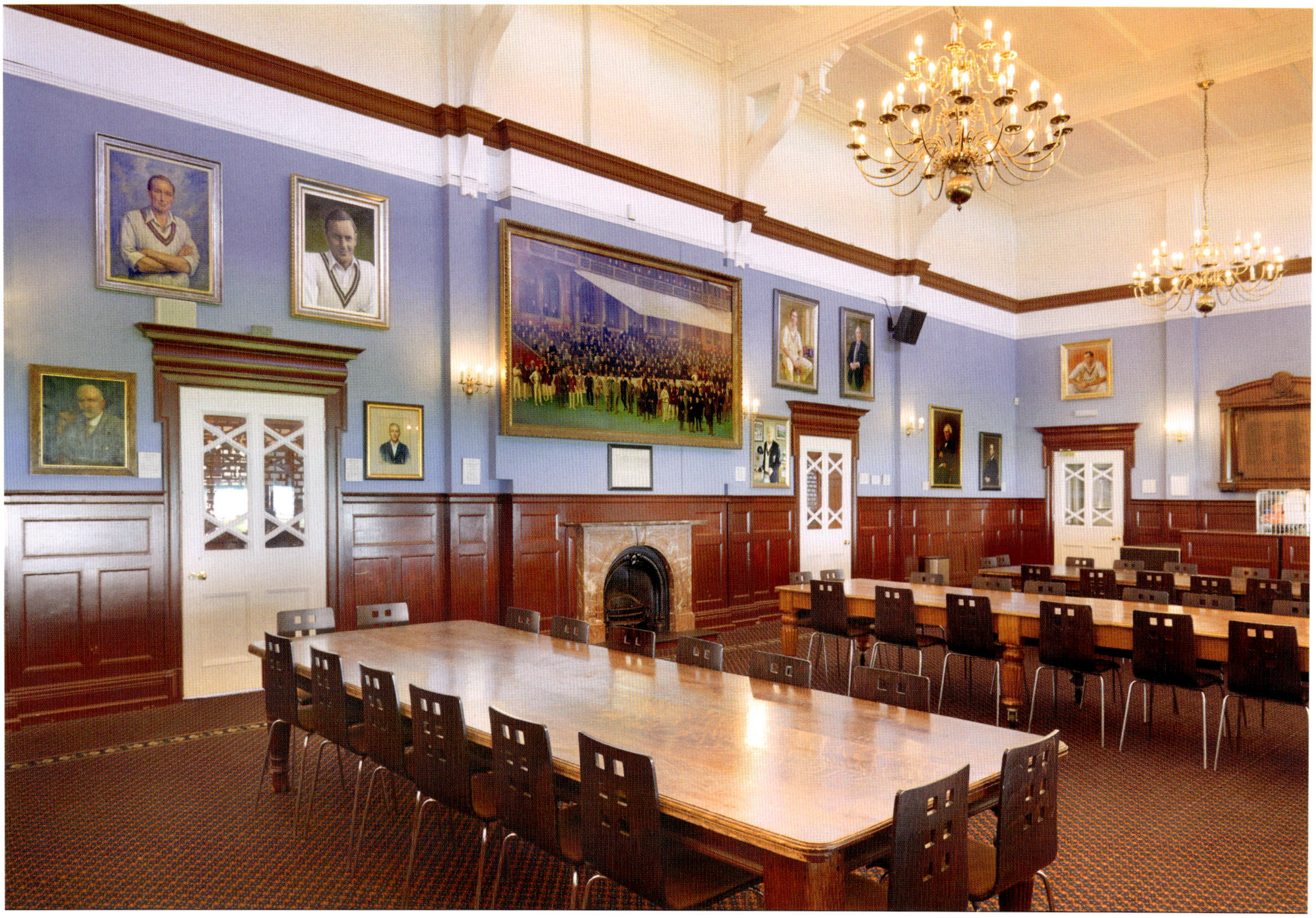

The famous Long Room in the Pavilion, which dates from 1898.

is owned by the Duchy of Cornwall and the connection with the business remains close. The Feathers form part of the Surrey CCC badge. The land was originally occupied by a market garden enclosed by an oval roadway, the same footprint that exists today.

Large panels on the inner wall on one side of the ground commemorate Surrey CCC player records and County Championship wins; the county's heyday was in the 1950s when it won seven consecutive county titles between 1952 and 1958, but it first won the County Championship back in 1890 and the Oval has been home to Surrey CCC since 1845.

The playing surface was believed to be the largest in England until the Rose Bowl replaced Hampshire's old County Ground in 2001. At the other end of the ground from the Pavilion is the OCS Stand, renamed the 1845 Stand in 2019, a much newer design.

For years its capacity was a little over 25,000, increasing to 28,000 in the 2020s. The One Oval Square development will see the Members' Pavilion extended and more space introduced above the Peter May Stand.

The Oval is unique in many ways. As well as its cricket history – it was the first ground in England to hold an international cricket match, for example (in 1880, versus Australia) – there is no other ground that has also hosted an FA Cup final. This was the first ever FA Cup final, played there in 1872. It can also claim the first international Rugby Union match to be held in England, played between England and Scotland in the same year.

That breadth of sporting coverage was largely the result of efforts by Charles Alcock, the first paid secretary of SCCC and a founding father of the Football Association. As well as having a room

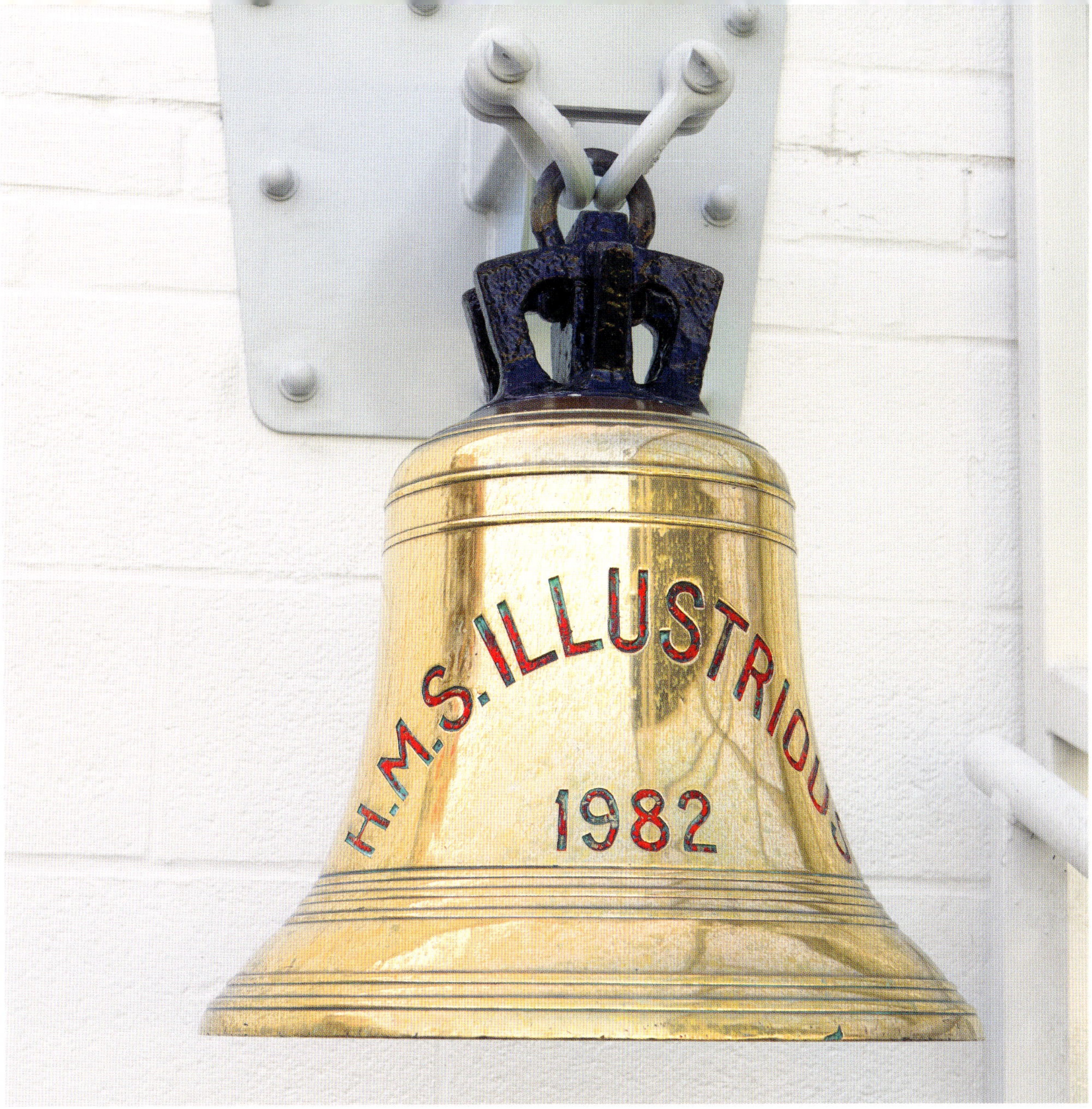

The bell was acquired from the decommissioned aircraft carrier HMS *Illustrious*. The bell is rung five minutes before the start of play on each day of a test match.

in the Pavilion named after him, there are more pictures of Alcock in the ground than of anyone else.

Also in the Pavilion is the Oval's Long Room, perhaps not as famous as its Lord's equivalent, and certainly without the formal dress code, but steeped in history. It dates from 1898.

A feature of the Kia Oval well known to any Surrey CCC member is its museum. As well as numerous bats, gloves and artefacts, autographed by leading cricketers who have played at the ground over the years, there are rare exhibits including the 'Chitty Bat', thought to be the first-ever cricket bat, a chain that was used to mark out the 22-yard wicket and an extensive cricketing library that includes two rare full sets of the *Wisden Cricketer's Almanack*, the Bible of cricket.

Another idiosyncrasy is the bell from the former Royal Navy aircraft carrier HMS *Illustrious*, which was put in place in late 2019 and is used to give the five-minute warning before play.

Finally, around the ground are scenes to which the TV cameras frequently pan when looking for context to their Oval coverage. The famous gas holder (gasometer) just outside the Oval, originally one of six, is a familiar sight to any Surrey or England cricket fan. It has been scheduled to be taken down to allow houses to be built but, because it is Grade II listed, it will then be rebuilt around the newly constructed housing development.

CONTACT INFORMATION

The Kia Oval,
Surrey County Cricket Club, Kennington, SE11 5SS
https://www.kiaoval.com/

LASSCO, Brunswick House

Brunswick House is the headquarters and flagship of LASSCO, the London Architectural Salvage and Supply Company. It is a 250-year-old mansion surviving as an island outpost in Vauxhall beside towering apartment blocks, a supermarket and one of the busiest and widest gyratory traffic systems in London. Its rooms contain hundreds of pieces salvaged from old buildings; chimneypieces and firegrates, doors, and street signs and lamp posts. Passengers riding on buses passing LASSCO can glimpse Italian statues in the courtyard and chandeliers in the upper rooms.

LASSCO Brunswick House serves different purposes. Some of its spaces are rooms made up into display areas for antiques, clocks and chandeliers, and furniture. Eclectic, sometimes eccentric and not always antique, there might be found at any one time a life-sized cutout of Tony Curtis from a cinema foyer alongside a delicate wirework birdcage. Ionic columns in imitation of the rarest of marbles stand salvaged from the unfinished conversion of Park Lane Playboy Club to a millionaire's residence.

Each room is minimally restored. There is a roof terrace and courtyards with statuary, fountains and garden curiosities. Other places – the saloon, smoking room, study parlour, library and cellar – may be hired for receptions and meetings. Throughout, nearly everything on display is for sale. Also in business at Brunswick House is a restaurant and bar.

A typically eclectic display room at LASSCO, including marble columns recovered from an old house in St James's, a pair of painted wooden columns from a fairground ride, an English Rococo Revival white Carrara marble chimneypiece and glass-and-gilt chandeliers.

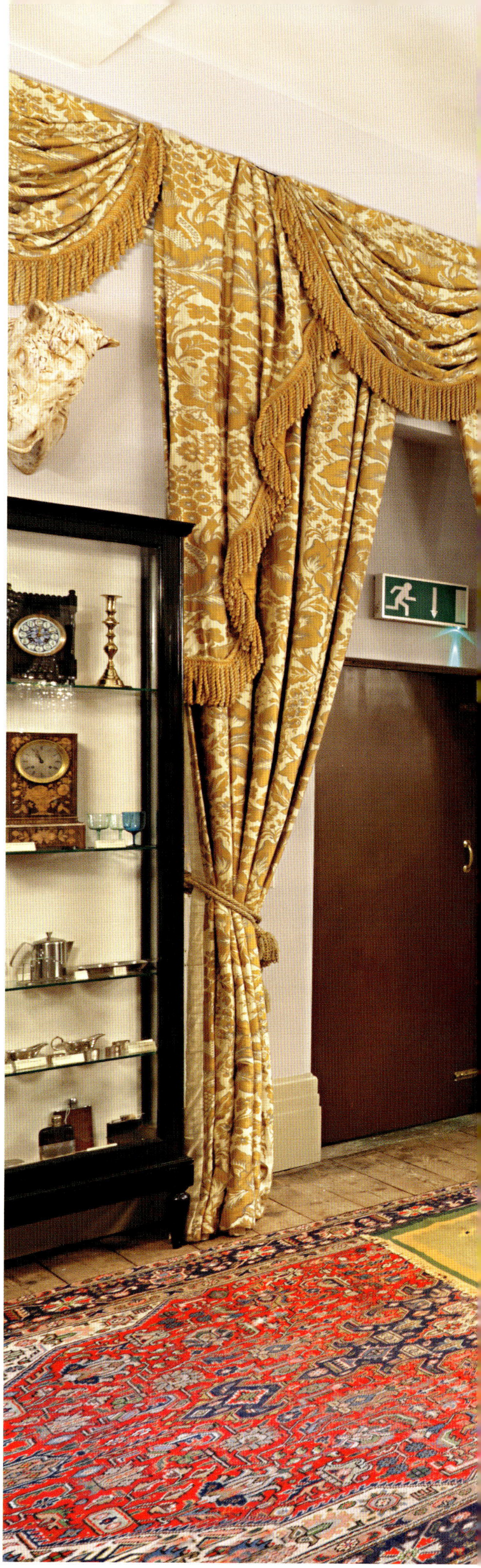

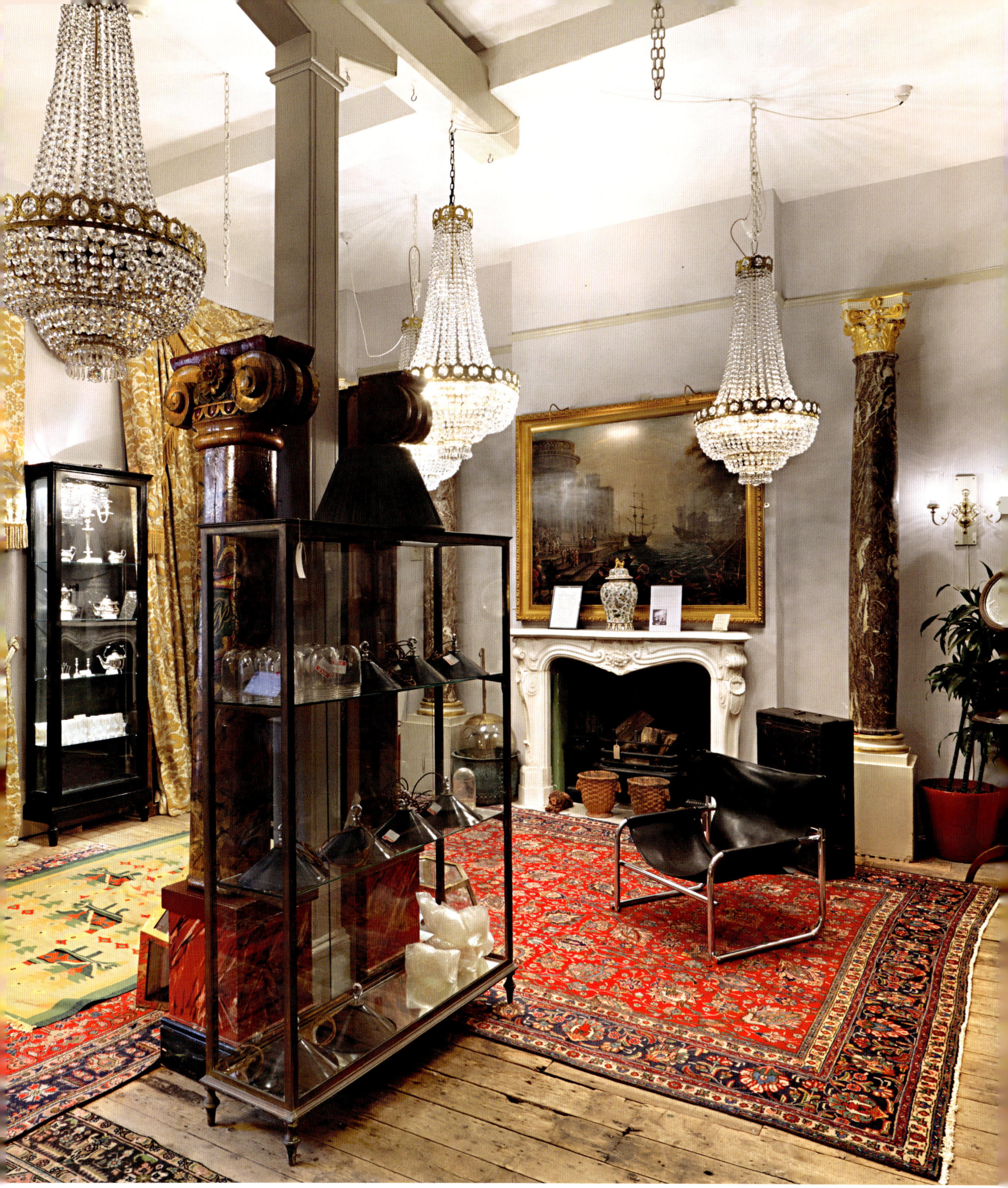

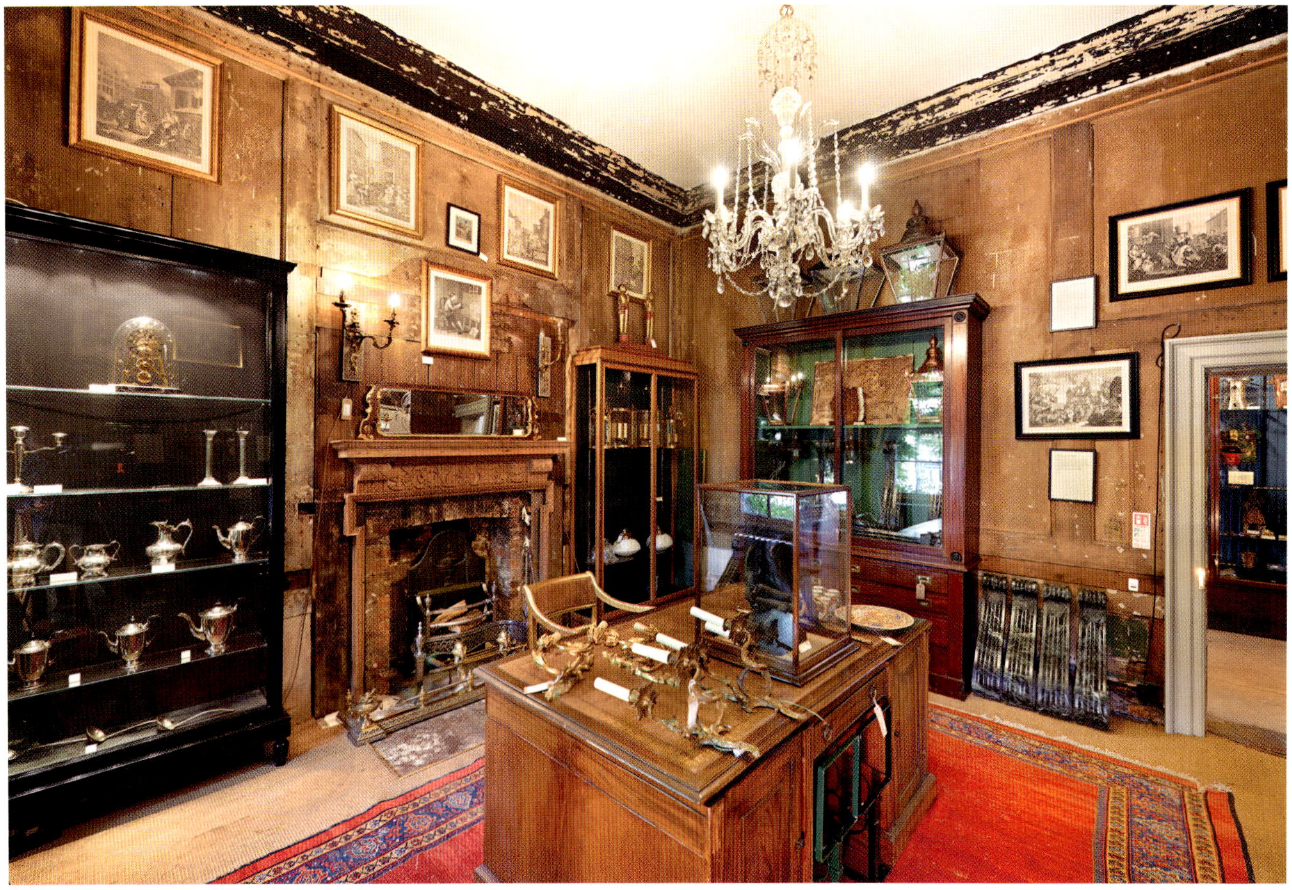

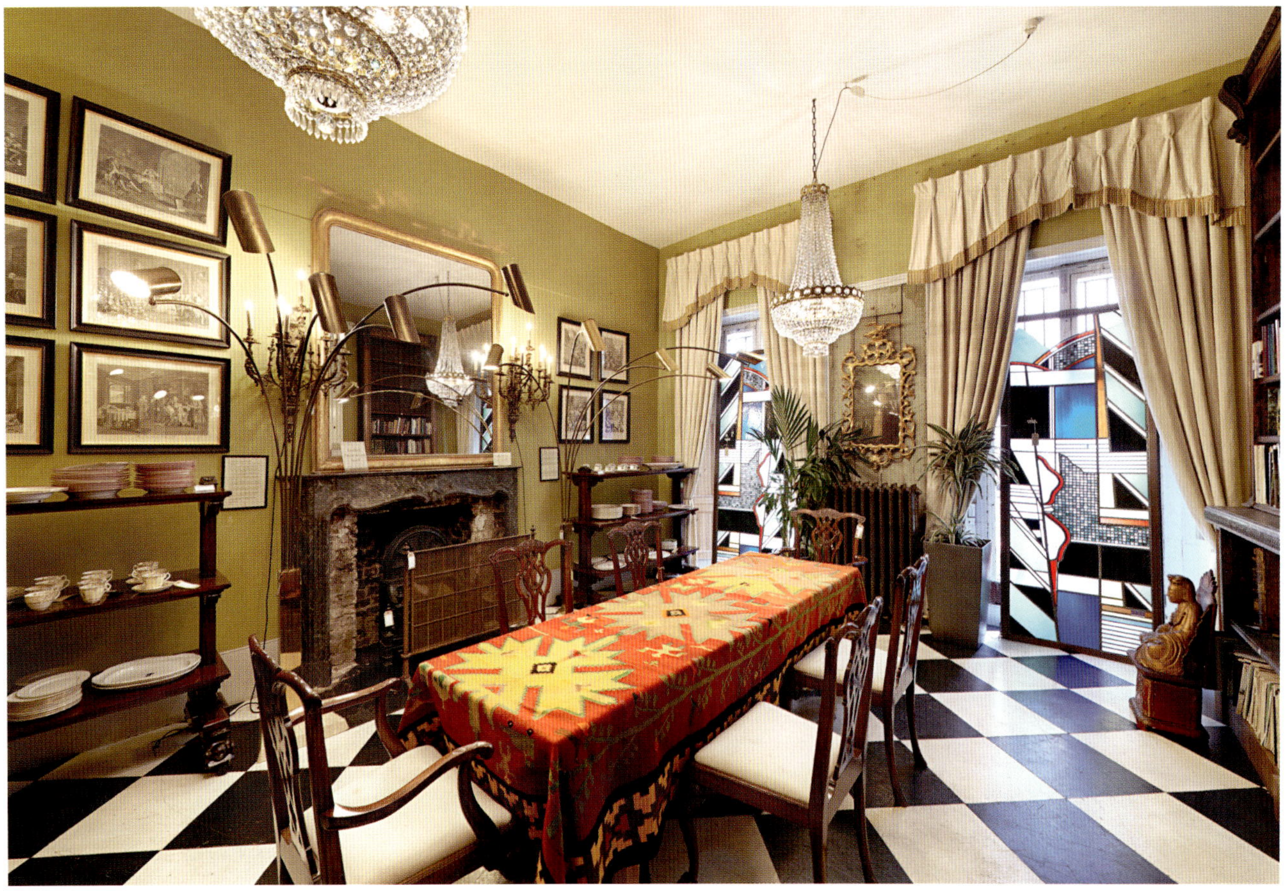

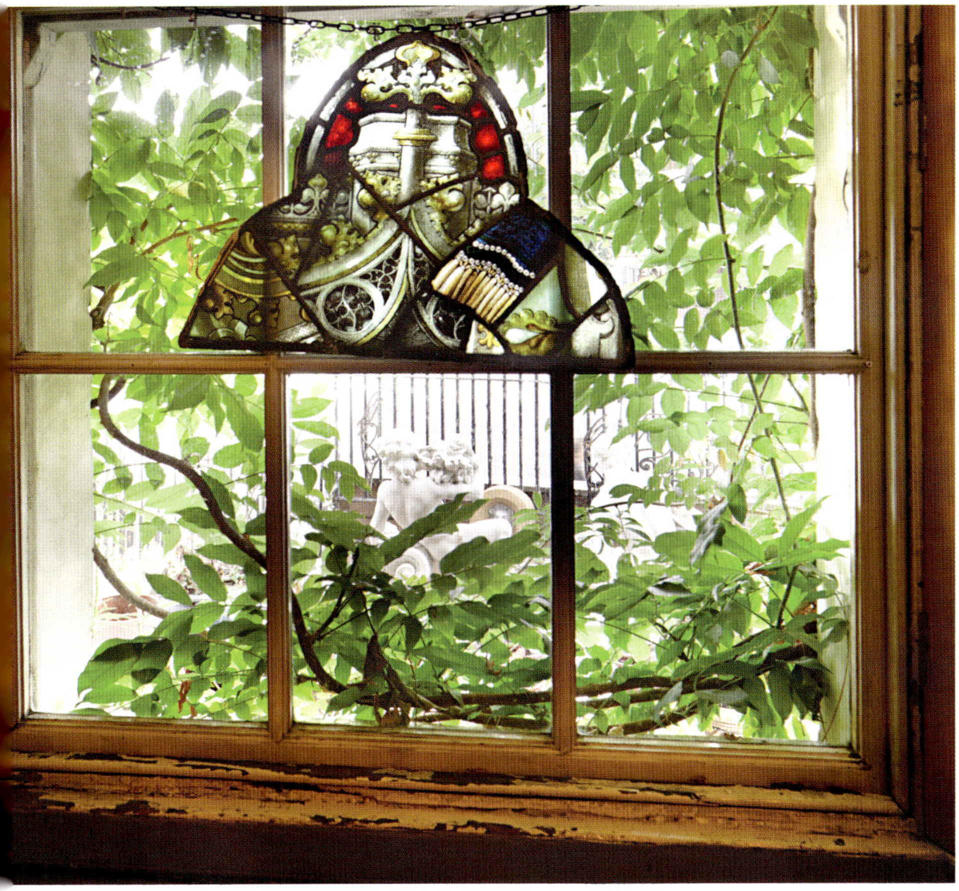

Opposite, above This office does double duty as a showroom at Brunswick House, with everything in the picture for sale.

Opposite, below This eclectic dining room display spans the styles. Every piece is labelled and for sale, including two sets of Hogarth prints: *Marriage à-la-mode* and *The Four Stages of Cruelty*.

Above A late-Victorian stained-and-painted trefoil, by Cottier & Co. of London, dated c.1890. It was removed from St George's Church, Perry Hill, Catford.

The saloon was once the drawing room of the Duke of Brunswick, and later the snooker room of the London South Western Railway Scientific & Literary Institute, and it is described as 'impressively shabby'. Below on the ground floor is the library, with its ceiling braced with what is reputed to be a piece of railway track against the weight of the snooker tables, and refitted with an elegant reclaimed fireplace. There are a series of cellars with ancient flagstones and old brickwork, which are the remains of an earlier building used as further display and entertainment areas.

Brunswick House dates from 1758, standing in what were once acres of parkland close to the river, going down to a mooring stage on the Thames. Part of the house was leased by the exiled aristocrat Freidrich Wilhelm, Duke of Braunschweig-Wolfenbüttel, this being anglicized to Brunswick. His German home had been overrun by Bonapartists, and his father killed in battle against Napoleon. All his adult life the Duke fought against Napoleon. He lived briefly at Brunswick House, returning to the fray on the continent in 1813 to be killed at the Battle of Quatre Bas just before Waterloo.

Brunswick House's pleasant location was quickly eroded by encroaching industry. The London South Western Railway built its first London terminus close alongside in 1838. Gasworks, a locomotive building works, Nine Elms engine shed and goods yards grew up around the house and alongside the river. A railway viaduct cut off the view southwards. Brunswick House, damaged and much neglected, was bought first by a gas company and then by the LSWR. The railways used its ground floor as goods yard offices from 1860, with a railwaymen's club on the upper two levels. A huge cold store was built close behind. In this landscape the survival of Brunswick House was freakish. The rail tracks and sheds surrounding it were built up in the nineteenth century and then run down in the mid-twentieth. When the Victorian gas works and rail yards were demolished, the building remained the British Railways Staff Association Club. The much-run-down area started to undergo regeneration in the 1990s, with the opening nearby of the MI6 headquarters building at Vauxhall Cross in 1994 and the apartment towers of St George Wharf in 2000. Brunswick House remained in the ownership of the railway social club until 2002.

It was purchased by in 2002 Adrian Amos, a pioneer of the business of architectural salvage, who had started the LASSCO firm at a redundant church in Shoreditch during the 1970s. LASSCO had owned a salvage yard at Bermondsey since 1999 for reclaimed building materials and Brunswick House was acquired to operate as showrooms and offices. The house was first restored from the ravages of squatters who had stripped much of the interior before LASSCO opened shop in 2005. It is a distinctive landmark where Wandsworth Road meets Nine Elms Lane alongside the bus station and the roaring one-way road system with five lanes of traffic. Brunswick House will continue to stand out in the regeneration of Vauxhall, close to the giant cube of the new US Embassy.

CONTACT INFORMATION

LASSCO,
Brunswick House, 30 Wandsworth Road, SW8 2LG
https://www.lassco.co.uk/

Crossness and Abbey Mills Pumping Stations

Crossness Pumping Station engine house is a splendid Romanesque industrial building which stands south of the Thames about 12 miles (19 km) east of Trafalgar Square. Its counterpart across the river in the East End is Abbey Mills, exotic in appearance. They are two conspicuous features of what remains one of London's hidden engineering secrets – its mid-Victorian sewer system.

The engine house at Crossness is a tribute to extensive restoration and preservation. The interior houses a remarkable octagonal pavilion with arched screens. Wrought iron and cast iron are used extensively for the capitals, columns, floors and spiral staircases, and there is much brasswork for details such as the handrails. Despite the use of so much metal, the decorations are delicate iron evocations of leaves, vines and flowers, in places intertwined with the Metropolitan Board of Works' monogram. Bright colours are used, as originally applied in 1865. Above lies the beam floor, and in the corners are four massive engines, each with a 52-ton flywheel.

At Abbey Mills, the main engine house, opened in 1868, is still in use. Its steam engines were replaced with electrical systems during the 1930s, and the electric motors and pumps remaining in the building now serve as a reserve system for Thames Water. Abbey Mills' ironwork was designed by the same architect as at Crossness, Charles Driver. The columns and arches are now painted in more muted colours. The building is often described as 'Byzantine'

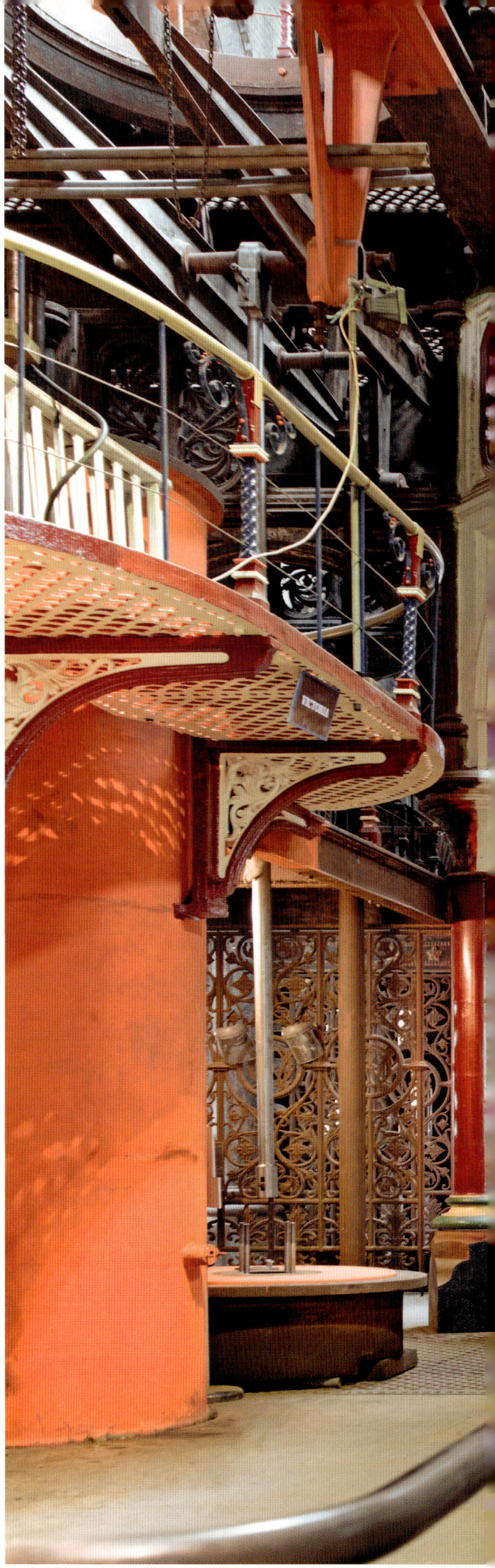

Main pump room, Crossness Pumping Station.

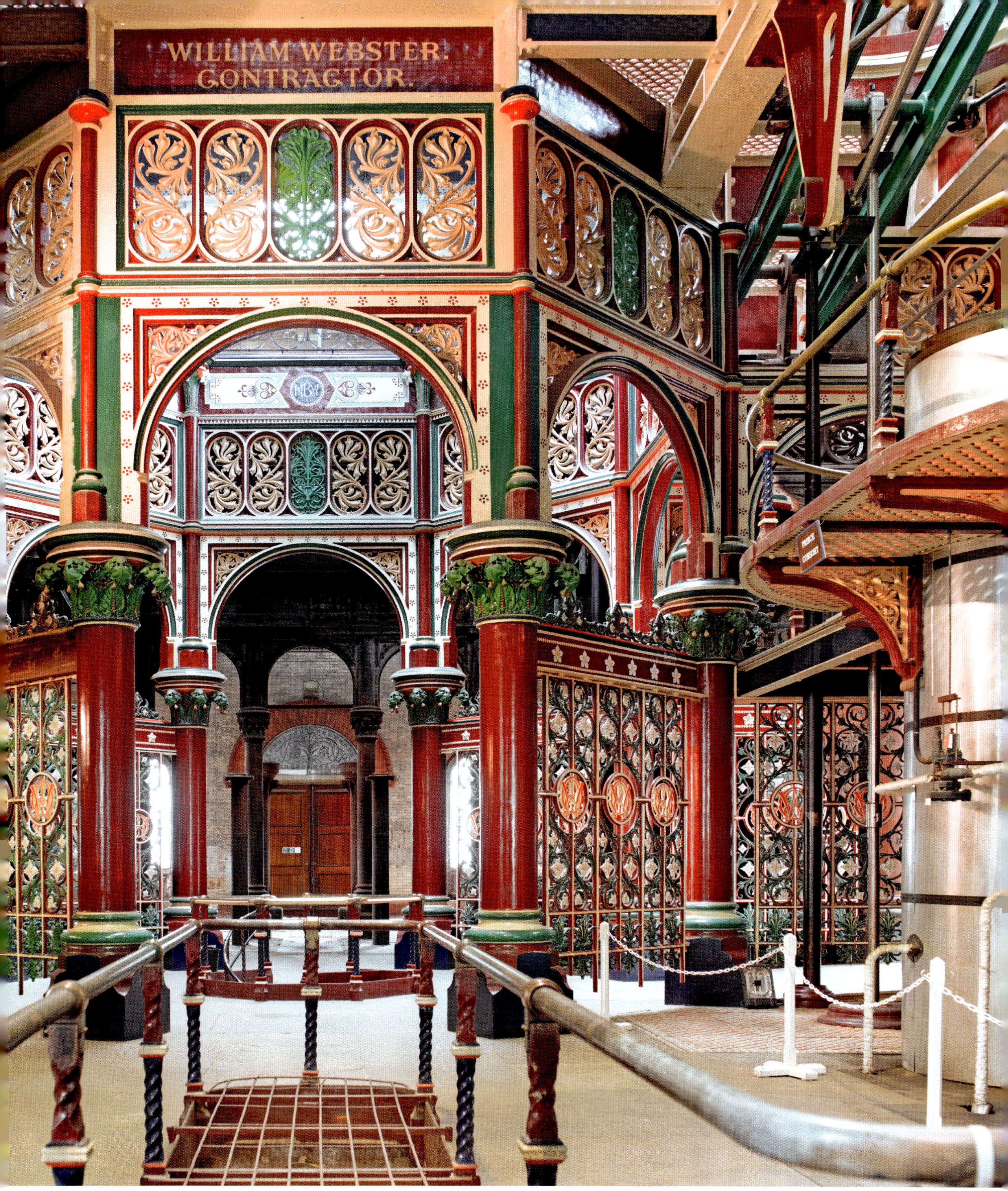
WILLIAM WEBSTER.
CONTRACTOR.

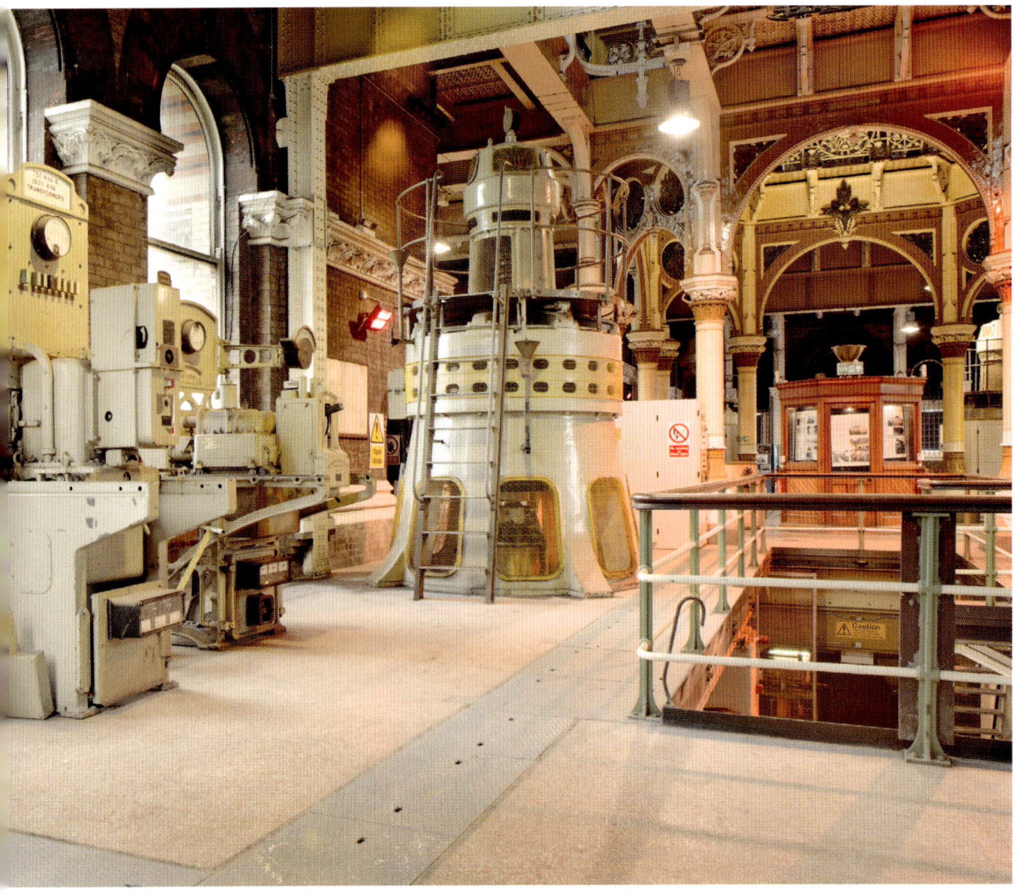

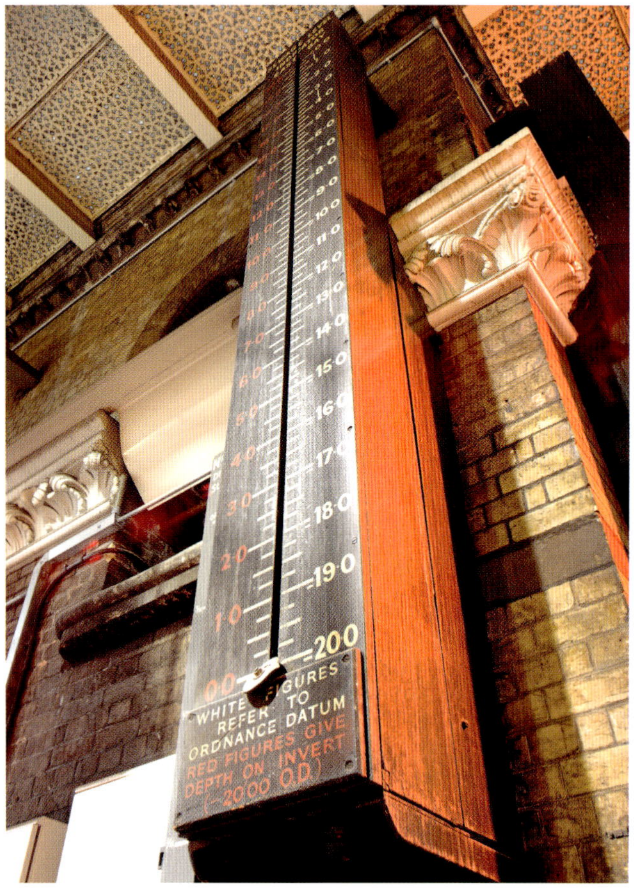

Above Pump room, Abbey Mills Pumping Station.

Above right Sewage level indicator, Abbey Mills Pumping Station.

Right Albert Edward fly wheel, Crossness Pumping Station.

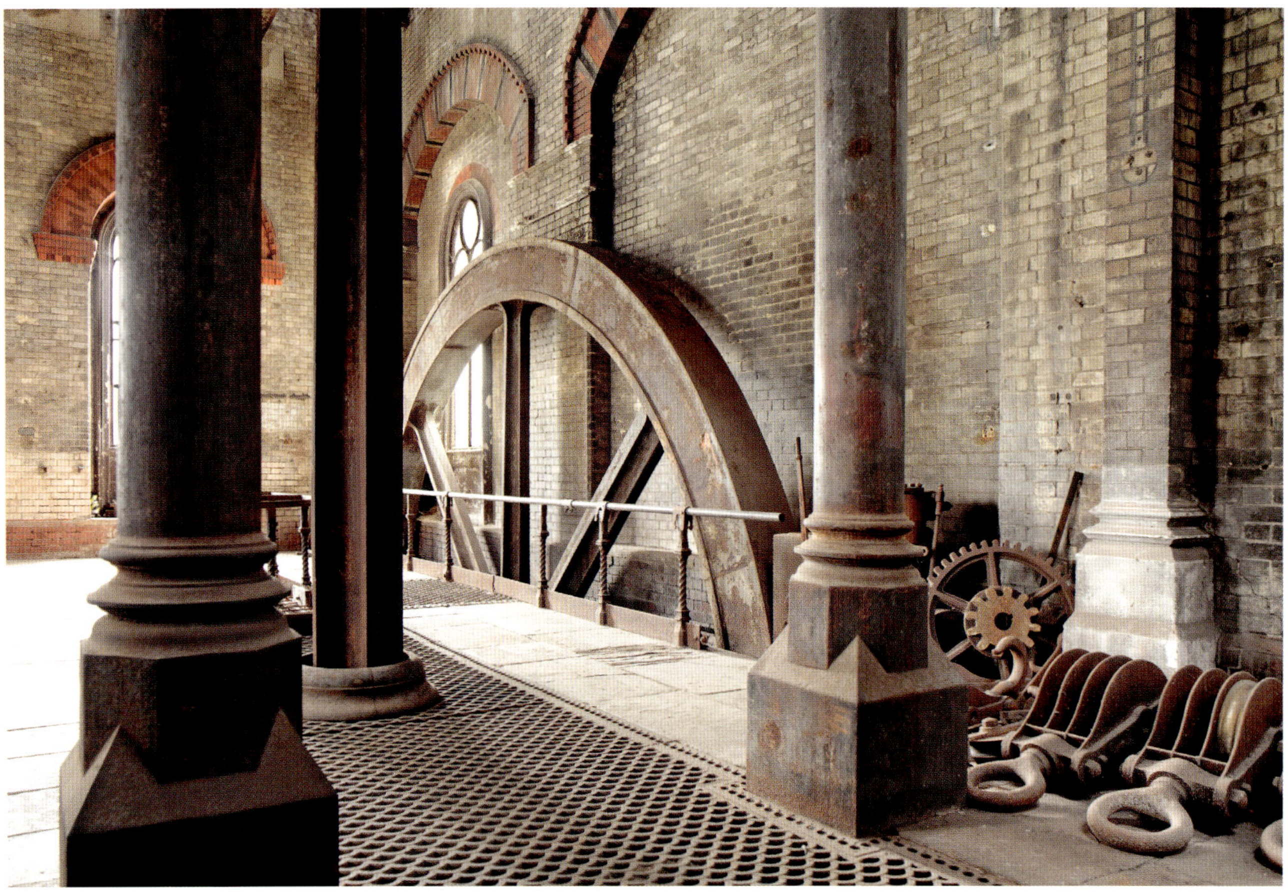

or 'gothic', but its style is hard to pin down precisely. The high dome and lantern are Russian in appearance and there were once two massive Moorish chimneys. Electrical control panels and instrumentation from a later age, now dated, do not look out of place in the Victorian engine house.

Behind the creation of both these buildings lay the desperate need to clean up the River Thames. In the early nineteenth century, the fact that contaminated water was the true cause of cholera, which was to kill more than 30,000 Londoners between 1830 and 1855, was imperfectly understood. It was not until the Great Stink of 1858, when the polluted Thames generated a stench so powerful that the Houses of Parliament were rendered barely habitable, that politicians took action.

The solution, designed by chief engineer to the Metropolitan Board of Works Sir Joseph Bazalgette, was typically Victorian in its ambition. A network of main sewer tunnels running parallel to the Thames would be built, collecting both waste water and surface water, and carrying it to outfalls far downriver. As the districts of London lie on different levels, the challenge was to lift much of the waste water to a level high enough to allow it to flow into the river. Three main intercepting sewers on the north side of the river at low, middle and high levels, and three on the south, would feed waste water into outfalls at Barking and at Crossness. Abbey Mills Pumping station was needed to raise the water from the lowest interceptor sewers to reservoirs, from where it could flow into the river.

On the south side, Crossness was able to discharge sewage directly into the river at high tide, but during low tide powerful pumping engines were needed to raise sewage water into a roofed reservoir (about the area of five football pitches) to await the change in the river level.

The Southern Outfall Sewer Pumping Station at Crossness lay on the edge of what was in 1865 a bleak marsh at Erith. To the west lay Woolwich Royal Arsenal, whose firing ranges, magazines and test areas were starting to sprawl over hundreds of acres of marsh, mostly closed, dangerous and secret – a place redacted from maps.

Abbey Mills stands close to Bromley-by-Bow and was further from the outlet. On completion in 1868 it was on the outer edge of London, with open country beyond. Within a year it was joined to the east by the gigantic Beckton Gas Works, a Hades-like collection of retorts, chimneys, gasometers and tar beds. Sewage from Abbey Mills flowed into the Northern Outfall Sewer, which curved closely around the gas works and discharged directly into the river at Barking. Here the concentration of unpleasantness was exceptional, and the outfalls at Barking and Crossness were frequently overpowering. This did briefly represent a kind of progress, because sewage was being shifted out of London to the downriver outlands, but soon the grim state of the banks raised another stink. A second phase of improvements was required as the realization grew that raw sewage could not be pumped into the Thames in the expectation that the tides would take it away.

From 1887 precipitation bed systems at Barking and Crossness came into operation to extract sludge from waste water. Sludge was loaded onto a fleet of purpose-built vessels, which steamed downriver to discharge it in the deepest parts of the estuary, a system which operated for more than a hundred years. The fleet of sludge carriers, numbering sixteen over time, performed that duty until EC rules outlawed dumping in 1998. Now all sewage is processed and some of it is incinerated at Crossness and Beckton.

As the sprawl of London caught up with Crossness, Woolwich Arsenal closed, and from 1967 Thamesmead town was developed. The original four giant simple engines had been updated to triple expansion compounds years before, but the last of them had been decommissioned by 1956. Too big to dismantle easily, the engines – named Prince Consort, Victoria, Albert Edward and Alexandra – together with the building housing them, remained intact but fell into dereliction. As years passed, it was discovered that the engines at Crossness are the largest remaining rotative beam engines in existence anywhere. After years of negotiation, and the establishment of a volunteer trust, work started on the restoration of the building and one engine in 1985. Prince Consort was the subject of a painstaking rebuild to working order by the Crossness Engines Trust, and was returned to steam in 2003. Work is proceeding on Victoria. Crossness is open to visitors four times each year for steaming demonstrations.

CONTACT INFORMATION

Crossness Pumping Station,
The Old Works, Thames Water STW, Bazalgette Way, SE2 9AQ
Abbey Mills Pumping Station,
Abbey Lane, Stratford, E15 2RW

Repton Boxing Club

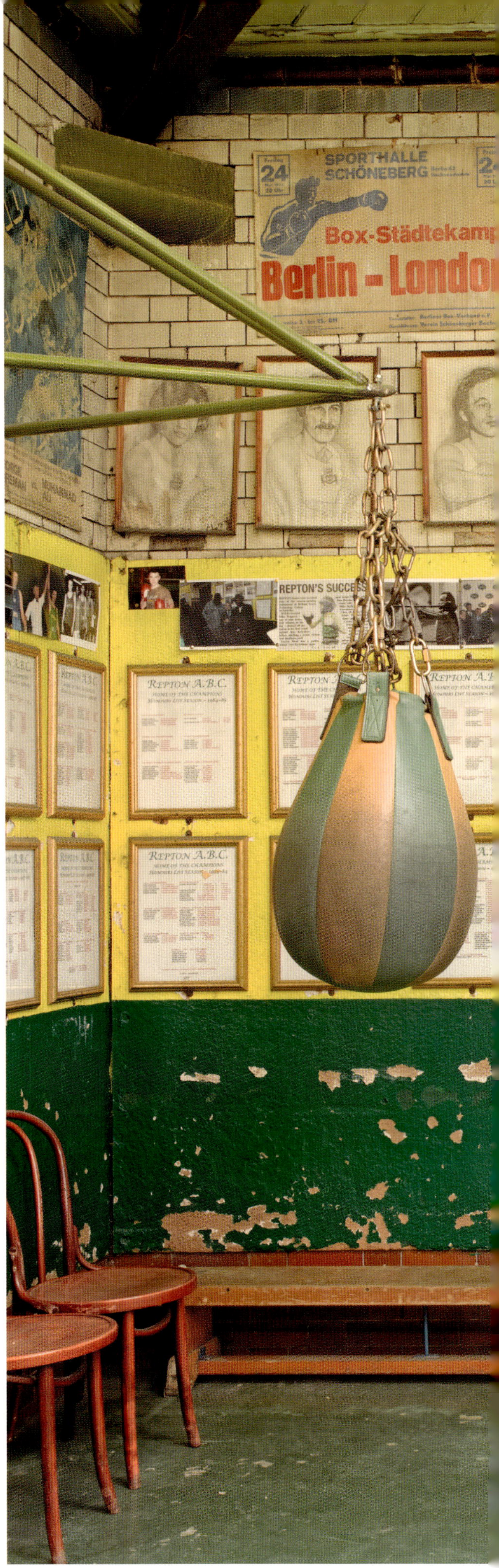

Wall-suspended punch bags alongside the ring, where mangles and washing machines once stood.

A fine Victorian bathhouse in Bethnal Green is home to the best-known amateur boxing establishment in Britain, Repton Boxing Club, with a history dating back to 1884 for the improvement of deprived boys of the East End. The area is now modernized and residentially desirable, but the club just off Brick Lane looks just as it might have done in the 1930s. There is a good patina on white glazed tile walls, distressed woodwork, yellowing bout bills, battered punchbags and a well-used square ring.

All this creates an authentic atmosphere for a casual visitor, but it is a little deceptive. Repton Boxing Club has been based at the Cheshire Street bathhouse since only 1978, having been housed at multiple locations in the East End previously. Boxing and the building represent two separate slices of East End culture.

Repton Boys' Club, as it was originally named, was founded through the philanthropy of Repton School. The precise reason why a public school based 130 miles (210 km) north of London in Derbyshire should adopt the East End is now obscure, but it was likely based on a combination of idealism and practicality. To the privileged classes in late-Victorian England the East End of London was the very definition of neediness and deprivation. A boys' club with a sporting side was seen as a way of alleviating hardship.

Connections between the school and club died had died away by 1971, but the name – by then Repton Boxing Club – continued, and its roll of honour has been impressive. The amateur club launched world

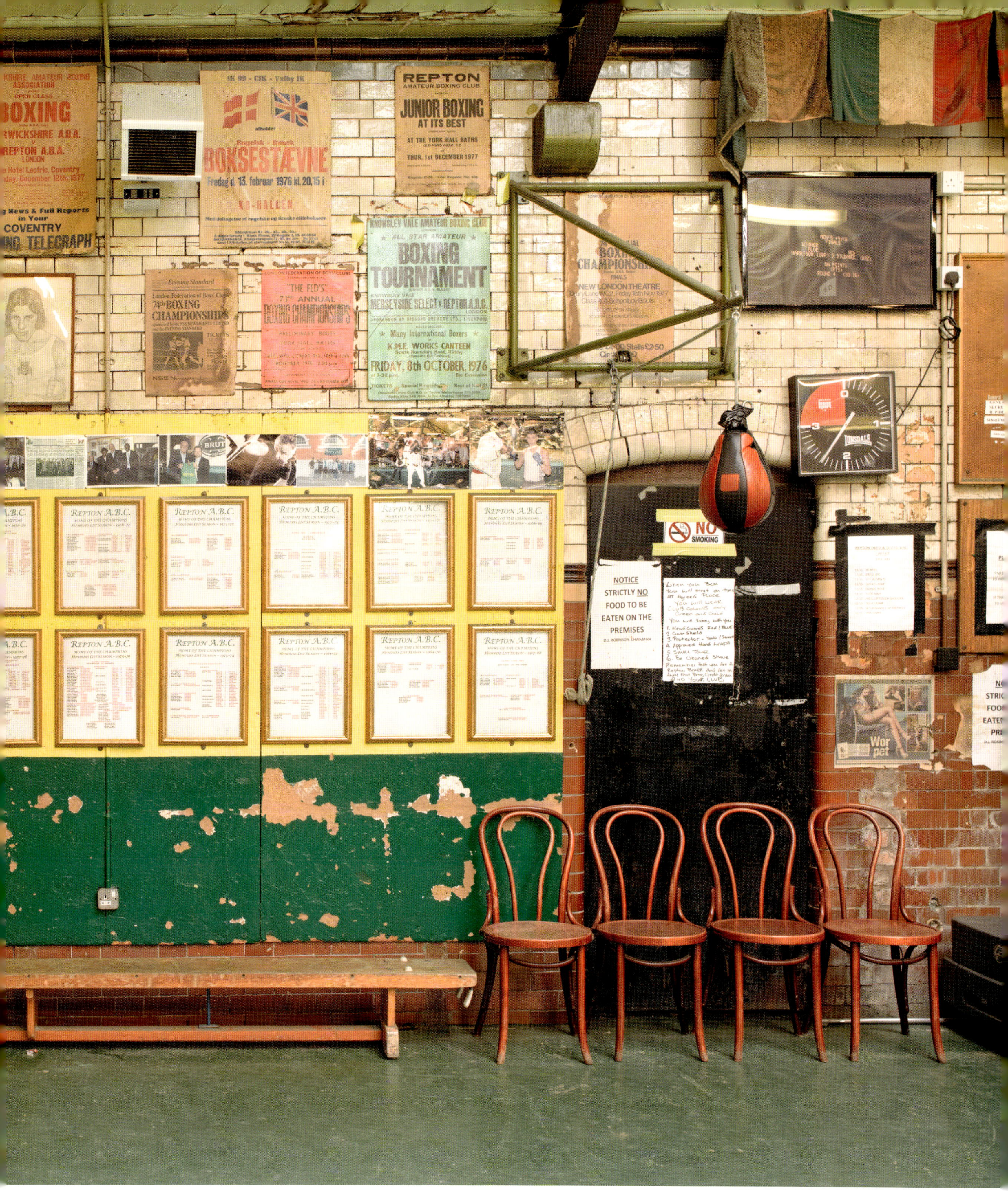
BOXING
COVENTRY
Engelsk - Dansk
BOKSESTÆVNE
Fredag d. 13. februar 1976 kl. 20,15 i
REPTON
AMATEUR BOXING CLUB
JUNIOR BOXING
AT ITS BEST
AT THE YORK HALL BATHS
THUR. 1st DECEMBER 1977
Evening Standard
74th BOXING CHAMPIONSHIPS
"THE FED'S"
73rd ANNUAL
BOXING CHAMPIONSHIPS
ALL STAR AMATEUR
BOXING TOURNAMENT
MERSEYSIDE SELECT v. REPTON A.B.C.
Many International Boxers
K.M.E. WORKS CANTEEN
FRIDAY, 8th OCTOBER, 1976
NEW LONDON THEATRE
REPTON A.B.C.
NO SMOKING
NOTICE
STRICTLY NO
FOOD TO BE
EATEN ON THE
PREMISES
LONSDALE

Club officials emphasize that Repton is the real thing, not a leisure centre or a fitness centre.

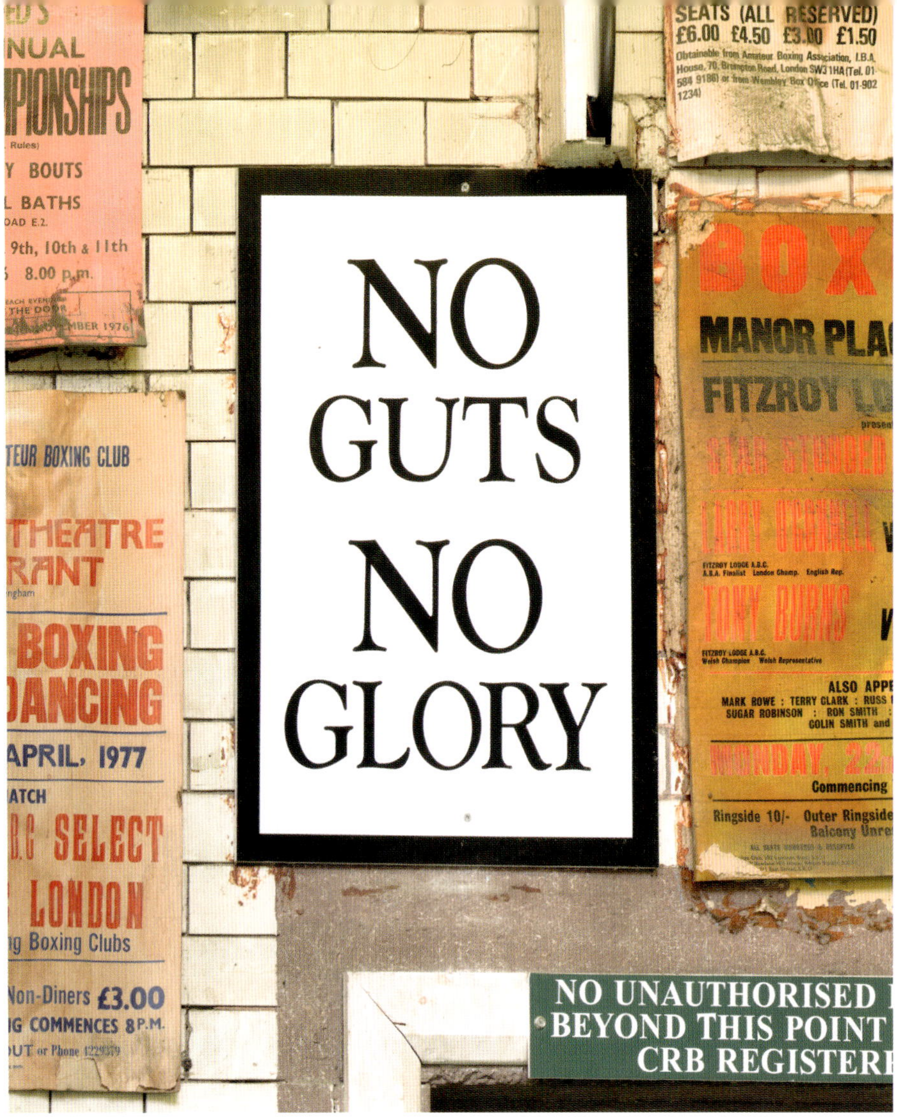

Welterweight champion John H. Stracey, Junior Middleweight champion Maurice Hope, Olympians Mickey Carter and Sylvester Mittee. World Middleweight champion Darren Barker started at Repton and Audley Harrison won the ABA Championship as a Repton fighter.

The club is shrewdly aware of the strong character of the place, preserving its 'retro' look and allowing it to be used as a location in *Lock, Stock and Two Smoking Barrels* and other films. Club officials also emphasize that Repton is the real thing, not a leisure centre or a fitness centre, but strictly for those who aspire to three rounds of action, with shirts on, and headguards worn. For the ambitious it may be a pathway to a shot at greatness, and for some boys it is said to be a steadying influence and a source of self-respect, which was one of the principles behind the founding of the club in 1884.

The surrounding bricks and mortar of the Bethnal Green Baths and Washhouse are the testament of the Second Public Baths and Washhouses Act of 1897. It provided baths for personal washing and facilities for laundering. Architect Robert Stephen Ayling specialized in social works that required high levels of hygiene, such as abattoirs and public conveniences. His design won praise at the time for providing space for prams, 'in which the washers usually bring their linen. In most of the London baths this been omitted, with the result that the waiting halls are often impassable'.

It is built from red brick and bands of Portland stone, with a curved gable end owing something to Flemish style, and its decorations include a relief of carved cherubs over the male and female entrances signed by scrolls held by cherubs, and at its eastern end is an oriel window buttressed by carved angels. Equipment once housed within the laundry included hand-powered mangles and some monumental belt-driven washing machines.

The need for public baths declined swiftly with facilities built into new housing after the Second World War, and the entire bathhouse building was falling into disuse by the 1970s. By coincidence, Repton Club's lease on space at the Bethnal Green Working Men's Club in nearby Pollard Row was coming to an end. With some financial aid from Tower Hamlets, the single-storey laundry washhouse part of the building was upgraded to accommodate the boxing club with no loss of sporting continuity.

As years passed, and as much of the building remained closed, the East End began to change. With the revitalized City of London lying close alongside and generating an increasing need for good accommodation, it was inevitable that the rest of the building would be transformed into desirable apartments.

CONTACT INFORMATION

Repton Boxing Club,
116 Cheshire Street, E2 6EG
https://www.reptonboxingclub.com/

Above The military slogan 'No Guts No Glory' inspires fierce sporting endeavour.

Opposite, above Cherubs, indicating separate bathing arrangements, remain on the largely unchanged exterior.

Opposite, below The Wall of Honour against the green and cream scheme inherited from the former Bethnal Green Bath and Wash House.

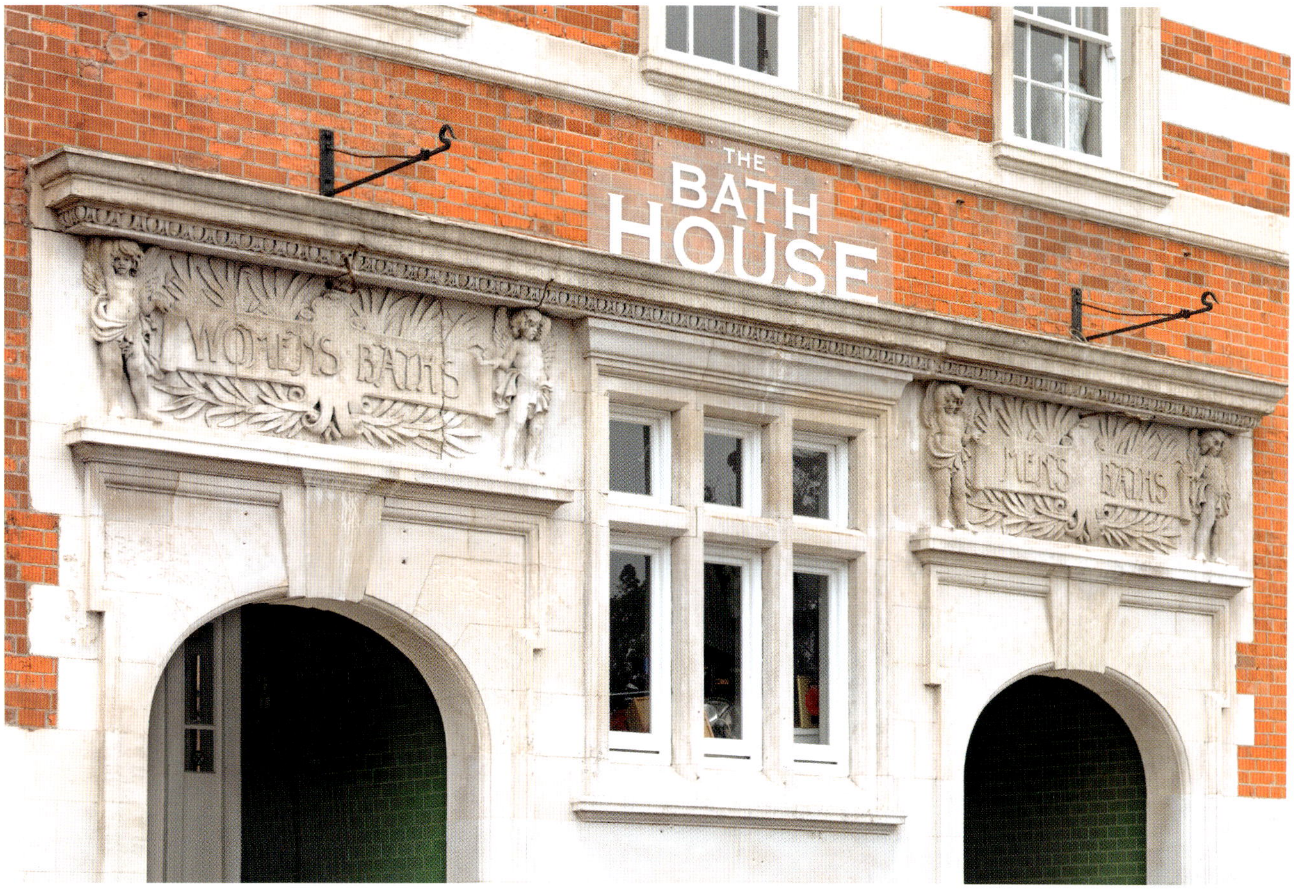
THE
BATH
HOUSE
WOMENS BATHS
MENS BATHS

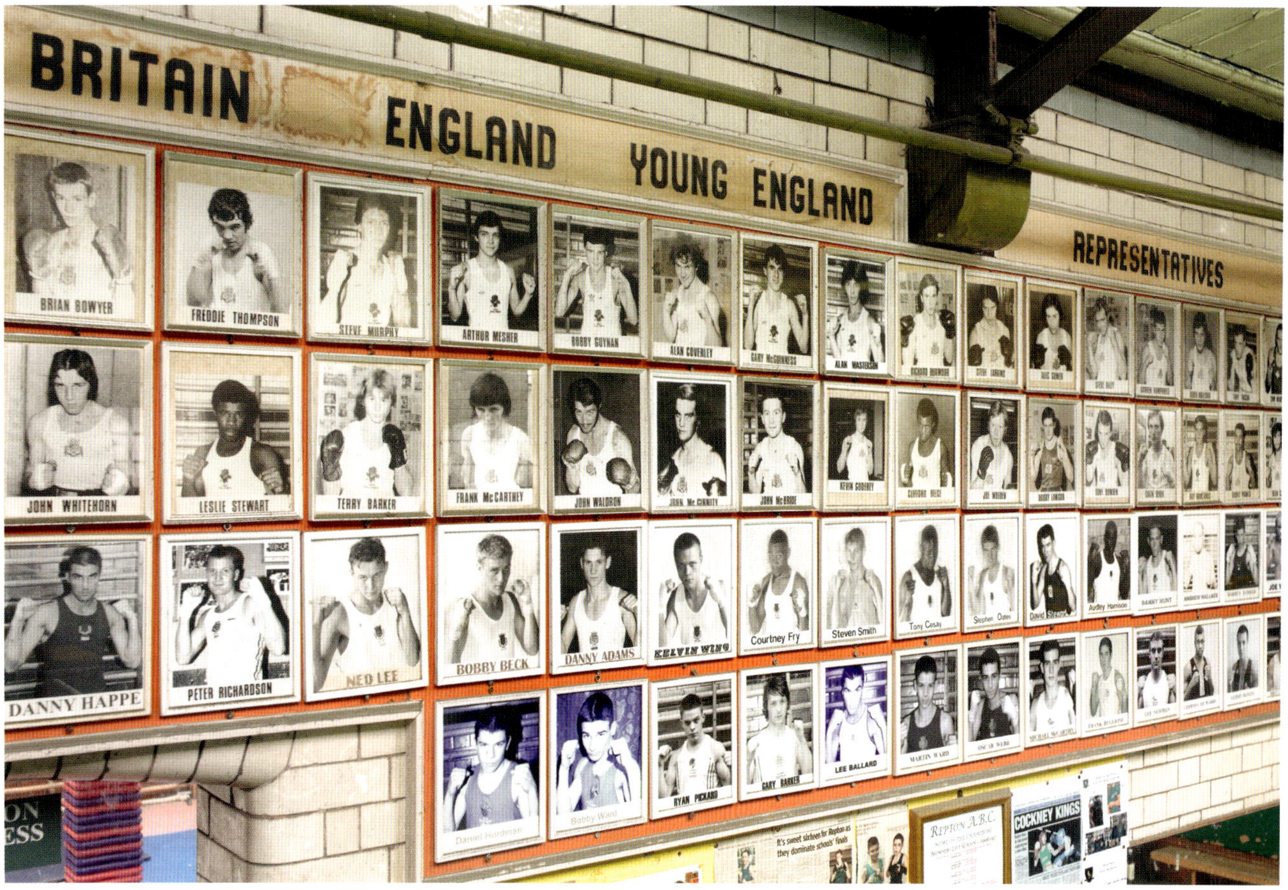
BRITAIN
ENGLAND
YOUNG ENGLAND
REPRESENTATIVES
BRIAN BOWYER
FREDDIE THOMPSON
STEVE MURPHY
ARTHUR MESHER
JOHN WHITEHORN
LESLIE STEWART
TERRY BARKER
FRANK McCARTHEY
JOHN WALDRON
DANNY HAPPE
PETER RICHARDSON
NED LEE
BOBBY BECK
DANNY ADAMS
KELVIN WING
Courtney Fry
Steven Smith
LEE BALLARD
COCKNEY KINGS

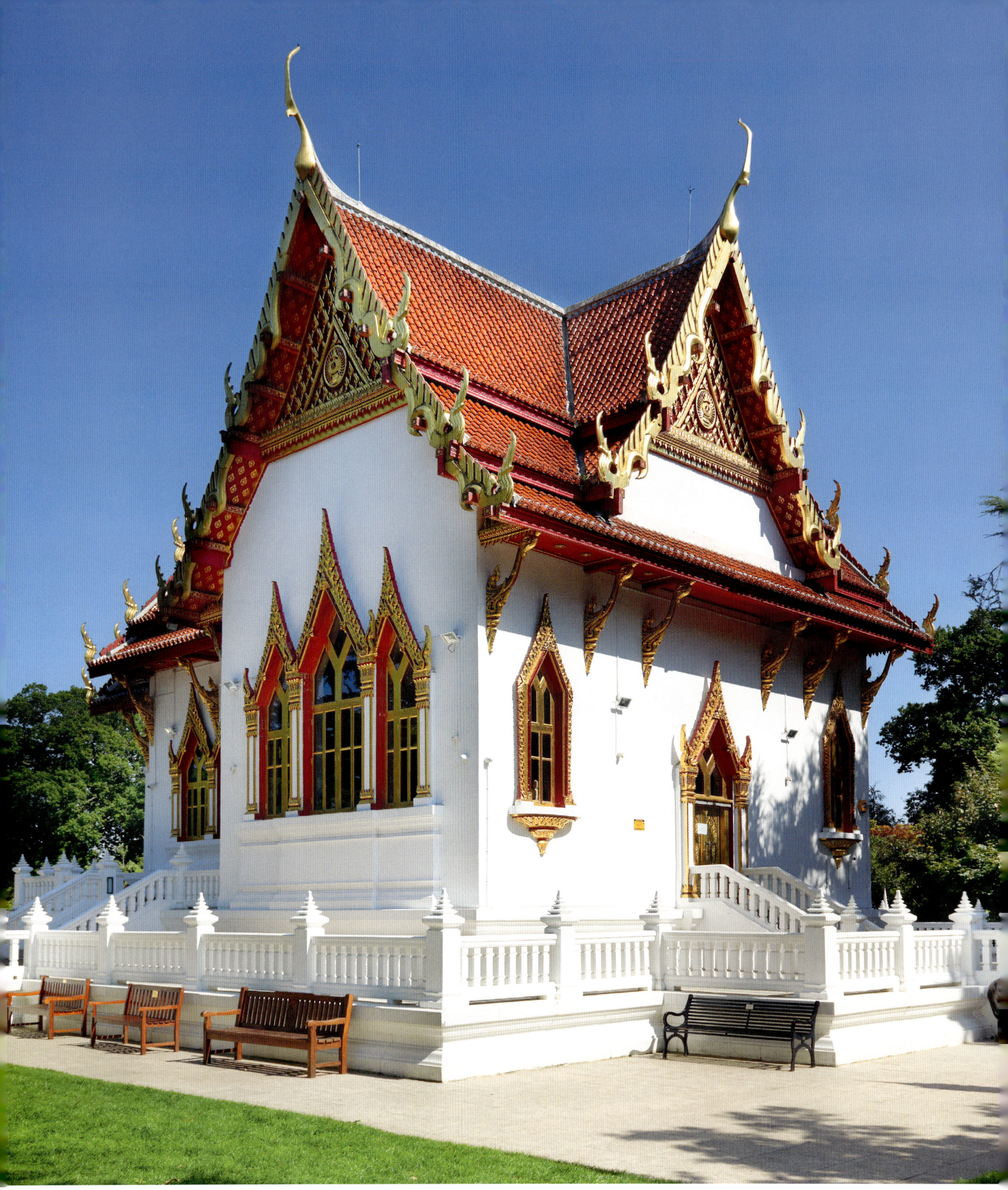

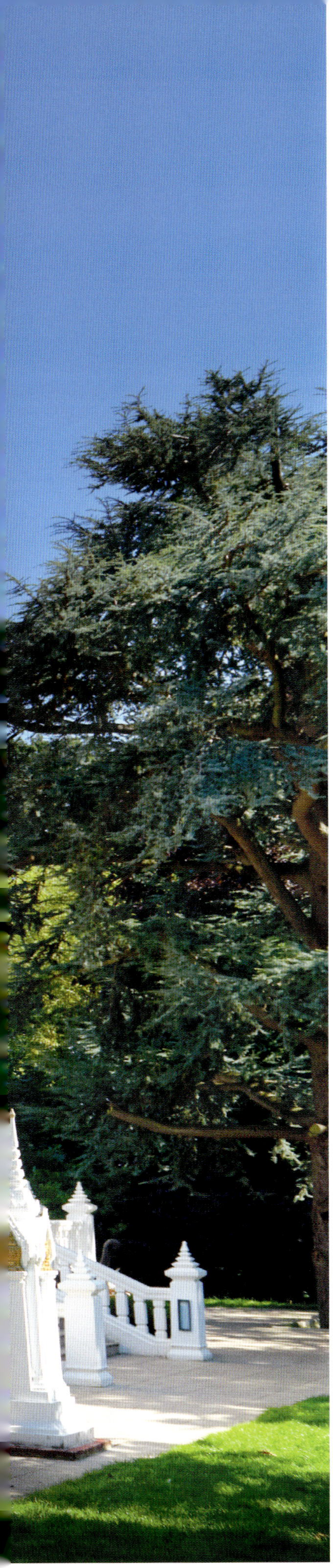

Wat Buddhapadipa Temple.

The Buddhapadipa Temple

Wat Buddhapadipa Temple is hidden in a wooded realm behind a suburban street just off Wimbledon Common. It follows the architectural style of Thai Buddhism, with white alls and multiple-tiered red roofs. The most distinctive and prominent features are gable boards bearing golden tassels and finials inspired by elements of the mythical Garuda bird, or serpentine Naga creature.

The old Barrogil Estate, purchased by the Thai government, came with a house, 4 acres (1.6 ha) of garden and an ornamental lake. The Temple was built here between 1979 and 1982 on an elevated lawn at the back of Barragil House, which became the monastic residence and office. There are three footbridges over water, a clocktower, a café, research centre and a memorial garden.

The temple building, properly known as *ubosot*, houses the shrine with three statues of the Buddha, the principal one of black bronze, more than 600 years old, the centre gold and the front green. These are flanked by flowers and candles of special significance and the backdrop shows a lofty Buddha reclining on a lotus leaf with Brahmas in the Brahma heavens below. Murals continue around the inside walls and these are the most extraordinary feature. Completed over an eight-year period up to 1992, the style is anachronistic and iconoclastic. The narrative is the life of Buddha, punctuated with modern elements such as a Space Shuttle, a golfer, Margaret Thatcher, George Bush and Superman.

CONTACT INFORMATION

The Buddhapadipa Temple,
14 Calonne Road, SW19 5HJ
https://buddhapadipa.com/

Wilton's Music Hall

The survival and conservation of Wilton's Music Hall, the oldest remaining musical hall anywhere, was a struggle that lasted fifty years and the scars can be clearly seen. That was the aim of the restorers, who in 2015 completed what has been described as 'a kind of invisible mending', which gave a sound structure and preserved an astonishing patina.

In the early 1850s, John Wilton built an entertainment hall behind three Georgian houses in Graces Alley, in the area between Whitechapel and Wapping. One of these properties was a pub known as The Mahogany Bar, which already had a concert room behind. Wilton soon acquired the lease on an adjoining house, and built a second, bigger auditorium in 1859, one of the first built specifically for emerging style of music hall entertainment.

It suffered a fire in 1877 and was rebuilt, but operated as a theatre for only four more years. One of the last turns was the legendary George Leybourne, performing in the character of the singing and dancing dandy 'Champagne Charlie'.

The hall was taken over by the Wesleyan Methodists, who reopened it as The Mahogany Bar Mission, after dispensing with the namesake wooden counter and bar where alcohol had been sold. Services were held in the theatre, and the building played a community role in chapters of East End history, including serving as a soup kitchen during the dockers' strike of 1889, and delivering relief to shelterers during the Blitz of 1940–1. The Methodists ran the mission until 1956,

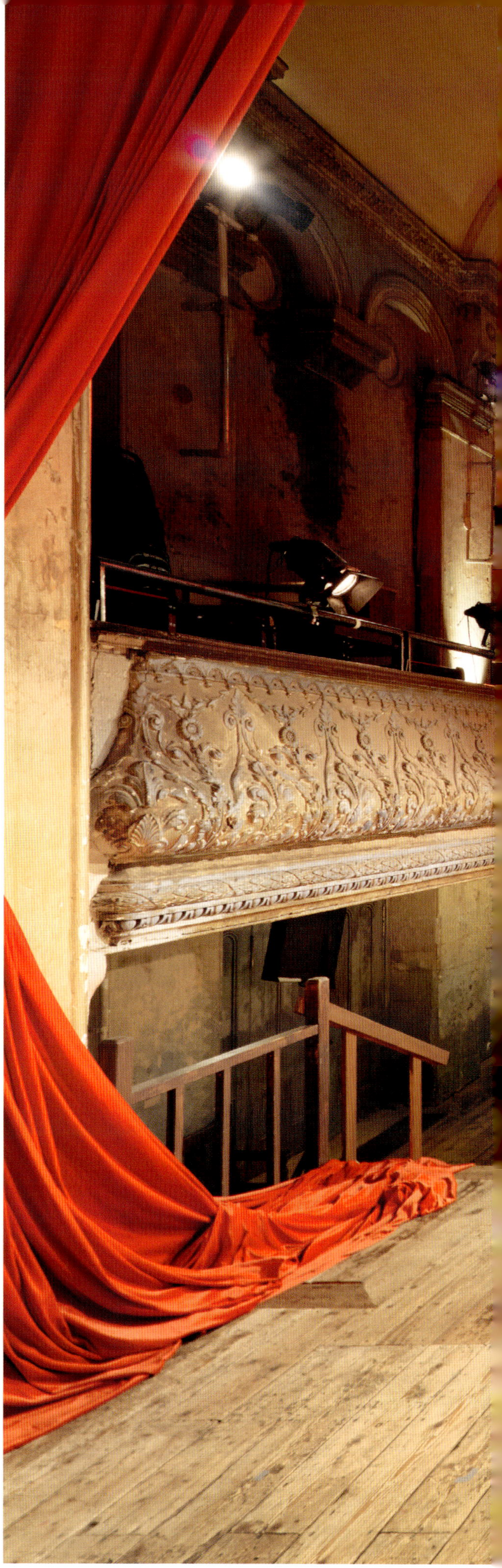

The view from the stage. The auditorium is in muted colours now. The gallery was once gilded and the alcoves filled with mirrors.

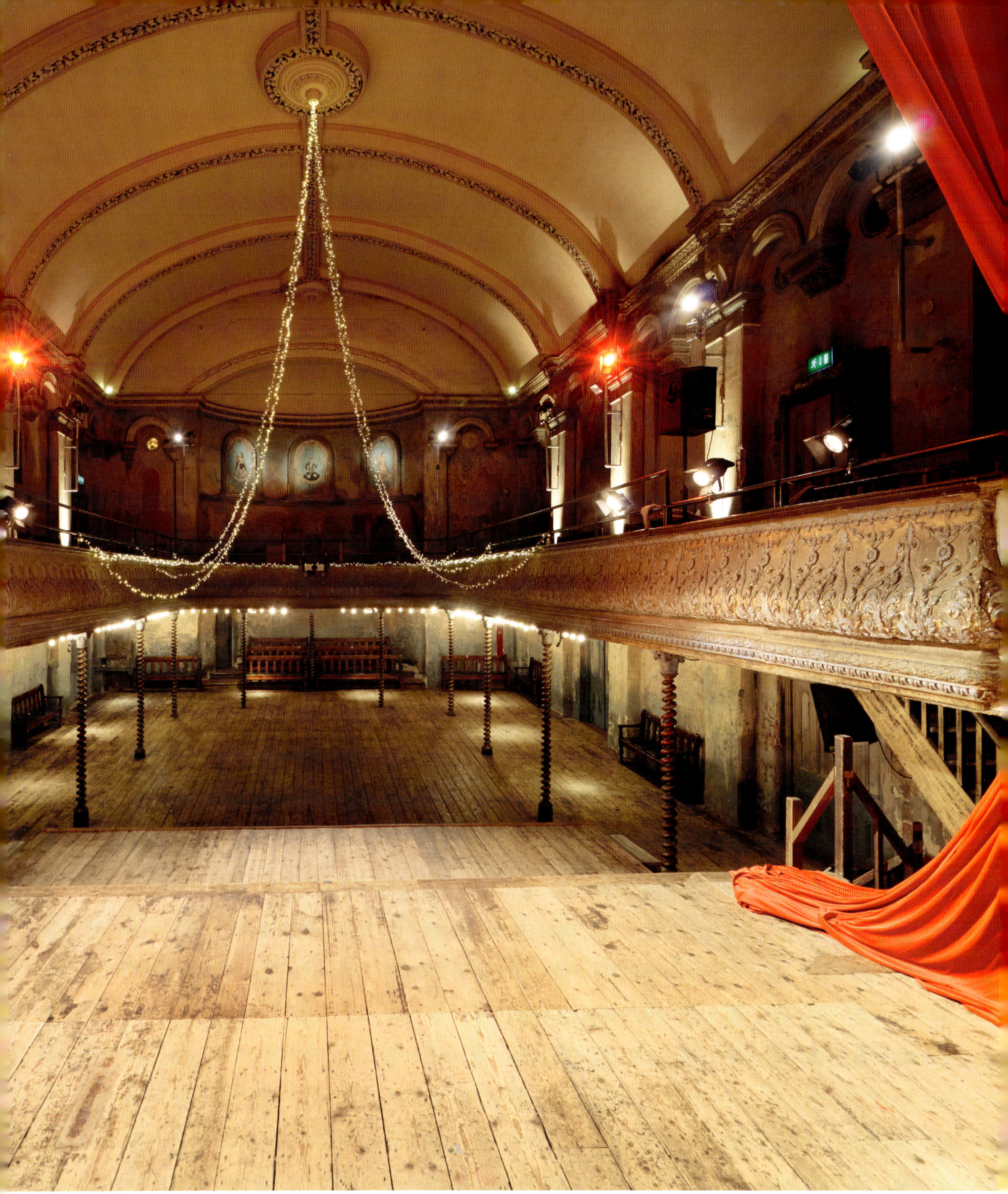

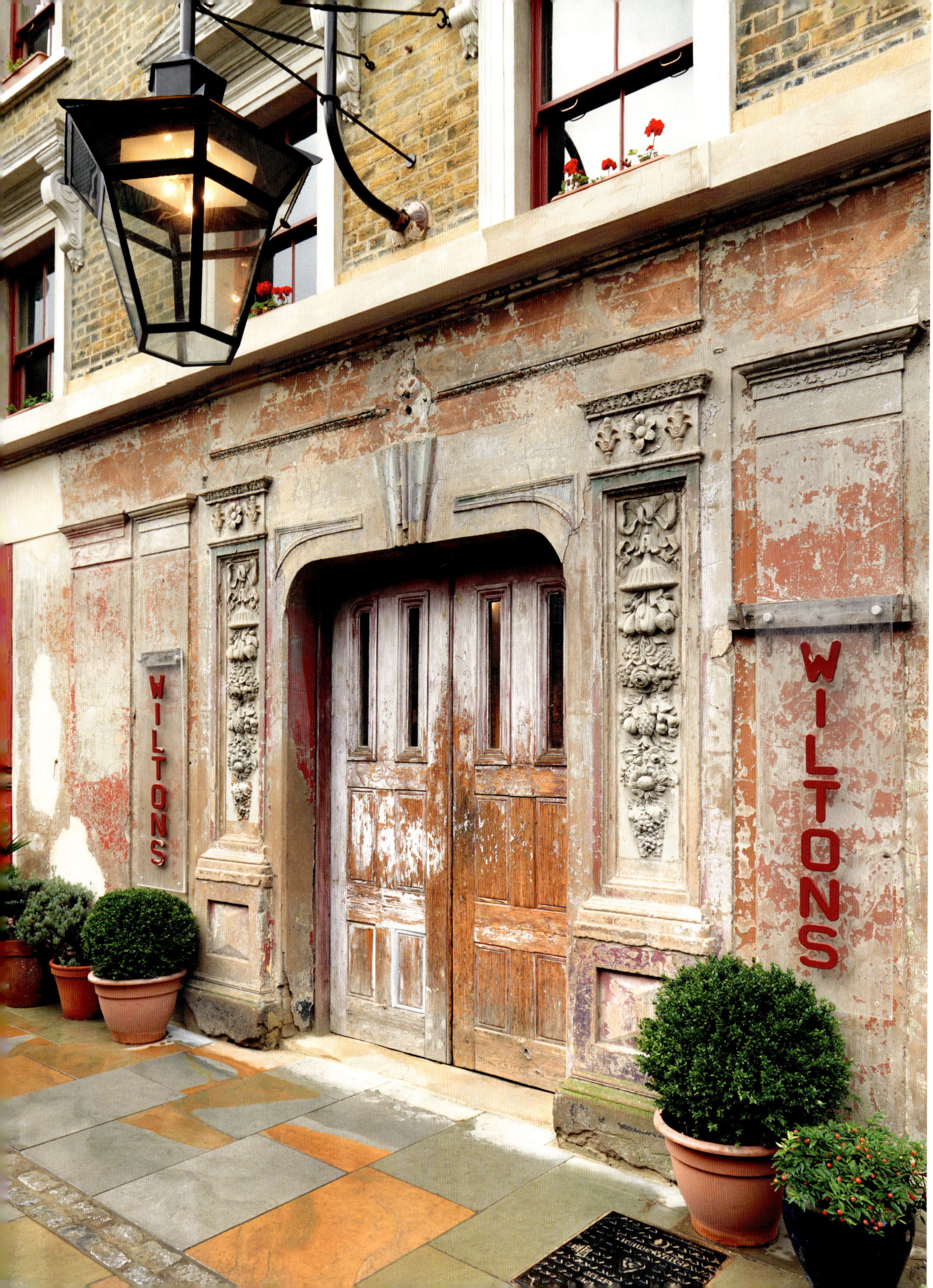
WILTONS
WILTONS

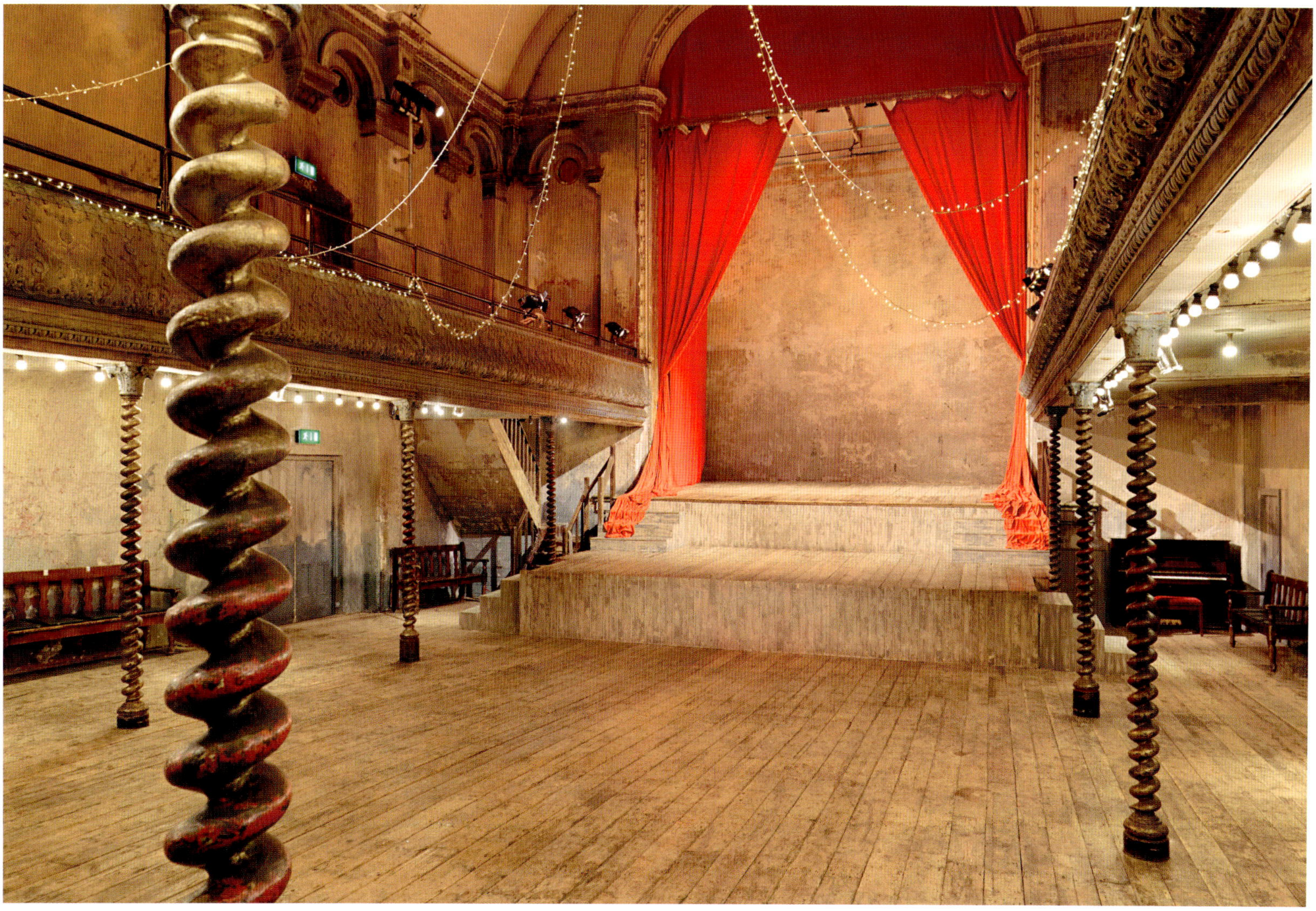

Opposite The gas-lit entrance was originally the door to a pub; Wilton's Music Hall is landlocked by surrounding buildings.

Above The helical-twist barley-sugar columns supporting the gallery date from 1859.

and afterwards the building operated as the Coppermill Rag-Sorting depot. Wilton's Music Hall should then have been swept away as part of a widespread slum clearance programme by London County Council in 1964, and demolition plans were drawn up. But at a public meeting for the closure, John Betjeman, poet laureate and pioneering conservationist, and theatre historian John Earle, spoke in support of keeping it. The building gained listed status in 1971, but the structure was semi-derelict. Fundraising efforts and restoration started and stalled. A trickle of piecemeal building work kept Wilton's standing, aided by a diet of film location and music video work.

Firstly, the London Music Hall Trust funded some work in in the 1980s and the building became a little more secure. A significant milestone was the first live act before an audience since 1881, a performance recitation of T.S. Eliot's *The Wasteland* in 1997 by Fiona Shaw, a staging that was praised for perfectly harnessing verse to Wilton's own poetic melancholy. The Wilton Music Hall Trust, formed in 2004, financed the restoration of the music hall itself in the 'conservative repair' style and the houses at the front were rebuilt. Nearly all the original features were retained, while introducing modern heating, electrical and lighting systems.

Wilton's Music Hall hosts opera, puppetry, classical music, cabaret, dance and magic shows, and also offers tours. These take place on some Mondays.

CONTACT INFORMATION

Wilton's Music Hall,
1 Graces Alley, E1 8JB
https://wiltons.org.uk/

Crystal Palace Subway

London's vast and intricate rail system has lost hardly any of its passenger-carrying tracks since the first lines opened in the 1830s. An ornate subway at Crystal Palace marks a rare exception: a beautiful isolated relic of a vanished branch line and a reminder of the huge exhibition hall it once served.

The vaulted subway of octagonal columns provided a pedestrian link from a lost terminus station. It was intended to channel passengers – first-class only – direct from the platforms to the main floor of the Palace through a courtyard and entrance steps. A 4 mile (6.4-km) branch had been built from the main line at Nunhead, providing trains to central London every half hour. Although there were three intermediate stations, the main justification for construction was the Crystal Palace itself. This Victorian showpiece built for the Great Exhibition at Hyde Park in 1851 had been re-erected on Sydenham Hill. Here, the prefabricated plate-glass, cast-iron and timber structure was enlarged as a tourist attraction housing a theatre and concert hall, shops and exhibitions.

The nearby Dulwich College estate exerted influence on the high-concept design of the subway and station, which became known as Crystal Palace High Level. The subway has fan vaults resembling church architecture, although here the vaults have no ribs. Patterns on the vaulting are picked out in red and cream bricks. On the ceiling, circular roundels in stone enclose more decorative brickwork and iron gaslight fittings. The subway was well lit. Overall it was 'designed to intrigue and excite, acting as a precursor to the treasures to be found in the Crystal Palace' in the words of conservators.

Crystal Palace was destroyed by fire on 30 November 1936, and the subway lost its purpose overnight. It entered a long twilight, becoming an air-raid shelter during the war. The branch line and High Level station closed in 1954 and the terminus was demolished seven years later.

Although locked away in recent years, it has attracted thousands of visitors on rare openings during heritage and festival days and Open House weekends. Paving has been replaced and grilles and gates fitted, and repairs to the flank walls authorized. In 2020, with funding in place for restoration and work underway, there are signs it is poised for rebirth, possibly as an event or exhibition space.

The Crystal Palace Subway survives in ornate isolation.

CONTACT INFORMATION

Crystal Palace Subway,
Crystal Palace Parade, Dulwich, SE19 1XX
https://www.crystalpalaceparktrust.org/pages/crystal-palace-subway

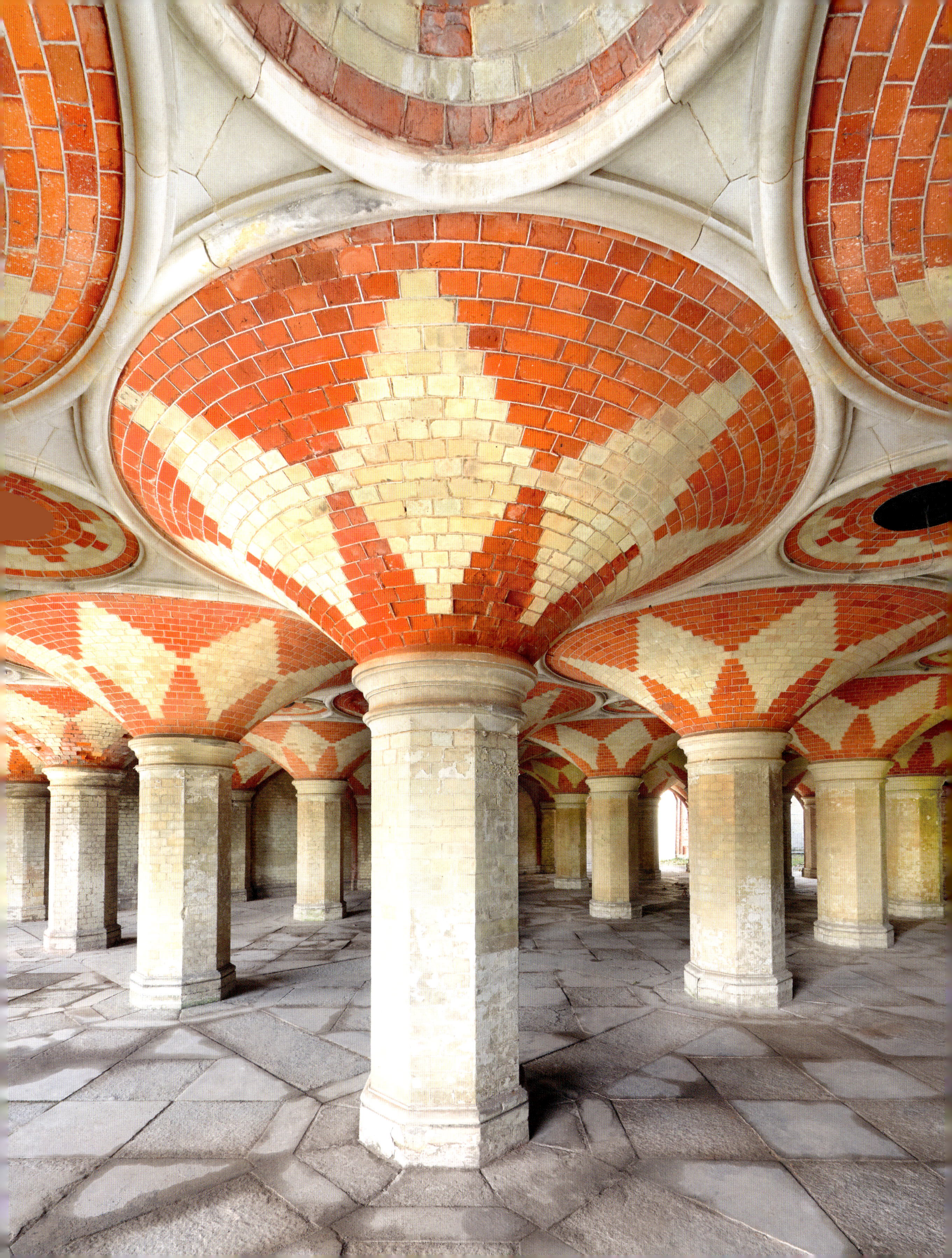

Index

Quarto

First published in 2026 by Frances Lincoln,
an imprint of the Quarto Group.
One Triptych Place, London, SE1 9SH, United Kingdom
T (0)20 7700 9000
www.Quarto.com

EEA Representation, WTS Tax d.o.o., Žanova ulica 3, 4000 Kranj, Slovenia www.wts-tax.si

Some material previously published in:
Unseen London, 2014, 2017
London Uncovered, 2016, 2018
London Explored, 2021

A catalogue record for this book is available from the British Library.

ISBN 978-1-80570-545-1
Ebook ISBN 978-1-80570-546-8

10 9 8 7 6 5 4 3 2 1

Design Sarah Pyke
Publisher Philip Cooper
Managing Editor Laura Bulbeck
Senior Editor Michael Brunström
Senior Designer Isabel Eeles
Senior Production Controller Rohana Yusof

Printed in Guangdong, China TT062026

FSC www.fsc.org MIX Paper | Supporting responsible forestry FSC® C016973